GREAT
BRITAIN'S
BEST TRIPS
36 AMAZING
ROAD TRIPS

Anthony Ham, Isabel Albiston, Oliver Berry, Joe Bindloss, Fionn Davenport, Belinda Dixon, Damian Harper, Anna Kaminski, Catherine Le Nevez, Andy Symington, Tasmin Waby, Kerry Walker, Luke Waterson, Neil Wilson

SYMBOLS IN THIS BOOK

MAP LEGEND

Routes
- Trip Route
- Trip Detour
- Linked Trip
- Walk Route
- Tollway
- Freeway
- Primary
- Secondary
- Tertiary
- Lane
- Unsealed Road
- Plaza/Mall
- Steps
- Tunnel
- Pedestrian Overpass
- Walk Track/Path

Boundaries
- International
- State/Province
- Cliff

Hydrography
- River/Creek
- Intermittent River
- Swamp/Mangrove
- Canal
- Water
- Dry/Salt/Intermittent Lake
- Glacier

Highway Markers
- M1 Motorway
- A44 Highway

Trips
- 1 Trip Numbers
- 9 Trip Stop
- Walking tour
- Trip Detour

Population
- Capital (National)
- Capital (State/Province)
- City/Large Town
- Town/Village

Areas
- Beach
- Cemetery (Christian)
- Cemetery (Other)
- Park
- Forest
- Reservation
- Urban Area
- Sportsground

Transport
- Airport
- Cable Car/Funicular
- London Tube station
- Metro station
- Parking
- Train/Railway
- Tram

Note: Not all symbols displayed above appear on the maps in this book

PLAN YOUR TRIP

ON THE ROAD

CONTENTS

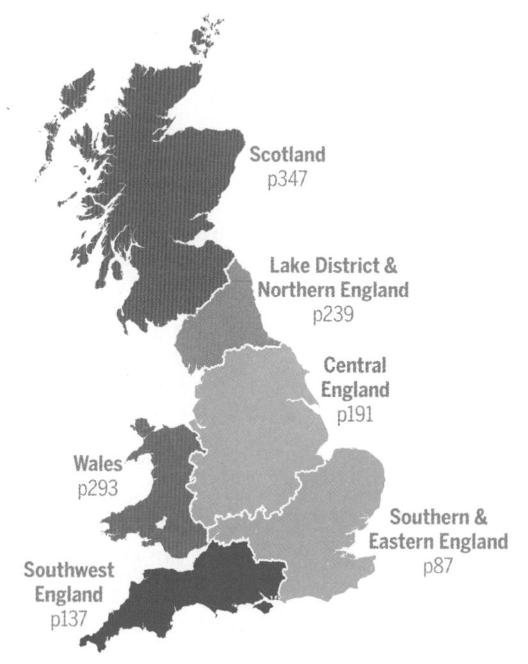

Scotland
p347
Lake District &
Northern England
p239
Central
England
p191
Wales
p293
Southern &
Eastern England
p87
Southwest
England
p137

Contents cont.

COVID-19

We have re-checked every business in this book before publication to ensure that it is still open after 2020's COVID-19 outbreak. However, the economic and social impacts of COVID-19 will continue to be felt long after the outbreak has been contained, and many businesses, services and events referenced in this guide may experience ongoing restrictions. Some businesses may be temporarily closed, have changed their opening hours and services, or require bookings; some unfortunately could have closed permanently. We suggest you check with venues before visiting for the latest information.

Classic Trips

Look out for the Classic Trips stamp on our favourite routes in this book.

CAOLAS CUMHANN

WELCOME TO GREAT BRITAIN

Great Britain overflows with unforgettable experiences and spectacular sights. There's the grandeur of Scotland's mountains; England's quaint villages and country lanes; and the haunting beauty of Welsh and West Country coasts. You'll also find wild northern moors, the elegant university towns of Oxford and Cambridge, and vibrant cities boasting everything from Georgian architecture to 21st-century art.

Our 36 drives take you through it all, leading you from one memorable experience to the next – prepare to encounter royal palaces, stone circles, gourmet hotspots, castles, stately homes, historic ships and enough literary locations to fill a book. From the world-famous to the well-hidden, our trips will help you discover all the elements that make Britain truly great.

History, cities, food, scenery, the arts – we've unearthed the best experiences and crafted them into superb drives. And if you've only got time for one trip, make it one of our 10 Classic Trips, which take you to the very best of Great Britain. Turn the page to get started.

Kylesku Bridge, Scotland

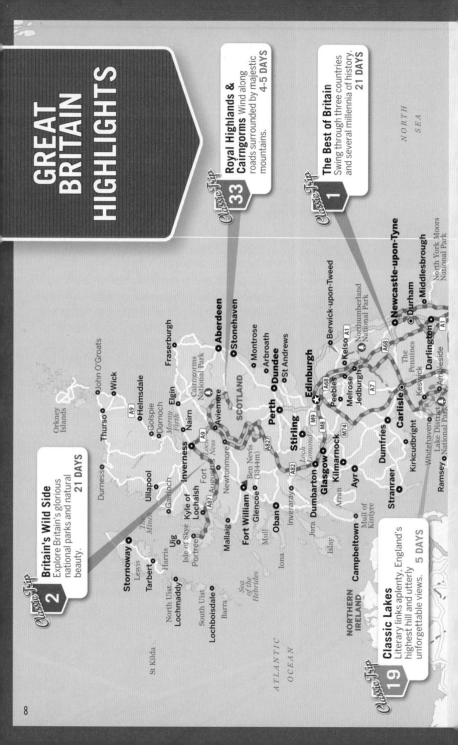

GREAT BRITAIN HIGHLIGHTS

Britain's Wild Side Explore Britain's glorious national parks and natural beauty. **21 DAYS**

Classic Trip 33

Royal Highlands & Cairngorms Wind along roads surrounded by majestic mountains. **4-5 DAYS**

Classic Trip 1

The Best of Britain Swing through three countries and several millennia of history. **21 DAYS**

Classic Trip 19

Classic Lakes Literary links aplenty, England's highest hill and utterly unforgettable views. **5 DAYS**

Orkney Islands
Durness
Thurso
John O'Groats
Wick
A9
Helmsdale
Golspie
Dornoch
Stornoway
Lewis
The Minch
Ullapool
St Kilda
Tarbert
Harris
North Uist
Lochmaddy
Uig
Gairloch
Moray Firth
Elgin
Fraserburgh
Isle of Skye
Kyle of Lochalsh
Inverness
Nairn
Portree
Cairngorms National Park
South Uist
Lochboisdale
A87
Fort Augustus
Loch Ness
Aviemore
Aberdeen
Barra
Mallaig
Newtonmore
Stonehaven
SCOTLAND
Sea of the Hebrides
Fort William
Ben Nevis (1344m)
Glencoe
Montrose
Mull
A827
Arbroath
ATLANTIC OCEAN
Oban
Perth
Dundee
Iona
St Andrews
Inveraray
A82
Stirling
Loch Lomond
Jura
Dumbarton
M9
Edinburgh
Islay
Glasgow
M8
A68
Berwick-upon-Tweed
Arran
Kilmarnock
Peebles
NORTHERN IRELAND
M74
Kelso
A1
Campbeltown
Ayr
Melrose
Jedburgh
Northumberland National Park
Mull of Kintyre
A7
Dumfries
A68
Stranraer
Newcastle-upon-Tyne
Carlisle
The Pennines
Durham
NORTH SEA
Kirkcudbright
Keswick
Middlesbrough
Whitehaven
Darlington
Ramsey
Lake District National Park
Ambleside
A1
North York Moors National Park

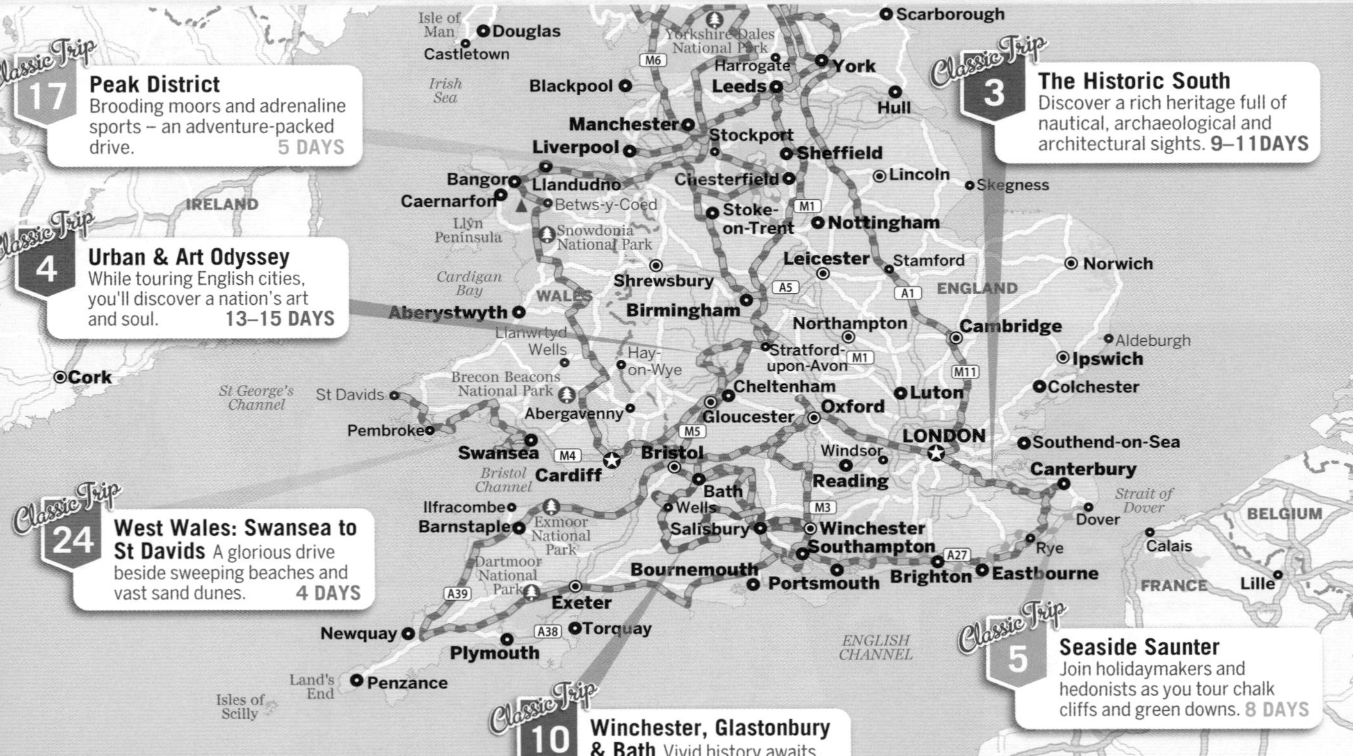
Classic Trip
17
Peak District
Brooding moors and adrenaline sports – an adventure-packed drive.
5 DAYS
Classic Trip
4
Urban & Art Odyssey
While touring English cities, you'll discover a nation's art and soul.
13–15 DAYS
Classic Trip
24
West Wales: Swansea to St Davids
A glorious drive beside sweeping beaches and vast sand dunes.
4 DAYS
Classic Trip
3
The Historic South
Discover a rich heritage full of nautical, archaeological and architectural sights.
9–11DAYS
Classic Trip
5
Seaside Saunter
Join holidaymakers and hedonists as you tour chalk cliffs and green downs.
8 DAYS
Classic Trip
10
Winchester, Glastonbury & Bath
Vivid history awaits, from stone circles to soaring cathedrals.
12-14 DAYS
Isle of Man
Douglas
Castletown
Irish Sea
IRELAND
Cork
St George's Channel
Cardigan Bay
WALES
ENGLAND
Scarborough
York
Harrogate
Yorkshire Dales National Park
M6
Blackpool
Leeds
Hull
Manchester
Stockport
Liverpool
Sheffield
Lincoln
Skegness
Bangor
Llandudno
Chesterfield
Caernarfon
Betws-y-Coed
Stoke-on-Trent
M1
Nottingham
Llŷn Peninsula
Snowdonia National Park
Leicester
Stamford
Norwich
Shrewsbury
A5
A1
Birmingham
Aberystwyth
Llanwrtyd Wells
Northampton
Cambridge
Aldeburgh
Hay-on-Wye
Stratford-upon-Avon
M1
Ipswich
M11
Brecon Beacons National Park
Cheltenham
Luton
Colchester
St Davids
Gloucester
Oxford
Abergavenny
M5
LONDON
Pembroke
Swansea
M4
Bristol
Windsor
Southend-on-Sea
Cardiff
Reading
Canterbury
Bristol Channel
Bath
Strait of Dover
Dover
Ilfracombe
Wells
M3
BELGIUM
Exmoor National Park
Barnstaple
Salisbury
Winchester
Calais
Southampton
Rye
A27
Dartmoor National Park
Bournemouth
Portsmouth
Brighton
Eastbourne
FRANCE
Lille
A39
Exeter
Newquay
A38
Torquay
Plymouth
ENGLISH CHANNEL
Land's End
Penzance
Isles of Scilly
0
200 km
0
100 miles
N
Caen

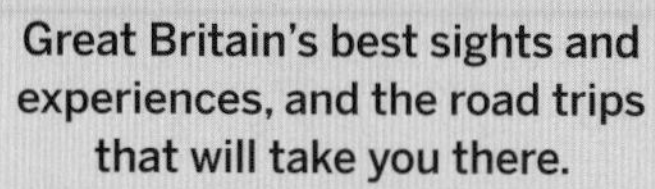
Great Britain's best sights and experiences, and the road trips that will take you there.

GREAT BRITAIN HIGHLIGHTS

Scottish Lochs & Mountains

Scotland's wild places abound in breathtaking views: spray-dashed coasts; glinting lochs; imposing mountains. The scenery here is truly awe-inspiring. Drive right into the views on **Trip 33: Royal Highlands & Cairngorms**, which delivers castles, peaks and wild landscapes galore – and the chance to explore the Royal Family's summer holiday haunts.

Trips    31 32 33 34 35

Torridon Hiking Beinn Alligin

Edinburgh Street performance for Edinburgh Fringe

Edinburgh

Famous for festivals, and especially lively in the summer, Edinburgh is a city of many moods. Glimpse them in a daffodil-framed castle silhouetted against a blue spring sky or on a chill December morning when the fog envelopes the spires of the Old Town. Discover your own version of the city on **Trip 1: The Best of Britain**, which sweeps the length of the country, from one blockbuster sight to the next.

Trip 1

The West Country

Britain's wild western corner is well worth the trip to the very end of England. Here tawny moors roll to jagged cliffs, ancient fishing ports tuck into spectacular cliffs, and sandy beaches stretch for miles. Find your favourite southwest spot on **Trip 14: Epic Cornwall**, which loops through Arthurian ruins, surfer bays and foodie ports.

Trips 11 12 13 14

Bath

Britain boasts many great cities, but Bath is the belle of the ball. The natural hot springs that bubble to the surface prompted the Romans to build a health resort here, while the Georgians turned the city into a fashionable watering hole. Soaking up Bath's sumptuous architecture is a highlight of **Trip 10: Winchester, Glastonbury & Bath**, a route also rich in cathedrals, ancient sites and myth.

Trips 1 3 10 15

JAN KRANENDONK / SHUTTERSTOCK © LEADINGLIGHTS / GETTY IMAGES ©

The Cotswolds Hikers approaching Broadway

BEST ROADS FOR DRIVING

A939 Scottish Highlands Drive beside ski slopes at roller-coaster Lecht Pass. **Trip** 33

A379 South Devon Beaches, first-gear bends and a straight-as-an-arrow coast road. **Trip** 13

A4086 Snowdonia Climb past the scree-scattered slopes of Pen-y-Pass. **Trip** 25

Off A896 Bealach na Ba Gradients of 25% and dramatic Isle of Skye views. **Trip** 32

B3157 Portland Glorious driving beside a fossil-rich shore. **Trip** 12

The Cotswolds

The most wonderful thing about the Cotswolds is that no matter where you go or how lost you get, you'll still end up in a village of honey-coloured stone complete with rose-clad cottages, an ancient pub and a view of the lush green hills. Find your very own slice of medieval England on **Trip 15: The Cotswolds & Literary England**, a tour of impossibly picturesque villages, with prestigious literary locations thrown in.

Trip 15

Wiltshire Stonehenge

Stonehenge

Mysterious and compelling, Stonehenge is Britain's most iconic ancient site. People have been drawn to this myth-laden ring of bluestones for the last 5000 years, and we still don't know quite why it was built. Come up with your own theories while gazing at the 50-ton megaliths on **Trip 3: The Historic South**, a voyage which charts a centuries-long timeline through Britain's compelling past.

Trips 1 3 10

BEST SEAFOOD STOPS

Wheeler's Oyster Bar Famously fabulous molluscs. **Trip** 6

Potted Lobster Bamburgh lobster and seafood platters. **Trip** 23

Crab House Cafe Super-fresh crustaceans and fish. **Trip** 12

Robson & Sons Kippers, just as the Queen likes them. **Trip** 23

Webbe's at the Fish Cafe Fabulous seafood down on the south coast. **Trip** 5

DAVID IONUT / SHUTTERSTOCK ©

HIGHLIGHTS

Oxford All Souls College

Wales Snowdonia National Park

Welsh Mountains

Rugged Wales has rocky mountain peaks, glacier-hewn valleys, sinuous shores, sparkling lakes, and charm-infused villages. The high point (literally) is Snowdonia, a wild and remote place offering hikes to lofty summits, adrenaline sports and off-the-beaten-track explorations. Tap into the wilderness vibe on **Trip 25: Snowdonia National Park**.

Trips 2 25 26 27

Cambridge

Adorned with exquisite architecture and steeped in tradition, Cambridge is a university town extraordinaire. The tightly packed core of ancient colleges, the picturesque riverside 'Backs' (college gardens) and the surrounding green meadows linger in your mind long after you leave. Prepare to fall more than a little in love on **Trip 8: Around the Cam**, which also explores the city's beautiful surrounds.

Trip 8

Oxford

For centuries, the brilliant minds and august institutions of Oxford University have made Oxford famous across the globe. Glimpse this revered world as you stroll hushed college quads and cobbled lanes roamed by cycling students. Touch base with your inner academic on **Trip 7: Royalty & the Thames Valley**, as it takes in prestigious southern sights.

Trips 1 3 7

HIGHLIGHTS

Northern Wildernesses

Poets and painters have long championed Britain's remote northern landscapes, which still hold a haunting appeal. Here you'll find moors, mountains, whaleback fells, Roman ruins and glistening lakes. Motor through this craggy corner of England, and take in its literary links, on **Trip 19: Classic Lakes**.

Trips 2 19 20 21 22 

Stratford-upon-Avon

The pretty English Midlands town of Stratford-upon-Avon is famed around the world as the birthplace of the nation's best-known dramatist, William Shakespeare. Today, the town's tight knot of Tudor streets forms a living map of Shakespeare's life and times. Visit his historic houses on a voyage around the pick of the country's top sights with **Trip 1: The Best of Britain**.

Trips    1 4 15

S-F / SHUTTERSTOCK ©

(left) **Stratford-upon-Avon** Birthplace of William Shakespeare;
(below) **Walltown** Hadrian's Wall

JUSTIN FOULKES / LONELY PLANET ©

Blenheim Palace

One of Britain's grandest stately homes, this early-18th century baroque confection is overpoweringly ornate. Objects d'art, ostentatious oil paintings and decadent decor fill grand rooms overlooking lavish grounds. Imagine living there when you drop by on **Trip 3: The Historic South**.

Trips  

BEST CASTLES & STATELY HOMES

Windsor Castle Nosey round the Queen's favourite home. **Trip** 7

Castle Howard Stunning, baroque setting for Brideshead Revisited. **Trips** 4 21

Beaumaris Castle A 13th-century masterpiece. **Trip** 28

Chatsworth House The exquisite 'palace of the Peak District'. **Trip** 17

Dover Castle Here, 12th-century defences meet secret WWII tunnels. **Trip** 5

Seasalter Oysters at the Sportsman Pub

History

In Great Britain the past is ever present. Everywhere lies evidence of a heritage stretching back thousands of years – from stone circles to palaces, via cathedrals, castles and stately homes. This history is a thread that runs through the entire country – it's one our trips help you explore.

3 **The Historic South** Stonehenge, Unesco-listed city Bath, sublime cathedrals and Napoleonic ships.

18 **Midlands Battlefields, Castles & Stately Homes** Indulge your inner royalty enthusiast and medieval knight.

22 **Hadrian's Wall** Haunting landscapes and Britain's blockbuster Roman site.

10 **Winchester, Glastonbury & Bath** Expect prehistoric monuments, cathedrals and Arthurian myths.

Mountains & Moors

Awe-inspiring mountains, wildly beautiful moors. Great Britain can claim superb landscapes – these are truly unforgettable drives, from Scotland's soaring Highlands and bewitching lochs to the more intimate peaks of Wales. In between you'll encounter the often-eerie beauty of the northern lakes and moors.

33 **Royal Highlands & Cairngorms** Spectacular scenery encircling the Queen's summer home.

19 **Classic Lakes** A feast of mountains, valleys and views.

25 **Snowdonia National Park** Adventure sports await all around the highest summit in Wales.

17 **Peak District** Ancient stone villages shelter among hills, valleys, gorges and lakes.

Coasts

This island nation is blessed by beautiful shores. Surfer hang-outs, expansive sand dunes, fossil-filled cliffs, golden beaches, geology-rich bays, remote islands, seafood havens and genteel resorts flanked by promenades and piers – they're all here. What's more they all link up into routes making for epic drives, where the sea is always by your side.

12 **Jurassic Coast** A photogenic cruise past age-old, sea-sculpted cliffs, stacks and bays.

23 **Northumbria** Castles and islands of singular beauty adorn the northwest coast.

24 **West Wales: Swansea to St Davids** Discover surf breaks, sand dunes and tranquil farms.

36 **Ferry-Hopping** Encounter beautiful beaches and laid-back island life in Scotland's Hebrides.

BAS MEELKER / SHUTTERSTOCK ©

Balmoral Castle A royal private residence

Urban Adventures

Britain's cities are among its most appealing assets – thriving urban areas rich in history, architecture, warmth and wit. It's often in these centres of contemporary culture that the country's diverse nature emerges; the experiences you have here may well prove some of the most memorable of your trip.

4 Urban & Art Odyssey Revelling in dynamic cities; a metropolitan dream.

1 The Best of Britain London, Bath, Cardiff, Oxford, Edinburgh – hard to beat.

5 Seaside Saunter Exploring coastal urban zones, from quaint Rye to gorgeous Brighton.

7 Royalty & the Thames Valley Chic Windsor, Henley and Oxford (plus Harry Potter too).

Art & Architecture

Britain's love affair with the arts has left a lasting legacy. You'll encounter it everywhere: from Shakespeare's birthplace to the Beatles' home town, via guerrilla artists and futuristic galleries. Architectural masterpieces pepper villages, land- and cityscapes .

15 The Cotswolds & Literary England Touring beautiful Bath, Cotswold villages and literary Stratford-upon-Avon.

8 Around the Cam Enchanting explorations of university-city Cambridge and its gorgeous surrounds.

3 The Historic South Three spectacular cathedrals, plus London and Bath's architectural delights.

4 Urban & Art Odyssey The pick of modern Britain's contemporary art.

Food & Drink

Britain boasts some seriously good food. Everywhere you'll enjoy the emphasis on all things local and seasonal – and often organic too. Regional treats include net-fresh seafood, succulent lamb and tangy cheese. And, once you've parked the car for the night, there's also craft beer, fine wines and whisky galore.

6 Kent: History, Art, Hops & Grapes Fine dining, oysters and breweries in England's rural south east.

13 South Devon Discover vineyards, the freshest seafood and a Michelin-starred eatery.

14 Epic Cornwall A county still in the vanguard of Britain's culinary renaissance – plus great pasties too.

35 Whisky Trails Spectacular Scottish scenery and scores of distilleries. Bliss.

NEED TO KNOW

CURRENCY
Pound sterling (£)

LANGUAGE
English; also Welsh and Scottish Gaelic

VISAS
Generally not needed for stays of up to six months. Britain is not a member of the Schengen Zone, so you will need to show your passport when arriving and leaving from the UK border.

FUEL
Urban petrol (gas) stations are plentiful; service stations are regularly spaced on motorways. Fill up before heading into rural areas, though, where they're scarcer. Expect to pay around £1.25 per litre.

RENTAL CARS
Avis (www.avis.co.uk)

Budget (www.budget.co.uk)

Europcar (www.europcar.co.uk)

Thrifty (www.thrifty.co.uk)

IMPORTANT NUMBERS
Emergency (☎112 or ☎999) Police, fire, ambulance, mountain rescue, coastguard

AA (☎0800 88 77 66) Roadside assistance

RAC (☎0330 159 0740) Roadside assistance

Climate

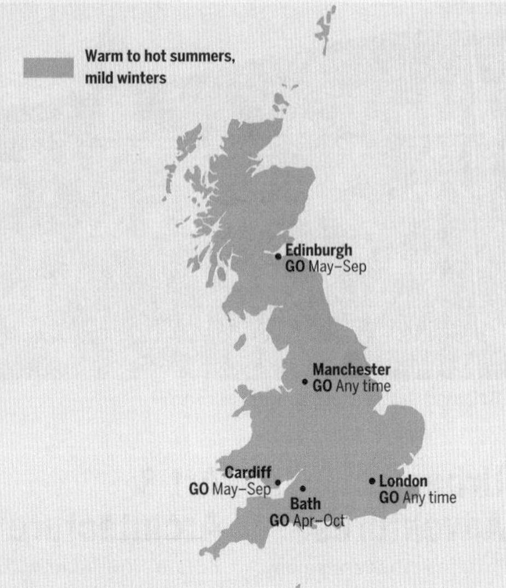

When to Go

High Season (Jun–Aug)
» Weather at its best. Accommodation rates peak – especially for August school holidays.

» Roads are busy, especially in seaside areas, national parks and popular cities such as Oxford, Bath, Edinburgh and York.

Shoulder (Mar–May, Sep & Oct)
» Crowds reduce. Prices drop.

» Weather often good. March to May has both sunny spells and sudden showers; September to October can feature balmy Indian summers.

» For outdoor activities in much of Scotland, May and September are the best months.

Low Season (Nov–Feb)
» Wet and cold. Snow falls in mountain areas, especially up north.

» Opening hours reduced October to Easter; some places shut for winter. Big-city sights (particularly London's) operate all year.

Your Daily Budget

Budget: Less than £60

» Dorm beds: £15–30

» Budget hotel double: under £65 (London under £100)

» Cheap cafe and pub meals: £7–11

Midrange: £60–120

» Double hotel or B&B room: £65–130 (London £100–200)

» Restaurant main meal: £12–22

Top End: More than £120

» Four-star hotel room: from £130 (London from £200)

» Three-course meal in a good restaurant: around £40

» Car rental per day: from £35

Eating

Restaurants From cheap and cheerful to Michelin-starred, covering all cuisines.

Pubs Serve reasonably priced meals, some are top notch.

Cafes Good daytime option for casual breakfasts, lunch or afternoon tea.

Vegetarian Find meat-free restaurants in towns and cities. But rural menus may contain just one 'choice'.

Sleeping

Hotels Anything from small, budget town houses to grand, boutique mansions.

B&Bs Range from a room in someone's house (with shared bathroom) to luxury spoils.

Inns Rooms above rural pubs; can be a cosy choice.

Hostels Bare-bones, often dorm-style accommodation.

Arriving in Great Britain

Heathrow airport Trains, London Underground (tube) and buses to central London from 5am to around midnight (night buses run later) £5.10– £25. Taxis to central London cost £50 to £100.

Gatwick airport Trains to central London from 4.30am to 1.35am £10– £20; 24hr buses (hourly) to central London from £10. Taxis to central London £100.

Mobile Phones

The UK uses the GSM 900/1800 network, which covers Europe, Australia and New Zealand, but isn't compatible with the North American GSM 1900, although most modern mobiles can function on both networks.

Internet Access

» Mobile broadband coverage is good in urban centres, but limited in rural areas – using a local SIM card helps keep data costs down.

» Most accommodation providers and many eateries have wi-fi access.

» Internet cafes (from £1 per hour) are rare away from tourist spots.

Money

ATMs ('cash machines') are common in cities and towns. Visa and MasterCard are widely accepted although some B&Bs take cash only.

Tipping

Restaurants Around 10%-15% in eateries with table service.

Pubs & Bars If you order and pay at the bar, tips are not expected. If you order at the table, your meal is brought to you, and you pay afterwards, then 10% is usual.

Taxis Roughly 10%.

Useful Websites

BBC (www.bbc.co.uk) National broadcaster.

Lonely Planet (www.lonelyplanet.com/great-britain) Destination info, hotel bookings, traveller forum and more.

Visit Britain (www.visitbritain.com) Comprehensive tourist information.

Opening Hours

In rural areas opening hours may be shorter between October and April; some places close completely.

Banks 9.30am to 4pm or 5pm Monday to Friday; some open 9.30am to 1pm Saturday.

Pubs & Bars Noon to 11pm Monday to Thursday, until 1am Friday and Saturday, 12.30pm to 11pm Sunday.

Shops 9am to 5.30pm or 6pm Monday to Saturday, and often 11am to 5pm Sunday. Cities have 24/7 convenience stores.

Restaurants Lunch is noon to 3pm, dinner 6pm to 9pm or 10pm (later in cities).

For more, see Great Britain Driving Guide (p426).

CITY GUIDE

LONDON

Britain's capital of cool is endlessly fascinating. Its multicultural streets and unique sights, together with the city's strong historical story, popular culture, architecture and art, create an irresistible metropolis. Add a world's worth of cuisines and you get a truly great city that's easy to love and hard to leave.

Buckingham Palace Band during a Changing of the Guard ceremony

Getting Around

London has a congestion charge to reduce central traffic. For prices and details of affected areas, see www.tfl.gov.uk/modes/driving/congestion-charge.

Alternatively, use TFL's frequent London Underground ('tube') and bus networks – see www.tfl.gov.uk.

Parking

Street parking is scarce and costly; wheel clampers are diligent. Few central hotels offer parking; if they do it comes at a premium. Q-Park (www.q-park.co.uk) and the NCP (www.ncp.co.uk) run numerous London car parks.

DAVID STEELE / SHUTTERSTOCK ©

Where to Eat

London is an undisputed dining destination. Top-notch Michelin-starred restaurants abound, but it's the A–Z diversity that's head-spinning. Sample it in the eclectic venues of the West End, South Bank, Hammersmith and Islington.

Where to Stay

Accommodation in London is expensive, but you might snag pre-booked deals in the central West End, edge-of-centre South Bank, traveller-friendly Earl's Court and still-cool Notting Hill.

Useful Websites

Lonely Planet (www.lonelyplanet.com/london) Bookings and more.

Visit London (www.visitlondon.com) The official visitor guide.

Transport for London (www.tfl.gov.uk) Essential tool for staying mobile.

Trips Through London: 

TOP EXPERIENCES

➡ Follow the Royals

From Buckingham Palace to the Royal Mews, via the Changing of the Guard – exploring London's regal landmarks is an A-list treat.

➡ Experience Park Life

London's green oases, among them Regent's Park and Hyde Park, are a joy; perfect places for strolling, picnicking and people-watching.

➡ Visit Theatreland

The world capital of theatre, London excels at both mammoth musicals and highbrow dramas. Top venues include the National, Shakespeare Globe and anywhere in the West End.

➡ Go Shopping

They may be posh – Harrods and Harvey Nichols. Or street stalls – Portobello Road, Spitalfields and Bourough Market. Either way they're great places to shop.

➡ Get Cultural

London's museums and galleries are simply superb. Must-sees include the National Portrait Gallery, the Tate Modern, the Victoria & Albert, Science and British museums

➡ Get Eating

From serious gastronomy to superb street food, London has it all. Fine neighbourhoods to get a taste include the West End, East End, Fitzrovia and Notting Hill.

➡ Bar-Hop

In London the pub is the hub of local social life – dip into it in sophisticated Soho, boho Hoxton, grungy Camden and neighbourhood-feel Notting Hill.

MURATART / SHUTTERSTOCK ©

Cardiff Panoramic view of Cardiff Bay

CARDIFF

Newly confident Cardiff delights in being one of Britain's leading urban centres. Stretching from ancient Cardiff Castle to the ultramodern architecture at Cardiff Bay, this city's aura of loving life is infectious – tap into it at a rugby match or in any of the thriving live-music venues, craft-beer pubs and endless bars.

Getting Around

Cardiff doesn't usually pose many difficulties for drivers, although most of the central city streets between Westgate St, Castle St and St David's are closed to traffic. Local bus services are extensive.

Parking

Car parks dot the city centre; it's also often possible to find free street parking in the suburbs. Pontcanna's Cathedral Rd has unrestricted parking, but gets busy in working hours.

Where to Eat

Appealing eateries cluster in the streets just south of Cardiff Castle. The chic Pontcanna district is another good foodie focus point, boasting bistros, gastropubs and modern Indian cuisine.

Where to Stay

Revelers love the plentiful budget and upmarket accommodation of central Cardiff. Light sleepers should head for Pontcanna and the Victorian townhouse B&Bs of leafy Cathedral Rd, just 20 minutes' walk from the city centre.

Useful Websites

Visit Cardiff (www.visitcardiff.com) The city's official tourism website.

Cardiff Bus (www.cardiffbus.com) Details the city's bus links.

Trips Through Cardiff:

Manchester Mackie Mayor food hall

MANCHESTER

The uncrowned capital of the north overflows with history and culture. World-class venues include the Imperial War Museum North, Manchester Art Gallery and the People's History Museum. But what makes Manchester really fun is the happy swirl of hedonism that lets you dine, drink and dance yourself into oblivion.

Getting Around

Central Manchester is relatively easy to navigate by car, but excellent public transport systems might prompt you to get out from behind the wheel. Three free bus routes loop around the centre, while frequent Metrolink trams shuttle to outlying areas.

Parking

Manchester has reasonable city-centre car parks and on-street parking provision, although demand can be high and charges can mount up. The city's on-street parking bays are usually free to use between 8pm and 8am; many of the bigger hotels have on-site parking too, although there can be an extra charge.

Where to Eat

Manchester's choice of restaurants is second only to London. Spinningfields, just off Deansgate, has some interesting spots while the Northern Quarter is great for off-beat cafes and organic eats. The city's Indian and Middle Eastern restaurants are legendary, while the outlying suburb of Didsbury is where in-the-know Mancunians like to dine.

Where to Stay

Numerous hotels aimed at business travellers and sports fans dot the city centre, placing you firmly in the heart of the action. More discerning visitors have a choice of designer digs and boutique lodgings. Beds are in short supply on home match days during the football season (August to May).

Useful Websites

Visit Manchster (www.visitmanchester.com) Official tourism website.

BBC Manchester (www.bbc.co.uk/manchester) News, weather and travel updates.

Restaurants of Manchester (www.restaurantsofmanchester.com) Reliable guide to the city's eateries.

Trips Through Manchester: 

EDINBURGH

Exquisite Edinburgh's quirky, come-hither nooks tempt you to explore. Draped across rocky hills, its cultured soul has seen it dubbed the Athens of the North. But this famously down-to-earth city also mocks artistic pretensions. Come here to delight in crowded pubs, decadent restaurants, beer-fuelled poets, foul-mouthed comedians and fun festivals.

Getting Around

A car in central Edinburgh is more of a liability than a convenience. There's restricted access on Princes St, George St and Charlotte Sq, and many streets are one way. Fortunately, as well as a handy tram line, the city has an extensive bus network.

Parking

Finding a parking place in the city centre is like striking gold. There's no parking on main roads into the city from 7.30am to 6.30pm Monday to Saturday. Large long-stay car parks are found at St James Centre, Greenside Pl, New St, Castle Tce and Morrison St.

DOMHNALL DODS / SHUTTERSTOCK ©

Edinburgh Royal Edinburgh Military Tattoo

TOP EXPERIENCES

➡ Stroll the Royal Mile

This mile-long street leads from Edinburgh Castle to the Palace of Holyroodhouse, via St Giles Cathedral and the Scottish Parliament, taking in scores of restaurants, street performers and bars.

➡ Climb Arthur's Seat

Scaling the summit of Edinburgh's 251m-high miniature mountains involves a hike through a former royal hunting ground. It also reveals wrap-around city views.

➡ Go on a Pub Crawl

Edinburgh's 19th- and early-20th-century pubs have often preserved their original decor and serve a staggering selection of malt whiskies.

➡ Get Cultural

In this arts-aware city you're spoilt for choice, from live music (traditional to indie) to theatre and comedy. Even if a festival isn't underway, there's always something going on.

Where to Eat

Fabulous-for-foodies Edinburgh has more restaurants per head of population than any other UK city. Top choices cluster around the High St (Royal Mile); good-value eats concentrate in Bruntsfield and Newington; for fine dining head for New Town and Leith.

Where to Stay

Edinburgh's sleep spots include boutique hotels and gorgeous B&Bs set in Victorian and Georgian town houses. Old Town accommodation is central but tends to be either very budget or fairly pricey. New Town choices can be cheaper and are still in the heart of things.

Useful Websites

This is Edinburgh (www.edinburgh.org) Official tourism website.

Edinburgh Festivals (www.edinburghfestivalcity.com) Info on the city's big events.

Trips Through Edinburgh: 1

Cloud-snagged mountains, wild moors, winding country lanes – Great Britain offers irresistible drives. Our guide to each region and its road trips will help you chose the very best routes and experiences.

Wales

Rugged, hauntingly beautiful and remote, Wales is a place to live Cardiff's city high-life or get well away from the crowds on sweeping sand-dunes and dramatic peaks.

Scale some mountains on Trip 25

Go barefoot beachcombing on Trip 24

Southwest England

The wild West Country makes for breathtaking drives: sea-carved shores, wildlife-rich moors, seafood ports and a lush landscape laced with myth.

Discover a powerful past on Trip 10

Enjoy awesome food and epic views on Trip 14

Scotland

Driving in Scotland is simply spectacular. Here mountains encircle glistening lochs, fairy-tale castles vie to be photographed, cities greet you with a whisky, and islands tempt you off shore.

Go ferry-hopping on Trip 36

Drink in fit-for-royalty Highland views on Trip 33

Lake District & Northern England

In this slice of northern England the scenery notches up a gear. From the so-scenic Lakes to dramatic, wind-blasted moors. And then there's the peerless Roman remnant that is Hadrian's Wall.

Discover lake-land literary connections on Trip 19

Motor across wild moorland on Trip 

Central England

Rolling hills and a rich heritage define the drives at Britain's core. Quaint villages usher in imposing castles and grand stately homes.

Explore a glorious Georgian cityscape on Trip 15

Encounter a right royal past on Trip 18

Southern & Eastern England

England's southern, eastern corner is full of charm. Here you can motor from cool-again resorts to exquisite university cities via a trail of castles, ancient villages and foodie pit stops.

Explore southern resort towns on Trip 

Get an English history fix on Trip 8

GREAT BRITAIN'S *Classic Trips*

NIKADA / GETTY IMAGES ©

What is a Classic Trip?

All the trips in this book show you the best of Great Britain, but we've chosen 10 as our all-time favourites. These are our Classic Trips – the ones that lead you to the best of the iconic sights, the top activities and the unique British experiences. Turn the page to see our cross-regional Classic Trips, and look for more Classic Trips on the following pages:

Above: Oxford University

Left: View from Castle Crag to Borrowdale, Lake District

Classic Trip

The Best of Britain

Journey through three countries and several millennia of history as you take in a greatest hits parade of Britain's chart-topping sights.

TRIP HIGHLIGHTS

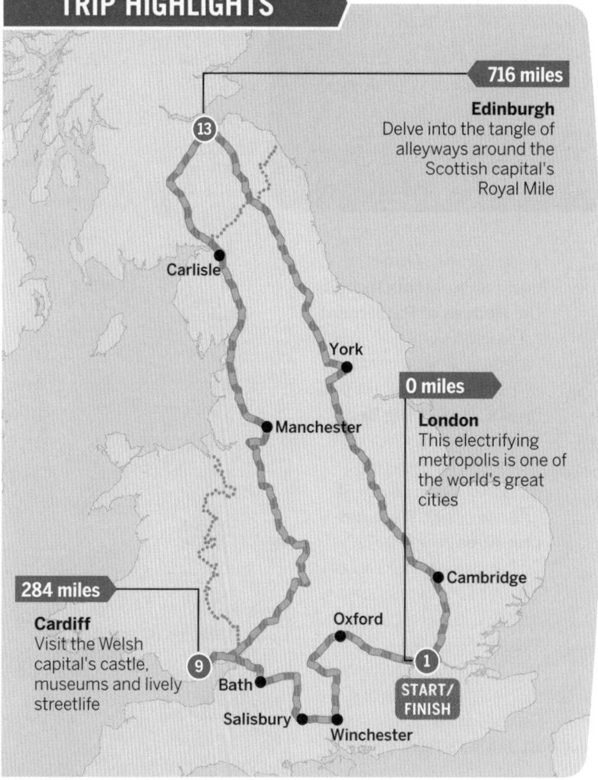

716 miles

Edinburgh
Delve into the tangle of alleyways around the Scottish capital's Royal Mile

0 miles

London
This electrifying metropolis is one of the world's great cities

284 miles

Cardiff
Visit the Welsh capital's castle, museums and lively streetlife

13 Carlisle York Manchester Cambridge Oxford 1 START/FINISH 9 Bath Salisbury Winchester

21 DAYS
1128 MILES / 1815KM

GREAT FOR...

BEST TIME TO GO

Myriad festivals take place between May and September.

Britain's biggest city spread below the London Eye.

Follow atmospheric footpaths through the world's largest stone circle at Avebury.

London View from the London Eye

Classic Trip

1 The Best of Britain

London's bright lights, blockbuster attractions, and stirring history bookend this epic expedition around the British mainland. In between, you'll explore ancient ruins and historic architecture, follow trails that lead from King Arthur to Shakespeare, and discover masterpiece-filled museums and galleries, all connected by quaint villages, patchworked farmland and glorious rolling green open countryside. Rest from life on the road with the best of British drinking, dining and nightlife.

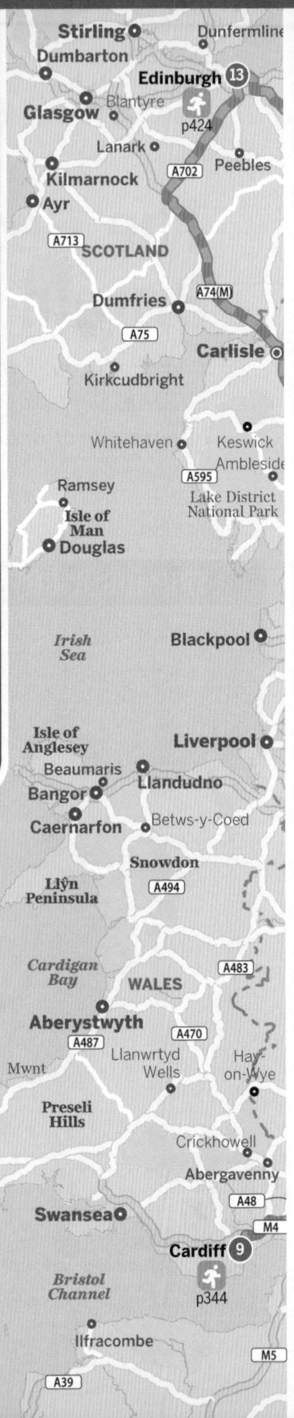

TRIP HIGHLIGHT

1 London

Prepare for your trip with at least a couple of days in Britain's most exhilarating city. Traversed by the serpentine River Thames, London is awash with instantly recognisable landmarks and open spaces, from **Trafalgar Square** (Charing Cross or Embankment) to the **London Eye** (www.londoneye.com; near County Hall, SE1; adult/child from £24.50/22; 10am-8.30pm, reduced hours in low season; Waterloo or Westminster). Other unmissable sights include the **Houses of Parliament** (tours 020-7219 4114; www.parliament.uk; Parliament Sq, SW1; Westminster), topped by clock tower **Big Ben** (www.parliament.uk/visiting/visiting-and-tours/tours-of-parliament/bigben; Bridge St; Westminster); **Westminster Abbey** (020-7222 5152; www.westminster-abbey.org; 20 Dean's Yard, SW1; adult/child £24/10, half price Wed 4.30pm; 9.30am-3.30pm Mon, Tue, Thu & Fri, to 6pm Wed, to 3pm Sat May-Aug, to 1pm Sat Sep-Apr; Westminster); **St James's Park** (www.

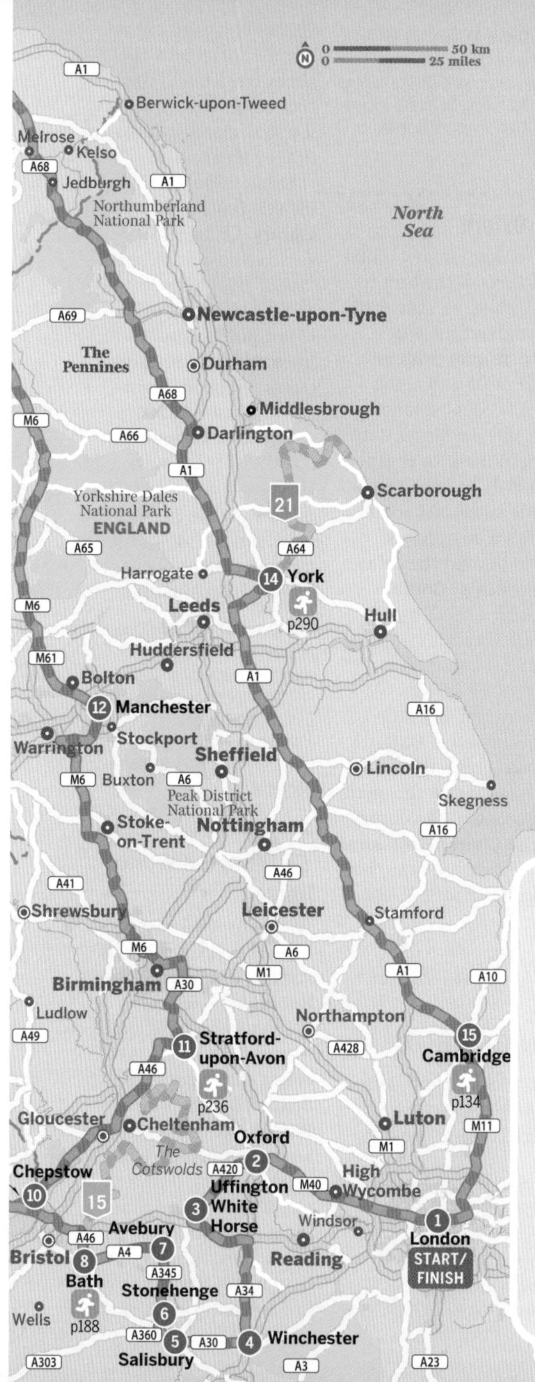

royalparks.org.uk/parks/st-jamess-park; The Mall, SW1; 5am-midnight; St James's Park or Green Park) and **Palace** (www.royal.uk/royal-residences-st-jamess-palace; Cleveland Row, SW1; Green Park); **Buckingham Palace** (0303 123 7300; www.rct.uk/visit/the-state-rooms-buckingham-palace; Buckingham Palace Rd, SW1; 9am-6pm mid-Jul–end Sep; Green Park or St James's Park); **Hyde Park** (www.royalparks.org.uk/parks/hyde-park; 5am-midnight; Marble Arch, Hyde Park Corner, Knightsbridge or Queensway); **Kensington Gardens** (0300 061 2000; www.royalparks.org.uk/parks/kensington-gardens; 6am-dusk; Queensway or Lancaster Gate) and **Palace** (www.hrp.org.uk/kensington-palace; Kensington Gardens, W8; adult/child £21.50/10.70, cheaper weekdays after 2pm; 10am-6pm, to 4pm Nov-Feb; High St Kensington); and **Tower Bridge** (020-7403 3761; www.towerbridge.org.

LINK YOUR TRIP

15 The Cotswolds & Literary England

From Bath, you can set out for a spin through the picturesque Cotswolds.

21 North York Moors & Coast

York is the starting point for a glorious drive through wild moorland and charming coastal villages.

uk; Tower Bridge, SE1; Ⓤ Tower Hill). World-leading, often-free museums and art galleries include the **Tate Modern** (☎020-7887 8888; www.tate.org.uk; Bankside, SE1; ⏲10am-6pm Sun-Thu, to 10pm Fri & Sat; Ⓤ Southwark) and the **British Museum** (☎020-7323 8000; www.britishmuseum.org; Great Russell St, WC1; ⏲10am-5pm, last entry 3.30pm; Ⓤ Tottenham Court Rd or Russell Sq).

London's drinking, dining and nightlife options are limitless (Soho and Shoreditch make great starting points), as are its entertainment venues, not least grand theatre stages such as **Shakespeare's Globe** (☎020-7401 9919; www.shakespearesglobe.com; 21 New Globe Walk, SE1; ⏲box office 10am-6pm; Ⓤ Blackfriars or London Bridge).

🛏 p47

The Drive » Take the M40 northwest through High Wycombe and the Chilterns Area of Outstanding Natural Beauty (AONB) to Oxford (59 miles in total).

❷ Oxford

The elegant honey-toned buildings of the university's colleges, scattered throughout the city, wrap around tranquil courtyards and along narrow cobbled lanes. The oldest colleges date back to the 13th century and little has changed inside since, although there's a busy, lively world beyond the college walls. **Christ Church** (☎01865-276492; www.chch.ox.ac.uk; St Aldate's; adult/child £15/14, pre-booking essential; ⏲10am-5pm Mon-Sat, from 2pm Sun) is the largest of all of Oxford's colleges, with the grandest quad. From the quad, you access 12th-century **Christ Church Cathedral** (☎01865-276150; www.chch.ox.ac.uk/cathedral; St Aldate's; ⏲10am-5pm Mon-Sat, from 2pm Sun), originally the abbey church and then the college chapel, before it was declared a cathedral by Henry VIII.

Other highlights include Oxford's **Bodleian Library** (☎01865-287400; www.bodleian.ox.ac.uk/bodley; Catte St; ⏲9am-5pm Mon-Sat, from 11am Sun), one of the oldest public libraries in the world; and Britain's oldest public museum, the 1683-established **Ashmolean Museum** (☎01865-278000; www.ashmolean.org; Beaumont St; ⏲10am-5pm Tue-Sun, to 8pm last Fri of month; 👪), second in repute only to London's British Museum.

The Drive » Head southwest on the A420 to Pusey and continue southwest on the B4508. You'll reach the car park for the White Horse 2.3 miles southwest of Uffington off the B4507, a 24-mile journey altogether.

❸ Uffington White Horse

Just below Oxfordshire's highest point, the highly stylised **Uffington White Horse** (NT; www.nationaltrust.org.uk; White Horse Hill; ⏲dawn-dusk) image is the oldest chalk figure in Britain, dating from the Bronze Age. It was created around 3000 years ago by cutting trenches out of the hill and filling them with blocks of chalk; local inhabitants have maintained the figure for centuries. Perhaps

TOP TIP: LONDON'S CONGESTION CHARGE

Central London levies a congestion charge from 7am to 10pm daily. Entering the 'C'-marked zone costs £15. You can pay online, at petrol stations or some shops.

In addition, if your car is not a new, cleaner, greener model, the Ultra Low Emission Zone (ULEZ) charge (£12.50) needs to be paid in the same zone 24/7.

You can pay online or over the phone. For full details, see the TFL website (www.tfl.gov.uk).

it was planned for the gods: it's best seen from the air above. It's a half-mile walk east through fields from the hillside car park.

The Drive » It's a 49-mile trip to Winchester: return to the B4507 and drive southeast to Ashbury and take the B4000 southeast to join the southbound A34.

4 Winchester

Set in a river valley, this ancient cathedral city was the capital of Saxon kings and a power base of bishops. It also evokes two of England's mightiest myth-makers: famous son Alfred the Great (commemorated by a **statue**) and King Arthur – a 700-year-old copy of the round table resides in Winchester's cavernous **Great Hall** (☎01962-846476; www.hants.gov.uk/greathall; Castle Ave; adult/child £3/free; ⏲10am-5pm), the only part of 11th-century Winchester Castle that Oliver Cromwell spared from destruction.

Winchester's architecture is exquisite, from the handsome Elizabethan and Regency buildings in the narrow streets to the wondrous **Winchester Cathedral** (☎01962-857200; www.winchester-cathedral.org.uk; The Close; adult/child £10/free; ⏲10am-4pm) at its core. One of southern England's most awe-inspiring buildings, the 11th-century cathedral has a fine Gothic facade and one of the longest medieval naves in Europe (164m). Other highlights including intricately carved medieval choir stalls, Jane Austen's grave (near the entrance, in the northern aisle) and one of the UK's finest illuminated manuscripts, the dazzling, four-volume Winchester Bible dating from the 12th-century. Book ahead for excellent tours of the ground floor, crypt and tower.

🛏 p47, p73, p151

The Drive » From Winchester, hop on the B3049 then the A30 for the 26-mile drive west to Salisbury.

5 Salisbury

Salisbury has been an important provincial city for more than a thousand years, and its streets form an architectural timeline ranging from medieval walls and half-timbered Tudor town houses to Georgian mansions and Victorian villas. Its centrepiece is the majestic 13th-century **Salisbury Cathedral** (☎01722-555150; www.salisburycathedral.org.uk; The Close; requested donation adult/child £7.50/3; ⏲9am-4pm Mon-Sat). This early English Gothic–style structure has an elaborate exterior decorated with pointed arches and flying buttresses, and is topped by Britain's tallest spire at 123m, which was added in the mid-14th century. Beyond the cathedral's highly decorative West Front, a small passageway leads into the 70m-long nave. In the north aisle look out for a fascinating medieval clock dating from 1386, probably the oldest working timepiece in the world. Don't miss the cathedral's original, 13th-century copy of the Magna Carta in the chapter house, or, if they've resumed, a 90-minute tower tour, which sees you climbing 332 vertigo-inducing steps to the base of the spire for jaw-dropping views across the city and the surrounding countryside.

The Drive » It's just 9.6 miles northwest from Salisbury via the A360 to other-worldly Stonehenge.

6 Stonehenge

Stonehenge (EH; ☎0370 333 1181; www.english-heritage.org.uk; near Amesbury; adult/child £21/13; ⏲9.30am-5pm, hours may vary; P) is one of Britain's most enduring archaeological mysteries: despite countless theories about the site's purpose, ranging from a sacrificial centre to a celestial timepiece, no one knows for sure what drove prehistoric Britons to expend so much time and effort on its construction. The first phase of building started around 3000 BCE, when

Classic Trip

BILLY STOCK / SHUTTERSTOCK ©

KIEV.VICTOR / SHUTTERSTOCK ©

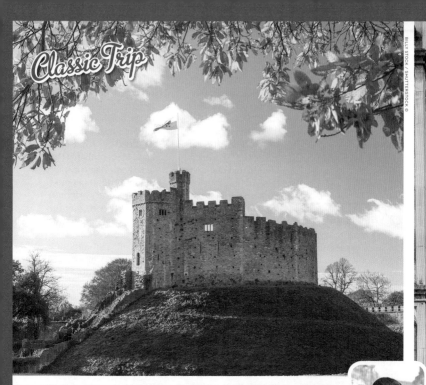

WHY THIS IS A CLASSIC TRIP
ANTHONY HAM, WRITER

Anything labelled Best of Britain has a lot to live up to, which this trip certainly does. The classy contemporary cities you'll visit here provide a nice counterpoint to so many sites where history is writ large upon the land. Throw in castles, cathedrals and Shakespeare's home town and you really will enjoy Britain's finest.

Above: Cardiff Castle
Left: Stonehenge
Right: Bodleian Library, Oxford University

the outer circular bank and ditch were erected. A thousand years later, an inner circle of granite stones, known as bluestones, was added.

An ultramodern makeover has brought an impressive visitor centre and the closure of an intrusive road (now restored to grassland). The result is a far stronger sense of historical context; dignity and mystery returned to an archaeological gem. A pathway frames the ring of massive stones. Although you can't walk in the circle, unless on a recommended **Stone Circle Access Visit** (☎0370 333 0605; www.english-heritage.org.uk; adult/child £47/28), you can get close-up views. Admission is through timed tickets – secure a place well in advance.

The Drive » Drive east to Durrington and take the A345 north, climbing over the grassy Pewsey Downs National Nature Reserve (home to another chalk figure, the Alton Barnes White Horse, dating from 1812), to reach Avebury (24 miles in total).

---

7 Avebury

With a diameter of 348m, **Avebury** (NT; ☎01672-539250; www.nationaltrust.org.uk; parking per day £7; ⏲dawn-dusk; P) is the largest stone circle in the world. It is also one of the oldest, dating from 2500 to 2200 BCE. Though it lacks the dramatic trilithons of its sister site Stonehenge, the massive

Classic Trip

stone circle is just as rewarding to visit. Today, more than 30 stones are in place (pillars show where missing stones would have been) and a large section of the village is actually inside the stones – footpaths wind around them, allowing you to really soak up the extraordinary atmosphere. Check whether the National Trust–run guided walks of the site (£3), which were suspended in 2020, have resumed.

The Drive » It's a 27-mile drive along the A4 past patchwork fields, country pubs and a smattering of villages to the Georgian streetscapes of Bath.

8 Bath

World Heritage–listed Bath was founded on top of natural hot springs and has been a tourist draw for some 2000 years. Its 18th-century heyday saw the construction of magnificent Georgian architecture from the 18th century. The best way to explore the city's Roman Baths complex and beautiful neoclassical buildings is on foot (p188).

Bath is known to many as a location in Jane Austen's novels, including *Persuasion* and *NorthOanger Abbey*. Although Austen lived in Bath for only five years, from 1801 to 1806, she remained a regular visitor and a keen student of the city's social scene. At the **Jane Austen Centre** (01225-443000; www.janeausten.co.uk; 40 Gay St; adult/child £12/6.20; 9.45am-5.30pm Apr-Oct, 10am-4pm Sun-Fri, 9.45am-5.30pm Sat Nov-Mar), guides in Regency costumes regale you with Austen-esque tales as you tour memorabilia relating to the writer's life in Bath.

p47. p73, p151, p203

The Drive » It's 56.5 miles from Bath to the Welsh capital. Take the A46 north and join the westbound M4 over the Severn Estuary on the six-lane, cable-stayed Second Severn Crossing bridge.

TRIP HIGHLIGHT

9 Cardiff

Between an ancient fort and ultramodern waterfront, Cardiff has been the capital of Wales since only 1955, but has embraced the role with vigour and is now one of Britain's leading urban centres, as you can see on a stroll (p344) through its compact streets.

Cardiff Castle (029-2087 8100; www.cardiffcastle.com; Castle St; adult/child £14.50/10, incl guided tour £19.50/14; 9am-6pm Mar-Oct, to 5pm Nov-Feb) has a medieval keep at its heart, but it's the later additions that really capture the imagination. Explore, and you may wind up concurring with the fortress's claim to be the most fascinating castle in Wales. Devoted mainly to art and natural history, the **National Museum Cardiff** (0300 111 2333; www.museum.wales/cardiff; Gorsedd Gardens, CF10 3NP; 10am-5pm Tue, Thu, Sat & Sun; P) fills a grand neoclassical building. It's both a part of the Welsh National Museum and one of Britain's best museums.

If you time it right, you can catch a fired-up rugby test at Cardiff's **Principality Stadium** (Millennium Stadium; tickets & tours 029-2082 2432; www.principalitystadium.wales; Westgate St; tours adult/child £13.75/9.90; tours 10am-5pm Mon-Sat, 10.15am-4pm Sun).

p47

The Drive » Take the A48 northeast for 32 miles, bypassing Newport, to riverside Chepstow.

10 Chepstow

Nestled in an S-bend in the River Wye, Chepstow (Welsh: Cas-gwent) was first developed as a base for the Norman conquest of southeast Wales, later prospering as a port for the timber and wine trades. As river-borne commerce gave way to the railways, Chepstow's importance diminished to reflect its name, which means 'market place' in Old English.

One of Britain's oldest castles, imposing **Chepstow Castle** (Cadw; ☎01291-624065; www.cadw.gov.wales; Bridge St; adult/child £6.50/3.90; ⏰10am-1pm & 2-5pm Wed-Sun Mar-Oct, to 4pm Nov-Feb; 👪) perches atop a limestone cliff overhanging the river, guarding the main river crossing from England into South Wales. Building commenced in 1067, less than a year after William the Conqueror invaded England, and it was extended over the centuries. Today there are plenty of towers, battlements and wall walks to explore. A cave in the cliff below the castle is one of many places where legend says King Arthur and his knights are napping until the day they're needed to save Britain.

The Drive » Farmland makes up most of this 68-mile drive. Head northeast on the A48 along the River Severn to Gloucester then continue northeast on the A46 to Stratford-upon-Avon.

⑪ Stratford-upon-Avon

Experiences linked to the life of Stratford's fêted son William Shakespeare range from the touristy (medieval re-creations and Bard-themed tearooms) to the humbling – Shakespeare's modest grave in **Holy Trinity Church** (☎01789-266316; www.stratford-upon-avon.org; Old Town; Shakespeare's grave adult/child £3/2; ⏰noon-2pm Mon-Thu, to 4pm Fri, 11am-4pm Sat) – and the sublime: a play by the **Royal Shakespeare Company** (RSC; ☎box office 01789-331111; www.rsc.org.uk; Waterside). One of the best ways to get a feel for the town's Tudor streets and willow-lined riverbanks is on foot (p236).

Combination tickets are available for the three houses associated with Shakespeare in town – Shakespeare's Birthplace (p79), Shakespeare's New Place (p79) and Hall's Croft. If you also plan to visit the childhood home of Shakespeare's wife, **Anne Hathaway's Cottage** (☎01789-338532; www.shakespeare.org.uk; Cottage Lane, Shottery; adult/child £12.50/8; ⏰9am-5pm Apr-Aug, to 4.30pm Sep & Oct, 10am-3.30pm Nov-Mar), and his mother's farm, **Mary Arden's Farm** (☎01789-338535; www.shakespeare.org.uk; Station Rd, Wilmcote; adult/child £15/10; ⏰10am-5pm Apr-Aug, to 4.30pm Sep & Oct; 👪), you can buy a

BRITAIN'S BEST FESTIVALS

Expect the following festivals to resume with gusto post-pandemic.

In London, see stunning blooms at the Royal Horticultural Society's **Chelsea Flower Show** (☎020-3176 5800; www.rhs.org.uk/chelsea; Royal Hospital Chelsea, Royal Hospital Rd, SW3; tickets £39.75-92.75; ⏰May; Ⓤ Sloane Sq); military bands and bear-skinned grenadiers during the martial pageant **Trooping the Colour** (www.householddivision.org.uk/trooping-the-colour; Horse Guards Parade, SW1; ⏰Jun; Ⓤ Westminster or Charing Cross); or steel drums, dancers and outrageous costumes at the famous multicultural Caribbean-style street festival **Notting Hill Carnival** (www.nhcarnival.org; ⏰Aug).

Wales' **National Eisteddfod** (Eisteddfod Genedlaethol Cymru; ☎08454-090900; www.eisteddfod.cymru; ⏰Aug) is descended from ancient Bardic tournaments. It's conducted in Welsh, but welcomes all entrants and visitors. It moves about each year, attracting some 150,000 visitors.

Edinburgh's most famous happenings are the **International Festival** (☎0131-473 2000; www.eif.co.uk; ⏰Aug-Sep) and **Fringe** (☎0131-226 0026; www.edfringe.com; ⏰Aug), but the city also has events throughout the year. Check the full list at www.edinburghfestivals.co.uk.

combination ticket covering all five properties.

Don't miss a pint with the locals at Stratford's oldest and most atmospheric pub, the 1470-built **Old Thatch Tavern** (www.oldthatchtavernstratford.co.uk; Greenhill St; ⌚11.30am-11pm Mon-Sat, from noon Sun; 📶).

The Drive » The fastest route from Stratford-upon-Avon to Manchester is to head northwest on Birmingham Rd and pick up the northbound M42, which becomes the M6. You'll see the hilly Peak District National Park to your east. It's a 116-mile journey; this stretch incurs road tolls that vary according to the time of day.

⓬ Manchester

A rich blend of history and culture is on show in this northern powerhouse's museums, galleries and innovative, multigenre art centres, such as **HOME** (☎0161-200 1500; www.homemcr.org; 2 Tony Wilson Pl, First St; tickets £5-25; ⌚box office noon-8pm, bar 10am-11pm Mon-Thu, to midnight Fri & Sat, 11am-10.30pm Sun; 🚌all city centre).

The **Manchester Art Gallery** (☎0161-235 8888; www.manchesterartgallery.org; Mosley St, M2 3JL; ⌚11am-4pm Thu-Sun; 🚊St Peter's Square) has a superb collection of British art and a hefty number of European masters. The older wing has an impressive selection that includes 37 Turner watercolours, as well as the country's best assemblage of Pre-Raphaelite art, while the newer gallery is home to 20th-century British art starring Lucien Freud, Francis Bacon, Stanley Spencer, Henry Moore and David Hockney. A wonderful collection of British watercolours are also displayed at Manchester's **Whitworth Art Gallery** (☎0161-275 7450; www.whitworth.manchester.ac.uk; University of Manchester, Oxford Rd, M15 6ER; ⌚10am-5pm Fri-Wed, to 9pm Thu; 🚌15, 41, 42, 43, 140, 143 or 147 from Piccadilly Gardens), which has an exceptional collection of historic textiles.

Manchester is famed for its rival football teams **Manchester United** (www.manutd.com) and **Manchester City** (www.mancity.com), and its **National Football Museum** (☎0161-605 8200; www.nationalfootballmuseum.com; Urbis Building, Cathedral Gardens, Corporation St, M4 3BG; adult/child £11/6, Manchester residents free; ⌚10am-4pm Thu-Sun; 🚊Victoria Station or Exchange Square) charts British football's evolution from its earliest days to the multibillion-pound phenomenon it is today.

The city is also world renowned for its live-music scene, with gigs in all genres most nights of the week.

LOU ARMOR / SHUTTERSTOCK ©

✕ 🛏 p47, p85, p211

The Drive » This trip's longest drive, at 216 miles, takes you northwest via the M61 and M6, passing between the Yorkshire Dales National Park to your east and the Lake District National Park to your west. Once you cross into Scotland the road becomes the A74 and climbs into the Southern Uplands, then becomes the A702 as it leads into Edinburgh.

Park-goers relaxing below Edinburgh Castle

TRIP HIGHLIGHT

⓭ Edinburgh

The Scottish capital is entwined with its landscape, with buildings and monuments perched atop crags and overshadowed by cliffs. From the Old Town's picturesque jumble of medieval tenements along the Royal Mile, its turreted skyline strung between the black, bull-nosed Castle Rock and the russet palisade of Salisbury Crags, to the New Town's neat neoclassical grid, the city offers a constantly changing perspective.

Along with a walk through the Old Town (p424), unmissable experiences here include visiting **Edinburgh Castle** (☎0131-225 9846; www.edinburghcastle.scot; Castle Esplanade, EH1 2NG; adult/child £17.50/10.50, audio guide £3.50/1.50; ⌚9.30am-6pm Apr-Sep, to 5pm Oct-Mar, last entry 1hr before closing; 🚌23, 27, 41, 42), which has played a pivotal role in Scottish history, both as a royal residence – King Malcolm Canmore (r 1058–93) and Queen Margaret first made their home here in the

11th century – and as a military stronghold; and climbing to the hilltop **Arthur's Seat** (Holyrood Park; 35) for city panoramas.

Edinburgh has 700-plus pubs, more per square mile than any other UK city. Sample a dram of Scottish whisky at icons like **Malt Shovel** (0131-225 6843; www.maltshovelinn-edinburgh.co.uk; 11-15 Cockburn St, EH1 1BP; 11am-11pm Mon-Wed, to midnight Thu & Sun, to 1am Fri & Sat; ; 6), with over 100 single malts behind the bar.

p47

The Drive » Drive southeast on the A68, passing through the Scottish Borders, and enter Northumberland National Park at the English border. Join the southbound A1 at Darlington, then take the eastbound A59 to York (191 miles altogether).

14 York

A magnificent ring of 13th-century walls encloses York's medieval spider's web of streets. At its heart lies the immense, awe-inspiring **York Minster** (01904-557200; www.yorkminster.org; Deangate; adult/child £11.50/free; 11am-4.30pm Mon-Thu, from 10am Fri & Sat, 12.30-2.30pm Sun). Constructed mainly between 1220 and 1480, it encompasses all the major stages of Gothic architecture. The transepts (1220–55) were built in Early English style; the octagonal chapter house (1260–90) and nave (1291–1340) in the Decorated style; and the west towers, west front and central (or lantern) tower (1470–72) in Perpendicular style.

Don't miss a walk on York's City Walls, which follow the line of the original Roman walls and give a whole new perspective on the city. Cover just the highlights (p290) or allow 1½ to two hours for the full circuit of 4.5 miles.

p47, p271

The Drive » From York, it's 156 miles to Cambridge. Take the A64 southwest to join onto the A1 heading southeast.

15 Cambridge

Surrounded by meadows, Cambridge is a university town extraordinaire, with a tightly packed core of ancient colleges and picturesque riverside 'Backs' (college gardens), which you can stroll around (p134).

The colossal neoclassical pile containing the **Fitzwilliam Museum** (www.fitzmuseum.cam.ac.uk; Trumpington St; by donation; 10am-5pm Tue-Sat, from noon Sun), locally dubbed 'the Fitz', was built to house the treasures that the seventh Viscount Fitzwilliam bequeathed to his old university. Standout exhibits include Roman and Egyptian grave goods, artworks by many of the great masters and some quirkier collections such as banknotes, literary autographs, watches and armour.

For the full Cambridge experience, rent a river boat from operators such as **Scudamore's Punting** (01223-359750; www.scudamores.com; Mill Lane; chauffeured punt trips per bench/boat from £70/120, 6-person punt hire from £51; 10am-7pm Mon-Fri, to 8pm Sat & Sun).

The Drive » Hop on the M11 for the 55-mile zip south to London.

LOCAL KNOWLEDGE: SCOTLAND'S CRAFT GIN

Scotland is famed around the world for its whisky, but Scottish craft gin (www.thescottishginsociety.com) is also hugely popular. Over 70% of gin consumed in the UK is produced in Scotland – there are more than 90 gin distilleries in the country, and nearly a dozen in the Edinburgh area. Bars all over the capital are offering cocktails based on brands such as Pickering's, 56 North, Edinburgh Gin and Holyrood.

Sleeping

London 1

Hoxton Shoreditch Hotel ££

(☎020-7550 1000; www.thehoxton.com/london/shoreditch/hotels; 81 Great Eastern St, EC2; r £109-260; ❄ 📶; Ⓤ Old St) In the heart of hip Shoreditch, this hotel takes the low-cost airline approach – book long enough ahead and you might pay just £109. The 210 renovated rooms are small but stylish, with TVs, desks, fridges with complimentary bottled water and milk, and breakfast (orange juice, granola, yoghurt and banana) delivered to your door.

Winchester 4

16a B&B £££

(☎07730 510663; www.16a-winchester.co.uk; 16a Parchment St; r £145-185; 📶) The word 'boutique' gets bandied around freely, but here it fits. The sumptuous conversion of this old dance hall sees an antique piano and honesty bar frame a wood-burning stove. Gorgeous bedrooms feature exposed brick, lofty ceilings, vast beds and baths on the mezzanines with views of the stars.

Bath 8

Grays Bath B&B £££

(☎01225-403020; www.graysbath.co.uk; 9 Upper Oldfield Park; r £125-185; P 📶) Boutique treat Grays is a beautiful blend of modern, pared-down design and family treasures, many picked up from the owners' travels. All the rooms are individual: choose from floral, polka dot or maritime stripes. Perhaps the pick is the curving, six-sided room in the attic, with partial city views.

Cardiff 9

Hotel Indigo Boutique Hotel ££

(☎0871 942 9104; www.ihg.com; Dominions Arcade, Queen St; r/ste from £62/103; 📶) The Indigo Hotel Group (IHG) has over a dozen hotels UK-wide, but only this one in Wales. Like other IHG offerings, it tailors itself uniquely to Cardiff and Welsh culture. Spacious rooms cleverly include aspects such as traditional Welsh fabrics above bed headboards, pictures of old industrial scenes and sheep decorating crockery. Insanely good value.

Manchester 12

King Street Townhouse Boutique Hotel £££

(☎0161-667 0707; www.eclectichotels.co.uk; 10 Booth St; r/ste from £180/£280; ❄ @ 📶 ≋; 🚌 all city centre) This beautiful 1872 Italian Renaissance–style former bank is now an exquisite boutique hotel with 40 bedrooms ranging from snug to suite. Furnishings are the perfect combination of period elegance and contemporary style. On the top floor is a small spa with an infinity pool overlooking the town hall; downstairs is a nice bar and restaurant. Online rates are cheaper.

Edinburgh 13

Southside Guest House B&B £££

(☎0131-466 6573; www.southsideguesthouse.co.uk; 8 Newington Rd, EH9 1QS; s/d from £145/180; 📶; 🚌 all Newington buses) Though set in a typical Victorian terrace, the Southside transcends the guesthouse category and feels more like a boutique hotel. Its seven stylish rooms, featuring the clever use of colours and modern furniture, ooze interior design. Breakfast is an event, with Buck's Fizz (cava mixed with orange juice) on offer to ease the hangover.

York 14

Lawrance Apartment ££

(☎01904-239988; www.thelawrance.com/york; 74 Micklegate; 1-/2-bed apt from £90/190; ❄ 📶) Set back from the road in a huddle of old red-brick buildings that once formed a factory, the Lawrance is an excellent find: super-swish serviced apartments with all mod cons on the inside and heritage character on the outside. Some apartments are split-level and all are comfy and spacious, with leather sofas, flatscreen TV and luxurious fixtures and fittings.

Classic Trip

Britain's Wild Side

Immerse yourself in wild Britain on this tri-country trip through glorious national parks and protected Areas of Outstanding Natural Beauty. There's barely a city in sight.

TRIP HIGHLIGHTS

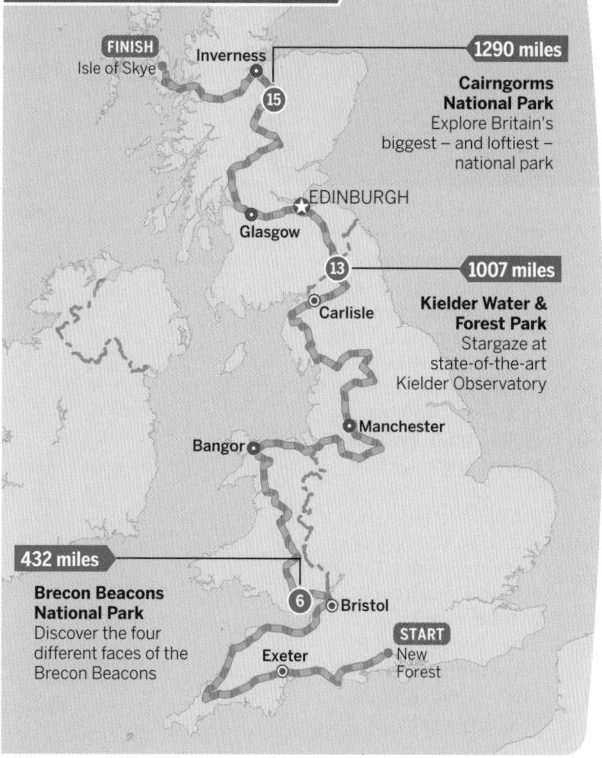

FINISH
Isle of Skye
Inverness
15
EDINBURGH
Glasgow
13
Carlisle
Manchester
Bangor
6
Bristol
Exeter
START
New Forest

1290 miles
Cairngorms National Park
Explore Britain's biggest – and loftiest – national park

1007 miles
Kielder Water & Forest Park
Stargaze at state-of-the-art Kielder Observatory

432 miles
Brecon Beacons National Park
Discover the four different faces of the Brecon Beacons

21 DAYS 1435 MILES / 2310KM

GREAT FOR...

BEST TIME TO GO

June to September offers the best conditions for outdoor activities.

Cornwall's Carnewas at Bedruthan at sunset.

Spot wild red deer, especially in autumn, at Exmoor National Park.

Exmoor National Park Home to one of Great Britain's largest wild red deer populations

Classic Trip

2 Britain's Wild Side

Leave the city lights behind on this adventure into Britain's wild natural heartland. On this intrepid trip you'll get up close to soaring mountain peaks, desolate moorland, sea-sprayed beaches, scalloped bays, lush hills, green dales, high, barren fells, and glassy lakes, some of which teem with wildlife. Along the way, get out and explore the breathtaking countryside on foot, bicycle, horseback and kayak.

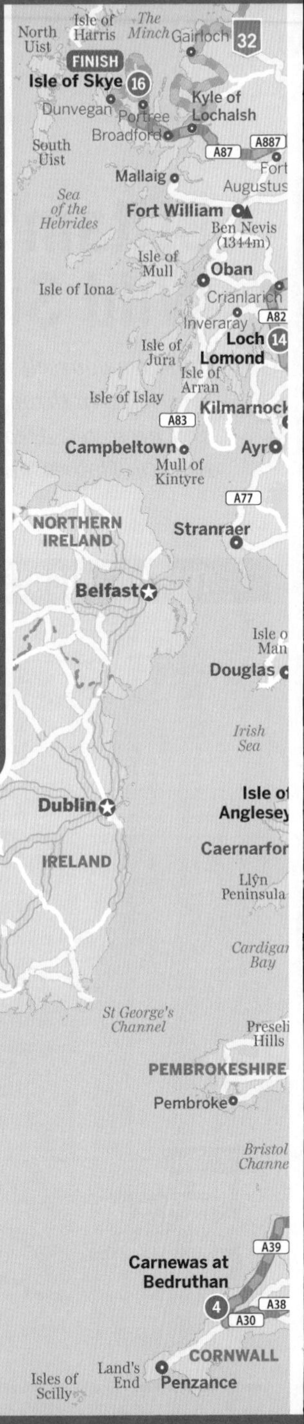

❶ New Forest

With typical, accidental, English irony the New Forest is anything but new – it was first proclaimed a royal hunting preserve in 1079. It's also not much of a forest, being mostly heathland ('forest' is from the Old French for 'hunting ground'). For an overview of New Forest, which was designated a national park in 2005, stop by the **New Forest Museum** (☎02380-283444; www.newforestcentre.org.uk; main car park, Lyndhurst; ⏰10.30am-4.30pm). Wild ponies mooch around pretty scrubland, deer flicker in the distance and rare birds flit among the foliage. Genteel villages dot the landscape, connected by a web of walking and cycling trails. **Lyndhurst tourist office** (☎01425-880020; www.thenewforest.co.uk; main car park, Lyndhurst; ⏰10.30am-4.30pm) stocks maps and guides; they're also available from its website. New Forest is also a popular spot for horse riding; **Burley Villa** (Western Riding; ☎01425-610278; www.burleyvilla.co.uk;

Bashley Common Rd, near New Milton) organises rides using traditional English and also Western saddle styles (per 90 minutes £54).

p61

The Drive » Take the A31 then the A35 southwest to Weymouth and Chesil Beach. Follow the Jurassic Coast northwest along the B3157 to Lyme Regis (81 miles in total).

2 Lyme Regis

Fossils regularly emerge from the unstable cliffs surrounding Lyme Regis, exposed by the landslides of a retreating shoreline, making this a key stop along the Unesco-listed Jurassic Coast.

For an overview, **Dinosaurland** (01297-443541; www.dinosaurland.

LINK YOUR TRIP

15 The Cotswolds & Literary England

New Forest is 48 miles southeast of Bath, from where you can travel through more picturesque British countryside in the Cotswolds.

32 Upper West Coast

The Isle of Skye's main town, Portree, is the departure point for a voyage through jaw-dropping Scottish highland and island scenery.

co.uk; Coombe St; adult/child £5/4; ⏲10am-5pm mid-Feb–mid-Oct, winter hours vary; 👪) overflows with fossilised remains; look out for belemnites, a plesiosaurus and an impressive locally found ichthyosaur. Kids love the lifelike dinosaur models, rock-hard tyrannosaur eggs and 73kg dinosaur dung.

Three miles east of Lyme, the **Charmouth Heritage Coast Centre** (☎01297-560772; www.charmouth.org; Lower Sea Lane, Charmouth; ⏲11am-4pm daily Easter-Oct, Fri-Mon Nov-Easter) runs one to seven fossil-hunting trips a week (adult/child £8/4). In Lyme itself, **Lyme Regis Museum** (☎01297-443370; www.lymeregismuseum.co.uk; Bridge St; up to 2 people £12, family £15; ⏲10am-4pm Wed-Sat) organises three to seven walks a week (up to six people £125). Book walks ahead.

The Drive » Drive west on the A3052 through the dazzling East Devon AONB to Exeter and take the B3212 up into Postbridge, a small village in the middle of Dartmoor National Park (52 miles all up).

❸ Dartmoor National Park

Covering 368 sq miles, this vast **national park** (☎01822-890414; www.visitdartmoor.co.uk) feels like it's tumbled straight out of a Tolkien tome, with its honey-coloured heaths, moss-covered boulders, meandering streams and eerie granite tors (hills). It's one of Britain's most wildly beautiful corners.

On sunny days Dartmoor is idyllic: ponies wander and sheep graze beside the road, as seen in Steven Spielberg's WWI epic *War Horse*. But Dartmoor is also the setting for Sir Arthur Conan Doyle's *The Hound of the Baskervilles,* and in sleeting rain and swirling mists the moor morphs into a bleak wilderness where tales of a phantom hound can seem very real. Be aware too that the military uses live ammunition in its training ranges.

Dartmoor is a haven for outdoor activities, including hiking, cycling, riding, climbing and white-water kayaking; the **Dartmoor National Park Authority** (DNPA; www.dartmoor.gov.uk) has detailed information. And there are plenty of rustic pubs to cosy up in when the fog rolls in.

🛏 p61

The Drive » Head west through Tavistock to pass through the Tamar Valley, another AONB, on the A390. At Dobwalls, pick up the A38 and drive west along the forested River Fowey to join the southwest-bound A30. Take the Victoria turn-off and travel northwest past Newquay Cornwall Airport to Carnewas at Bedruthan (62 miles altogether).

TOP TIP: WARNING: DARTMOOR MILITARY RANGES

Live ammunition is used on Dartmoor's training ranges. Check locations with the **Firing Information Service** (☎0800 458 4868; www.mod.uk/access) or tourist offices. Red flags fly at the edges of in-use ranges by day; red flares burn at night. Beware unidentified metal objects lying in the grass. Don't touch anything; report finds to the **Dartmoor Training Safety Officer** (☎01837-657210).

❹ Carnewas at Bedruthan

On Cornwall's surf-pounded coast loom the stately rock stacks of **Bedruthan** (Bedruthan Steps; NT; www.nationaltrust.org.uk). These mighty granite pillars have been carved out by thousands of years of wind and waves, and the area is now owned by the National Trust (NT). The beach itself is accessed via a steep staircase and is submerged at high tide – these were closed at the time of research due to restrictions associated with the coronavirus pandemic. Towards the north end is a rocky shelf known as Diggory's Island, which separates the main beach from another little-known cove.

The Drive » Drive east to join the northeast-bound A39, which runs parallel to the Cornish coast, to the town of Lynmouth in Exmoor National Park (94 miles in total).

5 Exmoor National Park

In the middle of Exmoor National Park is the higher moor, an empty, expansive, other-worldly landscape of tawny grasses and huge skies.

Exmoor supports one of England's largest wild red deer populations, best experienced in autumn when the annual 'rutting' season sees stags bellowing, charging at each other and clashing horns in an attempt to impress prospective mates. The Exmoor National Park Authority (ENPA; www.exmoor-nationalpark.gov.uk) runs regular wildlife-themed guided walks (free), which include evening deer-spotting hikes. Or head out on an organised jeep safari.

The open moors and a profusion of marked bridleways offer excellent hiking. Cycling is also popular; **Exmoor Adventures** (07976 208279; www.exmooradventures.co.uk; Old Bus Garage, Porlock Weir; P) runs a mountain-biking skills course (from £30) and also rents out bikes (per day £25).

The Drive » From Lynmouth to Libanus in the Brecon Beacons National Park it's 143 miles. Take the A39 east along the coast to join the M5 at Bridgwater. Take the Second Severn Crossing bridge and head west towards Cardiff to join the northwest-bound A470.

TRIP HIGHLIGHT

6 Brecon Beacons National Park

Brecon Beacons National Park (Parc Cenedlaethol Bannau Brycheiniog) ripples for 45 miles from the English border to near Llandeilo in the west. High mountain plateaus of grass and heather, their northern rims scalloped with glacier-scoured hollows, rise above wooded, waterfall-splashed valleys and green, rural landscapes.

Within the park there are four distinct regions: the wild, lonely **Black Mountain** (Mynydd Du)

HIKING EXMOOR

The open moors and a profusion of marked bridleways make Exmoor an excellent area for hiking. The best-known routes are the **Somerset & North Devon Coast Path**, which is part of the **South West Coast Path** (www.southwestcoastpath.org.uk), and the Exmoor section of the **Two Moors Way** (www.twomoorsway.org), which starts in Lynmouth and travels 102 miles south over Dartmoor to Ivybridge. From there a 15-mile extension leads to the south Devon coast at Wembury.

Another superb route is the **Coleridge Way** (www.coleridgeway.co.uk), which winds for 51 miles from Lynmouth to Nether Stowey, crossing Exmoor, the Brendon Hills and the Quantocks. Part of the 180-mile **Tarka Trail** (www.tarkatrail.org.uk) cuts through the park. The coastal section sweeps from Lynton to Bideford, before heading down into north Devon.

Check to see if walks run by the Exmoor National Park Authority (www.exmoor-nationalpark.gov.uk) are running. Past events include deer safaris, nightjar birdwatching walks and dark-sky strolls.

ENPA tourist offices also sell a great range of day-walk leaflets (£1).

Classic Trip

URBANCOW / GETTY IMAGES ©

ANDREAC77 / SHUTTERSTOCK ©

WHY THIS IS A CLASSIC TRIP

ANTHONY HAM, WRITER

This classic journey through wild Britain will leave you wondering how such diversity can possibly be within reach on one relatively short trip. Forests and cliffs, mountains and moors – Great Britain is one beautiful place, and this stirring exploration of lakes and national parks showcases the best that Britain's natural world has to offer.

Above: Mountain biking in Dartmoor National Park
Left: Mandarin duck, Brecon Beacons National Park
Right: Staircase at Bedruthan Steps

in the west, with its high moors and glacial lakes; **Great Forest** (Fforest Fawr), whose rushing streams and spectacular waterfalls form the headwaters of the Rivers Tawe and Neath; the **Brecon Beacons** (Bannau Brycheiniog) proper, a group of very distinctive, flat-topped hills that includes Pen-y-Fan (886m), the park's highest peak; and the rolling heathland ridges of the **Black Mountains** (Y Mynydd-doedd Duon) – not to be confused with the Black Mountain (singular) in the west. The park's main **visitor centre** (☎01874-624437; www.breconbeacons.org; Libanus; ⏰10am-4pm) has details of walks, hiking and biking trails, outdoor activities, wildlife and geology (call first to check it's open).

🛏 p61

The Drive » Drive north along the A470 to reach the southern boundary of Snowdonia National Park at Mallwyd (79 miles altogether).

7 Snowdonia National Park

Wales' best-known and most-visited slice of nature, Snowdonia National Park (Parc Cenedlaethol Eryri) became the country's first national park in 1951. Every year more than 350,000 people walk, climb or take the rack-and-pinion **railway** (☎01286-870223;

www.snowdonrailway.co.uk; A4086; adult/child return diesel £29/20, steam £37/27; ⏲9am-5pm mid-Mar–Oct) to the 1085m summit of Snowdon. The park's 823 sq miles embrace stunning coastline, forests, valleys, rivers, bird-filled estuaries and Wales' biggest natural lake. The **Snowdonia National Park Information Centre** (☎01690-710426; www.eryri-npa.gov.uk; Royal Oak Stables; ⏲9.30am-12.30pm & 1.30-4.30pm) is an invaluable source of information about walking trails, mountain conditions and more.

The Drive » Continue north on the A470 and take the A5 northwest to Bangor. Cross Robert Stephenson's 1850-built Britannia Bridge over the Menai Strait and take the A545 northwest to Beaumaris (a 72-mile trip).

8 Isle of Anglesey

The 276-sq-mile Isle of Anglesey (Ynys Môn) offers miles of inspiring coastline, hidden beaches and the country's greatest concentration of ancient sites.

Almost all of the Anglesey coast has been designated as an AONB (Area of Outstanding Natural Beauty). Beyond the handsome Georgian town of Beaumaris (Biwmares), there are hidden gems scattered all over the island. It's very much a living centre of Welsh culture, too, as you can see for yourself at **Oriel Ynys Môn** (☎01248-724444; www.orielmon.org; B5111, Rhosmeirch, Llangefni; ⏲10am-4pm Wed-Sun; P).

A great, introductory day walk from Beaumaris takes in the ancient monastic site of **Penmon Priory** (Cadw; www.cadw.gov.wales; B5109, Penmon; parking £3; ⏲10am-4pm; P), Penmon Point with views across to Puffin Island, and Blue Flag beach Llanddona.

✕ p61

The Drive » Return to the mainland and take the A55 northeast, crossing the border into England where the road becomes the M56. Continue northeast towards Manchester before turning off on the southeast-bound M6. At Sandbach turn east on the A534 and follow the signs to Leek, then take the A53 northeast before turning east towards Longnor then Bakewell (138 miles all up).

9 Peak District National Park

Founded in 1951, the Peak District was England's first national park and is Europe's busiest. But even at peak times, there are 555 sq miles of open countryside in which to soak up the scenery. Caving and climbing, cycling and, above all, walking (including numerous short walks) are the most popular activities. The **Peak District National Park Authority** (☎01629-816200; www.peakdistrict.gov.uk) has reams of information about the park and also operates several cycle-hire centres.

STARGAZING IN THE BRECON BEACONS

The Brecon Beacons is just one of a handful of places in the world to be awarded 'Dark-Sky Reserve' status. With almost zero light pollution, this is one of the UK's finest places for stargazing. Meteor showers, nebulae, strings of constellations and the Milky Way twinkle brightly in the night sky when the weather is clear. Among the 10 best spots are **Carreg Cennen** (Cadw; ☎01558-822291; www.cadw.gov.wales; Trapp; adult/child £5.50/3.50; ⏲9.30am-5pm), **Sugar Loaf** (Mynydd Pen-y-Fâl) and **Llanthony Priory** (Cadw; www.cadw.gov.wales; ⏲10am-4pm; P 🚻).

Visitor centres throughout the park can give you information about stargazing events, or check out www.breconbeacons.org/stargazing.

The charming town of Bakewell also has a helpful **tourist office** (☎01629-816558; www.visitpeakdistrict.com; Bridge St; ⏰10.30am-4pm).

🛏 p61

The Drive » From Bakewell take the A623 northwest towards Manchester and pick up the northbound M66, then at Burnley take the northeast-bound M65 to Skipton. Enter the Yorkshire Dales National Park on the B6265 to Grassington and head northwest on the B6265 to Aysgarth. Then take the A684 along the River Ure to Hawes (a total of 118 miles).

⑩ Yorkshire Dales National Park

Protected as a national park since the 1950s, the glacial valleys of the Yorkshire Dales (named from the old Norse word *dalr,* meaning 'valleys') are characterised by a distinctive landscape of high heather moorland, stepped skylines and flat-topped hills above valleys patchworked with drystone dykes and little barns. Hawes is home to the **Wensleydale Creamery** (www.wensleydale.co.uk; Gayle Lane; adult/child £1.95/free; ⏰10am-4pm; P 👪), producing famous Wensleydale cheese. In the limestone country of the southern Dales you'll encounter extraordinary examples of karst scenery (created by rainwater dissolving the underlying limestone bedrock).

TOP TIP: WALKING SAFETY TIPS

The British countryside can appear gentle, and often is, but conditions can deteriorate quickly. Year-round on the hills or open moors carry warm waterproof clothing, a map and compass, and high-energy food (eg chocolate) and drinks. If you're really going off the beaten track, leave your route details with someone.

The Drive » Head southwest on the B6255 to Ingleton. Take the A65 northwest to Sizergh then the A590 southwest to the Lake District's southern reaches at Newby Bridge. Drive north along Lake Windermere before veering northwest to Hawkshead (53 miles all up).

⑪ Lake District National Park

The Lake District (or Lakeland, as it's commonly known round these parts) is by far the UK's most popular national park. Ever since the Romantic poets arrived in the 19th century, its postcard panorama of craggy hilltops, mountain tarns and glittering lakes has stirred visitors' imaginations. It's awash with outdoor opportunities, from lake cruises to mountain walks.

Many people visit for the region's literary connections: among the many writers who found inspiration here are William Wordsworth, Samuel Taylor Coleridge, Arthur Ransome and, of course, Beatrix Potter, a lifelong lover of the Lakes, whose delightful former farmhouse, **Hill Top** (NT; ☎01539-436269; www.nationaltrust.org.uk/hill-top; garden adult/child £5/2.50; ⏰10am-5.30pm Jun-Aug, to 4.30pm Sat-Thu Apr, May, Sep & Oct, weekends only Nov-Mar), inspired many of her tales including *Peter Rabbit.*

🛏 p61

The Drive » Drive northwest on the A591 to join the A595 to Carlisle. Then take the A689 and A69 northeast to Walltown along Hadrian's Wall (72 miles altogether).

⑫ Hadrian's Wall

Hadrian's Wall is one of Britain's most revealing and dramatic Roman ruins, its 2000-year-old procession of abandoned forts, garrisons, towers and milecastles marching across the wild and lonely landscape of northern England. This wall was about defence and control, but this edge-of-empire barrier also symbolised the boundary of civilised order – to the north lay the unruly land of the marauding Celts, while to the south was the Roman world of orderly taxpaying, underfloor heating and bathrooms. There's an excellent visitor centre at **Walltown** (Northumberland National Park Visitor Centre; ☎01434-344396; www.northumberlandnationalpark.org.uk; Greenhead; ⏰10am-6pm daily Apr-Sep, to 5pm daily Oct, 10am-4pm Sat & Sun Nov-Mar). The finest sections of the wall run along the southern edge of remote **Northumberland National Park** (☎01434-605555; www.northumberlandnationalpark.org.uk), one of Britain's finest wilderness areas.

The Drive » Follow the B6318 northeast along Hadrian's Wall. Turn north on the B6320 to Bellingham. Continue northwest alongside the North Tyne river and Kielder Water lake to the village of Kielder (a 43-mile journey).

TRIP HIGHLIGHT

13 Kielder Water & Forest Park

Adjacent to Northumberland National Park, the Kielder Water & Forest Park is home to the vast artificial lake Kielder Water, holding 200 billion litres. Surrounding its 27-mile-long shoreline is England's largest plantation forest, with 150 million spruce and pine trees. Kielder Water is a water-sports playground (and midge magnet; bring insect repellent), and also has walking and cycling as well as great birdwatching. Comprehensive information is available at www.visitkielder.com.

The lack of population here helped see the area awarded dark-sky status by the International Dark Skies Association in 2013 (the largest such designation in Europe), with controls to prevent light pollution. For the best views of the Northumberland International Dark Sky Park, attend a stargazing session at state-of-the-art, 2008-built **Kielder Observatory** (☎0191-265 5510; www.kielderobservatory.org; Black Fell, off Shilling Pot; adult/child from £20/15; ⏰by reservation). Book ahead and dress warmly as it's seriously chilly here at night.

The Drive » It's a 139-mile drive from Kielder to Balloch on the southern shore of Loch Lomond. Head north into Scotland and join the A68 towards Edinburgh. Take the M8 to Glasgow and then the A82 northwest to Balloch.

14 Loch Lomond

Loch Lomond is mainland Britain's largest lake and, after Loch Ness, the most famous of Scotland's lochs. It's part of **Loch Lomond & the Trossachs National Park** (☎01389-722600; www.lochlomond-trossachs.org), which extends over a sizeable area, from Balloch north to Tyndrum and Killin, and from Callander west to the forests of Cowal.

JAROSLAV MORAVCIK / SHUTTERSTOCK ©

Loch Lomond Hikers descending Conic Hill

From Balloch, **Sweeney's Cruises** (☎01389-752376; www.sweeneyscruiseco.com; Balloch Rd, Balloch) offers, among other trips, a popular one-hour return cruise to the island of Inchmurrin (adult/child £12.50/8, nine times daily April to September, twice daily October to March). The quay is directly opposite Balloch train station. With departures from Tarbet and Luss on the loch's western shore, **Cruise Loch Lomond** (☎01301-702356; www.cruiselochlomond.co.uk; Tarbet; cruises adult/child from £12/7.50; ⏲8.30am-5.30pm late Mar-early Nov) runs short cruises and two-hour trips to Arklet Falls and Rob Roy's Cave (adult/child £15/9.50). There are also several options that involve drop-offs and pick-ups with a hike in between.

The Drive » Follow the A82 along Loch Lomond's western shoreline and pick up the northeast-bound A85 at Crianlarich, then the A827. Then take the northwest-bound A9 to Aviemore (a total of 141 miles).

Classic Trip

TRIP HIGHLIGHT

15 Cairngorms National Park

The vast Cairngorms National Park (www.cairngorms.co.uk) stretches from Aviemore in the north – which has a handy **tourist office** (01479-810930; www.visitaviemore.com; The Mall, Grampian Rd; 10am-4pm Sep-Jun, longer hours Jul & Aug) – to the Angus Glens in the south, and from Dalwhinnie in the west to Ballater and Royal Deeside in the east.

The park encompasses the highest landmass in Britain – a broad mountain plateau, riven only by the deep valleys of the Lairig Ghru and Loch Avon, with an average altitude of over 1000m and including five of the six highest summits in the UK. This wild mountain landscape of granite and heather has a sub-Arctic climate and supports rare alpine tundra vegetation and high-altitude bird species, such as snow bunting, ptarmigan and dotterel. Lower down, scenic glens are softened by beautiful open forests of native Scots pine, home to rare animals and birds such as pine martens, Scottish wildcats, red squirrels, ospreys, capercaillies and crossbills.

p61

The Drive » Take the A9 northwest to Inverness, then the southwest-bound A82 along Loch Ness. At Invermoriston join the westbound A887, which becomes the A87, and continue to Kyle of Lochalsh where you'll cross the Skye Bridge to the Isle of Skye. Continue along the A87 to reach Portree (145 miles all up).

16 Isle of Skye

The Isle of Skye (an t-Eilean Sgiathanach in Gaelic) takes its name from the old Norse *sky-a,* meaning 'cloud island', a Viking reference to the often-mist-enshrouded Cuillin Hills. It's a 50-mile-long patchwork of velvet moors, jagged mountains, sparkling lochs and towering sea cliffs. Lively Portree (Port Righ) has the island's only **tourist office** (01478-612992; www.visitscotland.com/destinations-maps/isle-skye; Bayfield Rd, IV51 9EL; 10am-4pm Mon-Sat year-round, longer hours Jun-Aug;).

Skye offers some of the finest walking in Scotland, including short, low-level routes. The sheltered coves and sea lochs around the coast of Skye provide magnificent sea-kayaking. **Whitewave Outdoor Centre** (01470-542414; www.white-wave.co.uk; 19 Linicro, Kilmuir, IV51 9YN; half-day kayak session per person £40-50; Mar-Oct) runs expeditions and courses for beginners and experienced paddlers to otherwise inaccessible places.

Skye's stunning scenery is the main attraction, but there are castles, crofting museums and cosy pubs and restaurants, along with dozens of art galleries and craft studios.

OUTER HEBRIDES

If you're not ready to return to the mainland after visiting the Isle of Skye, consider a trip to the Outer Hebrides (aka the Western Isles; Na h-Eileanan an Iar in Gaelic) – a 130-mile-long string of islands west of Skye. More than a third of Scotland's registered crofts are here, and no less than 60% of the population are Gaelic speakers. With limited time, head straight for the west coast of Lewis with its prehistoric sites, preserved black houses, beautiful beaches, and arts and crafts studios – the **Stornoway Tourist Office** (01851-703088; www.visitouterhebrides.co.uk; 26 Cromwell St, HS1 2DD; 10am-4pm daily Apr-Oct, closed Sun Nov-Mar) can provide a list. Ferries (car £31.65, driver and passenger £6.50 each) run once or twice daily from Uig on Skye to Lochmaddy (1¾ hours) and Tarbert (1½ hours).

Eating & Sleeping

New Forest 1

The Pig — Boutique Hotel £££

(01590-622354; www.thepighotel.com/brockenhurst; Beaulieu Rd, Brockenhurst; r £189-350; P, wifi) One of the New Forest's classiest hotels remains an utter delight: log baskets, croquet mallets and ranks of guest gumboots give things a country-house air; espresso machines and mini-larders lend bedrooms a luxury touch. The effortless elegance makes it feel like you've just dropped by a friend's (very stylish) rural retreat.

Dartmoor National Park 3

Tor Royal Farm — B&B ££

(01822-890189; www.torroyal.co.uk; Tor Royal Lane, near Princetown; s £70, d £85-115, tr £130; P, wifi) An easy-going, country-cottage-styled farmhouse packed with lived-in charm. Heritage-style rooms feature cream-and-white furniture, puffy bedspreads and easy chairs. They'll even rustle up an evening meal, probably featuring the farm's own reared beef or lamb.

Brecon Beacons National Park 6

Coach House — B&B ££

(01874-620043; www.coachhousebrecon.com; 12 Orchard St; d £89-150; wifi) This appealing 19th-century coaching inn is well attuned to the needs of walkers, with a drying room for hiking gear, generous breakfasts (including good vegetarian options), and packed lunches should you so wish. The six stylish, modern rooms, decorated in soothing taupes and creams, have ultra-comfy beds and great showers.

Isle of Anglesey 8

Tredici Italian Kitchen — Italian ££

(01248-811230; www.facebook.com/tredicikitchen; 13 Castle St; mains £14-16; 6-9pm Mon-Wed, noon-9pm Thu, noon-3pm & 6-9pm Fri & Sat) Occupying an intimate 1st-floor dining room above a quality butcher and grocer, Tredici has brought a touch of the Mediterranean to Anglesey. While local produce is used where possible (Halen Môn sea salt perks up the fries, and the mussels are from the Menai Strait), the figs, mozzarella and other pizza toppings and calzone fillings are imported from sunnier climes.

Peak District National Park 9

Rutland Arms Hotel — Hotel £££

(01629-812812; www.rutlandarmsbakewell.co.uk; The Square; d incl breakfast from £168; P, wifi, pets) Jane Austen is said to have stayed in room 2 of this aristocratic, 1804-built stone coaching inn while working on *Pride and Prejudice*. Its 33 rooms are in the main house and adjacent courtyard building; higher-priced rooms have lots of Victorian flourishes. Upmarket British classics (£14 to £23) such as pheasant and parsnip pie are served at its restaurant.

Lake District National Park 11

Yewfield — B&B ££

(01539-436765; www.yewfield.co.uk; Hawkshead Hill; s £90-115, d £100-145; P, wifi) This rambling Victorian mansion is one of the best options around Hawkshead, in a tranquil rural spot near **Tarn Hows** (NT; www.nationaltrust.org.uk/coniston-and-tarn-hows). It's veggie-only and ecofriendly (all heating and hot water comes from a biomass boiler supplied from the hotel's own woodland), and the handsome rooms are stocked with antiques. The spacious landscaped grounds are a highlight.

Cairngorms National Park 15

Cairngorm Hotel — Hotel ££

(01479-810233; www.cairngorm.com; Grampian Rd; s/d £75/110; P, wifi, family) Better known as 'the Cairn', this long-established hotel is set in the fine old granite building with the pointy turret opposite the train station. It's a welcoming place with comfortable rooms and a determinedly Scottish atmosphere, with tartan carpets and stags' antlers. There's live music on weekends, so it can get a bit noisy – not for early-to-bedders.

Classic Trip

The Historic South

England's rich heritage runs like a glittering seam through this remarkable road trip across the south. You'll discover sights nautical, archaeological and architectural as you clock up the miles.

TRIP HIGHLIGHTS

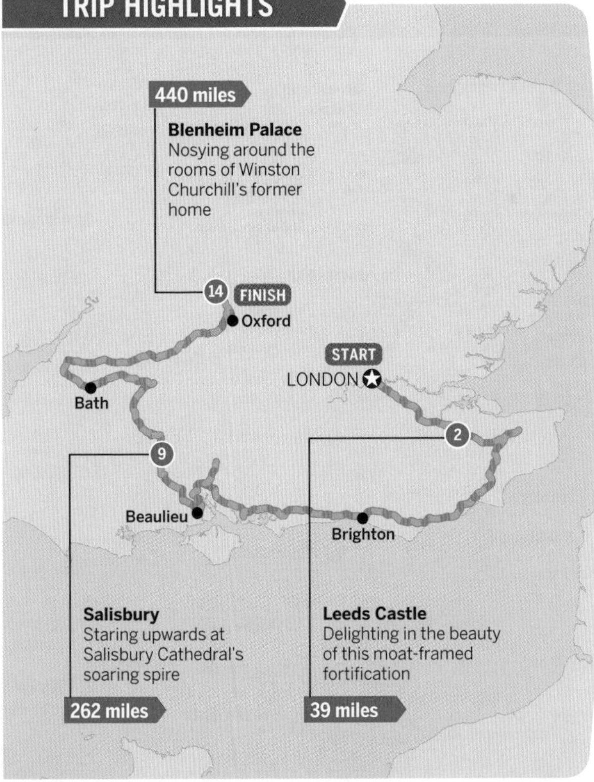

440 miles
Blenheim Palace
Nosying around the rooms of Winston Churchill's former home

14 FINISH
Oxford

START
LONDON

Bath

9

2

Beaulieu

Brighton

Salisbury
Staring upwards at Salisbury Cathedral's soaring spire
262 miles

Leeds Castle
Delighting in the beauty of this moat-framed fortification
39 miles

9–11 DAYS
450 MILES / 720KM

GREAT FOR...

BEST TIME TO GO

Spring and autumn. Plus summer if you don't mind more crowds.

ESSENTIAL PHOTO

Lounging in a punt with a backdrop of Oxford's divine buildings.

BEST FOR SURPRISES

The world's biggest stone circle: Avebury (not Stonehenge).

Leeds Castle A moat-ringed beauty, once home to Catherine of Aragon

Classic Trip

3 The Historic South

Stand by to tour some of the world's most beautiful castles and most memorable archaeological sites. Take in three of England's most impressive cathedrals, Georgian cityscapes, Churchill's palace and Oxford's spires. Discover guerilla art and this country's fine tradition of seaside kitsch. Motor to a car museum, explore unspoiled villages and encounter 14th-century fellow travellers' tales. And in doing so, take a road trip through the very best of Britain's past.

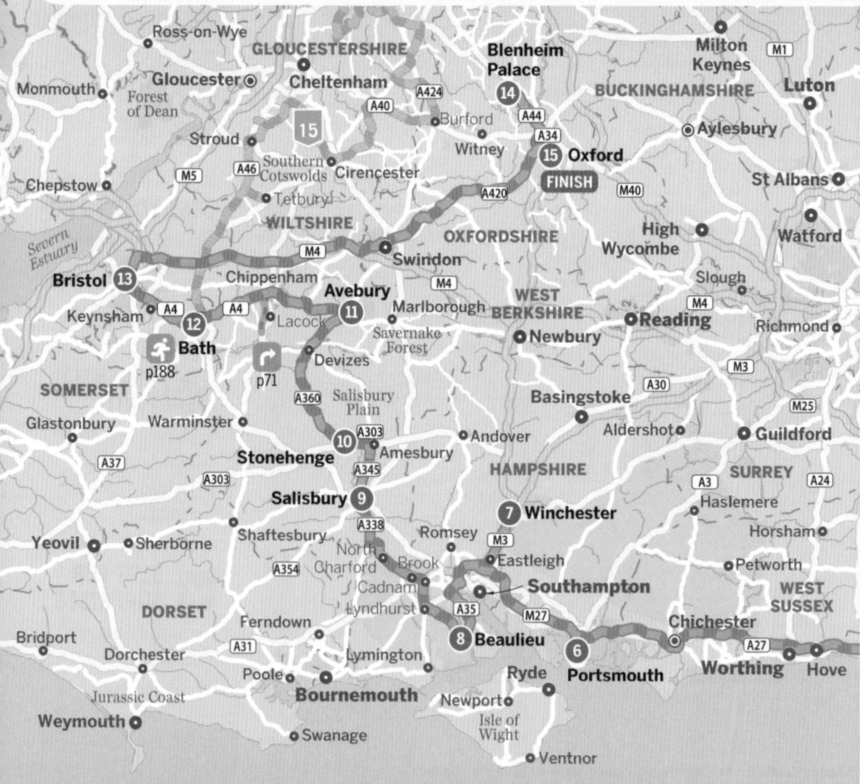

❶ London

Vibrant London is so packed with historic sights, it can be difficult to know where to start. Try the cathedral that is the capital's touchstone: **St Paul's** (☎020-7246 8357; www.stpauls.co.uk; St Paul's Churchyard, EC4; adult/child £17/7.20; ⌚8.30am-4.30pm Mon-Sat; Ⓤ St Paul's). Designed by Sir Christopher Wren in 1675 after the Great Fire, its vast dome is famed for avoiding Luftwaffe raids during the Blitz. Head inside and up 257 steps to the walkway called the Whispering Gallery, then to the Golden Gallery at the top for unforgettable London views. Next walk north to the **Museum of London** (☎020-7001 9844; www.museumoflondon.org.uk; 150 London Wall, EC2; ⌚10am-6pm; Ⓤ Barbican), where the capital's rich past is explored in riveting style. Then head east to elegant Tower Bridge to learn in its **exhibition** (☎020-7403 3761; www.towerbridge.org.uk; Tower Bridge, SE1; adult/child £10.60/5.30, incl Monument £12/5.50; ⌚9.30am-5pm; Ⓤ Tower Hill) just how they raise the arms – and the road – to let ships through.

The Drive » London's streets and suburbs meet bursts of the Kent countryside; you're heading for the A20 towards Sidcup, then the M20 towards Dover. Shortly after Maidstone leave the motorway behind, picking up A20 signs for Lenham and then Leeds Castle, some 40 miles from the capital.

TRIP HIGHLIGHT

❷ Leeds Castle

Immense and moat-ringed, for many **Leeds Castle** (www.leeds-castle.com; adult/child £27/18.50; ⌚10am-6pm Apr-Sep, to 5pm Oct-Mar; 👪) is one of the world's most romantic. The formidable, intricate structure balancing on two islands is known as something of a 'ladies

LINK YOUR TRIP

6 Kent: History, Art, Hops & Grapes

Encounter seashores, seafood and modern art on this Kentish cruise. Start at Margate, 17 miles northeast of Canterbury.

15 The Cotswolds & Literary England

Explore the enchanting Cotswold villages, then visit the home of the Bard himself. Join the fun at Tetbury, 50 miles west of Oxford.

Classic Trip

castle'. This stems from the fact that in its more than 1000 years of history, it has been home to a who's who of medieval queens, most famously Henry VIII's first wife, Catherine of Aragon.

The Drive » Next up is a 25-mile cruise, high up over the vast chalk ridge of the North Downs. Behind you stretch the villages and fields of the Weald of Kent. But you're headed northeast, largely along the A252/A28 – the Canterbury Rd which echoes the old pilgrim footpath to the cathedral city.

3 Canterbury

Canterbury tops the charts for English cathedral cities - and no wonder. Here medieval alleyways frame exquisite architecture, with **Canterbury Cathedral** (www.canterbury-cathedral.org; adult/child £12.50/8.50, tours adult/child £5/4, audio guide £4/3; ⏲10am-4.30pm Mon-Sat, 12.30-4.30pm Sun) the centrepiece. This towering Gothic masterpiece features fine stonework, a cavernous crypt and the site of English history's most famous murder: Archbishop Thomas Becket was killed here in 1170 after 'hints' from King Henry II, and has drawn pilgrims for more than 800 years since. Knowledgeable guides double up as energetic oarsmen at **Canterbury Historic River Tours** (☎07790 534744; www.canterburyrivertours.co.uk; King's Bridge; adult/child £12.50/7; ⏲10am-5pm Mar-Oct) for fascinating, multi-award-winning River Stour minicruises. For a taste of even older Canterbury, head to the mosaics of the **Roman Museum** (www.canterburymuseums.co.uk; Butchery Lane; adult/child £9/free; ⏲10am-5pm).

p73

The Drive » Now for a 35-mile drive. Head back up and over those creamy North Downs on the A28 towards Ashford. Then plunge down to roll, along the A2070, through the verdant valley of the Weald of Kent, then take the A259. Soon you're edging the flatlands of Romney Marsh and arriving at Rye.

4 Rye

Welcome to one of England's prettiest seaside towns. Here cobbled lanes, wonky Tudor buildings and tales of smugglers abound. The best place to start stretching your legs is **Mermaid Street**. It bristles with 15th-century timber-framed houses with quirky names such as 'The House with Two Front Doors' and 'The House Opposite'. The **Rye Heritage Centre** (☎01797-226696; www.ryeheritage.co.uk; Strand Quay; ⏲10am-5pm Apr-Oct, shorter hours Nov-Mar) offers themed walking tours.

The Drive » The next 50-mile leg sees you taking a string of A roads west. They lead past the woods and farms of the High Weald AONB and up another chalk ridge, this time the amphitheatre of hills known as the South Downs. Eventually, it's time to descend to Brighton on the shore.

THE CANTERBURY TALES

The Canterbury Tales is the best-known work of English literature's father figure: Geoffrey Chaucer (1342–1400). Chaucer was the first English writer to introduce characters – rather than 'types' – into fiction. They feature strongly in *The Canterbury Tales*, an unfinished series of 24 vivid stories told by a party of pilgrims travelling between London and Canterbury. The text remains a pillar of the literary canon. But more than that, it's a collection of rollicking good yarns of adultery, debauchery, crime and edgy romance, and is filled with Chaucer's witty observations about human nature.

5 Brighton

Famously hedonistic, exuberant and home to the UK's biggest gay scene, Brighton rocks the south. The bright and breezy seafront boasts the grand, century-old **Brighton Pier** (www.brightonpier.co.uk; Madeira Dr; ⌚11am-9pm Mon-Fri, 10am-10pm Sat, 10am-9pm Sun), complete with fairground rides, amusement arcades and candy-floss stalls. Stroll inland to the magnificent **Royal Pavilion** (☎03000-290900; http://brightonmuseums.org.uk/royalpavilion; Royal Pavilion Gardens; adult/child £15.50/9.50; ⌚9.30am-5.45pm Apr-Sep, 10am-5.15pm Oct-Mar), the glittering palace of Prince George (later King George IV). It's one of the most opulent buildings in England, and Europe's finest example of early-19th-century chinoiserie. Take in the Salvador Dalí sofa modelled on Mae West's lips at the **Brighton Museum & Art Gallery** (www.brightonmuseums.org.uk; Royal Pavilion Gardens; adult/child £6.20/3.60; ⌚10am-5pm Tue-Sun), then gear up for a lively night out by shopping amid the boutiques of the tightly packed **Brighton Lanes**.

p73, p99

The Drive » Next is a 50-mile blast due west, largely along A roads, to the historic port of Portsmouth. As the 170m-high Spinnaker Tower gets closer on the horizon, pick up signs for the Historic Dockyard Car Park.

DETOUR: BEACHY HEAD

Start: 4 Rye

An 8-mile detour off your route leads to a truly remarkable view. Around 25 miles west of Rye, peel off the A27 onto the A22 to Eastbourne. Head to the seafront to take the signed route that climbs to Beachy Head. Pick from several parking spots and follow the footpaths to the cliffs themselves. These 162m-tall sheer chalk faces are the highest point of cliffs that slice across the rugged coastline at the southern end of the South Downs. Far below sits a squat red-and-white-striped lighthouse. Appealing walks include the 1.5 mile hike west to the beach at Birling Gap.

6 Portsmouth

For a world-class collection of maritime heritage, head to **Portsmouth Historic Dockyard** (☎023-9283 9766; www.historicdockyard.co.uk; Victory Gate; all-attraction Explorer ticket adult/child/family £44/34/95, 1 attraction adult/child from £24/19, 3 attractions adult/child from £34/24; ⌚10am-5.30pm Apr-Oct, to 5pm Nov-Mar). The blockbuster draw is Henry VIII's favourite flagship, the **Mary Rose**. A £35-million, boat-shaped museum has now been built around her, giving uninterrupted views of the preserved timbers of her massive hull. Equally impressive is **HMS Victory**. Other nautical sights include the Victorian **HMS Warrior** and a wealth of imaginative museums. Round it all off by strolling around the defences in the historic **Point district**.

The Drive » Time to head inland; a 30-mile motorway cruise (the M27 then the M3) takes you to Winchester.

7 Winchester

Calm, collegiate Winchester is a mellow must-see. One of southern England's most awe-inspiring buildings, 11th-century **Winchester Cathedral** (☎01962-857200; www.winchester-cathedral.org.uk; The Close; adult/child £10/free; ⌚10am-4pm) adorns its core. It boasts a fine Gothic facade, one of the longest medieval naves in Europe (164m) and intricately carved medieval choir stalls, sporting everything from mythical beasts to a mischievous green man. Jane Austen's grave is near the entrance, in

Classic Trip

the northern aisle. The fantastical crumbling remains of **Wolvesey Castle** (EH; ☎0370 333 1181; www.english-heritage.org.uk; College St; ⏲10am-5pm Apr-Oct, to 4pm Sat & Sun Nov-Mar) sit nearby, as does one of England's most prestigious private schools: **Winchester College** (☎01962-621209; www.winchestercollege.org; College St), which you can visit on a tour.

🛏 p47, p73, p151

The Drive » Leave Winchester's ancient streets to take the motorways towards Southampton (initially the M3). After 14 miles turn off onto the A35 towards Lyndhurst. From here it's a 9-mile drive to Beaulieu through the New Forest's increasingly wooded roads.

8 Beaulieu

The vintage car museum and stately home at **Beaulieu** (☎01590-612345; www.beaulieu.co.uk; adult/child £25/10; ⏲10am-5pm) is centred on a 13th-century Cistercian monastery that passed to the ancestors of the current proprietors, the Montague family, after Henry VIII's 1536 monastic land-grab. Today its **motor museum** includes F1 cars and jet-powered land-speed record-breakers, as well as wheels driven by James Bond and Mr Bean. The **palace** began life as a 14th-century Gothic abbey gatehouse, and received a 19th-century Scottish baronial makeover from Baron Montague in the 1860s.

The Drive » The SatNav wants to start this 28-mile leg by routing you onto the A326. Resist! Opt for the A and B roads that winds through the villages of Lyndhurst, Cadnam, Brook and North Charford, revealing the New Forest's blend of woods and open heath. Eventually join the A338 to Salisbury. Soon an immense cathedral spire rises from the town.

TRIP HIGHLIGHT

9 Salisbury

Salisbury's skyline is dominated by the tallest spire in England, which soars from its central, majestic 13th-century cathedral (p39). This early English Gothic-style structure's elaborate exterior is decorated with pointed arches and flying buttresses, while its statuary and tombs are outstanding. Don't

WHY THIS IS A CLASSIC TRIP
ANTHONY HAM, WRITER

It doesn't get more classically British than this journey through the south. Quintessentially British seaside towns, at once quaint and kitsch, vie for attention with the cathedrals of Canterbury, Salisbury and Winchester. There's everyone's favourite archaeological ruin, and two towns – Bath and Bristol – that get that whole history-meets-modern-Britain cachet down perfectly.

Left: Winchester Cathedral
Right: National Motor Museum, Beaulieu

miss the daily tower tours (p39) and the cathedral's original, 13th-century copy of the Magna Carta. The surrounding **Cathedral Close** has a hushed, other-worldly feel. Nearby, the hugely important finds at **Salisbury Museum** (☎01722-332151; www.salisburymuseum.org.uk; 65 The Close; adult/child £8/4; ⏰11am-4pm Thu-Sun) include Iron Age gold coins, a Bronze Age gold necklace and the **Stonehenge Archer**, the bones of a man found in the ditch surrounding the stone circle.

🛏 p73, p151

The Drive ›› Next: a 10-mile drive taking you back 5000 years. The A345 heads north. Soon after joining the A303, detail a passenger to watch the right windows – the world's most famous stone circle will soon pop into view. The entry to the site is just beyond.

⑩ Stonehenge

Welcome to Britain's best-known archaeological site: Stonehenge (p39), a compelling ring of monolithic stones that dates, in parts, back to 3000 BCE. Head into the **Visitor Centre** to see 300 finds from the site and experience an impressive 360-degree projection of the stone circle through the ages and seasons. Next hop on a trolley bus (or walk; it's 1.5 miles) to the monument. There, as you stroll around it, play 'spot-the-stone': look out for the **bluestone horseshoe** (an inner semicircle), the **trilithon horseshoe** (sets of two vertical stones topped by a horizontal one) and the **Slaughter Stone** and **Heel Stone** (set apart, on the northeast side). Then try to work out what on earth it all means. Note that entrance is by timed ticket; secure yours well in advance.

The Drive ›› Now for a 24-mile, A-road meander through rural England. After dodging through Devizes, it's not long before signs point left to Avebury's main car park.

⑪ Avebury

A two-minute stroll from the car park (£7 per day) leads to a ring of stones that's so big an entire village sits inside. Fringed by a massive bank and ditch and with a diameter of 348m, Avebury (p41) is the largest stone circle in the world. Dating from 2500 to 2200 BCE, more than 30 stones are still in place and you can wander between them and clusters of other stones at will. Houses, the **Henge Shop** (☎01672-539229; www.hengeshop.com; High St; ⏰9.30am-5pm) and a pub, the **Red Lion** (☎01672-539266; www.oldenglishinns.co.uk; High St; ⏰11am-10pm Sun-Thu, to 11pm Fri & Sat), also nestle inside the circle.

The Drive ›› Next a cruise due west; as the A4 winds for 30 miles past fields and through villages to the city of Bath.

⑫ Bath

Sophisticated, stately and ever-so-slightly snooty, Bath is graced with some

STONEHENGE'S RITUAL LANDSCAPE

As you drive the roads around Stonehenge it's worth registering that the site forms part of a huge complex of ancient monuments. North of Stonehenge and running roughly east–west is the **Cursus**, an elongated embanked oval; the smaller **Lesser Cursus** is nearby. Two clusters of burial mounds, the **Old Barrow** and the **New Kings Barrow**, sit beside the ceremonial pathway **The Avenue**. This routeway cuts northeast of Stonehenge's **Heel Stone** and originally linked the site with the River Avon, 2 miles away. Theories abound as to what these sites were used for, ranging from ancient sporting arenas to processional avenues for the dead.

of the finest Georgian architecture anywhere in Britain. Wandering around the streets (p188) here is a real joy. For an insight into how the city came to look like it does, head to the **Museum of Bath Architecture** (☎01225-333895; www.museumofbatharchitecture.org.uk; The Countess of Huntingdon's Chapel, off the Paragon; adult/child £7/3.50; ⏲1-5pm Mon-Fri, 10am-5pm Sat & Sun mid-Feb–Nov). The **Bath Assembly Rooms** (NT; ☎01225-477789; www.nationaltrust.org.uk; 19 Bennett St; ⏲10.30am-6pm Mar-Oct, to 5pm Nov-Feb), where socialites once gathered, gives an insight into the Georgian world. To discover the city's culinary heritage head for **Sally Lunn's** (☎01225-461634; www.sallylunns.co.uk; 4 North Pde Passage; mains £7-13, afternoon tea £8-40; ⏲10am-8pm), which bakes the famous Bath Bunn (a brioche-meets-bread treat). For a free glass of the spring water that made the city rich, stop by the **Pump Room** (☎01225-477785; www.romanbaths.co.uk; Stall St; ⏲9.30am-5pm). Then perhaps soak yourself at **Thermae Bath Spa** (☎01225-331234; www.thermaebathspa.com; Hot Bath St; spa £37-42, treatments from £72; ⏲9am-9.30pm, last entry 7pm), with its steam rooms, waterfall showers and a choice of swimming pools (including a gorgeous rooftop one).

DETOUR: LACOCK

Start: ⑪ Avebury

Around 16 miles into your Avebury-to-Bath cruise, consider a detour south. Because a drive of just 4 extra miles leads to a real rarity: a medieval village that's been preserved in time. In Lacock, the sweet streets framed by stone cottages, higgledy-piggledy rooftops and mullioned windows are a delight to stroll around. Unsurprisingly, it's a popular movie location – it's popped up in the Harry Potter films, *The Other Boleyn Girl* and a BBC adaptation of *Pride and Prejudice*. The 13th-century former Augustinian nunnery of **Lacock Abbey** (NT; ☎01249-730459; www.nationaltrust.org.uk; Hither Way; adult/child £10/5; ⏲10.30am-5pm Mar-Oct, 11am-4pm Nov-Feb) is a must-see: its deeply atmospheric rooms and stunning Gothic entrance hall are lined with bizarre terracotta figures – spot the scapegoat with a lump of sugar on its nose. The **Fox Talbot Museum** (NT; ☎01249-730459; www.nationaltrust.org.uk; Hither Way; incl in Lacock Abbey admission; ⏲10.30am-5.30pm Mar-Oct, 11am-4pm Nov-Feb) features an intriguing display on early photography, while the **Sign of the Angel** (☎01249-730230; www.signoftheangel.co.uk; 6 Church St; s £85-115, d £115-145; P 📶 🐾) is a gorgeous, 15th-century restaurant-with-rooms.

🛏 p47, p73, p151, p203

The Drive » It's a 13-mile blast from Bath to Bristol along the A36/A4.

---

⑬ Bristol

In Bristol a fascinating seafaring heritage meets an edgy, contemporary vibe. The mighty **SS Great Britain** (☎0117-926 0680; www.ssgreatbritain.org; Great Western Dock, Gas Ferry Rd; adult/child/family £18/10/48; ⏲10am-6pm Apr-Oct, to 4.30pm Nov-Mar) sits on the city's waterfront. Designed in 1843 by engineering genius Isambard Kingdom Brunel, its interior has been impeccably refurbished, including the galley, the surgeon's quarters and a working model of the original steam engine. The whole vessel is contained in an air-tight dry dock, dubbed a 'glass sea'. At the **Bristol Museum & Art Gallery** (☎0117-922 3571; www.bristolmuseums.org.uk; Queen's Rd; ⏲10am-5pm Tue-Sun) take in the *Paint-Pot Angel* by world-famous street artist Banksy. In the suburb of **Clifton** explore Georgian architecture, especially in Cornwallis and Royal York Crescents. The **Clifton Observatory** (0117-974 1242; www.cliftonobservatory.com; Litfield Rd, Clifton Down; adult/child £2.50/1.50; 10am-5pm Mar-Oct, to 4pm Oct-Feb), meanwhile, features a rare camera obscura which offers incredible views of the deep fissure that is the Avon Gorge.

p73

The Drive ›› Travelling partly on the M4 and partly on A roads, the next 80-mile leg sees you skirting Oxford (for now) and arriving at the tree-lined avenue that leads to one of Britain's finest stately homes.

TRIP HIGHLIGHT

14 Blenheim Palace

Blenheim Palace (01993-810530; www.blenheimpalace.com; Woodstock; adult/child £28.50/16.50, park & gardens only £18.50/8.60; palace 10.30am-4.30pm, park & gardens 9.30am-6.30pm or dusk; P), a monumental baroque fantasy designed by Sir John Vanbrugh and Nicholas Hawksmoor, was built between 1705 and 1722. The house is filled with statues, tapestries, ostentatious furniture, priceless china and giant oil paintings. Highlights include the **Great Hall**, a soaring space topped by a 20m-high ceiling adorned with images of the first duke. Britain's legendary WWII prime minister, Sir Winston Churchill, was born here in 1874 – the **Churchill Exhibition** is dedicated to his life, work, paintings and writings. The house is encircled by vast, lavish **gardens** and **parklands**, parts of which were landscaped by the great Lancelot 'Capability' Brown. A minitrain (£1) whisks you to the **Pleasure Gardens**, which feature a yew **maze**, adventure playground, lavender garden and butterfly house.

The Drive ›› From Blenheim's grandeur, it's a 10-mile trip down the A44/A34/A4144 to Oxford's dreaming spires.

15 Oxford

One of the world's most famous university towns, the centre of Oxford is rich in history and studded with august buildings. The city has 38 colleges – Christ Church (p38) is the largest, with 650 students, and has the grandest quad. Christ Church was founded in 1524 by Cardinal Thomas Wolsey, and alumni include Albert Einstein and 13 British prime ministers. It's also famous as a location for the Harry Potter films. At the Ashmolean (p38), Britain's oldest public museum has had a modern makeover; interactive displays and glass walls revealing multilevel galleries help showcase treasures include Egyptian mummies, Indian textiles and Islamic art. Beautiful **Magdalen College** (01865-276000; www.magd.ox.ac.uk; High St; adult/child £7/6, pre-booking required; 10am-7pm late Jun-late Sep, 1pm-dusk rest of year) is worth a visit for its medieval chapel, 15th-century cloisters and 40-hectare grounds. Nearby, head to **Magdalen Bridge Boathouse** (01865-202643; www.oxfordpunting.co.uk; High St; chauffeured 4-person punts per 30min £30, punt rental per hour £22; 9.30am-dusk Feb-Nov) for a ride on a chauffeured punt.

p73, p115

Eating & Sleeping

Canterbury 3

ABode Canterbury Boutique Hotel ££

(☎01227-766266; www.abodecanterbury.co.uk; 30-33 High St; r from £74; 📶) The 72 rooms at this super-central hotel, the only boutique hotel in town, are graded from 'comfortable' to 'fabulous' (via 'enviable'), and for the most part live up to their names. They come with features such as handmade beds, chesterfield sofas, tweed cushions and beautiful modern bathrooms. There's a splendid champagne bar, restaurant and tavern, too.

Brighton 5

Artist Residence Boutique Hotel £££

(☎01273-324302; www.artistresidencebrighton.co.uk; 34 Regency Sq; d £120-290; 📶) Eclectic doesn't quite describe the rooms at this wonderful 24-room town-house hotel, set amid the splendour of Regency Sq. As befits the name, every bedroom is a hip blend of bold wall murals, bespoke and vintage furniture, rough wood cladding and in-room roll-top baths. The Set Restaurant downstairs enjoys a glowing reputation.

Winchester 7

Wykeham Arms Inn £££

(☎01962-853834; www.wykehamarmswinchester.co.uk; 75 Kingsgate St; s £84, d £144-194; P 📶) At 250-odd years of age, the Wykeham bursts with history – it used to be a brothel and also put Nelson up for a night (some say the events coincided). Creaking stairs lead to plush bedrooms that manage to be both deeply established and on-trend – sleigh beds meet jazzy fabrics, oak dressers sport stylish lights. Simply smashing.

Salisbury 9

Chapter House Inn £££

(☎01722-341277; www.thechapterhouseuk.com; 9 St Johns St; s £95-145, d £115-155; 📶) In this 800-year-old boutique beauty, wood panels and wildly wonky stairs sit beside duck-your-head beams. The cheaper bedrooms are swish but the posher ones are stunning, starring slipper baths and the odd heraldic crest. The pick is room 6, where King Charles is reputed to have stayed. Lucky him.

Bath 12

Queensberry Hotel £££

(☎01225-985086; www.thequeensberry.co.uk; 4 Russell St; r £235-323, ste £460-510; P 📶) Stylish but unstuffy Queensberry is Bath's best luxury spoil. In these Georgian town houses heritage roots meet snazzy gingham checks, bright upholstery, original fireplaces and free-standing tubs. It's witty (see The Rules on the website), independent (and proud of it), and service is first-rate.

Bristol 13

Riverstation British ££

(☎0117-914 4434; www.riverstation.co.uk; The Grove; bar/restaurant mains £14/17; ⏲10am-10pm Mon-Sat, to 6pm Sun) Riverstation's waterfront views are hard to beat, but it's the food that truly shines. Rich, classical flavours define dishes served up in the restaurant and less formal bar. Expect truffle-fragranced wild mushrooms for breakfast, seasonal risotto for lunch, and stone bass and samphire for dinner.

Oxford 15

Head of the River Hotel £££

(☎01865-721600; www.headoftheriveroxford.co.uk; Folly Bridge, St Aldate's; r incl breakfast £189; 📶) One of the more central Oxford hotels, this large and characterful place at Folly Bridge, immediately south of Christ Church, was originally a Thames-side warehouse. Each of its 20 good-sized rooms is individually decorated with contemporary flair, featuring exposed brickwork and/or tongue-and-groove panelling plus modern fittings. Rates include breakfast cooked to order in the (excellent) **pub** (☎01865-721600; www.headoftheriveroxford.co.uk; Folly Bridge, St Aldate's; ⏲8am-10.30pm Sun-Thu, to 11.30pm Fri & Sat) downstairs.

REP

Classic Trip

Urban & Art Odyssey

England's creative credentials are extraordinary, and touring cities from the southwest to the northeast, you'll undertake a journey through the nation's artistic soul.

TRIP HIGHLIGHTS

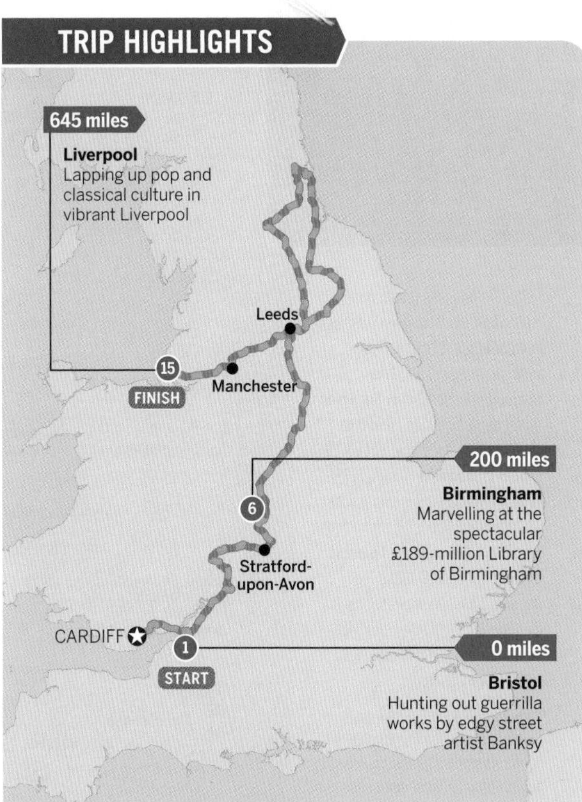

13–15 DAYS
645 MILES / 1030KM

GREAT FOR...

BEST TIME TO GO

Autumn avoids the worst of the weather on the northern legs.

ESSENTIAL PHOTO

Standing, arms outstretched, beside the 20m-high Angel of the North.

The classic lines on show at Great Malvern's Morgan Motor Company.

Birmingham Designed by Francine Houben, the Library of Birmingham is an architectural standout

Classic Trip

4 Urban & Art Odyssey

This exploration of England's urban and artistic soul makes for an exhilarating, creative drive. The visual art you'll see ranges from prehistoric chalk figures to old masters to sprayed-on street designs. Discover classical composers and design classics; exquisite bridges and hand-crafted motor cars. Experience film locations, stunning sculpture and pop culture ranging from the Beatles to football. And it all takes place against a beautiful backdrop.

TRIP HIGHLIGHT

1 Bristol

The creative, edgy city of Bristol is the perfect place to see works by the anonymous street artist Banksy. The central **Well Hung Lover** (Frogmore St) depicts an angry husband, a two-timing wife, and a naked man dangling from a window. The startling **Paint-Pot Angel** (think pink paint meets funerary monument) resides in the foyer of the Bristol Museum & Art Gallery (p71). Banksy's **Mild Mild West** (80 Stokes Croft) features a Molotov cocktail–wielding teddy bear facing three riot police, while his stencil of the **Grim Reaper** rowing a boat is now on the 1st floor of the city's **M Shed museum** (☎0117-352 6600; www.bristolmuseums.org.uk; Princes Wharf; ⊙10am-5pm Tue-Sun). The city's **tourist office** (☎0117-929 9205; www.visitbristol.co.uk; E-Shed, 1 Canons Rd; ⊙10am-5pm; 📶) sells an excellent Banksy info sheet (50p).

The Drive » It's a 45-mile drive along the M4 to Cardiff, a route enlivened by the cruise across the six-lane, cable-stayed

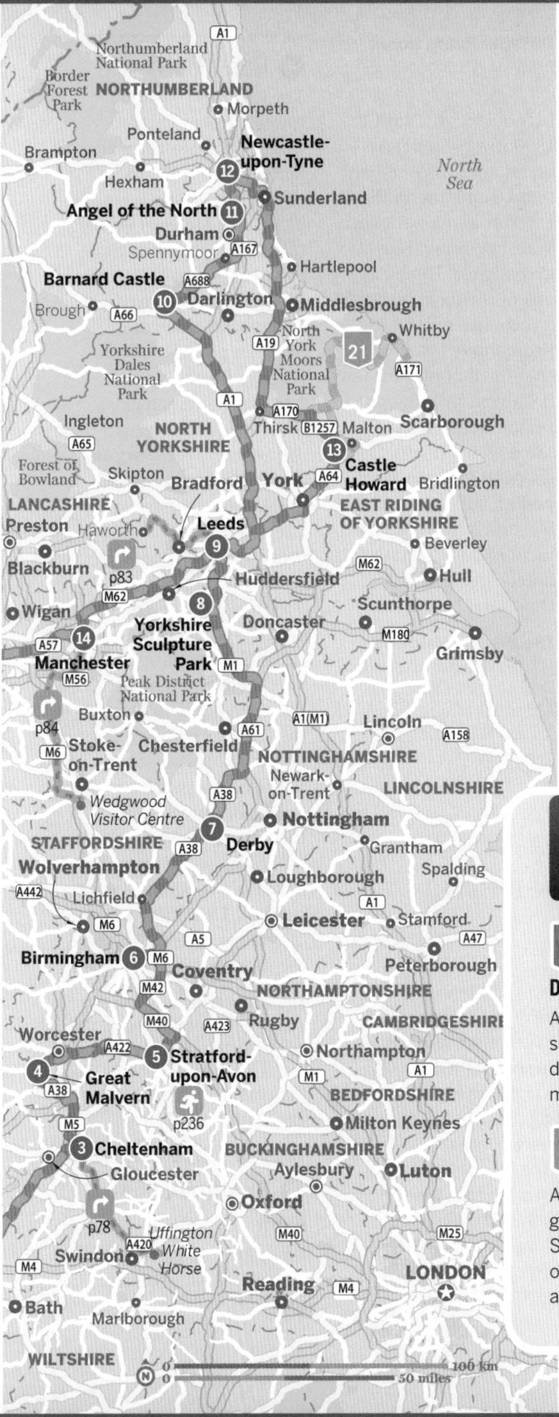

Second Severn Crossing bridge. In Cardiff, follow signs for City Centre car parks; Greyfriars and Westgate St are ideal.

2 Cardiff

The capital of Wales has a vibrant, confident air. And, in the National Museum Cardiff (p42), one of Britain's best museums. Highlights include a trio of Monet's *Water Lilies,* alongside his scenes of London, Rouen and Venice; Sisley's *The Cliff at Penarth* (the artist was married in Cardiff); Renoir's shimmering *La Parisienne;* a cast of Rodin's *The Kiss;* and Van Gogh's anguished *Rain: Auvers.* At nearby Cardiff Castle (p42) the artistic decor includes zodiac symbols in the winter smoking room, mahogany-and-mirrors in

LINK YOUR TRIP

24 West Wales: Swansea to St Davids

A cracking cruise along a spectacular stretch of surf-dashed coast. Starts 40 miles west of Cardiff.

21 North York Moors & Coast

A tour of Yorkshire's gorgeous moors and shores. Starts just 15 miles south of this trip's Castle Howard at York.

the bedrooms, and marble and acres of gold leaf in the Arab room. Cardiff is a great city to explore on foot (p344) – stroll 1 mile south to **Cardiff Bay** to take in the grand modern architecture of the **Wales Millennium Centre** (☎029-2063 6464; www.wmc.org.uk; Bute Pl, CF10 5AL, Cardiff Bay; ⏰10am-6pm, later on show nights).

The Drive » Head back over the Second Severn Crossing for the 70-mile jaunt up the M4/M5 to Cheltenham.

❸ Cheltenham

Gracious, 18th-century spa town Cheltenham offers some fine Regency buildings, including the **Pittville Pump Room** (☎0844-576 2210; www.pittvillepumproom.org.uk; Pittville Park; 👪). Built in 1830 it was modelled on an ancient Athenian temple and has a pillared exterior and a park with lake, lawns and blue-green gates. Famed as one of the most beautiful streets in England, the **Promenade** is a broad, tree-lined boulevard that is flanked by imposing period buildings that are now filled with fancy shops. It leads to **Montpellier**, with a village-like feel and a lively assortment of bars, restaurants, hotels, independent shops and boutiques.

The Drive » Make for the M5 to glide north for 14 miles before peeling off onto the A38 for the climb to hillside to Great Malvern, a further 11 miles away.

DETOUR: UFFINGTON WHITE HORSE

Start: ❸ Cheltenham

A 40-mile detour southeast from Cheltenham leads to the oldest chalk figure in Britain. The **Uffington White Horse** (p38) was created in the Bronze Age, some 3000 years ago, on the crest of Oxfordshire's highest point. A highly stylised horse image, it was crafted by cutting trenches out of the hill and filling them with blocks of chalk; local inhabitants have maintained the figure for centuries. From Cheltenham, head south on A roads towards Swindon, then join the A420 towards Oxford; the horse is signposted from that road. It's then a 0.5-mile walk east through fields from the National Trust car park to the chalk figure itself.

❹ Great Malvern

The gateway to the towering, 9-mile-long ridge of the Malvern Hills, Great Malvern is a picturesque spa town. The **Great Malvern Priory** (☎01684-561020; www.greatmalvernpriory.org.uk; Church St; ⏰9am-5pm) showcases designs ranging from Norman pillars via 15th-century tiles to surreal modernist stained glass. The town's other great attraction is the **Morgan Motor Company** (☎01684-573104; www.morgan-motor.com; Pickersleigh Rd; museum free, tours adult/child £24/12; ⏰museum 8.30am-5pm Mon-Thu, to 2pm Fri, tours by reservation), where Britain's famous sports cars are made. The firm has been handcrafting the vehicles since 1909, and you can still see the mechanics at work on two-hour guided tours of the unassuming shed-like buildings comprising the factory (pre-booking essential). Then view a fleet of vintage classics next to the museum.

The Drive » Time to leave the wooded ridge of the Malvern Hills behind on a 30-mile leg east; it's an A-road meander alongside green fields to Stratford-upon-Avon.

❺ Stratford-upon-Avon

Birthplace of the man who wrote some of the most quoted sentences in the English Language, for many a trip to Tudor Stratford is akin to a literary pilgrimage, and an opportunity to retrace his steps (p236). **Shakespeare's Birthplace** (☎01789-204016; www.shakespeare.org.uk; Henley St; adult/child £15/11; ⏲10am-4pm Mon-Fri, to 5pm Sat & Sun) has restored Tudor rooms and live presentations from famous Shakespearean characters. The playwright died in a house on the site of **Shakespeare's New Place** (☎01789-338536; www.shakespeare.org.uk; cnr Chapel St & Chapel Lane; adult/child £12.50/8; ⏲10am-5pm Apr-Aug, to 4.30pm Sep & Oct, to 3.30pm Nov-Feb) in 1616; an attractive Elizabethan knot garden occupies part of the grounds. Next visit Holy Trinity Church (p43), Shakespeare's final resting place. Look out for handsome 16th- and 17th-century tombs, some fabulous carved choir stalls and the grave of the Bard, with its ominous epitaph: 'cvrst be he yt moves my bones'.

The Drive » Make for the M40 to start your 40-mile drive north. This is true motorway territory; you'll navigate the M42 and the M6 before arriving in Birmingham. Head for the central Bull Ring Car Park.

TRIP HIGHLIGHT

6 Birmingham

Birmingham delivers a big-city vibe and culture by the truckload. Britain's second-biggest city is (rightly) hugely proud of its glittering £189 million **Library of Birmingham** (☎0121-242 4242; www.birmingham.gov.uk/libraries; Centenary Sq; ⏲ground fl 9am-9pm Mon & Tue, 11am-9pm Wed-Fri, to 5pm Sat, rest of bldg 11am-7pm Mon & Tue, to 5pm Wed-Sat). Designed by Francine Houben, it features a subterranean amphitheatre, spiralling interior, viewing decks and glass elevator to the 7th-floor 'secret garden' with panoramic city views. Nearby, Victoria Sq features civic architecture of another era in the 1870s-built **Council House**. To the west Centenary Sq is home to the art-deco **Hall of Memory War Memorial**. From there it's a short stroll to the **Birmingham Museum & Art Gallery** (☎0121-348 8000; www.birminghammuseums.org.uk; Chamberlain Sq; ⏲10am-5pm Sat-Thu, from 10.30am Fri) and its fine collection of Victorian art and major Pre-Raphaelite works by Rossetti and Edward Burne-Jones.

🛏 p85

The Drive » Time for more motorways (M6/M42), initially, on this 45-mile leg. After about 18 miles, though, it's onto the A38 for a more rural cruise to Derby.

7 Derby

One of the crucibles of the Industrial Revolution, these days Derby is home to cultural developments and a rejuvenated riverfront. The central **Quad** (☎01332-290606; www.derbyquad.co.uk; Market Pl; gallery free, cinema tickets adult/child £9/7; ⏲gallery 11am-5pm Mon-Sat, noon-5pm Sun), a striking modernist cube on Market Pl, contains a futuristic art gallery and an art-house cinema. A

ANTON_IVANOV / SHUTTERSTOCK ©

Stratford-upon-Avon Shakespeare's Birthplace

Classic Trip

ANGEL OF THE NORTH BY ANTONY GORMLEY. DAVIDGRAHAM86 / SHUTTERSTOCK ©

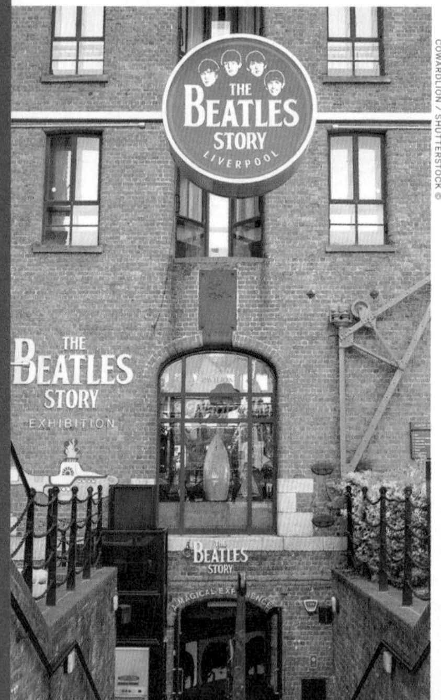

COWARDLION / SHUTTERSTOCK ©

WHY THIS IS A CLASSIC TRIP

ANTHONY HAM, WRITER

Classic Trips are about more than top sights and great drives; they also reveal deeper trends. The places you'll visit on this wide-ranging journey through urban and rural artscapes have either ancient roots or are modern in focus but they all go to the heart of Britain's enduring creativity. Some of the cities here – Cardiff, Newcastle, Manchester and Liverpool among them – have the country's most dynamic cultural offerings.

Above: Sculptor Antony Gormley's *Angel of the North*
Left: Beatles Story, Liverpool
Right: *Ultimate Form* by Barbara Hepworth, Yorkshire Sculpture Park

ULTIMATE FORM BY BARBARA HEPWORTH. DEBUSSY / SHUTTERSTOCK ©

short walk away, at the **Derby Museum & Art Gallery** (☎01332-641901; www.derbymuseums.org; The Strand; ⏰10.30am-4.30pm Tue-Sat, noon-4pm Sun), local history and industry displays include fine ceramics produced by Royal Crown Derby – get an even greater insight into this artistry at the **Royal Crown Derby Factory** (☎01332-712800; www.royal-crownderby.co.uk; 194 Osmaston Rd; museum & factory tour adult/child £5/2.50, museum only £2/1; ⏰museum 10am-4pm Mon-Sat, factory tours 11am & 1.30pm Mon-Thu, 11am Fri), which still produces some of the finest china in England. Pre-book for the factory tour.

🛏 p85

The Drive » Next a 60-mile drive, at first on the A38, then the A61, but largely via that great route north: the M1. Around 57 miles in, pick up signs for the Yorkshire Sculpture Park.

8 Yorkshire Sculpture Park

Yorkshire Sculpture Park (☎01924-832631; www.ysp.co.uk; Bretton Park, near Wakefield; £6; ⏰10am-6pm; P 👪) is one of England's most impressive collections of sculpture. It's scattered across the formidable 18th-century estate of Bretton Park, 200-odd hectares of lawns, fields and trees. A bit like the art world's equivalent of a safari park, the Yorkshire Sculpture Park showcases the work of dozens of sculptors both national and international. But the main focus of this outdoor gallery is the work of local kids Barbara Hepworth (1903–75), who was born in nearby Wakefield, and Henry Moore (1898–1986).

The Drive » Head due north again, but this time on a much shorter leg: 18 miles, largely up the M1. At Leeds, follow the signs for the City Centre.

9 Leeds

One of the UK's fastest-growing cities, Leeds is a vision of 21st-century urban chic. The **Leeds Art Gallery** (www.leeds.gov.uk/artgallery; The Headrow; 10am-4pm Tue-Sat) is packed with heavyweights – Turner, Constable, Stanley Spencer and Wyndham Lewis. Plus pieces by recent arrivals such as Antony Gormley, sculptor of the *Angel of the North*. Nearby, the **Henry Moore Institute** (www.henry-moore.org/hmi; The Headrow; 10am-5pm Tue-Sun) showcases the work of 20th-century sculptors. For a different culture fix, the **Victoria Quarter** (www.victorialeeds.co.uk; Vicar Lane;) delivers striking architecture in the form of mosaic paving, and stained-glass-roofed Victorian arcades. There's also cutting-edge fashion boutiques including Louis Vuitton, Vivienne Westwood and Swarovski, plus the flagship Harvey Nichols store.

p85

The Drive » Your art odyssey continues north, slicing between two national parks: the Yorkshire Dales and the North York Moors. Again, it's largely up the M1/A1. At about 58 miles in, turn off, first onto the A66 towards Brough, then to the town of Barnard Castle (13 miles). From there, signs point to the Bowes Museum.

10 Barnard Castle

Tucked in at the edge of the town of Barnard Castle, the **Bowes Museum** (01833-690606; www.thebowesmuseum.org.uk; Newgate; adult/child/family £14/5/30; 10am-5pm) is a monumental French-style château. Funded by the 19th-century industrialist John Bowes and opened in 1892, this brainchild of his Parisian actress wife, Josephine, was built by French architect Jules Pellechet. The aim was to display a collection the Bowes had travelled the world to assemble. The star attraction is the marvellous 18th-century mechanical swan, which performs every day at 2pm. If you miss it, a film shows it in action.

The Drive » A chance to bypass the motorway for a bit. Take the A688 through Bishop Auckland and Spennymoor for 23 miles. Then rejoin the A1 (M), towards Newcastle. Some 14 miles later take the A167 towards Gateshead South, and watch the windows for the towering Angel of the North. There's a free car park by the base.

11 Angel of the North

Nicknamed the Gateshead Flasher, the extraordinary 200-tonne, rust-coloured, winged human-form **Angel of the North** (www.gateshead.gov.uk; Durham Rd, Low Eighton) has loomed over the A1 (M) since 1998. Sir Antony Gormley's iconic work (which saw him knighted in 2014) stands 20m high, with a wingspan wider than a Boeing 767.

The Drive » Hop on the A167/B1318 for the 6-mile cruise into Newcastle City Centre. Just after 3 miles in, stand by to drive along one of England's most famous river crossings: the mighty Tyne Bridge. Head for a City Centre car park; those at Dean St, Akenside Hill or Painters Heugh are ideal.

12 Newcastle-upon-Tyne

Historic, sophisticated and bursting with nightlife, Newcastle is one of England's most appealing cities. Stroll to the Quayside to contemplate its most striking pieces of engineering. The imposing **Tyne Bridge**

(1925–28) resembles the Sydney Harbour Bridge – no wonder, both were built by the same firm, Dorman Long of Middlesbrough. The quaint **Swing Bridge** (1876), just to the west, pivots in the middle to let ships through. Next, walk 500m to the east over the gorgeous **Millennium Bridge** (2002). This opens like an eyelid to enable vessels to pass and leads to the **BALTIC – Centre for Contemporary Art** (☎0191-478 1810; www.baltic.art; Gateshead Quays; ⏲10.30am-6pm). Once a huge mustard-coloured grain store, this art gallery rivals London's Tate Modern. Rotating shows feature the work of some of the art world's biggest showstoppers. You'll also find artists in residence, a performance space, a cinema, a bar, a spectacular rooftop restaurant (bookings essential) and a 4th-floor outdoor platform and a 5th-floor viewing box, both with fabulous panoramas of the Tyne.

✕ p85, p279

The Drive » After hundreds of miles driving north, it's time to head 84 miles south. Drive back over the Tyne Bridge, making for the A19 towards York. At Thirsk take the A170 towards Helmsley. Peel off right onto the B1257 and follow the brown signs to Castle Howard; a route of rolling fields and woods.

⑬ Castle Howard

Grand, theatrical **Castle Howard** (☎01653-648333; www.castlehoward.co.uk; YO60 7DA; adult/child house & grounds £22/12, grounds only £12.95/8.50; ⏲house 10am-2pm Wed, Fri & Sat, grounds to 5.30pm daily, pre-booked tickets only; P) is one of the world's most beautiful buildings, instantly recognisable from its starring role in the 1980s TV series *Brideshead Revisited* and in the 2008 film of the same name. The great baroque house, which was commissioned in 1699, boasts a magnificent central cupola and plentiful treasures – the breathtaking Great Hall with its soaring Corinthian pilasters, Pre-Raphaelite stained glass in the chapel, and corridors lined with classical antiquities. A wander around the peacock-haunted grounds reveals views of the Howardian Hills and architect Sir John Vanbrugh's playful Temple of the Four Winds.

The Drive » Another near 90-mile stretch, this time heading southwest largely along the A64 towards Leeds and then the M62 to Manchester, eventually leaving the motorways to follow City Centre signs.

⑭ Manchester

Packed with history and culture, Manchester is the uncrowned capital of the north. Here, football is acknowledged as passion and art form in equal measure. The National Football Museum (p44) explores the evolution of the beautiful game, while engaging, hands-on displays include Football Plus, a series of interactive

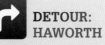

DETOUR: HAWORTH

Start: ⑬ Castle Howard

As you arrive at Leeds, en route from Castle Howard to Manchester, consider a 20-mile detour west, past Bradford to Haworth. This village set beside the moors of the South Pennines has an impeccable artistic pedigree. It was home to the Brontë sisters – Charlotte, Emily and Anne, responsible for *Jane Eyre, Wuthering Heights* and *The Tenant of Wildfell Hall* respectively. The house where they lived from 1820 to 1861 is now the **Bronte Parsonage Museum** (☎01535-642323; www.bronte.org.uk; Church St; adult/child £9.50/4; ⏲10am-5pm Wed-Sun). Rooms are decorated exactly as they were in the Brontë era, including Charlotte's bedroom, her clothes and her writing paraphernalia.

stations allowing you to test your skills in simulated conditions. A 500m walk south leads to the Manchester Art Gallery (p44) where a superb collection of British and European art includes 37 Turner watercolours, and the country's best assemblage of Pre-Raphaelite art. The 20th-century galleries include works by Lucien Freud, Francis Bacon, Stanley Spencer, Henry Moore and David Hockney. Next, hop on one of the city's swish trams to **MediaCityUK**, making for the **Lowry** (☎box office 0843-208 6000; www.thelowry.com; Pier 8, Salford Quays; ⏱10am-6pm, later during performances; 🚊Harbour City or Media-CityUK) to study 300 beautifully humanistic depictions of urban landscapes by LS Lowry (1887–1976), the local artist famous for painting matchstick figures amid the north's mill-dotted urban landscapes.

✖ 🛏 p47, p85, p211

The Drive » A final, 35-mile, motorway cruise: after the A57 (M), join the M62 to roll towards Liverpool, eventually picking up the brown tourist signs for the car parks at the Albert Dock.

TRIP HIGHLIGHT

⓯ Liverpool

A thriving city famous for music, football and wit, Liverpool also has, at **Albert Dock**, the country's largest collection of protected buildings. This World Heritage Site includes the **Tate Liverpool** (☎0151-702 7400; www.tate.org.uk/liverpool; Albert Dock; special exhibitions adult/child from £6/5; ⏱10am-5.50pm; 🚌all city centre), with its substantial checklist of 20th-century artists, plus exhibitions from the mother ship on London's Bankside. Just paces away, the **International Slavery Museum** (☎0151-478 4499; www.liverpoolmuseums.org.uk/ism; Albert Dock; ⏱10am-5pm Wed-Sun) is a clear, uncompromising and profoundly affecting depiction of slavery's unimaginable horrors. The nearby **Beatles Story** (☎0151-709 1963; www.beatlesstory.com; Albert Dock; adult/child £16/9; ⏱10am-4.30pm; 🚌all city centre) features plenty of genuine Fab Four memorabilia, a full-size replica Cavern Club (which was actually tiny) and the Abbey Rd studio where the lads recorded their first singles. A short walk north at **Pier Head** discover the trio of Edwardian buildings beloved by locals: the domed **Port of Liverpool Building** (1907), the Italian palazzo-style **Cunard Building** and the 1911 **Royal Liver Building**, crowned by Liverpool's symbol, a 5.5m copper **Liver Bird**.

🛏 p85

DETOUR: WEDGWOOD VISITOR CENTRE

Start: ⓮ Manchester

A 50-mile detour south from Manchester, largely via the M56/M6, leads to the **Wedgwood Visitor Centre** (☎01782-282986; www.worldofwedgwood.com; Wedgwood Dr, Barlaston ST12 9ER; factory tour & museum adult/child £10/8, museum only free; ⏱factory 10am-4pm Mon-Fri, museum to 5pm daily), 5 miles south of Stoke-on-Trent. The modern production plant for Josiah Wedgwood's porcelain empire, it also offers an insight into this whole area's defining industrial and artistic characteristic: ceramics – the region is still known as the Potteries to this day. Look out for extensive displays of historic pieces, including plenty of Wedgwood's delicate, neoclassical blue-and-white jasperware. The fascinating industrial process is revealed, and there's an interesting film on Josiah's life and work, including his involvement in canal-building and opposition to slavery.

Eating & Sleeping

Birmingham 6

St Pauls House Boutique Hotel ££

(01121-272 0999; www.saintpaulshouse.com; 15-20 St Paul's Sq; d from £99; P ❄) Overlooking a park in the Jewellery Quarter, this independent hotel has 34 fresh, contemporary rooms with welcoming touches, such as hot-water bottles in woollen covers. Upcycled decor in its hip bar (with live music Saturday nights and Sunday afternoons) and restaurant includes industrial-style ropes (as wall hangings and in furnishings) referencing the building's original use as a rope factory.

Derby 7

The Cow Inn £££

(01332-824297; www.cowdalbury.com; The Green, Dalbury Lees; d incl breakfast from £135; P) This whitewashed 19th-century inn 6.5 miles west of Derby has solid oak floors, stone walls and timber-lined ceilings. Its 12 individually styled rooms range from Victorian and art deco to retro vintage, and feature locally handcrafted mattresses and Egyptian cotton sheets. The bar-restaurant's stools are fashioned from milk cans; food is sourced within a 30-mile radius (mains £10.50 to £17.50).

Leeds 9

Quebecs Boutique Hotel ££

(0113-244 8989; www.quebecshotel.co.uk; 9 Quebec St; d/ste from £89/189; P) Victorian grace at its opulent best is the theme of Quebecs, a conversion of the former Leeds & County Liberal Club. The elaborate wood panelling and heraldic stained-glass windows in the public areas are mirrored by the grand design flourishes in the bedrooms, but it's a listed building (which means no double glazing) so expect some street noise.

Newcastle-upon-Tyne 12

Broad Chare Gastropub ££

(0191-211 2144; www.thebroadchare.co.uk; 25 Broad Chare; mains £9-27, bar snacks from £4; kitchen noon-2.30pm & 5.30-10pm Mon-Sat, noon-5pm Sun, bar 11am-11pm Mon-Sat, to 10pm Sun) English classics and splendid cask ales are served in the dark-wood bar and mezzanine of this perfect gastropub. Starters, such as crispy pig ears and venison terrine, are followed by mains that might include a divine grilled pork chop with black pudding and cider sauce.

Manchester 14

Mackie Mayor Food Hall ££

(www.mackiemayor.co.uk; 1 Eagle St; mains £9-15; 10am-10pm Tue-Thu, to 11pm Fri, 9am-11pm Sat, 9am-8pm Sun; all city centre) This restored former meat market is now home to a superb food hall with a fine selection of 10 individual traders. The pizzas from Honest Crust are divine; the pork-belly bao from Baohouse is done just right; Nationale 7 does wonders with a basic sandwich; and Tender Cow serves really tasty steaks. Dining is communal, across two floors.

Qbic Hotel £

(www.qbichotels.com/manchester; John Dalton House, Deansgate, M2 6JR; r from £60;) Qbic's ecofriendly hotel philosophy arrives in Manchester with aplomb in this brilliant budget option. The rooms are compact but cleverly designed, while the recycled furniture, refillable toiletries and glass carafes are just the most visible examples of its commitment to sustainability (there are also solar panels on the roof). Comfortable, convenient and eco-conscious – it's how all hotels should be.

Liverpool 15

Hope Street Hotel Boutique Hotel ££

(0151-709 3000; www.hopestreethotel.co.uk; 40 Hope St; r/ste from £110/175; @ ; all city centre) One of the best digs in town is this Scandi-chic hotel on the city's most elegant street. King-sized beds with Egyptian cotton, oak floors with underfloor heating, and sleek modern bathrooms are the norm in the original hotel as well as its new extension, where there's also a huge spa. Breakfast is £18.50.

BRIGHTON PIER
LITTER
LITTER

Southern & Eastern England

Tempting trails fan out all around London. After revelling in the capital's world-class sights, it's time to take to the road. Within an hour or two you'll be cruising down country lanes en route to fairy-tale castles and some of England's loveliest historic homes and most sun-kissed beaches.

In this corner of the land, road trips are peppered with heritage sights. Spectacular cathedrals are a short hop from rejuvenated seaside resorts, and university cities are just a quick trip from imposing baronial piles.

Whether you're cresting rolling chalk ridges, meandering beside salt marshes or tracing trails down rustic lanes, these are irresistible drives.

Brighton Brighton Pier

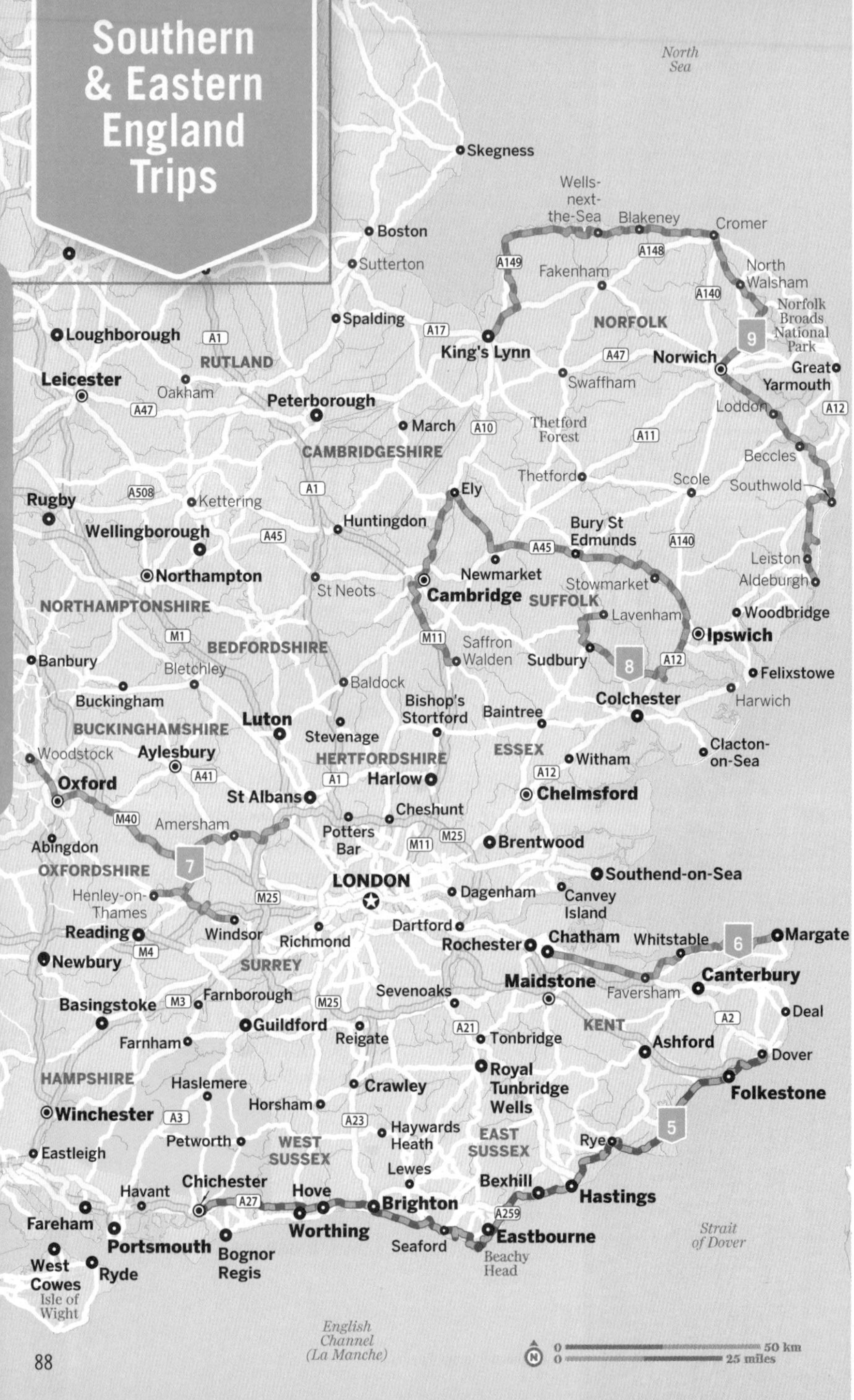
Southern & Eastern England Trips
North Sea
Skegness
Wells-next-the-Sea
Blakeney
Cromer
A148
A149
Fakenham
North Walsham
A140
Norfolk Broads National Park
9
NORFOLK
Boston
Sutterton
Spalding
A17
King's Lynn
A47
Norwich
Great Yarmouth
Swaffham
Loddon
A12
Loughborough
A1
RUTLAND
Leicester
Oakham
A47
Peterborough
March
A10
Thetford Forest
A11
Beccles
CAMBRIDGESHIRE
Thetford
Scole
Southwold
Rugby
A508
Kettering
A1
Ely
Wellingborough
A45
Huntingdon
Bury St Edmunds
A140
A45
Leiston
Northampton
St Neots
Newmarket
Stowmarket
Aldeburgh
NORTHAMPTONSHIRE
Cambridge
SUFFOLK
Lavenham
Woodbridge
M1
BEDFORDSHIRE
M11
Saffron Walden
Sudbury
Ipswich
Banbury
Bletchley
8
A12
Felixstowe
Baldock
Buckingham
Bishop's Stortford
Baintree
Colchester
Harwich
BUCKINGHAMSHIRE
Luton
Stevenage
Woodstock
Aylesbury
HERTFORDSHIRE
ESSEX
Witham
Clacton-on-Sea
A41
A1
Harlow
A12
Oxford
St Albans
Chelmsford
Cheshunt
M40
Amersham
Potters Bar
M25
M11
Brentwood
Abingdon
7
OXFORDSHIRE
LONDON
Southend-on-Sea
Henley-on-Thames
M25
Dagenham
Canvey Island
Windsor
Dartford
Reading
Richmond
Chatham
Whitstable
6
Margate
Rochester
M4
Newbury
SURREY
Maidstone
Canterbury
Faversham
Farnborough
Sevenoaks
M3
M25
Basingstoke
Deal
A2
Guildford
A21
KENT
Reigate
Tonbridge
Farnham
Ashford
Dover
Royal Tunbridge Wells
HAMPSHIRE
Haslemere
Crawley
Folkestone
Horsham
Winchester
A3
A23
5
Haywards Heath
EAST SUSSEX
Petworth
WEST SUSSEX
Rye
Eastleigh
Lewes
Chichester
Bexhill
Havant
Hove
Hastings
A27
Brighton
A259
Fareham
Worthing
Portsmouth
Bognor Regis
Seaford
Eastbourne
Strait of Dover
Beachy Head
West Cowes
Ryde
Isle of Wight
English Channel (La Manche)
N
0
50 km
0
25 miles

EXPOSE / SHUTTERSTOCK ©

Oxford Christ Church's Great Hall

5 **Seaside Saunter 8 Days**
Join holidaymakers and hedonists as you tour chalk cliffs and undulating downs.

6 **Kent: History, Art, Hops & Grapes 4 Days**
Hip resorts and foodie pit stops galore on a 'Garden of England' tour.

7 **Royalty & the Thames Valley 5–6 Days**
Pure class: a Queen's castle, a university city and Harry Potter sights.

8 **Around the Cam 6–7 Days**
From exquisite, collegiate Cambridge to magnificent medieval villages and countryside that inspired great masters.

9 **Suffolk-Norfolk Shore 8 Days**
Delight in fantastic seafood, bird-packed reserves, dune-backed beaches and some of England's grandest country houses.

DON'T MISS

Dover Castle

Hidden below Dover's famous medieval defences are a set of secret WWII tunnels. Compelling audiovisual displays brings them alive. Trip 5

Christ Church Cathedral

Christ Church's grand quad is world famous, but this 12th-century, vaulted cathedral is as glorious as it is serene. Trip 7

Shepherd Neame Brewery

Many people bypass Faversham, but seeing how this brewery's traditional ales are made makes it well worth a detour. Trip 6

Henry Blogg Museum

It may be bijou but the RNLI's life-saving exhibits on show here are absorbing, and include a full-sized lifeboat. Trip 9

Willy Lott's House

Visit the site of a world-famous painting – the setting for Constable's *The Hay Wain*. Trip 8

Classic Trip

Seaside Saunter

5

Along the southeast corner's underbelly, this string of shingle beaches, chalk cliffs, Victorian resorts and medieval castles constitutes a quintessentially British seaside escapade.

TRIP HIGHLIGHTS

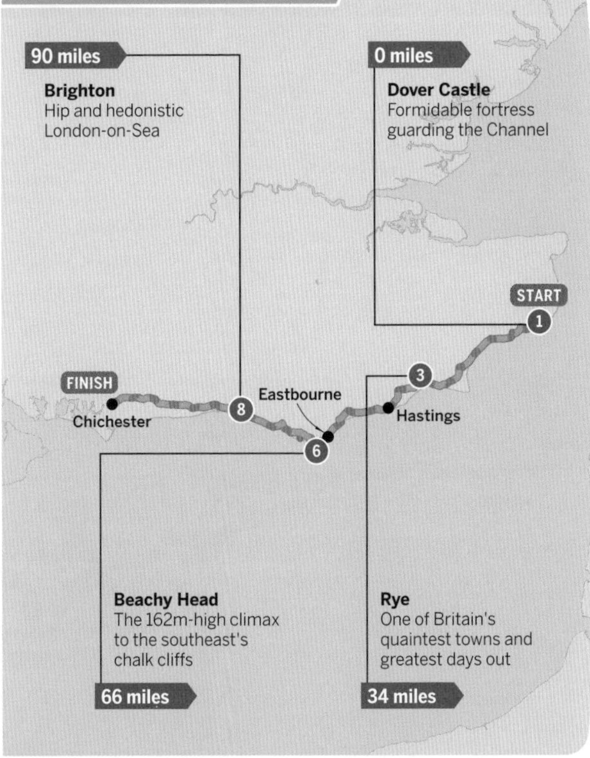

0 miles
Dover Castle
Formidable fortress guarding the Channel

34 miles
Rye
One of Britain's quaintest towns and greatest days out

66 miles
Beachy Head
The 162m-high climax to the southeast's chalk cliffs

90 miles
Brighton
Hip and hedonistic London-on-Sea

START 1 · 3 · Hastings · Eastbourne · 6 · 8 · FINISH Chichester

8 DAYS
123 MILES / 198KM

GREAT FOR...

BEST TIME TO GO

April to October, when the fickle British weather is at its warmest and driest.

ESSENTIAL PHOTO

The Seven Sisters chalk cliffs from Cuckmere Haven or Hope Gap.

BEST FOR SHOPPING

Brighton's Lanes and North Laine neighbourhoods have some of the UK'S best shopping.

Beachy Head Brilliant chalk cliffs that reach 162m high

Classic Trip

5 Seaside Saunter

This scenic saunter along the coast of Kent and Sussex takes you across undulating chalk cliffs, over rolling downs and through marshes, calling at some of the most famous names on the south's coastal map. London's riviera is stuffed with history and heritage, from the ancient remains of Roman and Norman invaders, to the more recent seaside legacies of holidaying Victorians.

TRIP HIGHLIGHT

1 Dover

The maritime city of Dover on the south coast, though bombed to pieces in WWII, possesses a principal chunk of Kent heritage – a huge **castle** (EH; www.english-heritage.org.uk; adult/child £17/10.20; ⏲10am-6pm Apr-Jul & Sep, 9.30am-6pm Aug, to 5pm Oct, 10am-4pm Sat & Sun Nov-Mar; P) that has guarded England's closest point to France since medieval times.

The 12th-century Great Tower, with walls up to 7m thick, is a medieval warren filled with interactive exhibits and light-and-sound shows that return visitors to the times of Henry II. The remains of a Roman lighthouse are also within the castle grounds.

The biggest draw, however, is the network of secret wartime tunnels. The claustrophobic chalk-hewn passageways were first excavated during the Napoleonic Wars and then expanded to house a

LINK YOUR TRIP

Kent: History, Art, Hops & Grapes

This North Kent route starts in Margate, just 22 miles north of Dover.

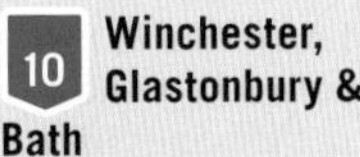

Winchester, Glastonbury & Bath

Chichester is 42 miles from historic Winchester.

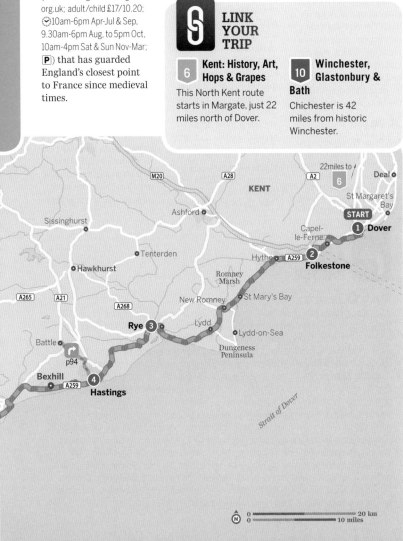

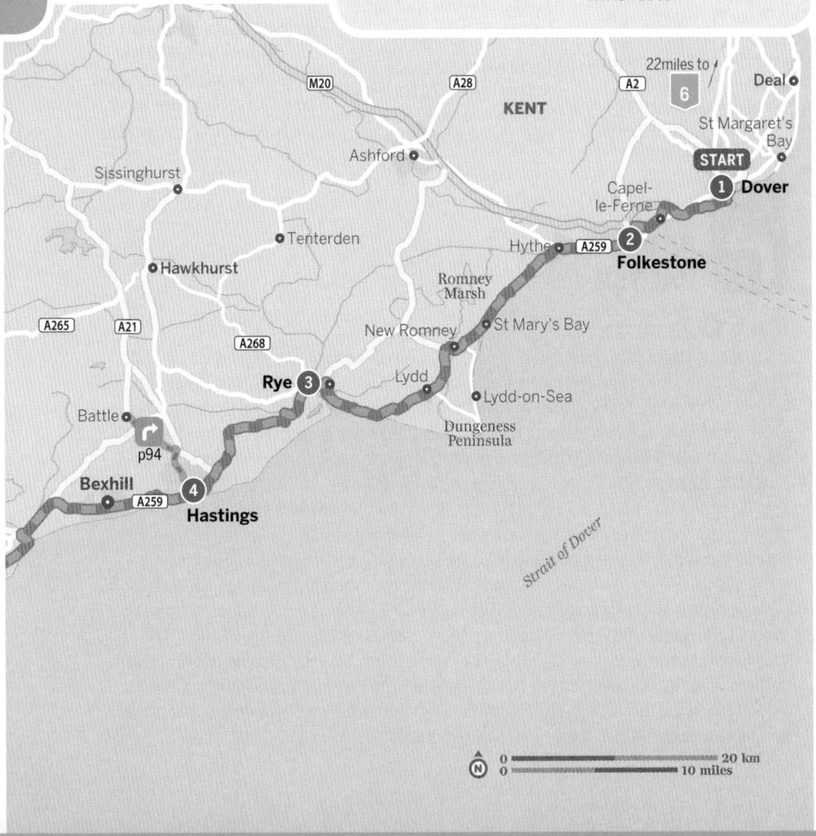

command post and hospital in WWII. The highly enjoyable 50-minute guided tour (every 20 minutes, included in the ticket price) tells the story of one of Britain's most famous wartime operations, code-named Dynamo, which was directed from here in 1940 and oversaw the evacuation of thousands from the beaches at Dunkirk.

 p99

The Drive » Follow London-bound foreign lorries out of Dover on the A20, which climbs steeply onto the chalk cliffs. After a couple of miles, find the turn-off for Capel-le-Ferne, home to a Battle of Britain Memorial. The suburbs of Folkestone, your next stop, lie just beyond (9 miles in total).

❷ Folkestone

This formerly grand resort was once a favourite stomping ground of royal bon viveur King Edward VII, but today is a wonderfully forgotten piece of England's seaside past. Stroll through the seafront Leas Coastal Park with its subtropical flora, then stop for fish and chips at the old fish market before ambling up through the Creative Quarter, Folkestone's old town, now home to artists' studios and craft shops.

The Drive » Satnavs may send you to the M20 but instead follow the coastal A259 to Hythe. This is the terminus of the idyllic Romney Hythe & Dymchurch narrow-gauge railway, worth a day off the road itself. At New Romney the road swings inland and crosses the Romney Marsh, a sweep of wetland flats dotted with grazing sheep and wind turbines. Total 25 miles.

TRIP HIGHLIGHT

❸ Rye

Possibly southern England's quaintest town, Rye is a little nugget of the past, a medieval settlement that looks like it's been sealed in amber. Cobbled lanes, mysterious passageways and crooked half-timbered Tudor buildings echo to tales of resident smugglers, ghosts and writers.

Aimless wandering and browsing are the way to go here, but the most picturesque scene is **Mer-**

DETOUR: BATTLE

Start: ❹ Hastings

If there's one date that seared itself into every English schoolchild's mind, it was 1066, the year of the most famous battle in the country's history – the Battle of Hastings, which saw invading French duke William of Normandy, aka William the Conqueror, score a decisive victory over local King Harold. This major bend in the road in English history actually took place 6 miles north of Hastings in what is now the town of Battle.

Battle Abbey (EH; www.english-heritage.org.uk; High St; adult/child £13.60/8.20; ⌚10am-6pm Apr-Sep, to 4pm Sat & Sun Oct-Mar) was built on the battlefield, a penance ordered by the pope for the loss of life incurred here. Only the foundations of the original church remain; the altar's position is supposedly the spot where King Harold famously took an arrow in his eye. Other impressive monastic buildings survive and make for atmospheric explorations. The battlefield's lush rolling hillsides do little to evoke the ferocity of the event, but high-tech interactive presentations and a film at the visitor centre, as well as blow-by-blow audio tours, do their utmost to bring the battle to life. You can now survey the battlefield from the rooftop viewing platform, a good place to start a visit. The biggest crowds turn up mid-October to witness the annual re-enactment on the original battlefield.

maid Street; American writer Henry James lived in **Lamb House** (NT; www.nationaltrust.org.uk; West St; adult/concession £7.90/3.95; ⏲11am-5pm Fri-Mon late Mar-Oct), while views over town extend from the tower of the **Church of St Mary the Virgin** (Church Sq; tower admission £3.50; ⏲9am-5.30pm Apr-Oct, to 4.30pm Nov-Mar).

 p99

The Drive » Just 12 miles separate Rye from your next stop west, Hastings. The A259 passes through chocolate-box-pretty Winchelsea – watch out for the steep hairpin turn below the village. There's another steep climb through the suburbs of Hastings before a quick descent back to sea level and Hastings' seafront.

4 Hastings

Forever associated with the Norman invasion of 1066, Hastings thrived as one of the Cinque Ports and, in its Victorian heyday, was one of the country's most fashionable resorts. After a period of steady postwar decline, the town has enjoyed a mini-renaissance.

The beach and restored pier are the biggest draws, but Hastings also has several worthwhile museums and bucketloads of independent shops. Away from the old town, the most intriguing neighbourhood is the **Stade** (Rock-A-Nore Rd), home to distinctive black clapboard structures known as Net Shops (built to store fishing gear back in the 17th century, but some now house fishmongers).

p99

The Drive » Follow the A259 along the coast as far as Bexhill, where architecture aficionados will want to see the De La Warr Pavilion in Bexhill-on-Sea. Stick to the A259 (as opposed to the A27) at Pevensey, site of a castle first built by the Romans – this will eventually bring you past Eastbourne's Sovereign Harbour and along Britain's most impressive seafront. Total distance 17 miles.

5 Eastbourne

'Britain's sunniest town' welcomes visitors with a grand seafront, white-washed late-Victorian hotels and palm trees lining the Channel, with the scene given focus by one of the country's finest Victorian **piers** (www.eastbournepier.com; ⏲24hr). Associated primarily with sedate retirement, Eastbourne has had a shot in the arm in recent years with huge Polish and student communities arriving to lower the average age considerably.

The traditional seaside duo of beach and pier are the main draws, but the **Towner Art Gallery** (☎01323-434670; www.townereastbourne.org.uk; Devonshire Park, College Rd; ⏲10am-5pm Tue-Sun) energises the town's artistic persona. The town is the start or end point for a hike along the 100-mile South Downs Way, which passes through the South Downs National Park.

The Drive » To reach Beachy Head (3.5 miles away), drive west along Eastbourne's seafront until the road turns inland and begins to climb. A brown tourist sign points the way to the famous cliff along a narrow road. There's ample parking around the area.

DETOUR: SOUTH DOWNS NATIONAL PARK

Start: 5 Eastbourne

The UK's newest national park is more than 600 sq miles of rolling chalk downs stretching west from Eastbourne to Winchester, a distance of about 100 miles. A long-distance hiking trail called the South Downs Way famously unfurls along its entire length – the ridge hike takes at least 10 days, consisting largely of breathtaking views. Many of the route's most interesting and prettiest locations can be found just west of Eastbourne and can be reached on a there-and-back day walk, or by using local buses.

Classic Trip

TRIP HIGHLIGHT

6 Beachy Head

At 162m tall, the cliffs of Beachy Head are the highest point of the chalky rock faces that slice across the coastline at the southern end of the South Downs. This is a spot of thrilling, windswept beauty, the brilliant white chalk rising high into the blue Sussex sky. At the foot of the cliffs stands a much-photographed, candy-striped lighthouse.

If you follow the clifftop path, you'll head down to the tiny seaside hamlet of **Birling Gap**, where the secluded beach is a sun-trap popular with locals and walkers taking a breather. You'll also find a handy National Trust–run cafe here.

On a darker note, Beachy Head is also known as one of Europe's most frequented suicide spots, with its own dedicated chaplaincy team whose job it is to talk people off the edge.

The Drive » Your next stop, the Seven Sisters, are best viewed from Cuckmere Haven, 6 miles west of Beachy Head. From the cliff top, head to Birling Gap then join the A259 at East Dean. Leave your car at the Cuckmere Inn in Exceat and walk 1 mile south to the sea, following the slow River Cuckmere.

7 Seven Sisters

The undulating chalk cliffs of the Seven Sisters create one of the southeast's classic views. The best vantage point is at Cuckmere Haven, the only spot on England's south coast where a river meets the sea with no town to keep it company. The pleasant walk from the car park at Exceat down to the shingle beach follows the crazily meandering River Cuckmere.

The Drive » Some 17 miles divide Cuckmere Haven from Brighton, your next stop. The A259 passes straight through Seaford and Newhaven, the latter home to an obscure cross-Channel ferry service. Nearer to Brighton, Rottingdean was home to Rudyard Kipling from 1897 to 1902. The A259 becomes Brighton seafront just beyond.

TRIP HIGHLIGHT

8 Brighton

Brighton warrants a couple of days' exploration. With its bohemian,

WHY THIS IS A CLASSIC TRIP
DAMIAN HARPER, WRITER

You're never far from London, but then you could be a million miles away. The brine is on the breeze as you roll past quaint fishing villages, vertiginous chalk cliffs, undulating hills, imposing castles and once-faded-but-revived Victorian resorts clinging to the coast. One moment you're staring out over miles of sea, the next you're wandering a warren of medieval lanes or stumbling across chunks of ancient Roman heritage.

Left: Royal Pavilion, Brighton
Right: Lighthouse at Beachy Head

Classic Trip

cosmopolitan and hedonistic vibe, Brighton is where England's seaside experience goes from cold to cool. Outside London it boasts the south's best shopping and nightlife and is the de facto gay capital of the UK.

Away from the beach, top billing goes to the **Royal Pavilion** (☎03000-290900; http://brightonmuseums.org.uk/royalpavilion; Royal Pavilion Gardens; adult/child £15.50/9.50; ⏲9.30am-5.45pm Apr-Sep, 10am-5.15pm Oct-Mar), the eye-popping palace party pad of Prince George, later Prince Regent and then King George IV. It's one of the most opulent buildings in England, packed with weird-and-wonderful interiors and outrageous chinoiserie.

The **i360 Tower** (☎03337-720360; www.britishairwaysi360.com; Lower King's Rd; adult/child £16.50/8.25; ⏲10am-7.30pm Sun-Thu, to 9.30pm Fri & Sat) rises from the point where the now-defunct West Pier used to make landfall. Take the huge glass doughnut 138m above the city for gobsmacking vistas of the coast.

p73, p99

The Drive » There are two routes you can take to reach Arundel, 23 miles to the west. The A259 and the A27 run parallel to each other – the latter is a much quicker option; the former a more interesting drive through Worthing and Littlehampton.

9 Arundel

Arguably the prettiest town in West Sussex, Arundel is clustered around a vast fairy-tale **castle** (www.arundelcastle.org; adult/child/family £15/5/35; ⏲10am-5pm Tue-Sun Easter-Oct), home to the dukes of Norfolk for centuries. An imposing bastion rising above the picturesque streets below, the castle was first built in the 11th century. Ransacked during the English Civil War, much – but not all – of the castle is the result of reconstruction between 1718 and 1900.

When you are done with the sights, Arundel's hilly streets overflow with antique emporiums, teashops, eateries and some excellent art galleries.

The Drive » A mere 11 miles separate Arundel from your final stop, the cathedral city of Chichester, the capital of West Sussex. The only feasible route is the fast A27 all the way.

10 Chichester

Founded by the Romans, this lively Georgian market town is still almost encircled by its Roman and medieval town walls. Away from the sights, Chichester has four pedestrianised shopping streets that meet at the Chichester Cross, the town's epicentre.

Chichester Cathedral (www.chichestercathedral.org.uk; West St; ⏲7.15am-6.30pm, free tours 11.15am & 2.30pm Mon-Sat) was begun in 1075 and largely rebuilt in the 13th century. The free-standing church tower went up in the 15th century; the spire dates from the 19th century, when its predecessor famously toppled over. Inside, three storeys of beautiful arches sweep upwards and Romanesque carvings are dotted around. Interesting features to track down include a smudgy stained-glass window added by artist Marc Chagall in 1978 and a glassed-over section of Roman mosaic flooring.

The **Novium** (☎01243-775888; www.thenovium.org; Tower St; ⏲10am-3pm Tue-Fri, to 4pm Sat) is Chichester's purpose-built museum, a home for the eclectic collections of the erstwhile District Museum, built around a set of Roman *thermae* (baths) discovered in the 1970s.

p99

Eating & Sleeping

Dover ❶

✕ Allotment British $$

(☎01304-214467; www.theallotmentrestaurant.com; 9 High St; mains £13.50-18; ⏲noon-9pm Tue-Sat, 12.30-4pm Sun) Dover's best dining spot sources fish and meat from around Canterbury, to be seasoned with herbs from the tranquil garden out back. Cleanse your palette with a Kentish wine in a relaxed, understated setting as you admire the view of the Maison Dieu (13th-century pilgrims' hospital) directly opposite through the exquisite stained-glass frontage.

Rye ❸

✕ Webbe's at the Fish Cafe Seafood $$

(☎01797-222226; www.webbesrestaurants.co.uk; 17 Tower St; mains £13-18; ⏲noon-2pm daily & 6-9.30pm Mon-Thu, 5.30-9.30pm Fri-Sun) Rye's best fish restaurant is a simple dining room flooded with natural light from large arched windows. The menu features local fish such as Rye Bay flounder in cider sauce and Rye cod in beer batter. The restaurant doubles as a cookery school and is the venue for the annual Scallop Week in March.

Jeake's House Hotel $$

(☎01797-222828; www.jeakeshouse.com; Mermaid St; r £100-225; P) Situated on Mermaid St, this 17th-century town house once belonged to US poet Conrad Aiken. The 11 rooms are named after writers who stayed here. The decor was probably slightly less bold then, missing the beeswaxed antiques and lavish drapery. Take a pew in the snug book-lined bar and, continuing the theme, enjoy breakfast in an 18th-century former Quaker chapel.

Hastings ❹

Swan House B&B $$$

(☎01424-430014; www.swanhousehastings.co.uk; 1 Hill St; s/d incl breakfast from £110/130; @) Inside its 15th-century timbered shell, this four-room place blends contemporary and vintage chic to perfection. Rooms feature organic toiletries, fresh flowers, hand-painted walls and huge beds. The guest lounge, where pale sofas, painted floorboards and striking modern sculptures rub shoulders with beams and a huge stone fireplace, is a stunner. Minimum two-night stay at weekends.

Brighton ❽

✕ Terre à Terre Vegetarian $$

(☎01273-729051; www.terreaterre.co.uk; 71 East St; mains from £16.95; ⏲noon-10pm Tue-Sun;) Take your taste buds around a meat-free world in this vegetarian restaurant, where inventive and flavourful dishes are meticulously plated in a casual and friendly ambience. The range is breathtaking, from wasabi-crusted cashews to fondue soufflé and steamed Szechuan buns, rounded off with salt caramel truffles. A daily afternoon-tea service includes a vegan option.

Hotel Pelirocco Hotel $$

(☎01273-327055; www.hotelpelirocco.co.uk; 10 Regency Sq; s/tw £59/84, d £99-155, tr/ste £165/249;) One of Brighton's sexiest and nuttiest places to stay, the Pelirocco is the ultimate venue for a flirty rock-and-roll weekend. Flamboyant rooms, some designed by artists, include the 'Lord Vader's Quarters', paying homage to *Star Wars;* the 'Do Knit Disturb' room, a knitted room with even a knitted telephone; the Rockabilly room, a shrine to 1950s nostalgia; a 'Modrophenia' room and a Bowie boudoir.

Chichester ❿

Chichester Harbour Hotel Boutique Hotel $$$

(☎01243-778000; www.chichester-harbour-hotel.co.uk; North St; s/d from £105/125;) An enticing option that boasts a stylish restaurant, this Georgian hotel has comfortable, period rooms spiced up with bold colours. Book well ahead.

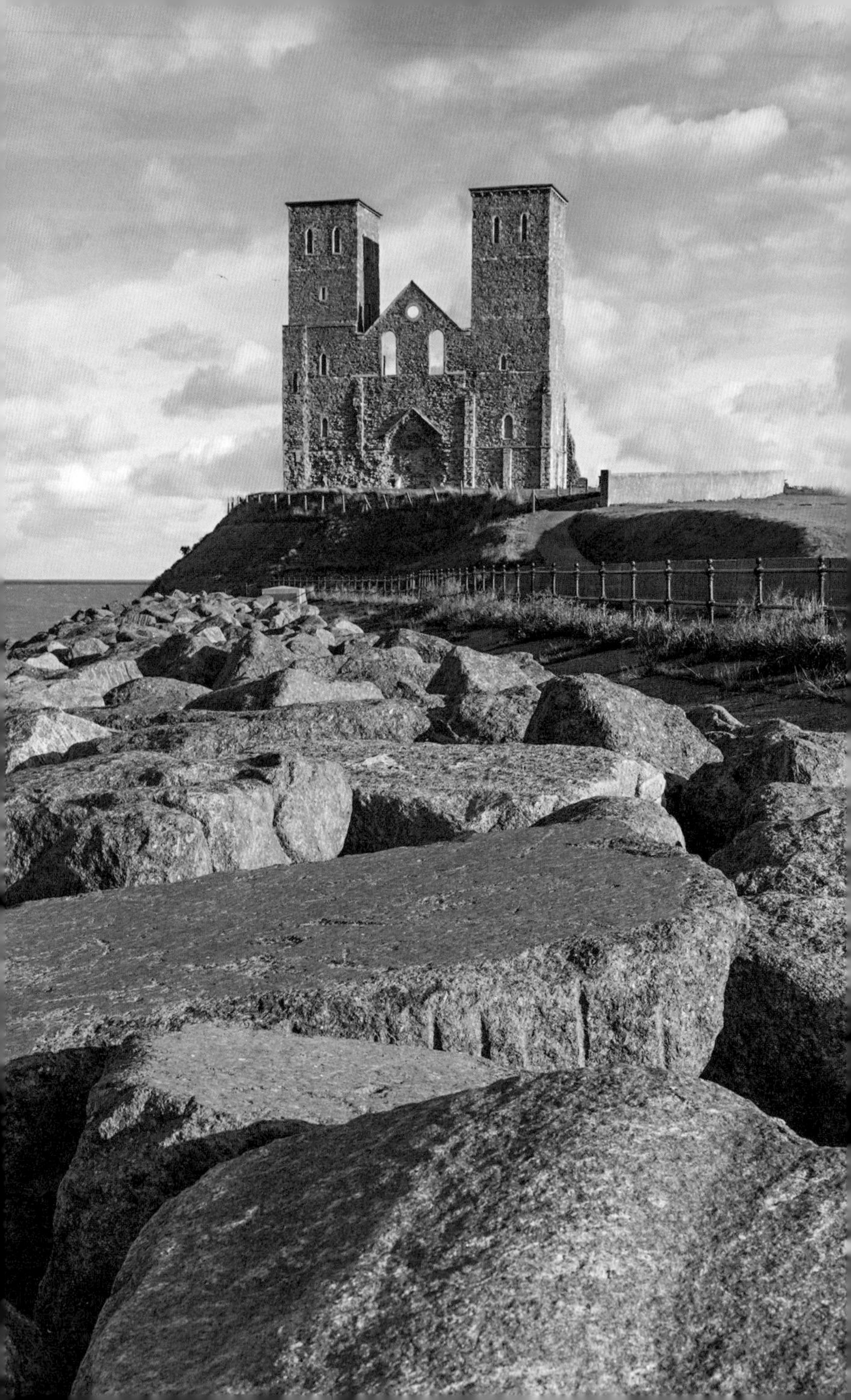

Kent: History, Art, Hops & Grapes

From Margate to Chatham, this eclectic route follows the north Kent coast, a stretch of shingle and shipyards, with rarely visited Roman heritage sites and seaside fun.

TRIP HIGHLIGHTS

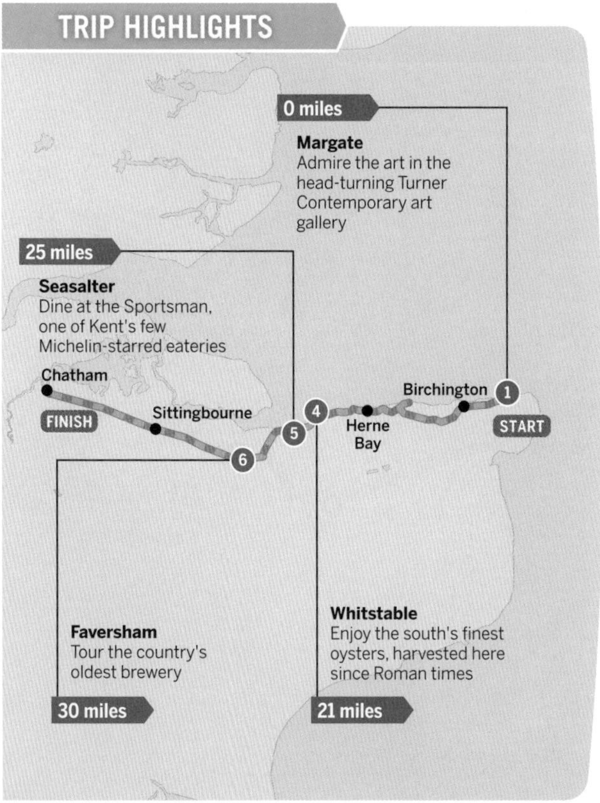

0 miles
Margate
Admire the art in the head-turning Turner Contemporary art gallery

25 miles
Seasalter
Dine at the Sportsman, one of Kent's few Michelin-starred eateries

Chatham
FINISH
Sittingbourne
Birchington
Herne Bay
START
1
4
5
6

Faversham
Tour the country's oldest brewery
30 miles

Whitstable
Enjoy the south's finest oysters, harvested here since Roman times
21 miles

4 DAYS
46 MILES / 74KM

GREAT FOR...

BEST TIME TO GO

April to October sees the mildest temperatures, least rainfall and most sun.

ESSENTIAL PHOTO

The Reculver towers rising high above the sea is one of the Kent coast's most memorable images.

BEST FOR FOODIES

The Sportsman Pub and Fordwich Arms are Michelin-starred and superb.

Reculver Ruins of a deserted 12th-century church

6 Kent: History, Art, Hops & Grapes

From Margate's seafront to the oyster houses of gentrified Whitstable, from the shipping heritage of Chatham to Britain's oldest brewery in Faversham, the theme along Kent's north coast is local tradition. Kent is the 'Garden of England' and produces the tastiest of ingredients – most notably here, the country's finest hops – but on this trip you'll also discover what a vital role the sea has played in the county's traditional life.

TRIP HIGHLIGHT

1 Margate

This grand old seaside town, with fine-sand beaches, artistic associations and the famous **Dreamland** (www.dreamland.co.uk; Marine Tce; entry £5, rides £1.50-5; 10am-6pm, days vary throughout the year;) amusement park, endured a long period of decline but has bounced back splendidly in recent years. There's no greater symbol of this rejuvenation than the eye-catching **Turner Contemporary**

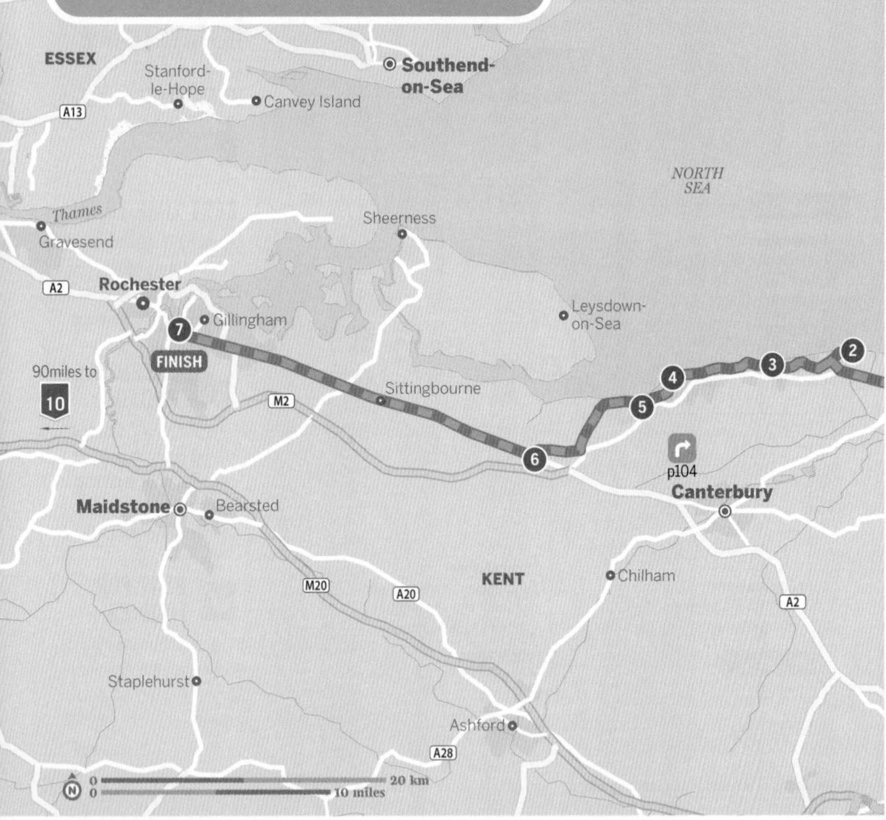

(☎01843-233000; www.turnercontemporary.org; Rendezvous; ⏰10am-5pm Wed-Sun) art gallery, bolted together on the site of the seafront guesthouse where artistic genius and pioneer JMW Turner used to stay. Top-notch contemporary installations by high-calibre artists such as Tracey Emin (who grew up in Margate) and Alex Katz are on the gallery menu.

Add a bevy of superb restaurants and boho cafes to the carefully curated junk emporia and period architecture of the rejuvenated old town and Margate has even emerged with a new and fashionable nickname: Shoreditch-on-Sea, in honour of the London hipster ghetto.

✕ 🛏 p107

The Drive » From Margate seafront head west along Canterbury Rd until you come to the roundabout junction with the A299. Turn right and follow this until you see the turn-off for Reculver. The journey is around 12 miles.

2 Reculver

When the Romans first arrived in Britain they built two fortresses at either end of the strategic Wantsum Channel, a stretch of water that divided the Isle of Thanet from the mainland. The channel silted up in the 16th century, but the ruins of the fortresses remain – Richborough near Sandwich, and Reculver here on the north Kent coast. The Roman remnants here are not as impressive as the ruins of the 12th-century church, the twin towers of which can be seen for miles along the coast. This was part of an Anglo-Saxon monastery but today the site, with the sea creeping ever closer, is deserted.

The Drive » Just 4.5 miles divide Reculver and Herne Bay, your next stop. Don't take the A299; follow instead the back roads along the coast through residential areas and with the occasional sea view.

3 Herne Bay

The seaside town of Herne Bay may be light on sights but it does have a long shingle beach that extends for miles either side of town. The shingle shelves ever so gradually into the North Sea, making this ideal territory for water sports and hot-weather water fun. The Reculver Country Park, a wild stretch of rocky shore backed by cliffs, operated by the Kent Wildlife Trust, lines the coast west of the town.

The Drive » Herne Bay and Whitstable are almost joined

LINK YOUR TRIP

5 Seaside Saunter
It's just 22 miles from Margate to Dover, the start of an epic route along the south coast.

10 Winchester, Glastonbury & Bath
It looks a long way on the map, but it's only two hours (103 miles) from Chatham to Winchester.

at the hip, but the drive from the centre of one to the centre of the other is still 5 miles. The best route is to head onto the A299 then turn off at Tankerton, the local main road morphing eventually into Whitstable's high street.

TRIP HIGHLIGHT

4 Whitstable

Oysters, weatherboard houses, a shingle beach, an old-fashioned high street and an easy-going vibe – these are the things that attract so many Londoners to Whitstable, just a few miles north of Canterbury. It's most famous for its oysters, best sampled at **Wheeler's Oyster Bar** (01227-273311; www.wheelersoysterbar.com; 8 High St; dozen oysters from £12, mains from £7.50; 10am-

DETOUR: CANTERBURY

Start: 4 Whitstable

It's an easy 8-mile drive south from Whitstable (follow the B2205 south from Whitstable to the roundabout and then take the A290) to Canterbury, a chart-topping English cathedral city and one of southern England's biggest attractions. Many consider the World Heritage–listed cathedral that dominates its centre to be one of Europe's finest, and the town's narrow medieval alleyways, riverside gardens and ancient city walls are a joy to explore. But Canterbury isn't just a showpiece for the past – it's a bustling, busy place with an energetic student population and a wide choice of contemporary bars, restaurants, venues and independent shops.

Canterbury Cathedral (www.canterbury-cathedral.org; adult/child £12.50/8.50, tours £5/4, audio guide £4/3; 10am-4.30pm Mon-Sat, 12.30-4.30pm Sun) is a rich repository of over 1400 years of Christian history, and the Church of England's mother ship is a truly extraordinary place. This Gothic cathedral, the highlight of the city's World Heritage Sites, is southeast England's top tourist attraction as well as a very active place of worship. It's also the site of one of English history's most famous murders: Archbishop Thomas Becket violently met his maker here in 1170. Allow at least two hours to do the cathedral justice.

Of the city's other sites, the **Roman Museum** (www.canterburymuseums.co.uk; Butchery Lane; adult/child £9/free; 10am-5pm) is a subterranean archaeological site that affords fascinating glimpses into everyday life in Canterbury almost two millennia ago. Stroll a reconstructed Roman marketplace and rooms, including a kitchen, and examine Roman mosaic floors. Almost everything you see here was only discovered after WWII bombs delivered impromptu excavation. A highlight is the almost entirely intact Roman soldier's helmet dating from Caesar's invasion, unearthed near the village of Bridge in 2012. It's the most complete example ever found in the UK.

For a different perspective of the city's history, take a River Stour cruise with **Canterbury Historic River Tours** (07790 534744; www.canterburyrivertours.co.uk; King's Bridge; adult/child £12.50/7; 10am-5pm Mar-Oct). Knowledgeable guides double as energetic oarsmen on these fascinating, multi-award-winning trips, which depart from King's Bridge.

p107

PADMAYOGINI / SHUTTERSTOCK ©

Whitstable Participants in the annual Whitstable Oyster Festival

4pm Thu-Tue), which has been serving the fabled molluscs since 1856. The town holds an annual oyster festival in late July. The modest local **museum** (☎01227-264742; www.whitstablemuseum.org; 5 Oxford St; adult/child £3/free; ⏰10.30am-4.30pm Thu-Sat, 10.30am-4.30pm Wed-Sat during school holidays) has glass cases examining Whitstable's oyster industry, the Crab & Winkle Railway that once ran from Canterbury, and the local fishing fleet, as well as a corner dedicated to actor Peter Cushing, star of several Hammer Horror films and the town's most famous resident, who died in 1994.

✕ 🛏 p107

The Drive » It's 4 miles to the next stop, the Sportsman Pub. From Whitstable centre follow Joy Lane until it becomes Faversham Rd – this will take you all the way to Seasalter, the village home of the Michelin-starred tavern.

TRIP HIGHLIGHT

5 Seasalter

The anonymous village of Seasalter would barely deserve mention without the **Sportsman Pub** (www.thesportsmanseasalter.co.uk; Faversham Rd, Seasalter; five-course tasting menu £60; ⏲restaurant noon-2pm & 7-9pm Tue-Sat, 12.30-2.45pm Sun), one of East Kent's two eateries decorated with a Michelin star (held for 12 years). Local ingredients from sea, marsh and woods are crafted by Whitstable-born chef Stephen Harris into taste-packed Kentish creations that have food critics drooling. Oysters dominate the starter line-up, fish the mains menu. All the butter, salt and cured meats here are made by the chef himself. It's a real treat and proof that Michelin-standard food can be served in an informal bar setting and at an affordable price.

The Drive » From the culinary delights of Seasalter take the 5-mile drive east to Faversham for one of Kent's drinking highlights. From the Sportsman Pub take Seasalter Rd south until just after Goodnestone, then turn right onto Whitstable Rd – this will take you into Faversham.

TRIP HIGHLIGHT

6 Faversham

The little-visited but pleasant old market town of Faversham is packed with architecture from medieval times right up to the present day. Light on top-tier sights, it does have one big draw – the **Shepherd Neame Brewery** (☎01795-542016; www.shepherdneame.co.uk; 10 Court St, Faversham; tours £14; ⏲2pm daily), Britain's oldest and the pride of Kent for its traditional ales brewed from the county's unrivalled hops. There are brewery tours, ale samplers' suppers, beer-and-food-matching evenings, but you'll have to book ahead for all of these as they're very popular. Otherwise Shepherd Neame ale is available across the county, the most famous brand being the aptly named Spitfire.

The Drive » Faversham to Chatham is the longest uninterrupted stretch on this route, at 19 miles. Shun the M2 for the 'old' A2, the original Roman road that runs almost arrow-straight from Canterbury to the River Medway.

7 Chatham

On the Medway riverfront, the **Chatham Historic Dockyard** (☎01634-823800; https://thedockyard.co.uk; Dock Rd; adult/child £25/15; ⏲10am-6pm Apr-Oct, to 4pm mid-Feb–Mar & Nov), a candidate for Unesco World Heritage status, occupies a third of what was once the Royal Navy's main dock facility. It is possibly the most complete 18th-century dock in the world and has been transformed into a maritime museum examining the Age of Sail. Exhibits include well-restored ships, exhibitions on a variety of shipbuilding themes and a working steam railway.

Eating & Sleeping

Margate 1

Angela's — Seafood $$

(01843-319978; www.angelasofmargate.com; 21 The Parade; mains £12-21; noon-2.30pm & 5.45-10pm Tue-Sat) Simple white-fronted Angela's casts its net wide over local and visiting diners seeking top-notch seafood. Built on a sustainable ethic and run by lovely staff, the restaurant serves delightful goodies from the brine. The menu changes daily but expect goodies like smoked haddock chowder, Whitstable rock oysters, mussels with cider and garlic, or ray wing with leek, rosemary and smoked paprika.

Reading Rooms — B&B $$$

(01843-225166; www.thereadingrooms margate.co.uk; 31 Hawley Sq; r incl breakfast £190;) Occupying an unmarked 18th-century Georgian town house on a tranquil square just five minutes' walk from the sea, this luxury two-bedroom boutique B&B is an elegant treat. Antique white-painted rooms with waxed wooden floors and beautiful French antique reproduction furniture contrast with the 21st-century bathrooms fragrant with luxury cosmetics. Breakfast is served in your room. Bookings essential.

Whitstable 4

Samphire — Modern British $$

(01227-770075; www.samphirewhitstable.co.uk; 4 High St; mains £9-20; 8am-9.30pm Sun-Tue & Thu, 9am-9.30pm Wed, 8am-10pm Fri & Sat) The shabby-chic jumble of tables and chairs, big-print wallpaper and blackboard menus create the perfect stage for meticulously crafted mains containing East Kent's most flavour-packed ingredients. An interesting side dish is its namesake samphire, an asparagus-like plant that grows on sea-sprayed rocks and cliffs, often found on menus in these parts.

Hotel Continental — Hotel $$

(01227-280280; www.hotelcontinental.co.uk; 29 Beach Walk; r from £75, huts from £85;) The bright and breezy quarters at this elegant seaside art deco building sport light-painted wood cladding, brilliant white beds and sparkling bathrooms. There's a decent restaurant and bar on the premises. The hotel also runs the Fishermen's Huts by the beach, a dozen-or-so former fishermen's stores that have been charmingly converted to accommodate visitors.

Canterbury: Detour

Fordwich Arms — British $$$

(01227-710444; www.fordwicharms.co.uk; King St, Fordwich; mains £30-32, tasting menu £75, set lunch/dinner £35/50; noon-2.30pm & 6-9pm Tue-Sat, noon-4pm Sun;) By the River Stour in England's smallest town (population 400), this pub is elevated by both views from the riverside terrace and a twinkling Michelin star. With its 1930s bar, the restaurant, under the leadership of head chef Daniel Smith, has caused a Kentish stir. Each dish is a work of art, employing fresh creativity and locally sourced ingredients.

Expect such delightful choices as rock oysters and mignonette dressing, line-caught turbot, mussels, cabbage, smoked bacon and *vin jaune* or roast duck with parsnip, pickled walnut and quince. Vegetarian menus are also available. The home-baked bread with home-churned butter is very moreish. Fordwich is 3.5km east of Canterbury, south of the A28.

House of Agnes — Hotel $$

(01227-472185; www.houseofagnes.co.uk; 71 St Dunstan's St; r incl breakfast £70-145;) This rather wonky 13th-century beamed inn, mentioned in Dickens' *David Copperfield*, has eight themed rooms bearing names such as 'Marrakesh' (Moorish), 'Venice' (carnival masks), 'Boston' (light and airy) and 'Canterbury' (antiques, four-poster, heavy fabrics). If you prefer your room to have straight lines and right angles, there are eight less exciting, but no less comfortable, 'stable' rooms in the garden annexe.

Royalty & the Thames Valley

West of London's bright lights, venture into a rewarding world of timeworn castles, literary legends, glorious gardens, Harry Potter frenzy and architectural wizardry.

TRIP HIGHLIGHTS

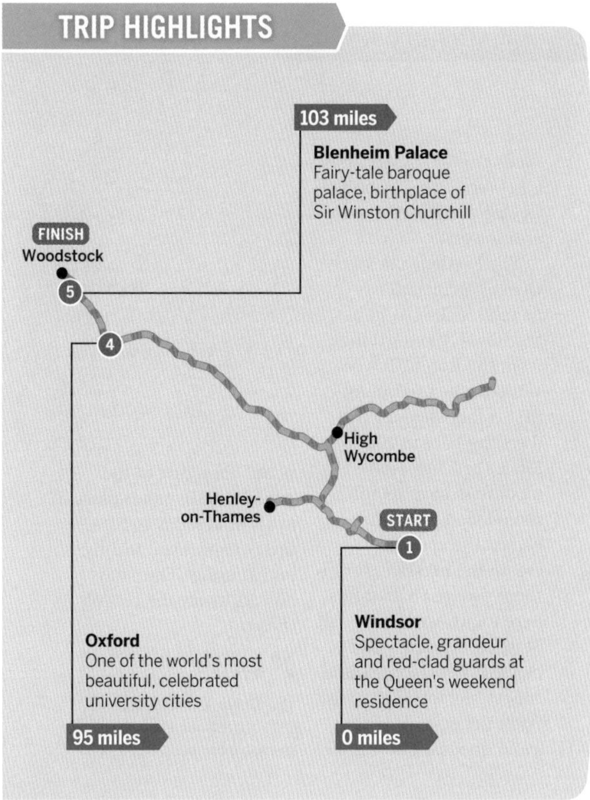

103 miles

Blenheim Palace
Fairy-tale baroque palace, birthplace of Sir Winston Churchill

FINISH
Woodstock

5

4

High Wycombe

Henley-on-Thames

START

1

Oxford
One of the world's most beautiful, celebrated university cities

95 miles

Windsor
Spectacle, grandeur and red-clad guards at the Queen's weekend residence

0 miles

5–6 DAYS
105 MILES / 169KM

GREAT FOR...

BEST TIME TO GO

Anytime; particularly April to July, for warmer weather and flower-filled gardens.

ESSENTIAL PHOTO

Any of Oxford's sandstone landmarks: the Bridge of Sighs, the Radcliffe Camera or one of the Colleges.

BEST FOR FAMILIES

Disappearing into Harry Potter's magical world at Warner Bros Studio Tour.

Oxford Bridge of Sighs at Oxford University

7 Royalty & the Thames Valley

Zigzagging from whimsical Windsor to scholarly Oxford, this richly varied trip whisks you off to some of south England's most magical destinations. You'll find royal fanfare and the world's oldest continually occupied fortress in Windsor, one of the country's most magnificent stately homes at Blenheim, and architectural wonders, academic buzz and historical curiosities in Oxford. Then there's Henley-on-Thames' rowing extravaganza, Woodstock's prosperous charm and, for detouring adventurers, landscaped Stowe.

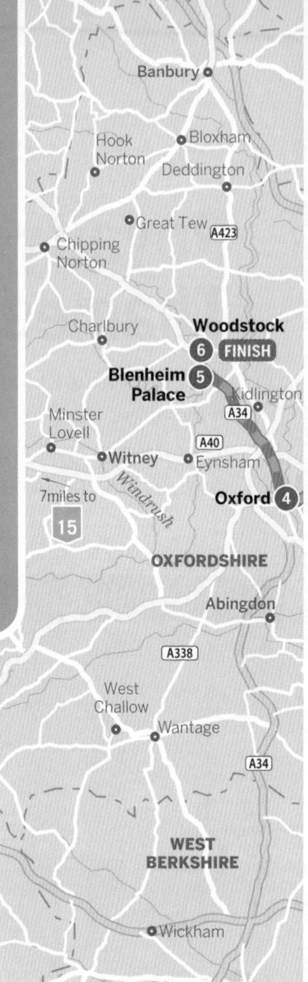

TRIP HIGHLIGHT

1 Windsor

Flaunting royal pomp at every turn, from the ceremonious changing of the guards to the magnificent outdoors treasure that is **Windsor Great Park** (☎01753-860222; www.windsor-greatpark.co.uk; Windsor; ⏲dawn-dusk), Windsor has a rather surreal atmosphere. Crowning the Thames-side town is **Windsor Castle** (☎03031-237304; www.royalcollection.org.uk; Castle Hill; adult/child £23.50/13.50; ⏲10am-5.15pm Mar-Oct, to 4.15pm Nov-Feb; 👪; 🚌702 from London Victoria, 🚆London Waterloo-Windsor & Eton Riverside, 🚆London Paddington-Windsor & Eton Central via Slough), a majestic vision of battlements and towers.

The castle is one of the Queen's principal residences; if she's at home, the Royal Standard flies from the Round Tower. William the Conqueror first established a royal dwelling here in 1080. Since then successive monarchs have rebuilt, remodelled and refurbished the complex to create the massive, sumptuous palace that stands here today, with its lavish State Apartments and beautiful St George's and Albert Memorial chapels. Book tickets online to avoid queues. The triumphant changing of the guard usually takes place at 11am Monday to Saturday from April to July, and Tuesday, Thursday and Saturday the rest of the year.

✕ 🛏 p115

The Drive » This section of the drive involves some inevitable big roads, but they'll

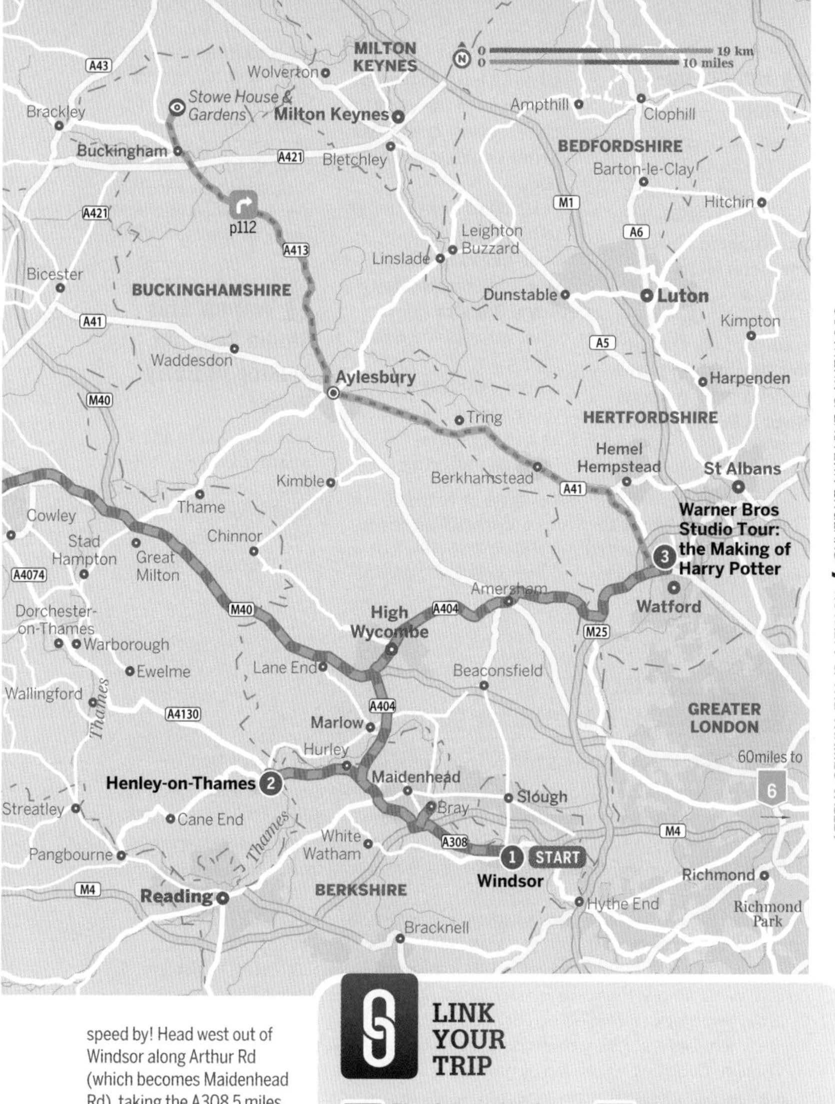

speed by! Head west out of Windsor along Arthur Rd (which becomes Maidenhead Rd), taking the A308 5 miles northwest to bypass the M4 motorway. Follow signs onto the A404(M), head 3.5 miles northwest and exit onto the A4130. It's 6 miles northwest to Henley-on-Thames.

LINK YOUR TRIP

15 The Cotswolds & Literary England

Head 20 miles west from Oxford to Burford to get lost in this in-depth tour of the dreamy gold-tinged Cotswolds.

6 Kent: History, Art, Hops & Grapes

From Windsor, skirt 70 miles around London's southern edge to meet this culture-fuelled jaunt at Chatham.

❷ Henley-on-Thames

Standing elegantly beside the Thames, Henley is an attractive commuter town of red-brick and half-timbered houses, characterful pubs, lovely riverside saunters and a long-established rowing tradition. For the full low-down, drop into the excellent, modern **River & Rowing Museum** (☎01491-415600; www.rrm.co.uk; Mill Meadows; adult/child £12.50/10; ⏰10am-4pm Thu-Mon; P 👪), where the airy 1st-floor galleries tell the story of rowing as an Olympic sport, alongside striking boat displays that include the early 19th-century *Royal Oak,* Britain's oldest racing boat.

If you're lucky enough to be visiting in July, book ahead for the world-famous **Henley Royal Regatta** (www.hrr.co.uk; tickets £25-32, on-site parking £34; ⏰early Jul), a high-calibre rowing tournament that doubles as a major social fixture for England's elite.

The Drive » Whizz 10.5 miles northeast from Henley to High Wycombe (A4130 and A404). It's mostly major roads into London from here, but for a prettier, more rural drive, continue 15 miles northeast along the A404, passing Amersham, through the Chilterns Area of Outstanding Natural Beauty. Join the M25; 5 miles northeast is Warner Bros Studio Tour (signposted).

❸ Warner Bros Studio Tour: the Making of Harry Potter

Whether you're a fair-weather fan or a full-on Potterhead, this magical **studio tour** (☎0345 084 0900; www.wbstudiotour.co.uk; Studio Tour Dr,

DETOUR: STOWE HOUSE & GARDENS

Start: ❸ Warner Bros Studio Tour: The Making of Harry Potter

From the Harry Potter studios, it's a rewarding 41-mile diversion northwest to Stowe, home to some of England's most spectacularly beautiful gardens. Take the A41 23 miles northwest to Aylesbury, then the A413 16 miles northwest to Buckingham. From here, brown signs lead along fabulous 1.5-mile-long tree-lined Stowe Ave to Stowe.

Covering 160 hectares, Stowe's glorious **gardens** (NT; ☎01280-817156; www.nationaltrust.org.uk; New Inn Farm; adult/child £10/5; ⏰10am-5pm mid-Feb–Oct, to 4pm Nov–mid-Feb; P) were shaped in the 18th century by Britain's greatest landscape gardeners. Among them was master landscape architect Lancelot 'Capability' Brown, who kick-started his career at Stowe. The gardens are best known for their many temples and follies, commissioned by the super-wealthy Richard Temple (1st Viscount Cobham), whose family motto was *Templa Quam Dilecta* (How Delightful are Your Temples). Paths meander past lakes, bridges, temples, fountains and cascades, and through Capability Brown's Grecian Valley.

Lording over the gardens, neoclassical Stowe House is now an exclusive private school. Although rooms are left bare (the house's contents were sold off to rescue the original owners from financial disaster), the sheer scale and ornamentation of the building is impressive.

From Stowe, head 32 miles southwest via the A421, A43, M40 and A34 to Oxford to rejoin the main route. This detour totals 72 miles; you'll need at least half a day to explore Stowe properly.

WD25; adult/child £47/38; ⌚8.30am-10pm, hours vary Oct-May; P ♿) is worth its out-the-way Watford location and admittedly hefty-sounding admission price. You'll need to pre-book your visit for an allocated time slot; arrive 20 minutes beforehand and allow two to three hours inside. It starts with a short film before you're ushered through giant doors into the film studios – the first of many 'wow' moments.

You're then free to explore the rest of the complex, including a large hangar featuring all the most familiar interior sets (Dumbledore's office, the Gryffindor common room, Hagrid's hut), another starring Platform 9¾ and the Hogwarts Express, and an outdoor section displaying Privet Drive, the purple triple-decker Knight Bus, Sirius Black's motorbike and a shop selling butterbeer (sickly sweet).

Other highlights include a stroll down Diagon Alley, but the most enchanting treat is saved for last – a shimmering, gasp-inducing 1:24 scale model of Hogwarts.

The Drive » Exit the major M25 5 miles southwest of Watford and backtrack along the scenic A404, past Amersham, to High Wycombe. Zip 17 miles northwest on the M40, take the A40 5 miles west and follow Oxford signs. Driving and parking in central Oxford is near impossible; use one of five Park & Ride car parks around the city edge (£2 to £4 per day, plus bus fare).

Watford Warner Bros Studio Tour: the Making of Harry Potter

TRIP HIGHLIGHT

4 Oxford

One of the world's most famous university cities, Oxford is a beautiful, privileged place, and deserves at least two days on your itinerary. Loved by literary greats JRR Tolkien, CS Lewis and Oscar Wilde, it's steeped in history and studded with august honey-toned buildings, yet maintains a young, lively studenty feel.

The university's 38 colleges are scattered throughout the city, the oldest dating back to the 13th century. Seek out your own corner of studious calm, but don't miss extraordinary, wealthy **Magdalen College** (☎01865-276000; www.magd.ox.ac.uk; High St; adult/child £7/6, pre-booking required; ⌚10am-7pm late Jun-late Sep, 1pm-dusk rest of year), peaceful and exclusive All Souls College (if visitors are allowed in again), and magnificent, popular **Christ Church** (☎01865-276492; www.chch.ox.ac.uk; St Aldate's; adult/child £15/14, pre-booking essential; ⌚10am-5pm Mon-Sat, from 2pm Sun), with the grandest of quads. Christ Church is Oxford's largest college, famous as a location for the Harry Potter films (check out the Great Hall and staircase) and for its wonderful vaulted **cathedral** (☎01865-276150; www.chch.ox.ac.uk/cathedral; St Aldate's; ⌚10am-5pm Mon-Sat, from 2pm Sun).

Explore the fantastic **Ashmolean Museum** (☎01865-278000; www.ashmolean.org; Beaumont St; ⌚10am-5pm Tue-Sun, to 8pm last Fri of month; ♿)

and stroll down exquisite Catte St, flanked by golden colleges, the steeped 1914 **Bridge of Sighs** (Hertford Bridge; New College Lane), the relatively unadorned (but historically important) **University Church of St Mary the Virgin** (☎01865-279111; www.university-church.ox.ac.uk; High St; church free, tower £5; ⏲10am-6pm Mon-Sat, from noon Sun), and the striking, circular, columned **Radcliffe Camera** (☎01865-287400; www.bodleian.ox.ac.uk; Radcliffe Sq; tours £15; ⏲tours 9.15am Wed & Sat, 11.15am & 1.15pm Sun). Also here is Oxford's **Bodleian Library** (☎01865-287400; www.bodleian.ox.ac.uk/bodley; Catte St; ⏲9am-5pm Mon-Sat, from 11am Sun), one of the oldest public libraries in the world and quite possibly the most impressive one you'll ever see; admission is by guided tour.

Outstanding buildings aside, punting is a quintessential, unmissable Oxford experience: **Magdalen Bridge Boathouse** (☎01865-202643; www.oxfordpunting.co.uk; High St; chauffeured 4-person punts per 30min £30, punt rental per hour £22; ⏲9.30am-dusk Feb-Nov) is the most central location to take to the water. Oxford's many literary-linked pubs, such as the **Turf Tavern** (☎01865-243235; www.turftavern-oxford.co.uk; 4-5 Bath Pl; ⏲noon-10pm; 📶) and **Eagle & Child** (☎01865-302925; www.nicholsonspubs.co.uk/theeagleandchildoxford; 49 St Giles; ⏲11am-10pm Mon-Sat, noon-10pm Sun), provide the perfect post-punt retreat.

✕ 🛏 p73, p115

The Drive » It's a quick 8-mile trip northwest on the A44 to Blenheim Palace, which has a sprawling free car park.

TRIP HIGHLIGHT

5 Blenheim Palace

Absolutely worth travelling for, **Blenheim Palace** (☎01993-810530; www.blenheimpalace.com; Woodstock; adult/child £28.50/16.50, park & gardens only £18.50/8.60; ⏲palace 10.30am-4.30pm, park & gardens 9.30am-6.30pm or dusk; P), one of Britain's greatest stately homes, is a monumental baroque fantasy, designed by Sir John Vanbrugh and Nicholas Hawksmoor, and built between 1705 and 1722. The land and funds to build the house were granted to John Churchill, duke of Marlborough, by a grateful Queen Anne, after his victory over the French at the 1704 Battle of Blenheim. Sir Winston Churchill was born here in 1874. Now a Unesco World Heritage Site, Blenheim (*blen*-num) is home to the 12th duke.

Leave enough time and energy to walk the lavish **gardens and parklands**, parts of which were landscaped by the great Lancelot 'Capability' Brown.

The Drive » Leaving Blenheim Palace you'll emerge on the A4095. Turn left, skirting the splendid palace grounds, and, from the roundabout, signs lead 1 mile northwest into Woodstock.

---

6 Woodstock

Though the main reason to swing by Woodstock is, of course, to visit nearby Blenheim Palace, the town itself is blessed with a delightful, affluent centre dotted with old pubs, antique stores, fine stone houses and several luxuriously stylish hotels. It's well worth exploring, and makes the perfect final overnight stop to your trip.

If you're craving a stroll, the **Wychwood Way** (www.wychwoodproject.org/cms/node/24) is a historic, 37-mile loop route from Woodstock through an ancient royal forest, divided into manageable sections for those who fancy tackling a smaller part.

Eating & Sleeping

Windsor 1

✕ Fat Duck — Modern British $$$

(☎01628-580333; www.thefatduck.co.uk; High St; degustation menu per person £250-325; ⏰lunch from noon, dinner from 7pm Tue-Sat) Arguably Britain's most famous restaurant, the Fat Duck is the flagship property of Heston Blumenthal. A pioneer of 'molecular' cuisine, he transformed the place from a rundown pub into a three-starred restaurant that was once voted the world's best. Reserve your 'ticket' in advance and enjoy a journey-themed, seasonally changing set menu. Drinks and service are charged in addition to the dining price.

✕ Two Brewers — Pub Food $$

(☎01753-855426; www.twobrewerswindsor.co.uk; 34 Park St; mains £15-26; ⏰11.30am-10pm Mon-Sat, noon-10pm Sun) This atmospheric 18th-century inn, at the gateway to Windsor Great Park, serves tasty, well-prepped food ranging from soups, salads and fishcakes to steak, cod loin and cheeseboards. Sunny benches front the flower-covered exterior; inside are low-beamed ceilings, dim lighting and a roaring winter fire.

Macdonald Windsor Hotel — Hotel $$$

(☎03448-799101; www.macdonaldhotels.co.uk/Windsor; 23 High St; r from £185; P Wi-Fi Pets) The cream of Windsor's crop, this floral-scented hotel may look small from the front, but beyond its revolving door you'll find 120 elegant rooms. Rich, deep reds and purples add a plush feel to the resolutely modern decor, while service hits a perfect friendly and professional note. Some rooms have castle glimpses.

Alma House — B&B $$

(☎01753-862983; www.almahouse.co.uk; 56 Alma Rd; s/d from £60/80; Wi-Fi) Within this pretty Victorian town house, half a mile southwest of the castle, the four smart rooms feature comfy beds, abundant light and tasteful cream or purple decor. Three rooms, including the similarly homey annexe room out back, accommodate families. Breakfast is a minimal self-service continental spread.

Oxford 4

✕ Vaults & Garden — Cafe $

(☎01865-279112; www.thevaultsandgarden.com; University Church of St Mary the Virgin, Radcliffe Sq; mains £9-10.50; ⏰9am-5pm; Wi-Fi Vegetarian) This beautiful lunch venue spreads from the vaulted 14th-century Old Congregation House of the University Church into a garden facing the Radcliffe Camera. Come early and queue at the counter to choose from wholesome organic specials. Breakfast and afternoon tea (those scones!) are equally good.

✕ Magdalen Arms — British $$

(☎01865-243159; www.magdalenarms.co.uk; 243 Iffley Rd; mains £14-42; ⏰11am-10pm Tue-Sat, to 9pm Sun; Vegetarian Family) A mile beyond Magdalen Bridge, this extra-special neighbourhood gastropub has won plaudits from the national press. A friendly, informal spot, it offers indoor and outdoor space for drinkers, and dining tables further back. From vegetarian specials such as broad-bean tagliatelle to the fabulous sharing-size steak-and-ale pie, everything is delicious, with gutsy flavours.

Oxford Coach & Horses — B&B $$$

(☎01865-200017; www.oxfordcoachandhorses.co.uk; 62 St Clement's St; s/d £130/150; P Wi-Fi) A former 18th-century coaching inn, this fabulous English-Mexican-owned boutique B&B hides behind a fresh powder-blue exterior, just a few metres from the Cowley Rd action. The eight light-filled rooms are cosy, spacious and styled in soothing pastels with exposed beams. The converted ground floor houses an airy, attractive breakfast room.

Old Bank Hotel — Hotel $$$

(☎01865-799599; www.oldbank-hotel.co.uk; 91-94 High St; r from £230; P Wi-Fi) Slap bang in the centre of Oxford (front rooms overlook the University Church), this grand hotel is liberally scattered with contemporary art and offers 42 elegant, spacious, pale-hued rooms. Sleek pads feature sensor lighting and Nespresso machines; others are less flashy but comfortable and characterful. For spectacular views, splash out on glossy junior suite 45.

Around the Cam

Settle in for a grand tour though the heart of old England; a trip that meanders through countryside that inspired old masters, to ancient villages and a spectacular university city.

TRIP HIGHLIGHTS

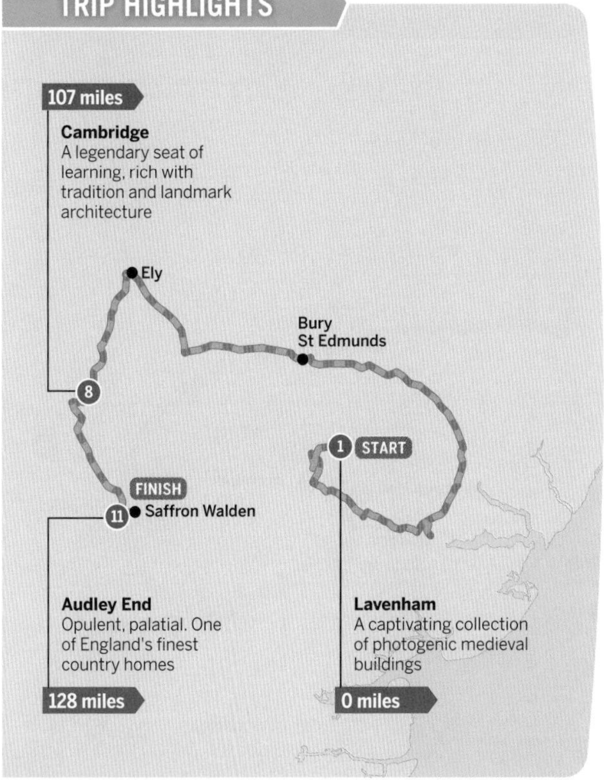

107 miles

Cambridge
A legendary seat of learning, rich with tradition and landmark architecture

Ely

Bury St Edmunds

8

1 START

FINISH

11 Saffron Walden

Audley End
Opulent, palatial. One of England's finest country homes

128 miles

Lavenham
A captivating collection of photogenic medieval buildings

0 miles

6–7 DAYS
130 MILES / 210KM

GREAT FOR...

BEST TIME TO GO

Mid-June to September brings fine weather and longer opening hours.

ESSENTIAL PHOTO

The Flatford Mill view that has hardly changed since Constable's time.

BEST FOR CULTURE

One of the world's most important centres of learning: historic Cambridge.

Cambridge Historic, architecturally rich, and easily explored on foot

8 Around the Cam

On this road trip, you'll take a journey not just into English history, but into landscapes that define what it means to be English. Stops include a spectacular cathedral, wonky villages of leaning timbered houses, scenery immortalised by famous painters, and some of England's grandest stately homes. Then there's Cambridge, a bewitching university city where history and tradition seem to emanate from the bicycle-crowded streets.

TRIP HIGHLIGHT

1 Lavenham

One of England's most immaculately preserved medieval towns, the former wool-trade centre of Lavenham is dominated by beautiful timbered houses that tip and lean at crazy angles. If it's open, browse the museum inside whitewashed **Lavenham Guildhall** (NT; ☎01787-247646; www.nationaltrust.org.uk; Market Pl; adult/child £9.30/4.65; ⏲10.30am-4pm Wed-Sun), a superb example of close-

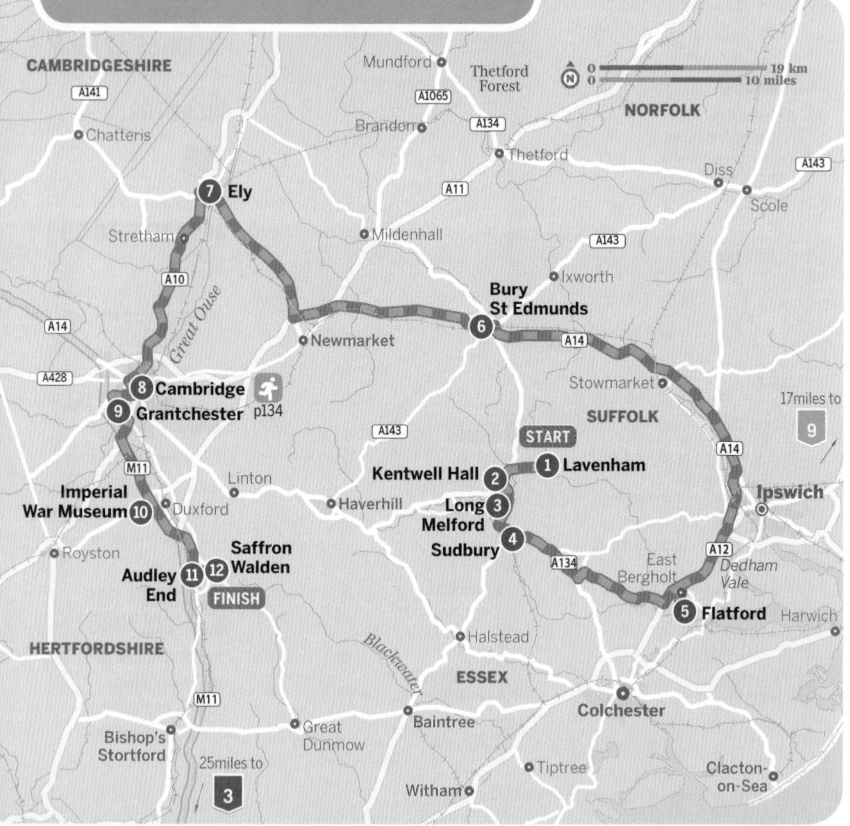

studded, timber-framed, early 16th-century architecture, and caramel-coloured, 14th-century **Little Hall** (☎01787-247019; www.littlehall.org.uk; Market Pl; adult/child £4/free; ⊙2-4pm Sat & Sun), where rooms have been restored to their period splendour. Even if the museums are closed, the whole town is a living museum of medieval architecture – drop into the 15th-century church of **St Peter & St Paul** (www.lavenhamchurch.onesuffolk.net; Church St; ⊙10am-4pm), with its churchyard of skull and cherub gravestones.

p123

The Drive » Your first leg is a 5-mile countryside cruise southwest, initially along the B1071, then Bridge St Rd, towards Long Melford. Turn right onto the A134 then again onto the A1092; seconds later you'll reach the long, tree-lined driveway to Kentwell Hall.

2 Kentwell Hall

Gorgeous, turreted, Tudor-era **Kentwell Hall** (☎01787-310207; www.kentwell.co.uk; adult/child £10.75/7.50; ⊙hours vary; P) may date from the 1500s, but it's still used as a private home, lending it a wonderfully lived-in feel. The mansion is framed by a rectangular moat and lush gardens, and during Tudor re-enactment events, the whole estate bristles with bodices, codpieces and hose. Opening hours are erratic: in 2020, the gardens (only) were open from noon to 4pm Wednesday to Sunday – call for the latest information.

The Drive » Continue south once you exit Kentwell Hall to waft alongside Long Melford's famous village green, passing a medieval hospital and the village church, with its fine 15th-century stained glass.

3 Long Melford

The charming village of Long Melford has a second ace up its sleeve: the romantic Elizabethan mansion of **Melford Hall** (NT; ☎01787-379228; www.nationaltrust.org.uk; Hall St; P), which from the outside has changed little since it entertained Queen Elizabeth I in 1578. Inside, there's a panelled banqueting hall, masses of Regency and Victorian finery, and a display on Beatrix Potter, who was a cousin of the owners. Call for current hours and prices.

The Drive » Continue south through the village to get back onto the A134/131 for the 6-mile stretch to Gainsborough's House in the town of Sudbury.

4 Sudbury

Today a quiet little market town, Sudbury was the 18th-century birthplace of the painter Thomas Gainsborough. His family home, **Gainsborough's House** (☎01787-372958; www.gainsborough.org; 46 Gainsborough St), now houses the world's largest collection of his work. The museum was closed for renovations at the time of writing, but when it reopens, look out for the exquisite *Portrait of Harriett; Viscountess Tracy*, with its delicate portrayal of drapery.

The Drive » The road onwards winds through bucolic, hedgerow-framed fields for 18 miles, following the A131/134, then the B1068. There's a brief zoom on the A12 to reach the B1070 through East Bergholt; turn off to the right for Flatford.

5 Flatford

If this languid landscape looks familiar, thank local boy John Constable – his romantic visions of springtime fields and

LINK YOUR TRIP

Suffolk-Norfolk Shore

A glorious cruise along a sublime stretch of sandy, marsh-backed shore. Starts 45 miles east of Bury St Edmunds at Aldeburgh.

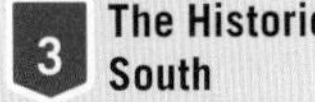

The Historic South

An exploration of the pick of southern England's heritage sights. Starts in London, 60 miles south of Saffron Walden.

babbling brooks were inspired by this serene corner of the country. Centred on the historic mill that features in *The Hay Wain*, the tiny hamlet of **Flatford** (NT; 01206-298260; www.nationaltrust.org.uk; Bridge Cottage, near East Bergholt; parking £5; 10am-6pm Apr-Oct, to 3.30pm Sat & Sun Nov-Mar; P) is now a National Trust–run window onto Constable's time. Check if you can enter tiny Bridge Cottage, with its restored interior, then stroll past **Flatford Mill**, where the view across the millpond to **Willy Lott's House** has hardly changed since 1821.

The Drive » Retrace your route back to the A12, then zip along A roads (the A14 and A134) to curve round into Bury St Edmunds; 35 miles in all.

6 Bury St Edmunds

History-rich Bury is a delight to explore. In the picturesque **Abbey Gardens** (Mustow St; dawn-dusk), the mighty walls of a once-vast abbey have crumbled and eroded into fantastical shapes. Next door, partly 16th-century **St Edmundsbury Cathedral** (01284-748720; www.stedscathedral.org; Angel Hill; by donation; 10am-4pm Mon-Sat) was once just a small part of the enormous abbey; look inside to see if tours of the 45m-high tower have resumed. You'll detect brewing smells from the **Greene King Brewery** as you loop round to reach the fascinating but macabre **Moyse's Hall** (01284-706183; www.moyseshall.org; Cornhill; adult/child £5/3; 10am-5pm Mon-Sat, noon-4pm Sun;) museum.

 p123

The Drive » Pick up the A14 towards Newmarket, turning off 15 miles later to head northwest onto the A142. From here it's a 12-mile cruise through the flat Fenland landscape, with

Ely Cathedral's towering spire beckoning you onwards.

7 Ely

Sleepy Ely's city status is conferred by **Ely Cathedral** (01353-667735; www.elycathedral.org; The Gallery; adult/child £8/free; 10am-4pm Mon-Sat, 1-3.30pm Sun), dubbed the 'Ship of the Fens' because its spire rises like a mast above the flat Fens. Inside, gaze up to see the 14th-century Octagon that transfers the weight of the tower onto vast columns, then enter the Lady Chapel, preserved in the ravaged

FAMOUS CAMBRIDGE STUDENTS

The honour roll of famous Cambridge students and academics is an international who's who of high achievers. This is the town where Newton refined his theory of gravity, where Whipple invented the jet engine, where Stephen Hawking penned *A Brief History of Time* and where Crick and Watson discovered DNA. Alongside Britain's favourite comedians – everyone from Rowan Atkinson to the Monty Python team found an audience thanks to the university's Footlights Dramatic Club – you'll find 98 Nobel Prize winners, 13 British prime ministers, nine archbishops of Canterbury and an immense number of scientists, poets and authors.

Ely The octagonal tower of Ely Cathedral

state in which it was left at the end of the English Civil War. A few minutes' walk away, timbered **Oliver Cromwell's House** (☎01353-662062; www.olivercromwellshouse.co.uk; 29 St Mary's St; adult/child £5.20/3.50; ⏲10am-5pm Apr-Oct, 11am-4pm Nov-Mar) is where the man who initiated that war (and executed a king) lived in the mid-1600s. It's now an engaging museum.

 p123

The Drive » This one's simple: 16 miles south along the A10, through the low-lying Fens to Cambridge. Make for the car park under the Grand Arcade in the centre.

TRIP HIGHLIGHT

8 Cambridge

Awash with exquisite medieval and Regency architecture and oozing tradition, Cambridge is a perfect city to explore on foot (p134). There are more than 30 colleges here; perhaps the greatest and grandest is King's College with its extravagant chapel (p134). Climb the tower of Great St Mary's Church (p135) for eagle-eye views over the college rooftops, and take a punt trip along the River Cam. Don't miss the fabulous **Fitzwilliam Museum** (www.fitzmuseum.cam.ac.uk; Trumpington St; by donation; ⏲10am-5pm Tue-Sat, from noon Sun), with its Roman and Egyptian grave goods, pottery and old-master paintings, and intriguing **Kettle's Yard** (☎01223-748100; www.kettlesyard.co.uk; Castle St; ⏲11am-5pm Wed-Sun), with its eccentric artworks assembled by a former curator from the Tate in London.

p123

The Drive » Take a 4-mile drive south through Cambridge's streets – you're making for the A603, aka the Fen Causeway. Soon, take the left to Grantchester, via Grantchester

Rd, and roll into the Orchard Tea Garden car park.

9 Grantchester

With its thatched cottages, flower-filled gardens, breezy meadows and classic cream teas, Grantchester is the picture-postcard image of England and the setting for a popular TV detective show. The quintessentially English **Orchard Tea Garden** (01223-840230; www.theorchardteagarden.co.uk; 47 Mill Way; lunch mains £6-10; 9am-6pm Apr-Oct, to 4pm Wed-Sun Nov-Mar), beside the church, has deckchairs spread beneath the apple trees and reassuringly calorific cakes and light lunches. It was a favourite haunt of the Bloomsbury Group, who came to camp, picnic, swim and push back social boundaries.

The Drive » Leaving Grantchester, snake south via the A1134 onto the speedy M11, southbound. Leave it at junction 10, heading for Duxford, then pick up signs for the Imperial War Museum. It's a trip of 7 miles in all.

10 Imperial War Museum

Plane-spotters will be in aviation heaven at Europe's biggest **aircraft museum** (01223-835000; www.iwm.org.uk; Duxford; adult/child including donation £19.80/9.90; 10am-6pm; P), with around 200 vintage aircraft – including many veterans of WWI and WWII – spread across a series of enormous hangars. You'll see everything from dive bombers to biplanes, Spitfires, Hurricanes and the Concorde, which was moved here after ending service in 2003 and can be explored on free tours.

The Drive » Another short drive, this time just under 10 miles on minor roads: first the A505, then the A1301, before the B1383 leads lazily to Audley End.

TRIP HIGHLIGHT

11 Audley End

Palatial in scale, the fabulous early Jacobean **Audley End House** (EH; 01799-522842; www.english-heritage.org.uk; off London Rd; adult/child £19/11.40; timed visits 10am-3pm; P) was clearly designed to place its creator, the first earl of Suffolk, at the top table of the English gentry. The house eventually did become a royal palace when it was purchased by Charles II in 1668. The rooms inside are lavishly decorated with heirloom furniture, oil paintings, priceless silverware, woodcarvings and taxidermy. Also swing by the lavish gardens, designed by Capability Brown, including a walled kitchen garden full of traditional varieties.

The Drive » Blink and you'd miss the final leg – a fraction under 2 miles. Head east from Audley End via Spring Hill and Audley End Rd, into the picturesque streets of Saffron Walden.

12 Saffron Walden

The dainty 12th-century market town of Saffron Walden is a delightful knot of half-timbered houses, narrow lanes, crooked roofs and ancient churches. It gets its name from the purple saffron crocus (the source of the world's most expensive spice), which was cultivated in the surrounding fields between the 15th and 18th centuries. Swot up on local history in the **Saffron Walden Museum** (01799-510333; www.saffronwaldenmuseum.org; Museum St; adult/child £2.50/free; 10am-5pm Tue-Sat, from 2pm Sun;) then swan over to the restored Victorian **Bridge End Gardens** (Bridge End; 8am-4pm Mon-Thu, to noon Fri), an elegant sprawl of water features, gazebos and manicured hedges.

p123

Eating & Sleeping

Lavenham 1

Swan at Lavenham Hotel $$$

(01787-247477; www.theswanatlavenham.co.uk; High St; r £110-180, ste from £210; P) Marvellously medieval, the stylish Swan is Lavenham's signature place to stay – a bent and leaning timbered coaching inn, with flawless service, fine modern British cuisine and rooms decorated in soothing colours and bound by a latticework of ancient beams. The house spa offers a full range of relaxing treatments in rooms lit by candles and sunlight.

Bury St Edmunds 6

Old Cannon Pub $$

(01284-768769; www.oldcannonbrewery.co.uk; 86 Cannon St; 11am-11pm;) In this microbrewery, gleaming mash tuns (malt mashing vats) sit alongside the bar, where you can quaff the end results – try the feisty Gunner's Daughter (ABV 5.5%) or Powder Monkey (4.75%). Help your ale down with solid pub grub (mains £12 to £18), served noon to 3pm and 5.30pm to 8.30pm Monday to Friday, noon to 6.30pm Saturday and noon to 6pm Sunday.

Chantry Hotel $$$

(01284-767427; www.chantryhotel.com; 8 Sparhawk St; r £120-175; P @) This family-run town-house B&B has the feel of a country hotel, with a gorgeous collection of four-poster, metal-framed and antique timber beds, set in inviting rooms with the odd original Georgian feature. There's a convivial lounge and tiny bar to help guests feel right at home.

Ely 7

Almonry Cafe $

(01353-666360; off High St; cream tea £6, light meals from £7; 9am-4pm Mon-Sat, from 11am Sun) This elegant tearoom and restaurant sits in neatly pruned gardens at the back of the cathedral compound, serving cream teas, sandwiches and a few more ambitious mains – chicken breast stuffed with brie and asparagus, squash and chickpea burgers and the like. The cathedral views are sublime.

Cambridge 8

Pint Shop Modern British $$

(01223-981070; www.pintshop.co.uk; 10 Peas Hill; 2/3 courses £22/26; noon-9pm Mon-Wed, to 10pm Thu-Sat, to 6pm Sun) Popular Pint Shop is part craft-beer sampling house, part hearty kitchen. Wash down tasty pub grub (charred salmon, burgers, flatbread kebabs) with artisan ciders, ales and fruit beers (including coconut, passionfruit and mango).

Worth House B&B $$

(01223-316074; www.worth-house.co.uk; 152 Chesterton Rd; s/d/tr from £100/110/150; P) The welcome is warm and the rooms are delightful at this friendly, upbeat B&B. In the rooms, cool greys and whites meet flashes of colour, bathrooms have a hint of glam and the breakfast is a feast.

Saffron Walden 12

Eight Bells Pub Food $$

(01799-522790; www.theeightbellssaffronwalden.com; 18 Bridge St; mains £15-26; noon-3pm & 6-10pm Mon-Sat, noon-6pm Sun;) Medieval meets design mag at this historic 16th-century pub, where ancient timbers collide above walls crammed with mismatched paintings. The menu is more traditional, with steaks, roasts (including nut) and posh burgers.

Suffolk-Norfolk Shore

Chart the changing character of the English coastline, from dignified resorts to a wild sweep of sandy beaches, backed by dunes and endless marshes where myriad bird species gather.

TRIP HIGHLIGHTS

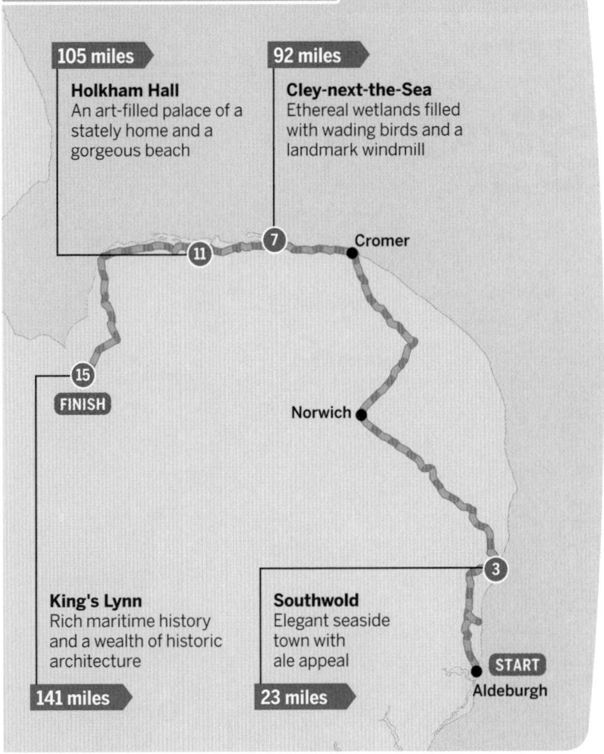

105 miles

Holkham Hall
An art-filled palace of a stately home and a gorgeous beach

92 miles

Cley-next-the-Sea
Ethereal wetlands filled with wading birds and a landmark windmill

11

7

Cromer

15

FINISH

Norwich

3

King's Lynn
Rich maritime history and a wealth of historic architecture

141 miles

Southwold
Elegant seaside town with ale appeal

23 miles

START

Aldeburgh

8 DAYS
141 MILES / 227KM

GREAT FOR...

BEST TIME TO GO

Spring through to summer for finer weather; autumn for quieter beaches.

ESSENTIAL PHOTO

Grassy dunes and an endless sweep of sand at Holkham National Nature Reserve.

BEST FOR ROYALTY

Her Majesty the Queen's country estate: Sandringham.

King's Lynn A statue of George Vancouver outside Custom House, built in 1683

9 Suffolk-Norfolk Shore

Prepare to see another side to the English seaside, as you motor from Suffolk's piers to North Norfolk's dune-backed shore. The distances aren't great but the pit stops are: scenic drives lead to creeks full of bobbing boats; salt marshes teem with fluttering and wading birds; and hidden beaches lurk behind grass-topped dunes. If you've only experienced the English seaside full of gambling arcades and fairground rides, prepare to be surprised.

1 Aldeburgh

The coastal town of Aldeburgh (*orld*-bruh) floats in a charming time warp. Along the pebbly shore, wooden sheds sell ocean-fresh seafood hauled in by the boats perched on the beach, while sightseers stroll along the prom with nary a slot machine in sight. Look out for the town museum in **Moot Hall** (www.aldeburghmuseum.org.uk; Market Cross Pl; adult/child £3/1; ⌚1-4pm Apr-Oct, 1-4pm Sat & Sun Nov-Mar), a medieval merchant's house on the seafront

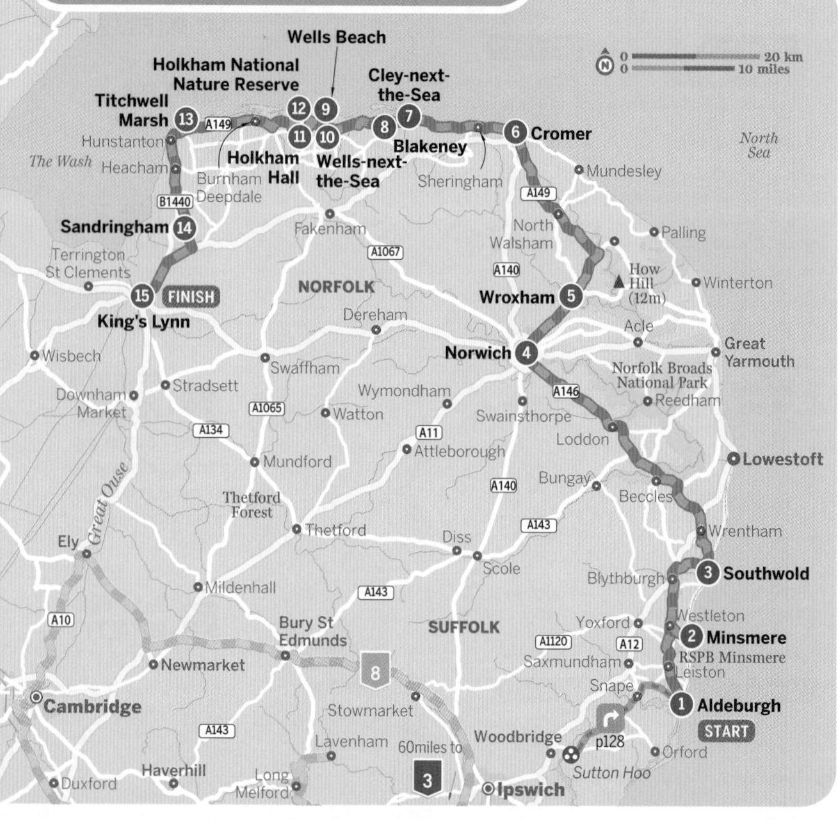

made from ancient oak beams and herringbone brick. Take a wander north along the pebbles towards Thorpeness to view the sculpture known as the **Scallop**, celebrating composer Benjamin Britten's links to the town.

The Drive » This first short hop is an 11-mile trip north into the marshes. Take the rural B1122, then the B1125 to Westleton, then Mill Rd and Sheepwash Lane to the Royal Society for the Protection of Birds (RSPB) Minsmere car park.

2 Minsmere

The nature reserve at **RSPB Minsmere** (RSPB; www.rspb.org.uk; near Westleton; adult/child £9/5; reserve dawn-dusk, visitor centre 10am-4pm; P) near Dunwich is home to one of England's rarest birds, the bittern, along with dozens of other resident and migratory bird species, best spotted in the autumn, when the marshes and pools come alive with birdlife. Trails run through the reeds that line the foreshore to hides that offer prime spotting opportunities. The reserve borders the National Trust–administered **Dunwich Heath** (NT; www.nationaltrust.org.uk; Dunwich; parking £6; 10am-5pm), another fine spot for coastal bird-watching.

The Drive » From Minsmere return to Westleton and continue to the A12 to cross the River Blyth, then peel off right onto the A1095 and rumble through rolling farmland to Southwold, a trip of 12 miles. Park up near the pier.

TRIP HIGHLIGHT

3 Southwold

Lovely Southwold has been a favourite retreat for well-heeled Londoners since the Regency period, thanks to its lovely sandy beach, pebble-walled cottages, clifftop promenade and rows of beachfront bathing huts. First built in 1899, the 190m-long **pier** (01502-722105; www.southwoldpier.co.uk; North Pde; pier 10am-7pm, to 5pm winter) is worth a visit for a peek at the Under the Pier Show, a kooky collection of handmade amusement machines combining daft fun with political satire. The malty smells that waft around the centre of town come from the Victorian-era **Adnams** (01502-727225; www.adnams.co.uk; Adnams Pl; tours £20; tours daily Mar-Sep) brewery, which produces some of East Anglia's most popular ales. Book ahead for hour-long tours of the high-tech kit and a tutored tasting of the house brews.

p133

The Drive » Pick up the B1127, then join the A146 for a 30-mile cruise to Norwich. Norfolk's roads are famously straight but they dip into gullies and rise over bridges like a roller coaster, hence the typically East Anglian 'Hidden Dip!' and 'Humpback Bridge' warning signs.

4 Norwich

Norwich (norr-ich) – the affluent and easy-going home of TV's Alan Partridge – is one of East Anglia's most historic cities, and its winding, part-pedestrianised streets are crammed with ancient flint churches and venerable timbered buildings that speak volumes about the wealth that the wool trade brought to Norfolk in the medieval period. The magnificent **Norwich Cathedral** (01603-218300; www.cathedral.org.uk; 65 The Close; donations requested; 10am-4pm Mon-Fri, 10am-3pm Sat, 1-3pm Sun) has England's second-highest spire, a fan-vaulted ceiling and fantastical ceiling

LINK YOUR TRIP

8 Around the Cam
A history-rich meander through Fenland countryside to historic university city Cambridge. Join it 45 miles west of Aldeburgh at Bury St Edmunds.

3 The Historic South
A cross-country dive into Britain's fascinating past, taking in blockbuster heritage sights. Starts in London, 100 miles southwest of Aldeburgh.

DETOUR: SUTTON HOO

Start: 1 Aldeburgh

From Aldeburgh, it's well worth taking the A1094, B1069 and A1152 for 15 miles southwest to the remarkable archaeological site of **Sutton Hoo** (NT; 01394-389700; www.nationaltrust.org.uk; near Woodbridge; adult/child £8/4; 10.30am-3.30pm Sat-Wed; P). In 1939 a tumulus was excavated to reveal the decayed hull of an enormous Anglo-Saxon ship containing the lavish grave goods and earthly remains of the Anglo-Saxon king Raedwald, who ruled over East Anglia until AD 625. The massive effort that went into Raedwald's burial gives some idea of his high status, and the intricate craftsmanship of the treasures he was buried with transformed perceptions of what was previously thought to be a primitive 'dark age'. As well as visiting a royal cemetery of yet-to-be-excavated tumuli surrounding the ship burial site, you can see a full-scale reconstruction of the grave ship and reproductions of Raedwald's remarkable jewelled sword, helmet and shield (the originals are displayed in London's British Museum). Stroll over to Tranmere House to see archive footage of the original archaeological excavation.

bosses in its vast cloisters. Take a wander through the ancient **Tombland** district to gorgeous **Elm Hill**, and nip into **Looses Emporium** (01603-665600; www.loosesemporium.co.uk; 23-35 Magdalen St; 10am-5pm Mon-Fri, 9am-6pm Sat, 10am-4pm Sun) to browse for antiques, heirlooms and chintz. If it's open, browse the displays in 12th-century **Norwich Castle** (01603-495897; www.museums.norfolk.gov.uk; Castle Hill); if not, head over to the **Sainsbury Centre for Visual Arts** (01603-593199; www.scva.ac.uk; University of East Anglia/UEA; 9am-6pm Tue-Fri, 10am-5pm Sat & Sun; 22, 25, 26) at the university for African and Asian treasures, and artworks by Bacon, Giacometti, Henry Moore and others. About 15 miles north of Norwich, **Blickling Hall** (NT; 01263-738030; www.nationaltrust.org.uk; Blickling; adult/child £10/5; house noon-4pm, grounds 10am-4pm; P), ancestral seat of the Boleyn family (of Anne Boleyn fame) is a worthwhile detour.

p133

The Drive » Next, an easy 8-mile drive northeast to Wroxham along the A1151, slicing past fields painted in vivid colours in summer by terracotta-coloured earth and vivid yellow oilseed rape (used to make vegetable oil).

5 Wroxham

Signs in the shape of sailboats signal your arrival at Wroxham, gateway to the Norfolk Broads. Head for the twin humpbacked bridges dividing Wroxham from twin-town Hoveton, where **Broads Tours** (01603-782207; www.broadstours.co.uk; The Bridge, Wroxham; boat hire per hour/day from £21/130, tours adult/child from £9.50/6; 8am-5.30pm Mar-Oct) can book you onto a one- to two-hour boat trip around the waterways, or let you loose on a rented boat for self-guided day explorations. One charming boat-trip stop is **Toad Hole Cottage** (01692-678763; www.howhilltrust.org.uk; How Hill; 10am-5pm Easter-Oct) at How Hill, a restored eel-catchers' cottage on the edge of marshes traversed by nature trails and dotted with 'skeleton mills' that were once used to drain sections of the swamps.

The Drive » It's hedgerows, fields and leafy lanes for most of the next 20 miles (via the A1151 and A149), passing through a string of pretty villages and small market towns. After a burst of woodland, you'll hit the main road into Cromer.

6 Cromer

The once-fashionable Victorian resort of Cromer still flourishes as a busy fishing port, famous for the sweet-tasting brown crabs that are hauled in daily during the March to October crabbing season. The long, cliff-edged seafront is lined with fishing boats and the tractors that pull them onto the pebbles, and the beach sees some impressive swell for surfers. The town itself is a friendly mix of seaside chintz and Victorian elegance, complete with a vintage **pier** (01263-512495; www.cromerpier.co.uk; Esplanade; 10am-dusk). Just east is the **Henry Blogg Museum** (RNLI Lifeboat Museum; 01263-511294; www.rnli.org; The Gangway; 10am-5pm Tue-Sun Apr-Sep, to 4pm Oct, Nov, Feb & Mar), devoted to the lifeboats, where you can take a hands-on lesson in Morse code and semaphore flag signals. For something more ambitious, rent a surfboard from **Glide Surf School** (01263-805005; www.glidesurfschool.co.uk; Esplanade; lessons adult/child £27/32, board hire per day from £17; 9.30am-5.30pm Mon-Sat, to 4pm Sun Apr-Oct, 10am-4pm Sat & Sun Nov-Mar) on the seafront and brave the breakers. In the streets leading back from the shore, seek out **Davies** (01263-512727; 7 Garden St; crab £3.50-6; 8.30am-5pm Mon-Sat, 10am-4pm Sun), where the Cromer crab is caught by the owner's day boat and boiled, cracked and dressed on-site.

p133

The Drive » Time for an 11-mile cruise through the villages of brick-edged flint houses that define the Norfolk coast. The A149 peels west along Cromer's seafront, affording frequent sea views. At Salthouse the scenery changes – the road dips down to a wide sweep of flat, reed-filled marshland, edged to the north by a distant ridge of dunes, hiding the beach beyond.

TRIP HIGHLIGHT

7 Cley-next-the-Sea

As the name suggests, the sleepy, flint-stone village of Cley (pronounced 'cly') huddles near the shore, but the breakers lie far beyond a sea of reeds. Just east of Cley, the **Cley Marshes** (01263-740008; www.norfolkwildlifetrust.org.uk; near Cley-next-the-Sea; adult/child £4.50/free; reserve dawn-dusk, visitor centre 10am-5pm Mar-Oct, to 4pm Nov-Feb; P) are one of England's premier birdwatching sites, with a network of walking trails and bird hides that offer excellent chances of spotting marsh harriers, bitterns and bearded reedlings, alongside 300 other species. Wander down signposted lanes to reach the postcard-pretty **windmill** (now a lovely B&B), sitting serenely beside reed beds, and grab a bite from **Picnic Fayre** (01263-740587; www.picnic-fayre.co.uk; High St; snacks from £3; 9am-4pm Mon-Sat, from 10am Sun), a deli crammed full of imaginative variations on English picnic classics.

p133

The Drive » It's just a 1½-mile jaunt past hedges and houses to Blakeney. Once in the village, follow signs to Blakeney Quay.

THE NORFOLK BROADS

These vast wetlands were formed when the rivers Wensum, Bure, Waveney and Yare flooded gaping holes created by 12th-century crofters digging for peat. In the process, a vast and valuable wetland ecosystem was created – as well as a playground for leisure boating, with tourism taking off here in a big way in the Victorian period. Now protected as a national park, the tangled waterways of the Broads are home to some of the UK's rarest plants and birds – attracting legions of boaters and birdspotters. The best way to explore is by rented self-drive 'day boat', easily arranged in Wroxham.

❽ Blakeney

The pretty village of Blakeney was once a busy fishing and trading port before its harbour silted up. These days visitors come to sit beside the creek, watching the boats bob between the mudflats, and take trips to **Blakeney National Nature Reserve** (NT; ☎01263-740241; www.nationaltrust.org.uk; ⊙dawn-dusk), a curving sandspit lined with marshes, providing a home for myriad seabirds and a huge colony of common and grey seals. Seals can be spotted year-round at **Blakeney Point**; take a trip to see them with **Bishop's Boats** (☎01263-740753; www.bishopsboats.com; Blakeney Quay; adult/child £13/7; ⊙1-4 boats daily Mar-Oct) from the quayside at Blakeney.

The Drive » Head west on the A149, which weaves through villages of flint-fronted houses, passing through a gentle landscape of salt mashes and meadows. Some 8 miles later, in Wells-next-the-Sea, head down the mile-long straight road that borders the banked sea defences to the car park near the beach.

❾ Wells Beach

Stroll north from the car park and follow the boardwalk past the lifeboat station on the point to one of Norfolk's finest beaches: a sweeping curve of dune-backed sand, lined with pastel-coloured beach huts on stilts. The shore stretches for miles to the west, offering long, uplifting and often windy walks. Closer to the boardwalk, the shallow water is perfect for paddling. Grab a snack near the car park at the weatherboard **Wells Beach Cafe** (www.holkham.co.uk; Wells Beach; mains from £5; ⊙10am-5pm Mon-Fri, from 9am Sat & Sun; 📶👪).

The Drive » Head back down Beach Rd to the centre of Wells, and park up near the quay (£4.50 per day).

❿ Wells-next-the-Sea

In charming Wells-next-the-Sea (known locally just as Wells), rows of attractive Georgian houses and flint cottages snake down to a busy, boat-lined fishing quay bordered by creeks and marshes. Take a peek at what the boats are hauling in, then wander inland to explore the pretty back lanes around tiny Buttlands park. Head to Stiffkey Rd to board the charming **Wells & Walsingham Railway** (☎01328-711630; www.wwlr.co.uk; Stiffkey Rd; adult/child return £9.50/7.50; ⊙4-5 trains daily Mar-Nov), the world's longest 10.25in narrow-gauge railway. This tiny loco puffs for 5 picturesque miles (30 minutes) to the village of Little Walsingham, an ancient Catholic pilgrimage site centred on the ruins of the Reformation-ravaged Walsingham Priory.

CLARE LOUISE JACKSON / SHUTTERSTOCK ©

🛏 p133

The Drive » The A149 plots your route onwards, tracing the marsh-fringed coast for 2 miles through a flat, open landscape. You'll know you've reached Holkham by the neat houses built to accommodate workers at the stately Holkham Hall, which is a 400m drive to the right.

TRIP HIGHLIGHT

⓫ Holkham Hall

Holkham Hall (☎01328-713111; www.holkham.co.uk; adult/child £17/8.50, parking £4; ⊙noon-4pm Sun, Mon

Wells Beach Colourful beach huts

& Thu Mar-Oct, grounds daily 9am-5pm, to 4pm Nov-Mar; P) was the ancestral seat of the Earls of Leicester and the current earl still lives in the palatial Palladian mansion, constructed by Earl Thomas Coke in the 18th century. The perfectly symmetrical, Italianate house was essentially constructed as a display case for the earl's astonishing collection of classical sculpture and painting, assembled during a grand tour of Europe from 1712 to 1718. Guided visits explore the guest rooms, with their original tapestry and *cafoy* (fabric) wall coverings, and the warren of hidden passageways used by servants.

The Drive » Head back up the drive from Holkham Hall and park over the road in the car park on Lady Anne's Drive (£2 per hour), then stroll north on the earth and boardwalk trail to the beach (a mile in all).

12 Holkham National Nature Reserve

The track from the car park runs through pine forests and over salt marshes to a distant line of dunes hiding the marvellous beach at **Holkham National Nature Reserve** (www.holkham.co.uk; parking per hour/day £2/9; car park 6am-6pm;). This 14-sq-mile nature reserve throngs with birdlife (easily spotted from hides dotted behind the shore) and the endless sweep of fine golden sand is one of England's most beautiful coastal vistas.

The Drive » Running west, the A149 follows a winding, undulating route, passing a picturesque windmill at Burnham Overy, before crossing the marshes at the mouth of the River Burn. There are multiple villages here with the name Burnham – stick to the A149, which turns back towards the coast and weaves through Burnham Deepdale and Titchwell village to reach Titchwell Marsh nature reserve – a 10-mile leg in all.

⑬ Titchwell Marsh

At **RSPB Titchwell Marsh** (RSPB; ☎01485-210779; www.rspb.org.uk; Titchwell; adult/child £5/2.50; ⏰9.30am-5pm Mar-Oct, to 4pm Nov-Feb; P) nature reserve, sandbars, marshes and lagoons attract vast numbers of birds, including pied avocets, marsh harriers, Eurasian bitterns and bearded reedlings in summer. In winter the marshes throng with wading birds and countless ducks and geese, plus plenty of visitors touting binoculars and long lenses. There's good eating and a pretty beach nearby in Brancaster Staithe.

✕ p133

The Drive » Take the A149 onwards through the flatlands, past the broad sweep of golf-course-framed sea at Hunstanton, before peeling off onto the B1440 for the gentle cruise to Sandringham, 15 miles from Titchwell Marsh.

⑭ Sandringham

Both monarchists and republicans will find fuel for their respective positions at the Queen's lavish country **estate** (☎01485-545400; www.sandringhamestate.co.uk; adult/child £15.30/7.50 plus booking fee; ⏰10am-4pm selected dates Apr-Oct; P; 🚌35). Built in homage to much older stately homes, this elegant Victorian manor is set in 25 hectares of beautifully landscaped gardens, and the sumptuous reception rooms – still regularly used by the royals and open on selected summer dates – contain a wealth of objets d'art and glinting gifts from European and Russian royal families. Sandringham was built in 1870 by the then Prince and Princess of Wales (who later became King Edward VII and Queen Alexandra) and the house's features and furnishings remain much as they were in Edwardian times. It's surreal to imagine generations of royals treating this grand house as just a family home. The stables today house a flag-waving museum filled with royal memorabilia. The superb vintage-car collection includes the very first royal motor from 1900.

The Drive » From Sandringham, it's a 10-mile hop along well-signposted A and B roads to King's Lynn.

TRIP HIGHLIGHT

⑮ King's Lynn

Historically one of England's most important ports, King's Lynn was long known as 'the Warehouse on the Wash' after the nearby bay at the mouth of the River Great Ouse. In its heyday, it was said you could cross from one side of the river to the other by simply stepping from boat to boat. Start exploring at the 15th-century town hall now housing **Stories of Lynn** (☎01553-774297; www.storiesoflynn.co.uk; Saturday Market Pl; adult/child £3.95/1.95; ⏰10am-4.30pm), a lively town museum covering everything from mercantile history to crime and punishment, then follow a genteel row of town houses along Queen St to Purfleet Quay, where a statue of Charles II crowns the **Custom House**, built in 1683. Continue along King St, past the 15th-century **St George's Guildhall** (www.shakespearesguildhalltrust.org.uk; 29 King St; ⏰10am-2pm Mon-Sat), where Shakespeare reputedly performed, and a succession of courtyards crowded with medieval merchants' warehouses. Beyond is charming **True's Yard** (☎01553-770479; www.truesyard.co.uk; North St; adult/child £3/1.50; ⏰10am-4pm Tue-Sat), where two restored fisher's cottages explore the lives and traditions of King's Lynn's fisherfolk, who lived packed like sardines into buildings such as these.

🛏 p133

Eating & Sleeping

Southwold 3

Sutherland House Hotel $$$

(☎01502-724544; www.sutherlandhouse.co.uk; 56 High St; r from £175; P Wi-Fi) Past guests at this former mayor's residence include the prince who later became James II, and the earl of Sandwich. Modern-day travellers can enjoy a hint of the same extravagant lifestyle in sumptuous rooms with pargeted ceilings, exposed beams and free-standing baths.

Norwich 4

3 Princes B&B $$$

(☎01603-622699; www.3princes-norwich.co.uk; 3 Princes St; s/d from £89/185; Wi-Fi) A handsome old town house with a walled, tree-shaded courtyard garden, 3 Princes puts you in the medieval heart of the city, yards from lovely Elm Hill. Behind the historic exterior, the wood-floored rooms come in a modernist colour scheme of greys and whites, with small swatches of blue from cushions and bedspreads.

Cromer 6

Red Lion Inn $$

(☎01263-514964; www.redlioncromer.co.uk; Brook St; s/d/ste from £68/125/145; P Wi-Fi) Coloured floor tiles, wooden banisters and stained glass signal this seafront inn's 18th-century heritage, but stylish, sea-themed rooms bring the package bang up to date. All bedrooms come with bathtubs. You can see the sea from the dreamy deluxe suite (room 7), which also has its own sea-facing balcony.

Cley-next-the-Sea 7

Cley Windmill B&B $$$

(☎01263-740209; www.cleywindmill.co.uk; High St; d £159-295, apt per week from £495; P) If you've ever fancied staying in a windmill, you won't find one much lovelier than this fully intact, 19th-century gem. The curiously shaped but cosy rooms are named after their former working lives, and many look directly over reed-filled salt marshes. A cute four-person self-catering cottage sits just next door.

Wells-next-the-Sea 10

Old Custom House B&B $$

(☎01328-711463; www.eastquay.co.uk; East Quay; s/d from £100/120, ste s/d £110/130; P Wi-Fi) This stately but comfortable white house by the quay has worn timbers, alcoves full of books and gorgeous creek views. Choose from snug 'Captain's Quarters' rooms or the grand four-poster suite. It also has two cute self-catering cottages for longer stays.

Titchwell Marsh 

White Horse Modern British $$

(☎01485-210262; www.whitehorsebrancaster.co.uk; Main Rd, Brancaster Staithe; mains £14-26; noon-9pm; P Wi-Fi) Backing onto a sweep of marshland, the White Horse celebrates Norfolk seafood in all its myriad forms: locally smoked salmon and prawns, saffron-pickled cockles, Brancaster oysters, dressed Cromer crab. It also serves plenty of local meats and poultry. Dine inside or under a marquee in the garden; the sharing seafood platter (£62) is a veritable feast.

King's Lynn 15

Bank House Boutique Hotel $$

(☎01553-660492; www.thebankhouse.co.uk; King's Staithe Sq; s £85-120, d £115-220; P Wi-Fi) A statue of Charles I casts an eye over arrivals to this handsome Georgian town house near the quay, but inside the rooms are modern and fun-filled, with lots of soft upholstery and eye-pleasing splashes of colour.

Set behind arched windows in a wood-floored annexe, the house brasserie (dishes £14 to £25, open noon to 8pm) serves seriously good modern British food.

STRETCH YOUR LEGS CAMBRIDGE

Start/Finish: Grand Arcade

Distance: 2.5 miles

Duration: 3 hours

Historic Cambridge is best explored on foot. This tour takes in prestigious colleges, magnificent chapels and a punt on the River Cam; check the latest college opening times and prices before you set off.

Take this walk on Trips

Grand Arcade

You won't find much history in Cambridge's glitzy Grand Arcade, but it's one of the few places you can park centrally.

The Walk » Head for the Downing St exit, and turn right towards Pembroke St then left on Trumpington St.

Fitzwilliam Museum

This colossal neoclassical treasure house (p121) was one of the first public art museums in Britain. There are obvious parallels to the British Museum, and highlights include Roman, Egyptian and Cypriot grave goods, artworks by great masters and one of the country's finest collections of ancient, medieval and modern pottery.

The Walk » About-turn and go north on Trumpington St to the corner with Pembroke St for a sweet, sticky rest stop.

Fitzbillies

Cambridge's oldest bakery, **Fitzbillies** (www.fitzbillies.com; 52 Trumpington St; mains £5-15; 8.30am-5pm Mon-Fri, 9am-5.30pm Sat & Sun) has a soft, doughy place in the hearts of generations of students. Its stock-in-trade is sticky Chelsea buns and cream teas, served packed to go or in the attached cafe.

The Walk » Continue north on Trumpington St and dip left onto Silver St for a glimpse of the rickety-looking wooden Mathematical Bridge, then continue north to reach King's Pde.

King's College Chapel

The grandiose 16th-century **King's College Chapel** (01223-331100; www.kings.cam.ac.uk; King's Pde; adult/child £10/8; 9.30am-3.15pm Mon-Sat, 1.15-2.30pm Sun term time, 9.30am-4.30pm rest of year) is one of England's most extraordinary Gothic monuments. During services, the sound of the choir rises to an almost impossibly intricate fan-vaulted ceiling – think of it as a firework display, expressed as architecture.

The Walk » You'll see your next stop just north along King's Pde, rising proudly above the surrounding buildings.

Great St Mary's Church

The grand facade of **Great St Mary's** (☎01223-747273; www.gsm.cam.ac.uk; Senate House Hill; tower per person/family £6/16; ⏰11am-5pm Tue-Sun) was largely the result of a major expansion from 1478 to 1519, but the best thing about this imposing Gothic church is the **tower**, which offers awe-inspiring views over Cambridge's dreaming spires.

The Walk » Cross King's Pde and duck down Senate House Passage to marvel at the occult-looking Porta Honoris, side gate to Gonville & Caius College, then continue on Trinity St.

Trinity College

The largest of Cambridge's colleges, elegant **Trinity College** (☎01223-338400; www.trin.cam.ac.uk; Trinity St) is reached through an epic Tudor gateway, topped by a stern-looking statue of Henry VIII. Beyond lies the sweeping Great Court, the biggest of its kind, and (if it's open) the renowned **Wren Library**, containing 55,000 books dated before 1820.

The Walk » Continue north past St John's College, then turn left onto Bridge St to reach the river. Rent a punt from Quayside to see another side of the Cambridge colleges.

The Backs

The rear ends of the grand colleges along King's Pde spill onto the riverbanks in a long sweep of parks, gardens and even grazing pastures for livestock. Known as **The Backs**, the parklands can be explored on foot when the colleges are open, but are best viewed from a punt on the river, passing under a succession of elegant bridges, including the famous **Bridge of Sighs**.

The Walk » Returning your punt to the depot, retrace your steps to reach Sidney St, then duck right onto Pety Cury to reach the north entrance to the Grand Arcade.

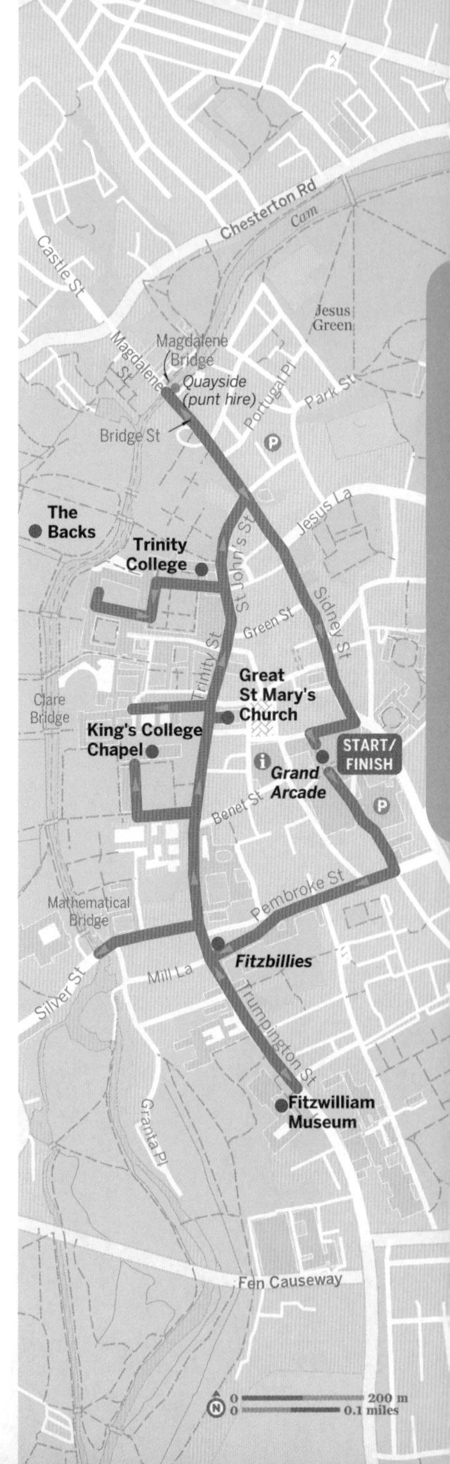

Southwest England

Sunsets and echoes of happy holidays beckon you to Britain's southwest. This captivating region has long drawn waves of road-trippers, tempted by rural charm, alternative vibes, sweeping moors and wild shores. Famous as holiday hot spots (avoid the bank-holiday jams), the routes around Cornwall and south Devon see wind-whipped cliffs linking dreamy beaches, foodie enclaves, grand gardens and salty fishing ports. Dorset's Jurassic Coast offers breathtaking geology and road-lined shores. Exmoor's jagged cliffs and wild moorland deliver memorable cruising. Meanwhile hipsters, hippies and history fans should beeline for the routes out of Winchester, heading west.

Lulworth Cove A narrow-mouthed crescent of white cliffs
AVRESA / SHUTTERSTOCK ©

Southwest England

10 Winchester, Glastonbury & Bath 12–14 Days
Vivid history awaits: monumental stone circles, soaring cathedrals and glorious Roman baths.

11 North Devon & Exmoor National Park 3–4 Days
Steep roads and switchbacks link rugged cliffs and big-sky moors.

12 Jurassic Coast 7 Days
A ribboning route leading west beside fishing ports and sea-sculpted shores.

13 South Devon 4 Days
Prepare for lido swims, historic homes, fabulous food and tucked-away bays.

14 Epic Cornwall 10 Days
Expect surfer beaches, iconic eco projects, remote headlands and very sandy feet.

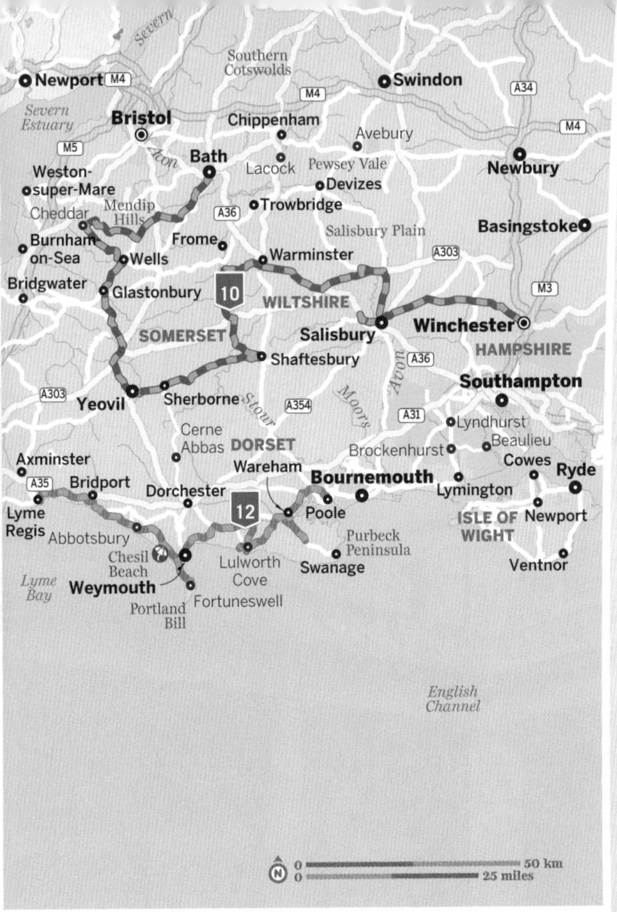

Clovelly Boats in the harbour of this historic village

DON'T MISS

Encounter Cornwall

A kayaking trip on the enchanting River Fowey, passing pastel-coloured fishers' cottages and thriller writer Daphne du Maurier's home. Trip 14

Lido Swimming

Two gorgeous, jazz-age, saltwater pools tempt you to dive in for open-air, sea-view swims. Trip 13

Tout Quarry

Head here for an extraordinary array of sculptures-in-situ – fantastical designs carved into the rock of a limestone quarry. Trip 12

Porlock Hill

A brake-burning descent down a 25% gradient – look out for the escape lanes and 'try your brakes' signs. Trip 11

Cerne Giant

One of Britain's rudest sights: a 60m-high, well-endowed chalk figure etched into the Dorset hills. He hasn't got a stitch on... Trip 10

Classic Trip

Winchester, Glastonbury & Bath

Prepare to cruise through England's cultural heartland. Discover archaeological wonders, serene cathedrals, imposing castles, stately homes, Georgian streets and Roman baths.

TRIP HIGHLIGHTS

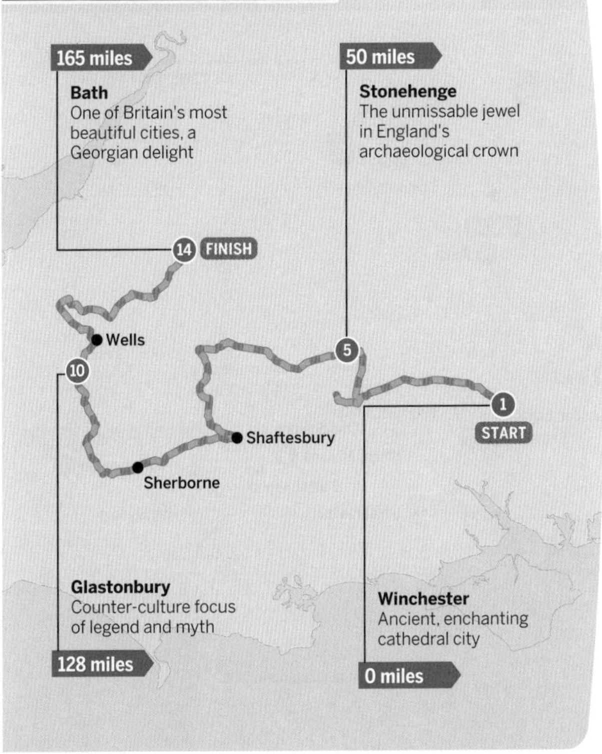

165 miles
Bath
One of Britain's most beautiful cities, a Georgian delight

50 miles
Stonehenge
The unmissable jewel in England's archaeological crown

14 FINISH
Wells
10
5
1 START
Shaftesbury
Sherborne

Glastonbury
Counter-culture focus of legend and myth
128 miles

Winchester
Ancient, enchanting cathedral city
0 miles

12–14 DAYS
165 MILES / 265KM

GREAT FOR...

BEST TIME TO GO

March to June to get better weather and fewer crowds.

ESSENTIAL PHOTO

Standing beside the massive 5000-year-old monument at Stonehenge.

BEST CITYSCAPES

The exquisite, ancient architecture in Unesco World Heritage city Bath.

Bath Roman baths

Classic Trip

10 Winchester, Glastonbury & Bath

This is a trip for encountering England's most extraordinary constructions. You'll circle the 5000-year-old stones at Stonehenge, prowl the still-stunning Roman baths in Bath and wonder at the soaring cathedrals at Salisbury and Wells. Add a safari park, stalactite-filled caverns and a saucy chalk figure, and it's your chance to tour the essence of old England and experience her best archaeological and architectural sights.

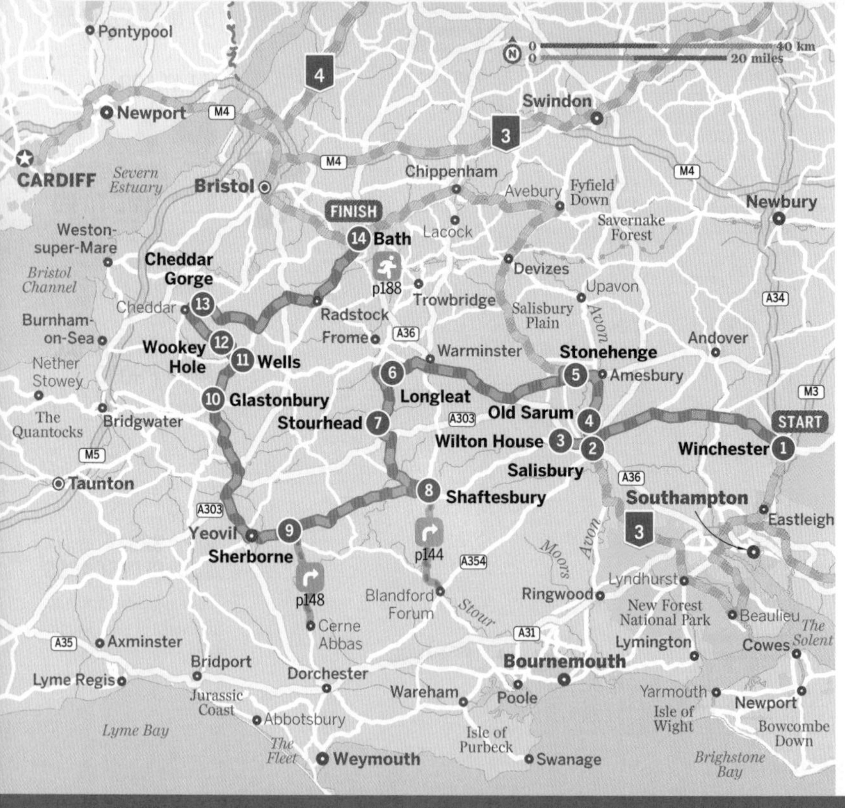

TRIP HIGHLIGHT

1 Winchester

Calm, collegiate Winchester is a mellow must-see. The past still echoes strongly around the flint-flecked walls of this ancient cathedral city, which has been the power base of bishops and a capital to Saxon kings. Start with an exploration of 11th-century **Winchester Cathedral** (☎01962-857200; www.winchester-cathedral.org.uk; The Close; adult/child £10/free; ⏲10am-4pm). One of southern England's most awe-inspiring buildings, it boasts a fine Gothic facade, one of the longest medieval naves in Europe (164m) and a fascinating jumble of features from all eras. Highlights include the intricately carved medieval choir stalls, which sport everything from mythical beasts to a mischievous green man. Check the website to see if you can book on a crypt or tower tour and whether one of the UK's finest illuminated manuscripts, the dazzling **Winchester Bible,** will be on display. Next, stroll 10 minutes west to Winchester's 11th-century **Great Hall** (☎01962-846476; www.hants.gov.uk/greathall; Castle Ave; adult/child £3/free; ⏲10am-5pm). It holds the **Round Table**, a copy of the mythical piece of furniture that King Arthur and his knights reputedly sat around. Although it's actually thought to have been made some 700 years after King Arthur died, it's impressive nonetheless.

🛏 p47, p73, p151

The Drive » Pick up the 'Salisbury A30' signs for a 31-mile, often-dual-carriageway cruise. Eventually Salisbury Cathedral's soaring spire glides into view. Head for one of the central car parks signed from the ring road.

TOP TIP: STONEHENGE TICKETS

Stonehenge operates by pre-booked, timed tickets, even for English Heritage and National Trust members entitled to free admission. To be sure you can visit when you want, book your ticket well in advance.

LINK YOUR TRIP

4 Urban & Art Odyssey

Just 14 miles northwest of Bath, Bristol is the launch pad for an exciting exploration of some of Britain's best cities for culture.

3 The Historic South

Even more history awaits on this tour of southern England's big-name heritage sights, which links to the final stop: Bath.

2 Salisbury

The 790-year-old cathedral that points your way into the city was constructed in the early English Gothic style. **Salisbury Cathedral** (☎01722-555150; www.salisburycathedral.org.uk; The Close; requested donation adult/child £7.50/3; ⏲9am-4pm Mon-Sat) boasts the tallest spire in Britain (at 123m) and an elaborate exterior boasting pointed arches, flying buttresses and a highly decorative West Front. The 70m-long nave houses a 1386 medieval clock, which is probably the oldest working timepiece in the world. The Cathedral's prized **Magna Carta** is one of only four surviving original copies of the historic agreement made in 1215 between King John and his barons. If it's not on display, look out for the high resolution facsimile in the North Transept. Like all sights in this trip, you may need to pre-book your visit to Salisbury Cathedral; check the website beforehand.

p73, p151

The Drive ›› From Salisbury, it's a 3-mile cruise west to gorgeous Wilton House.

3 Wilton House

Stately **Wilton House** (01722-746700; www.wilton-house.co.uk; Wilton; house & grounds adult/child £15.50/8; 11.30am-5pm Sun-Thu May-Aug; P) provides an insight into the rarefied world of the British aristocracy. One of England's finest stately homes, the earls of Pembroke have lived here since 1542. Highlights are the Single and Double Cube Rooms, designed by the pioneering 17th-century architect Inigo Jones. Look out for magnificent period furniture, frescoed ceilings and elaborate plasterwork; they frame paintings by van Dyck, Rembrandt and Joshua Reynolds. That will be why *The Madness of King George*, *Sense and Sensibility* and *Pride and Prejudice* were shot here.

The Drive ›› Peel back east on the A36 towards Salisbury, before darting north on the A345 to Old Sarum. Total distance? Some 6 miles.

4 Old Sarum

The huge ramparts of **Old Sarum** (EH; 01722-335398; www.english-heritage.org.uk; Castle Rd; adult/child £5.90/3.50; 10am-5pm Apr-Oct, to 4pm Nov-Mar; P) sit on a grass-covered mound. It began life as a hill fort during the Iron Age, and was later occupied by the Romans, but by the mid-11th century it was an important town, and the first cathedral was built in 1092. Today it's a place to wander grassy defences, see the original cathedral's stone foundations and look across the Wiltshire countryside to the spire of the present Salisbury Cathedral.

The Drive ›› Hop back onto the A345, joining the tour buses for the 10-mile blast (via the A303) to Stonehenge. You'll see the stone circle, suddenly, thrillingly, on the right; carry on to the signposted visitor centre, beyond.

TRIP HIGHLIGHT

5 Stonehenge

One of England's most recognisable sights, ancient **Stonehenge** (EH; 0370 333 1181; www.english-heritage.org.uk; near Amesbury; adult/child £21/13; 9.30am-5pm, hours may vary; P) has had an ultra-modern makeover, bringing an impressive visitor centre, the closure of an intrusive road and a far stronger sense of historical context. A pathway frames the ring of massive stones and, although you can only walk in the circle itself on a Stone Circle Access Visit (p41), you can get close-up views of a striking sight – the remaining

DETOUR: BLANDFORD FORUM

Start: 8 Shaftesbury

A 13-mile drive south of Shaftesbury, largely along the B3081/2 leads to the architectural oddity that is Blandford Forum. In 1731 the whole town was consumed in a fire and the subsequent rebuild (by leading architects the Bastard brothers) resulted in a rarity: a town centre that dates from just one period. A short stroll pretty much anywhere here rewards the eye – a good route sees you starting at central **Market Place**, beside the cupola-crowned **Parish Church of St Peter and St Paul**; the imposing **town hall** sits nearby. To the west, **Salisbury St** heads up past bow windows and mathematical tiling. The **Plocks** darts off to the right to reveal more grand buildings, before The Close and **Church Walk** lead you back, 30 minutes later, to the start.

NEIL LANG / SHUTTERSTOCK ©

Longleat Giraffes at Britain's first safari park

sets of stones, some forming huge doorways, others towering towards the sky. The **visitor centre** (EH; ☎0370 333 1181; www.english-heritage.org.uk; incl access to Stonehenge adult/child £21/13; ⏲9.30am-5pm, hours may vary) charts the site's 5000-year past; it also sees you standing in the middle of a 360-degree projection of the stone circle through the ages and seasons – complete with midsummer sunrise and swirling starscape. The visitor centre is 1.5 miles from the stones. A fleet of trolley buses makes the 10-minute trip – you can also walk via a 2.6-mile circular trail through the ancient landscape.

The Drive » Next comes a 20-mile drive as the A303/A36 slices through the high chalk plateau of Salisbury Plain. After Warminster, follow the signs for Longleat.

6 Longleat

Half ancestral mansion, half safari park, **Longleat** (☎01985-844400; www.longleat.co.uk; near Warminster; adult/child £26/19; ⏲10am-5pm, hours may vary; P) was transformed into Britain's first safari park in 1966, turning Capability Brown's landscaped grounds into an amazing drive-through zoo, populated by a menagerie of animals more at home in the African wilderness than the fields of Wiltshire. There's a throng of attractions, too: the historic house, animatronic dinosaur exhibits, narrow-gauge railway, mazes, pets' corner, butterfly garden and bat cave.

The Drive » Time for a meander off the main roads as the B3092 winds gently past ploughed fields and through woodland and scattered villages to Stourhead, 10 miles away.

7 Stourhead

Overflowing with vistas, temples and follies, **Stourhead** (NT; ☎01747-841152; www.nationaltrust.org.uk; Mere; gardens adult/child £13/6.50; ⏲gardens 9am-5pm; P) is landscape gardening at its finest. The magnificent 18th-century gardens spread across the valley, with a picturesque 2-mile garden circuit taking you past ornate follies, around a centrepiece lake and to the Georgian Temple of Apollo. A 3.5-mile walking detour leads from near the Pantheon to a 50m-high folly called King Alfred's Tower.

The Drive » Keep heading south, as more B roads snake for 11 miles beside pastoral meadows and hogbacked

Classic Trip

MARCHAUGH / SHUTTERSTOCK ©

ABCBRITAIN / SHUTTERSTOCK ©

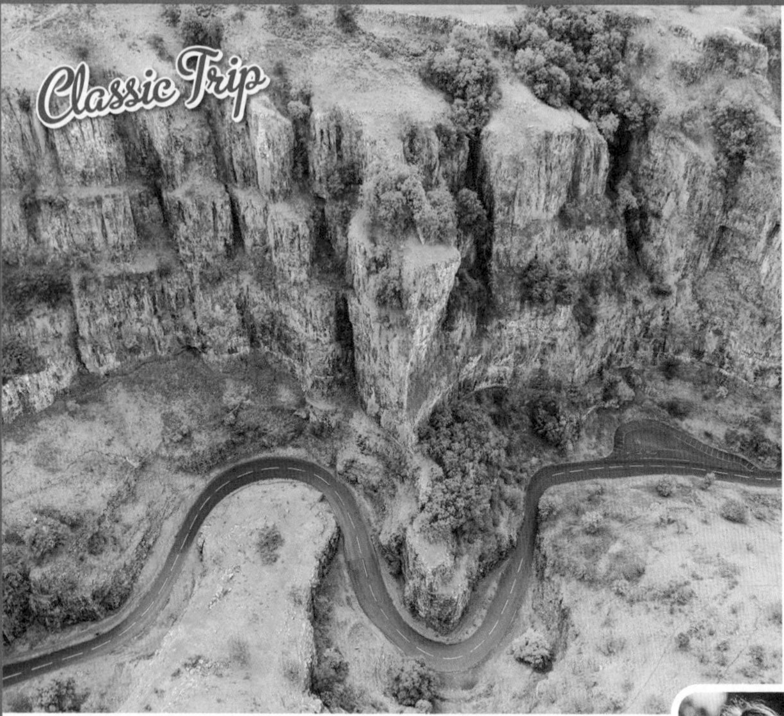

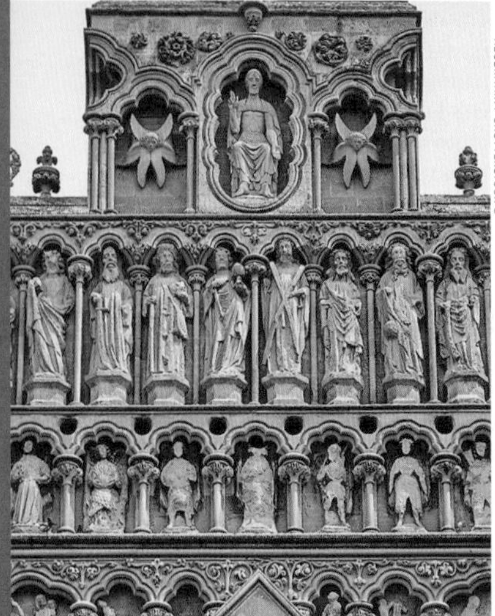

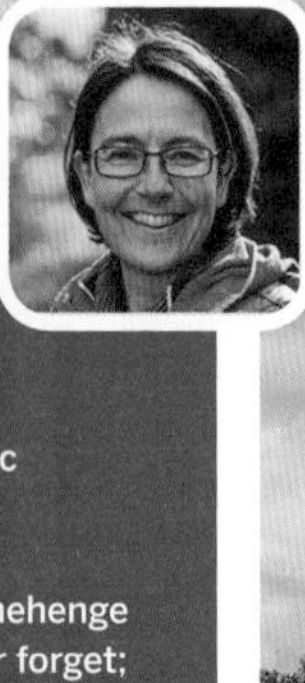

WHY THIS IS A CLASSIC TRIP

BELINDA DIXON, WRITER

For me, this trip is a classic because it delivers truly memorable moments. Encountering mighty Stonehenge is an experience you never forget; the beauty of the cathedrals also lingers in the mind. The drives are special too, taking in high plateaus, ancient villages, stylish cities and chalk plains. It's a trip into the heart of this country's heritage, which reveals how that history still echoes around England today.

Above: Cheddar Gorge
Left: Wells Cathedral
Right: Glastonbury Abbey

CHRISDORNEY / SHUTTERSTOCK ©

hills. Then climb the ridge to Shaftesbury.

8 Shaftesbury

The appealing market town of Shaftesbury circles around the ruins of **Shaftesbury Abbey** (01747-852910; www.shaftesburyabbey.org.uk; Park Walk; donation requested; 10am-4pm Sat & Sun Apr-Oct). Once England's largest and richest nunnery, it was founded in 888 by King Alfred the Great; Alfred's daughter, Aethelgifu, was its first abbess. Most of the buildings were dismantled by Henry VIII, but you can still spot the foundations amid swathes of grass and wildflowers, and hunt out the medieval-inspired herb and fruit-tree collections. A few paces away sits **Gold Hill**, an often-photographed, painfully steep, quaint cobbled slope, lined by chocolate-box cottages.

p151

The Drive » Join the A30 as it swoops down out of town and undulates besides fields for 17 miles to Sherborne. As you approach, follow signs for the town's short-stay parking.

9 Sherborne

Sherborne gleams with mellow, orangey-yellow stone, which has been used to build a cluster of 15th-century buildings and the impressive **Sherborne Abbey**

(☎01935-812452; www.sherborneabbey.com; Abbey Cl; suggested donation £4; ⏲check website for hours) at their core. At the height of its influence, this magnificent building was the central cathedral of 26 succeeding Saxon bishops. Established early in the 8th century, it became a Benedictine abbey in 998 and functioned as a cathedral until 1075. The church has mesmerising fan vaulting that's the oldest in the country, a central tower supported by Saxon-Norman piers and an 1180 Norman porch.

One mile east, on the outskirts of town, sits impressive **Sherborne New Castle** (☎01935-812072; www.sherbornecastle.com; New Rd; adult/child £9/free; ⏲10am-5pm Apr-Sep; P). Sir Walter Raleigh began building this fine stately home in 1594, but only got as far as the central block before being imprisoned by James I. James promptly sold the castle to Sir John Digby, who added the splendid wings you see today. In 1753 the grounds received a mega-makeover at the hands of landscape-gardener extraordinaire Lancelot 'Capability' Brown, who added a massive lake and the 12-hectare waterside gardens.

🛏 p151

The Drive » Time to head north for 20 miles; an A- and B-road blend that winds past a patchwork of fields. As you near Glastonbury, look out for the iconic hump of Glastonbury Tor rising out of the pan-flat landscape.

TRIP HIGHLIGHT

⑩ Glastonbury

Thanks to converging ley lines and ranks of legends, Glastonbury is England's premier counterculture town. It centres around the scattered ruins of **Glastonbury Abbey** (☎01458-832267; www.glastonburyabbey.com; Magdalene St; adult/child £8.60/4.70; ⏲9am-8pm Jun-Aug, to 6pm Mar-May, Sep & Oct, to 4pm Nov-Feb), which was once one of England's great seats of ecclesiastical power. Today's striking ruins include some of the nave walls, the remains of St Mary's chapel, and crossing arches. A 20-minute stroll southeast leads to the reputedly holy waters of the **Chalice Well** (☎01458-831154; www.chalicewell.org.uk; Chilkwell St; adult/child £4.60/2.30; ⏲10am-6pm Apr-Oct, to 4.30pm Nov-Mar) and then **Glastonbury Tor** (NT; ☎01278-751874; www.nationaltrust.org.uk; ⏲24hr), a vast mound that's the focal point of Arthurian legends and is home to a ruined medieval chapel. The half-hour hike to the top reveals wrap-around views.

🛏 p151

The Drive » From Glastonbury it's a relatively routine 6-mile cruise up the A39 to Wells.

DETOUR: CERNE GIANT

Start: ⑨ Sherborne

An 11-mile detour south from Sherborne (along the B3145 and A352) leads to a truly eye-opening sight. The **Cerne Giant** (NT; ☎01297-489481; www.nationaltrust.org.uk; Cerne Abbas; ⏲24hr; P) is a 60m-high, 51m-wide depiction of a man, etched into a chalk hillside. Nude, full frontal and notoriously well endowed, he's revealed in a state of excitement that wouldn't be allowed in most magazines. Once you've got over his assets, ponder his age: some claim he's Roman, but the first historical reference comes in 1694, when three shillings were set aside for his repair.

⓫ Wells

England's smallest city boasts one of her grandest medieval buildings: **Wells Cathedral** (Cathedral Church of St Andrew; ☎01749-674483; www.wellscathedral.org.uk; Cathedral Green; requested donation adult/child £6/5; ⏰7am-7pm Apr-Sep, to 6pm Oct-Mar), a gargantuan Gothic confection built in stages between 1180 and 1508. Highlights include a **West Front** decorated with more than 300 carved figures, and some fine scissor arches. In the surrounding **Cathedral Close**, hunt out the 14th-century cobbled **Vicar's Close**, then make for the nearby **Bishop's Palace** (☎01749-988111; www.bishopspalace.org.uk; Market Pl; adult/child £9/4.50; ⏰10am-6pm Apr-Oct, to 4pm Nov-Mar), a moat-ringed, 13th-century manor house with state rooms, a ruined great hall and delightful gardens, complete with natural springs.

✕ p151

The Drive » Peeling out of town on the A371, it's a mere 3 miles to Wookey Hole.

⓬ Wookey Hole

Yes, the **Wookey Hole** (☎01749-672243; www.wookey.co.uk; Wookey Hole; adult/child £20/16; ⏰10am-5pm Apr-Oct, to 4pm Nov-Mar, closed Mon-Fri Dec–mid-Feb; P) limestone caverns are incredibly touristy (the local legend of a witch inhabiting them is played for all it's worth), but the caves themselves are rightly famous for striking stalagmites and stalactites, one of which is the infamous witch herself, purportedly turned to stone by a local priest.

The Drive » Continue northwest for 8 miles through a string of villages on the A371, which skirts the Mendip Hills on the right (you'll be up there later). Once in Cheddar, continue through the village, following signs to Cheddar Gorge.

TOP TIP: GLASTONBURY TRAFFIC

To many, Glastonbury is synonymous with the **Glastonbury Festival** (www.glastonburyfestivals.co.uk), a majestic and often-mud-soaked extravaganza of music and culture that attracts over 150,000 people in mid-June. If you're not festival-bound, avoid the area then as traffic jams can be horrendous.

⓭ Cheddar Gorge

Pick any one of the parking spots in **Cheddar Gorge** (☎01934-742343; www.cheddargorge.co.uk; Cheddar Gorge; adult/child £20/15; ⏰10am-5pm, to 5.30pm late July-Aug) then get out and explore. Carved out by glacial meltwater during the last Ice Age, these limestone cliffs form England's deepest natural canyon, in places towering 138m above the twisting B3135. Of the gorge's caves, **Cox's Cave** and **Gough's Cave** are the easiest to reach, and are decorated with impressive stalactites and stalagmites. The 274-step staircase known as **Jacob's Ladder** leads to a spectacular viewpoint over the gorge and a 3-mile clifftop trail. Admission covers parking, Jacob's Ladder and entry to the caves.

The Drive » The short drive up the gorge itself is along a twisting, sometimes single-track road that cuts through towering rock formations. At the top, the B3135 becomes a rolling, field-framed route across the roof of the Mendip plateau. Next, a series of A roads cut down from the hills and on to Bath, some 20 miles from Cheddar Gorge.

TRIP HIGHLIGHT

⓮ Bath

Home to some of Britain's grandest Georgian architecture, Bath is also one of the nation's most beautiful cities. On the southern fringes sits 18th-century **Prior Park** (NT; ☎01225-833977; www.nationaltrust.org.uk; Ralph

Classic Trip

Allen Dr; adult/child £7.50/3.75; ⏲10am-5.30pm daily Feb-Oct, 10am-4pm Sat & Sun Nov-Jan; P). Partly designed by landscape architect Capability Brown, the grounds of this exquisite 18th-century estate feature cascading lakes and a graceful Palladian bridge, one of only four such structures in the world (look out for the period graffiti, some of which dates back to the 1800s). Of the estate's lovely pathways, the pick is the **Bath Skyline**, a 6-mile circular trail offering truly inspirational views.

Get back in the car for the 1-mile cruise to Bath itself. Here a walk around the streets is richly rewarded. The **Museum of Bath Architecture** (☎01225-333895; www.museumofbatharchitecture.org.uk; The Countess of Huntingdon's Chapel, off the Paragon; adult/child £7/3.50; ⏲1-5pm Mon-Fri, 10am-5pm Sat & Sun mid-Feb–Nov) explores the stories behind the construction of the most striking structures, and features antique tools and a 1:500 scale model of the city. Bath is also famously a location featured in Jane Austen's novels including *Persuasion* and *Northanger Abbey*. The writer was a city resident for five years and remained a regular visitor and keen student of the city's social scene. In the **Jane Austen Centre** (☎01225-443000; www.janeausten.co.uk; 40 Gay St; adult/child £12/6.20; ⏲9.45am-5.30pm Apr-Oct, 10am-4pm Sun-Fri, 9.45am-5.30pm Sat Nov-Mar), guides in Regency costumes regale you with Austenesque tales as you tour memorabilia relating to her life in Bath.

🛏 p47, p73, p151, p203

BATH'S HISTORY

Legend has it King Bladud, a Trojan refugee and father of King Lear, founded Bath some 2800 years ago when his pigs were cured of leprosy by a dip in the muddy swamps. The Romans established the town of Aquae Sulis in AD 44 and built the extensive **Roman Baths** complex and a temple to the goddess Sulis-Minerva.

Long after the Romans decamped, the Anglo-Saxons arrived, and in 944 a monastery was founded on the site of the present **Bath Abbey**. Throughout the Middle Ages, Bath was an ecclesiastical centre and a wool-trading town, but it wasn't until the early 18th century that Ralph Allen and the celebrated dandy Richard 'Beau' Nash made Bath the centre of fashionable society. Allen developed the quarries at Coombe Down, constructed **Prior Park** and employed the two John Woods (father and son) to create Bath's signature buildings.

During WWII Bath was hit by the Luftwaffe during the so-called Baedeker raids, which targeted historic cities in an effort to sap British morale. Several houses on the **Royal Crescent** and the **Circus** were badly damaged, and the city's **Assembly Rooms** were gutted by fire, though all have since been restored.

In 1987 Bath became the only city in Britain to be declared a Unesco World Heritage Site in its entirety, leading to many subsequent wrangles over construction and development, most recently concerning the design of the redeveloped **Thermae Bath Spa** and **SouthGate** shopping centre.

Eating & Sleeping

Winchester 1

16a B&B $$$

(☎07730 510663; www.16a-winchester.co.uk; 16a Parchment St; r £145-185; wifi) The word 'boutique' gets bandied around freely, but here it fits. The sumptuous conversion of this old dance hall sees an antique piano and honesty bar frame a wood-burning stove. Gorgeous bedrooms feature exposed brick, lofty ceilings, vast beds and baths on the mezzanines with views of the stars.

Salisbury 2

St Ann's House B&B $$

(☎01722-335657; www.stannshouse.co.uk; 32 St Ann St; d £65-90; wifi) Utter elegance reigns at 18th-century St Ann's, where cast-iron fireplaces, mini-chandeliers and sash windows cosy up to warm colours and well-chosen antiques. Breakfast goodies include locally baked bread and homemade orange and star anise marmalade.

Shaftesbury 8

Fleur de Lys Hotel $$$

(☎01747-853717; www.lafleurdelys.co.uk; Bleke St; s £90-110, d £100-160, tr £170-180; P @ wifi) In this bijou, delightfully romantic hotel, soft lighting shines on satin fabrics and plump cushions, while mini-fridges, homemade biscuits and freshly ground coffee keep pamper levels high.

Sherborne 9

Cumberland House B&B $$

(☎01935-817554; www.bandbdorset.co.uk; Greenhill; d £80-85; P wifi) Artistry emanates from these history-rich rooms – bright scatter rugs sit on flagstone floors, and lemon and oatmeal walls undulate between wonderfully wonky beams. Gourmet breakfasts include freshly squeezed orange juice, fresh-fruit compote and homemade granola.

Glastonbury 10

Magdalene House B&B $$

(☎01458-830202; www.magdalenehouseglastonbury.co.uk; Magdalene St; s £80-110, d £95-110, tr £140; P wifi) Artfully decorated Magdalene used to be a school run by Glastonbury's nuns, and one room still overlooks the abbey grounds. Each of the tall, light rooms is an array of olive, oatmeal and other soft tones, while tasteful artworks give it all a restful feel.

Wells 11

Goodfellows European $$

(☎01749-673866; www.goodfellowswells.co.uk; 5 Sadler St; dinner mains £14-24; ⏲10am-3pm Tue-Sat, noon-3pm Sun & Mon, 6-9pm Wed-Sat) There's a choice of eating options in Goodfellows' three vibrant rooms: the continental cafe menu offers cakes, pastries and light lunches (from £6), or book for an evening fine-dining experience – £33 gets you three classy courses, while the five-course seafood tasting menu (£50) is an absolute treat.

Bath 14

Haringtons Hotel $$

(☎01225-461728; www.haringtonshotel.co.uk; 8 Queen St; r £120-200; P wifi pets) If Bath's classical trappings aren't to your taste, head for this strictly modern city-centre crash pad, with vivid colour schemes, clashing wallpapers and a fun, young vibe. The location is fantastic, with the central sights just a few minutes' walk away.

North Devon & Exmoor National Park

Stand by for a rip-roaring roller coaster of a ride along a cliff-framed shore. You'll negotiate precipitous inclines and hairpin bends, and marvel at jaw-dropping sea views.

TRIP HIGHLIGHTS

50 miles

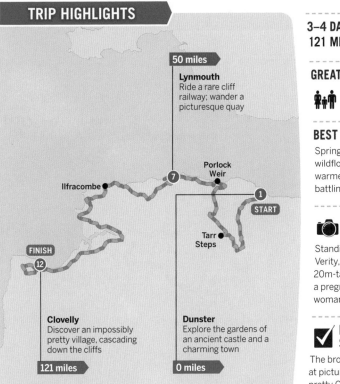

Lynmouth
Ride a rare cliff railway; wander a picturesque quay

Porlock Weir

Ilfracombe

7

1

START

Tarr Steps

FINISH

12

Clovelly
Discover an impossibly pretty village, cascading down the cliffs

121 miles

Dunster
Explore the gardens of an ancient castle and a charming town

0 miles

3–4 DAYS 121 MILES / 195KM

GREAT FOR...

BEST TIME TO GO

Spring brings wildflowers; summer, warmer seas; autumn, battling stags.

ESSENTIAL PHOTO

Standing beside Verity, Damien Hirst's 20m-tall statue of a pregnant, naked woman in Ilfracombe.

BEST SURF SPOT

The broad sandy beach at picture-postcard-pretty Croyde.

Clovelly A picturesque hillside village

11 North Devon & Exmoor National Park

It's the kind of road trip cars were made for. From quaint villages you'll climb to open moorland topped by an overarching sky. Here single-track roads wind between free-roaming ponies; you might even spot wild deer. Motor down to picturesque quays, burn your brakes on white-knuckle descents, then bump along toll roads. Coal-black cliffs fill your windscreen en route to surfing beaches and quaint swimming coves. It's an unforgettable drive.

TRIP HIGHLIGHT

1 Dunster

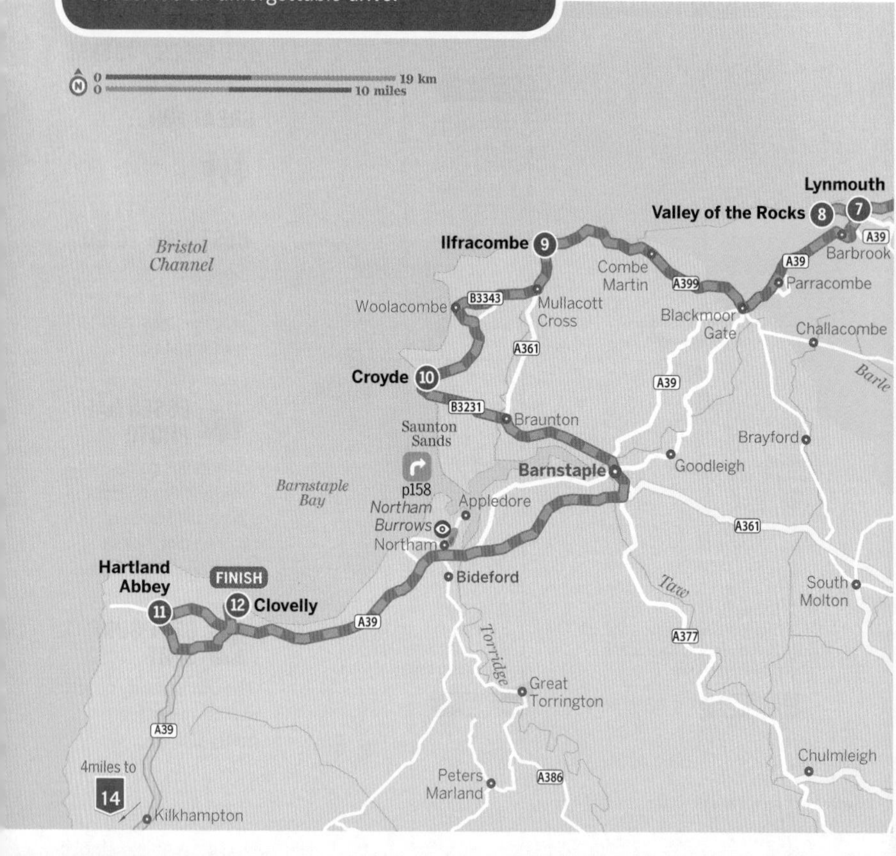

The pretty town of Dunster is a tempting tangle of cobbled streets and bubbling brooks. It's presided over by rose-stone, 13th-century **Dunster Castle** (NT; ☎01643-821314; www.nationaltrust.org.uk; Castle Hill; gardens adult/child £8/4; ⏰11am-5pm Mar-Oct; P); check whether you need to pre-book a visit. The colourful terraced gardens have views across Exmoor's shores and

lead to an 18th-century **watermill**, which still has most of its original working mechanisms. A short walk leads to picturesque **St George's Church**; a 16th-century **dovecote** sits just behind.

🛏 p159

The Drive ›› Motoring 15 miles south along the A396, a steep wooded ridge rises to the west. But on this stretch you're not driving on the higher moor; that comes later. Instead it's a rolling route through tree-framed valleys.

2 Dulverton

Dulverton is a quintessential Exmoor market town. Sitting at the base of the Barle Valley, it's home to a collection of gun sellers, fishing-tackle stores and gift shops. It's a pleasing place at which to stock up on picnic foods at the **Exclusive Cake Co** (☎01398-324131; www.exclusivecakecompany.co.uk; Northmoor Rd; snacks from £3; ⏲7am-2pm Mon-Fri, from 9am Sat) and pick up local books at the **tourist office** (☎01398-323841; www.visit-exmoor.co.uk; 7 Fore St; ⏲10am-4pm Apr-Oct, reduced hours Nov-Mar).

✕ p159

The Drive ›› From the centre of town, take the B3223 north towards Exford (also signed Tarr Steps). Soon woods clear and after rattling across a couple of cattle grids you're onto the open, undulating moor. Five miles out of Dulverton follow signs to Tarr Steps, a mile away down steep, winding lanes. Park at the car park, continuing 450m on foot.

3 Tarr Steps

Exmoor's most famous landmark, **Tarr Steps** (P) is an ancient stone clapper bridge shaded by gnarled old trees. Its huge slabs are propped up on stone columns embedded in the River Barle. Local folklore aside (which declares it was used by the Devil for sunbathing), it first

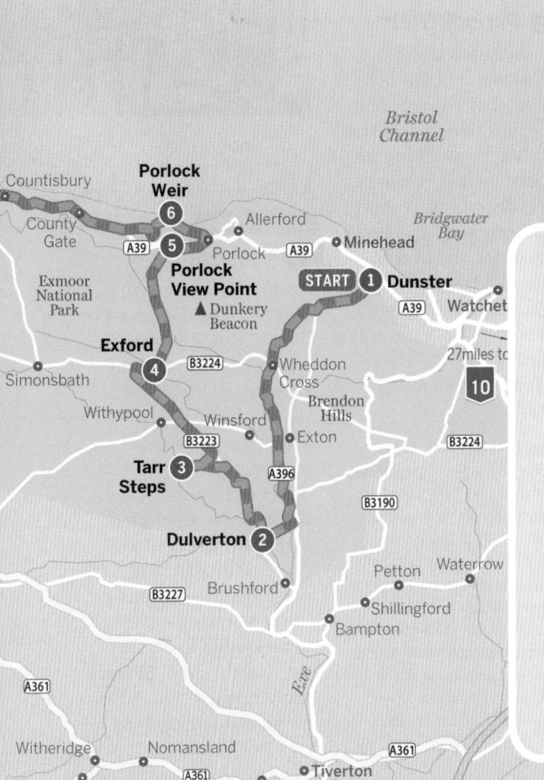

LINK YOUR TRIP

14 Epic Cornwall

From Clovelly, head 17 miles southwest to Bude to link up with a charismatic, spray-dashed drive around the end of England.

10 Winchester, Glastonbury & Bath

A history-rich tour of the west's best big-name cultural sights. Pick it up 40 miles east of Dunster at Glastonbury.

pops into the historical record in the 1600s, and had to be rebuilt after 21st-century floods. A few paces away, **Tarr Farm** (☎01643-851507; www.tarrfarm.co.uk; Tarr Steps, TA22 9QA; s/d £90/160; P 📶🐾) is a charming inn that dishes up snacks and meals strong on local fish and game.

The Drive » Back up the hill, peel left, following signs for Exford. It's a 7-mile roof-of-the-moor meander, with swathes of honey-brown bracken unfolding on either side. Cross the bridge by the Exmoor White Horse Inn, parking beside the village green.

❹ Exford

There's not much to Exford, but what there is defines quaint. This tiny village clusters around a pleasant muddle of cottages and slate-roofed houses. Time then to stroll beside the rushing River Exe and sip a drink on the terrace of the waterfront pub.

The Drive » Next, a 6-mile leg. Head up the hill with the village green to your left, signed Porlock. It's another steep climb (you'll feel your ears pop) that's rewarded with a prolonged burst of open moor. Eventually the sea slides into view in your windscreen. Soon after, you meet the A39; cross it to stop in the car park.

❺ Porlock View Point

Rarely, surely, has a car park offered such captivating views. The sweep of beach far below frames Porlock Bay; the headland at its eastern (right hand) edge is Hurlstone Point. The shoreline on the horizon, dotted with cliffs and toy-sized structures, is actually the coast of South Wales.

The Drive » Turn left at the car-park entrance for a second-gear descent down the infamous, 25%-gradient **Porlock Hill**; expect hairpin bends, escape lanes and 'try your brakes' signs. Once in Porlock village, turn left to Porlock Weir. In all, a 4-mile drive.

❻ Porlock Weir

At the charismatic breakwater of Porlock Weir, an arching pebble beach frames a pint-sized harbour – watching small boats navigate their way in is absorbing. A short walkway stretches beside the water and over the lock to a tiny terrace of cottages clinging to a slender spit of sea-framed land. A pub, cafes and gift and art shops sit nearby.

The Drive » Take the lane between the Ship Inn and the Locanda On The Weir hotel. It cuts sharply right, signed Worthy. At the toll gate pay £2. A bouncing road climbs through woods; sea glimpses emerge below. The A39 rolls along a moorland plateau to spectacular sea views. As the road plunges, signs speak volumes: 'Rockfalls', '12% gradient'. It's 12 miles in all.

PETER TITMUSS / SHUTTERSTOCK ©

TRIP HIGHLIGHT

❼ Lynmouth

Bustling Lynmouth is tucked in amid steep, tree-lined slopes. A busy harbour leads west to a **cliff railway** (☎01598-753486; www.cliffrailwaylynton.co.uk; The Esplanade, Lynmouth; 1 way adult/child £3/2; ⏰11am-4pm). This extraordinary piece of 1890s water-powered engineering sees two connected cars shuttle up and down the sloping cliffs. They deliver you to hill-town **Lynton** to head to the churchyard of **St Mary the Virgin** (Church Hill) for views of precipitous

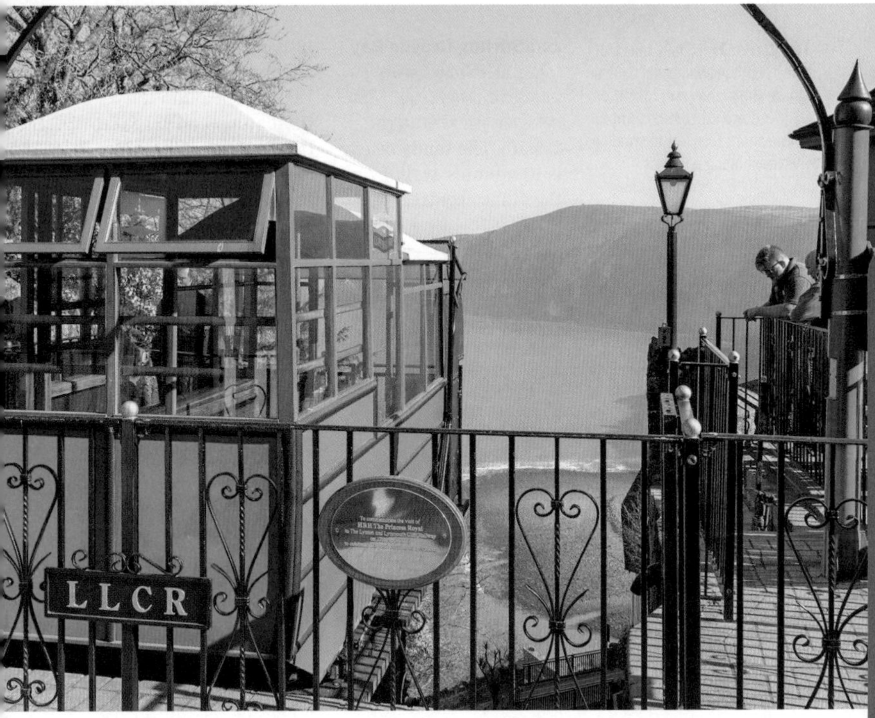

Lynmouth A cliffside railway connects Lynmouth with Lynton

Countisbury Hill (the one you've just driven down). Hop back on the cliff railway and back to your car.

✕ 🛏 p159

The Drive » Now, a 2-mile drive. From Lynmouth seafront take the right fork up the hill for another set of 25% gradient switchbacks. Ignore the turn for Simonsbath and pick up the Valley of the Rocks signs. Soon you're heading into a deep, broad dip, framed by towering rocks.

---

8 Valley of the Rocks

Welcome to a perfect pit stop for a dramatic stroll. The awesome geology in the shoreside **Valley of the Rocks** includes formations dubbed the **Devil's Cheesewring** and **Ragged Jack**. Look out too for feral goats, wandering the tracks.

The Drive » Head back into Lynton, picking up signs to Ilfracombe, initially along a climbing A39 (signed Barnstaple). At Blackmoor Gate turn right onto the A399, heading down Combe Martin's long High St, to emerge at Ilfracombe. It's 20 miles in all.

---

9 Ilfracombe

In Ilfracombe steep headlands plummet down to pint-sized beaches, and paths cling to sheer cliffs. At the harbour mouth Damien Hirst's towering, 20m-high statue, **Verity** (The Pier), depicts a naked pregnant woman holding aloft a spear. On the seaward side her skin is peeled back, revealing sinew and foetus. On the other side of the harbour, beside the Royal National Lifeboat Institution (RNLI) lifeboat house, hunt out the **S&P** (☎01271-865923; www.sandpfish.co.uk; 1 The Cove; dishes £6-15, seafood platters £64; ⏰10am-4pm Mon-Sat, 11am-4pm Sun) cafe. Opt for some cockles or go all out for a bumper seafood platter.

🛏 p159

The Drive » Initially take the A361 south. At Mullacott Cross, ignore the satnav and take the B3343 down into Woolacombe. At the shore turn left to shadow the coast along a web of unclassified lanes, then pick up signs for Croyde. A 10-mile leg in all.

10 Croyde

The cheerful, chilled village of Croyde is Devon's surf central. Thatched roofs peep out over racks of wetsuits, and cool types in board shorts sip beer beside 17th-century inns. **Ralph's** (01271-890147; Hobb's Hill; surfboard & wetsuit hire per 4/24hr £12/18, bodyboard & wetsuit £10/15; 9am-dusk mid-Mar–Dec) hires out surf equipment. Lessons are provided by **Surf South West** (01271-890400; www.surfsouthwest.com; Croyde Burrows car park; half-/full day £35/65; mid-Mar–mid-Nov) and **Surfing Croyde Bay** (0800 188 4860; www.surfingcroydebay.co.uk; Freshwell Camping; half-/full day £35/70). The sandy beach is 10 minutes' walk from the village centre.

p159

The Drive » Time to cover some miles – 33 to be exact. The B3231 winds west, revealing the 3-mile sweep of Saunton Sands. After Barnstaple, the A39 (aka the 'Atlantic Hwy') glides southwest. After Higher Clovelly the B3248 branches off to Hartland village; your next stop is 1.5 miles further on.

11 Hartland Abbey

History seems to flow from the walls of enchanting **Hartland Abbey** (01237-441496; www.hartlandabbey.com; near Hartland; house adult/child £12.50/5.50, gardens & grounds £9/4.50; grounds 11am-5pm Sun-Thu Apr-Sep; P). Built in the 12th century, it was a monastery until Henry VIII grabbed it in the Dissolution and gave it to the sergeant of his wine cellar. His descendants, the Stucley family, still live in the abbey today. It's encircled by a fernery, walled garden, camellia garden and woodland walks.

The Drive » A 6.5-mile leg, largely retracing your route to Higher Clovelly. From there pick up signs to Clovelly village.

TRIP HIGHLIGHT

12 Clovelly

Picture-postcard-pretty **Clovelly** (01237-431781; www.clovelly.co.uk; adult/child £8/4.60; 9am-5pm, book visits in advance; P) is privately owned, so park up beside the hilltop visitor centre and pay your admission. Then walk down cobbled streets so steep cars can't cope – supplies are brought in by sledge; spot these big bread baskets on runners leaning outside homes. Look out for the former home of Charles Kingsley, author of the children's classic *The Water Babies*, the atmospheric fisher's cottage and the twin chapels.

p159

DETOUR: NORTHAM BURROWS

Start: 12 Clovelly

A detour of just 3 miles off the A39 between Barnstaple and Clovelly leads to a vast, wildlife-rich expanse. The 253-hectare **Northam Burrows** (01237-479708; www.torridge.gov.uk/northamburrows; Northam; parking per day £4.50; pedestrians 24hr, cars 7am-10pm Mar-Oct, to 6pm Nov-Feb; P) reserve encompasses grassy plains, dunes, salt marshes, a sandy shore and grazing sheep and horses. It's home to wheatear, linnet, stonechat, curlew and little egret. A pebble ridge sits between the burrows and 2-mile-long Westward Ho! beach, forming a natural sea defence.

Eating & Sleeping

Dunster 1

Millstream Cottage B&B $$

(01643-822413; www.millstreamcottagedunster.co.uk; 2 Mill Lane; s £65, d £80-90) In the 1600s this was Dunster's workhouse. Now it's a sweet-as-pie guesthouse with country-cottage-style rooms with beams, pine doors and stone fireplaces. Breakfasts treats include porridge, toast with Exmoor jams and smoked haddock and poached eggs.

Dulverton 2

Woods Bistro $$

(01398-324007; www.woodsdulverton.co.uk; 4 Bank Sq; mains £13-19; bar noon-3pm & 7-11pm, food noon-2pm & 7-9.30pm) With its deer antlers, hunting prints and big wood-burning stove, multi-award-winning Woods is Exmoor to its core. No surprise then to find menus with full-bodied ingredients: expect confit leg of guinea fowl, slow-roast lamb shoulder, and asparagus and wild garlic risotto. The clutch of tables outside and in the flower-framed courtyard garden are first-come, first-served.

Lynmouth 7

Ancient Mariner Pub Food $$

(01598-752238; www.bathhotellynmouth.co.uk; The Harbour, Lynmouth; mains £12-19; 10-11.30am, noon-4pm & 5.30-9pm;) The Mariner brings a burst of shipwreck chic to Lynmouth, thanks to a copper bar top, curved ship's decking, covered outdoor seating and a figurehead that isn't entirely clothed. Drink it all in while tucking into a stacked-high Mariner Burger, complete with Exmoor ale and black-treacle-braised brisket, onion jam and blue-cheese mousse.

Bath Hotel Hotel $$

(01598-752238; www.bathhotellynmouth.co.uk; The Harbour, Lynmouth; d £90-145, ste £155;) The Bath Hotel has been a feature of the town since Victorian times. These days it's a swish affair with premium rooms featuring gorgeously nautical styling, Victorian curios, supremely comfortable beds and expansive harbour and headland views. The 'Austerity' rooms are much less snazzy – but they're also £50 cheaper.

Ilfracombe 9

Norbury House B&B $$

(01271-863888; www.norburyhouse.co.uk; Torrs Park; d £110-130, tr £135;) Each of the rooms in this gorgeous guesthouse is done up in a different style: choose from pop art, art deco or contemporary chic. Fabulous furnishings, light-filled interiors, charming hosts and cracking sea-and-town views seal the deal.

Croyde 10

Biffen's Kitchen Street Food $

(www.biffenskitchen.com; Ocean Pitch Campsite, Moor Lane; dishes £4.50-7; 8.30-10.30am Tue-Sun, 5-8pm Wed-Sat mid-Apr–Sep;) Inspired by surf-themed street food, the eponymous Biff set up this snack shack in 2019 after ditching a London marketing job to ride north Devon's waves. Expect chipotle jackfruit tacos, jerk chicken curry and plenty of beach-bum flair.

Clovelly 12

Red Lion Inn $$$

(01237-431237; www.stayatclovelly.co.uk/red-lion; The Quay; d £170-195;) Welcome to the best of Clovelly's brace of inns. To a superb waterside position add quaint, airy rooms with a choice of aspects: opt for big, blue sea views, or an equally sweet outlook across the harbour – the style is plush vintage-chic either way.

Jurassic Coast

On this road trip to remember, the route ribbons along a World Heritage–listed shore. Expect gorgeous bays, iconic castles and a windscreen full of views.

TRIP HIGHLIGHTS

70 miles

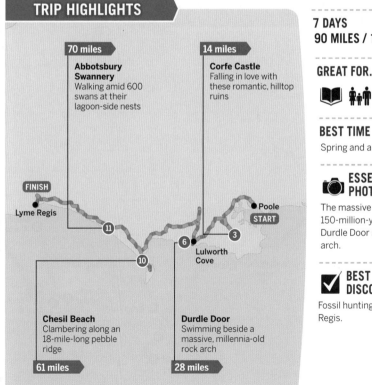

Abbotsbury Swannery
Walking amid 600 swans at their lagoon-side nests

14 miles

Corfe Castle
Falling in love with these romantic, hilltop ruins

FINISH
Lyme Regis
11
10
6
Lulworth Cove
3
Poole
START

Chesil Beach
Clambering along an 18-mile-long pebble ridge

61 miles

Durdle Door
Swimming beside a massive, millennia-old rock arch

28 miles

7 DAYS
90 MILES / 145KM

GREAT FOR...

BEST TIME TO GO

Spring and autumn.

ESSENTIAL PHOTO

The massive 150-million-year-old Durdle Door stone arch.

BEST DISCOVERIES

Fossil hunting in Lyme Regis.

Durdle Door Portland stone arch

12 Jurassic Coast

One of the west's best drives, this route rolls up chalk ridges, through thatched villages and along sea-fringed roads. It takes in vast beaches, unforgettable swim spots, a soaring rock arch and fossils galore. History is everywhere: from fairy-tale castles to an art-packed quarry. Prepare for the pick of Dorset's sights and sea-view sunsets as you keep heading west.

1 Poole

The attractive historic buildings in the old port of Poole include the Tudor **King Charles pub** on Thames St, the cream **Old Harbour Office** (1820s) next door and the impressive red-brick **Custom House** (1813) opposite. A few yards away, the **Waterfront Museum** (☎01202-262600; www.boroughofpoole.com/museums; 4 High St; ⏰10am-1pm & 2-5pm Apr-Oct) is a beautifully restored 15th-century warehouse housing a 2300-year-old,

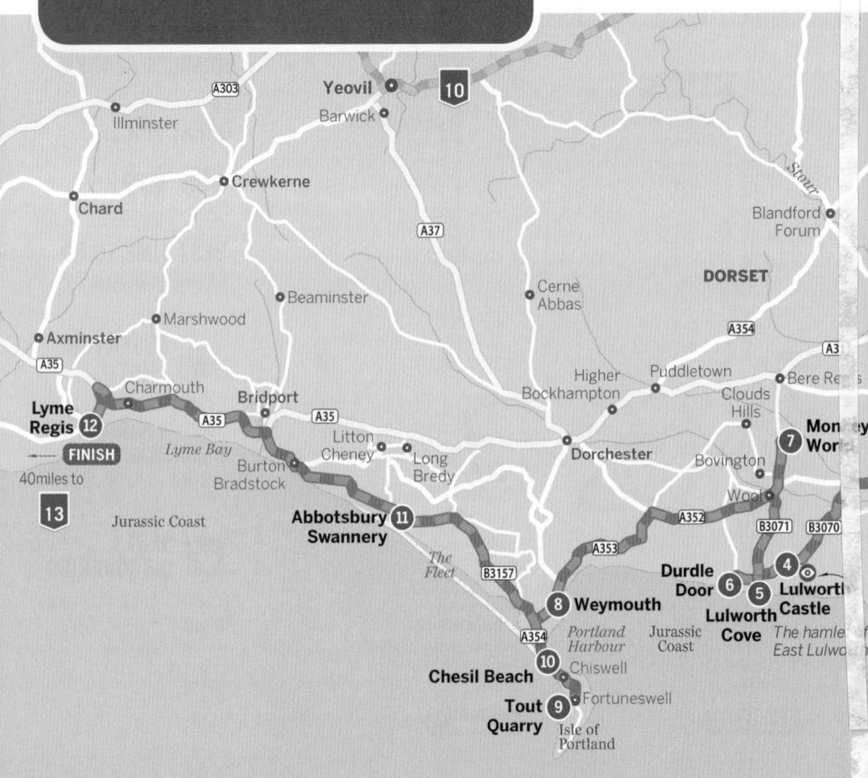

10m-long, 14-tonne Iron Age logboat dredged up from Poole Harbour. From Poole Quay, boats shuttle to the wooded nature reserve of **Brownsea Island** (NT; ☎01202-707744; www.nationaltrust.org.uk; Poole Harbour; ferry & admission adult/child £17.50/9.50; ⏲9am-5.30pm late Mar-Oct), just offshore.

🛏 p167

The Drive » Pick up signs for the A350 to Dorchester/Blandford, then peel off onto the A351 to Wareham for a 10-mile drive.

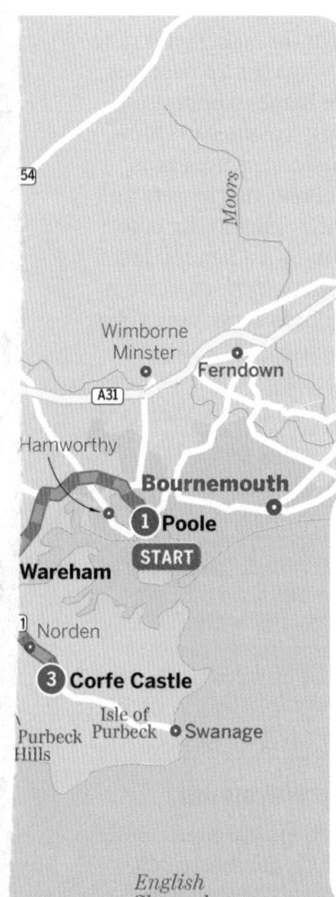

2 Wareham

The Saxons built sturdy Wareham in the 10th century, and their legacy lingers in surviving remnants of the market town's defensive walls – explore them on the 45-minute **Walls Walk**, or make a beeline for one section: the 11th-century **St Martin's on the Walls** (North St; ⏲3-5pm Mon, 10am-noon Fri) church at the top of North St. It features a 12th-century fresco and a marble effigy of TE Lawrence (aka Lawrence of Arabia), who lived locally.

The Drive » Continue south on the A351, a tree-lined but unremarkable drive. Unremarkable, that is, until 4 miles on, when the startling, shattered hilltop ruins of mighty Corfe Castle leap into view.

TRIP HIGHLIGHT

3 Corfe Castle

From the National Trust (NT) car park, walk two minutes to **Corfe Castle** (NT; ☎01929-481294; www.nationaltrust.org.uk; The Square; adult/child £10/5; ⏲10am-6pm Apr-Sep, to 5pm Mar & Oct, to 4pm Nov-Feb) itself. Once home to Sir John Bankes, Charles I's right-hand man, the castle was besieged by Cromwellian forces in the English Civil War. In 1646 the plucky Lady Bankes directed a six-week defence, and the castle fell only after being betrayed from within. The Roundheads then gunpowdered Corfe Castle apart; turrets and soaring walls still sheer off at precarious angles – the splayed-out gatehouse looks like it's just been blown up.

The Drive » Put Corfe Castle in your rear-view mirror, heading back towards Wareham then onto the B3070 to East Lulworth (some 10 miles). Rattle over the cattle grid and into Lulworth Castle's grounds.

4 Lulworth Castle

Creamy, dreamy **Lulworth Castle** (EH; ☎01929-400352; www.

LINK YOUR TRIP

10 Winchester, Glastonbury & Bath

Stonehenge, soaring cathedrals and the sumptuous city of Bath. Pick it up at Sherborne, 27 miles north of Weymouth.

13 South Devon

Some 50 miles southwest of this trip's end, Torquay leads to a charming tour of historic ports, an eco-town, a vineyard and Agatha Christie's home.

lulworth.com; adult/child £6/4, parking £3; ⏲10.30am-5pm Sun-Fri Apr-Dec) looks more like a French chateau than a traditional English castle; it was built in 1608 as a hunting lodge, and has survived extravagant owners, extensive remodelling and a fire in 1929. Tour the reconstructed kitchen and cellars; if the tower has reopened, take in sweeping coastal views.

The Drive » Turn right for a 3-mile dawdle along rural roads, past a military tank camp and through West Lulworth, to the main visitor centre car park at Lulworth Cove.

5 Lulworth Cove

At the village of Lulworth Cove, a pleasing jumble of thatched cottages and fishing gear leads down to the eponymous bay – a perfect, narrow-mouthed crescent of white cliffs. After admiring the views, pop into the **visitor centre** (☎01929-400587; www.lulworth.com; main car park; ⏲10am-5pm Easter-Sep, to 4pm Oct-Easter) to learn how rock types and erosion have shaped this remarkable shore. Then walk two minutes to see geology in action at the **Lulworth Crumple**, where layers of rock form dramatically zigzagging folds.

🛏 p167

The Drive » It's back uphill, turning left with the brown signs to Durdle Door – a steep 1-mile climb beside hummocky hills. Head into the campsite; your Lulworth Cove parking ticket is valid at either of the two car parks furthest from the shore.

TRIP HIGHLIGHT

6 Durdle Door

The walk from the car park that brings the **Durdle Door** (www.lulworth.com; near Lulworth Cove, BH20 5PU; parking half-/full day £5/10) into view is well worth the effort. This immense, sea-fringed, 150-million-year-old Portland stone arch was created by a combination of massive earth movements and erosion. Today it's framed by shimmering bays; bring a swimsuit and head down the hundreds of steps for an unforgettable dip. The beaches and car park here can get busy. To be sure of a parking place in summer, book ahead, or visit early in the day.

The Drive » Next, an 8-mile drive. Head up the B3070/3071 to Wool. After Wool train station turn right, across the tracks, to pick up signs featuring the cute, long-tailed residents of your next stop: Monkey World.

7 Monkey World

Monkey World (☎01929-462537; www.monkeyworld.co.uk; Longthorns, BH20 6HH; adult/child/family £16/11/32; ⏲10am-5pm; P) overflows with the 'aah' factor. The sanctuary's 26 hectares are home to bounding, noisy colonies of chimpanzees, orang-utans, gibbons, marmosets and some ridiculously cute ring-tailed lemurs. Most have been rescued from primate smuggling rings, circuses, laboratories, working on beaches, or being mistreated as pets.

The Drive » Head back through Wool, then join the A352/353 for the 15-mile cruise through rolling hills southwest to Weymouth. There, pass the reed-filled lagoons of the bird reserve and ranks of B&Bs to park up on the seafront or beside the waterfront Pavilions theatre.

8 Weymouth

Historic harbour, 3-mile beach, candy-striped kiosks – welcome to

TOP TIP: FIRING RANGES

The picturesque Purbeck Hills are also tank live-firing ranges: road signs warn: '! Sudden Gunfire'. Our route avoids restricted areas, but the ranges *are* sometimes accessible. A southerly Corfe Castle to East Lulworth route (offering sea glimpses and tank remnants) is often open holidays and weekends; call 01929-404714 to check.

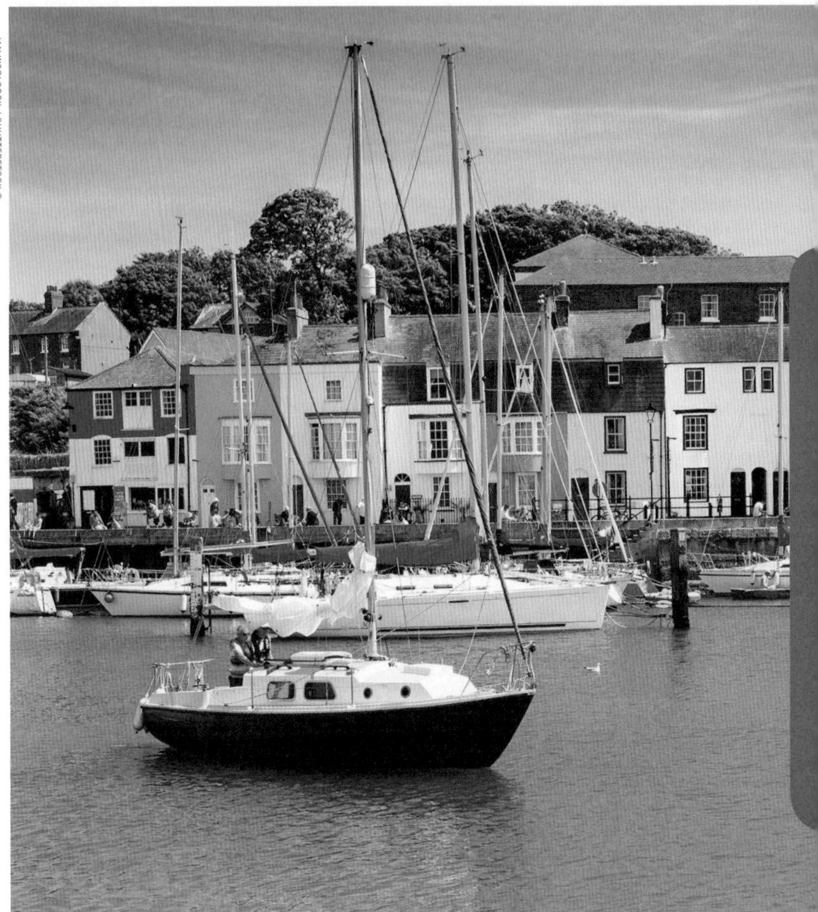
IAN WOOLCOCK / SHUTTERSTOCK ©

Weymouth Boats gathered in the Old Harbour

the kitsch-rich seaside resort of Weymouth. The nostalgia-inducing offerings along the fine sandy shore could see you renting a deckchair or pedalo. A grid of sweet streets leads to an **old harbour** packed with fishing boats. The cannon-studded defences of 19th-century **Nothe Fort** (☎01305-766626; www.nothefort.org.uk; Barrack Rd; adult/child £8/2; ⏰11am-4pm Apr-Oct) sit nearby. Then head out to **Sandworld** (☎07411 387529; www.sandworld.co.uk; Lodmoor Country Park, Preston Beach Rd; adult/child £7.75/5.75; ⏰10am-3.30pm) to see lifelike sand sculptures of fairy-tale castles, sly dragons and scenes from blockbuster films.

🛏 p167

The Drive » Join the A354 south to Portland. The long straight road onto the isle is an exhilarating stretch, sweeping between a vast harbour and a high-ridged pebble beach. The twisting climb through Chiswell on the Fortuneswell road reveals Portland's unique character: remote, rugged, sometimes bleak, but beautiful. At the hill's crest follow the signs to Tout Quarry Park (around 7 miles in all).

9 Tout Quarry

Portland's white limestone has been quarried for centuries and features in some of the world's finest buildings, such as the British Museum and St Paul's Cathedral. The disused workings of **Tout Quarry** (near Fortuneswell; ⌚dawn-dusk; P) now house more than 50 sculptures carved into the rock in situ. It results in a fascinating combination of raw materials, the detritus of the quarrying process and the beauty of chiselled works. Stroll to the cliffs at the quarry's edge for 180-degree views down to the awe-inspiring sweep of Chesil Beach.

p167

The Drive » Retrace your route down off the plateau (passengers can delight in drinking in the remarkable views) and back along the thin road to the mainland. Near the end, head left into the Chesil Beach car park; in total a mere 3 miles away.

TRIP HIGHLIGHT

10 Chesil Beach

One of Britain's most breathtaking beaches, Chesil is 18 miles long, 15m high and moving inland at the rate of 5m a century. The stones on this mind-boggling, 100-million-tonne pebble ridge range from pea-sized in the west to hand-sized here in the east. The **Chesil Beach Centre** (Fine Foundation; ☎01305-206191; www.dorsetwildlifetrust.org.uk; Ferrybridge; parking per hour £1; ⌚10am-5pm Easter-Sep, to 4pm Oct-Easter; P) details its ecosystem. From the car park an energy-sapping hike up sliding pebbles leads to the constant surge and rattle of waves on stones and dazzling views of the sea, with the thin pebble line and the expanse of the Fleet Lagoon behind.

p167

The Drive » Time to drive the road you saw from Portland: a 9-mile sweep along the B3157, rolling beside undulating fields and hills. In the midst of the thatched-cottage-rich village of Abbotsbury, turn sharp left for the Swannery.

TRIP HIGHLIGHT

11 Abbotsbury Swannery

Every May some 600 free-flying swans choose to nest at **Abbotsbury Swannery** (☎01305-871858; www.abbotsbury-tourism.co.uk; New Barn Rd, Abbotsbury; adult/child £10/5; ⌚10am-5pm late Mar-Oct), which shelters in the Fleet Lagoon. Wandering the network of trails winding between the swans' nests is an awe-inspiring experience that's punctuated by occasional territorial displays (think snuffling coughs and stand-up flapping), ensuring that even the liveliest children are stilled.

The Drive » Continue through Abbotsbury for another glorious, second-gear climb, pausing at the lay-bys for cracking views back onto Chesil Beach. Next, a ridgetop roller coaster of a road, framed by green fields and an improbably wide bay. Some 20 miles later you descend into Lyme Regis.

12 Lyme Regis

Beach-framed and quaint, Lyme Regis is one of Dorset's most delightful towns. It's also fantastically fossiliferous – rock-hard relics of the past pop out repeatedly from the surrounding cliffs, exposed by the landslides of a retreating shore. Delve into that heritage at **Lyme Regis Museum** (☎01297-443370; www.lymeregismuseum.co.uk; Bridge St; up to 2 people £12, family £15; ⌚10am-4pm Wed-Sat). The museum also tells the story of local teenager Mary Anning who, in 1814, found the first full ichthyosaur skeleton near Lyme Regis, propelling the town onto the world stage. An incredibly famous fossilist in her day, Miss Anning did much to pioneer the science of modern-day palaeontology. To find your own fossils, go on a guided walk run by the museum or the nearby **Charmouth Heritage Coast Centre** (☎01297-560772; www.charmouth.org; Lower Sea Lane, Charmouth; ⌚11am-4pm daily Easter-Oct, Fri-Mon Nov-Easter).

p167

Eating & Sleeping

Poole 1

Merchant House B&B $$$

(01202-661474; www.themerchanthouse.org.uk; 10 Strand St; s £110, d £140-160) Tucked one street back from Poole Quay, tall, red-brick Merchant House is boutiquery at its best. Hefty wooden sculptures, wicker rocking chairs and crisp linen ensure it's stylish; the odd teddy bear keeps it cheery, too.

Lulworth Cove 5

Lulworth Cove Inn Inn $$$

(01929-400333; www.lulworth-coveinn.co.uk; Main Rd; d £135-150; P) One to delight your inner beachcomber. In this veritable vision of driftwood-chic, whitewashed floorboards and aquamarine panels frame painted wicker chairs and roll-top baths. Add cracking sea views, a mini roof terrace and top-quality gastropub grub (mains £13 to £17, food served from noon to 9pm) and you have an irresistible inn.

Rudds of Lulworth B&B $$$

(01929-400552; www.ruddslulworth.co.uk; Main Rd; d £85-185, ste £160-200;) An idyllic setting, pared-down designs, top-notch linen and pamper-yourself toiletries combine to make this a memorable place to stay, especially if you opt for a room with Lulworth Cove views. Or just lounge beside the pool, which also overlooks that circle of bay.

Weymouth 8

Roundhouse B&B $$

(01305-761010; www.roundhouse-weymouth.com; 1 The Esplanade; d £105-125;) The decor here is as gently eccentric as the owner – interiors combine snazzy modern art with comfy sofas and bursts of purple and bright blue. But the big draw is the view – you can see both the beach out front and the harbour behind from all bedrooms.

Tout Quarry 9

Queen Anne House B&B $$

(01305-820028; www.queenannehouse.co.uk; 2 Fortuneswell; s/d £70/95;) It's impossible to know which room to pick: White, with skylight, beams and a hobbit-esque door; Lotus, with its grand furniture; ornate Oyster with its half-tester bed; or Garden, a suite with a French bath and mini-conservatory. It doesn't matter, though – they're all great value and gorgeous.

Chesil Beach 10

Crab House Cafe Seafood $$

(01305-788867; www.crabhousecafe.co.uk; Ferrymans Way, Wyke Regis; mains £14-30; noon-2.30pm & 6-9pm Wed-Sat, noon-3.30pm Sun) This is where the locals head on hot summer days, to sit beside Fleet Lagoon in beach-shack-chic, tucking into fresh-as-it-gets seafood. Fish is enlivened by chilli, curry, lemon and herbs, crab comes spicy Chinese-style or whole for you to crack, and the oysters are served with either pesto and parmesan or bacon and cream.

Lyme Regis 12

Lyme Townhouse B&B $$

(01929-400252; www.lyme-townhouse.co.uk; 8 Pound St; d £105-135;) With stylish decor and luxury flourishes, this good-value guesthouse is hard to resist. Most of the seven rooms are on the small size (as signalled by the categories Super-Snug and Snug), but the central location, sea glimpses and views onto the town make it hard to beat.

South Devon

Green, gentle and gorgeous, the coastline of south Devon is simply made for a road trip – from salty seaports to classic sandy beaches.

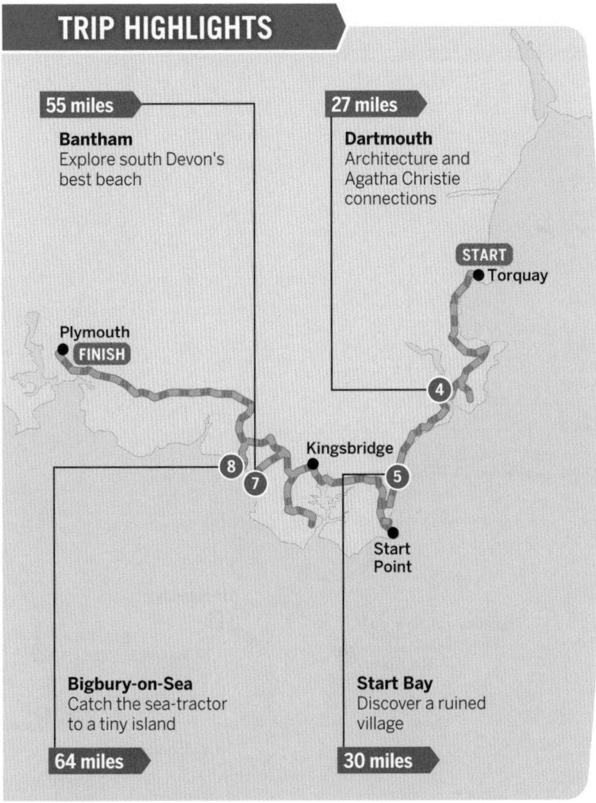

TRIP HIGHLIGHTS

4 DAYS 104 MILES / 167KM

GREAT FOR...

BEST TIME TO GO

Early summer (June or July).

ESSENTIAL PHOTO

A Sherman tank selfie at Slapton Ley.

BEST FOR FAMILIES

Bodyboarding at Bantham Beach.

Start Point Photogenic lighthouse looks over Devon's south coast

13 South Devon

From old seaside villages and thatched cottages to quaint harbours and riverside towns, south Devon serves up the essence of rural, coastal England. It's a wonderful landscape to drive through – a patchwork of green fields, old farms, pebble beaches, art deco swim spots and sudden flashes of bright blue sea. Take your time, pack a picnic and revel in the drive.

1 Torquay

Sometimes dubbed the heart of the English Riviera, this classic seaside resort is the perfect place to begin a south Devon tour. With its palm trees and russet-red cliffs, there's a dash of elegance to Torquay's seafront, though windbreakers and buckets and spades define most of the town's 20-odd beaches. The best thing to do is just embrace it: take a trip on Babbacombe's funicular **railway** (☎01803-328750; www.babbacombecliffrailway.

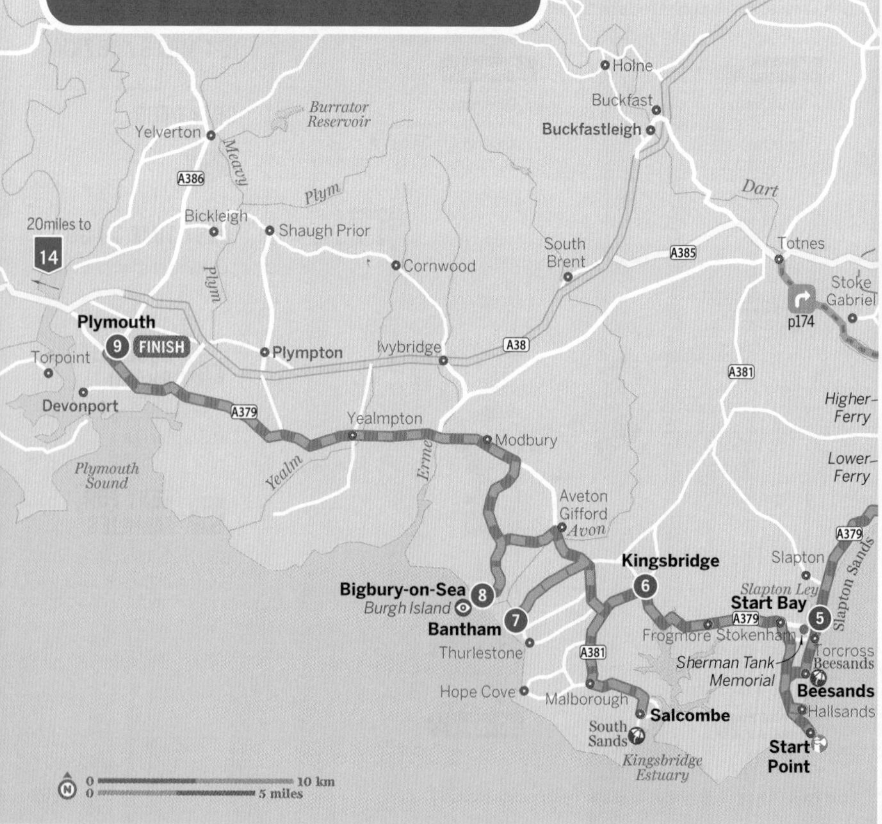

co.uk; Babbacombe Downs Rd; adult/child return £2.90/2.10; ⏲9.30am-4.30pm Feb-Oct, hours may vary), soak up the kitsch miniatures of the **Babbacombe Model Village** (☎01803-315315; www.model-village.co.uk; Hampton Ave, Babbacombe; adult/child £12.50/10.50; ⏲10am-6pm Fri-Mon, to 6.30pm Tue-Thu Apr-Aug, to 5.30pm Sep, to 5pm Oct, to 4pm Nov-Mar; P), and take a sunset stroll along Paignton Pier, candyfloss in hand.

p175

The Drive » The easiest route is just to follow the main coast road around the bay to Paignton and Brixham (partly the A379); it's a pleasant 9.5-mile drive, though you'll inevitably run into jams in summertime.

2 Brixham

This horseshoe-shaped harbour is as salty and shipshape as it gets. The market sells more than £40 million of fish a year, making it England's biggest by value of fish sold. A replica of Francis Drake's globetrotting ship, the **Golden Hind** (☎01803-856223; www.goldenhind.co.uk; The Quay; adult/child £7/5; ⏲10am-4.30pm Mar-Oct), is moored along the historic harbour, while gorgeous art deco, open-air **Shoalstone Pool** (☎07799 414702; www.shoalstonepool.com; Berry Head Rd; requested donation adult/family £2/5; ⏲10am-6pm May-Sep) is built into natural rock to the east of the breakwater.

The Drive » Follow signs out of Brixham pointing you towards Dartmouth. Once you reach the signpost showing you've reached Kingswear, turn left, following the brown tourist signs for Coleton Fishacre (initially it'll also be signed Lower Ferry). It's 16 miles in all.

3 Coleton Fishacre

Echoes of the Jazz Age still ring through the beguiling art deco estate of **Coleton Fishacre** (NT; ☎01803-842382; www.nationaltrust.org.uk; Brownstone Rd, near Kingswear; adult/child £8/4; ⏲10.30am-5pm mid-Feb–Oct, 11am-4pm Sat & Sun Nov & Dec; P). The croquet terrace leads to deeply shelved subtropical gardens and suddenly revealed vistas of the sea. If the house's interior has reopened after distancing measures, you'll also see original Lalique tulip uplighters, comic bathroom tiles and a stunning saloon.

The Drive » Backtrack along the road to take the first sign to Kingswear along the B3205 (some 2 miles). This will take you down to the Dartmouth-Kingswear Lower Ferry, the latest incarnation of a service that's been running since the 14th century.

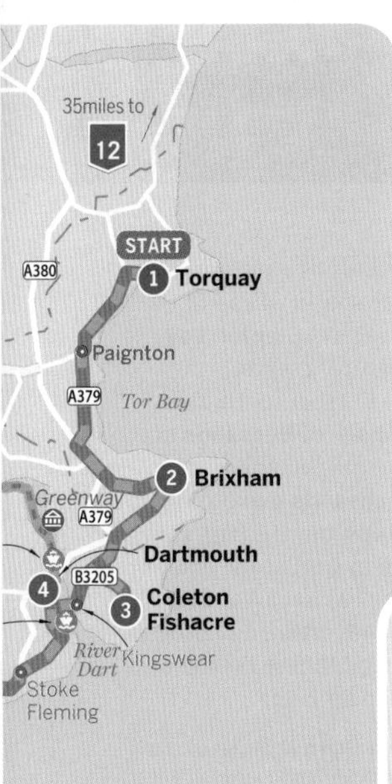

LINK YOUR TRIP

14 Epic Cornwall
From Plymouth, it's just a quick jaunt across the Tamar Bridge into Cornwall: head 45 miles north to reach Bude.

12 Jurassic Coast
More epic coastal adventures await further to the east – it's 53 miles from Torquay to Lyme Regis.

TRIP HIGHLIGHT

4 Dartmouth

South Devon isn't short on photogenic seaports, but Dartmouth still manages to dazzle. Its boat-filled estuary and quaint 17th- and 18th-century architecture are framed by green hills and the bright-blue waters of the River Dart. It's a place to explore at leisure – don't miss the half-timbered houses of South Embankment, Fairfax Pl and Duke St, and the punch-drunk buildings of the **Butterwalk**. Book ahead for a **river cruise** (01803-882811; www.greenwayferry.co.uk; adult/child return £9.50/7; 5-8 ferries daily mid-Mar–Oct) over to **Greenway** (NT; 01803-842382; www.nationaltrust.org.uk; Greenway Rd, Galmpton; gardens adult/child £8/4; 10.30am-5pm mid-Feb–Oct, 11am-4pm Sat & Sun Nov & Dec), where thriller writer Agatha Christie dreamt up some of her best-loved tales.

p175

The Drive » The next stage of the drive, along the coastal A379 past shingly beaches and green fields, offers glorious views. It's easy to navigate as far as the Slapton Ley nature reserve (7 miles away) and Torcross, but it's very easy to get lost along the minor roads leading south to Hallsands, Beesands and Start Point. Bring a decent road map.

TRIP HIGHLIGHT

5 Start Bay

Surging down the coast towards Start Point, the first essential stop is **Slapton Sands** (a pebble ridge, despite the name). Rehearsals for the D-Day landings here in 1944 went disastrously wrong when an attack by German E-Boats resulted in more than 800 Allied deaths. A Sherman tank stands as a memorial at the southern end of the peaceful **Slapton Ley** nature reserve.

Further south, the village of **Beesands** and the ruined village of **Hallsands** make good stops, but the best views lie in wait at the end of the bay's road at **Start Point**, where a photogenic lighthouse bookends a slender ridge.

The Drive » Backtrack along the backroads to the A379, then turn left towards Kingsbridge (10 miles from Start Point). From here it's pleasant driving through fields and farmland onto the A381 to Salcombe (a further 7 miles).

TOP TIP: DARTMOUTH–KINGSWEAR FERRIES

There are two car ferries that shuttle across the River Dart. The **Lower Ferry** (www.southhams.gov.uk; per car/pedestrian £6/1.50; 7.10am-10.45pm) is a floating platform that's pulled and pushed along by a tug boat; it runs from Kingswear, right into Dartmouth's town centre. The **Higher Ferry** (07866 531687; www.dartmouthhigherferry.com; per car/pedestrian 1 way £6.70/70p; 6.30am-10.50pm Mon-Sat, from 8am Sun) chugs across the river on Dartmouth's northern edge, avoiding the centre of town.

Dartmouth The boat-filled harbour is one of Dartmouth's many attractions

6 Kingsbridge & Salcombe

Though they're on the same river estuary, the neighbouring towns of Kingsbridge and Salcombe feel very different. Kingsbridge has the vibe of a sleepy country town, with weekly markets and lots of independent shops. A few miles further south, Salcombe is an altogether more chi-chi affair: a muddle of winding lanes, old cottages and sandy coves. Salcombe's **South Sands** (P) beach is the perfect place for a swim. Either hop on the **South Sands Ferry** (☎07831 568684; www.southsandsferry.co.uk; Whitestrand Quay; adult/child 1 way £4.50/3.50; ⊙9.45am-5.30pm Apr-Oct) or walk up Fore St, then continue south for 2 miles, sticking to the waterfront. Or hire a sit-on-top **kayak** (☎07834 893191; www.salcombekayaks.co.uk; per week from £90) and explore the estuary. Round the day off with dinner at the **Crab Shed** (☎01548-844280; www.crabshed.com; Fish Quay, Gould Rd; mains £11-21; ⊙noon-2.30pm & 6-9pm) seafood shack.

🛏 p175

The Drive » Follow the A381 back the way you came, but don't turn off to Kingsbridge; stay on the A381 (signed to Plymouth/Modbury A379) and follow it till you see a roundabout with a left turn to Bantham Beach (8 miles all up).

TRIP HIGHLIGHT

7 Bantham

It's certainly got stiff competition, but some say that at low tide the beach at Bantham might just be Devon's best. Backed by dunes, ringed by golden sand and with stunning views across the water to Burgh Island, it's certainly a

DETOUR: TOTNES

Start: 4 Dartmouth

The counter-culture town of Totnes has a fine **castle** (EH; 01803-864406; www.english-heritage.org.uk; Castle St; adult/child £6/3.50; 10am-4pm daily Apr-Oct, to 3pm Sat & Sun Nov-Mar) and is awash with Tudor architecture and interesting shops, but there are two other irresistible reasons to visit – a meal at the nearby **Riverford Field Kitchen** (01803-227391; https://fieldkitchen.riverford.co.uk; Wash Farm; 3-course brunch/lunch/dinner £20/28/32; sittings 10am Sat, 12.30pm & 7pm daily, noon & 3.30pm Sun;), a farm that hosts lavish feasts of locally grown produce, and the 324-hectare **Dartington Estate** (01803-847000; www.dartington.org; dawn-dusk; P) on the outskirts of town, which has a deer park, walking trails and riverbanks from which you can kayak and swim. Totnes is 15 miles' drive northwest from Dartmouth.

p175

beauty – and perfect picnic territory. It also happens to have the best surf on the south Devon coast, and thanks to **Bantham Surfing Academy** (www.banthamsurfingacademy.co.uk), it's a good place to hire kit and learn the basics.

The Drive » Return to the roundabout and turn left onto the A379, signed to Aveton Gifford. Follow this road through the countryside until you see the left turn onto the B3392 to Bigbury. It's a gorgeous drive down to the sea from here. It's 9 miles all up.

TRIP HIGHLIGHT

8 Bigbury-on-Sea

At Bigbury-on-Sea elegant town houses line the hills down to a sandy beach that is expansive at low tide. From here you can hop across to **Burgh Island**, a 10-hectare outcrop of rock that's home to a circular footpath and a stunning art deco hotel. At low tide you can walk across to the island, but it's more fun at high tide, when you have to catch the sea-tractor (single £2), with its passenger platform perched 6ft above the waves.

The Drive » Return to the A379 and follow signs to Plymouth, about 21 miles away through the countryside.

9 Plymouth

Some knock Plymouth's post-Blitz rebuild, but the port city has much to tempt visitors. Displays at the **Box** (01752-304774; www.theboxplymouth.com; Tavistock Pl; 10am-5pm Tue-Sun), a shimmering, £46-million museum, include 14 massive, suspended ships' figureheads. In the historic **Barbican** area, wonky buildings and cobbled lanes surround the **Mayflower Steps**, which mark the departure of the Pilgrim Fathers to North America. Stroll up to the cafe-dotted grassy headland called the **Hoe** to look out over a beautiful natural harbour. You can paddle out to it on guided trips with **Ocean City Kayaking** (07376 954991; www.oceancityseakayaking.com; Tinside Beach; half-/full day from £60/110), but don't miss a bracing dip in curving, art deco **Tinside Lido** (01752-261915; www.everyoneactive.com/centre/tinside-lido; Hoe Rd; adult/child £5/4; noon-5.30pm Mon-Fri, from 10am Sat, Sun & school holidays late May-early Sep), an open-air saltwater pool set into the shore.

p175

Eating & Sleeping

Torquay 1

Number 7 — Seafood $$

(01803-295055; www.no7-fish.com; 7 Beacon Tce; mains £14-22; noon-1.45pm Wed-Sat, 7-9pm Mon-Sat) Excellent, no-fuss fish is the order of the day at this small family-run bistro. Super-fresh crab, lobster, scallops and cod steaks can be seared, grilled or roasted, and laced with garlic butter or dusted with Moroccan spices.

Cary Arms — Boutique Hotel $$$

(01803-327110; www.caryarms.co.uk; Babbacombe Beach; d £125-365, ste £355-470; P) In a dreamy spot beside Babbacombe's sands, this heritage hotel has more than a hint of a New England beach retreat. Bright, light-filled rooms with white furniture shimmer with style, but for the best view book a stylish beach 'hut', complete with Smeg fridge, mezzanine bedroom and knockout beach-view patio.

Dartmouth 4

Alf Resco — Cafe $

(01803-835880; www.cafealfresco.co.uk; Lower St; dishes from £7; 7am-2pm;) This indie cafe is the preferred hang-out for a variety of discerning Dartmouthians, from yachties and families to riverboat crews, all tucking into cracking coffee, copious all-day breakfasts, granola pots, smoked fish platters, healthy salads and gooey cakes.

Bayard's Cove — B&B $$$

(01803-839278; www.bayardscoveinn.co.uk; 27 Lower St; d £114-190, f £165-320;) Crammed with character and bursting with beams, Bayard's Cove's seven rooms have you sleeping within whitewashed stone walls and beside huge church candles. The lavish family suites feature grand double beds and kids' cabins, complete with bunk beds and tiny TVs. There are even estuary glimpses from the rooms.

Totnes: Detour

Dartington Hall — B&B $$

(01803-847150; www.dartington.org; Dartington Estate; s/d from £55/90; P) The wings of this idyllic ancient manor house have been carefully converted into rooms that range from heritage themed to deluxe modern. Ask for one overlooking the grassy, cobble-fringed courtyard, and settle back for a truly tranquil night's sleep.

Kingsbridge & Salcombe 6

Fortescue — Pub $$$

(01548-842868; www.thefortsalcombe.co.uk; Union St, Salcombe; d incl breakfast £135-160; P) The bedrooms may be above a busy town-centre locals' pub, but they're a treat. The exposed stone speaks of the building's 300-year history; chunky wooden headboards and pristine bathrooms bring things bang up to date.

Plymouth 9

Harbour — Seafood $$

(01752-228556; www.harbourbarbican.co.uk; 21 Sutton Harbour; mains £12-22; 11am-9pm) With harbour-view picture windows in an airy, open-plan dining room, and a takeaway hatch, Harbour is a sound seafood choice whatever the weather. And it's not just fish and chips – expect monkfish curry, clam chowder and scallop burgers.

Residence One — B&B $$

(01752-262318; www.bistrotpierre.co.uk; 7 Royal William Yard; d £105-140, ste £165) Your chance to sleep in the former digs of an admiral. The exquisite rooms in this listed building team fluffy duvets and sea-chic styling with original shutters and cast-iron radiators. And all just a few steps from the shore.

Epic Cornwall

Buckle up, roll down the windows and have the camera ready – this round-Cornwall road trip is a photogenic parade of sea, cliff and countryside.

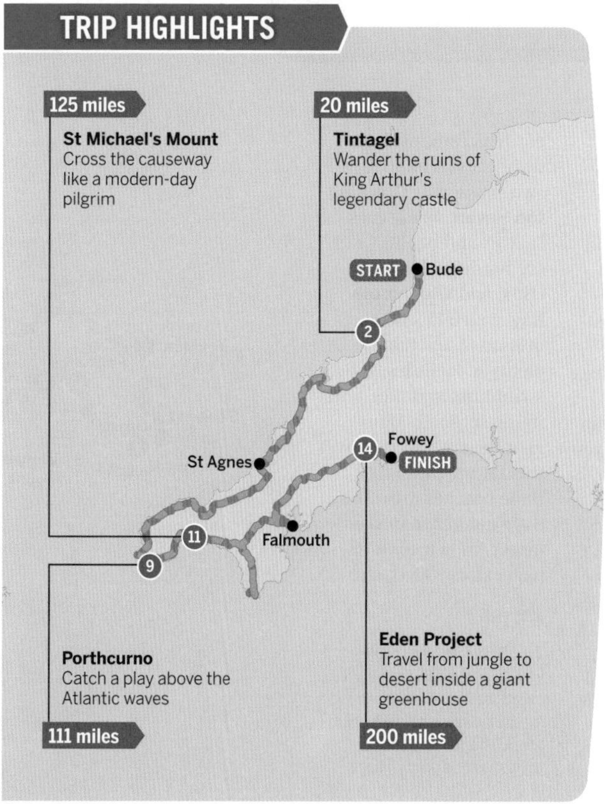

TRIP HIGHLIGHTS

125 miles
St Michael's Mount
Cross the causeway like a modern-day pilgrim

20 miles
Tintagel
Wander the ruins of King Arthur's legendary castle

START Bude

2

St Agnes

14 Fowey FINISH

11

Falmouth

9

Porthcurno
Catch a play above the Atlantic waves
111 miles

Eden Project
Travel from jungle to desert inside a giant greenhouse
200 miles

10 DAYS
207 MILES / 333 KM

GREAT FOR...

BEST TIME TO GO

Summer holidays bring traffic; try spring or autumn.

ESSENTIAL PHOTO

The fairy-tale battlements of St Michael's Mount.

BEST ACTIVITIES BEACH

(Arguably) Watergate Bay.

St Michael's Mount Historic tidal island in Mount's Bay

14 Epic Cornwall

There can be few corners of Britain where scenery packs such an eyes-wide, heart-in-the-mouth, jaw-on-the-floor punch as Cornwall. This unforgettable adventure travels right the way round Britain's most westerly county: top-to-bottom, coast-to-coast. Along the way you'll encounter sparkling beaches, surf bays and seaside ports galore, as well as curiosities such as a clifftop theatre and a trio of space-age biomes. It's wild and wonderful out west, as you're about to find out.

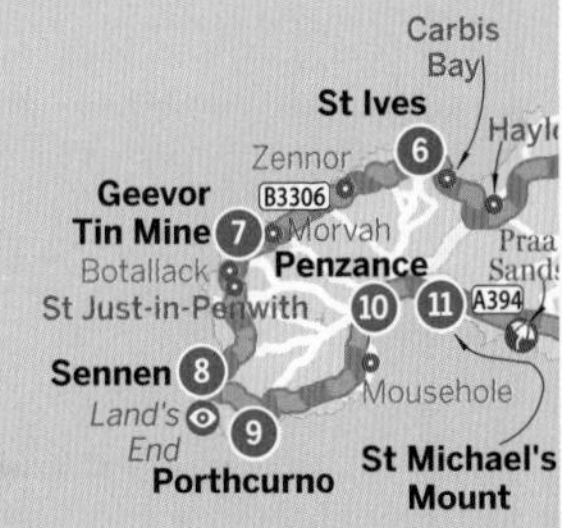

❶ Bude

This breezy sea town makes a great place to start your cruise around Cornwall – or Kernow, as it's known to locals. The town is surrounded by beaches: the family favourite is Summerleaze, right in the centre of town. If you don't feel up to tackling the waves, you can take a dip in the bracing waters of **Bude Sea Pool** (www.budeseapool.org; Summerleaze Beach; 24hr). This saltwater lido was built into an existing rock bowl back in the 1930s. It means you can swim in the sea but are sheltered from its force.

More beaches can be found north and south of town, ranging from tiny coves to impressive sweeps such as **Crackington Haven**, where rock shelves and pebbly sand are bordered by black cliffs, and **Widemouth Bay**, which has hectares of sand at low tide, plenty of facilities, good swimming and lifeguards in the summer. Many visitors never quite travel this far north, so the Bude beaches are often a little quieter than their better-known counterparts along the coast.

p187

The Drive » Head south, initially on the A39 (sometimes called the Atlantic Hwy on road signs). Soon you cut right, onto the B3263, following signs to Boscastle, a pretty village

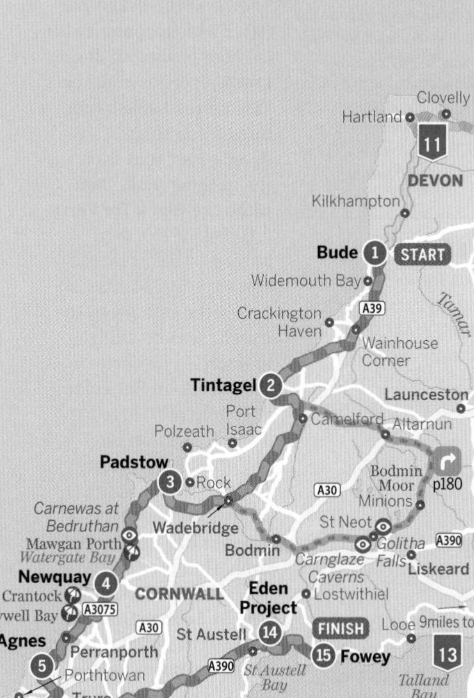

with an even prettier harbour. From there the road tracks the coast all the way to Tintagel, a distance of some 20 miles.

TRIP HIGHLIGHT

2 Tintagel

Cornwall's most legend-strewn location is the crumbling clifftop castle of **Tintagel** (EH; ☎01840-770328; www.english-heritage.org.uk; Castle Rd; adult/child £14.50/8.70; ⏲10am-5pm), rumoured to be the birthplace of England's most heroic of heroes, King Arthur. In truth, there's more fiction than fact in that – the present castle is largely the work of Richard, Earl of Cornwall, who built a base here during the 1230s. But there's no denying the truly epic setting – a fairy-tale ruined

LINK YOUR TRIP

13 South Devon

From the stark drama of Cornwall to the gentler countryside of Devon – it's a 38-mile drive from Fowey to Plymouth.

11 North Devon & Exmoor

Before exploring Cornwall's coasts, take in under-explored Exmoor and its famous starry skies. From Clovelly, it's just an 18-mile hop across the Cornish border to Bude.

fortress teetering above black cliffs and booming surf. An elegant new footbridge now spans a plunging 60m gully, linking the two sides of the medieval castle and re-creating a land bridge that existed 500 years ago. Take a blustery wander among the ruins, then head down at low tide to explore the beach and the murky **Merlin's Cave**.

It's also worth walking over to teeny St Materiana Church, which dates back to the 12th century and occupies a dramatic position atop Glebe Cliff. Look out for signs from the castle.

The Drive » The most scenic route to Padstow is to explore the backroads via Polzeath and Rock, but it's easy to get lost, so we route you south to the main A39 to follow it past Wadebridge, then turn off towards Padstow. It's a drive of 21 miles this way; there's a large car park above town.

DETOUR: BODMIN MOOR

Start: 2 Tintagel

Sprawling over an area of some 77 sq miles along Cornwall's eastern edge, Bodmin Moor might not be everyone's idea of classic Cornwall, but it has a bleak, magisterial beauty all of its own. Pockmarked with heaths and granite hills, including Cornwall's highest point, Brown Willy (420m), it's a desolate place that works on the imagination – for years there have been reported sightings of the Beast of Bodmin, a large, black, cat-like creature, though no one's ever managed to snap a decent picture.

It's a fine place for hiking and cycling, and is strewn with many beauty spots such as the underground slate chambers of **Carnglaze Caverns** (☎01579-320251; www.carnglaze.com; near St Neot; adult/child £8/5; ⌚10am-5pm, to 8pm Aug; 👪🐾) and tumbling **Golitha Falls** (near Redgate). It's also home to the Jamaica Inn, made famous by Daphne du Maurier's novel of the same name – though it's been ruthlessly modernised since the author's day.

There are various routes onto the moor. Try heading from Tintagel to just northeast of Camelford, and circling east then southwest across the moor from there.

3 Padstow

Famous for its foodie culture thanks to celebrity chef Rick Stein, Padstow has to rank as one of north Cornwall's prettiest ports. It's beautifully situated on the Camel Estuary, opposite the treacherous sandbank known as the Doom Bar (after which a popular local beer is named). It's a lovely place for a wander: explore the backstreets, browse the shops, dangle your toes over the harbour wall, then catch the **Black Tor Ferry** (☎01841-532239; www.padstow-harbour.co.uk; adult/child single £3/1.50, bikes £4) across the estuary to the chi-chi seaside village of **Rock** – a favourite of the poet John Betjeman, who holidayed here as a child, and now one of Cornwall's priciest patches of real estate. Nearby, the sands of **Daymer Bay** are perfect sunbathing territory. While there, hunt out tiny **St Enodoc Church**. Betjeman adored this chapel so much he asked to be buried here; it doesn't take long to find his headstone – it's a surprisingly ornate affair.

🛏 p187

The Drive » Head around the Padstow peninsula, initially following signs towards Trevone. After Trevose Head comes a roller-coaster coast, dipping and swerving past a string of stunning white-sand beaches. Soon a line of dramatic rock towers loom out of the surf: called Carnewas at Bedruthan (or Bedruthan Steps), they make for a great photo op. Then comes party-town Newquay. Total distance? 10 miles.

❹ Newquay

Welcome to Cornwall's surf central. Impressive beaches on the eastern outskirts of town include **Mawgan Porth**, while at nearby **Watergate Bay** the **Extreme Academy** (☎01637-860840; www.extremeacademy.co.uk; Watergate Bay) offers lessons in surfing and stand-up paddleboarding. It also runs three-hour SUP tours (£45), where you snorkel, stop for a cup of tea and look out for spider crabs. Or just hire a wetsuit (per three hours £8) and surfboard (per three hours from £8) and have a play in the waves on your own.

Newquay itself is a love-it-or-hate-it affair. Brash and busy, it's notorious for its nightlife, but it is home to several beautiful beaches, most notably the magnet for British surfers: Fistral. Although purists scoff that it's way too busy to be worth surfing these days – and they may be right – its consistent swell and close-to-town facilities make it a fine place for beginners and novices.

The Drive » The best road along this stretch of coast is the A3075, which passes detours to the photogenic beaches at Crantock and Holywell Bay. Take the turn-off to Perranporth (perhaps stopping to gaze at its sweeping beach), then follow the B3285 out of town past Perranporth Airfield and into St Agnes (12 miles in total).

LOCAL KNOWLEDGE: THE CAMEL TRAIL

If you fancy swapping four wheels for two, try cycling along the old Padstow–Bodmin railway line. It was closed in the 1950s, but re-emerged decades later as the **Camel Trail** (☎0300 1234 202; www.cornwall.gov.uk/cameltrail). It's now Cornwall's most popular cycle route. The main section starts in Padstow and heads east through Wadebridge (5.75 miles), but the full trail runs on all the way to Poley Bridge on Bodmin Moor (18 miles). Bikes can be booked from **Trail Bike Hire** (☎01841-532594; www.trailbikehire.co.uk; unit 6, South Quay; per day adult/child from £15/10; ⏲9am-5pm) at the Padstow end, or from **Bridge Bike Hire** (☎01208-813050; www.bridgebikehire.co.uk; off Commissioners Rd; per day adult/child from £14/10; ⏲10am-5pm) at the Wadebridge end. Most people ride the route from Padstow and back, so it's quieter (and much, much easier to find parking) if you start from the Wadebridge side.

❺ St Agnes

Pretty St Agnes, once a centre for Cornwall's tin industry, is strewn with reminders of its mighty mining past. At the beautiful beach of **Chapel Porth** (NT; ☎01872-552412; www.nationaltrust.org.uk; parking per day £4; P), on the west side of St Agnes Head, a trail leads up to the abandoned mine at **Wheal Coates**, towering above heather-covered cliffs and rust-red rock. Hiking trails radiate all around from here, including a path that leads to the panoramic hilltop called the **Beacon**. Alternatively, you can just head back down to the car park for a hot cup of tea and ice cream with a dollop of clotted cream at the beach cafe.

The Drive » There are some wonderful backroads to explore from here, but they're a maze, so the easiest option is to take the road back to Chiverton Cross and join the main A30, which will zip you all the way past Hayle. From there, follow signs to St Ives. It's 24 miles stop to stop.

❻ St Ives

Few spots in Cornwall have such a wow factor as St Ives. Occupying a graceful curving bay, framed by a jumble of slate rooftops, dazzling blue water and white beaches, it's postcard perfect – so it's not hard to see why artists find themselves drawn here. Among them was the abstract sculptor Barbara

Hepworth, who made her home here in the 1930s. Her **house and studio** (☎01736-796226; www.tate.org.uk/stives; Barnoon Hill; joint ticket with Tate St Ives adult/child £12/free; ⏰10am-5.20pm Mar-Oct, to 4pm Nov-Feb) have remained almost untouched since her death and the adjoining garden contains several of her most notable sculptures, many of which were inspired by the elemental forces she discovered in her adopted Cornish home: rock, sea, sand, wind, sky. There are galleries and studios scattered along St Ives' warren of backstreets, but the flagship is the **Tate St Ives** (☎01736-796226; www.tate.org.uk/stives; Porthmeor Beach; adult/child £9.50/free, joint ticket with Barbara Hepworth Museum £12/free; ⏰10am-5.20pm, last admission 4pm), which displays key works by St Ives artists such as Barbara Hepworth, Terry Frost, Peter Lanyon and Patrick Heron, and has recently been impressively extended.

After soaking up some art and culture, head for one of the town's beaches to soak up some sun. There's **Porthmeor**, opposite the Tate, or little **Porthgwidden** around the headland, with an excellent beach cafe, but most people favour **Porthminster**, a curl of white sand not far from the train station, home to the sophisticated **Porthminster Beach Café** (☎01736-795352; www.porthminstercafe.co.uk; Porthminster Beach; mains £15-22; ⏰9am-10pm).

✕ 🛏 p187

The Drive » An epic 11-mile stretch of tarmac lies in store. Take the road up Higher Stennack onto the B3306, signed Zennor. From here the wilds of Penwith's moors open up all around; you'll pass ancient fields, rock formations and abandoned mine stacks, all framed by the sea to your right.

DETOUR: GWITHIAN & GODREVY TOWANS

Start: 6 St Ives

Four miles east of St Ives, across the Hayle Estuary, the dune-backed flats of Gwithian and Godrevy unfurl in a golden curve that joins together at low tide to form Hayle's '3 miles of golden sand'. This is one of Cornwall's most glorious beach panoramas, fringed by hectares of rock pools and grassy dunes (known in Cornish as *towans*) and, at the northern end, the lighthouse that inspired Virginia Woolf's stream-of-consciousness class *To The Lighthouse*. Don't miss it.

Pick up a healthy, homemade takeaway snack at the excellent **Godrevy Cafe** (☎01736-757999; Godrevy Towans; mains £4-9; ⏰10am-5pm) and settle down to enjoy the views.

7 Geevor Tin Mine

Penwith is one of Cornwall's wildest corners but was once a mining heartland. Hardly surprising then that it features heavily in the BBC's barnstorming series *Poldark*, an 18th-century historical drama with a mining subplot. To get a true taste of a miner's life, head for **Geevor Tin Mine** (☎01736-788662; www.geevor.com; Pendeen; adult/child £16.10/9; ⏰9am-5pm Sun-Thu, hours may vary), where you can view the original machinery used to sort the minerals and ores, before taking a guided tour into some of the underground shafts.

Other photogenic ruins dot the area. One mile west of Geevor sits **Levant Mine** (NT; ☎01736-786156; www.nationaltrust.org.uk; Trewellard, Pendeen), with its working beam engine. Visits were suspended in 2020; ask whether they've resumed. Two miles southwest of Geevor, **Botallack** (NT; Crowns Engine House; ☎01736-786934; www.nationaltrust.org.uk) clings to the cliffs. This dramatic complex of crumbling mine workings is one of the most atmospheric sights from Cornwall's

INSPIRED BY MAPS / SHUTTERSTOCK ©

Porthcurno Watching a performance in the carved amphitheatre

industrial past. The main mine stack teeters on the cliff edge above a cauldron of surf. It's famously photogenic and *Poldark* fans will recognise the views. The National Trust website has a 1-mile, looped walking trail taking in Botallack.

The Drive » From the tin sites around Geevor, hop back on the B3306. Cruise through the mining village of St Just before joining the A30 and following signs to Sennen. A drive of around 8 miles in all.

8 Sennen

Many secret beaches await in Cornwall for those intrepid enough to find them, but with its white sands unfurling right from the road, the pretty village of Sennen is rather easier to find. Sennen is also a great launch pad for hiking the coast path around to **Land's End** (a 2.5-mile walk each way). This is where mainland Britain comes to a screeching halt. Though it's now home to an uninspiring theme park, there's still something thrilling about standing on Britain's westernmost point: you'll see cliffs, seagulls and lighthouses, and on a clear day, perhaps, glimpse the silhouettes of the **Isles of Scilly**, 28 miles west.

The Drive » You'd have to try really hard to get lost from here: there's only one road from Sennen to Porthcurno, the B3315, for 5 miles. Follow the signs to Porthcurno and the Minack Theatre.

TRIP HIGHLIGHT

9 Porthcurno

Forget Stratford-upon-Avon or London's West End: if you're looking for Britain's most dramatic place to watch a play, you'll find it above the beach of Porthcurno. Dreamt up by an eccentric theatre lover called

Rowena Cade, and inspired by the amphitheatres of ancient Greece, the **Minack** (☎01736-810181; www.minack.com; performance tickets £10-40, adult/child £6/3) was painstakingly carved out from the granite cliffs during the 1930s and '40s. It now hosts a season of plays throughout the summer: on a clear night it's utterly magical, though experienced theatregoers remember to pack a cushion, a picnic and rain gear in case the Cornish weather decides to stage an unscheduled appearance. Down below you'll find sandy **Porthcurno beach**, one of the best coves in west Cornwall for swimming and sunbathing.

The Drive » The prettiest route is to follow the B3315 to Penzance, which passes the lovely village of Mousehole and the busy fishing harbour of Newlyn en route. It's around 10 miles this way.

⑩ Penzance

The salty seafront town of Penzance is pretty much the end of the line for Cornwall (and the last stop for the railway from London Paddington). Established as a fishing and trading port, Penzance has a blustery, lived-in charm, and has resisted the gentrification that's taken over many of Cornwall's other seaside towns. Reminders of its seafaring heyday can be found along Chapel St, which is lined with grand Georgian mansions and some cracking pubs.

Further down towards the seafront is the town's pride and joy: the **Jubilee Pool** (☎01736-369224; www.jubileepool.co.uk; Western Promenade Rd; main pool adult/child £4.25/3, geothermal pool £11.75/8; ⏲10am-5pm Tue-Sun early Jun-Nov, winter hours vary), a glorious seawater lido that was built in 1935. A bold statement of art deco styling – sleek, sharp and whitewashed – it's the perfect backdrop for bracing, shoreside al fresco bathing. Sections now have geothermal heating – book well ahead for a much warmer, 35°C dip.

🛏 p187

The Drive » Head out of Penzance on the A30, cross through a couple of roundabouts and follow signs to Marazion on the A394. It's a 4-mile drive.

TRIP HIGHLIGHT

⑪ St Michael's Mount

As you approach Penzance, catching your first sight of **St Michael's Mount** (NT; ☎01736-710507; www.stmichaelsmount.co.uk; Marazion; castle adult/child £11.50/5.50, gardens adult/child £8.50/4; ⏲hours vary) is an unforgettable experience: it looks like something from the pages of Harry Potter. A cluster of spires and battlements looming up from a rocky island in the middle of Mount's Bay, the fairytale building dates back to the 1100s, and has variously served as an abbey, a fortress, a prison and a trading port. Later it became the ancestral seat of the St Aubyn family, and is now administered by the National Trust. Highlights include the stately great hall and subtropical gardens, but the crossing is almost the best part: at low tide, you can walk across a cobbled causeway from the nearby town of **Marazion**. Check the website to see if distancing regulations mean you have to book a timed visiting slot and walk across the causeway at low tide. If none are in force you may also be able to hop on a boat (adult/child £2/1) to visit at high tide.

The Drive » From Marazion the A394 runs past the busy beach at Praa Sands all the way to Helston, gateway town to the Lizard. You can take a direct route from Helston on the A3083 straight to Lizard Point (20 miles), but there are countless detours along the way if you have time.

⑫ The Lizard

Despite its name, you won't spot too many reptiles on this back-of-beyond peninsula (the word is actually thought to derive from the Cornish *lys ardh,* meaning high court or high fortress). What you will spy is mile after mile of cliffs, beaches, coves and moors – this is another of Cornwall's wildest corners, where summer wildflowers blaze, choughs wheel over the clifftops, and countless ships have come to grief on the unforgiving rocks. The coastline is strewn with quaint little fishing villages such as Cadgwith and Coverack on the east side of the peninsula. On the west side gorgeous bays include **Church Cove** near Gunwalloe, which was used as a ready-made backdrop in *Poldark*.

Some 11 miles south, **Kynance Cove** (NT; ☎01326-222170; www.nationaltrust.org.uk; The Lizard, TR12 7PJ; P) is truly stunning at low tide – a picturesque concoction of turquoise water, white surf and rocky islands. The cliffs around the cove are rich in serpentine, a red-green rock popular with Victorian trinket makers. The island opposite the cove is called **Asparagus Island**, as wild asparagus can be foraged here in spring and summer. Drinks and snacks are available at Kynance's ecofriendly **beach cafe** (☎01326-290436; www.kynancecovecafe.co.uk; Kynance Cove; mains £5-14; ⏰9am-5.30pm). The cove gets busy in summer, try to arrive before 11am.

Nearby is the sea-smacked headland at Lizard Point, with its striking **lighthouse** (☎01326-290202; www.trinityhouse.co.uk/lighthouse-visitor-centres/lizard-lighthouse-visitor-centre; Lizard Point). Check to see whether lighthouse tours have resumed.

TOM MEAKER / SHUTTERSTOCK ©

Falmouth National Maritime Museum

The Drive » Backtrack to Helston and continue east on the A394 – not the most exciting 25 miles of road, but the fastest way from here to Falmouth.

13 Falmouth

Truro might by the county's capital, but Falmouth surely stakes a claim as Cornwall's coolest town. Thanks to its deepwater harbour, this historic port was once a bustling hub for Britain's maritime trade, welcoming clippers and tall ships from all over the globe. It's now home to Cornwall's only university (based at nearby Penryn), meaning it's awash with trendy bars, hip coffee shops and excellent restaurants. It also has the western outpost of the **National Maritime Museum** (☎01326-313388; www.nmmc.co.uk; Discovery Quay; adult/child £14/7; ⏰10am-5pm), which presents a fascinating collection of boats and maritime memorabilia in innovative ways.

Out on the town's headland you'll find **Pendennis Castle** (EH; ☎01326-316594; www.english-heritage.org.uk; Castle Dr; adult/child £12/7.30; ⏰10am-5pm; P), an imposing Tudor fortress built by Henry VIII to guard the entrance to Falmouth Harbour in partnership with its sister castle across the bay in St Mawes. It's an atmospheric location, and you can wander round the gun decks and battlements. Don't be too perturbed if you hear a deafening crack at midday – it'll just be the noonday gun going off with a bang.

p187

The Drive ›› We're taking the most direct route to Eden: the A39 to Truro, then the A390 to St Austell, and another 4 miles further to the Eden Project. It's a pleasant but uneventful drive of 30 miles. Count on an hour, longer if there's traffic.

TRIP HIGHLIGHT

14 Eden Project

At first glance it looks like something from a sci-fi film set – two gigantic glass biomes, glittering in the sunlight at the bottom of a disused clay pit. But you haven't stumbled onto the set of the latest Ridley Scott movie – you've just arrived at the **Eden Project** (01726-811911; www.edenproject.com; Bodelva, PL24 2SG; adult/child £28.50/15; 9.30am-6pm; P), a pioneering eco-initiative that aims to re-create habitats from around the globe inside its oversized greenhouses. From tropical jungle to dry desert, soaring palms to spiky cactus, it sometimes feels a bit like wandering through a scene from *Jurassic Park*. Recent additions including a canopy walkway and a zip-wire have added extra thrills and spills.

The Drive ›› Follow the road back towards St Austell, but after you reach the A390, follow signs to Par and then the A3082 to Fowey. Once you pass Par, it's a lovely drive through quiet countryside. In total it's around 7 miles.

15 Fowey

The last stop on your Cornish road trip is the riverside town of Fowey. It's another postcard-perfect scene, a jumble of pastel-coloured town houses, fishers' cottages and winding alleyways, all backed by the wooded banks of the River Fowey. The best way to see it is from the water: book ahead for one of the memorable three-hour guided kayaking trips run by **Encounter Cornwall** (07976 466123; www.encountercornwall.com; The Boatshed, Golant; adult/child £30/20). These see you gliding up creeks and backwaters, spotting egrets, kingfishers and seals. End the day with a pint of ale and a plate of fish and chips at the quayside **King of Prussia** (01726-833694; www.kingofprussiafowey.co.uk; 3 Town Quay; 11am-11pm). Thank you Cornwall, or *meur ras*, as they say round here – it's been a blast.

p187

CORNISH PASTIES

There's nothing more local to tuck into for lunch than a Cornish pasty. Half-moon shaped, stuffed with steak and vegetables and sealed with a decorative crimp on the side, they've been a staple here since the 13th century. They're said to have been created as a portable lunch for tin miners: the crust was designed to allow the miners' filthy fingers to grip the pasty without contaminating their food. When waves of impoverished Cornish miners emigrated in the mid-1800s, they took their pasty techniques with them, particularly to Australia and the USA – today you can still pop out for a pasty in places as far from Cornwall as Adelaide and Arizona.

Annually, pasty production employs thousands, and brings millions of pounds into Cornwall's economy. In 2011 the savoury was finally awarded protected status by the European Commission, meaning only those actually made in Cornwall, according to a traditional recipe, can be called 'Cornish pasties'.

Everyone has their favourite pasty shops: two of our top tips are the **Chough Bakery** (01841-533361; www.thechoughbakery.co.uk; 1-3 The Strand; pasties £3-5; 9am-5pm Mon-Sat) in Padstow and **Ann's Pasties** (01326-572282; www.annspasties.co.uk; 18 Tresprison Business Park; pasties £3.10; 10.30am-2pm Mon-Sat) in Helston, both endorsed by Rick Stein, no less.

Eating & Sleeping

Bude 1

Beach at Bude Hotel **$$$**

(01288-389800; www.thebeachatbude.co.uk; Summerleaze Cres; incl breakfast d £125-215, ste £195-355; P) Space, style and broad views steal the show at the Beach at Bude. Pale wood furniture, Lloyd Loom chairs and peach-and-taupe colours conjure the feel of a New England beach cabin. The suites sleep four.

Padstow 3

Treverbyn House B&B **$$$**

(07534 095961; www.treverbynhouse.com; Station Rd; d £135-140; P) The sweeping views of Padstow's sandy estuary from this gorgeous guesthouse linger long in the memory. Choose from yellow- or green-themed rooms or a romantic turret hideaway. Either way you get oriental rugs, brass bedsteads and a table on the terrace at which to enjoy breakfasts of homemade jams and smoked kippers.

St Ives 6

Porthgwidden Beach Cafe Cafe **$$**

(01736-796791; www.porthgwiddencafe.co.uk; Porthgwidden; mains £10-16; 9am-10pm) Head to the dreamy terrace beside Porthgwidden's beach huts to savour classy dishes like smoked-haddock chowder or spicy dressed crab.

Saltwater B&B **$$**

(07391 086299; www.saltwaterstivesbb.co.uk; 3 Belmont Tce; d £110-150, tr £130-180;) It's driftwood-chic all the way at Saltwater, where bright blue and yellow bedrooms have USB charging points; most also have sea views. It's a few minutes' walk from Porthmeor and offers surfboard hire and breakfast in bed.

Penzance 10

Venton Vean B&B **$$**

(01736-351294; www.ventonvean.co.uk; Trewithen Rd; d £98-105, tr £142;) The picture of a modern B&B, finished in stylish greys and blues, with stripped wood floors, bay windows and a keen eye for design. The sumptuous breakfast choice includes pancakes, smoked Newlyn fish and avocado on sourdough toast.

Falmouth 13

Highcliffe B&B **$$**

(01326-314466; www.highcliffefalmouth.com; 22 Melvill Rd; s £65, d £105-150, ste £145-160; P) Vintage furniture and upcycled design pieces give each of the soothing rooms here an individual feel. The pick of the bunch is the light-filled Attic Penthouse, with skylight windows overlooking Falmouth Bay. Room-service breakfasts in picnic baskets might feature toasted muffins, pancakes with bacon, or homemade granola with compote.

Fowey 15

Coriander Cottages Apartment **$$$**

(01726-834998; www.foweyaccommodation.co.uk; Penventinue Lane; 1-bed cottages £130-150; P) A delightfully rural cottage complex on the outskirts of Fowey, with ecofriendly accommodation in open-plan, self-catering barns, all with quiet country views. The stone barns have been beautifully modernised, and use a combination of solar panels, ground-source heating and rainwater harvesting to reduce environmental impact. Handily, cottages are available per night, so you're not restricted to weekly stays.

STRETCH YOUR LEGS BATH

Start/Finish: SouthGate

Distance: 2.5 miles

Duration: Three hours

Bath's cityscape is simply sumptuous. So stunning, it has World Heritage status. On this walk you'll encounter architecture ranging from Roman baths to a medieval cathedral to exquisite Georgian designs.

Take this walk on Trips

SouthGate

Head into Bath, following signs to SouthGate car park.

The Walk » Exit into St Lawrence St, heading north to join Stall St. Then cut right down Abbeygate St towards the Roman Baths.

Roman Baths

The Romans built this **bathhouse** (01225-477785; www.romanbaths.co.uk; Abbey Church Yard; adult £16-23, child £8.50-15.50; 9.30am-5pm Nov-Feb, 9am-5pm Mar–mid-Jun, Sep & Oct, 9am-9pm mid-Jun–Aug) above three natural hot springs. They emerge at a toasty 46°C (115°F), forming one of the best-preserved ancient Roman spas in the world. A tour reveals the steaming **Great Bath**, bathing pools and changing rooms.

The Walk » it's a few steps east to Bath Abbey.

Bath Abbey

The building of **Bath Abbey** (01225-422462; www.bathabbey.org; Abbey Church Yard; suggested donation adult/child £5/2.50; 9.30am-5.30pm Mon, 9am-5.30pm Tue-Fri, to 6pm Sat, 12.15-1.45pm & 4-6.30pm Sun) started after 1499, making it England's last great medieval church. On the striking **west facade** angels climb up and down stone ladders; find out more on **tower tours** (01225-422462; www.bathabbey.org; adult/child £8/4; 10am-4pm Mon-Sat).

The Walk » Cross the square south of Bath Abbey, then wind onto Parade Gardens, passing the rushing weir to gracious Pultney Bridge (1773). Then make your way to Green St.

Old Green Tree

Duck into the tiny, traditional **Old Green Tree** (01225-448259; 12 Green St; 11am-11pm Mon-Sat, noon-6.30pm Sun) pub for real ales and soups and casseroles (noon to 3pm Tuesday to Sunday).

The Walk » Turn right into elegant Milsom St. Then head, via George St, into trendy Bartlett St.

Assembly Rooms

When they opened in 1771, Bath's **Assembly Rooms** (NT; 01225-477789; www.

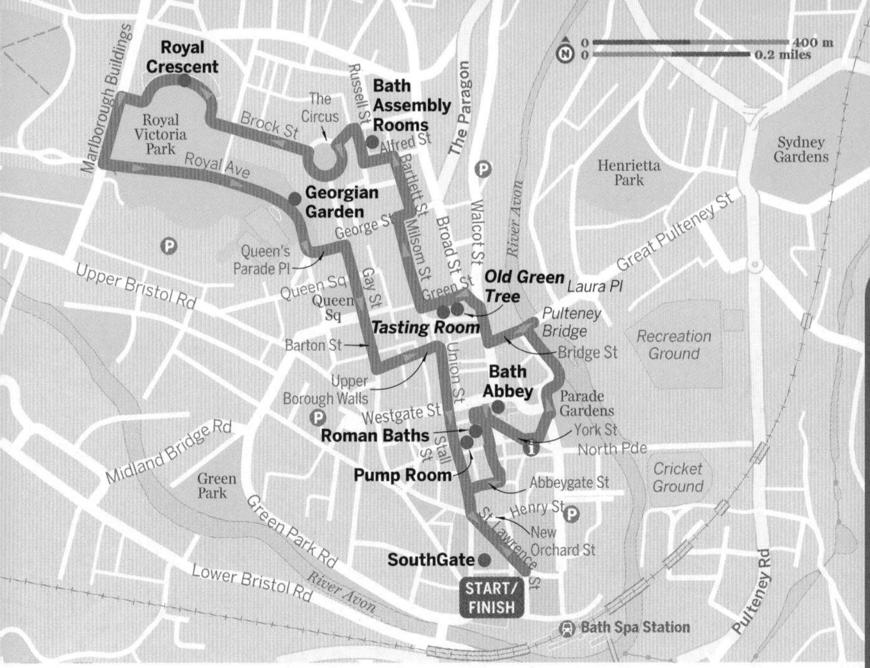

nationaltrust.org.uk; 19 Bennett St; ⌚10.30am-6pm Mar-Oct, to 5pm Nov-Feb) were where fashionable socialites gathered to waltz, play cards and listen to chamber music. Tour the card room, tearoom and ballroom, lit by the original 18th-century chandeliers.

The Walk » Next, the Circus (1768), a ring of 33 honey-coloured, semicircular terraces. From there, gracious Brock St gradually reveals Bath's exquisite Royal Crescent.

Royal Crescent

The imposing **Royal Crescent** curls around private lawns. Designed by John Wood the Younger and built between 1767 and 1775, the houses appear perfectly symmetrical from the outside, but the owners were allowed to tweak the interiors, so no two are quite the same.

The Walk » From the Crescent's far end, stroll back along Royal Ave. Just before the Royal Pavilion Cafe, cut left, up a short flight of steps, to the gate in the wall leading into the Georgian Garden.

Georgian Garden

The period plants and gravel walkways of the tiny, walled **Georgian Garden** (☎01225-394041; off Royal Ave; ⌚9am-7pm) provide intriguing insights into what would have lain behind the Circus' grand facades.

The Walk » Skirt Georgian Queen Sq. Just before the elaborate Theatre Royal (1805), turn left into Upper Borough Walls. It marks medieval Bath's northern edge. From here it's a short stroll to the Pump Room.

Pump Room

The grand **Pump Room** (☎01225-477785; www.romanbaths.co.uk; Stall St; ⌚9.30am-5pm) features an ornate spa from which Bath's famous hot springs flow. Ask staff for a glass (50p); it's mineraly and startlingly warm – an impressive 38°C (100°F).

The Walk » Cut down Stall St, back into St Lawrence St and back to your car.

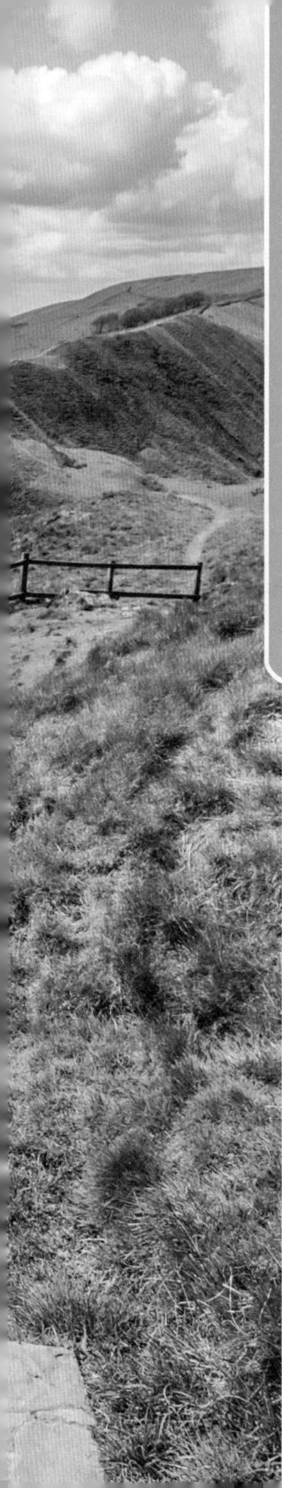

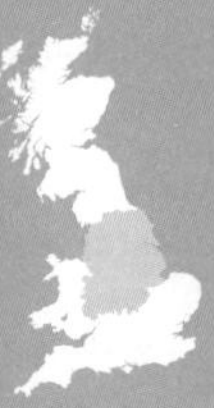

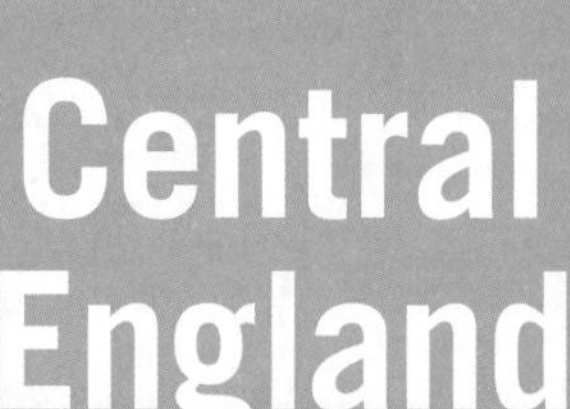

Central England

Routes in this region reveal the heart of Britain, showcasing literature, landscape and history. Drive here and you'll explore the Cotswold Hills, a rolling ridge of quintessentially English villages built out of honey-coloured stone. They lead you to Stratford-upon-Avon, a town with a plethora of Shakespearean links.

History lies at every turn: the sites of battles that dethroned monarchs; the castles that helped keep kings on the throne; some of England's finest stately homes; the industrial heritage that forged a nation. And each just a short drive away.

Then there's the Peak District National Park. Here, the motoring is bewitching, winding from limestone dales to wilderness moors.

Peak District National Park Mam Tor
KIMBERLEYJANE / SHUTTERSTOCK ©

Central England
NORTH YORKSHIRE
0 40 km
0 20 miles
Yorkshire Dales National Park
Skipton
Harrogate
York
EAST RIDING OF YORKSHIRE
Keighley
Leeds
Bradford
Selby
Beverley
Halifax
Hull
Goole
Humber
Huddersfield
Scunthorpe
DONCASTER
Wigan
Bolton
Barnsley
Holmfirth
Doncaster
St Helens
Manchester
ROTHERHAM
Liverpool
Warrington
Stockport
Damflask Reservoir
Maltby
Gainsborough
Bebington
Peak District National Park
Sheffield
Worksop
LINCOLNSHIRE
Ellesmere Port
Macclesfield
CHESHIRE
Lincoln
Buxton
Chesterfield
Chester
Clwydian Range
Bakewell
Southport
Newark-on-Trent
Sandbach
Matlock
Leek
Wrexham
Stoke-on-Trent
Tissington
NOTTINGHAMSHIRE
Nottingham
Whitchurch
Longton
Grantham
Oswestry
STAFFORDSHIRE
DERBYSHIRE
Derby
Stafford
Loughborough
Melton Mowbray
Newport
Burton-upon-Trent
Shrewsbury
Welshpool
Cannock
Telford
Lichfield
Coalville
Stamford
Snailbeach
LEICESTERSHIRE
Leicester
Rutland Water
Wolverhampton
Walsall
Hinckley
Church Stretton
Dudley
Birmingham
Kidderminster
Coventry
NORTHAMPTONSHIRE
Clun
Ludlow
WORCESTERSHIRE
Brixworth
Wellingborough
Warwick
Leominster
WARWICKSHIRE
Northampton
Bromyard
Worcester
Stratford-upon-Avon
Bedford
Great Malvern
Hereford
Evesham
Chipping Campden
BEDFORDSHIRE
Banbury
Milton Keynes
Talgarth
Buckingham
Moreton-in-Marsh
Brecon Beacons National Park
Ross-on-Wye
GLOUCESTERSHIRE
BUCKINGHAMSHIRE
OXFORDSHIRE
Luton
Gloucester
Cheltenham
Aylesbury
Abergavenny
Monmouth
Forest of Dean
Burford
Witney
St Albans
Stroud
Oxford
HERTFORDSHIRE
Cirencester
Cwmbran
Severn
Abingdon
Watford
Chepstow
Tetbury
High Wycombe
Beaconsfield
Newport
Swindon
CARDIFF
Bristol
WEST BERKSHIRE
Chippenham
Severn Estuary
Fyfield Down
Reading
Clevedon
Marlborough
Newbury
Bath
Weston-super-Mare
Bristol Channel
Devizes
Basingstoke
Guildford
Burnham-on-Sea
Wells
Warminster
HAMPSHIRE
15
16
17
18
A59
A1
A65
M62
M180
A580
A628
M56
A15
M1
A55
M6
A1(M1)
A34
A515
A523
A41
A38
A518
A46
M6
A1
A47
A442
A49
A45
A423
M1
A438
A435
M50
M5
A6
M40
A5
A40
A46
M4
M5
A4
M4
A338
M3

A G BAXTER / SHUTTERSTOCK ©

Gloucester Gloucester Cathedral

15 **The Cotswolds & Literary England 7–8 Days**
The essential England: impossibly pretty villages and the birthplace of the Bard.

16 **Central England Industrial Powerhouse 4 Days**
History-rich mines, factories and mills; this is where modern England was made.

17 **Peak District 5 Days**
Brooding moors, rocky hills and adrenaline sports – an adventure-packed drive.

18 **Midlands Battlefields, Castles & Stately Homes 5 Days**
A drive-through timeline of English history, in all its scheming, bloody, greedy glory.

DON'T MISS

No 1 Royal Crescent

Every tourist goes to Bath's architectural triumph. But by entering this tall town house you'll also glimpse the period lifestyle. Trip 15

City of Caves Tour

Worm your way deep under Nottingham to discover a WWII air-raid shelter, pub cellars and a Victorian slum. Trip 18

Morgan Motor Company

England's most elegant sports cars have been handcrafted here since 1909. Watch the mechanics at work on a two-hour tour. Trip 16

Gloucester Cathedral

A less well-known ecclesiastical gem that's among the best examples of English Perpendicular Gothic style (it's been in Harry Potter films too). Trip 15

Haddon Hall

An enticing example of a medieval manor house, 12th-century Haddon Hall is rich in stone turrets and well-worn beams. Trip 17

The Cotswolds & Literary England

On this bucolic spin into the heart of the Cotswolds, you'll traverse five counties, wander time-warped, gold-washed villages, feast on local produce and pay your respects to William Shakespeare.

TRIP HIGHLIGHTS

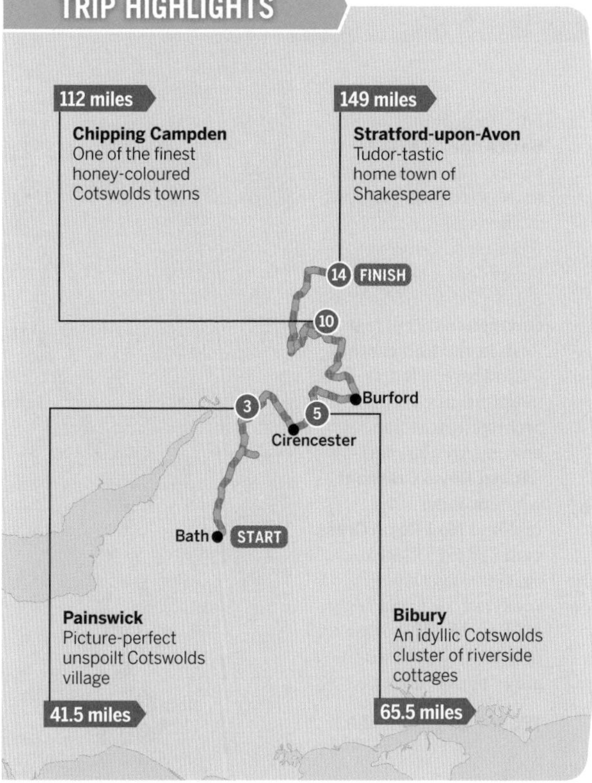

112 miles

Chipping Campden
One of the finest honey-coloured Cotswolds towns

149 miles

Stratford-upon-Avon
Tudor-tastic home town of Shakespeare

14 FINISH

10

Burford

3

5

Cirencester

Bath START

Painswick
Picture-perfect unspoilt Cotswolds village

41.5 miles

Bibury
An idyllic Cotswolds cluster of riverside cottages

65.5 miles

7–8 DAYS
149 MILES / 240KM

GREAT FOR...

BEST TIME TO GO

April, May, June and September, for better weather, minus summer crowds.

ESSENTIAL PHOTO

Broadway Tower perched spectacularly on the crest of the escarpment.

BEST FOR HISTORY

Getting lost in majestic Sudeley Castle.

Winchcombe Sudeley Castle

15 The Cotswolds & Literary England

From the less-travelled, superbly pretty villages of the southwestern Cotswolds to the impossibly beautiful gold-coloured streets of the classic northern Cotswolds, this trip threads through the core of one of England's most desirable regions. Glimpse Georgian grandeur in Bath, marvel at Painswick's sleepy beauty, unearth Roman history in Cirencester, stroll Chipping Campden's honey-hued lanes and wrap up in dramatic Tudor style at Stratford-upon-Avon, home of the illustrious Bard.

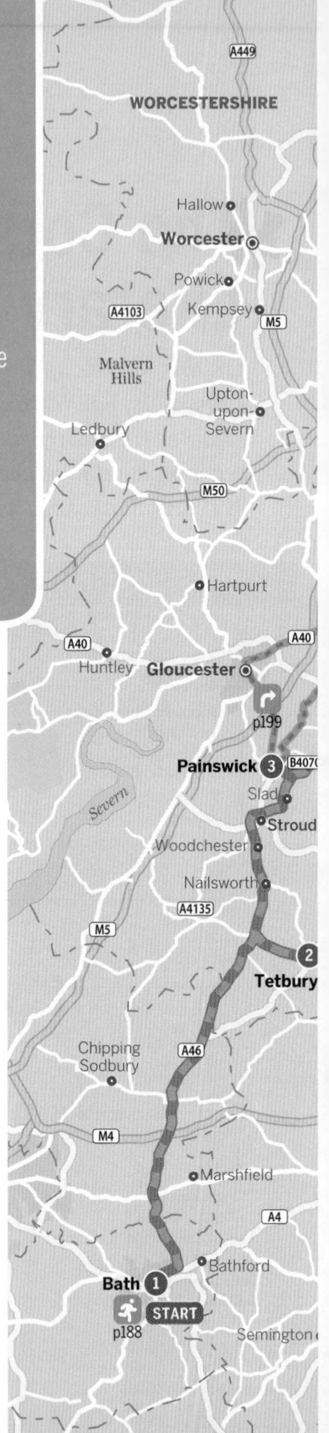

1 Bath

A star among Britain's most beautiful cities, Bath boasts splendid honey-toned Georgian buildings coupled with one of the world's most unspoilt Roman bath-houses. It's a lovely place to explore on foot. Jane Austen set *Persuasion* and *Northanger Abbey* here.

The busy, brilliantly preserved **Roman Baths** (☎01225-477785; www.romanbaths.co.uk; Abbey Church Yard; adult £16-23, child £8.50-15.50; ⏲9am-9pm mid-Jun–Aug, 9.30am-5pm Nov-Feb, 9am-5pm Mar–mid-Jun, Sep & Oct) bubble up at 46°C, surrounded by 18th- and 19th-century buildings. Handsome **Bath Abbey** (☎01225-422462; www.bathabbey.org; Abbey Church Yard; suggested donation adult/child £5/2.50; ⏲9.30am-5.30pm Mon, 9am-5.30pm Tue-Fri, to 6pm Sat, 12.15-1.45pm & 4-6.30pm Sun) emerged in its current form in the 15th century.

Nowhere is Bath's magnificent Georgian architecture as fine as on semicircular, park-fringed **Royal Crescent**, where wonderfully restored **No 1 Royal Crescent** (☎01225-428126; www.no1royalcrescent.org.uk; 1 Royal Cres; adult/child/family £11/5.40/27; ⏲10am-5pm) provides a peek into the glitzy period lifestyle.

🛏 p47, p73, p151, p203

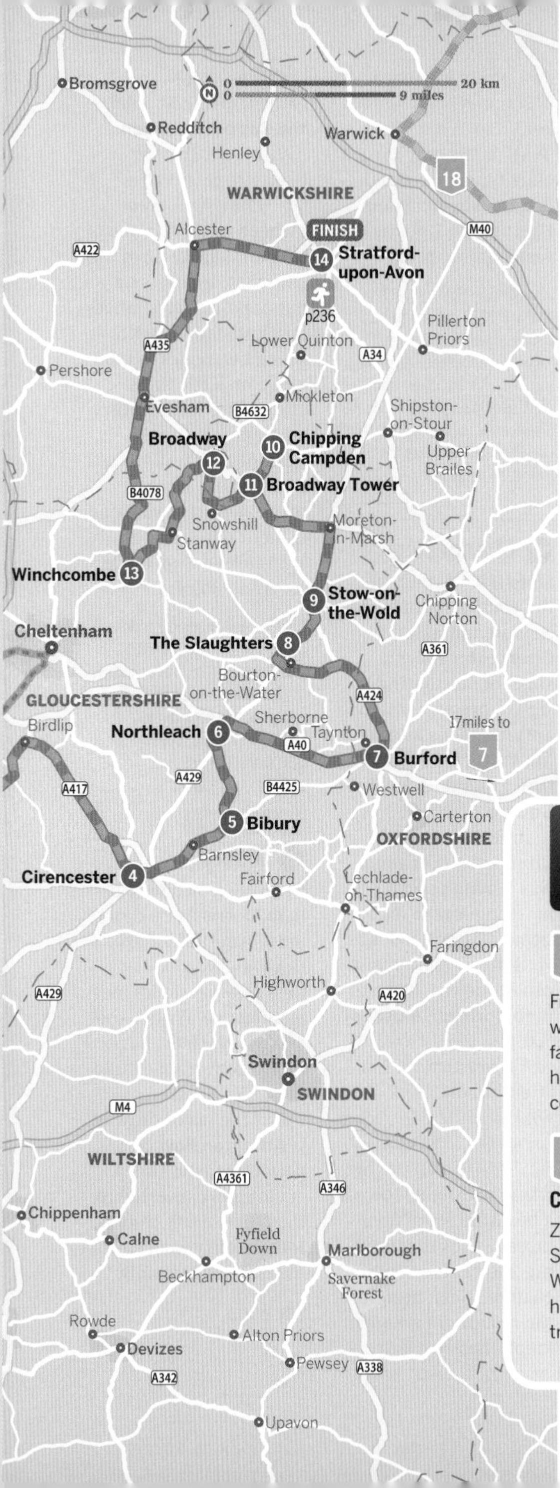

Bromsgrove
0 20 km
0 9 miles
Redditch
Henley
Warwick
18
WARWICKSHIRE
Alcester
FINISH
M40
A422
14 Stratford-upon-Avon
p236
Pillerton Priors
A435
Lower Quinton
A34
Pershore
Mickleton
Evesham
B4632
Shipston-on-Stour
Broadway 12
10 Chipping Campden
Upper Brailes
11 Broadway Tower
B4078
Snowshill
Stanway
Moreton-in-Marsh
Winchcombe 13
9 Stow-on-the-Wold
Chipping Norton
Cheltenham
The Slaughters 8
A361
Bourton-on-the-Water
GLOUCESTERSHIRE
A424
Sherborne
Birdlip
Northleach 6
Taynton
17miles to 7
A40
7 Burford
A429
B4425
Westwell
A417
5 Bibury
Carterton
OXFORDSHIRE
Barnsley
Cirencester 4
Fairford
Lechlade-on-Thames
Faringdon
A429
Highworth
A420
Swindon
SWINDON
M4
WILTSHIRE
A4361
A346
Chippenham
Calne
Fyfield Down
Marlborough
Beckhampton
Savernake Forest
Rowde
Alton Priors
Devizes
Pewsey
A338
A342
Upavon

The Drive » Bath's London Rd joins the A46; follow 'Stroud' signs. Drive 24 miles north on the A46 into Gloucestershire. The countryside becomes increasingly bucolic and the road narrower as you enter the southern Cotswolds. Turn east onto the A4135; after 4 miles, you'll reach Tetbury.

2 Tetbury

Sitting prettily in the Cotswolds' southwestern reaches, Tetbury was once a wealthy wool town. Its easily strolled sandy-gold centre is a delightful tangle of lively streets flanked by medieval cottages, grand town houses, antique shops and a 17th-century **Market House** (Market Pl). The Georgian Gothic Church of St Mary the Virgin & St Mary Magdalen

LINK YOUR TRIP

7 Royalty & the Thames Valley

From Burford, drive 20 miles west to Oxford to explore fantastical worlds, royal hang-outs and bookish colleges.

18 Midlands Battlefields, Castles & Stately Homes

Zip 9 miles northwest from Stratford-upon-Avon to Warwick to pick up this history-rich central England trip.

has a towering spire (a 19th-century replica of its medieval original) and a dramatic interior of 18th-century dark-oak box pews.

In spring and summer visit Prince Charles' **Highgrove** (☎0303-123 7310; www.highgrovegardens.com; Doughton; tours £27.50; ⏲Apr-Sep; P), a mile southwest of town, for its gorgeous organic gardens.

The Drive » Head 4 miles west from Tetbury on the A4135, then 6 miles north on the A46. Wiggle around Stroud onto the B4070, then it's 3 miles northeast through green-clad Slad Valley – follow 'Painswick' signs 1 mile northwest to Painswick. You'll pass through little Slad, once the beloved home of writer Laurie Lee: stop for a refreshment at the Woolpack Inn.

TRIP HIGHLIGHT

❸ Painswick

Hilltop Painswick is the Cotswolds' most perfectly formed village. At its heart stands 14th-century **St Mary's Church** (www.beaconbenefice.org.uk/painswick; New St; ⏲9.30am-dusk), a resplendent Perpendicular Gothic creation surrounded by 18th-century tabletop tombs and 99 clipped yew trees.

Stroll Painswick's slender, twisting streets, passing ancient honey-coloured homes and medieval inns. Just north of town, the exquisite folly-dotted **Painswick Rococo Garden** (☎01452-813204; www.rococogarden.org.uk; off B4073; adult/child £10/4.90; ⏲10.30am-5pm mid-Jan–Oct; P 👪) is the only garden of its type in England, designed by Benjamin Hyett in the 1740s as a vast 'outdoor room'.

The Drive » Backtrack to the B4070, head 6 miles northeast and, at Birdlip, follow 'Cirencester' signs onto the A417. It's a 10-mile spin southeast past green fields to Cirencester, where signposted Brewery Car Park has central (short-term) parking.

❹ Cirencester

Self-styled capital of the southern Cotswolds, elegant and affluent Cirencester hides a stash of fascinating sights, pretty boutiques, antique shops and striking Victorian architecture around its **Market Square**.

In Roman times, Cirencester (Corinium) was Britain's second-most-important settlement after London. Well-preserved remains can be viewed at the superb **Corinium Museum** (☎01285-655611; www.coriniummuseum.org; Park St; adult/child £5.60/2.70; ⏲10am-5pm Mon-Sat, 2-5pm Sun Apr-Oct, 10am-4pm Mon-Sat, 2-4pm Sun Nov-Mar; 👪), where highlights include a beautiful set of floor mosaics plus the towering 2nd-century 'Jupiter column'. Next, head to the remains of a Roman amphitheatre nearby.

Cirencester's cathedral-like **St John the Baptist's Church** (☎01285-659317; www.cirenparish.co.uk; Market Sq; ⏲10am-4pm), commenced in 1100, is one of England's largest parish churches. It boasts an outstanding Perpendicular Gothic tower with flying buttresses (c 1400) and a majestic three-storey, late-15th-century south porch. In the light-filled interior you'll find soaring arches, magnificent fan vaulting, a Tudor nave and the 1535 Boleyn Cup, made for Anne Boleyn.

The Drive » Wind 8 miles northeast to Bibury on the tree-lined B4425, traversing mellow, well-heeled Barnsley and peaceful countryside interspersed with sprawling Cotswolds panoramas.

TRIP HIGHLIGHT

❺ Bibury

Once described by William Morris as England's most beautiful village, tiny Bibury embodies the Cotswolds at its most picturesque. With a knot of narrow streets flanked by attractive stone buildings, it's popular.

But the major draw is **Arlington Row**: a perfectly rustic sweep of cottages converted in the 17th century from a 14th-century wool store. Access is by foot only.

🛏 p203

DETOUR: GLOUCESTER & CHELTENHAM

Start: 3 Painswick

Gloucester's spectacular **cathedral** (01452-528095; www.gloucestercathedral.org.uk; 12 College Green; 10am-5pm) is among the first and most exquisite examples of the English Perpendicular Gothic style, with a 14th-century, fan-vaulted Great Cloister so enchanting and beautiful that it features in the first, second and sixth *Harry Potter* films. The cathedral also contains Edward II's tomb, a magnificently elaborate work in alabaster created after the king died in suspicious circumstances at nearby Berkeley Castle. From Painswick, head 6 miles northwest on the B4073 to Gloucester; there's plenty of signposted parking.

A 10-mile drive east on the A40 from Gloucester brings you to the handsome Regency town of Cheltenham, a flourishing 18th-century spa resort on the western fringe of the Cotswolds. Fine accommodation and restaurants make Cheltenham an attractive overnight stop.

Cheltenham's **Promenade** is a wide, tree-lined boulevard flanked by imposing period buildings and flower-filled gardens. Also worth a look if it has re-opened (online only at the time of research) is Cheltenham's excellent museum, **The Wilson** (01242-387488; www.cheltenhammuseum.org.uk; Clarence St; 9.30am-5.15pm Mon-Sat, 11am-4pm Sun), which depicts local life through the ages and has wonderful displays on William Morris and the Arts and Crafts movement. Modelled on an ancient Athenian temple, the **Pittville Pump Room** (0844-576 2210; www.pittvillepumproom.org.uk; Pittville Park;) is the town's outstanding Regency building.

Allow a one-day detour, then from Cheltenham motor 10 miles southwest back to Painswick on the A46. Alternatively, rejoin the main route at Cirencester, 15 miles southeast (A417), or at Winchcombe, 8 miles northeast (B4632).

The Drive » We'll be sticking to gorgeous, slim, classic-Costwolds country lanes here. Head west out of Bibury on the Ablington road, starting outside Bibury's Swan Hotel. After 1 mile, turn north, following signs for 5 miles to Northleach.

6 Northleach

Little visited, underappreciated and, therefore, well worth a stop on your Cotswolds itinerary, Northleach has been a small market town since 1227. Its centre is made up of late-medieval cottages, imposing merchants' stores and half-timbered Tudor houses.

The grand **Church of St Peter & St Paul** (www.northleach.org; Church Walk), a masterpiece of the Cotswold Perpendicular style, is testimony to Northleach's wool-era wealth; its chancel, 30m tower and unusual font date to the 14th century.

A short drive from town, nestled in the Cotswolds countryside, the **Chedworth Roman Villa** (NT; 01242-890256; www.nationaltrust.org.uk; Yanworth; adult/child £10.50/5.25; 10am-5pm Apr-Oct, to 4pm mid-Feb–Mar & Nov; P) is a well-preserved sight with idyllic rural views. Pre-book your tickets as there was limited visitor capacity at the time of research.

The Drive » It's a quick 10-mile drive east along the (admittedly unexciting) A40, crossing into Oxfordshire, to Burford. Parking here can be tricky: head for an official car park first, then look for a spot hidden down a side street if they're full.

7 Burford

Tumbling steeply downhill to the River Windrush, Burford is usually one of the Cotswolds' busiest villages, little changed since its high-flying wool-era days. It makes a picturesque overnight stop thanks to its remarkable mix of stone cottages, gold-tinged town houses, chintzy tearooms, ancient pubs, antiques shops and delicatessens.

Commenced in 1175 and added to over the years, Burford's **St John the Baptist's Church** (www.burfordchurch.org; Church Lane) has survived reformers and Roundheads (supporters of parliament against the king in the English Civil War) with its fan-vaulted ceiling, Norman west doorway, 15th-century spire and several grand tombs intact.

If you're craving a stretch after all that driving, there are some good signposted walks.

The Drive » It's time to tackle the wonderfully scenic, undulating northern Cotswolds. Hop on the A424 northwest; after 6 miles, follow 'Little Rissington' signs east. Drive 900m, turn right, then immediately left, continuing 3 miles through Little Rissington and picturesque Bourton-on-the-Water onto the A429. Skip a mile northwest, take the signposted 'The Slaughters' turn-off and 650m west is Lower Slaughter.

8 The Slaughters

Blissfully charming, the tranquil chocolate-box villages of Upper and Lower Slaughter are the perfect introduction to the golden-stone delights of the northern Cotswolds. Their names are derived from the Old English 'sloughtre' ('slough' or 'muddy place').

The River Eye meanders peacefully through the villages, flanked by classic honey-washed houses and manors and Lower Slaughter's **Old Mill** (☎01451-820052; www.oldmill-lowerslaughter.com; Lower Slaughter; ⏲10am-6pm Mar-Oct, to dusk Nov-Feb) museum and tearoom.

✖ p203

The Drive » Back on the A429, Stow-on-the-Wold is 2.5 miles northeast past rippling fields, along what was once the Roman Fosse Way.

9 Stow-on-the-Wold

Welcome to the Cotswolds' highest town, strategically positioned at 244m on the junction of six roads. Stow has long been an important market town, with thin alleyways (originally for funnelling sheep) feeding into a sprawling market square lined with graceful stone buildings, cute tearooms, a medieval-era church and old-world pubs.

The Drive » Rejoin the A429 and head 4.5 miles north to busy Moreton-in-Marsh, known for its local food shops and Tuesday farmers market. From Moreton, take the A44 6 miles northwest, climbing through tiny Bourton-on-the-Hill. Exit onto the B4081, following signs to Chipping Campden, 2.5 miles north of the A44.

TRIP HIGHLIGHT

10 Chipping Campden

Chipping Campden is one of the Cotswolds' most exquisitely beautiful

THE COTSWOLD WAY

As you travel through the Cotswolds, you'll undoubtedly spot happy hikers meandering along. One of the region's most popular long-distance walks (followed at times by this drive) is the 102-mile Cotswold Way (www.nationaltrail.co.uk/cotswold-way). The route rambles from Chipping Campden to Bath via the northwestern and southwestern Cotswolds, passing through some lovely countryside and tiny villages, with no major climbs or difficult stretches. It's easily accessible from many points en route, such as Broadway, Chipping Campden or Winchcombe, if you fancy tackling a shorter section.

Broadway Broadway Tower

towns and home to many English A-listers.

Elegant High St is flanked by a perfectly picturesque array of stone cottages, fine terraced houses, ancient inns, historic homes and the 14th-century **Grevel House** (High St; closed to the public), with a marvellous Perpendicular Gothic–style gabled window. The premier attraction is the highly photogenic 17th-century **Market Hall** (NT; www.nationaltrust.org.uk/market-hall; High St), an open-sided, timber-roofed pillared building that looks like a cross between a barn and a chapel.

Imposing **St James' Church** (01386-841927; www.stjameschurchcampden.co.uk; Church St), built in the late 15th century in Perpendicular Gothic style on wool-trade riches, has an impressive tower and some graceful 17th-century monuments. Just outside, the **Court Barn Museum** (01386-841951; www.courtbarn.org.uk; Church St; adult/child £5/free; 10am-5pm Wed-Sun Apr-Oct, to 4pm Nov-Mar) gives a detailed insight into Chipping Campden's important connection with the Arts and Crafts movement: architect and designer Charles Robert Ashbee moved his Guild of Handicraft here from East London in 1902.

p203

The Drive » Drive 1 mile northwest on the A44, crossing into the Cotswolds' Worcestershire pocket. Follow 'Broadway Tower' signs 1 mile southwest to the top of the escarpment.

11 Broadway Tower

A crenulated 18th-century Gothic folly, **Broadway Tower** (01386-852390; www.broadwaytower.co.uk; Middle Hill; adult/child £8/4, with separate Nuclear Bunker tours; 10am-5pm; P) stands on the windswept crest of the escarpment, offering all-encompassing views from the top. Victorian polymath William Morris once summered here. It's also on the Cotswold Way: a 2-mile path links it to St Eadburgha's Church, a mile south of Broadway.

The Drive » Continue 1 mile south from Broadway Tower and turn right (southwest). Signs soon lead the 1-mile way to pretty little Snowshill, famed for featuring in Bridget Jones's Diary. If you're visiting in June or July, you'll pass gorgeously purple fields carpeted with blooming lavender. From Snowshill, it's 2.5 miles north to Broadway.

12 Broadway

Huddling beautifully at the foot of a sloping escarpment, Broadway has one of the lengthiest high streets in England. A quintessentially Cotswolds village, it reels in visitors with its golden cottages, art galleries, boutiques, foodie stops and plush hotels.

Set inside a grand converted coaching inn, the **Broadway Museum & Art Gallery** (☎01386-859047; www.ashmoleanbroadway.org; Tudor House, 65 High St; adult/child £5/2; ⊙10am-5pm Tue-Sun Feb-Oct, to 4pm Tue-Sun Nov & Dec, closed Jan) has fascinating displays of local crafts, antiques and history spanning the 17th century to the present day. Collections include Winchcombe pottery, vintage furniture, ornate tapestries and paintings by Reynolds and Gainsborough.

The Drive » The fastest Broadway-to-Winchcombe route is the B4632 southwest; we're turning off 3 miles southwest of Broadway to detour through picture-perfect Stanton (signposted). Next, track 1 mile south on the road that parallels the Cotswold Way to stunning little Stanway, famous for its fabulous Jacobean mansion. Turn west onto the B4077, then southwest onto the B4632; it's 3.5 miles to Winchcombe.

13 Winchcombe

Once capital of the Anglo-Saxon kingdom of Mercia and a prominent Cotswolds town until the Middle Ages, Winchcombe retains its workaday bustle amid half-timbered houses, gold-stone buildings and ancient inns. It's also a popular walkers' hang-out.

Winchcombe's main attraction, spectacular **Sudeley Castle** (☎01242-604244; www.sudeleycastle.co.uk; adult/child £12/5; ⊙10.45am-5pm mid-Mar–Oct; P 👪) has welcomed many a monarch over its thousand-year history, including Richard III, Henry VIII and Charles I. It's most famous as the home and final resting place of Catherine Parr (Henry VIII's widow), who lived here with her fourth husband, Thomas Seymour. You'll find Catherine's tomb in the castle's Perpendicular Gothic St Mary's Church, making this the only private house in England where a queen is buried. Outside lie 10 splendid gardens.

✕ p203

The Drive » Take the B4078 north for 7 miles, then zip along the A46 for 21 miles to Stratford-upon-Avon. Stratford has plenty of central parking, though town car parks charge high fees.

TRIP HIGHLIGHT

14 Stratford-upon-Avon

A distinctly Tudor town with a fanatical following, Stratford-upon-Avon is a fascinating place to wander, and a fittingly famous final stop on your itinerary: the birth and burial place of the greatest of Englisvh scribes, William Shakespeare (1564–1616).

Kick off your Shakespeare story at **Shakespeare's Birthplace** (☎01789-204016; www.shakespeare.org.uk; Henley St; adult/child £15/11; ⊙10am-4pm Mon-Fri, to 5pm Sat & Sun), where the world's most popular playwright spent his childhood. In Stratford's medieval **Holy Trinity Church** (☎01789-266316; www.stratford-upon-avon.org; Old Town; Shakespeare's grave adult/child £3/2; ⊙noon-2pm Mon-Thu, to 4pm Fri, 11am-4pm Sat), you can see the unexpectedly modest, much-visited grave of William Shakespeare, with its menacing epitaph: 'cvrst be he yt moves my bones'.

Book ahead to join the world-renowned **Royal Shakespeare Company** (RSC; ☎box office 01789-331111; www.rsc.org.uk; Waterside) at one of its legendary productions. From here on, you're in the hands of the Bard.

🛏 p203

Eating & Sleeping

Bath ❶

Queensberry Hotel £££

(☎01225-985086; www.thequeensberry.co.uk; 4 Russell St; r £235-323, ste £460-510; P) Stylish but unstuffy Queensberry is Bath's best luxury spoil. In these Georgian town houses heritage roots meet snazzy gingham checks, bright upholstery, original fireplaces and free-standing tubs. It's witty (see The Rules on the website), independent (and proud of it), and service is first-rate.

Prices shoot up on Friday and Saturday nights. Valet parking is £7. The hotel's Olive Tree Restaurant is excellent, too.

Bibury ❺

New Inn Pub ££

(☎01285-750651; www.new-inn.co.uk; Main St, Coln St Aldwyns; r incl breakfast £119-149; P) The jasmine-clad 16th-century New Inn, 2.5 miles southeast of Bibury, offers 14 spacious and atmospheric bedrooms divided between the main pub building and a neighbouring cottage. Idiosyncratic contemporary stylings include bold colours, fluffy throws, smart furnishings and the odd free-standing bathtub, while the pub itself, with its exposed beams, is the place for a burger and beer.

The Slaughters ❽

Atrium at Lords of the Manor Modern British £££

(☎01451-820243; www.lordsofthemanor.com; Upper Slaughter; 3-/7-course dinner £72.50/£90; noon-1.30pm Sat & Sun, 6.45-9pm daily; P) Set inside a romantic countryside manor, this acclaimed restaurant concocts imaginative, beautifully presented dishes with French touches and plenty of quality local produce. The neighbouring and more relaxed dining space, aptly named The Dining Room, also serves popular afternoon teas, as well as a casual bar lunch.

Chipping Campden ❿

Eight Bells Inn Pub ££

(☎01386-840371; www.eightbellsinn.co.uk; Church St; r incl breakfast £99-143;) This friendly and atmospheric 14th-century inn offers six bright, modern rooms with iron bedsteads, soothing neutral decor, flowery wallpaper and warm accents. Room 7 – there's no number 4 – with its chunky old-world beams, is especially striking. The cosy pub downstairs serves contemporary country cooking.

Winchcombe ⓭

5 North St Modern European £££

(☎01242-604566; www.5northstreetrestaurant.co.uk; 5 North St; 2-/3-course lunch £26/32, 3-/7-course dinner £54/74; 12.30-1.30pm Tue-Sun, plus 7-9pm Wed-Sat;) This veteran gourmet restaurant is a treat from start to finish, from its splendid 400-year-old timbered exterior to the elegant, inventive creations you eventually find on your plate. Marcus Ashenford's cooking is rooted in traditional seasonal ingredients, but the odd playful experiment (think duck-egg pasta or malt ice cream) adds that extra magic. Vegetarians can enjoy a separate £45 menu.

Stratford-upon-Avon ⓮

Townhouse Boutique Hotel £££

(☎01789-262222; www.stratfordtownhouse.co.uk; 16 Church St; d incl breakfast from £140;) Some of the dozen rooms at this exquisite hotel have free-standing claw-foot bathtubs, and all have luxurious bedding and Temple Spa toiletries. The building is a centrally located 400-year-old gem with a first-rate **restaurant** (☎01789-262222; www.stratfordtownhouse.co.uk; 16 Church St; mains £13-21; kitchen noon-3pm & 5-9.30pm Mon-Fri, noon-9.30pm Sat, to 8pm Sun, bar 8am-midnight Mon-Sat, to 10.30pm Sun;). Light sleepers should avoid room 1, nearest the bar. There's a minimum two-night stay on weekends.

PAUL DANIELS / SHUTTERSTOCK ©

Central England Industrial Powerhouse

As you drive from the vibrant northern city of Manchester to bucolic, hilly Great Malvern, you'll encounter Britain's industrial heritage at every turn, from former mines to fascinating, factory-housed museums.

TRIP HIGHLIGHTS

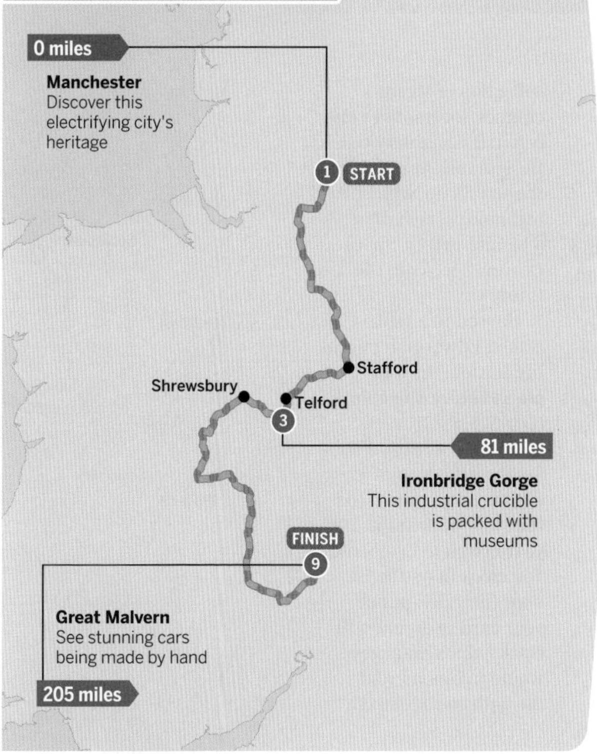

0 miles

Manchester
Discover this electrifying city's heritage

1 START

Stafford

Shrewsbury

Telford

3

81 miles

Ironbridge Gorge
This industrial crucible is packed with museums

FINISH

9

Great Malvern
See stunning cars being made by hand

205 miles

4 DAYS
197 MILES / 317KM

GREAT FOR...

BEST TIME TO GO

May to September are the most pleasant months.

ESSENTIAL PHOTO

The arched Iron Bridge that first showcased cast-iron technology.

BEST FOR HISTORY

Steam engines, locomotives and original factory machinery at Manchester's Science & Industry Museum.

Ironbridge Gorge The world's first iron bridge

16 Central England Industrial Powerhouse

The Industrial Revolution's humble beginnings took place deep in the English countryside: the wooded riverbanks of Ironbridge Gorge are where cast iron was first mass-produced, and today the gorge teems with the factories' legacies, including its namesake bridge. Other industries you'll encounter along this attraction-packed route include pottery, cars, aircraft and cider producers (including one that supplies the Houses of Parliament).

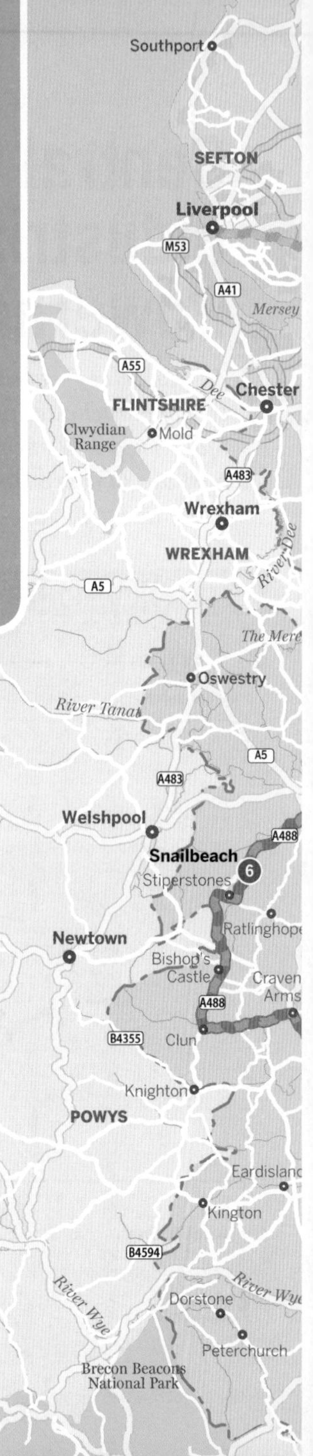

TRIP HIGHLIGHT

1 Manchester

Manchester has a rich blend of history and culture along with a hedonistic swirl of epicurean and entertainment venues.

This northern powerhouse's industrial legacy is explored at the excellent **Science & Industry Museum** (MOSI; ☎0161-832 2244; www.scienceandindustrymuseum.org.uk; Liverpool Rd, M3 4FP; suggested donation £4, special exhibits £6-10; ⏰10am-5pm Wed-Sun; 🚻; 🚌1 or 3, 🚊Deansgate-Castlefield), set within the enormous grounds of the old Liverpool St Station, the oldest rail terminus in the world. The large collection of steam engines, locomotives and original machinery tells the story of the city from the sewers up, while new technology (including a virtual-reality 'Space Descent') looks to the future.

Housed in a refurbished Edwardian pumping station, the **People's History Museum** (☎0161-838 9190; www.phm.org.uk; Left Bank, Bridge St, Spinningfields, M3 3ER; ⏰10am-5pm Tue-Sun) tells the story of Britain's 200-year march to democracy. You clock in on the 1st floor (literally: punch your card in an old mill clock, which managers would infamously fiddle with so as to make employees work longer) and plunge into the heart of Britain's struggle for rights, labour reform and fair pay.

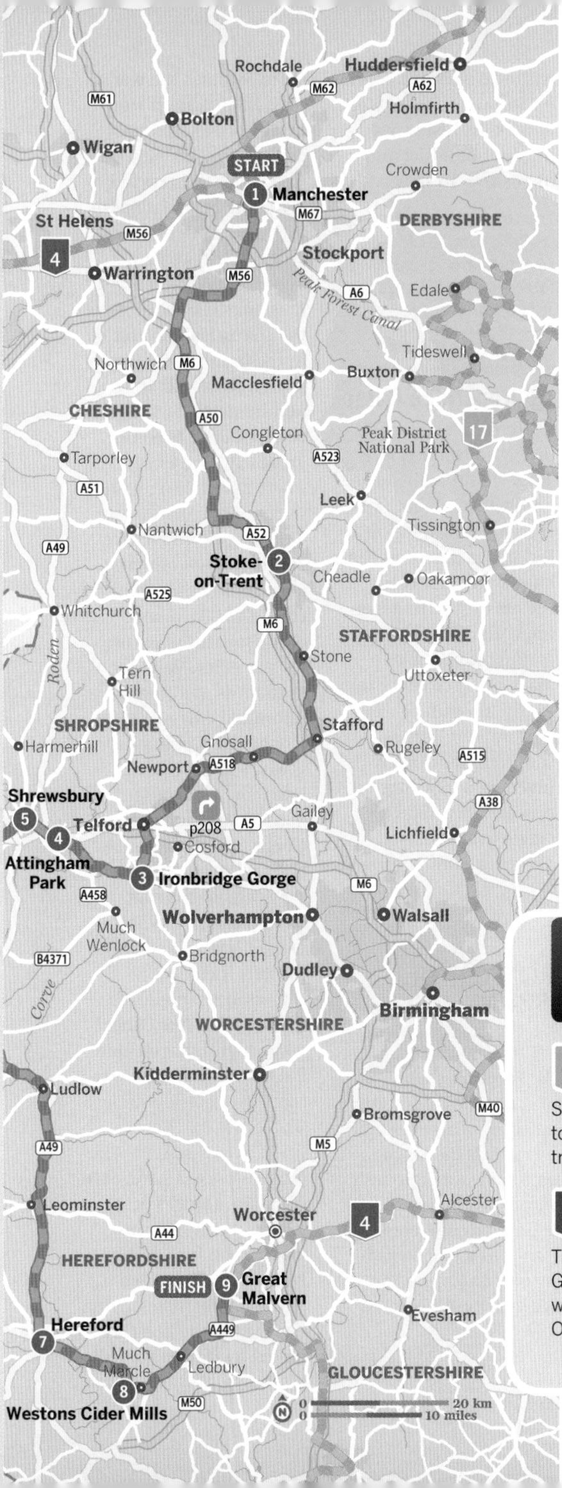

✕ 🛏 p47, p85, p211

The Drive » It's 45 miles south to Stoke-on-Trent. Take Princess Rd to Manchester Airport, where it becomes the M56, and connect to the southbound M6.

❷ Stoke-on-Trent

Situated at the heart of the Potteries – the famous pottery-producing region of Staffordshire – Stoke-on-Trent is famed for its ceramics. Don't expect cute little artisanal producers: this was where pottery shifted to mass production during the Industrial Revolution, and Stoke today is a sprawl of industrial townships tied together by flyovers and bypasses.

For a good overview, visit the **Potteries**

LINK YOUR TRIP

17 Peak District

Head 23 miles east of Stoke-on-Trent via the A52 to pick up the Peak District trip in Ashbourne.

4 Urban & Art Odyssey

The end point of this trip, Great Malvern, intersects with the Urban & Art Odyssey.

Museum & Art Gallery (01782-236000; www.stoke-museums.org.uk; Bethesda St, Hanley; 10am-5pm Mon-Sat, 11am-4pm Sun), which houses an extensive ceramics display, from Toby jugs and jasperware to outrageous ornamental pieces. Other highlights include displays on the WWII Spitfire, created by the Stoke-born aviator Reginald Mitchell.

Active potteries that you can visit in the greater area include the **Wedgwood factory** (01782-282986; www.worldofwedgwood.com; Wedgwood Dr, Barlaston ST12 9ER; factory tour & museum adult/child £10/8, museum only free; factory 10am-4pm Mon-Fri, museum to 5pm daily). The modern production centre for Josiah Wedgwood's porcelain empire displays historic pieces, including plenty of Wedgwood's delicate, neoclassical blue-and-white jasperware. A film on Josiah's life and work details his involvement in canal-building and opposition to slavery.

The Drive » Drive 36 miles southwest, via the late-20th-century town of Telford (named for civil engineer Thomas Telford), to Ironbridge Gorge.

TRIP HIGHLIGHT

3 Ironbridge Gorge

It's hard to believe this peaceful, wooded river gorge could really have been the birthplace of the Industrial Revolution. But it was here that Abraham Darby perfected the art of smelting iron ore with coke in 1709, making it possible to mass-produce cast iron for the first time.

Abraham Darby's son, Abraham Darby II, invented a new forging process for producing single beams of iron, allowing Abraham Darby III to astound the world with the first-ever **iron bridge** (www.ironbridge.org.uk; bridge 24hr, tollhouse 10am-5pm), constructed in 1779. The bridge remains the focal point of this World Heritage Site, and 10 very different museums tell the story of the Industrial Revolution in the buildings where it took place. All are administered by the **Ironbridge Gorge Museum Trust** (01952-433424; www.discovertelford.co.uk/visitironbridge; The Wharfage; 10am-5pm). You'll save considerably by buying a passport ticket (adult/child £25/15) at any of the museums or the tourist office. Valid for 12 months, it allows unlimited entry to all of Ironbridge Gorge's sites.

Start at the Gothic riverside warehouse-housed **Museum of the Gorge** (www.ironbridge.org.uk; The Wharfage; 10am-5pm), which offers an outstanding overview using film, photos and exhibits including a 12m-long 3D model of the town in 1796. Other gorge highlights include the **Museum of Iron** (www.ironbridge.org.uk; Wellington Rd; adult/child £9.95/6.95, incl Darby Houses £11.95/7.95; 10am-4pm Wed-Sun), set in Abraham Darby's original iron foundry. As iron-making fell into decline, Ironbridge diversified into manufacturing china pots, using the fine clay mined around Blists Hill.

DETOUR: COSFORD ROYAL AIR FORCE MUSEUM

Start: 3 Ironbridge Gorge

The famous **Cosford Royal Air Force Museum** (01902-376200; www.rafmuseum.org.uk; Shifnal, TF11 8UP; 10am-5pm Mar-Oct, to 4pm Nov-Feb) is run by the Royal Air Force, whose pilots steered many of the winged wonders here across the skies. Among the 70 aircraft on display are the Vulcan bomber (which carried Britain's nuclear deterrent) and the tiny helicopter-like FA330 Bachstelze glider that was towed behind German U-boats to warn them of enemy ships. You can also try out a Black Hawk simulator. It's 13 miles east of Ironbridge via the A4169.

Learn more at the **Coalport China Museum** (www.ironbridge.org.uk; Coalport High St; adult/child £9.95/6.95; ⌚10am-4pm daily mid-Mar–Sep, closed Mon Oct–mid-Mar), dominated by a pair of towering bottle kilns.

✕ 🛏 p211

The Drive » Head west out of Ironbridge on the B4380 along the River Severn; Attingham Park is 11 miles away.

4 Attingham Park

Built in imposing neoclassical style in 1785, **Attingham Park** (NT; ☎01743-708123; www.nationaltrust.org.uk; Atcham, SY5 6JP; adult/child £13/6.50; ⌚house 11am-4.30pm mid-Mar–early Nov, grounds dawn-dusk year-round) looks like something straight out of a period drama with its grand columned facade, manicured lawns, and stagecoach turning circle in the courtyard. The landscaped grounds swirl around an ornamental lake and are home to some 300 fallow deer. The restored walled garden is a picture.

The Drive » Cross to the southern bank of the River Severn; it's a quick 5-mile drive northwest to Shrewsbury.

5 Shrewsbury

A jumble of winding medieval streets and timbered Tudor houses leaning at precarious angles around its 16th-century **Old Market Hall** (www.oldmarkethall.co.uk; The Square), Shrewsbury was a crucial front in the conflict between English and Welsh in medieval days, and is the birthplace of Charles Darwin (1809–82). He's commemorated by a **statue** (Castle Gates) outside the town library, formerly the Shrewsbury School, where he was educated.

Hewn from flaking red Shropshire sandstone, **Shrewsbury Castle** (☎01743-358516; www.soldiersofshropshire.co.uk; Castle St; castle adult/child £4.50/2, grounds free; ⌚10.30am-5pm Mon-Wed, Fri & Sat, to 4pm Sun Apr–mid-Sep, to 4pm Mon-Wed, Fri & Sat mid-Feb–Mar & mid-Sep–mid-Dec) contains the Shropshire Regimental Museum. There are fine views from Laura's Tower and the battlements.

Shrewsbury Medieval street near Old Market Hall

The Drive » Follow the A488 southwest from Shrewsbury through rolling green countryside, and take the first left after the town of Minsterley to Snailbeach (which, despite its name, is not a beach), on the edge of the Shropshire Hills – a 12-mile journey all up.

6 Snailbeach

You'll see relics including an abandoned pumping house, explosives magazine, disused railway lines and rusting machinery such as an ore crusher at the former lead- and silver-mining village of **Snailbeach** (☎07716 116732; www.shropshiremines.org.uk; Shop Lane, Snailbeach SY5 0NX; site free, mine tours adult/child £15/5; ⌚site 24hr, tours by reservation Sun & Thu Apr-Oct). Self-guided trails let you explore the site, or you can join a guided tour that takes you deep into the mine. Waterproof footwear is a must; hard hats and lamps are provided.

The Drive » Drive southwest through the village of Stiper-stones to the town of Bishop's Castle (home to the 1642-founded Three Tuns Brewery). Continue south on the A488 to the black-and-white village of Clun. From here, it's 18 miles east via the B4368 to the market town of Ludlow, then 23 miles south via the A49 to Hereford (59 miles all up).

7 Hereford

Surrounded by apple orchards and rolling pastures at the heart of the Marches, straddling the River Wye, Hereford is famed for its prime steaks and its cider – you can learn about the local tipple at the **Cider Museum & King Offa Distillery** (☎01432-354207; www.cidermuseum.co.uk; Pomona Pl). Displays cover cider-making history and you can sample the delicious modern brews. Look for the fine costrels (minibarrels) used by agricultural workers to carry their wages, which were partially paid in cider.

Soaring **Hereford Cathedral** (☎01432-374200; www.herefordcathedral.org; 5 College Cloisters, Cathedral Close; cathedral entry by donation, Mappa Mundi £6; ⏲cathedral 10am-3pm Mon-Sat, noon-3pm Sun, Mappa Mundi 10am-3pm Mon-Sat) is home to the extraordinary Mappa Mundi, a single piece of calfskin vellum intricately painted with some rather fantastical assumptions about the layout of the globe in around 1290. The same wing contains the world's largest surviving chained library of rare manuscripts manacled to the shelves.

🛏 p211

The Drive » It's 16 miles southeast along the A438 through countryside and farming villages to Westons Cider Mills, just under a mile west of the tiny village of Much Marcle. Much of the journey shadows the River Wye.

8 Westons Cider Mills

Cider producers are scattered throughout the Herefordshire countryside. One of the most prestigious is **Westons Cider Mills** (☎01531-660108; www.westons-cider.co.uk; The Bounds, Much Marcle HR8 2NQ; tours adult/child £12.50/5; ⏲9am-5pm Mon-Fri, from 10am Sat & Sun) – its house brew is served in the Houses of Parliament. Informative tours (1½ hours) start at 11am, 12.30pm, 2pm and 3.30pm Monday to Friday, with free cider and perry tastings. There's also a fascinating bottle museum.

The Drive » The final stretch of this trip is also the prettiest. Take the A449 northeast, via the postcard-perfect black-and-white Tudor town of Ledbury, up into the wooded hills to Great Malvern (13 miles in total).

TRIP HIGHLIGHT

9 Great Malvern

Tumbling down the side of a forested ridge about 7 miles southwest of Worcester is the spa town of Great Malvern.

The 11th-century **Great Malvern Priory** (☎01684-561020; www.greatmalvernpriory.org.uk; Church St; ⏲9am-5pm) is packed with remarkable features, from original Norman pillars to surreal modernist stained glass. The choir is enclosed by a screen of 15th-century tiles and the monks' stalls are decorated with delightfully irreverent 14th-century misericords, depicting everything from three rats hanging a cat to the mythological reptile, the basilisk. Charles Darwin's daughter Annie is buried here.

For road-trippers, though, the real treat is the **Morgan Motor Company** (☎01684-573104; www.morgan-motor.com; Pickersleigh Rd; museum free, tours adult/child £24/12; ⏲museum 8.30am-5pm Mon-Thu, to 2pm Fri, tours by reservation), which has been handcrafting elegant sports cars since 1909. You can still see the mechanics at work on two-hour guided tours (book ahead), and view vintage classics adjacent to the museum. If you want to swap your wheels for one of these machines (at least for a while), it's possible to rent one (per day from £235, including insurance).

🍴 🛏 p211

Eating & Sleeping

Manchester 1

Mackie Mayor Food Hall ££

(www.mackiemayor.co.uk; 1 Eagle St; mains £9-15; 10am-10pm Tue-Thu, to 11pm Fri, 9am-11pm Sat, 9am-8pm Sun; all city centre) This restored former meat market is now home to a superb food hall with a fine selection of 10 individual traders. The pizzas from Honest Crust are divine; the pork-belly bao from Baohouse is done just right; Nationale 7 does wonders with a basic sandwich; and Tender Cow serves really tasty steaks. Dining is communal, across two floors.

Kimpton Clocktower Hotel Hotel ££

(0161-288 2222; www.kimptonclocktowerhotel.com; Oxford St, M60 7HA; r from £90; ; St Peter's Square) Beyond the triple-height lobby of this 19th-century beaut are 270 newly refurbished loft-style rooms that are incredibly popular with both leisure and business visitors alike. From the lobby you can access the wonderful **Refuge** (0161-233 5151; www.refugemcr.co.uk; Oxford St; 8am-midnight Mon-Wed, to 1am Thu, to 2am Fri & Sat, to 11.30pm Sun; all city centre) restaurant and bar.

Ironbridge Gorge 3

D'arcys at the Station Mediterranean ££

(01952-884499; www.darcysironbridge.co.uk; Ladywood; mains £11.50-15; 6-9.30pm Wed-Sat) Just over the bridge by the river, the handsome old station building is the backdrop for flavoursome Mediterranean dishes, from Moroccan chicken to Cypriot kebabs and Tuscan bean casserole. Kids aged over 10 are welcome.

Library House B&B ££

(01952-432299; www.libraryhouse.com; 11 Severn Bank; s/d from £75/100;) Up an alley off the main street, this lovingly restored Georgian library building built in 1730 is hugged by vines, backed by a beautiful garden and decked out with stacks of vintage books, curios, prints and lithographs. There are three charmingly well-preserved, individually decorated rooms, named Milton, Chaucer and Eliot. The affable dog whipping around is Millie.

Hereford 7

Castle House Boutique Hotel £££

(01432-356321; www.castlehse.co.uk; Castle St; s/d/ste from £140/175/200;) In a regal Georgian town house where the Bishop of Hereford once resided, this tranquil 16-room hotel has two sophisticated restaurants using ingredients sourced from its own nearby farm, a sunny garden spilling down to Hereford's former castle moat, and magnificent rooms and suites. Another eight newer rooms (some wheelchair accessible) are a short walk away at 25 Castle St.

Great Malvern 9

Fig Tree Mediterranean ££

(01684-569909; www.thefigmalvern.co.uk; 99b Church St; breakfast dishes £6.50-9.50, mains lunch £8.50-13, dinner £16.50-24; 10am-2pm & 5.30-9.30pm Tue-Sat;) Tucked down an alleyway off Church St, this 19th-century former stable serves hearty breakfasts (including vegan options), and Mediterranean-inspired fare at lunch (eg focaccia, pastas and salads) and dinner (chorizo-stuffed squid, lamb souvlaki with tzatziki and saffron rice). Don't miss its signature almond-and-lemon polenta cake with fig ice cream.

Abbey Hotel Hotel £££

(01684-892332; www.sarova-abbeyhotel.com; Abbey Rd; d/f from £139/179;) Tangled in vines like a Brothers Grimm fairy-tale castle, this stately property has 103 elegant rooms in a prime location by the local-history museum and priory.

Family rooms have fold-out sofa beds.

ANN TAYLOR-HUGHES / GETTY IMAGES ©

Classic Trip

Peak District

This adventure-packed trip plunges you into the heart of the Peak District National Park and offers boundless opportunities to get out of your car and into the invigorating landscapes.

TRIP HIGHLIGHTS

113 miles

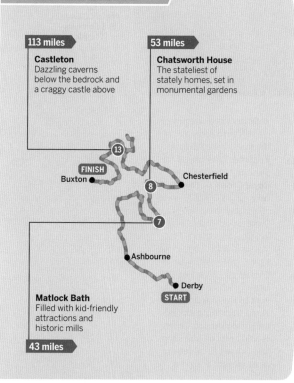

Castleton
Dazzling caverns below the bedrock and a craggy castle above

53 miles

Chatsworth House
The stateliest of stately homes, set in monumental gardens

FINISH
Buxton
13
8
Chesterfield
7
Ashbourne
Derby
START

Matlock Bath
Filled with kid-friendly attractions and historic mills

43 miles

5 DAYS
135 MILES / 217KM

GREAT FOR...

BEST TIME TO GO

Easter to September lets you enjoy the best weather.

ESSENTIAL PHOTO

The dramatic view up through steep-sided Winnats Pass.

BEST FOR OUTDOORS

Spectacular walking trails fan out around Edale.

Peak District National Park Cycling the Tissington Trail

Classic Trip

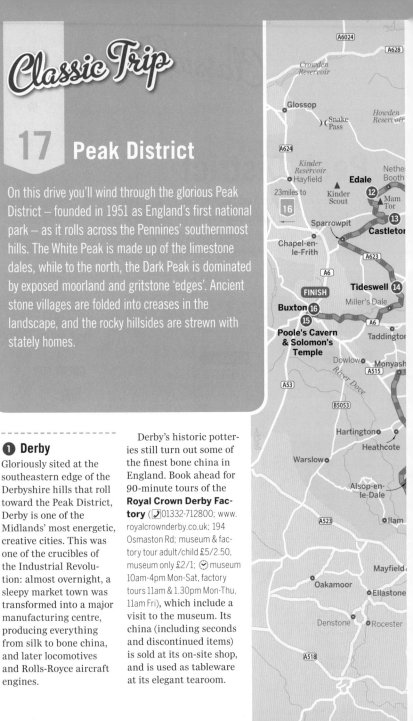

17 Peak District

On this drive you'll wind through the glorious Peak District – founded in 1951 as England's first national park – as it rolls across the Pennines' southernmost hills. The White Peak is made up of the limestone dales, while to the north, the Dark Peak is dominated by exposed moorland and gritstone 'edges'. Ancient stone villages are folded into creases in the landscape, and the rocky hillsides are strewn with stately homes.

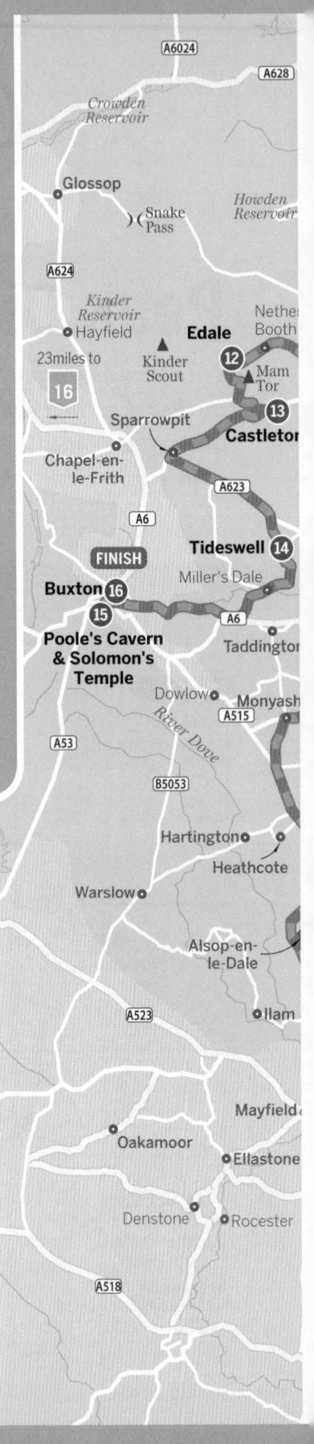

1 Derby

Gloriously sited at the southeastern edge of the Derbyshire hills that roll toward the Peak District, Derby is one of the Midlands' most energetic, creative cities. This was one of the crucibles of the Industrial Revolution: almost overnight, a sleepy market town was transformed into a major manufacturing centre, producing everything from silk to bone china, and later locomotives and Rolls-Royce aircraft engines.

Derby's historic potteries still turn out some of the finest bone china in England. Book ahead for 90-minute tours of the **Royal Crown Derby Factory** (01332-712800; www.royalcrownderby.co.uk; 194 Osmaston Rd; museum & factory tour adult/child £5/2.50, museum only £2/1; museum 10am-4pm Mon-Sat, factory tours 11am & 1.30pm Mon-Thu, 11am Fri), which include a visit to the museum. Its china (including seconds and discontinued items) is sold at its on-site shop, and is used as tableware at its elegant tearoom.

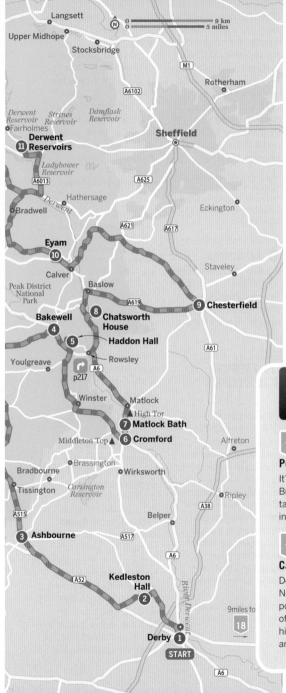

The **Derby Museum & Art Gallery** (☎01332-641901; www.derbymuseums.org; The Strand; ⏰10.30am-4.30pm Tue-Sat, noon-4pm Sun) also has ceramics produced by Royal Crown Derby, along with an archaeology gallery.

✖ 🛏 p85, p225

The Drive » Drive through Derby's outskirts along Kedleston Rd, which gives way to farmland just before the turn-off to Kedleston Hall (5 miles in total).

2 Kedleston Hall

Sitting pretty in vast landscaped grounds, the neoclassical mansion **Kedleston Hall** (NT; ☎01332-842191; www.nationaltrust.org.uk; Kedleston Rd, Quarndon DE22 5JH; house & gardens

LINK YOUR TRIP

16 Central England Industrial Powerhouse

It's a 30-mile drive from Buxton to Manchester to take a spin through British industrial history.

18 Midlands Battlefields, Castles & Stately Homes

Derby is a 15-mile hop from Nottingham, the starting point for discovering some of the country's most historic battlefields, castles and stately homes.

adult/child £13.60/6.80, garden only £10/5; ⏲house noon-5pm Sat-Thu Feb-Oct, garden 10am-5pm Feb-Oct, to 4pm Nov-Jan) is a must for fans of stately homes. Entering the house through a grand portico, you'll reach the breathtaking Marble Hall with massive alabaster columns and statues of Greek deities.

The Curzon family has lived here since the 12th century but the current wonder was built by Sir Nathaniel Curzon in 1758. Meanwhile, the poor old peasants in Kedleston village had their humble dwellings moved a mile down the road, as they interfered with the view. Ah, the good old days...

Highlights include Indian treasures amassed by Viceroy George Curzon and a domed, circular saloon modelled on the Pantheon in Rome, as well as 18th-century-style pleasure gardens.

The Drive » Head west along Buckhazels Lane and join Ashbourne Rd (aka the A52) to drive northwest into Ashbourne (10 miles all up).

3 Ashbourne

Perched at the southern edge of the Peak District National Park, Ashbourne is a pretty patchwork of steeply slanting stone streets lined with cafes, pubs and antique shops.

The main attraction is the chance to walk or cycle along the **Tissington Trail**, part of NCN Route 68, which runs north for 13 miles to Parsley Hay. The track climbs gently along the tunnels, viaducts and cuttings of the disused railway line that once transported local milk to London.

The Drive » It's 17 miles from Ashbourne to Bakewell. Drive north into the rolling countryside (carpeted with daffodils in spring) along Buxton Rd as it winds up through the hills and valleys of the White Peak region.

LOCAL KNOWLEDGE: ROYAL SHROVETIDE FOOTBALL

Some people celebrate Mardi Gras aka Shrove Tuesday (the last day before Lent) by eating pancakes or dressing up in carnival finery. But Ashbourne marks the occasion with a riotous game of football, where the ball is wrestled as much as kicked from one end of town to the other by crowds of revellers.

Following 12th-century rules, villagers are split into two teams – those from north of the river and those from south – and the 'goals' are two millstones, set 3 miles apart. Participants are free to kick, carry or throw the ball, though it's usually squeezed through the crowds like a rugby scrum. Sooner or later, players and the ball end up in the river. Local shops board up their windows and the whole town comes out to watch or play.

Fearless visitors are welcome to participate in the melee but, under a quirk of the rules, only locals are allowed to score goals.

4 Bakewell

The Peak District's second-largest town (after Buxton), Bakewell is filled with storybook stone buildings. The town is ringed by famous walking trails and stately homes, but it's probably best known for its famous Bakewell Pudding, a pastry shell filled with jam and frangipane invented here in 1820.

Up on the hill above Rutland Sq, **All Saints Church** (www.bakewell-church.co.uk; South Church St; by donation; ⏲9am-5pm Apr-Oct, to 4pm Nov-Mar) is packed with ancient features, including a 14th-century font, a pair of Norman arches, heraldic tombs, and a collection of crude stone gravestones and crosses dating from the 12th century.

Nearby, the **Old House Museum** (☎01629-813642; www.oldhousemuseum.org.uk; Cunningham Pl; adult/child £5/2.50; ⏰10.30am-4pm Wed-Sat late Mar-early Nov) explores local history. Check out the Tudor loo and the displays on wattle and daub, a traditional technique for building walls using woven twigs and cow dung.

 p225

The Drive » From Bakewell it's just 2 miles southeast along Haddon Rd, following the River Wye, to Haddon Hall.

5 Haddon Hall

With stone turrets, time-worn timbers and walled gardens, **Haddon Hall** (☎01629-812855; www.haddonhall.co.uk; Haddon Rd, DE45 1LA; adult/child £18.50/free; ⏰10.30am-5pm daily late Mar-Sep, Fri-Mon Oct, to 4pm daily Dec) looks exactly like a medieval manor house should. Founded in the 12th century, it was expanded and remodelled throughout medieval times. The 'modernisation' stopped when the house was abandoned in the 18th century. Spared from the more florid excesses of the Victorian period, Haddon Hall has been used as the location for numerous period blockbusters (such as *Elizabeth*).

The Drive » From Haddon Hall's car park, take your first right (south) onto the B5056 to Grange Mill, then take the A5012 southeast down along a deep gully to Cromford Mill (10.5 miles in total).

DETOUR: CAUDWELL'S MILL

Start: 5 Haddon Hall

In the village of Rowsley, the chugging, grinding, water-powered **Caudwell's Mill** (☎01629-734374; www.caudwellsmill.co.uk; Rowsley, DE4 2EB; ⏰9am-5pm Mon-Sat, 10am-4pm Sun) still produces flour the old-fashioned way (20 different types are for sale, along with eight different oat products as well as yeast and biscuits). There are various craft workshops here and a tearoom.

From Haddon Hall, Caudwell's Mill is 1.5 miles east via the A6 along the river.

6 Cromford Mill

Founded in the 1770s by Richard Arkwright, a leading inventor and entrepreneur during the early Industrial Revolution, the **Cromford Mill** (☎01629-823256; www.cromfordmills.org.uk; Mill Lane, Cromford; adult/child £10/free; ⏰10am-5pm) was the first modern factory, producing cotton on automated machines powered by a series of waterwheels along the River Derwent. This prototype inspired a succession of mills, ushering in the industrial age.

The Drive » It's a mile-long drive north along the River Derwent to Matlock Bath (not to be confused with the larger, workaday town of Matlock 2 miles to Matlock Bath's north).

TRIP HIGHLIGHT

7 Matlock Bath

Unashamedly tacky, Matlock Bath looks like a seaside resort that somehow lost its way and ended up at the foot of the Peak District. Following the River Derwent through a sheer-walled gorge, the main promenade is lined with amusement arcades, tearooms, fish-and-chip shops and pubs. Family-friendly attractions here include **Heights of Abraham** (☎01629-582365; www.heightsofabraham.com; Dale Rd; adult/child £19/13; ⏰10am-5pm mid-Mar–early Nov; 👪). A spectacular cable-car ride (accessible with admission ticket only) from the bottom of the gorge brings you to this hilltop leisure park, which has cave and mine tours and fossil exhibitions.

The enthusiast-run **Peak District Lead Mining Museum** (☎01629-583834;

Classic Trip

JO JONES / SHUTTERSTOCK ©

JO JONES / SHUTTERSTOCK ©

WHY THIS IS A CLASSIC TRIP

CATHERINE LE NEVEZ, WRITER

What makes this trip a true classic is its diversity. England's first national park isn't simply an outdoors playground (though there's plenty to do, including incredible walking, so pack your hiking boots!). History lessons here span grand manors to Industrial Revolution–era mills and the site of the Dambusters testing ground. And when you've finished exploring for the day, you can unwind in cosy open-fire-warmed country pubs.

Above: Hiking the Great Ridge trail, between Castleton and Edale
Left: All Saints Church, Bakewell
Right: Haddon Hall

www.peakdistrictleadmining-museum.co.uk; The Grand Pavilion, South Pde; museum adult/child £5.50/3.50, mine £6.50/4, combined ticket £10/6; ⏲11am-3.45pm Wed, Sat & Sun Apr-Oct, Sat & Sun Nov-Mar; 👪) provides an educational introduction to Matlock Bath's mining history.

✕ 🛏 p225

The Drive » Continue north through the valley along the River Derwent and follow the road northeast up into the hills to Chatsworth House, a 9.5-mile journey.

TRIP HIGHLIGHT

8 Chatsworth House

Known as the 'Palace of the Peak', vast **Chatsworth House** (☎01246-565300; www.chatsworth.org; DE45 1PP; house & gardens adult/child £23/12.50, gardens only £14/7.50, playground £7, park free; ⏲9.30am-5.30pm late May-early Sep, shorter hours mid-Mar–late May & early Sep-early Jan) has been occupied by the earls and dukes of Devonshire for centuries. Inside, the lavish apartments and mural-painted staterooms are packed with priceless paintings and period furniture. The house sits in 25 sq miles of grounds and ornamental gardens, some landscaped by Lancelot 'Capability' Brown. Kids will love the farmyard adventure playground.

The manor was founded in 1552 by

the formidable Bess of Hardwick and her second husband, William Cavendish, who earned grace and favour by helping Henry VIII dissolve the English monasteries. Mary, Queen of Scots was imprisoned at Chatsworth on the orders of Elizabeth I in 1569.

Look out for the portraits of the current generation of Devonshires by Lucian Freud.

Also on the estate is an exceptional **farm shop** (www.chatsworth.org; Pilsley, DE45 1UF; dishes £6.50-15.50; cafe 9am-5pm Mon-Sat, 10am-5pm Sun, shop 9am-6pm Mon-Sat, 11am-5pm Sun;) – one of the best in the UK – and an attached cafe, as well as a handful of other eateries and shops.

The Drive » From Chatsworth House it's 9.7 miles to Chesterfield. Head north along Bakewell Rd to Baslow, then east along the A619 and descend through the forested valley.

9 Chesterfield

Busy Chesterfield is worth a stop to see the astonishing crooked spire rising atop **St Mary & All Saints Church** (01246-206506; www.crookedspire.org; Church Way; spire tours adult/child £6/4; church 9am-4pm Mon-Sat). Dating from 1360, the 68m-high spire is twisted in a right-handed corkscrew and leans several metres southwest. It's the result of the lead casing on the south-facing side having buckled in the sun. Learn more at the engaging **Chesterfield Museum & Art Gallery** (01246-345727; www.chesterfield.gov.uk; St Mary's Gate; 10am-4pm Mon & Thu-Sat), which documents Chesterfield's history as a Roman fort through to the present today.

The Drive » Take the B6051 northwest through open farmland to Owler Bar. Head west on the B6054 through the Dark Peak region and along the side of the sheer gritstone escarpment Froggatt Edge to Calver, from where Eyam is 2 miles northwest (a 16-mile journey in total).

10 Eyam

Quaint little Eyam (ee-em), a former lead-mining village of sloping streets and old cottages backed by rows of green hills, has a poignant history that's all the more resonant in light of the global Covid-19 pandemic. In 1665 the town was infected by the dreaded Black Death plague, carried here by fleas on a consignment of cloth from London, and the village rector, William Mompesson, convinced villagers to quarantine themselves. Some 270 of the village's 800 inhabitants succumbed, leaving surrounding villages relatively unscathed. Vivid displays on the Eyam plague are the centrepiece of the engaging **Eyam Museum** (01433-631371; www.eyam-museum.org.uk; Hawkhill Rd; adult/child £3/2.50; 10am-4pm Tue-

TOP TIP: CYCLING IN THE PEAK DISTRICT

The **Peak District National Park Authority** (01629-816200; www.peakdistrict.gov.uk) operates several cycle-hire centres at **Ashbourne** (01335-343156; Mapleton Rd, DE6 2AA; per half-/full day standard bike from £14/17, electric bike £32/36; 9.30am-5pm Mar-Oct, shorter hours Nov-Feb), **Derwent Reservoirs** (01433-651261; Fairholmes, S33 0AQ; per half-/full day standard bike £14/17, electric bike £32/36; 9.30am-4.30pm early Feb-early Nov) and **Parsley Hay** (01298-84493; Parsley Hay, SK17 0DG; per half-/full day standard bike £14/17, electric bike £32/36; 10am-4.30pm mid-Feb–early Nov), renting out road, mountain, tandem and electric bicycles as well as kids' bikes. You can hire a bike from one location and drop it off at another for no extra charge.

Sun Easter-Oct), alongside exhibits on the village's history of lead mining and silk weaving. Many victims of the village's 1665 Black Death plague outbreak were buried at **Eyam Parish Church** (St Lawrence's Church; www.eyamchurch.org; Church St; by donation; 9am-6pm Easter-Sep, to 4pm Oct-Easter). Stained-glass panels and moving displays tell the story of the outbreak.

Scenic walking trails surround the village. An interesting short walk leads to **Mompesson's Well**, where supplies were left during the Black Death plague by friends from other villages (paid for using coins sterilised in vinegar).

p225

The Drive » Drive west along Main Rd and turn north on the B6049, passing through the villages of Bradwell and Thornhill, to Snake Rd. Cross the two bridges spanning Ladybower Reservoir and head northwest along the western bank to Derwent Reservoir (16 miles in total).

11 Derwent Reservoirs

The upper reaches of the Derwent Valley were flooded between 1916 and 1935 to create three huge reservoirs – the Ladybower, Derwent and Howden Reservoirs – to supply Sheffield, Leicester, Nottingham and Derby with water. These constructed lakes soon proved their worth – the Dambusters squadron carried out practice runs over Derwent Reservoir before unleashing their 'bouncing bombs' on the Ruhr Valley in Germany in WWII. Their exploits are detailed in the **Derwent Dam Museum** (01433-650953; www.dambusters.org.uk; Fairholmes, S33 0AQ; 10am-4.30pm Mon-Fri, 9.30am-5.30pm Sat & Sun Apr-Oct, shorter hours Nov-Mar).

These days, the reservoirs are popular destinations for walkers, cyclists and mountain bikers – and lots of ducks, so drive slowly!

The Drive » Return to Thornhill and take Hope Rd west to the village of Hope, then turn north on Edale Rd through a wide valley dominated by Dark Peak slopes until you reach Edale (14 miles altogether).

DAVO FOSTER / SHUTTERSTOCK ©

Derwent Valley Derwent Reservoir

12 Edale

Surrounded by majestic Peak District countryside, this cluster of stone houses is an enchanting place to pass the time. Walking is the number-one drawcard, with plenty of diverting strolls for less-committed hill walkers.

As well as trips to Hollins Cross and Mam Tor, on the ridge dividing Edale from Castleton, you can walk north onto the Kinder Plateau, dark and brooding in the mist, gloriously high and open when the sun's out. This was the setting for a famous act of civil disobedience by ramblers in 1932 that paved the way for the legal 'right to roam' and the creation of England's national parks.

A fine circular walk starts by following the

Pennine Way through fields to Upper Booth, then up a path called Jacobs Ladder and along the southern edge of Kinder, before dropping down to Edale via the steep rocky valley of Grindsbrook Clough, or the ridge of Ringing Roger.

p225

The Drive » Leave Edale to the southwest and climb the steep hill of Mam Tor, before descending precipitous Winnats Pass to Castleton (4.7 miles in total).

ALEXEY FEDORENKO / SHUTTERSTOCK ©

TRIP HIGHLIGHT

13 Castleton

Castleton's village streets are lined with leaning stone houses, with walking trails criss-crossing the surrounding hills. Topping the ridge to the south, a 350m walk from the town centre, sits crag-like **Peveril Castle** (EH; 01433-620613; www.english-heritage.org.uk; adult/child £7.60/4.60; 10am-5pm Wed-Sun Easter-Oct, to 4pm Sat & Sun Nov-Easter). Constructed by William Peveril, son of William the Conqueror, the castle was used as a hunting lodge by Henry II, King John and Henry III.

The bedrock below is riddled with fascinating caves. The most convenient, **Peak Cavern** (01433-620285; www.peakcavern.co.uk; Peak Cavern Rd, S33 8WS; adult/child £15/8; 10am-5pm daily Apr-Oct, Sat & Sun Nov-Mar), is easily reached by a pretty streamside 250m walk south of the village centre. Dramatic limestone formations are lit with fibre-optic cables.

Just over half a mile west of Castleton, claustrophobe's nightmare **Speedwell Cavern** (01433-623018; www.

LOCAL KNOWLEDGE: THE PEAK DISTRICT – WHAT'S IN A NAME?

No one knows how the Peak District got its name – certainly not from the landscape, which has hills and valleys, gorges and lakes, wild moorland and gritstone escarpments, but no peaks. The most popular theory is that the region was named for the Pecsaetan, the Anglo-Saxon tribe who once populated this part of England.

Castleton View from Peveril Castle over Castleton

speedwellcavern.co.uk; Winnats Pass, S33 8WA; tour £17; ⏲10am-5pm daily Apr-Oct, Sat & Sun Nov-Mar) is reached via an eerie boat ride through flooded tunnels.

Captivating **Treak Cliff Cavern** (☎01433-620571; www.bluejohnstone.com; Buxton Rd, S33 8WP; adult/child £12.50/6; ⏲9am-4.30pm Mar-Oct, to 3.30pm Nov-Feb), just under a mile west of Castleton's village centre, has a forest of stalactites and exposed seams of colourful Blue John Stone.

Up the southeastern side of Mam Tor, 2 miles west of Castleton, **Blue John Cavern** (☎01433-620638; www.bluejohn-cavern.co.uk; Old Mam Tor Rd, S33 8WH; adult/child £14/7; ⏲9.30am-4pm Mon-Fri, to 5pm Sat & Sun Apr-Oct, to dusk Nov-Mar) is a maze of natural caverns.

The Drive » Retrace your route up spectacular Winnats Pass and head southwest to Sparrowpit. Turn southeast onto the A623 and follow it to Tideswell (a total of 9.5 miles).

14 Tideswell

Dominating the former lead-mining village of Tideswell, the massive parish church of St John the Baptist – aka the **Cathedral of the Peak** (☎01298-871317; www.tideswellchurch.org; Commercial Rd, Tideswell; ⏲8.30am-5.30pm) – has stood here virtually unchanged since the 14th century. Look out for the wooden panels inscribed with the Ten Commandments and grand 14th-century tomb of local landowner Thurston de Bower, depicted in full medieval armour.

The Drive » Take the B6049 south to join the forested A6 (you'll see clouds of snowdrops and bluebells in early spring), which shadows the River Wye to Poole's Cavern (9 miles all up).

Classic Trip

15 Poole's Cavern

The magnificent natural limestone **Poole's Cavern** (☎01298-26978; www.poolescavern.co.uk; Green Lane; adult/child £11/5.50; ⌚10am-4.30pm, tours 10am-4pm every 20min Mar-Oct, 10.30am, 12.30pm & 2.30pm Mon-Fri, every 20min Sat & Sun Nov-Feb) is reached by descending 28 steps; the temperature is a cool 7°C. Tours last 50 minutes.

From the cavern's car park, a 20-minute walk leads up through Grin Low Wood to Solomon's Temple, a ruined tower with fine views over the town.

The Drive » The last stretch is also the shortest: from Poole's Cavern it's just 1 mile northeast along the A515 to Buxton.

16 Buxton

The 'capital' of the Peak District National Park, albeit just outside the park boundary in the rolling hills of the Derbyshire dales, Buxton built its fortunes on its natural warm-water springs, which attracted health tourists in Buxton's turn-of-the-century heyday.

Buxton's extravagant baths were built in Regency style in 1854 and are fronted by the **Crescent** (☎01298-213577; www.buxtoncrescentexperience.com; The Crescent; ⌚10am-4.30pm Mon-Sat, to 4pm Sun), a grand, curving facade inspired by the Royal Crescent in Bath. Its pump room, which dispensed the town's spring water for nearly a century, has displays showcasing Buxton's thermal springs heritage spanning their Roman discovery to today. Within the complex is a five-star hotel and lavish spa including the original Victorian baths with naturally heated 28 °C water.

Adjoining Buxton's turreted **Opera House** (☎01298-72190; www.buxtonoperahouse.org.uk; Water St; tours £10; ⌚tours by reservation) are the 23-acre **Pavilion Gardens** (www.paviliongardens.co.uk; St John's Rd; ⌚9am-6pm Jul & Aug, shorter hours Sep-Jun) with domed pavilions; concerts take place in the bandstand throughout the year.

The **Buxton Tram** (☎01298-79648; www.discoverbuxton.co.uk; adult/child £8/5; ⌚by reservation late Mar–Oct) is a vintage milk float that takes you on a 12mph, hour-or-so circuit of the centre on its entertaining 'Wonder of the Peak' tour.

In a handsome Victorian building, the **Buxton Museum & Art Gallery** (☎01629-533540; www.derbyshire.gov.uk/leisure/buxton-museum/buxton-museum-and-art-gallery.aspx; Terrace Rd; ⌚10am-5pm Tue-Sat year-round, plus noon-4pm Sun Easter-Sep) displays local historical bric-a-brac and curiosities.

✕ 🛏 p225

CAVING & CLIMBING

The limestone sections of the Peak District are riddled with caves and caverns, including the series of 'showcaves' in Castleton, Buxton and Matlock Bath. For caving (or potholing) trips, your first port of call should be the website www.peakdistrictcaving.info. **Peaks and Paddles** (☎07896 912871; www.peaksandpaddles.org; canoeing & caving from £55, abseiling from £25; ⌚by reservation) runs expeditions.

England's top mountaineers train in this area, which offers rigorous technical climbing on a series of limestone gorges, exposed tors (crags) and gritstone 'edges' that extend south into the Staffordshire Moorlands. Gritstone climbing in the Peak District is predominantly on old-school trad routes, requiring a decent rack of friends, nuts and hexes. Bolted sport routes are found on several limestone crags in the Peak District, but many use ancient pieces of gear and most require additional protection. Tourist offices throughout the Peak District can supply information.

Eating & Sleeping

Derby 1

Farmhouse at Mackworth Inn ££

(01332-824324; www.thefarmhouseatmackworth.com; 60 Ashbourne Rd; d/f incl breakfast from £90/110; P) The Farmhouse at Mackworth is just 2.5 miles northwest of Derby in undulating countryside, with the bonus of plentiful free parking. The designer inn's 10 rooms have checked fabrics, rustic timber cladding and chrome fittings, plus amenities including Nespresso machines and fluffy robes. There's a fabulous bar and a restaurant with a Josper charcoal oven (mains £12 to £32).

Bakewell 4

Old Original Bakewell Pudding Shop Bakery, Cafe £

(www.bakewellpuddingshop.co.uk; The Square; dishes £8-13; 9am-5pm) One of those that claims to have invented the Bakewell Pudding, this place has a lovely 1st-floor tearoom with exposed beams. It serves light meals and afternoon teas on tiered trays.

Rutland Arms Hotel Hotel £££

(01629-812812; www.rutlandarmsbakewell.co.uk; The Square; d incl breakfast from £168; P) Jane Austen is said to have stayed in room 2 of this aristocratic, 1804-built stone coaching inn while working on *Pride and Prejudice*. Its 33 rooms are in the main house and adjacent courtyard building; higher-priced rooms have lots of Victorian flourishes. Upmarket British classics (£14 to £23) such as pheasant and parsnip pie are served at its restaurant.

Matlock Bath 7

Hodgkinson's Hotel & Restaurant Hotel ££

(01629-582170; www.hodgkinsons-hotel.co.uk; 150 South Pde; s/d/f incl breakfast from £60/110/155; P) The eight rooms at this central Grade II–listed Victorian beauty conjure up Matlock's golden age with antique furnishings, cast-iron fireplaces, flowery wallpaper, handmade soaps and goose-down duvets. The restaurant (open Tuesday to Saturday evenings; two-/three-course menus £28/32) has just 18 seats, so bookings are advised. From April to September there's a minimum two-night stay on weekends.
Arrive early to nab one of its five parking spaces.

Eyam 10

Miner's Arms Pub ££

(01433-630853; www.theminersarmseyam.co.uk; Water Lane; s/d from £45/70;) Although its age isn't immediately obvious, this traditional village inn was built shortly before the Black Death hit Eyam in 1665. Inside you'll find beamed ceilings, affable staff, a blazing open fire, comfy en-suite rooms and good-value pub food (mains £11 to £15.50).

Edale 12

Stonecroft B&B ££

(01433-670262; www.stonecroftguesthouse.co.uk; Grindsbrook; s/d from £65/110; P) This handsomely fitted-out 1900s stone house has three comfortable guest rooms (two doubles, one single). Host Julia's organic breakfasts are gluten-free, with vegetarian and vegan options; packed lunches (£7.50) and Friday- and Saturday-evening meals (£35) available by request when booking. Bike rental costs £25 per half-day. Pick-up from the train station can be arranged. Kids aren't permitted.

Buxton 16

Old Hall Hotel Historic Hotel ££

(01298-22841; www.oldhallhotelbuxton.co.uk; The Square; s/d incl breakfast from £69/89;) There's a tale to go with every creak of the floorboards at this history-soaked establishment, supposedly the oldest hotel in England. Among other esteemed residents, Mary, Queen of Scots stayed here from 1576 to 1578, albeit against her will. The rooms still retain their grandeur (some have four-poster beds), and there are several bars, lounges and dining options.

Midlands Battlefields, Castles & Stately Homes

English history unfolds in all its pomp and ceremony along this journey through the country's heart where royal battles were fought, castles were besieged and the aristocracy built palatial manors.

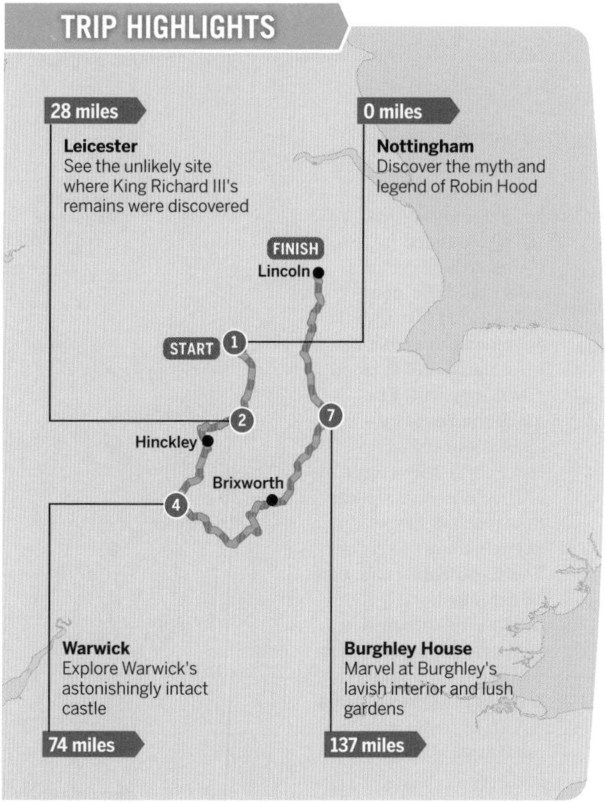

TRIP HIGHLIGHTS

0 miles
Nottingham
Discover the myth and legend of Robin Hood

28 miles
Leicester
See the unlikely site where King Richard III's remains were discovered

74 miles
Warwick
Explore Warwick's astonishingly intact castle

137 miles
Burghley House
Marvel at Burghley's lavish interior and lush gardens

FINISH
Lincoln
START 1
2
Hinckley
Brixworth
4
7

5 DAYS
214 MILES / 344KM

GREAT FOR...

BEST TIME TO GO

June to September sees the best weather and fewest closures.

ESSENTIAL PHOTO

Newton's apple tree that inspired his theory of gravity.

BEST FOR FAMILIES

Relive medieval times at Warwick Castle.

Warwick Warwick Castle

18

Midlands Battlefields, Castles & Stately Homes

This grand tour begins and ends with famed castles, and stops at a third mighty fortress en route. In between, you'll see the field where Richard III became the last English king to die in battle, learn the extraordinary story of the recent discovery of his long-lost remains in a city car park, and wander the opulent corridors of stately homes and their magnificently landscaped gardens and deer-roamed grounds.

TRIP HIGHLIGHT

1 Nottingham

Nottingham is synonymous with mythologised outlaw Robin Hood. A bronze **statue** (Castle Rd) of the woodsman stands in the former moat of **Nottingham Castle** (www.nottinghamcastle.org.uk; Lenton Rd). Founded by William the Conqueror, the original castle was held by a succession of English kings before falling in the English Civil War. Its 17th-century manor-house-like replacement contains a local-history museum and art gallery. Carved into the cliff beneath the castle, **Ye Olde Trip to Jerusalem** (☎0115-947 3171; www.triptojerusalem.com; Brewhouse Yard, Castle Rd; ⌚11am-11pm Sun-Thu, to midnight Fri & Sat; 📶), founded in 1189, claims to be England's oldest pub. For more Robin Hood history, take an entertaining, highly informative Robin Hood Town Tour with **Ezekial Bone Tours** (☎07941 210986; www.ezekialbone.com; Robin Hood Town Tour adult/child £14.50/8; ⌚Robin Hood Town Tour 2pm Sat Mar-Oct). Tours of nearby Sherwood Forest can also be arranged.

The city's bedrock is riddled with caves, which you can delve into on tours of the **City of Caves** (☎0115-952 0555; www.nationaljusticemuseum.org.uk/

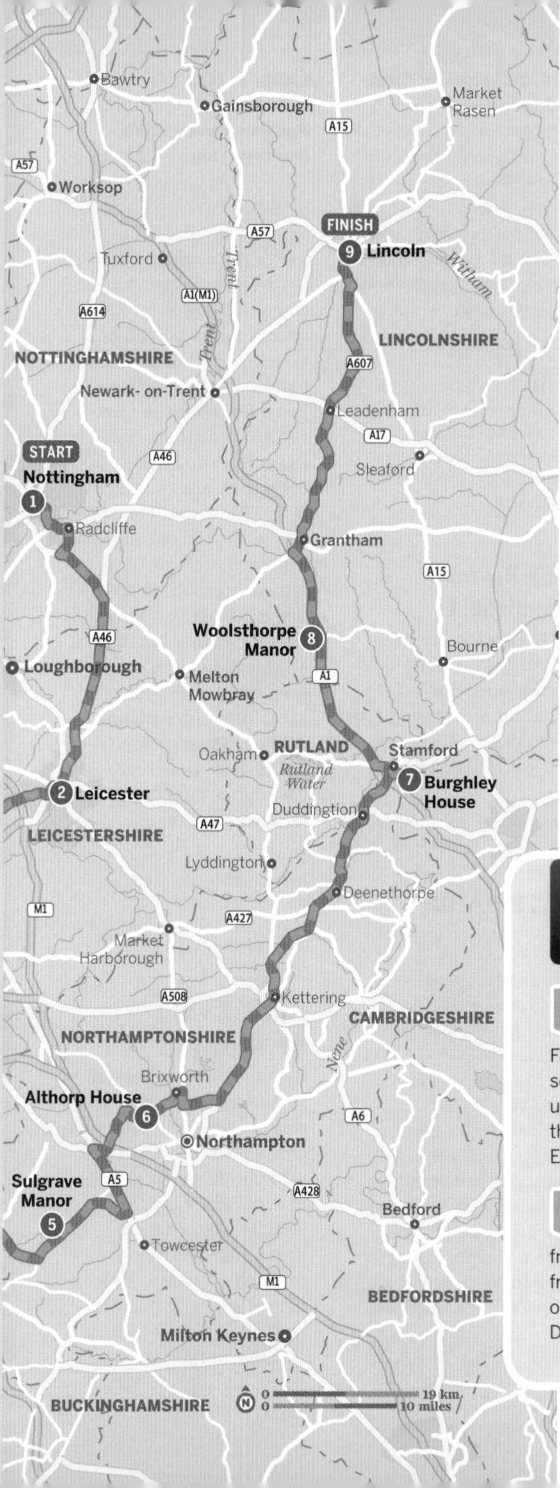

venue/city-of-caves; Garner's Hill; adult/child £8.75/7.65, incl National Justice Museum £17.60/15.10; ⏲ tours 10am-4pm). Tours lead you through a WWII air-raid shelter, a medieval underground tannery, several pub cellars and a mock-up of a Victorian slum dwelling. Book ahead for a timeslot.

✕ 🛏 p235

The Drive » It's an easy 28 miles' drive south to Leicester. The A46, which travels through a dark-green patchwork of dairy and crop fields, makes a more scenic alternative to the speedier but busier M1.

TRIP HIGHLIGHT

2 Leicester

Built over the buried ruins of two millennia of history, Leicester (*les*-ter) suffered at the hands of the Luftwaffe and

LINK YOUR TRIP

15 The Cotswolds & Literary England

From Warwick, it's 8 miles southwest to Stratford-upon-Avon for a spin through quintessentially English rolling countryside.

17 Peak District

It's a 15-mile hop west from Nottingham to Derby, from where you can strike out into the glorious Peak District National Park.

post-war planners, but a massive influx of textile workers from India and Pakistan since the 1960s has transformed the city into a bustling global melting pot.

The astonishing 2012 discovery and 2013 identification of the remains of King Richard III in a Leicester car park sparked a flurry of developments, including a spiffing visitor centre on the site, **King Richard III: Dynasty, Death & Discovery** (www.kriii.com; 4a St Martin's Pl; adult/child £9.25/4.75; ⌚10am-4pm Sun-Fri, to 5pm Sat), which details the University of Leicester's archaeological dig and identification, and lets you view the site of the grave in which he was found. The discovery also led to the restoration of the **Leicester Cathedral** (☎0116-261 5357; www.leicestercathedral.org; Peacock Lane; by donation; ⌚11am-3pm Wed-Sat, noon-3pm Sun), where the king was reburied in 2015; you can visit his grave, which is topped by a contemporary limestone tomb.

✕ 🛏 p235

The Drive » Travel through open farmland for 14 miles west, via the A47, to Sutton Cheney, where you'll see the turn-off to the site of the Battle of Bosworth.

❸ Bosworth Battlefield

Given a few hundred years, every battlefield ends up simply a field, but the site of the Battle of Bosworth – where Richard III met his maker in 1485 – is enlivened by the entertaining **Bosworth Battlefield Heritage Centre** (☎01455-290429; www.bosworthbattlefield.org.uk; Ambion Lane, Sutton Cheney CV13 0AD; adult/child £8.95/5.75, guided walk £4.50/3; ⌚heritage centre 10.30am-4pm Sat-Wed, grounds dawn-dusk), full of skeletons and musket balls. Although it lasted just a few hours, the Battle of Bosworth marked the end of the Plantagenet dynasty and the start of the Tudor era. This was where the mortally wounded Richard III famously proclaimed: 'A horse, a horse, my kingdom for a horse.' (Actually, he didn't: the quote was invented by that great Tudor propagandist William Shakespeare.) Enthusiasts in period costume re-enact the battle each August.

The Drive » It's 32 miles southwest from Bosworth, via the M69 (skirting the southeastern edge of Coventry) and the A46, to Warwick.

TRIP HIGHLIGHT

❹ Warwick

Regularly name-checked by Shakespeare, Warwick was the ancestral seat of the earls of Warwick, who played a pivotal role in the Wars of the Roses. Despite a devastating fire in 1694, Warwick remains a treasure-house of medieval architecture with rich veins of history and charming streets,

DETOUR: CHARLECOTE PARK

Start: ❹ Warwick

From Warwick, you can take a short 8.5-mile side trip southwest, via Stratford Rd and the southbound A429, to **Charlecote Park** (NT; ☎01789-470277; www.nationaltrust.org.uk; Loxley Lane, Charlecote CV35 9ER; house & garden adult/child £11.45/5.70, garden only £8/4; ⌚house 11am-4.30pm Thu-Tue mid-Mar–Oct, noon-3.30pm Thu-Tue mid-Feb–mid-Mar, noon-3.30pm Sat & Sun Nov & Dec, garden 9am-5pm Mar-Oct, to 4.30pm Nov-Feb). A youthful Shakespeare allegedly poached deer in the grounds of this lavish Elizabethan pile on the River Avon, and fallow deer still roam the grounds today. The interiors were restored from Georgian chintz to Tudor splendour in 1823. Highlights include Victorian kitchens, filled with culinary moulds, and an original 1551 Tudor gatehouse.

GARY PERKIN / SHUTTERSTOCK ©

Warwick Medieval re-enactment at Warwick Castle

dominated by the soaring turrets of **Warwick Castle** (☎01926-495421; www.warwick-castle.com; Castle Lane; castle adult/child £20/17, castle & dungeon £30/17; ⏰10am-5pm Apr-Sep, to 4pm Oct-Mar; P). Founded in 1068 by William the Conqueror, the ancestral home of the earls of Warwick remains impressively intact, and the Tussauds Group has filled the interior with flamboyant, family-friendly attractions that bring the castle's rich history to life. Waxworks populate the private apartments; there are also jousting tournaments, daily trebuchet firings, themed evenings and a dungeon. Discounted online tickets provide fast-track entry. You can even stay here – atmospheric **accommodation options** (☎0871 097 1228; www.warwick-castle.com; Warwick Castle; tower ste/lodge/glamping per night from £588/172/145; ⏰tower ste & lodge year-round, glamping Easter-Sep; P 📶) span tower suites to lodges at its riverside Knight's Village and themed tents in its 'glamping' ground.

✕ 🛏 p235

TRABANTOS / SHUTTERSTOCK ©

The Drive » Take Gallows Hill Rd southeast out of Warwick and continue southeast through farmland of potato and cabbage crops along with golden fields of flowering canola. It's 27 miles in total to Sulgrave Manor.

5 Sulgrave Manor

The impressively preserved Tudor mansion **Sulgrave Manor** (☎01295-760205; www.sulgravemanor.org.uk; Manor Rd, Sulgrave OX17 2SD; adult/child £7.20/3.60; ⏰11am-5pm Thu, Fri & Sun Apr-Sep) was built by Lawrence Washington in 1539. The Washington family lived here for almost 120 years before Colonel John Washington, the great-grandfather of America's first president George Washington, sailed to Virginia in 1656.

The Drive » From Sulgrave Manor it's a 21-mile drive northeast via Northampton Rd and the A5 to another famous family home, Althorp House.

6 Althorp House

The ancestral home of the Spencer family, **Althorp House** (☎01604-770107; www.spencerofalthorp.com; A428, Althorp NN7 4HQ; adult/child £14/7; ⏰11am-4pm Aug) – pronounced 'altrup' – is the final resting place of Diana, Princess of Wales, commemorated by a memorial. The outstanding art collection features works by Rubens, Gainsborough and van Dyck. Hours are seasonal and tickets are limited; pre-book by phone or online.

The Drive » Leaving Althorp House, head northeast, passing through the charming ivy-clad stone villages of Church Brampton and Chapel Brampton. You'll skirt the larger towns of Kettering and Corby, as well as the southern edge of Stamford, before reaching Burghley House (42 miles all up).

Stamford Burghley House

TRIP HIGHLIGHT

7 Burghley House

Set in more than 810 hectares of grounds, landscaped by Capability Brown, resplendent **Burghley House** (☎01780-752451; www.burghley.co.uk; Barnack Rd; house & garden adult/child £17/9, garden only £9.50/5.50, park free; ⏰house 10.30am-5pm Wed-Sun Apr-early Oct, garden 10.30am-1pm & 2-4.30pm daily Apr-Oct, park 7am-6pm daily year-round), pronounced 'bur-lee', was built by Queen Elizabeth I's chief adviser William Cecil, whose descendants still live here. It bristles with cupolas, pavilions, belvederes and chimneys; the lavish staterooms are a particular highlight. In early September the renowned Burghley Horse Trials take place here.

The estate is 1.3 miles southeast of Stamford, one of England's prettiest towns, with elegant streets lined with honey-coloured limestone buildings and hidden alleyways dotted with alehouses, interesting eating outlets and small independent boutiques. A forest of historic church spires rises overhead and the gently gurgling River Welland meanders through the town centre. It's a favourite with film-makers seeking the postcard vision of England, and has appeared in everything from *Pride and Prejudice* to *The Da Vinci Code*.

The Drive » It's a 17-mile trip from Burghley House via the A1 to Woolsthorpe Manor.

8 Woolsthorpe Manor

Sir Isaac Newton fans may feel the gravitational pull of the great man's birthplace, **Woolsthorpe Manor** (NT; ☎01476-862823;

www.nationaltrust.org.uk; Water Lane, NG33 5NR; house & grounds adult/child £9.20/4.60, grounds only £4.10/2.90; ⏰11am-5pm Wed-Mon mid-Mar–Oct, Fri-Sun Nov–mid-Mar). The humble 17th-century house contains reconstructions of Newton's rooms; the apple that inspired his theory of gravity allegedly fell from the tree in the garden. There's a nifty kids' science room and a cafe.

The Drive » The final 33-mile stretch of this trip, via the High Dike road, takes you past cauliflower, corn and wheat fields. At Waddington, look out to your right to see fighter jets landing at its famous RAF air base. As you approach Lincoln, you'll see its cathedral spires and castle crenulations rising up on the ridgeline to the north.

❾ Lincoln

Ringed by historic city gates – including the **Newport Arch** (Bailgate) on Bailgate, a relic from the original Roman settlement – Lincoln's historic centre is a tangle of cobbled medieval streets surrounding a colossal 12th-century **cathedral** (☎01522-561600; www.lincolncathedral.com; Minster Yard; cathedral adult/child £8/4.80 Mon-Sat; ⏰10am-4pm Mon-Sat, 11am-3.30pm Sun). Towering over the city like a medieval skyscraper, it's a breathtaking representation of divine power on earth. The great tower rising above the crossing is the third highest in England at 83m, but in medieval times, a lead-encased wooden spire added a further 79m, topping even the great pyramids of Giza. One-hour guided tours (included in admission) take place at least twice daily Monday to Saturday; there are also tours of the roof and tower (£5; book in advance).

Nearby **Lincoln Castle** (☎01522-554559; www.lincolncastle.com; Castle Hill; castle day ticket adult/child £14/7.50, walls only £10/5.50, grounds free; ⏰10am-5pm Apr-Sep, to 4pm Oct-Mar) was one of the first castles erected by the victorious William the Conqueror to keep his new kingdom in line, and offers awesome views over the city and miles of surrounding countryside. A major restoration program has opened up the entire castle walls and given the 1215 Magna Carta (one of only four copies) a swanky, subterranean new home. One-hour guided tours, included in castle admission, depart from the eastern gate – check the blackboard for times.

The lanes that topple over the edge of Lincoln Cliff are lined with Tudor town houses, ancient pubs and quirky independent stores. Flanking the River Witham at the base of the hill, the new town is less absorbing but the revitalised Brayford Waterfront development is a popular spot to watch the boats go by.

✕ 🛏 p235

Eating & Sleeping

Nottingham ❶

Delilah Fine Foods Deli, Cafe £

(☎0115-948 4461; www.delilahfinefoods.co.uk; 12 Victoria St; dishes £4-15, platters £19-26; ⏰9am-5pm Wed-Mon;) Impeccably selected cheeses (more than 150 varieties), pâtés, meats and more from artisan producers are available to take away or eat on-site at this foodie's fantasy land, housed in a grand former bank with mezzanine seating. It doesn't take reservations but you can pre-order customised hampers for a gourmet picnic.

Lace Market Hotel Boutique Hotel £££

(☎0115-948 4414; www.lacemarkethotel.co.uk; 29-31 High Pavement; s/d/ste incl breakfast from £76/140/194; P) In the heart of the gentrified Lace Market, this elegant Georgian town house has 42 sleek rooms with state-of-the-art furnishings and amenities, some with air-conditioning. Its adjoining pub, the **Cock & Hoop** (www.lacemarkethotel.co.uk; 25 High Pavement; ⏰noon-11pm Sun-Thu, to midnight Fri & Sat), serves real ales and traditional pub food all day.

Leicester ❷

Bobby's Indian £

(☎0116-266 0106; www.bobbys-restaurant.co.uk; 154-156 Belgrave Rd; dishes £5-7.50; ⏰11am-9pm Mon, Wed & Thu, to 10pm Fri, 10am-10pm Sat & Sun;) The top pick along Leicester's Golden Mile – lined with sari stores, jewellery emporiums and curry houses – is Bobby's, a 1970s-established institution serving all-vegetarian classics.

Belmont Hotel Hotel ££

(☎0116-254 4773; www.belmonthotel.co.uk; 20 De Montfort St; s/d/f/ste from £71/90/115/125; P @) Owned and run by the same family for four generations, the 19th-century Belmont has 74 stylish, contemporary, individually designed rooms and a fantastic location overlooking leafy New Walk. Family rooms have a double bed and bunks. Its restaurant is highly regarded; the two bars, Jamie's and Bowie's, open to a terrace and a conservatory respectively.

Warwick ❹

Old Coffee Tavern British ££

(☎01926-679737; www.theoldcoffeetavern.co.uk; 16 Old Sq; mains £10.50-15.50; ⏰kitchen 7am-10pm Mon-Fri, noon-10pm Sat, to 8pm Sun, bar 7am-11pm Mon-Thu, to 12.30am Fri, 8am-12.30am Sat, to 10pm Sun;) An 1880-built beauty with many of its Victorian features intact, this tavern was originally established as a teetotal alternative to Warwick's pubs. Today you can order real ales, craft ciders, cocktails and wines, along with elevated versions of British classics like toad-in-the-hole and chicken-and-ham-hock pie. Upstairs are 10 stylish oyster-toned guest rooms (doubles including breakfast from £125).

Lincoln ❾

Castle Hotel Boutique Hotel ££

(☎01522-538801; www.castlehotel.net; Westgate; s/d/coach house incl breakfast from £90/120/220; P) Each of the Castle Hotel's 18 rooms have been exquisitely refurbished in olive, truffle and oyster tones, as has its family-friendly four-person coach house. It was built on the site of Lincoln's Roman forum in 1852; the red-brick building's incarnations variously included a school and a WWII lookout station. Take advantage of great-value dinner, bed and breakfast deals with its award-winning restaurant **Reform** (☎01522-538801; www.reformrestaurant.co.uk; Castle Hotel, Westgate; mains £15-25; ⏰noon-2.30pm & 7-9pm Wed-Sat, noon-3pm Sun).

STRETCH YOUR LEGS STRATFORD-UPON-AVON

Start/Finish: Gower Memorial

Distance: 1.7 miles

Duration: Two hours

A willow-lined river and wonky black-and-white Tudor architecture set the stage for retracing the footsteps of the Bard at his birthplace, school room, home and final resting place, as well as the world-renowned theatres where his works come to life.

Take this walk on Trips

Gower Memorial

Designed by aristocratic sculptor Lord Ronald Gower, the multi-sculpture **Gower Memorial** (Bancroft Gardens, Bridge Foot), in the beautiful Bancroft Gardens, features the characters of Hamlet as well as the Bard himself.

The Walk » Follow Bridge St northwest and continue on Henley St to Shakespeare's Birthplace (500m in total).

Shakespeare's Birthplace

The jury is still out on whether Shakespeare's Birthplace (p202) is really where the Bard was born but devotees have been scratching their signatures onto the windows since at least the 19th century. Behind a modern facade are restored Tudor rooms, live presentations from famous Shakespearean characters, and an engaging Shakespeare exhibition.

The Walk » Continue northwest along Henley St. Turn southwest onto Windsor St; the American Fountain is just across the intersection on your left (260m all up).

American Fountain

Created by George W Childs in 1887 to mark Queen Victoria's Golden Jubilee, the ornate Victorian Gothic **American Fountain** (Market Sq, Rother St) clock tower was unveiled by the great Shakespearean actor Henry Irving (his tribute to the Bard is inscribed in the stonework).

The Walk » Take Rother St southwest and turn east onto Ely St. At Chapel St, turn southwest; New Place is on your left (450m in total).

Shakespeare's New Place

When Shakespeare retired, he swapped London's bright lights for a comfortable town house at **New Place** (☎01789-338536; www.shakespeare.org.uk; cnr Chapel St & Chapel Lane; adult/child £12.50/8; ⏰10am-5pm Apr-Aug, to 4.30pm Sep & Oct, to 3.30pm Nov-Feb), where he died of unknown causes in April 1616. The house was demolished in 1759, but there's an Elizabethan knot garden, and a major

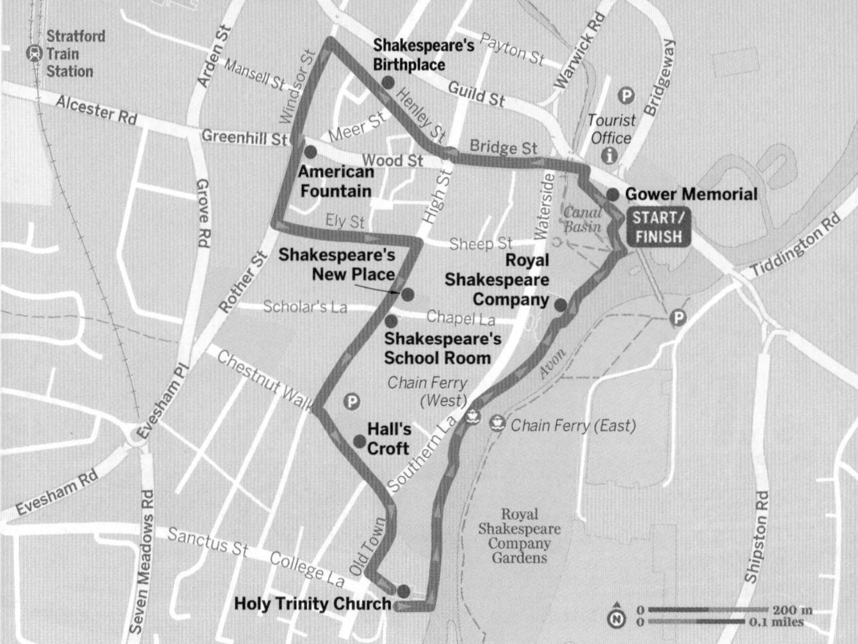

restoration project has uncovered Shakespeare's kitchen.

The Walk » It's a 50m stroll southwest along Chapel St, which becomes Church St, to Shakespeare's School Room.

Shakespeare's School Room

Shakespeare's alma mater, King Edward VI School, incorporates a vast black-and-white timbered building, dating from 1420, that was once the town's guildhall. Upstairs in **Shakespeare's School Room** (☎01789-203170; www.shakespearesschoolroom.org; King Edward VI School, Church St; adult/child £8.50/5.50, combination ticket with MAD Museum £13.10/8.60; ⏲11am-5pm) you can sit in on mock-Tudor lessons.

The Walk » Head southwest along Church St, then turn southeast onto Old Town; Hall's Croft is on your left (400m in total).

Hall's Croft

Shakespeare's daughter Susanna and her husband, respected doctor John Hall, lived in the handsome Jacobean town house **Hall's Croft** (☎01789-338533; www.shakespeare.org.uk; Old Town; adult/child £8.50/5.50; ⏲10am-5pm Apr-Aug, to 4.30pm Sep & Oct, 11am-3.30pm Nov-Feb).

The Walk » Continue southeast for 220m on Old Town; you'll see Holy Trinity Church on your left.

Holy Trinity Church

The Bard's final resting place is within Holy Trinity Church (p202).

The Walk » Take the riverside path north, passing the hand-wound, summer-operating Chain Ferry that yo-yos across the Avon, to the Royal Shakespeare Theatre (500m all up).

Royal Shakespeare Theatre

One of three stages belonging to the Royal Shakespeare Company (p202), the Royal Shakespeare Theatre has witnessed legendary thespians' performances.

The Walk » It's 200m northeast along the river from the theatre to the Gower Memorial.

Lake District & Northern England

Inspirational landscapes deliver inspirational drives. And this swathe of northern England has long been a muse to many. Wordsworth, the Brontës and Beatrix Potter all drew on its natural splendour, and every bend in the road still reveals extraordinary views. In the west, the Lake District National Park gifts you the classic Lakes experience: craggy hilltops, glittering water and mountain tarns. Point the car east to discover the pretty villages and wilderness moors of Yorkshire's Dales. Head still further east to encounter historic York and a coast full of charm. To the north lie thriving Newcastle-upon-Tyne, Northumberland's otherworldly beaches and the Roman remains of Hadrian's Wall.

Keswick Rowboats and the Keswick Launch
DANIEL_KAY / SHUTTERSTOCK ©

Lake District & Northern England

ANDREW ROLAND / SHUTTERSTOCK ©

Grasmere Rolling hills outside the village

19 **Classic Lakes 5 Days**
Literary links aplenty, England's highest hill and utterly unforgettable views.

20 **Yorkshire Dales 3–4 Days**
A classy spa town and thrilling climbs up England's most spectacular roads.

21 **North York Moors & Coast 4–5 Days**
Combines medieval York, wild moorlands, stately Castle Howard and salty fishing ports.

22 **Hadrian's Wall 3–4 Days**
An evocative, fort-studded route tracing the length of these unique Roman remains.

23 **Northumbria 3–4 Days**
Fishing ports, castles, a sacred island and breathtaking stretches of sand.

DON'T MISS

Tynemouth
Hanging ten at one of the best surf spots in England at this vast, Blue Flag golden beach. Trip 23

North Yorkshire Moors Railway
Hopping on a train at the station immortalised as Hogsmeade in the Harry Potter films. Trip 21

Hardknott Pass & Wrynose Pass
Driving England's two steepest road routes – where gradients reach 30%. Trip 19

Chesters Roman Fort & Museum
Roaming the superbly preserved living quarters of a cavalry unit, based at Hadrian's Wall. Trip 22

Tan Hill Inn
Sipping a drink and getting a warm welcome at Britain's highest pub (elevation 528m). Trip 20

Classic Trip

Classic Lakes

Beloved of poets and painters, this road trip takes in the scenic wonders of the UK's largest and loveliest national park.

TRIP HIGHLIGHTS

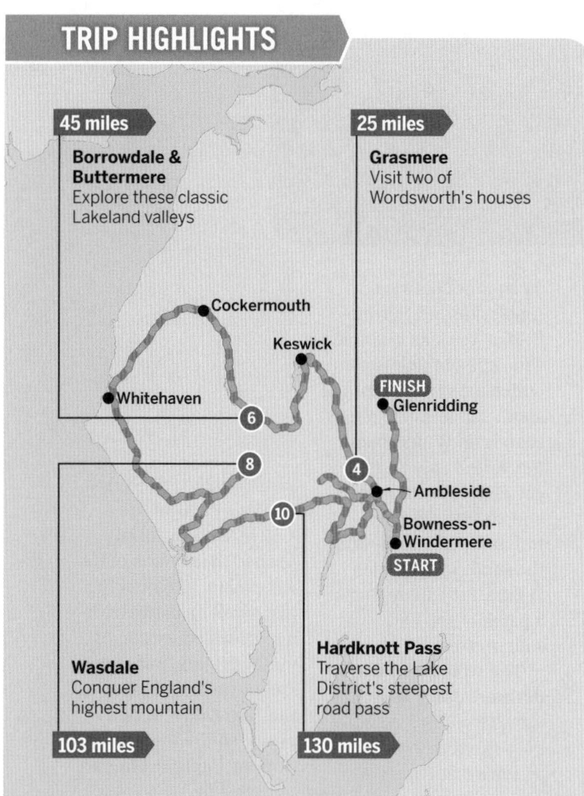

5 DAYS
162 MILES / 260KM

GREAT FOR...

BEST TIME TO GO

Summer and Easter can be hectic in the Lakes; spring and autumn are best.

ESSENTIAL PHOTO

Striking a pose in Wasdale, surrounded by England's highest hills.

BEST FOR FAMILIES

Bike trails, sculptures and zip lines at Grizedale Forest.

Wasdale Valley A dramatic Ice-Age valley

Classic Trip

19 Classic Lakes

William Wordsworth, Samuel Taylor Coleridge and Beatrix Potter are just a few of the literary luminaries who have fallen in love with the Lake District. It's been a national park since 1951, and is studded by England's highest hills (fells), including the highest of all, Scafell Pike. This drive takes in lakes, forest, hills and valleys, with country houses, hill walks and cosy pubs thrown in for good measure.

1 Bowness-on-Windermere

At 10.5 miles long, Windermere is the largest body of water in England: more a loch than a lake. It's also one of the most popular places in the Lake District, and has been a tourist centre since the late 19th century, especially for lake cruises.

Windermere gets its name from the old Norse, 'Vinandr mere' (Vinandr's lake; so 'Lake Windermere' is actually tautologous). Encompassing 5.7 sq miles between Ambleside and Newby Bridge, the lake is a mile wide at its broadest point, with a maximum depth of about 220m. There are 18 islands on Windermere: the largest is Belle Isle, encompassing 16 hectares and an 18th-century Italianate mansion, while the smallest is Maiden Holme, little more than a patch of soil and a solitary tree.

The wonderful **Windermere Jetty Museum** (☎01539-637940; www.lakelandarts.org.uk/windermere-jetty-museum; Rayrigg Rd; adult/child £9/4.50; ⏰10am-5pm Mar-Oct, 10.30am-4.30pm Nov-Feb), finally opened after years of development, explores the history of cruising with a glorious collection of vintage boats, punts and steam yachts – including the *Esperance*, which provided the inspiration for Captain Flint's

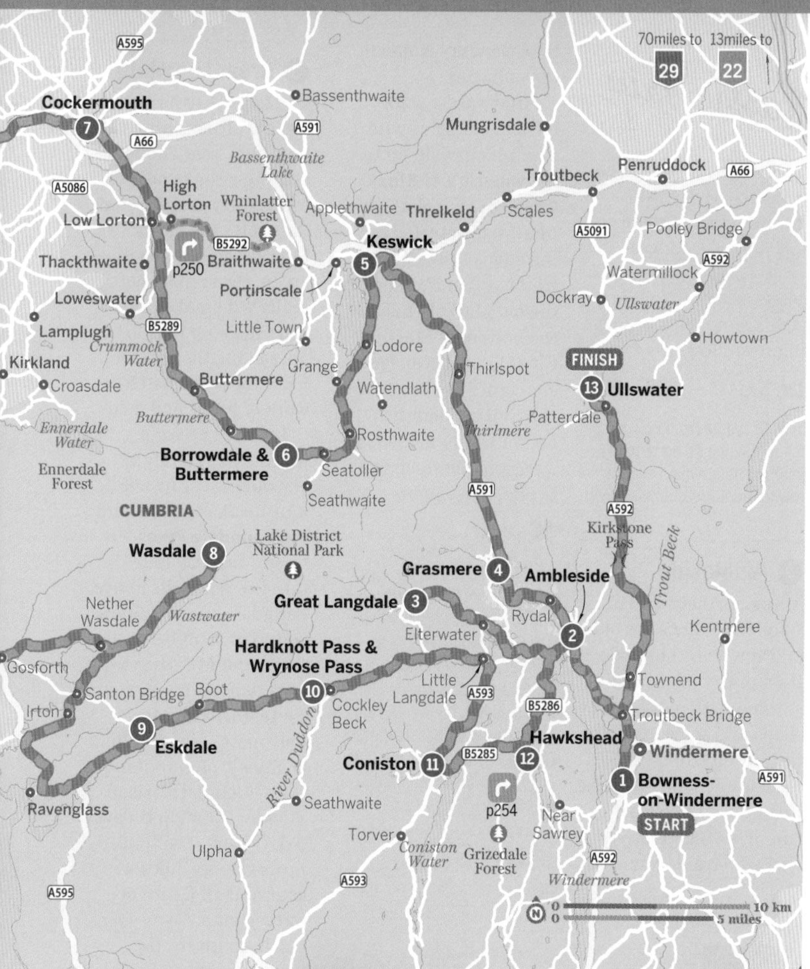

houseboat in Arthur Ransome's *Swallows and Amazons*. Best of all, you can take your own trip aboard the 1902 *Osprey* or the 1930 *Penelope II*. There's simply no more stylish way to see Windermere.

LINK YOUR TRIP

22 Hadrian's Wall

From Windermere, head north to Carlisle to explore Roman England's most ambitious structure.

29 The Borders

The Lake District is an obvious launch pad for travels north of the Scottish border; Glasgow is 130 miles from Ullswater.

Alternatively, **Windermere Lake Cruises** (01539-443360; www.windermere-lakecruises.co.uk; cruises from £9.50) offers sightseeing trips departing from Bowness Pier.

p255

The Drive » From Bowness, follow Rayrigg Rd north until it joins the A591, which rolls all the way to Ambleside, 6 miles north.

2 Ambleside

At the northern end of Windermere lies the old mill town of Ambleside. It's a pretty place, well stocked with outdoors shops and some excellent restaurants: don't miss a meal at the fabulous Lake Road Kitchen (p255), run by an imaginative chef who trained at the legendary Noma in Copenhagen.

Afterwards, work off some calories with a half-hour walk up to the waterfall of **Stock Ghyll Force**, a clattering 18m-high waterfall on the edge of town. The trail is signposted behind the old Market Hall at the bottom of Stock Ghyll Lane. If you feel energetic, you can follow the trail beyond the falls up Wansfell Pike (482m), a reasonably steep walk of about two hours.

p255

The Drive » Take the A593 west towards Skelwith Bridge, and follow signs to Elterwater and Great Langdale. It's a wonderful 8-mile drive that gets wilder and wilder the deeper you head into the valley. There's a large car park beside the Old Dungeon Ghyll Hotel, but it gets busy in summer; there's usually overflow parking available in a nearby field.

3 Great Langdale

The Lake District has some truly stunning valleys, but Great Langdale definitely ranks near the top. As you pass through the pretty village of **Elterwater** and its village green, the scenery gets really wild and empty. Fells stack up like dominoes along the horizon, looming over a patchwork of barns and fields.

If you're up for a hike, then you might consider tackling the multipeak circuit around the **Langdale Pikes** – a tough, full-day hike into the wild fells above Langdale, which allows you to pick off between three and five summits depending on your route, including the four main 'Pikes' of Pike O' Stickle (709m), Loft Crag (682m), Harrison Stickle (736m) and Pavey Ark (700m). You'll need proper boots, hiking gear and an Ordnance Survey map.

Alternatively, the more sedentary option is to just admire the views over a pint of locally brewed ale from the cosy bar of the **Old Dungeon Ghyll** (01539-437272; www.odg.co.uk; Great Langdale; s £62.50, d £116-135; P), a classic hikers' haunt.

The Drive » Retrace the road to Ambleside and head north to Grasmere on the A591 for 5 miles.

TOP TIP: NATIONAL TRUST MEMBERSHIP

Being a member of the **National Trust** (NT; www.nationaltrust.org.uk) comes in very handy in the Lake District. The Trust owns several key attractions, including Hill Top and the Beatrix Potter Gallery near Hawkshead, Wordsworth House in Cockermouth and Fell Foot and Wray Castle near Windermere. Best of all, you get to park for free at all the NT's car parks – handy in celebrated beauty spots like Buttermere, Borrowdale, Wasdale, Gowbarrow Park and Tarn Hows.

TRIP HIGHLIGHT

4 Grasmere

The lovely little village of Grasmere is inextricably linked with the poet William Wordsworth, who made it his home in the late 18th century and never left unless he really had to. Two of his houses are now open to the public. The most famous is **Dove Cottage** (01539-435544; www.wordsworth.org.uk; adult/child £9.50/4.50; 9.30am-5.30pm Mar-Oct, 10am-4.30pm Nov, Dec & Feb), a tiny house where he lived with his sister Dorothy, wife Mary and three children between 1798 and 1808. Guided tours explore the house, and next door the Jerwood Museum has lots of memorabilia and original manuscripts relating to the Romantic poets.

A little way south of Grasmere is the house where Wordsworth spent most of his adult life, **Rydal Mount** (01539-433002; www.rydalmount.co.uk; adult/child £7.50/4, grounds only £5; 9.30am-5pm Apr-Oct, 11am-4pm Wed-Sun Nov, Dec, Feb & Mar). It's still owned by the poet's descendants, and is a much grander affair than Dove Cottage: you can have a look around the library, visit the poet's attic study and wander around the gardens he designed. Below the house, **Dora's Field** is filled with daffodils in springtime; it was planted in memory of Wordsworth's daughter, who died of tuberculosis.

If you have a sweet tooth, you'll also want to pick up a souvenir at **Sarah Nelson's Gingerbread Shop** (01539-435428; www.grasmeregingerbread.co.uk; Church Cottage; 9.15am-5.30pm Mon-Sat, 12.30-5pm Sun), which still makes its gingerbread to a recipe formulated in 1854.

p255

The Drive » From Grasmere, continue north on the A591. You'll pass through the dramatic pass known as Dunmail Raise, where a great battle is said to have taken place between the Saxons and the Celtic king Dunmail, who was slain near the pass. Stay on the road past the lake of Thirlmere all the way to Keswick (13 miles).

5 Keswick

Another of the Lake District's classic market towns, Keswick is a place that revolves around the great outdoors. Several big fells lie on its doorstep, including the imposing lump of **Skiddaw** and the dramatic ridge of **Blencathra**, but it's the lake of **Derwentwater** that really draws the eye: it was said to be Beatrix Potter's favourite, and she supposedly got the idea for Squirrel Nutkin while watching red squirrels frolicking on its shores.

The **Keswick Launch** (01768-772263; www.keswick-launch.co.uk; round-the-lake pass adult/child/family £11/5.70/27.50) travels out around the lake year-round: you could combine it with an easy hike up to the top of **Catbells** (451m), a favourite first-time fell for many walkers. The views of the lake and the distant hills are absolutely breathtaking.

Back in town, don't miss a visit to **George Fisher** (01768-772178; www.georgefisher.co.uk; 2 Borrowdale Rd; 9am-5.30pm Mon-Sat, 10am-4pm Sun), the most famous outdoors shop in the Lake District: if you need a new pair of hiking boots, this is definitely the place to come.

p255

The Drive » The drive into Borrowdale on the B5289 is a beauty, passing several pretty villages as it travels through the valley. You can't get lost en route to Honister Pass (10 miles from Keswick) – there's only one road to take; Buttermere lies on the other side of the pass. You'll want to stop for numerous photos on the way.

TRIP HIGHLIGHT

6 Borrowdale & Buttermere

South of Keswick, the B5289 tracks along the eastern side of Derwentwater and enters the bucolic valley of Borrowdale, a classic Lakeland canvas of fields, fells, streams and endless

JUSTIN FOULKES / LONELY PLANET ©

RICHARD WHITCOMBE / SHUTTERSTOCK ©

WHY THIS IS A CLASSIC TRIP

OLIVER BERRY, WRITER

For classic English scenery, nowhere quite compares to the Lake District. With its fells and waterfalls, valleys and villages, lakes and meadows, it's like a postcard that's come to life. It's visited by some 13 million people every year, but it's still easy to find peace and serenity – whether it's rowing across a lake, cycling through the countryside or standing atop a fell. Pack spare memory cards – you'll need them.

Above: Hiker atop Haystacks, looking over Buttermere
Left: Hiking up Scafell Pike
Right: Shoppers and tourists in Keswick

drystone walls. It's worth stopping off to see the geological oddity of the **Bowder Stone**, a huge boulder deposited by a glacier, and for a quick hike up to the top of **Castle Crag**, which has the best views of the valley.

Then it's up and over the perilously steep **Honister Pass**, where the Lake District's last working **slate mine** (☎01768-777230; www.honister.com; mine tour adult/child £17.50/9.50, all-day pass incl mine tour & classic/extreme via ferrata £55/47; ⏲10am-5pm) is still doing a thriving trade. You can take a guided tour down into the mine or brave the heights along the stomach-upsetting via ferrata, and pick up slate souvenirs in the shop.

Nearby Buttermere has a sparkling twinset of lakes, **Buttermere** and **Crummock Water**, and is backed by a string of impressive fells. The summit of **Haystacks** is a popular route: it was the favourite fell of Alfred Wainwright, who penned the definitive seven-volume set of guidebooks of the Lake District's fells between the 1950s and '70s. It's a two- to three-hour return walk from Buttermere.

The Drive » From Buttermere village, bear left on the B5289 signed towards Loweswater and Crummock Water, which continues into the Lorton Valley. At Low Lorton, stay on the B5289, which continues 4 miles

to Cockermouth. (Total distance: 11 miles.)

7 Cockermouth

Grasmere might be Wordsworth central, but completists will want to visit the poet's **childhood home** (NT; ☎01900-824805; www.nationaltrust.org.uk/wordsworth-house; Main St; adult/child £8.80/4.40; ⏰11am-5pm Sat-Thu Mar-Oct) in Cockermouth. Now owned by the National Trust, it's been redecorated in period style according to details published in Wordsworth's own father's accounts: you can wander round the drawing room, kitchen, pantry and garden, and see the rooms where little Willie and his brother John slept. Costumed guides wander around the house for added period authenticity. Outside is the walled kitchen garden mentioned in Wordsworth's autobiographical epic *The Prelude*.

The Drive » Head west on the A66 and detour onto the A595, which tracks the coast all the way to Whitehaven. To reach Wasdale (35 miles all up), turn off at Gosforth, and then follow signs to Nether Wasdale and Wasdale Head. It's quite easy to miss the turning, so keep your eyes peeled; satnavs can be very unreliable here.

TRIP HIGHLIGHT

8 Wasdale

Wild Wasdale is arguably the most dramatic valley in the national park. Carving its way for 5 miles from the coast, it was gouged out by a long-extinct glacier during the last Ice Age; if you look closely you can still see glacial marks on the scree-strewn slopes above Wastwater. It's a truly dramatic drive that feels rather like heading into the depths of a remote Scottish glen: in terms of mountain scenery, it's probably the most impressive stretch of road this side of the Highlands.

Most people come for the chance to reach the summit of **Scafell Pike**, England's highest point (978m); it's a tough six- to seven-hour slog, but the views from the top are quite literally as good as they get (assuming the weather plays ball, of course).

Afterwards, reward yourself with a meal at the **Wasdale Head Inn** (☎01946-726229; www.wasdale.com; s/d/tr £60/120/180; P 📶), a gloriously olde-worlde hostelry with lashings of mountain heritage: it was here that the sport of rock climbing was pioneered in the mid-19th century.

The Drive » Retrace your route to Gosforth, and take the coast road (A595) south to Ravenglass and follow signs to Eskdale (22 miles). Alternatively, there's a shortcut into Eskdale via Nether Wasdale and Santon Bridge, but it's easy to get lost, especially if you're relying on satnav; a good road map is really handy here.

DETOUR: WHINLATTER FOREST PARK

Start: 6 Buttermere

Encompassing 4.6 sq miles of pine, larch and spruce, **Whinlatter** (www.forestry.gov.uk/whinlatter) is England's only true mountain forest, rising sharply to 790m about 5 miles from Keswick. The forest is a designated red squirrel reserve; you can check out live video feeds from squirrel cams at the visitor centre. It's also home to two exciting mountain-bike trails and a treetop assault course. You can hire bikes next to the visitor centre.

To get to Whinlatter Forest Park from Buttermere, look out for the right turn onto the B5292 at Low Lorton, which climbs up to Whinlatter Pass.

9 Eskdale

The valley of Eskdale was once a centre for mineral mining, and a miniature steam train was built to carry ore down from the hillsides to the coast. Now known as the **Ravenglass & Eskdale Railway** (☎01229-717171; www.ravenglass-railway.co.uk; adult/child return £18/12; 👪) (or La'al Ratty to locals), its miniature choo-choos are a beloved Lakeland attraction. They chuff for 7 miles along the valley from the station at Ravenglass to the final terminus at Dalegarth, stopping at several stations in between. Nearby, the **Boot Inn** (☎019467-23224; www.thebooteskdale.co.uk; Boot; mains £10-18) makes a pleasant stop for lunch.

The Drive » Since you're driving, the most sensible idea is to park near Dalegarth Station, ride the train to Ravenglass and back, and then set off for Hardknott Pass. There's only one road east. Take it and get ready for a hair-raising, white-knuckle drive. It's 6 (very steep!) miles from Eskdale to Hardknott Pass.

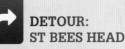

DETOUR: ST BEES HEAD

Start: 7 Cockermouth

Cumbria's coastline might not have the white sandy beaches of Wales or the epic grandeur of the Scottish coast, but it has a bleak beauty all of its own – not to mention a renowned seabird reserve at **St Bees Head** (RSPB; stbees.head@rspb.org.uk), where you can spot species including fulmars, herring gulls, kittiwakes and razorbills – as well as England's only nesting black guillemots at nearby Fleswick Bay. Just try and forget the fact that one of the UK's largest nuclear reactors, Sellafield, is round the corner.

The village of St Bees lies 5 miles south of Whitehaven, and the headland is signposted from there.

TRIP HIGHLIGHT

10 Hardknott Pass & Wrynose Pass

At the eastern end of Eskdale lie England's two steepest road passes, Hardknott and Wrynose. Reaching 30% gradient in some places, and with precious few passing places on the narrow, single-file road, they're absolutely not for the faint-hearted or for nervous drivers – but the views are amazing, and they're doable if you take things slow (although it's probably best to leave the caravan or motor home in the garage). Make sure your car has plenty of oil and water, as you'll do much of the road in 1st gear, and the strain on the engine can be taxing. Take it slow, and take breaks – you need to keep your focus on the road ahead.

From Eskdale, the road ascends via a series of very sharp, steep switchbacks to the remains of **Hardknott Fort**, a Roman outpost where you can still see the remains of some of the walls. Soon after you reach **Hardknott Pass** at 393m (1289ft). The vistas here are magnificent: you'll be able to see all the way to the coast on a clear day. Next you'll drop down into Cockley Beck before continuing the climb up to **Wrynose Pass** (393m/1289ft). Near the summit is a small car park containing the **Three Shire Stone**, where the counties of Cumberland, Westmorland and Lancashire historically met. Then it's a slow descent down through hairpins and corners to the packhorse Slaters Bridge and on into the valley of **Little Langdale**. Phew! You made it.

The Drive » Once you reach Little Langdale, follow the road east until you reach the A593, the main road between Skelwith Bridge and Coniston. Turn right and follow it for 5 miles.

Classic Trip

11 Coniston

South of Ambleside, the old mining village of Coniston is dominated by its hulking fell, the **Old Man of Coniston**, an ever-popular objective for hikers, but it's perhaps best known for the world speed record attempts made here by father and son Malcolm and Donald Campbell between the 1930s and 1960s. Though they jointly broke many records, in 1967 Donald was tragically killed during an attempt in his jetboat *Bluebird;* the little **Ruskin Museum** (☎015394-41164; www.ruskin-museum.com; adult/child £6.50/3.25; ⏱10am-4.30pm mid-Mar–mid-Nov) has the full story.

Coniston Water is also said to have been the inspiration for Arthur Ransome's classic children's tale, *Swallows and Amazons*. The best way to explore is aboard the **Steam Yacht Gondola** (NT; ☎01539-0432733; www.nationaltrust.org.uk/steam-yacht-gondola; Coniston Jetty; cruises adult/child/family £17/8.50/38), a beautifully restored steam yacht built in 1859. It travels over the lake to the stately home of **Brantwood** (☎01539-441396; www.brantwood.org.uk; gardens only adult/child £6.20/free; ⏱10.30am-5pm), owned by the Victorian polymath, critic, painter and inveterate collector John Ruskin. The house is packed with furniture and crafts, and the gardens are glorious.

🛏 p255

The Drive » Heading north from Coniston, turn right onto the B5285 up Hawkshead Hill. You'll pass Tarn Hows and the Drunken Duck en route to Hawkshead, about 4 miles east.

12 Hawkshead

If you're searching for the perfect chocolate-box lakeland village, look no further – you've found it in Hawkshead, an improbably pretty confection of whitewashed cottages, winding lanes and slate roofs. It's car-free, so you can wander at will: don't miss the **Beatrix Potter Gallery**, which has a collection of the artist's original watercolours and botanical paintings (she had a particular fascination with fungi).

Nearby, it's worth making a detour to have a stroll around the lake of **Tarn Hows** (NT; www.nationaltrust.org.uk/coniston-and-tarn-hows) – a bucolic place, but one that's artificially created (it was made by joining three neighbouring tarns in the 19th century).

HILL TOP

Two miles from Hawkshead in the tiny village of Near Sawrey, the idyllic cottage at **Hill Top** (NT; ☎01539-436269; www.nationaltrust.org.uk/hill-top; garden adult/child £5/2.50; ⏱10am-5.30pm Jun-Aug, to 4.30pm Sat-Thu Apr, May, Sep & Oct, weekends only Nov-Mar) is the most famous house in the whole of the Lake District. It belonged to Beatrix Potter, and was used as inspiration for many of her tales: the house features directly in *Samuel Whiskers, Tom Kitten, Pigling Bland* and *Jemima Puddle-Duck,* and you will doubtless recognise the kitchen garden from *Peter Rabbit.*

Following her death in 1943, Beatrix bequeathed Hill Top (along with more than 1600 hectares of land) to the National Trust, with the proviso that the house be left with her belongings and decor untouched. The house formed the centrepiece for celebrations to mark the author's 150th birthday in 2016.

It's probably the Lake District's most popular attraction, however, so don't expect to have it all to yourself...

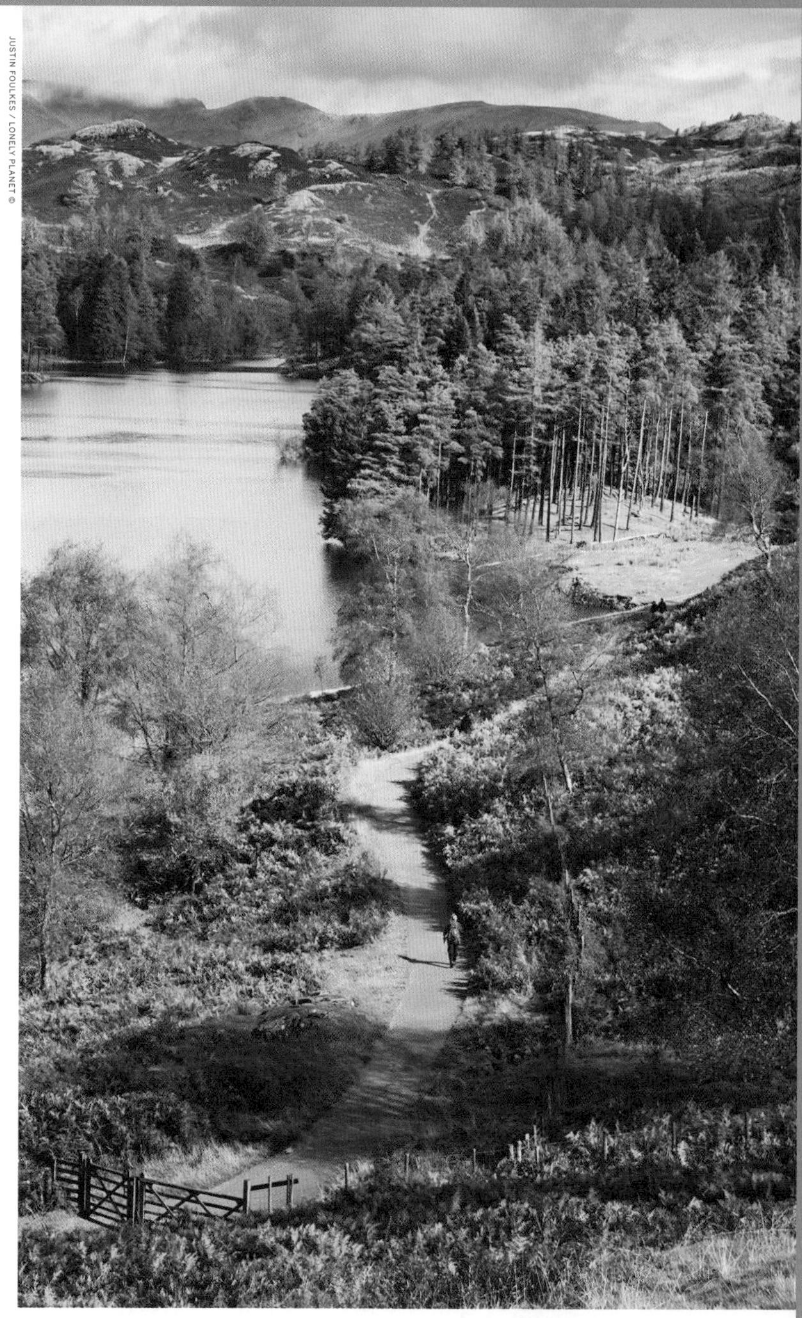

JUSTIN FOULKES / LONELY PLANET ©

Hawkshead Walking around Tarn Hows lake

After your walk, pop in for lunch at the Lake District's finest dining pub, the wonderfully named Drunken Duck.

p255

The Drive » Head back to Ambleside and then follow the A591 back towards Windermere. Just before you reach it, take the turn-off onto the A592 to Troutbeck Bridge, which climbs up to the lofty Kirkstone Pass – at 454m this is the highest mountain pass in Cumbria that's open to road traffic. It's steep, but it's a main A road so it's well maintained.

DETOUR: GRIZEDALE FOREST

Start: 12 Hawkshead

Stretching for more than 2400 hectares across the hilltops between Coniston Water and Esthwaite Water, **Grizedale Forest** (www.forestry.gov.uk/grizedale) is a wonderful place for a wander. It's criss-crossed by cycling trails, and is also home to more than 40 outdoor sculptures created by artists since 1977, including a xylophone and a man of the forest. There's an online guide at www.grizedalesculpture.org. As you leave the Hawkshead car park, you'll immediately see a brown sign for Grizedale, heading right onto North Lonsdale Rd. Just follow the brown signs from here – it's 3 miles' drive from the village.

13 Ullswater

From the windlashed heights of Kirkstone Pass, the A592 loops down towards the last stop on this jaunt around the Lake District: stately Ullswater, the national park's second-largest lake (after Windermere). It's an impressive sight, its silvery surface framed by jagged fells and plied by the puttering **Ullswater 'Steamers'** (☎01768-482229; www.ullswater-steamers.co.uk; cruise 'all piers' pass adult/child £16.80/10.10); you can also hire your own vessels from the Glenridding Sailing Centre.

As you skirt up the lake's western edge, it's worth stopping for a walk around **Gowbarrow Park** (NT; www.nationaltrust.org.uk), where there's a clattering waterfall to admire called **Aira Force**, and impressive displays of daffodils in springtime (Wordsworth dreamt up his most famous poem while walking nearby).

For an epic end to the trip, strap on your hiking boots and tackle the famous ridge climb via Striding Edge to the summit of **Helvellyn**, the Lake District's third-highest mountain at 950m. You'll need a head for heights, but you'll feel a real sense of achievement: you've just conquered perhaps the finest hill walk in all of England.

Eating & Sleeping

Bowness-on-Windermere ❶

Rum Doodle B&B ££

(☎01539-445967; www.rumdoodlewindermere.com; Sunny Bank Rd, Windermere Town; d £79-139; P 📶) Named after a classic travel novel about a fictional mountain in the Himalaya, this B&B zings with imagination. Its rooms are themed after places and characters in the book, with details such as book-effect wallpaper, vintage maps and old suitcases. Top of the heap is the Summit, snug under the eaves with a separate sitting room. Two-night minimum in summer.

Ambleside ❷

Lake Road Kitchen Bistro £££

(☎01539-422012; www.lakeroadkitchen.co.uk; Lake Rd; 5-/8-course tasting menu £65/90; ⏲6-9.30pm Wed-Sun) Quite simply one of the hottest places to dine in the Lakes. Its Noma-trained head chef, James Cross, explores 'cold climate' cooking (think Scandi-inspired, impeccably presented and laced with experimental ingredients aplenty). From shore-sourced seaweed to pickled vegetables and forest-picked mushrooms, the flavours are constantly surprising – and the stripped-back styling feels very appropriate.

Grasmere ❹

Forest Side Boutique Hotel £££

(☎01539-435250; www.theforestside.com; Keswick Rd; r £189-369; P 📶) This boutique beauty – a former hunting lodge – is hard to top for luxury. Renovated at huge expense by hotelier Andrew Wildsmith, it's a design temple: crushed-velvet sofas, Zoffany fabrics, stag heads and 20 country-chic rooms from 'Cosy' to 'Master'. Its restaurant is Michelin-starred, and the grounds (including a working kitchen garden) are gorgeous.

Keswick ❺

Cottage in the Wood Hotel £££

(☎01768-778409; www.thecottageinthewood.co.uk; Braithwaite; lunch/dinner menu £40/55; ⏲lunch 12.30-1.30pm, dinner 6.30-9.30pm; P 📶) Under chef Ben Wilkinson, this Michelin-starred coaching inn en route to Whinlatter Pass has become Keswick's premier dining destination. The food is seasonal, flavoursome and delicately presented – the Taste Cumbria menu (themed around Stream, Woodland, Coasts and Fells) is an inventive delight. If you fancy making a night of it, sleek rooms survey woods and countryside.

Coniston ⓫

Bank Ground Farm B&B ££

(☎01539-441264; www.bankground.com; East of the Lake Rd; d from £110; P) This lakeside farmhouse has literary cachet: Arthur Ransome used it as the model for Holly Howe Farm in *Swallows and Amazons*. Parts of the house date back to the 15th century, so the rooms are snug. Some have sleigh beds, others exposed beams. The tearoom is a beauty, and there are cottages for longer stays. Two-night minimum.

Hawkshead ⓬

Drunken Duck Pub Food £££

(☎01539-436347; www.drunkenduckinn.co.uk; Barngates; mains £24; ⏲noon-2.30pm & 6-8.45pm; P 📶) Long one of the Lakes' premier dining destinations, the Drunken Duck is a blend of historic pub and fine-dining restaurant. On a wooded crossroads on the top of Hawkshead Hill, it's renowned for its luxurious food and home-brewed ales, and the flagstones and sporting prints conjure a convincing country atmosphere. Book well ahead.

If you fancy staying, you'll find the rooms (£125 to £250) are as fancy as the food. The pub's tricky to find: drive along the B5286 from Hawkshead towards Ambleside and look for the brown signs.

R A KEARTON / GETTY IMAGES ©

Yorkshire Dales

This roller coaster of a route leads you through the finest scenery in the Yorkshire Dales, from pretty villages and country pubs to limestone crags and windswept moors.

TRIP HIGHLIGHTS

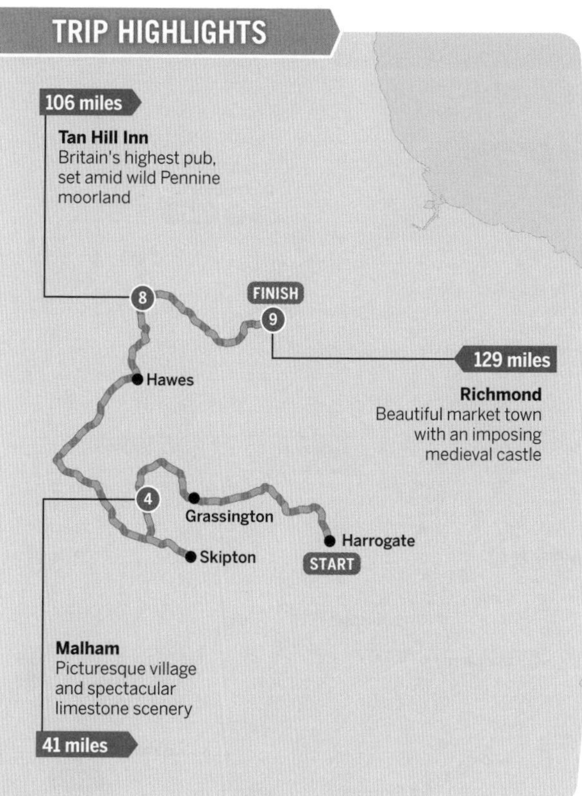

3–4 DAYS 129 MILES / 208KM

GREAT FOR...

BEST TIME TO GO

May and June see wildflowers add a splash of colour to the scenery.

ESSENTIAL PHOTO

The view north from the summit of Buttertubs Pass.

BEST FOR OUTDOORS

Hiking to the top of Malham Cove's spectacular cliff.

Richmond Market square seen from Richmond Castle

20 Yorkshire Dales

The winding road over the Buttertubs Pass – a favourite of TV motoring programmes and a highlight of the Yorkshire *grand départ* of 2014's Tour de France cycling race – is regularly voted the most spectacular road in England. This trip adds a second thrilling road climb, from Arncliffe to Malham, to link six of the national park's most beautiful dales in a tour de force of scenic splendour.

❶ Harrogate

The quintessential Victorian spa town, prim and pretty Harrogate has long been associated with a kind of old-fashioned Englishness – it is fitting that the town's most famous visitor was crime novelist Agatha Christie, who fled here incognito in 1926 to escape her broken marriage. It was also Queen Victoria's favourite spot for a spa break.

Wander around the **Montpellier Quarter** (www.montpellierharrogate.com), an area of

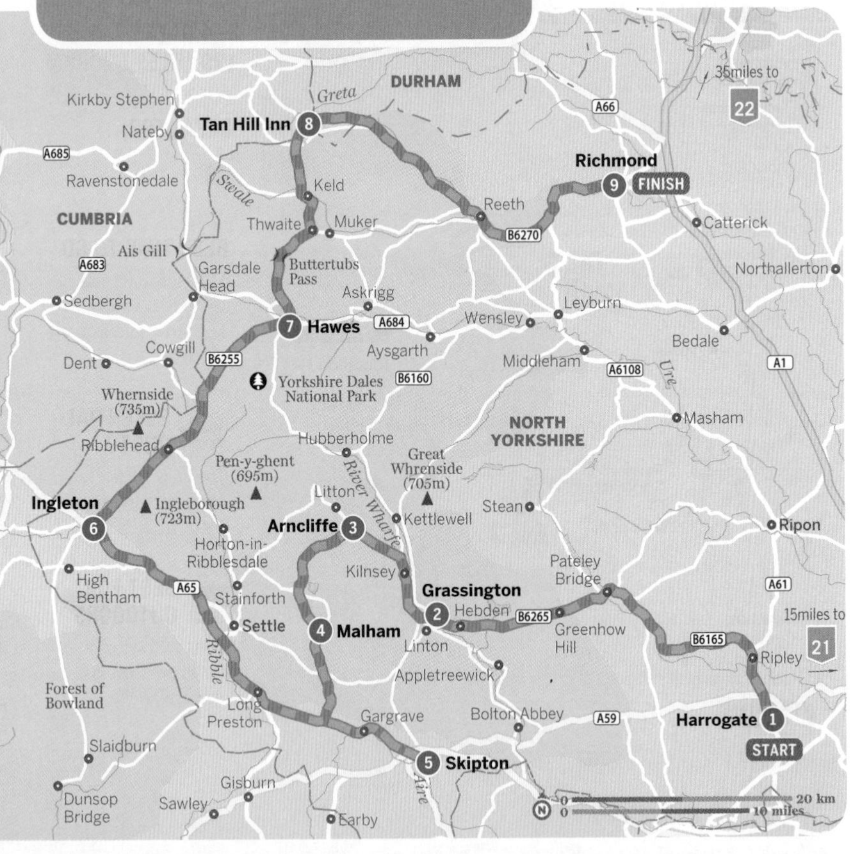

pedestrianised streets lined with restored 19th-century buildings that are now home to art galleries, antique shops, fashion boutiques, cafes and restaurants, and learn all about the town's history in the ornate **Royal Pump Room Museum** (www.harrogate.gov.uk; Crown Pl; adult/child £3/1; ⏲10.30am-5pm Mon-Sat, 2-5pm Sun Apr-Oct, to 4pm Nov-Mar), built in 1842 over the most famous of the town's sulphurous springs.

If you feel like sampling the waters for yourself, take a dip in the town's ornate **Turkish Baths** (☎01423-556746; www.turkishbathsharrogate.co.uk; Parliament St; Mon from 6pm & Tue-Thu £19, Mon & Fri £23, Sat & Sun £32, guided tour per person £5; ⏲check website), a Victorian's idea of a Moorish bathhouse. A range of watery delights are on offer here: hot rooms, steam rooms, a plunge pool and so on, plus use of the original wooden changing cubicles and historic Crapper toilets. Opening hours are quite complex (bathing sessions are alternately mixed and single sex) – check the website for details. There's also a fascinating guided tour of the building (9am Monday, Wednesday and Friday).

p263

The Drive » Head north out of Harrogate on the A61. After 4 miles turn left at Ripley onto the B6165 to the pretty town of Pately Bridge, then continue on the B6265 as it climbs high over Craven Moor before entering the Yorkshire Dales National Park and descending to Grassington (total 24 miles).

LINK YOUR TRIP

21 North York Moors & Coast

From Richmond it's a quick 47-mile blast down the M1 to link with our tour of Yorkshire's other national park.

22 Hadrian's Wall

One hour's drive north from Richmond (47 miles) is Newcastle, where you can begin a tour of Britain's most famous Roman legacy.

2 Grassington

The perfect base for hiking the south Dales, Grassington's handsome Georgian centre teems with walkers and visitors throughout the summer months, soaking up an atmosphere that – despite the odd touch of faux rusticity – is as attractive and traditional as you'll find in these parts.

p263

The Drive » Head north out of Grassington and follow the B6160 along Wharfedale for a few miles. Soon after passing the massive limestone overhang of Kilnsey Crag on your left, take the minor road on the left to Arncliffe, just 8 miles from Grassington. As you enter the village turn left to find the village green.

3 Arncliffe

The tiny village of Arncliffe sits in the heart of scenic Littondale, its neat stone houses ranged around the village green. On the north side of the green is the **Falcon Inn** (www.thefalconinnarncliffe.co.uk; Arncliffe; ⏲noon-11pm Mon-Sat, to 10.30pm Sun), the original for the Woolpack pub in the popular UK TV series *Emmerdale*. It's a lovely rustic inn where beer is still served from a jug on the counter.

The Drive » Exit the far end of the village green, cross the bridge and turn sharp left to follow the steep, twisting, single-track road that climbs up the valley of Cowside Beck (beware of wandering sheep). At a fork near Malham Tarn bear left and after 400m, at another junction, continue straight across and descend steeply into Malham (9 miles).

TRIP HIGHLIGHT

4 Malham

Malham is set within the largest area of limestone country in England, stretching west from Grassington to Ingleton – a distinctive landscape pockmarked with potholes, dry valleys, limestone pavements and gorges. Two of the most spectacular features – Malham Cove and Gordale Scar – are within walking distance of Malham's centre.

The huge rock amphitheatre known as **Malham Cove** is ringed with 80m-high vertical cliffs. In the wake of the last Ice Age, this was a waterfall to rival Niagara; today it is a playground for rock climbers. Peregrine falcons nest here in spring, when the Royal Society for the Protection of Birds (RSPB) sets up a birdwatching lookout. You can hike up the steep steps on the left-hand side of the cove to see the extensive limestone pavement above the cliffs.

For a longer walk, follow the 5-mile circular **Malham Landscape Trail** (www.malhamdale.com), which continues on to spectacular **Gordale Scar**, a deep limestone canyon with scenic cascades, then leads to the remains of an Iron Age settlement and Janet's Foss waterfall.

p263

The Drive » Continue south on the minor road from Malham (it can be very busy on summer weekends) to the A65, and turn left to reach Skipton in 11 miles.

5 Skipton

This busy market town on the southern edge of the Dales takes its name from the Anglo-Saxon *sceape ton* (sheep town) – no prizes for guessing how it made its money. Skipton's pride and joy is the broad and bustling **High Street**, one of the most attractive shopping streets in Yorkshire. Monday, Wednesday, Friday and Saturday are market days, bringing crowds from all over and giving the town something of a festive atmosphere.

No visit to Skipton is complete without a cruise along the Leeds–Liverpool Canal, which runs through the middle of town. **Pennine Cruisers** (01756-795478; www.penninecruisers.com; The Wharf, Coach St; per person £4; 10.30am-dusk Mar-Oct) runs half-hour trips to Skipton Castle and back.

p263

The Drive » Head northwest from Skipton along the A59 onto the busy A65, and continue to Ingleton, 24 miles away. Turn off the main road and follow signs for Village Centre, and then Waterfalls Walk.

6 Ingleton

The village of Ingleton, perched precariously above a river gorge, is the caving capital of England. It sits at the foot of one of the country's most extensive areas of limestone, crowned by the dominating peak of Ingleborough and riddled with countless potholes and cave systems.

The town is the starting point for a famous Dales hike, the circular, 4.5-mile **Waterfalls Trail** (www.ingletonwaterfallstrail.co.uk), which passes through native oak woodland on its way past a series of spectacular waterfalls on the Rivers Twiss and Doe (allow three to four hours).

The Drive » Follow the B6255 northeast from Ingleton. Beyond Chapel-le-Dale you'll see the spectacular 30m-high, 400m-long Ribblehead Viaduct on your left. The road continues over bleak Gayle Moor and down to Hawes (17 miles). Leave the car in the car park beside the national park centre at the eastern end of the village.

NICK BRUNDLE / SHUTTERSTOCK ©

Ingleton Walking the Waterfalls Trail

7 Hawes

Hawes is the beating heart of Wensleydale, and a thriving and picturesque market town (market day is Tuesday) with several antique, art and craft shops, with the added attraction of its own waterfall in the village centre. Beside the car park is the **Dales Countryside Museum** (01969-666210; www.dalescountrysidemuseum.org.uk; Station Yard; adult/child £4.80/free; 10am-5pm Feb-Dec; P), a beautifully presented social history of the area that explains the forces shaping the landscape, from geology to lead mining to land enclosure.

At the other end of the town is the **Wensleydale Creamery** (www.wensleydale.co.uk; Gayle Lane; adult/child £1.95/free; 10am-4pm; P), devoted to the production of the animated TV characters Wallace and Gromit's favourite crumbly white cheese. You can drop into the visitor centre, watch cheesemakers in action, and then try-before-you-buy in the shop. There's also a rather good cafe, Calvert's Restaurant.

About 1.5 miles north of Hawes is 30m-high **Hardraw Force** (www.hardrawforce.com; Hardraw; adult/child £4/2; P), the highest unbroken waterfall in England, but by international standards not that impressive (except after heavy rain). Access is via a lovely landscaped walk (400m) from the car park behind the Green Dragon Inn. There's an admission fee (coins only) to access the walk, and a cafe selling local ice cream.

p263

The Drive » The 13-mile route from Hawes to the Tan Hill Inn is one of the most scenic in the Dales. Turn right and right again out of the car park (signposted Muker) and follow the minor road over the Buttertubs Pass. Turn left on the B6270 to Keld, then right on the minor road signposted West Stonesdale and Tan Hill.

TRIP HIGHLIGHT

8 Tan Hill Inn

Sitting in the middle of nowhere at an elevation of 528m (1732ft), the **Tan Hill Inn** (01833-628246; www.tanhillinn.com; Tan Hill, Swaledale; 8am-11.30pm Jul & Aug, 9am-9.30pm Sep-Jun;) is Britain's highest pub. Despite its isolation it's an unexpectedly comfortable and welcoming hostelry, with an ancient fireplace in the atmospheric, stone-flagged public bar, and an assorted menagerie of dogs, cats and even sheep wandering in and out of the building. An important watering hole on the Pennine Way, the inn offers real ale on tap and decent pub grub.

The Drive » Head east from Tan Hill on a wild and lonely single-track road that cuts across the high Pennine moors then descends through Arkengarthdale to the picturesque village of Reeth. Follow the B6270 along Swaledale through classic Dales scenery patchworked with drystone dykes and little barns, then the A6108 for the final stretch to Richmond (total 23 miles).

TRIP HIGHLIGHT

9 Richmond

The handsome market town of Richmond is one of England's best-kept secrets, perched on a rocky outcrop overlooking the River Swale and guarded by the ruins of massive **Richmond Castle** (EH; www.english-heritage.org.uk; Tower St; adult/child £6.90/4.10; 10am-5pm Wed-Sun). A maze of cobbled streets radiates from the broad, sloping market square (market day is Saturday), lined with elegant Georgian buildings and photogenic stone cottages, with glimpses of the surrounding hills and dales peeking through the gaps. It's a fine spot to end your Yorkshire adventure.

Another important Richmond landmark is the **Georgian Theatre Royal** (www.georgiantheatre-royal.co.uk; Victoria Rd; adult/child £5/2; tours hourly 10am-4pm Mon-Sat mid-Feb–mid-Nov). Built in 1788, this is the most complete Georgian playhouse in Britain. It closed in 1848 and was used as an auction house into the early 20th century, reopening as a working theatre again in 1963 after a period of restoration. Fascinating tours (starting on the hour) include a look at the country's oldest surviving stage scenery, painted between 1818 and 1836.

p263

MOUNTAIN BIKING IN SWALEDALE

Swaledale – the quietest and least visited of the Dales – stretches west from Richmond, its wild and rugged beauty in sharp contrast to the softer, greener dales to the south. It's hard to imagine that only a century ago this was a major lead-mining area. When the price of ore fell in the 19th century, many people left to find work in England's burgeoning industrial cities, while others emigrated – especially to Wisconsin in the USA – leaving the valley almost empty, with just a few lonely villages scattered along its length.

The many rough tracks that criss-cross the moors and hillsides around the pretty village of Reeth, at the junction of Swaledale and Arkengarthdale, make this part of the Dales a paradise for mountain bikers, with dozens of miles of off-road trails to explore. The **Dales Bike Centre** (01748-884908; www.dalesbikecentre.co.uk; Fremington; mountain bike/e-bike per day from £40/50; 9am-5pm), just east of Reeth, can rent you a bike and provide local trail maps.

Eating & Sleeping

Harrogate 1

Bijou B&B ££

(☎01423-567974; www.thebijou.co.uk; 17 Ripon Rd; s/d from £54/74; P) Bijou by name, bijou by nature – this jewel of a Victorian villa sits firmly at the boutique end of the B&B spectrum, with a grand piano to tinkle on in the lounge and bottles of Prosecco for £12 a pop in the honesty bar. It's just a bit of a schlep up the hill from the conference centre.

Grassington 2

Corner House Cafe Cafe £

(☎01756-752414; www.cornerhousegrassington.co.uk; 1 Garr's Lane; mains £7-10; 10am-4pm;) This cute little white cottage, just uphill from the village square, serves good coffee and unusual homemade cakes (citrus and lavender-syrup sponge is unexpectedly delicious), as well as tasty made-to-order sandwiches and lunch specials such as Dales lamb hotpot or chicken and chorizo gratin. Breakfast, served till 11.30am, ranges from cinnamon toast to the full-English fry-up.

Devonshire Fell Hotel ££

(☎01756-718111; www.devonshirefell.co.uk; Burnsall; r from £95; P) This former gentleman's club for mill owners in the scenic village of Burnsall has a very contemporary feel and spacious rooms, many with beautiful valley views. The conservatory (used as a restaurant, breakfast room and for afternoon tea) has a stunning outlook. It's 3 miles southeast of Grassington, which can be reached via a walking path by the river.

Malham 4

Lister Barn B&B £££

(☎01729-830444; www.listerarms.co.uk; Cove Rd; d £120-165; P) The Lister Arms pub in Malham runs this chic barn conversion on the main road through the village, with eight modern rooms centred on a lovely open-plan communal area with free herbal teas and a log burner to huddle around after long walks. One room is suitable for wheelchair users and there are two family rooms with bunks and a separate bedroom.

Skipton 5

Pinfold Guesthouse ££

(☎07510-175270; www.thepinfoldskipton.co.uk; Chapel Hill; r £60-80; P) This petite, room-only guesthouse has three light and airy, oak-beamed rooms with a lovely fresh country feel. Forgive the tiny shower rooms, because the excellent location around the corner from Skipton Castle more than compensates. The Littondale room has its own entrance, parking and small grassy patio. The Little Pinfold Cottage, a one-room self-catering cottage across the street, has been added.

Hawes 7

Green Dragon Inn Inn ££

(☎01969-667392; www.thegreendragoninnhardraw.com; Hardraw; d/ste £90/110; P) A lovely old pub with flagstone floors, low timber beams, ancient oak furniture and Theakston on draught, the Dragon serves up a tasty steak-and-ale pie and offers B&B in pleasant, simple rooms behind the pub, as well as a pair of fancy suites above the bar. It's 1 mile northwest of Hawes.

Richmond 9

Frenchgate Hotel Boutique Hotel ££

(☎01748-822087; www.thefrenchgate.co.uk; 59-61 Frenchgate; s/d incl breakfast from £98/148; P) Nine elegant bedrooms occupy the upper floors of this converted Georgian town house, with flash touches such as memory-foam mattresses and heated marble floors in luxurious bathrooms. Parts of the house date to 1650, so we can forgive a crack here or peeling paint there. Downstairs there's an excellent restaurant (three-course dinner £39), an oasis of a garden and a private rear car park.

№ 1264
B-1
WH TBY

MILOSZ MASLANKA / SHUTTERSTOCK ©

North York Moors & Coast

This varied tour takes in ancient architecture, wild moorland scenery, picture-postcard villages (complete with steam trains!) and a classic seaside resort...with macabre literary connections.

TRIP HIGHLIGHTS

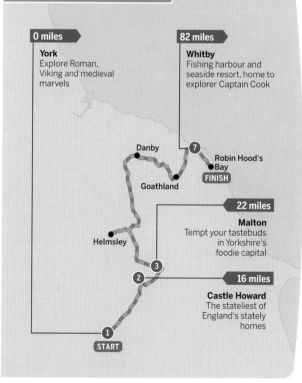

0 miles
York
Explore Roman, Viking and medieval marvels

82 miles
Whitby
Fishing harbour and seaside resort, home to explorer Captain Cook

Danby
Goathland
Robin Hood's Bay
FINISH

22 miles
Malton
Tempt your tastebuds in Yorkshire's foodie capital

Helmsley

16 miles
Castle Howard
The stateliest of England's stately homes

START

4–5 DAYS
87 MILES / 140KM

GREAT FOR...

BEST TIME TO GO

The moors look their best in August when the heather is in bloom.

ESSENTIAL PHOTO

A steam train passing through Goathland station.

BEST FOR FOODIES

Browsing the market and delicatessens in Helmsley.

Goathland North Yorkshire Moors Railway

21

North York Moors & Coast

The Blakey Ridge road out of Hutton-le-Hole just keeps climbing and climbing, leaving behind the medieval city of York and the aristocratic spendour of Castle Howard to enter a world of windswept heather moorland, wandering sheep, lonely stone crosses and ancient footpaths. Stop in a Yorkshire food haven and then the bustling fishing harbour of Whitby, with its Gothic abbey and links to Bram Stoker's Dracula.

TRIP HIGHLIGHT

1 York

Nowhere in northern England says 'medieval' quite like York, a city of extraordinary cultural and historical wealth that has lost little of its pre-industrial lustre. At its heart lies the immense, awe-inspiring **York Minster** (☎01904-557200; www.yorkminster.org; Deangate; adult/child £11.50/free; ⏰11am-4.30pm Mon-Thu, from 10am Fri & Sat, 12.30-2.30pm Sun), the largest medieval cathedral in

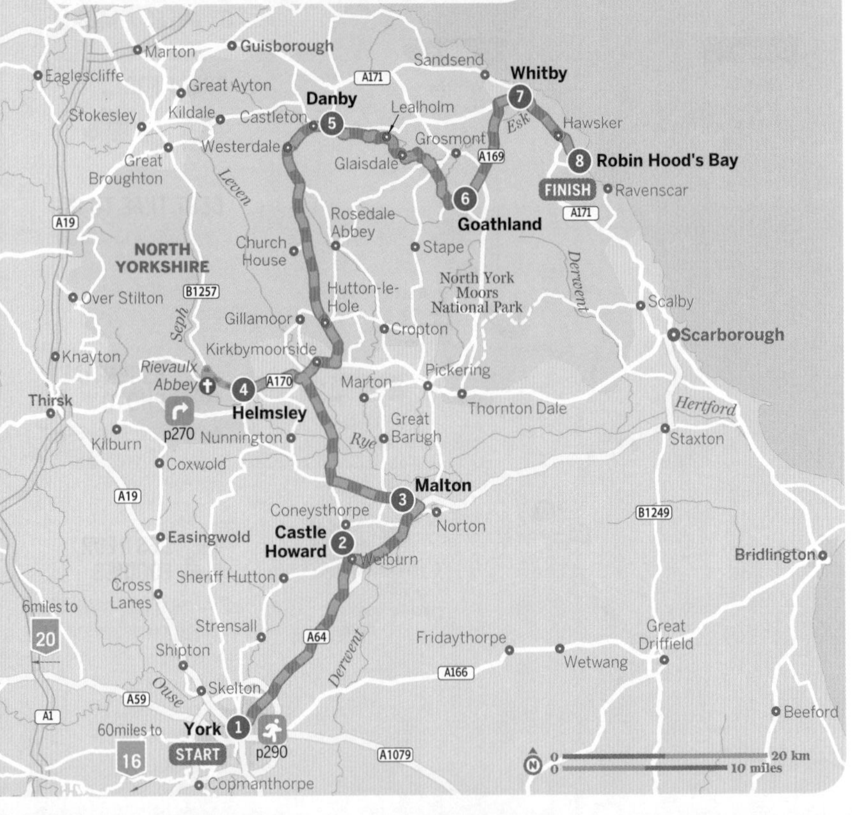

all of northern Europe, and one of the world's most beautiful Gothic buildings. If this is the only cathedral you visit in England, you'll still walk away satisfied.

While many railway museums are the sole preserve of lone men in anoraks comparing dog-eared notebooks and getting high on the smell of machine oil, coal smoke and nostalgia, York's **National Railway Museum** (www.railwaymuseum.org.uk; Leeman Rd; 10am-5pm Wed-Sun; P) is different. The biggest in the world, with more than 100 locomotives, it is so well presented and crammed with fascinating stuff that it's interesting even to folk whose eyes don't mist over at the thought of a 4-6-2 A1 Pacific class thundering into a tunnel.

Interactive multimedia exhibits aimed at bringing history to life often achieve exactly the opposite, but the much-hyped **Jorvik Viking Centre** (ticket reservations 01904-615505; www.jorvikvikingcentre.co.uk; Coppergate; adult/child £12.50/8.50, with Barley Hall £15/10, with Dig £15.50/12, 3-site ticket £18/12.50; 10am-5pm Apr-Oct, to 4pm Nov-Mar) manages to pull it off with aplomb. Thoroughly restored and reimagined following flood damage in 2015, it's a smells-and-all reconstruction of the Viking settlement unearthed here during excavations in the late 1970s, experienced via a 'time-car' monorail that transports you through 9th-century Jorvik (the Viking name for York). You can reduce time waiting in the queue by booking your tickets online.

And don't miss the chance to walk (p290) York's magnificent circuit of 13th-century City Walls.

The Drive » Head northeast out of York on the A64. After 11 miles, at Barton Hill, turn left on the signposted minor road to Castle Howard. After 1.7 miles of twisting and turning, the road becomes arrow-straight as it enters the castle's landscaped grounds, and passes through a monumental gate to reach the visitors' car park (16 miles in total).

LINK YOUR TRIP

20 Yorkshire Dales

Head west for 22 miles from York to Harrogate to discover the scenic delights of the Yorkshire Dales.

16 Central England Industrial Powerhouse

A 71-mile drive southwest from York on the A64 and M62 leads to Manchester, starting point for our tour of Britain's industrial heritage.

TRIP HIGHLIGHT

2 Castle Howard

Stately homes may be two a penny in England, but you'll have to try pretty damn hard to find one as breathtakingly stately as **Castle Howard** (01653-648333; www.castlehoward.co.uk; YO60 7DA; adult/child house & grounds £22/12, grounds only £12.95/8.50; house 10am-2pm Wed, Fri & Sat, grounds to 5.30pm daily, pre-booked tickets only; P), a work of theatrical grandeur and audacity set in the rolling Howardian Hills. This is surely one of the world's most beautiful buildings, instantly recognisable from its starring role as Sebastian Flyte's home in both screen versions of Evelyn Waugh's 1945 paean to the English aristocracy, *Brideshead Revisited*. You'll need at least two hours to do the place justice; admission is by pre-booked ticket only.

The Drive » Continue north from Castle Howard for half a mile, and take a right onto Hepton Hill. Follow the road for 5 miles until you reach Malton (5.5 miles in total).

3 Malton

The sweet market town of Malton was dubbed Yorkshire's food capital by legendary late Italian chef Antonio Carluccio,

JACK COUSIN / SHUTTERSTOCK ©

and with good reason. For a town of its size the food scene is fabulous, with overflowing delis such as **Malton Relish** (☎01653-699389; www.maltonrelish.co.uk; 58 Market Pl; dishes £4-9; ⏰9am-5.30pm Mon-Sat, 10am-4pm Sun) championing produce from the moors, wolds and dales; pint-sized artisan food and drink businesses; and food-focused tours.

Although there are no specific sights to speak of, the town does have some lovely Georgian architecture and independent shops – like York, Malton has a crooked **Shambles**, now crammed with vintage shops, where butchers would have once slaughtered the lambs brought in for the town's sheep markets.

The town also has connections to Charles Dickens, who regularly visited a friend here and wrote *A Christmas Carol* here on one of his trips.

✕ p271

The Drive » Take the narrow B1257 northwest (watch for the sharp bend at Hovingham) for 15 miles to Helmsley (total 15 miles).

❹ Helmsley

Helmsley is a classic North Yorkshire market town, a handsome huddle of old stone houses, historic coaching inns and a cobbled market square (market day is Friday), all basking under the watchful gaze of a sturdy Norman **castle** (EH; www.english-heritage.org.uk; Castlegate; adult/child £7.90/4.70; ⏰10am-6pm Apr-Sep, to 5pm Oct, to 4pm Fri-Sun Nov-Mar; P). It's also a bit of a foodie town, sporting several good coffee shops, a couple of quality delicatessens on the main square and some

Malton Yorkshire's food capital

renowned restaurants in the surrounding area

South of Helmsley lies the superb ornamental landscape of **Duncombe Park estate** (www.duncombepark.com; adult/child £5/3; ⏲10.30am-5pm Sun-Fri Apr-Aug), laid out in 1718 for Thomas Duncombe (whose son would later build Rievaulx Terrace). Wide grassy walkways and terraces lead through woodland to mock-classical temples, while longer walking trails are set out in the landscaped parkland, now protected as a nature reserve.

✕ 🛏 p271

The Drive » Drive east from Helmsley on the A170 and, just past Kirkbymoorside, turn left on the minor road to the picturesque village of Hutton-le-Hole. Continue on the Blakey Ridge road, which climbs high over the moors, peaking at 418m near the remote Lion Inn before swooping steeply down to Danby (total 23 miles).

5 Danby

Danby is a compact stone-built village set deep amid the moors at the head of Eskdale. It's home to the **Moors National Park Centre** (☎01439-772737; www.northyorkmoors.org.uk; Lodge Lane,; parking 2/24hr £3/5.50; ⏲10am-5pm; 👪), the national park's headquarters, which has interesting exhibits on the natural history of the moors as well as a cafe. There are several short circular walks from the village, but a more challenging objective is **Danby Beacon**, a stiff 2 miles uphill to a stunning 360-degree panorama across the moors. Or you can cheat, and just drive your way up.

🛏 p271

The Drive » Head east from Danby on steep and twisting minor roads winding along

DETOUR: RIEVAULX ABBEY

Start: 4 Helmsley

In the secluded valley of the River Rye, amid fields and woods loud with birdsong, stand the magnificent ruins of **Rievaulx Abbey** (EH; www.english-heritage.org.uk; adult/child £11/6.60; 10am-6pm Apr-Sep, to 5pm Oct, to 4pm Sat & Sun Nov–mid-Feb, daily Mar; P), pronounced 'ree-voh'. The extensive remains give a wonderful sense of the size and complexity of the community that once lived here, and their story is fleshed out in a series of fascinating exhibits in a new museum and visitor centre. On the hillside above the abbey is **Rievaulx Terrace**, built in the 18th century by Thomas Duncombe II as a place to admire views of the abbey (separate admission fee).

Rievaulx is 3 miles west of Helmsley, signposted off the B1257.

gorgeous Eskdale, passing through the villages of Lealholm and Glaisdale before reaching Egdon Bridge, where you turn right and follow signs to Goathland (13 miles).

6 Goathland

This picture-postcard halt on the **North Yorkshire Moors Railway** (NYMR; www.nymr.co.uk; Park St; Pickering-Whitby day-rover ticket adult/child £35/20; Easter-Oct, reduced service Nov-Easter) stars as Hogsmeade train station in the Harry Potter films, and the village appears as Aidensfield in the British TV series *Heartbeat*. It's also the starting point for lots of easy and enjoyable walks, often with the chuff-chuff-chuff of passing steam engines in the background.

The Drive » Continue east from Goathland then north on the A169, pausing at Blue Bank parking area to take in the sweeping view of the North Yorkshire coast, before descending into Whitby (total 9 miles).

TRIP HIGHLIGHT

7 Whitby

Whitby is both a busy fishing port and a traditional seaside resort that has managed to retain much of its 18th-century character. The narrow streets and alleys of the old town hug the riverside, now lined with restaurants, pubs and cute little shops. Keeping a watchful eye over the whole scene are the atmospheric ruins of **Whitby Abbey** (EH; www.english-heritage.org.uk; East Cliff; adult/child £10/6; 10am-6pm Apr-Sep, to 5pm Oct, to 4pm Nov-Mar; P).

James Cook, one of the best-known explorers in history, lived here – his life is celebrated in the **Captain Cook Memorial Museum** (www.cookmuseumwhitby.co.uk; Grape Lane; adult/child £6.50/free; 9.45am-5pm Apr-Oct, 11am-4pm mid-Feb–Mar) – and the famous horror story of Dracula was written by Bram Stoker while holidaying in Whitby in 1897.

Whitby is famous for its seafood and the town is home to several award-winning fish-and-chip shops, so grab some takeaway and enjoy it while you sit on a harbourside bench.

p271

The Drive » Head 5.5 miles south from Whitby on the A171 and B1447 to Robin Hood's Bay.

8 Robin Hood's Bay

The picturesque fishing village of Robin Hood's Bay (www.robin-hoods-bay.co.uk) is one of the prettiest spots on the Yorkshire coast. Leave your car at the parking area in the upper village and walk downhill to Old Bay: a maze of narrow lanes and passages is dotted with tearooms, pubs, craft shops and artists' studios. At low tide you can go onto the beach and fossick around in the rock pools.

Eating & Sleeping

York 1

Chopping Block at Walmgate Ale House British ££

(www.thechoppingblock.co.uk; 25 Walmgate; mains £14-18; 5-10pm Tue-Fri, noon-10pm Sat, to 9pm Sun;) This restaurant above a pub wears its Yorkshire credentials with pride. Local produce underpins the menu, which turns out mainly meat dishes (lamb shoulder, confit of duck leg, pork belly), given a French-flavoured gourmet twist, that are fine examples of contemporary British cuisine. Vegetarian options include tasty dishes like pea pancakes with spiced cauliflower.

Grays Court Historic Hotel £££

(01904-612613; www.grayscourtyork.com; Chapter House St; d £180-240, ste £265-300; P) This medieval mansion with just 11 rooms feels like a country-house hotel. It's set in lovely gardens with direct access to the city walls, and bedrooms combine antique furniture with modern comfort and design. The oldest part of the building was built in the 11th century, and King James I once dined in the Long Gallery. It also offers one or two surprises: walls lined with modern travel portrait photography, and an excellent restaurant.

Malton 3

Talbot Yard Food Hall £

(www.visitmalton.com/talbot-yard-food-court; Yorkersgate; dishes £4-7; hours vary) Across the road from the Talbot Hotel, this huddle of converted stables has been reimagined as an extraordinary food court housing the stuff of gourmands' dreams. Here you'll find the only UK shop from award-winning macaron master Florian Poirot, and the home base of artisan Yorkshire bakery Blue Bird, among others. Come for gelato, posh pork pies, freshly ground coffee, Chelsea buns and macarons.

Talbot Yard is the main focus of the **Malton Artisan Food Tour**, but it's also easy to browse independently, and is perfect for picnic fodder.

Helmsley 4

Hare Inn Modern British £££

(01845-597769; www.thehare-inn.com; Scawton; tasting menu £85, half-board package from £167; noon-2.30pm & 6-9pm Wed-Sat; P) Drowsing in a secluded hamlet 4 miles west of Helmsley, the Hare is a 21st-century restaurant in a 13th-century inn, where gourmet dining is relaxed, informal and even fun. There's no à la carte, just a seasonal tasting menu, and only seven tables; bookings must be made in advance. In 2019 a couple of guest rooms were added.

Danby 5

Duke of Wellington Inn ££

(01287-660351; www.dukeofwellingtondanby.co.uk; s/d from £50/90; P) The Duke of Wellington is a fine traditional pub in the middle of Danby village; it serves good beer and bar meals, and has eight guest bedrooms with appealingly countrified decor. Dating from the 18th century, the pub was used as a recruitment centre during the Napoleonic Wars (hence the name).

Whitby 7

Magpie Cafe Seafood ££

(01947-602058; www.magpiecafe.co.uk; 14 Pier Rd; mains £13-28; 11.30am-9pm;) The Magpie flaunts its reputation for serving the 'World's Best Fish and Chips'. Damn fine they are too, but the world and his dog knows about it and summertime queues can stretch along the street. Takeaway fish and chips cost £7.95; the sit-down restaurant is more expensive, but offers a wide range of seafood dishes, from grilled sea bass to paella.

Hadrian's Wall

Follow in the Romans' mighty footsteps as you trace the length of this enormous, enduring wall, built between 122 and 128 CE to separate the Romans and Scottish Picts.

TRIP HIGHLIGHTS

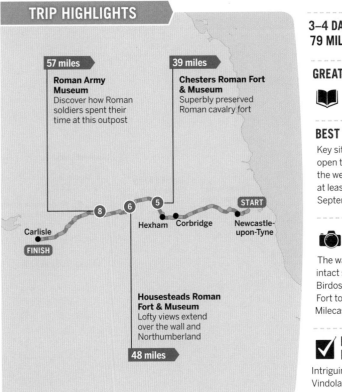

57 miles
Roman Army Museum
Discover how Roman soldiers spent their time at this outpost

39 miles
Chesters Roman Fort & Museum
Superbly preserved Roman cavalry fort

48 miles
Housesteads Roman Fort & Museum
Lofty views extend over the wall and Northumberland

Carlisle
FINISH
Hexham
Corbridge
Newcastle-upon-Tyne
START

3–4 DAYS
79 MILES / 127KM

GREAT FOR...

BEST TIME TO GO

Key sites generally open throughout the week between at least Easter and September.

ESSENTIAL PHOTO

The wall's longest intact stretch, from Birdoswald Roman Fort to Harrow's Scar Milecastle.

BEST FOR HISTORY

Intriguing exhibits at Vindolanda's museum.

22 Hadrian's Wall

Traversing the island's narrow neck, you'll encounter this extraordinary feat of engineering first-hand. Every Roman mile (0.95 miles) had a gateway guarded by a small fort (milecastle), with two observation turrets between them, and many of these remain. A series of southern forts (which may predate the wall) were developed as bases, and 16 lie astride it. Preserved remains and intriguing museums punctuate the route, along with easily accessible remnants of the wall.

1 Newcastle-upon-Tyne

Against a dramatic backdrop of Victorian elegance and industrial grit, this fiercely independent city harbours a spirited mix of heritage and urban sophistication. You can expect excellent art galleries, exceptional restaurants and, of course, interesting bars: Newcastle-upon-Tyne is renowned throughout Britain for its thumping nightlife.

Newcastle is an ideal place for a debrief on the

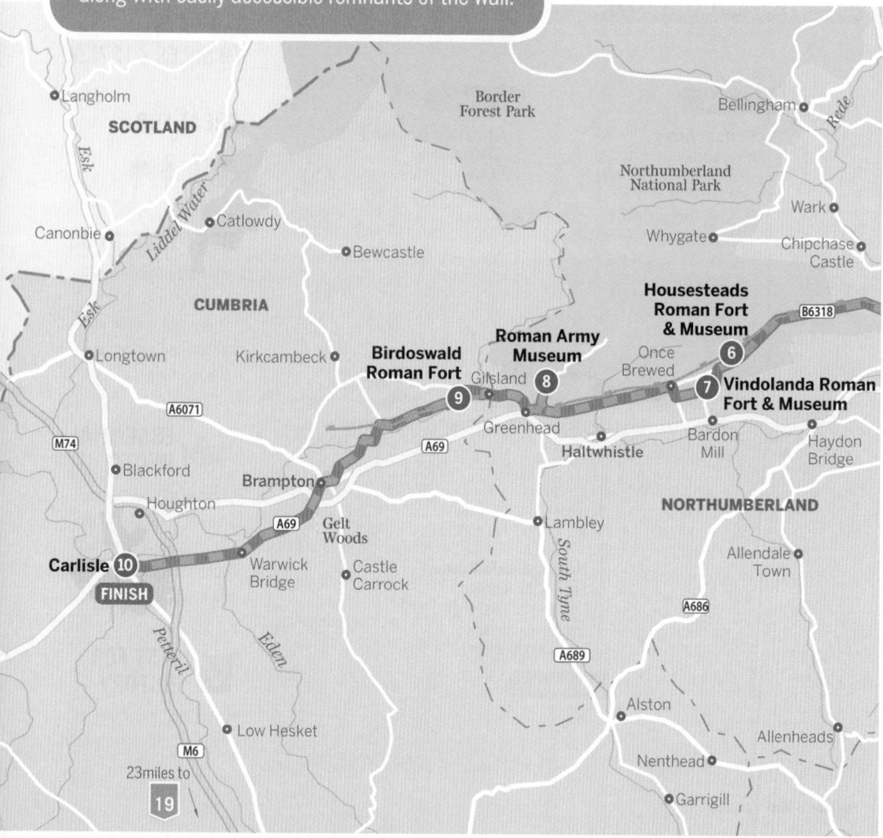

area's Roman legacies. The **Discovery Museum** (☎0191-232 6789; www.discoverymuseum.org.uk; Blandford Sq; ⏲10am-4pm Mon-Fri, 11am-4pm Sat & Sun), housed in the vast former Co-operative Wholesale Society building, has displays on Pons Aelius (Roman Newcastle) as well as every subsequent era throughout the city's history.

At the **Great North Museum** (☎0191-208 6765; www.greatnorthmuseum.org.uk; Barras Bridge; general admission free, planetarium adult/child £3.75/2; ⏲10am-5pm Mon-Fri, to 4pm Sat, 11am-4pm Sun), a fantastic interactive model of Hadrian's Wall shows every milecastle and fortress.

p85, p279

The Drive » Take the A193 and A187 for 5 miles east to Segedunum.

2 Segedunum

The last strong post of Hadrian's Wall was the fort of **Segedunum**

LINK YOUR TRIP

23 Northumbria
Newcastle-upon-Tyne is also the starting point for a spectacular journey along the Northumberland coast to the Scottish border.

19 Classic Lakes
It's 43 miles south from Carlisle, via the M6 and A592, to Ullswater, where you can take the picturesque Classic Lakes drive in reverse.

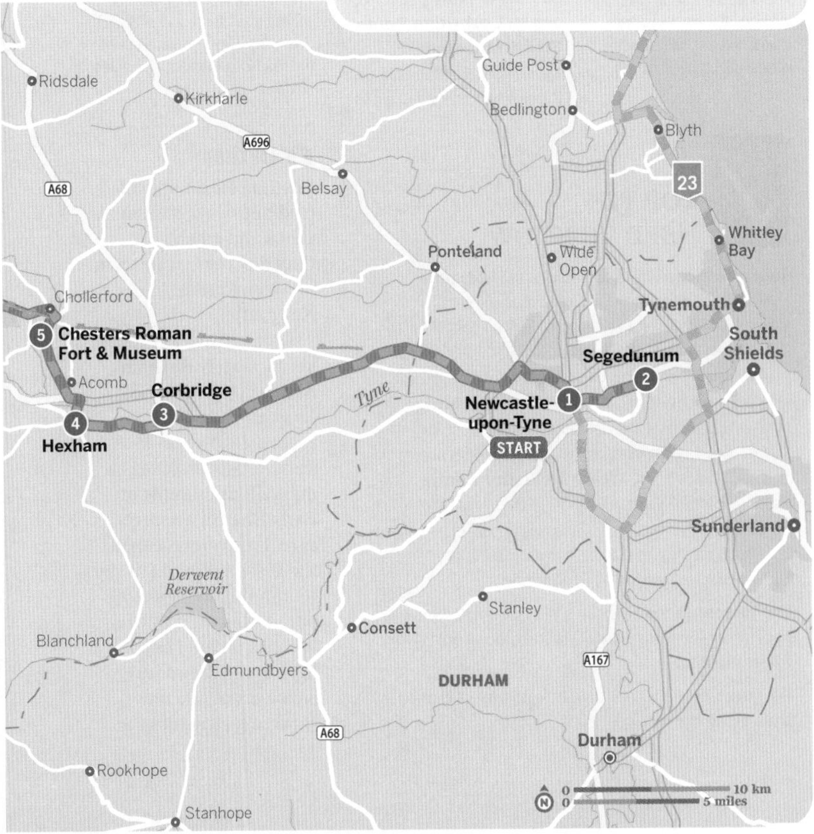

(☎0191-278 4217; www.segedunumromanfort.org.uk; Buddle St, Wallsend; adult/child £4.95/free; ⏰10am-4pm Jun–mid-Sep, to 3pm mid-Sep–early Dec & mid-Jan–May), at the 'wall's end', now the Newcastle suburb of Wallsend. Beneath the 35m-high tower, which you can climb for terrific views, is an absorbing site that includes a reconstructed Roman bathhouse (with steaming pools and frescoes) and a museum offering a fascinating insight into life during Roman times.

The Drive » Hop on the A167 ring road and head west on the A69. You'll soon enter a patchwork of farmland. After 19 miles, take the B6530 into Corbridge (23 miles in total).

3 Corbridge

Above a green-banked curve in the Tyne, Corbridge's shady, cobbled streets are lined with old-fashioned shops and pubs. It's been inhabited since Saxon times when there was a substantial monastery; many of the town's charming buildings feature stones plundered from the nearby Roman garrison town of Corstopitum.

What's left of Corstopitum lies about half a mile west of Market Pl on Dere St, once the main road from York to Scotland. Now preserved as the **Corbridge Roman Site & Museum** (EH; www.english-heritage.org.uk; Corchester Lane; adult/child £9/5.40; ⏰10am-5pm), it's the oldest fortified site in the area, predating the wall itself by some 40 years. Most of what you see here dates from around 200 CE, when the fort had developed into a civilian settlement and was the main base along the wall. You get a real sense of the domestic heart of the town from the visible remains. The museum displays Roman sculpture and carvings, including the amazing 3rd-century Corbridge Lion.

p279

The Drive » From Corbridge, set out southwest on the B6321. Cross the River Tyne and follow the road into Hexham (4.3 miles all up).

TOP TIP: NEED TO KNOW

Tourist offices There are offices in **Hexham** (☎01670-620450; www.visitnorthumberland.com; Queen's Hall, Beaumont St, Hexham; ⏰9am-5pm Mon-Fri, 9.30am-5pm Sat), **Haltwhistle** (☎01434-321863; www.visitnorthumberland.com; Mechanics Institute, Westgate; ⏰10am-4.30pm Mon-Fri, to 1pm Sat) and **Corbridge** (☎01434-632815; www.visitnorthumberland.com; Hill St; ⏰10am-4.30pm Mon-Sat Apr-Sep, 11am-4pm Wed, Fri & Sat Oct-Mar). The **Walltown Visitor Centre** (Northumberland National Park Visitor Centre; ☎01434-344396; www.northumberlandnationalpark.org.uk; Greenhead; ⏰10am-6pm daily Apr-Sep, to 5pm daily Oct, 10am-4pm Sat & Sun Nov-Mar) is located at Greenhead.

Online resources Hadrian's Wall Country (www.hadrianswallcountry.co.uk) is the official portal for the entire area.

Parking Costs £10 per day; tickets are valid at all sites along the wall.

4 Hexham

Bustling Hexham's cobbled alleyways have more shops and amenities than any other wall town between Carlisle and Newcastle.

Dominating tiny Market Pl, stately **Hexham Abbey** (☎01434-602031; www.hexhamabbey.org.uk; Beaumont St, Hexham; by donation; ⏰10am-4pm) is a marvellous example of Early English architecture. It cleverly escaped the Dissolution of 1537 by rebranding as Hexham's parish church, a role it still has today. The highlight is the 7th-century Saxon crypt, the only surviving element of St

Wilfrid's Church, built with inscribed stones from Corstopitum in 674.

The Drive » From the River Tyne's northern bank, take the A69 west for just under a mile. Turn northwest onto the A6079 and cross the single-lane stone bridge over the North Tyne to the village of Chollerford. Turn left (west) on to the B6318; Chesters Roman Fort & Museum is half a mile ahead on your left (6.8 miles altogether).

TRIP HIGHLIGHT

5 Chesters Roman Fort & Museum

Now the **Chesters Roman Fort & Museum** (EH; ☎01434-681379; www.english-heritage.org.uk; Chollerford; adult/child £9/5.40; ⏰10am-6pm daily Apr-Sep, to 5pm daily Oct, 10am-4pm Sat & Sun Nov–mid-Feb, 10am-4pm Wed-Sun mid-Feb–Mar), this Roman cavalry fort's superbly preserved remains are set among idyllic green woods and meadows. Originally constructed to house up to 500 troops from Asturias in northern Spain, they include part of a bridge (best appreciated from the eastern bank), four gatehouses, a bathhouse and an underfloor heating system. The museum has a large Roman sculpture collection.

The Drive » Head west on the B6318 uphill to Housesteads Roman Fort & Museum (9 miles in total). As you drive, keep a lookout for crumbling remains of the wall.

TRIP HIGHLIGHT

6 Housesteads Roman Fort & Museum

Hadrian's Wall's most dramatic site – and the best-preserved Roman fort in the whole country – is the **Housesteads Roman Fort & Museum** (EH; ☎01434-344363; www.english-heritage.org.uk; Haydon Bridge; adult/child £9/5.40; ⏰10am-6pm Apr-Sep, to 5pm Oct, to 4pm Nov-Mar), set high on a ridge and covering 2 hectares. From here you can survey the moors of Northumberland National Park and the snaking wall, with a sense of awe at the landscape and the unmistakable aura of the Roman lookouts.

Up to 800 troops were based at Housesteads at any one time. Its remains include an impressive hospital, granaries with a carefully worked out ventilation system, and barrack blocks. Most memorable are the spectacularly situated communal flushable latrines. Information boards show what the individual buildings would have looked like in their heyday. There's a scale model of the entire fort in the small museum at the ticket office.

The Drive » It's a short, well-signposted 2-mile hop southwest from Housesteads Roman Fort & Museum to Vindolanda.

7 Vindolanda

The extensive site of **Vindolanda** (☎01434-344277; www.vindolanda.com; Bardon Mill; adult/child/family £8/4.75/22.80; ⏰10am-5pm) offers a fascinating glimpse into the daily life of a Roman garrison town. The time-capsule museum is just one part of this large, extensively excavated site, which includes impressive parts of the fort and town (excavations continue) and reconstructed turrets and a temple.

Highlights of the Vindolanda museum displays include leather sandals, signature Roman toothbrush-flourish helmet decorations, and numerous writing tablets returned from the British Library. These include a student's marked work ('sloppy'), and a parent's note with a present of socks and underpants (things haven't changed – in this climate you can never have too many).

🛏 p279

The Drive » Rejoin the B6318 at the small hamlet of Once Brewed and turn west. Below you to the south you'll see the village of Haltwhistle – one of the places that claims to be the geographic centre of the British mainland, although the jury is still out. The Roman Army Museum is ahead on your right (7 miles all up).

TRIP HIGHLIGHT

8 Roman Army Museum

On the site of the Carvoran Roman Fort, the revamped **Roman Army Museum** (☎01697-747485; www.vindolanda.com/roman-army-museum; Greenhead; adult/child/family £6.89/3.80/19; ⏰10am-5pm) has three galleries covering the Roman army and the expanding and contracting empire; the wall (with a 3D film illustrating what the wall was like nearly 2000 years ago and today); and colourful background detail to Hadrian's Wall life (such as how the soldiers spent their R&R time in this lonely outpost of the empire).

The Drive » It's 4.7 miles to the Birdoswald Roman Fort. Continue along the B6318 through the hamlets of Greenhead and Gilsland, crossing the River Irthing; Birdoswald is on your left.

9 Birdoswald Roman Fort

The remains of the once-formidable **Birdoswald Roman Fort** (EH; ☎01697-747602; www.english-heritage.org.uk; Gilsland, Greenhead; adult/child £9/5.50; ⏰10am-6pm daily Apr-Sep, to 5pm daily Oct, 10am-4pm Sat & Sun Nov–mid-Feb, 10am-4pm Wed-Sun mid-Feb–Mar) are set on an escarpment overlooking the beautiful Irthing Gorge. The longest intact stretch of wall extends from here to Harrow's Scar Milecastle.

The Drive » Head southwest to the small village of Lanercost, where you'll see the raspberry-coloured ruins of the Lanercost Priory, before crossing the River Irthing and entering the town of Brampton. Continue west on the A689 to Carlisle (17 miles all up).

10 Carlisle

Carlisle has history and heritage aplenty. Precariously perched on the frontier between England and Scotland, in the area once ominously dubbed the 'Debatable Lands', it's a city with a notoriously stormy past: sacked by the Vikings, pillaged by the Scots, and plundered by the Border Reivers, the city has been on the frontline of England's defences for more than 1000 years.

Reminders of the past are evident in the great crimson **Carlisle Castle** (EH; ☎01228-591922; www.english-heritage.org.uk/visit/places/carlisle-castle; Castle Way; adult/child £11.20/6.40; ⏰10am-5pm) and **Carlisle Cathedral** (☎01228-548151; www.carlislecathedral.org.uk; 7 The Abbey; suggested donation £3; ⏰10am-3pm Mon-Sat, noon-3pm Sun), built from the same rosy-red sandstone as most of the city's houses. On English St are two massive circular towers that once flanked the city's gateway.

Carlisle's **Tullie House Museum** (☎01228-618718; www.tulliehouse.co.uk; Castle St; adult/child £10/free; ⏰10am-3pm Tue-Sat) covers the city's past, from its Roman foundations onwards. The highlight is the Roman Frontier Gallery, which uses a mix of archaeological exhibits and interactive displays to tell the story of the Roman occupation of Carlisle. The Border Galleries cover the city's history, from the Bronze Age through to the Border Reivers, the Jacobite Rebellion and the Industrial Revolution. There's an awesome view of the castle from the rooftop lookout.

✕ 🛏 p279

Eating & Sleeping

Newcastle-upon-Tyne 1

Blackfriars — British ££

(☎0191-261 5945; www.blackfriarsrestaurant.co.uk; Friars St; mains £15-32; ⏲noon-2.30pm & 5.30-8.30pm Mon-Thu, noon-2.30pm & 5-8.30pm Fri & Sat, noon-4pm Sun;) A 13th-century friary is the atmospheric setting for 'modern medieval' cuisine. Beautiful stained-glass windows frame the dining room; in summer tables are set up in the cloister garden. Consult the table-mat map for the provenance of your cod, wood pigeon or rare-breed pork. Everything else is made from scratch on site, including breads, pastries, ice creams and sausages. Bookings recommended.

Jesmond Dene House — Boutique Hotel ££

(☎0191-212 3000; www.jesmonddenehouse.co.uk; Jesmond Dene Rd; d from £125; P @) Large bedrooms at this exquisite 40-room property are furnished in a modern interpretation of the Arts and Crafts style and have stunning bathrooms complete with underfloor heating, as well as the latest tech; some have private terraces. The fine-dining **restaurant** (☎0191-212 5555; mains £17-33, 2-/3-course menus £23.50/27.50, afternoon tea £29.50; ⏲7-10am, noon-5pm & 7-9pm Mon-Thu, to 9.30pm Fri, 7.30-10.30am, noon-5pm & 7-9.30pm Sat, 7.30-10.30am & noon-9pm Sun) is sublime; dinner, bed and breakfast packages are available.

Corbridge 3

Corbridge Larder — Deli £

(☎01434-632948; www.corbridgelarder.co.uk; 18 Hill St; mains £4-10; ⏲9am-5pm Mon-Sat, 10am-4pm Sun) Gourmet picnic fare at this fabulous deli includes bread, over 100 varieties of cheese, chutneys, cakes, chocolates and wine (you can get hampers made up) as well as made-to-order sandwiches, pies, quiches, tarts, and antipasti and meze delicacies. Upstairs from the wonderland of provisions there's a small sit-down cafe serving dishes such as Moroccan spiced chicken.

Lord Crewe Arms — Inn £££

(☎01434-677100; www.lordcrewearmsblanchland.co.uk; The Square, Blanchland; d from £175; P) An 1165-built abbot's house in the honey-stone North Pennines village of Blanchland, 11 miles south of Corbridge, shelters some of this entrancing inn's 21 rooms, while others are located in former miners' cottages. Rates almost halve outside high season. Non-guests can dine on outstanding Modern British fare and drink in the vaulted bar, the Crypt, with a monumental medieval fireplace.

Vindolanda 7

Ashcroft — B&B ££

(☎01434-320213; www.ashcroftguesthouse.co.uk; Lanty's Lonnen, Haltwhistle; s/d from £77/89; P) British B&Bs don't get better than this elegant Edwardian vicarage surrounded by nearly a hectare of beautifully manicured terraced lawns and gardens. Some rooms open to private balconies and terraces and all have soaring ceilings and 21st-century gadgets. Breakfast (included) is cooked on a cast-iron Aga and served in a grand dining room.

Carlisle 10

David's — British ££

(☎01228-523578; www.davidsrestaurant.co.uk; 62 Warwick Rd; 2-/3-course menus lunch £17.95/22.95, dinner £22.95/27.95; ⏲noon-1.30pm & 6-9pm Tue-Sat) For many years this town-house restaurant has been the address for formal dining in Carlisle. It majors in rich, traditional dishes with a strong French influence: duo of venison, pan-fried turbot, roast chicken with champ mash. The feel is formal, so dress appropriately. À la carte only on Friday and Saturday evenings.

Northumbria

This drive along northeast England's stirring coastline from Newcastle-upon-Tyne to the Scottish border runs through the medieval kingdom of Northumbria, passing desolate beaches, wind-worn castles and magical islands.

TRIP HIGHLIGHTS

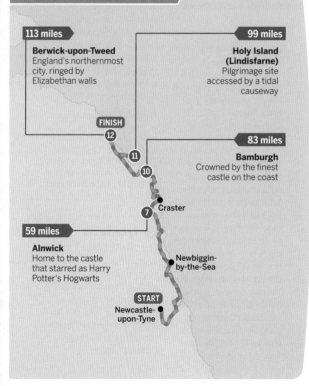

113 miles
Berwick-upon-Tweed
England's northernmost city, ringed by Elizabethan walls

99 miles
Holy Island (Lindisfarne)
Pilgrimage site accessed by a tidal causeway

83 miles
Bamburgh
Crowned by the finest castle on the coast

59 miles
Alnwick
Home to the castle that starred as Harry Potter's Hogwarts

FINISH
12
11
10
Craster
7
Newbiggin-by-the-Sea
START
Newcastle-upon-Tyne

3–4 DAYS
113 MILES / 182KM

GREAT FOR...

BEST TIME TO GO

Birdwatching is best from March to July.

ESSENTIAL PHOTO

Ethereal priory ruins on Holy Island (Lindisfarne).

Warkworth's castle and boat-accessed hermitage.

Holy Island (Lindisfarne) Lindisfarne Castle

23 Northumbria

Newcastle is renowned for its culture and nightlife, but once you hit the open road the pace drops down several gears. Wild and remote, this area is sparsely populated: charming, castle-crowned villages are strung along miles of wide, sandy beaches that you might just have all to yourself. Along the way you'll encounter incredible birdlife and fresh-as-it-gets seafood hauled in at traditional fishing ports.

1 Newcastle

Vibrant Newcastle is famed for its nightlife, but there's plenty to see by day too, including museums showcasing the region's Roman heritage.

Newcastle Castle (☎0191-230 6300; www.newcastlecastle.co.uk; Castle Garth; adult/child £8.50/5; ⏰10am-5pm) – the stronghold that gave the city its name – has been largely swallowed up by the train station, leaving only a few remaining fragments including the square Norman keep and the Black Gate. Exhibits cover the history of the city, its castle and its residents from Roman times onwards. The 360-degree city views from the keep's rooftop are superb.

Walking Newcastle's streets, you'd never know the extraordinary **Victoria Tunnel** (☎0191-230 4210; www.ouseburntrust.org.uk; Victoria Tunnel Visitor Centre, 55 Lime St; tours adult/child £8/4.50; ⏰by reservation) runs for 2.5 miles beneath your feet. Built between 1839 and 1842 as a coal-wagon thoroughfare, it was used as an air-raid shelter during WWII. Volunteer-led two-hour tours take you through an atmospheric 700m-long level section. Book ahead as numbers are limited, and wear good shoes and a washable jacket for the limewashed walls.

🛏 p289

The Drive » Cross the Tyne Bridge (which closely resembles the Sydney Harbour Bridge – both were built by the same company around the same time) and take the A167 south through Gateshead for 6.5 miles to the Angel of the North. There's a free car park by the base.

2 Angel of the North

Nicknamed the Gateshead Flasher, the **Angel of the North** (www.gateshead.gov.uk; Durham Rd, Low Eighton) – an extraordinary 200-tonne, rust-coloured, winged human frame – has loomed improbably over the A1 (M) motorway since 1998. Sir Antony Gormley's iconic work (which saw him knighted in 2014) stands 20m high, with a wingspan wider than a Boeing 767.

The Drive » Head southeast on the A1 to pick up the northbound A194 and pass under the River Tyne through the Tyne Tunnel (one-way toll £1.80). After you resurface, take the A193 to Tynemouth (14 miles in total).

3 Tynemouth

The mouth of the Tyne is one of the best surf spots in England, with great all-year breaks off an immense, crescent-shaped Blue Flag beach, which occasionally hosts the National Surfing Championships.

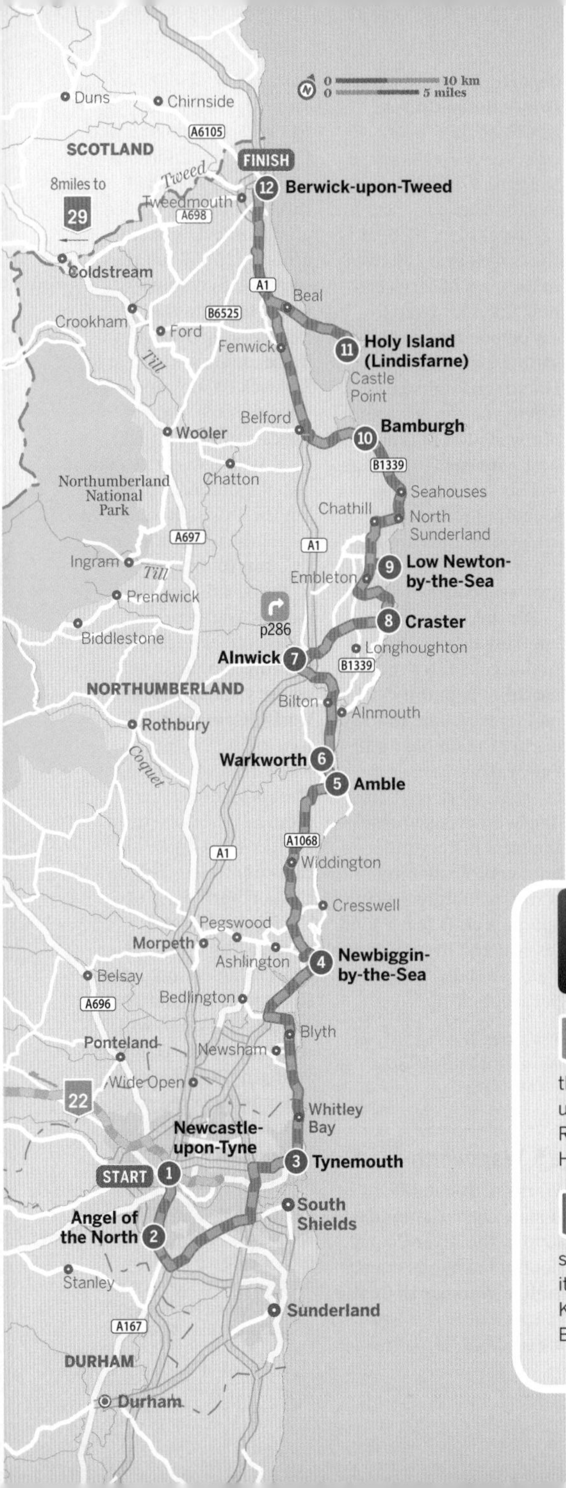

For all your surfing needs, try **Tynemouth Surf Company** (☎0191-258 2496; www.tynemouthsurf.co.uk; Grand Pde; group surf lesson per person £30; ⏰shop 10am-5pm, surf lesson 1pm Sat & Sun Mar-Nov), which also provides two-hour group lessons (when the surf's up) from March to November. The adjoining chilled surf cafe morphs into a cool bar and live-music venue at night.

Built by Benedictine monks on a strategic bluff above the Tyne mouth in the 11th-century ruins, **Tynemouth Priory** (EH; www.english-heritage.org.uk; Pier Rd; adult/child £6.90/4.10; ⏰10am-5pm) was ransacked during the Dissolution in 1539. The military took over for four centuries, only leaving in 1960, and to-day the skeletal remains of the priory church sit alongside old military

LINK YOUR TRIP

22 Hadrian's Wall

Newcastle is also the jumping-off point for an unforgettable drive through Roman history along Hadrian's Wall.

29 The Borders

From this trip's final stop, Berwick-upon-Tweed, it's 24 miles southwest to Kelso to drive the Scottish Borders trip in reverse.

installations, their guns aimed out to sea at an enemy that never came.

Opposite the priory, village-like Front St runs inland from the ocean and is lined with restaurants, cafes and arty shops.

p289

The Drive » Drive north along the coast to the town of Blyth and join the northbound A189 to Newbiggin-by-the-Sea (16.3 miles altogether).

4 Newbiggin-by-the-Sea

Rising above the North Sea 300m offshore from Newbiggin's North Beach, British sculptor Sean Henry's immense 2007 bronze creation **The Couple** (North Beach, Newbiggin-by-the-Sea), measuring 12m high by 20m wide, depicts a man and woman standing on a pier-like structure looking out to sea. Its installation was part of a major regeneration of the area, which included shifting 500,000 tonnes of sand to the beach here to prevent erosion.

The Drive » Rejoin the A189 and head northwest to pick up the northbound A1068 through patchworked farmland to Amble (a 13-mile trip).

5 Amble

The fishing port of Amble has a boardwalk along the seafront and is the departure point for **Dave Gray's Puffin Cruises** (01665-711975; www.puffincruises.co.uk; Amble Harbour, Amble; adult/child £10/5; by reservation Apr-Oct). An ex–Royal Navy lifeboat that saved over 130 lives in its years of service now takes birdwatchers on one-hour cruises sailing around Coquet Island (no landing), where you can see some of the 20,000 puffins that nest here each March, as well as other bird species including Eider ducks, kittiwakes and rare Roseate terns, and the island's grey seal colony.

For three days from late May to early June, Amble celebrates the hatching of puffin chicks on Coquet Island in town during the **Amble Puffin Festival** (www.amblepuffinfest.co.uk; late May-early Jun), with events including local history talks, guided birdwatching walks, exhibitions, watersports, a craft fair, a food festival and live music, as well as a daily teddy bear parachute drop.

The Drive » It's just 1.7 miles north along the River Coquet to Warkworth.

6 Warkworth

Warkworth's huddle of houses cluster around a loop in the River Coquet, dominated by the craggy ruin of **Warkworth Castle** (EH; www.english-heritage.org.uk; Castle Tce, Warkworth; adult/child £7.90/4.70, incl Hermitage £11.30/6.80; 10am-5pm). Looking like the ultimate sandcastle you'd see at the beach, this honey-stone edifice atop a hillock was built around 1200. From the 14th to 17th centuries, it was home to the Percy family (whose descendants still live at Alnwick Castle), and was pivotal in the Wars of the Roses and the English Civil War. It became a national monument in 1915 but the Duke's Rooms remained under the family's control until 1987.

Half-a-mile's walk west of Warkworth Castle (no car access), the tiny, magical 14th-century chapel **Warkworth Hermitage** (EH; www.english-heritage.org.uk; Castle Tce, Warkworth; adult/child £5/3, with Warkworth Castle £11.30/6.80; 11am-4pm Mon & Sun Apr-Oct) is carved into the rock on the northern bank of the River Coquet. It's accessed by a short boat ride (included in admission); ring the brass bell and the ferryman will row you across. Dappled sunlight illuminates the moss-covered ruin's interior. Look for the stone-carved nativity scene in the window.

The Drive » Continue northwest on the A1068. On your right you'll see the pastel-shaded estuary town of Alnmouth. It's a total of 7.6 miles from Warkworth to Alnwick.

WONDERLUSTPICSTRAVEL / SHUTTERSTOCK ©

Alnwick Alnwick Garden's Grand Cascade

TRIP HIGHLIGHT

7 Alnwick

Northumberland's historic ducal town, Alnwick (pronounced 'annick') is an elegant tangle of narrow cobbled streets beneath the colossal medieval **Alnwick Castle** (01665-511178; www.alnwickcastle.com; The Peth; adult/child £8/free; 10am-5pm Apr-Sep, 10am-4pm Oct). The imposing ancestral home of the Duke of Northumberland has changed little since the 14th century. It's a favourite set for film-makers and starred as Hogwarts for the first couple of *Harry Potter* films. Various free tours include several focusing on *Harry Potter* (check the website for broomstick training times on weekends) and other productions that have used the castle as a backdrop, including British comedy series *Blackadder* and period drama *Downton Abbey*. For the best views of the castle's exterior, take The Peth to the River Aln's northern bank and follow the woodland trail east.

Nearby is spectacular **Alnwick Garden** (www.alnwickgarden.com; Denwick Lane; adult/child £13/5; 10am-6pm Apr-Oct, hours vary rest of year). This 4.8-hectare walled beauty incorporates a series of magnificent green spaces surrounding the breathtaking Grand Cascade – 120 separate jets spurting some 30,000L of water down 21 weirs.

If you're familiar with the renaissance of the WWII 'Keep Calm and Carry On' slogan, it's thanks to the wonderfully atmospheric second-hand bookshop **Barter Books** (01665-604888; www.barterbooks.co.uk; Alnwick Station, Wagon Way Rd; 9am-6pm) in Alnwick's

DETOUR: CHILLINGHAM CASTLE

Start: 7 Alnwick

Steeped in history, warfare, torture and ghosts, 13th-century **Chillingham Castle** (☎01668-215359; www.chillingham-castle.com; Chillingham; castle adult/child £10.50/6.50, Chillingham Wild Cattle £8.50/4, castle & Chillingham Wild Cattle £17.50/6.50; ⏰castle noon-5pm Apr-Oct, Chillingham Wild Cattle tours 10am, 11.30am, 1.45pm & 3.15pm Apr-Oct) is said to be one of the country's most haunted places, with spectres from a phantom funeral to Lady Mary Berkeley seeking her errant husband. Owner Sir Humphry Wakefield has passionately restored the castle's extravagant medieval staterooms, stone-flagged banquet halls and grisly torture chambers. It's possible to stay at the medieval fortress in one of eight self-catering apartments where the likes of Henry III and Edward I once snoozed. Doubles start from £100.

The grounds are home to some 100 Chillingham wild cattle, thought to be the last descendants of the aurochs that once roamed Britain until becoming all but extinct during the Bronze Age, making them one of the world's rarest breeds of any species. Tours lasting one hour are led by a park warden; wear sturdy shoes.

From Alnwick, it's a 14-mile journey: take the B6346 northwest through forest and farmland to Chillingham.

Victorian former railway station. While converting the station, the owner came across a set of posters – the framed original is above the till – and turned it into a successful industry. Coal fires, velvet ottomans, reading rooms and a cafe make this one of Britain's great bookstores. As you browse the crammed bookshelves, the silence is interrupted only by the tiny toy train that runs along the track above your head.

🛏 p289

The Drive » Head northeast through rolling farmland and hidden glens to the little seaside village of Craster (7.3 miles in total), where you'll see fishing boats moored in the harbour and the ruins of Dunstanburgh Castle beyond.

8 Craster

Sandy, salty Craster is a small, sheltered fishing village that's famous for its kippers. In the early 20th century 2500 herring were smoked here daily. The kippers still produced today by **Robson & Sons** (☎01665-576223; www.kipper.co.uk; Haven Hill; kippers per kg from £9; ⏰9am-4.30pm Mon-Fri, to 3.30pm Sat, 11am-3.30pm Sun) are said to grace the Queen's breakfast table. Four generations have operated this traditional fish smokers. It's best known for its kippers, but also smokes salmon and other fish.

The dramatic 1.5-mile walk along the coast from Craster (not accessible by car) is the most scenic path to moody, weather-beaten **Dunstanburgh Castle** (EH; www.english-heritage.org.uk; Dunstanburgh Rd; adult/child £5.90/3.50; ⏰10am-6pm daily Apr-Aug, to 5pm daily Sep, to 4pm daily Oct, 10am-4pm Sat & Sun Nov-Mar). Its construction began in 1314 and it was strengthened during the Wars of the Roses, but then left to crumble, before falling into ruin by 1550. Parts of the original wall and gatehouse keep are still standing and it's a tribute to its builders that so much remains.

✕ p289

The Drive » This section of the drive skirts the edge of beautiful Embleton Bay, a pale wide arc of sand that stretches from Dunstanburgh past the endearing, sloping village of Embleton and curves in a broad vanilla-coloured strand around to end at Low Newton-by-the-Sea. En route, several side roads lead down to the water. From Craster, it's a 5.9-mile journey.

9 Low Newton-by-the-Sea

This tiny whitewashed, National Trust–preserved village centres on its village green adjoining the brewery-pub the **Ship Inn** (☎01665-576262; www.shipinnnewton.co.uk; Low Newton-by-the-Sea; mains lunch £6.50-9, dinner £13-29; ⏰11am-7pm Sun-Tue, to 9.30pm Wed-Sat).

Behind the bay is a path leading to the Newton Pool Nature Reserve, an important spot for breeding and migrating birds such as black-headed gulls and grasshopper warblers. There are a couple of hides where you can peer out at them. You can continue walking along the headland beyond Low Newton, where you'll find Football Hole, a delightful hidden beach between headlands.

The Drive » Bamburgh is just 11 miles north of Low Newton-by-the-Sea via the small villages of Beadnell and Seahouses (the departure point for the Farne Islands). Between Beadnell and Seahouses you'll have a sweeping view of the white-sand beach on your right; after Seahouses, the dunes rise up between the road and the shore.

TRIP HIGHLIGHT

10 Bamburgh

High up on a basalt crag, Northumberland's most dramatic castle looms over the quaint village's clutch of houses centred around a pleasant green.

Bamburgh Castle (☎01668-214515; www.bamburghcastle.com; Links Rd; adult/child £11.75/5.75; ⏰10am-5pm daily early Feb-early Nov, 11am-4.30pm Sat & Sun early Nov-early Feb) was built around a powerful 11th-century Norman keep by Henry II. The castle played a key role in the border wars of the 13th and 14th centuries, and in 1464 was the first English castle to fall during the Wars of the Roses. It was restored in the 19th century by the great industrialist Lord Armstrong, and is still home to the Armstrong family. Its name is a derivative of Bebbanburgh, after the wife of Anglo-Saxon ruler Aedelfrip, whose fortified home occupied this basalt outcrop 500 years earlier. Antique

FARNE ISLANDS

The otherwise unmemorable village of Seahouses, between Low Newton-by-the-Sea and Bamburgh, is the jumping-off point for the **Farne Islands** (NT; ☎01289-389244; www.nationaltrust.org.uk; adult/child excl boat transport £34.80/17.40, cheaper outside breeding season; ⏰by reservation, season & conditions permitting Mar-Oct).

During breeding season (roughly May to July) you can see feeding chicks of 20 seabird species (including puffin, kittiwake, Arctic tern, eider duck, cormorant and gull), and some 6000 grey seals, on this rocky archipelago 3 miles offshore. Four boat operators, contactable through **Seahouses' tourist office** (☎01670-625593; www.visitnorthumberland.com; Seafield car park, Seahouses; ⏰9.30am-4pm Thu-Tue Apr, 9.30am-4pm daily May-Oct), depart from Seahouses' dock, including **Billy Shiel** (☎01665-720308; www.farne-islands.com; Harbour Rd, Seahouses; adult/child excl island landing fees 2½hr tour £20/15, 6hr tour £40/25; ⏰by reservation Apr-Oct).

Crossings can be rough (impossible in bad weather); wear warm, waterproof clothing and an old hat to guard against the birds!

Inner Farne is the more interesting of the two islands accessible to the public (along with Staple Island); its tiny chapel (1370; restored 1848) commemorates St Cuthbert, who lived here for a spell and died here in 687.

furniture, suits of armour, priceless ceramics and artworks cram the castle's rooms and chambers, but top billing goes to the neo-Gothic King's Hall with wood panelling, leaded windows and hefty beams supporting the roof.

p289

The Drive » It's 16 miles to Holy Island (Lindisfarne). Check tide times at www.holy-island.info – the island is only accessible at low tide. You must park in the signposted car park (£5.50 per day). A shuttle bus (£2 return) runs from the car park to the castle every 20 minutes from Easter to September; alternatively, it's a level 300m walk to the village.

TRIP HIGHLIGHT

11 Holy Island (Lindisfarne)

There's something otherworldly about this tiny, 2-sq-mile island. Connected to the mainland by a narrow causeway that only appears at low tide, cut off from the mainland for about five hours each day, it's fiercely desolate and isolated, little changed from when St Aidan arrived to found a monastery in 635.

As you cross the empty flats, it's easy to imagine the marauding Vikings who repeatedly sacked the settlement between 793 and 875, when the monks finally took the hint and left. They carried with them the illuminated Lindisfarne Gospels (now in the British Library in London) and the miraculously preserved body of St Cuthbert, who lived here for a couple of years.

The skeletal, red and grey ruins of **Lindisfarne Priory** (EH; www.english-heritage.org.uk; adult/child £7.90/4.70; ⌚10am-5pm, times vary with tides) are an eerie sight and give a glimpse into the isolated life of the Lindisfarne monks. The later 13th-century St Mary the Virgin Church is built on the site of the first church between the Tees and the Firth of Forth. The adjacent museum displays the remains of the first monastery and tells the story of the monastic community before and after the Dissolution.

Built atop a rocky bluff in 1550, tiny **Lindisfarne Castle** (NT; www.nationaltrust.org.uk; adult/child £7.30/3.60; ⌚11am-5pm Tue-Sun late May-Sep, 10am-4pm Easter-late May & Oct) was extended and converted by Sir Edwin Lutyens from 1902 to 1910 for Edward Hudson, the owner of *Country Life* magazine – you can imagine some of the decadent Gatsby-style parties that graced its alluring rooms.

🛏 p289

The Drive » Again, check tide times before leaving the island. Every year drivers are caught midway by the incoming tide and have to abandon their cars. From the island, it's 14 miles north to beautiful Berwick-upon-Tweed.

TRIP HIGHLIGHT

12 Berwick-upon-Tweed

England's northernmost city is a picturesque fortress town, cleaved in two by the River Tweed and spanned by historic bridges. Between 1174 and 1482 this fought-over settlement changed hands 14 times between the Scots and the English.

Only a small fragment remains of the once-mighty border castle but you can walk almost the entire length of Berwick's hefty Elizabethan **walls** (EH; www.english-heritage.org.uk; ⌚dawn-dusk), begun in 1558 to reinforce an earlier set built during the reign of Edward II. The mile-long walk is a must, with wonderful, wide-open views.

Eating & Sleeping

Newcastle 1

Grey Street Hotel Boutique Hotel ££

(0191-230 6777; www.greystreethotel.co.uk; 2-12 Grey St; d/ste from £49.50/67.50;) On the city centre's most elegant street, this beautiful Grade II–listed former bank has been adapted for contemporary needs, including triple glazing on the sash windows, wall-sized murals and splashes of colour. Its 49 individually designed rooms have big beds and stylish colour combinations; some have giant black-and-white photographs covering one wall.

Tynemouth 3

Grand Hotel Heritage Hotel ££

(0191-293 6666; www.grandhoteltynemouth.co.uk; Grand Pde; d/f incl breakfast from £87/108; P @) Built in 1872, this was the one-time summer residence of the Duke and Duchess of Northumberland. Many of the rooms in the main building and neighbouring town house overlook the beach (sea views cost £10 extra); some have four-poster beds and spa baths. Its Victorian-style real-ale pub, drawing room serving high tea and brasserie are excellent. Book well ahead.

Alnwick 7

Alnwick Lodge B&B, Campground ££

(01665-604363; www.alnwicklodge.com; West Cawledge Park, A1; tent sites from £15, glamping incl linen £45-60, B&B s £45-55, d & tw £62-130; P) Three miles south of Alnwick's centre, this gorgeous Victorian farmstead has 15 antique-filled rooms with quirky touches like free-standing, lidded baths. Cooked breakfasts are served around a huge circular banqueting table. You can also go 'glamping' in restored gypsy caravans, wagons and shepherds' huts (with shared bathrooms), or pitch up on the sheltered meadow.

Craster 8

Jolly Fisherman Gastropub ££

(016650-576461; www.thejollyfishermancraster.co.uk; Haven Hill; mains lunch £8-15, dinner £12-26; 11am-8.30pm Mon-Sat, noon-7pm Sun Apr-Oct, to 5pm Sun Nov-Mar) Crab (in soup, sandwiches, fish platters and more) is the speciality of this gastropub, but it also has a variety of fish dishes, as well as a house burger and steaks served with beef-dripping chips. A strong wine list complements its wonderful real ales. There's a blazing fire in the bar and a beer garden overlooking Dunstanburgh Castle.

Bamburgh 10

Potted Lobster Seafood ££

(01668-214088; www.thepottedlobster.co.uk; 3 Lucker Rd; mains £14-28, half-/full lobster £22/39, seafood platter for 2 £69; noon-9pm Jul & Aug, noon-3pm & 6-9pm Sep-Jun) Bamburgh lobster – served as a creamy egg and brandy thermidor stuffed in the shell; grilled with garlic and parsley butter; or poached and served cold with wild garlic mayo – is the star of this nautical-styled gem. Seafood platters for two, piled high with lobster, Lindisfarne oysters, Craster crab, pickled herring and more, come with hand-cut chips and crusty home-baked bread.

Holy Island (Lindisfarne) 11

Crown & Anchor Inn ££

(01289-389215; www.holyislandcrown.co.uk; Market Pl; s/d from £60/70) A cornerstone of the island's social life, this venerable pub has brightly coloured guest rooms and solid pub food, but the biggest winner is the beer garden with a postcard panorama of the castle, priory and harbour.

STRETCH YOUR LEGS YORK

Start/Finish: Monk Bar

Distance: 2.5 miles

Duration: Two to three hours

York is a city that is best explored on foot, and this walk takes in the most impressive parts of the town's medieval walls, fascinating Roman remains, a 13th-century castle and the most picturesque street in Britain.

Take this walk on Trips

Monk Bar

The 700-year-old Monk Bar is the best preserved of York's medieval city gates, with twin turrets and a dozen cross-shaped arrow slits. Inside you will find the **Richard III Experience**, a museum that sets out the case of the murdered 'Princes in the Tower' and invites you to judge whether their uncle, Richard III, killed them.

The Walk » Climb the steps to the top of the city wall and head northwest – check out the Instagrammable views of York Minster. Turn the corner, and descend to the street at Bootham Bar, across from York City Art Gallery.

York City Art Gallery

York's **art gallery** (☎01904-687687; www.yorkartgallery.org.uk; Exhibition Sq; adult/child £8/free; ⏰11am-4pm Wed-Sun; 👪) houses an exhibition dedicated to British ceramics, where the **Wall of Pots** displays more than 1000 pieces dating from Roman times to the present day. As well as an impressive collection of old masters, there are works by LS Lowry, Picasso, Grayson Perry and David Hockney.

The Walk » Exit the gallery via its rear entrance and turn left into Museum Gardens.

Museum Gardens

In these peaceful gardens you can see the ruins of St Mary's Abbey, dating from 1270 to 1294, and the **Multangular Tower**, a part of the city walls that was once the western tower of the Roman garrison's defensive ramparts. In the middle of the gardens, the **Yorkshire Museum** houses a superb exhibition on Roman York.

The Walk » Leave the gardens by the main gate on Museum St, and turn right to cross Lendal Bridge, built in 1863. On the far side climb back up to the top of the city walls and follow them round to Micklegate Bar.

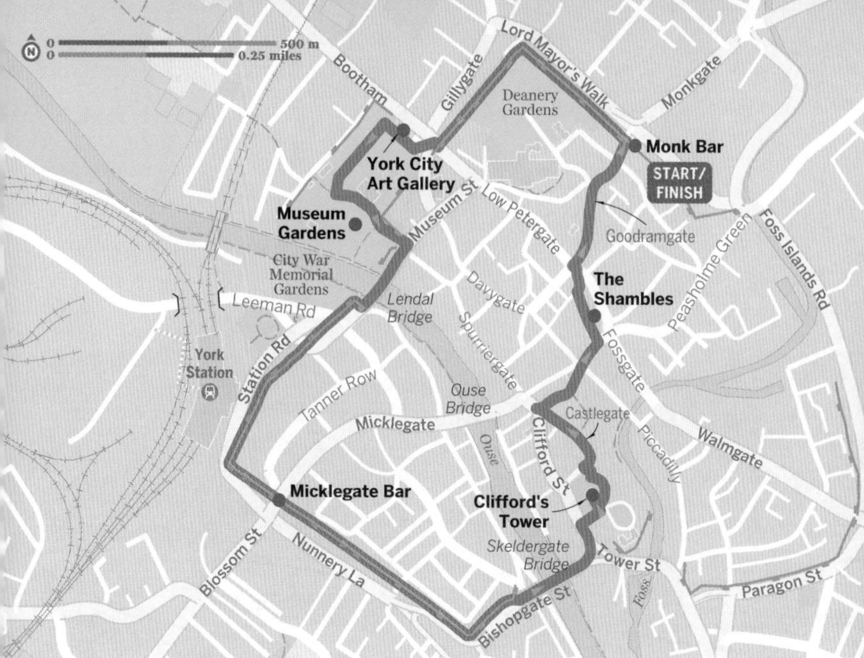

Mickelgate Bar

Micklegate Bar was the most important and impressive of York's city gates, where the severed heads of traitors were once displayed on spikes. It houses the **Henry VII Experience**, a museum exploring the reign of Henry VII (r 1485–1509), the first Tudor king of England, who defeated Richard III at the Battle of Bosworth Field, the climax of the Wars of the Roses.

The Walk » Continue along the top of the city walls until you have to descend and cross the River Ouse again at Skeldergate Bridge. Turn left on Tower St and climb the stairs to Clifford's Tower.

Clifford's Tower

All that remains of York Castle is this evocative **stone tower** (EH; www.english-heritage.org.uk; Tower St; adult/child £5.90/3.50; ⌚10am-6pm Apr-Sep, to 5pm Oct, to 4pm Nov-Mar), a highly unusual four-lobed design built into the keep after the original one was destroyed in 1190 during anti-Jewish riots. An angry mob forced 150 Jews to be locked inside the tower and the hapless victims took their own lives rather than be killed. There's not much to see inside, but the views over the city are excellent.

The Walk » Continue along Castlegate on the far side of the tower, and head right on Coppergate and Pavement to reach the south end of The Shambles.

The Shambles

The Shambles takes its name from the Saxon word *shamel*, meaning 'slaughterhouse' – in 1862 there were 26 butcher shops on this street. Today the butchers are long gone, but this narrow cobbled lane, lined with 15th-century Tudor buildings that overhang so much they seem to meet above your head, is the most picturesque in Britain.

The Walk » From the far end of The Shambles bear right across King's Sq and along Goodramgate to return to Monk Bar.

Wales

Learn to dodge sheep and reverse like a pro on single-track lanes with views to make your heart sing. Wales is road-trip heaven, whether you're negotiating rugged mountain passes and lonely moors, or cruising along the glorious coast.

Leave Cardiff behind and you'll soon be driving along the surf-dashed shores of the Gower Peninsula or deep into the Brecon Beacons.

Swing north to reach an often overlooked enclave of villages, castles and soaring hills – and delightfully literary Hay-on-Wye.

Further north still, routes ramble through grand seaside resorts and past towering cliffs, while Snowdonia National Park dishes up a feast of outdoor adventures and mountain vistas.

Rhossili Bay Parasailing over Worms Head promontory
BILLY STOCK / SHUTTERSTOCK ©

Wales

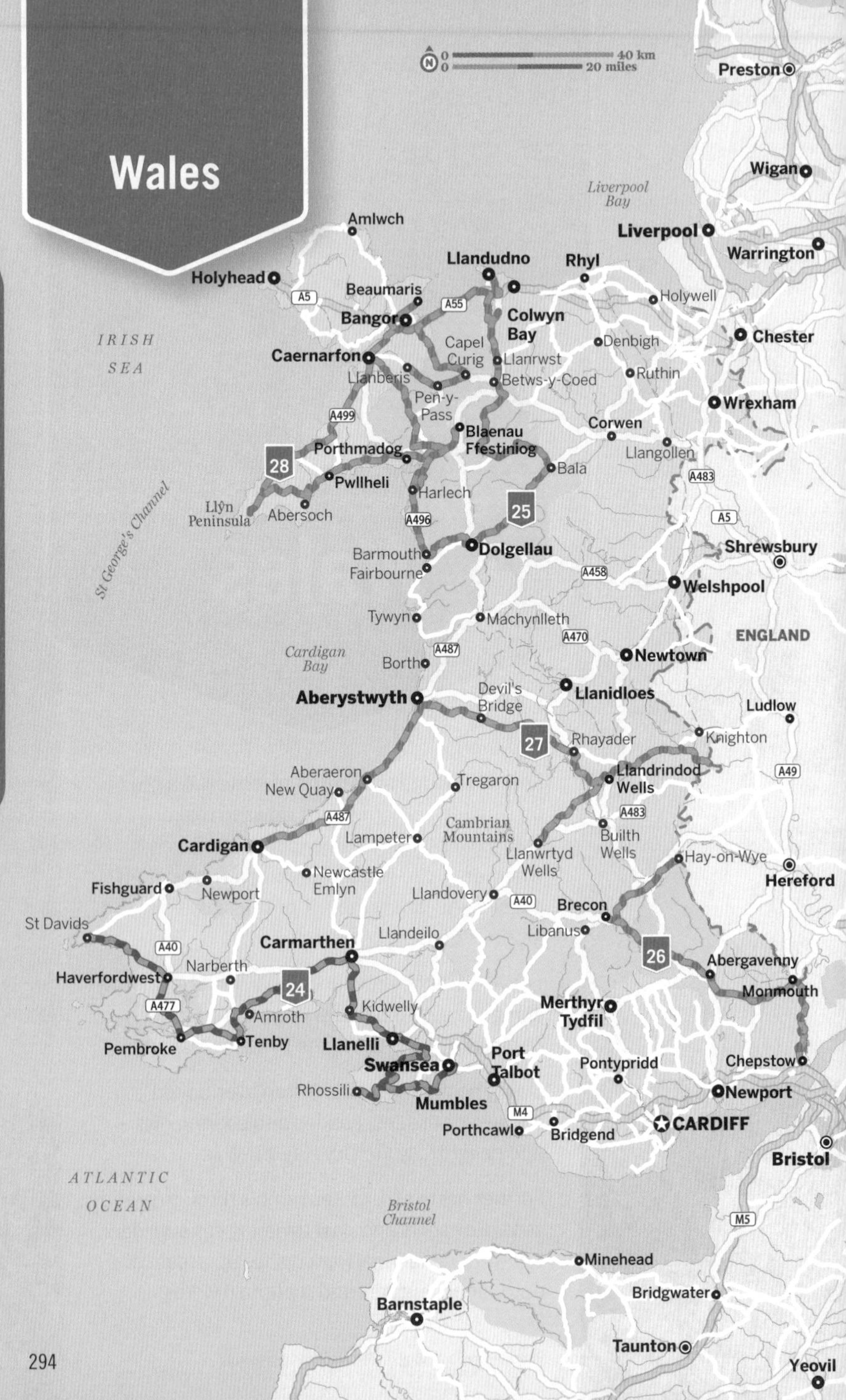

0 40 km
0 20 miles
Preston
Wigan
Liverpool Bay
Liverpool
Warrington
Amlwch
Llandudno
Rhyl
Holyhead
Beaumaris
A5
A55
Holywell
Bangor
Colwyn Bay
Chester
IRISH SEA
Capel Curig
Denbigh
Caernarfon
Llanrwst
Llanberis
Ruthin
Betws-y-Coed
Pen-y-Pass
Wrexham
A499
Blaenau Ffestiniog
Corwen
Porthmadog
Llangollen
28
Bala
A483
Pwllheli
Harlech
St George's Channel
Llŷn Peninsula
Abersoch
25
A5
A496
Dolgellau
Shrewsbury
Barmouth
Fairbourne
A458
Welshpool
Tywyn
Machynlleth
ENGLAND
A470
Cardigan Bay
A487
Borth
Newtown
Aberystwyth
Devil's Bridge
Llanidloes
Ludlow
27
Rhayader
Knighton
Aberaeron
Llandrindod Wells
A49
New Quay
Tregaron
A487
A483
Cambrian Mountains
Lampeter
Cardigan
Builth Wells
Llanwrtyd Wells
Hay-on-Wye
Hereford
Fishguard
Newcastle Emlyn
Newport
Llandovery
A40
Brecon
St Davids
Libanus
Llandeilo
Carmarthen
A40
26
Abergavenny
Narberth
Haverfordwest
24
Monmouth
A477
Kidwelly
Merthyr Tydfil
Amroth
Pembroke
Tenby
Llanelli
Port Talbot
Chepstow
Swansea
Pontypridd
Rhossili
Newport
Mumbles
M4
CARDIFF
Porthcawl
Bridgend
Bristol
ATLANTIC OCEAN
Bristol Channel
M5
Minehead
Bridgwater
Barnstaple
Taunton
Yeovil

ARJEN DE RUITER / SHUTTERSTOCK ©

Braich-y-Pwll Headland with a view to the island of Bardsey

24 West Wales: Swansea to St Davids 4 Days
A glorious blast west beside sweeping beaches and vast sand dunes.

25 Snowdonia National Park 4 Days
Prepare for dramatic drives through Wales' spectacular mountain heartlands.

26 Landscapes & Literature Across Southeast Wales 3 Days
Memorable touring through picturesque valleys, a bookish town and high, high hills.

27 Wilderness Wales 4 Days
An off-the-beaten track exploration of the wilderness at Wales' heart.

28 Northwest Wales 4 Days
Imposing castles and sensational coasts on some of Wales' best touring routes.

DON'T MISS

Braich-y-Pwll

Many visitors don't get as far as this wind-buffeted headland. Shame; they miss the spectacular views to the pilgrim's island of Bardsey. Trip 28

Conwy Town Walls

Conwy is feted for its 13th-century castle, but it also enthrals with Britain's most complete set of medieval town walls. Trip 25

The Whitebrook

Exceptional, inventive cuisine ensures in-the-know gourmets are happy to track down the Whitebrook amid a maze of country lanes. Trip 26

Kidwelly Castle

Wales is the world's most castellated country, and the battlements of lesser-known Kidwelly are an absolute joy to clamber around. Trip 24

Classic Trip

West Wales: Swansea to St Davids

This route links two distinctly Welsh cities – Wales' second largest and the UK's tiniest – by way of Wales' two most famously beautiful tracts of coast.

TRIP HIGHLIGHTS

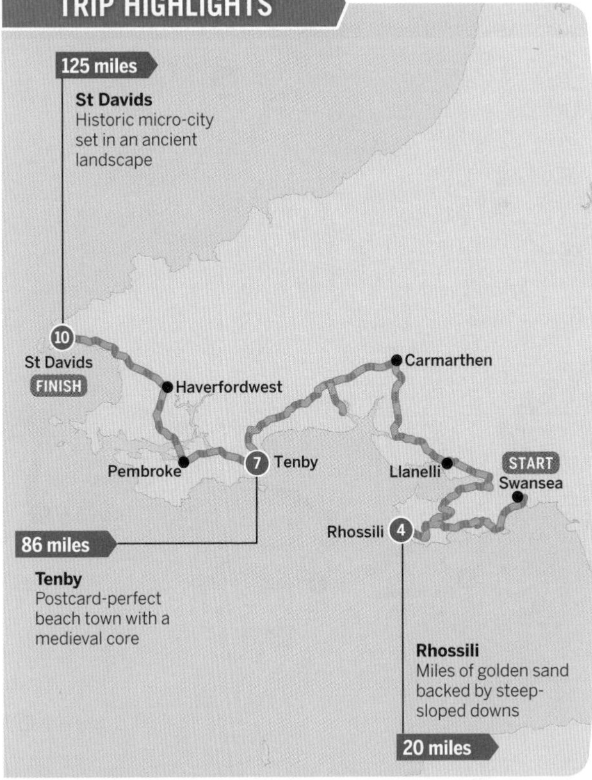

125 miles

St Davids
Historic micro-city set in an ancient landscape

10 St Davids FINISH

Haverfordwest

Carmarthen

Pembroke

7 Tenby

Llanelli

START Swansea

Rhossili 4

86 miles

Tenby
Postcard-perfect beach town with a medieval core

Rhossili
Miles of golden sand backed by steep-sloped downs

20 miles

4 DAYS
129 MILES / 207KM

GREAT FOR...

BEST TIME TO GO

June, July and August offer the best beach weather; in April, May or September the jaw-dropping sandy beaches have fewer crowds.

ESSENTIAL PHOTO

The view of Three Cliffs Bay from Pennard Castle.

BEST FOR FAMILIES

Splashing about on the beach at Tenby.

Pembrokeshire Green Bridge of Wales

Classic Trip

24 West Wales: Swansea to St Davids

The broad sandy arc of Swansea Bay is only a teaser for what is to come. Escape the city sprawl, and the majesty of the Welsh coast immediately begins to assert itself. Waves crash against sheer cliffs painted from a rapidly changing palate of grey, purple and inky black. In between are some of Britain's very best beaches: glorious sandy stretches and remote coves alike.

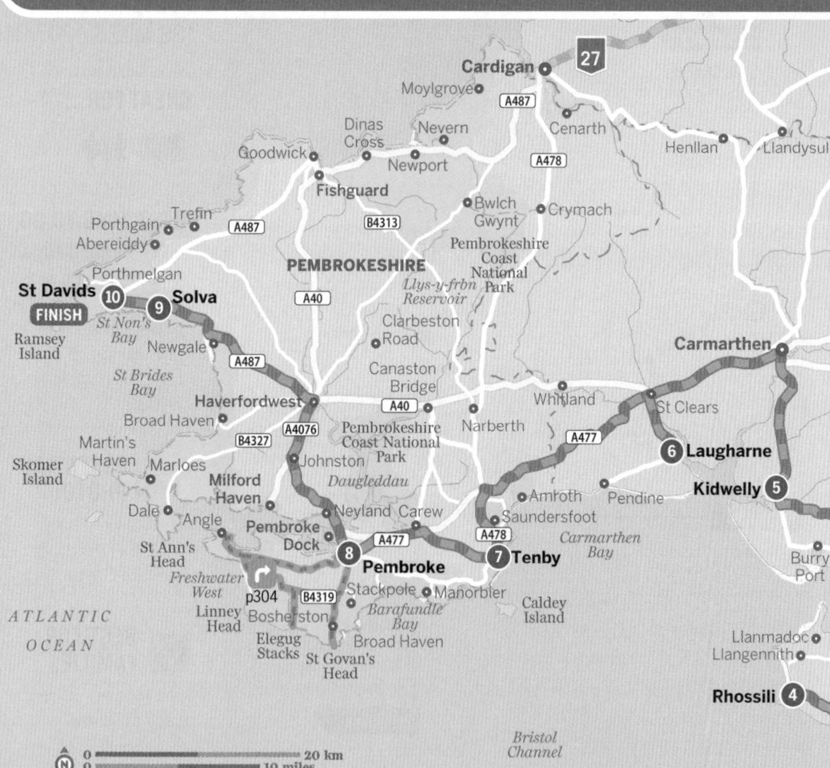

❶ Swansea

Wales' second city has its own workaday charm and an enviable setting on 5-mile-long, sandy Swansea Bay. An active bar scene is enthusiastically supported by a large student population, while a new brace of affordable ethnic eateries and swimmingly good seafood restaurants have improved the city's once drab dining options no end. Literature lovers will relish the handsome Uplands area where the country's best-known writer Dylan Thomas was born, bred, inspired and inebriated.

Fuel up on everything from wondrous Welsh cakes to tantalising Thai food at one of the nation's best markets, **Swansea Market** (www.swanseaindoormarket.co.uk; Oxford St; ⌚8.30am-4.30pm Mon-Sat), then dive into the whizz-bang **National Waterfront Museum** (☎0300 111 2333; www.museum.wales/swansea; South Dock Marina, Oystermouth Rd; ⌚11am-4pm Thu, Sat & Sun). Dylan Thomas fans can tour the district surrounding his **birthplace** (☎01792-472555; www.dylanthomasbirthplace.com; 5 Cwmdonkin Dr, Uplands, SA2 0RA; adult/child £8/6; ⌚10.30am-4.30pm), explore his legacy at the **Dylan Thomas Centre** (☎01792-463980; www.dylanthomas.com; Somerset Pl; ⌚10am-4.30pm) and visit some of the (many!) pubs he famously frequented.

🛏 p306

The Drive » Broad Oystermouth Rd traces the edge of Swansea Bay, changing its name to Mumbles Rd halfway along. It's only 4 miles from central Swansea to the heart of The Mumbles strip.

❷ Mumbles

Swansea's swanky seaside suburb sprawls along the western curve of Swansea Bay and terminates in the pair of rounded hills which may have gifted the area its unusual name (from the French *Les Mamelles* – 'the breasts'). The Norman fortress of **Oystermouth Castle** (☎01792-635478; www.swansea.gov.uk/oystermouthcastle; Castle Ave) stands guard over the fashionable Newton Rd and seafronting Mumbles Rd with their spread of tempting restaurants and bars.

Pick up an ice cream at **Joe's** (☎01792-368212; www.joes-icecream.com; 526 Mumbles Rd; ⌚10.30am-5.30pm Mon, from 10am Tue-Fri, to 6.30pm Sat & Sun),

LINK YOUR TRIP

26 Landscapes & Literature Across Southeast Wales

It's an 80-minute (50-mile) drive from Abergavenny to Swansea via Merthyr Tydfil along the southern edge of the Brecon Beacons.

27 Wilderness Wales

From St Davids it's a simple matter of continuing up a scenic stretch of the Pembrokeshire coast to Cardigan, 35 miles away.

a Swansea institution founded by an Italian immigrant in 1922, and take a stroll along the waterside promenade to the Victorian **pier** (☎01792-365200; www.mumbles-pier.co.uk; Mumbles Rd; 🕒noon-10pm Mon-Fri, 10am-10pm Sat & Sun). There's a pretty little sandy beach tucked just beneath it. If you're peckish, there are some good cafes and restaurants spread along the waterfront, some serving the region's highly regarded seafood, and plenty of pubs and bars too.

p306

The Drive » From the Mumbles it's 6 miles to Parkmill on the Gower Peninsula. Head uphill on Newton Rd, following the Gower signs. Eventually the houses give way to fields and, at the village of Murton, a sharp right-hand turn leads to the B4436 and on to the A4118, the main Gower road.

---

❸ Parkmill

The spectacular coastal landscape of the Gower Peninsula was recognised by officialdom when it was declared the UK's first 'Area of Outstanding Natural Beauty' in 1956.

In the gateway village of Parkmill, historic mill buildings have been converted into the **Gower Heritage Centre** (☎01792-371206; www.gowerheritagecentre.co.uk; adult/child £6.75/5.75; 🕒10am-5.30pm; 👪). Despite its worthy-sounding name, it's a great place to take kids, incorporating a petting zoo and a puppet theatre. Nearby **Parc-le-Breos** contains the remains of a 5500-year-old burial chamber.

However, the real reason to stop in Parkmill is to take a stroll to **Three Cliffs Bay**. Recognised as one of Britain's most beautiful sandy beaches, Three Cliffs has a memorable setting, with a ruined 13th-century castle above and a triple-pointed rock formation framing a natural arch at its eastern end.

The Drive » From Parkmill, head west along the A4118, following the signs to Rhossili. Eventually the road turns left towards the village of Scurlage and the Rhossili turn-off. All up, it's a distance of 10 miles along good roads, but it's quite likely you'll be sporadically stuck behind a slow-moving campervan or tractor.

TRIP HIGHLIGHT

❹ Rhossili

The three miles of surf-battered golden sands of **Rhossili Bay** make it the Gower Peninsula's most spectacular strand. Rhossili village at the southern end of the beach makes the best casual stop. There's a National Trust **visitor centre** (☎01792-390707; www.nationaltrust.org.uk/rhossili-and-south-gower-coast; Coastguard Cottages; 🕒11am-5pm daily Mar-Sep, Fri-Sun Oct) here, and the excellent Bay Bistro & Coffee House (p306). Beware of swimming here: tides can make it dangerous.

This end of the beach is abutted by **Worms Head**, a dragon-shaped promontory which turns into an island at high tide and is home to seals and many seabirds. It's safe to explore on foot for 2½ hours either side of low tide. Don't get cut off by incoming tides!

Surfers tend to prefer Llangennith, near the north end of the beach, as a base.

p306

The Drive » It's only 31 miles from Rhossili to Kidwelly, but allow an hour as the first part of the journey zigzags along tiny byways on the Gower Peninsula's northern edge. Before and after navigating the scraggly outskirts of Llanelli, it's a pleasantly rural drive.

---

❺ Kidwelly

Castles are a dime a dozen in this part of Wales – a legacy of a time when Norman 'Marcher' lords were given authority and a large degree of autonomy to subjugate the Welsh in the south and along the English border. The cute little Carmarthenshire town of

Kidwelly has a particularly well-preserved example.

Originally erected in 1106, only 40 years after the Norman invasion of England, **Kidwelly Castle** (Cadw; 01554-890104; www.cadw.gov.wales; Castle Rd; adult/child £5.10/3.10; 10am-1pm & 2-5pm Wed-Sun) got its current configuration of imposing stone walls in the 13th century. Wander around and explore its remaining towers and battlements, or just stop by to take a photo of the grey walls looming above the peaceful river far below.

Extensive **Pembrey Country Park** (01554-742435; www.pembreycountrypark.wales; parking 2hr/all day £3/5.50; 6am-10pm;) is 5 miles south of Kidwelly. With 500 acres of trail-crossed woods abutting one of Wales' longest sandy beaches, you could spend hours mooching about here.

The Drive » From Kidwelly, motor north along the A484 through the green fields of Carmarthenshire. At Carmarthen, a pleasant but unremarkable county town, switch to the A40 dual carriageway to St Clears, and then follow the A4066 south to the becalmed estuary town of Laugharne: 21 miles in total.

6 Laugharne

While shooting down the highway between Carmarthen and Tenby, it's worth considering taking a left at St Clears to visit the town of Laugharne (pronounced '*larn*') on the Taf estuary. Perched picturesquely above the reed-lined shore, **Laugharne Castle** (Cadw; 01994-427906; www.cadw.gov.wales; cnr King & Wogan Sts; adult/child £3.80/2.20; 10am-1pm & 2-5pm Thu-Mon) is a hefty 13th-century fortress, converted into a mansion in the 16th century.

Swansea may have been Dylan Thomas' birthplace, but Laugharne is where he lived out his final years, getting inspiration for his classic play for voices *Under Milk Wood*. Many fans make the pilgrimage here to visit the **boathouse** (01994-427420; www.dylanthomasboathouse.com; Dylan's Walk; adult/child £4.75/3.75; 2-5pm Fri-Mon) where he lived, the shed where he wrote and his final resting place in the graveyard of St Martin's Church. Also worth a visit is cosy **Brown's Hotel** (King St), one of his favourite watering holes. Then there is the **Dylan Thomas Birthday Walk** (www.laugharnetownship-wcc.gov.uk), taking you on a trail around the town and nearby estuary to spots associated with the poet.

Laugharne is situated 4 miles off the highway: allocate a few hours to explore it properly. Although you can continue southwest from here on narrow roads, you're better off backtracking to the A477 to get to Tenby.

The Drive » Twenty miles of verdant farmland separate Laugharne from Tenby via the A477 and then, once you hit Kilgetty, the A478.

LOCAL KNOWLEDGE: ST DAVID'S DAY

St David's Day is to the Welsh what St Patrick's Day is to the Irish – a day to celebrate one's essential Welshness, albeit somewhat more soberly than Ireland does. If you're in Wales on 1 March, there's no better place to be than the saint's own city, St Davids. Around the cathedral, a host of golden daffodils flower seemingly right on cue; people pin leek, daffodil or red dragon badges to their lapels; streets are strung with flags bearing the black-and-gold St David's cross; and *cawl* (a traditional soupy stew) is consumed in industrial qualities. You should also visit the cathedral, where the saint's remains lie (year-round) in a recently restored shrine.

Classic Trip

LUKASZ PAJOR / SHUTTERSTOCK ©

RADEK STURGOLEWSKI / SHUTTERSTOCK ©

WHY THIS IS A CLASSIC TRIP

LUKE WATERSON, WRITER

Traversing two of Wales' most acclaimed beauty spots (the Gower Peninsula and the Pembrokeshire Coast), this journey also offers up a couple of urban extremes in the form of a large post-industrial city (Swansea) and its near antithesis, an ancient settlement that is Britain's smallest and most westerly city (St Davids). Meander there via time-lost fishing villages, thickset fortresses and serendipitous sandy beaches.

Above: Tenby
Left: St David's Cathedral, St Davids
Right: Oystermouth Castle, the Mumbles

BILLY STOCK / SHUTTERSTOCK ©

TRIP HIGHLIGHT

7 Tenby

Sandy, family-friendly beaches spread out in either direction from this pretty pastel-hued resort town tumbling over the headland above. Pembrokeshire's (if not Wales') premier seaside resort it is, but Tenby's eclectic blend of architecture and steep twisty streets, still part-wrapped by Norman walls, almost evoking Greek island towns at times, impress most.

The beaches are the major attraction here, plus the variety of eateries stashed away amidst the sinuous cobbled streets. The other big draws – the sea-bashed crag of **St Catherine's Island** (www.saintcatherinesisland.co.uk; adult/child £5/2.50; late Mar-Dec) topped by its bombastic fort, along with the **Tenby Boat Trips** (07980-864509; www.tenbyboattrips.co.uk; Tenby Harbour; Apr-Oct;) out to Caldey Island, home to seals, seabirds, beaches and a community of Cistercian monks – are lovely additional strings to Tenby's bow.

p306

The Drive » From Tenby, it's a short, sweet 10-mile hop to Pembroke. From the town centre, head west on Greenhill Rd, go under the railway bridge and turn right at the roundabout. Follow Hayward Lane (the B4318) through a

patchwork of fields until you reach the Sageston roundabout. Turn left onto the A477, and then veer left on the A4075 (or plump for the equally distanced but quieter A4139 via Jameston, where enticing lanes shoot off to the likes of Manorbier and Freshwater East beaches).

8 Pembroke

Pembroke is dominated by hulking **Pembroke Castle** (☎01646-681510; www.pembroke-castle.co.uk; Main St; adult/child £7/6; ⏰10am-5pm; 👪), which looms over the end of the town's main street. The fortress is best viewed from the Mill Pond, a pretty lake which forms a moat on three sides of the headland from which the castle rises. Pembroke played a leading role in British history as the birthplace of the first Tudor king, Henry VII. The castle is in extremely good condition, with lots of well-preserved towers, dungeons and wall walks to explore.

A strip of mainly Georgian and Victorian buildings leads down from the castle, including some good pubs and the excellent **Food at Williams** (☎01646-689990; 18 Main St; light bites £3.50-8, mains £8.50-16; ⏰9am-3pm Mon-Sat, from 10am Sun; 📶) cafe.

🛏 p307

The Drive » The 24-mile journey to Solva heads through the port town of Pembroke Dock, crosses the Daugleddau estuary and then traverses Pembrokeshire's nondescript county town Haverfordwest. Exit Haverfordwest on the A487, trundling through farmland

DETOUR: WEST OF PEMBROKE

Start: 8 Pembroke

The remote peninsula that forms the bottom lip of the long, deep-sea harbour of Milford Haven has some of the Pembrokeshire Coast's most dramatic geological features and blissful little beaches. An especially lovely area includes the golden sands of **Barafundle Bay** and **Broad Haven South**, and a network of walking tracks around **Bosherston Lily Ponds**.

The B4319 winds south from Pembroke to Bosherston. Continue past Bosherston to the coast and a short, steep path leads to the photogenic shell of **St Govan's Chapel** (☎01646-662367), wedged into a slot in the cliffs just above the pounding waves. Sadly, the coast here and just west is part of a military firing range: when red flags are flying there's no public access to some of the Pembrokeshire Coast's most arresting natural sights – neither the chapel, nor **Elegug Stacks**, nor the gigantic arch known as the Green Bridge of Wales.

After sidestepping the firing range, the road continues on to **Freshwater West** – a moody, wave-battered stretch of coast that has provided a brooding backdrop for movies such as *Harry Potter and the Deathly Hallows* and Ridley Scott's *Robin Hood*. It's widely held to be Wales' best surf beach, but also one of the most dangerous for swimmers.

From Pembroke, it's just over 6 miles to Barafundle Bay (heading southeast) or 8 miles to Freshwater West (heading west). For all these sights, you could easily make a day of it. Best is to take the B4319 heading south from Pembroke; Bosherston and the Elegug Stack Rocks are reached from narrow country lanes branching off it. The B4319 continues past Freshwater West and terminates at the B4320, where you can turn right to return to Pembroke.

before reaching the coast at Newgale, a vast sandy surf beach backed by a high bank of pebbles. From here the road more or less shadows the coast.

Solva Colourful streetscape

9 Solva

Clustered around a long, hook-shaped harbour, Solva is the classic Welsh fishing village straight out of central casting. Pastel-hued cottages line the gurgling stream running through its lower reaches, while Georgian town houses cling to the cliffs above. When the tide's out, the water disappears completely from the harbour, leaving the sailing fleet striking angular poses on the sand.

Lower Solva is the part of interest to travellers. Amble about antique shops and galleries, settle in somewhere cosy for a meal or walk a section of the Pembrokeshire Coast Path which approaches its most exquisite around Solva. Our favourite eatery for its sheer novelty is MamGu Welshcakes (p307), a lively cafe specialising in wacky takes on the typical Welsh sweet snack of Welshcakes.

If you need to shed some calories afterwards, a 1-mile walk will take you upstream to the **Solva Woollen Mill** (☎01437-721112; www.solvawoollenmill.co.uk; Middle Mill; ⏰10am-5.30pm Mon, to 4pm Tue-Fri), the oldest working mill of its kind in Pembrokeshire.

✕ 🛏 p307

The Drive » You really can't go wrong on the 3-mile drive to St Davids. Just continue west.

TRIP HIGHLIGHT

10 St Davids

A city only by dint of its prestigious cathedral, pretty St Davids feels more like an oversized village. Yet this little settlement looms large in the Welsh consciousness as the hometown of its patron saint and has a very special vibe as a result.

Mesmeric **St David's Cathedral** (www.stdavidscathedral.org.uk; The Pebbles; ⏰10am-3pm Mon-Sat, 1-4pm Sun) stands on the site of the saint's own 6th-century religious settlement. Wonderful stone and wooden carvings decorate the interior, and there's a treasury and historic library hidden within.

St David was born at **St Non's Bay**, a ruggedly attractive section of coast with a holy well and a cute little chapel, a short walk from the centre of town. If it's a swim or surf you covet, head to broad, beautiful **Whitesands Bay** (Porth Mawr), although there are other quieter beaches dotted between the headlands hereabouts.

Also not to be missed are the city's distinguished bunch of cafes and restaurants, which are ever-ready to sate weary travellers' bellies.

But do not just dally in St Davids now that you have come this far west. Get out and roam the emerald-green, undulating landscape around as it bows to sandy and stony bays where you will truly feel the significance of the Welsh word *'Penfro'* which explains how Pembrokeshire gets its name. The meaning? 'Land's end.'

✕ 🛏 p307

Eating & Sleeping

Swansea 1

Dylan Thomas Birthplace — Guesthouse $$$

(☎01792-472555; www.dylanthomasbirthplace.com; 5 Cwmdonkin Dr, Uplands, SA2 0RA; r from £179) Dylan Thomas fans now have the unique opportunity to stay in the house where the poet was born and spent his first 23 years. The house has been diligently maintained in period style, and you'll have the choice of staying in the bedrooms once occupied by Nancy (his sister), DJ and Florrie (his parents), and of course Dylan himself.

Booking a room entails exclusive use of the house, so solo travellers will get it all to themselves! At the time of research there is a two-night minimum stay, although the price given is for one/two people for one night.

Mumbles 2

Môr — Seafood $$

(☎07932 385217; www.mor-mumbles.co.uk; 620 Mumbles Rd; mains £12-20; ⏰5.30-9pm Tue, 12.30-3.30pm & 5.30-9pm Wed-Sat, 12.30-8pm Sun) Some of the area's scrummiest seafood is proffered at this slick restaurant, such as succulent sea bass with bacon and dashi, although there is also turf beside the surf on the menu. Book in advance. 'Môr' in Welsh simply means sea.

Tides Reach Guest House — B&B $$

(☎01792-404877; www.tidesreachguesthouse.com; 388 Mumbles Rd; s/d from £65/80; P 📶) Tides Reach has maintained the same friendly service and delicious breakfasts across the years. Some rooms have sea views; we dig sea-facing Room 6. Two-night minimum stays can apply in peak periods.

Rhossili 4

Bay Bistro & Coffee House — Bistro $

(☎01792-390519; www.thebaybistro.co.uk; mains £7-15; ⏰10am-4pm Mon-Fri, 9am-5pm Sat & Sun; 🖉) This buzzy beach cafe has a sunny terrace, good surfy vibrations and the kind of drop-your-panini views that would make anything taste good – although the roster of burgers, sandwiches, salads, cakes and coffee stands up well regardless. On summer evenings it opens for alfresco meals.

Tenby 7

Plantagenet House — Modern British $$$

(☎01834-842350; www.plantagenettenby.co.uk; Quay Hill; mains lunch £10-12, dinner £25-28; ⏰noon-2.30pm & 6-9pm, reduced hours in winter; 🖉 👪) Atmosphere-wise, this place sure has the wow factor, ramping up the romance with cheek-by-jowl tables and candlelight. Tucked down an alley in Tenby's oldest house, parts of which date to the 10th century, it's dominated by an immense 12th-century Flemish chimney hearth. Tenby-caught fish, seafood and local organic beef are seasoned with freshly picked herbs, and the wine list is second to none.

Penally Abbey — Hotel $$$

(☎01834-843033; www.penally-abbey.com; Penally; r from £165; P 📶 🐾) One of Pembrokeshire's most alluring escapes, this ivy-wreathed fantasy of a Strawberry Gothic country house sits on a hillside amid acres of gardens and woodland, with soul-stirring views across Carmarthen Bay. Rooms blend calm colours and contemporary style with period charm, arched windows, embroidered white bedspreads and espresso machines. Built on the site of an ancient abbey in the village of Penally, it is 2 miles southwest of Tenby along the A4139.

For romance, top billing goes to the superior double with four-poster bed and dreamy views across the bay to Caldey Island. The country house's restaurant, **Rhosyn** (01834-843033; www.penally-abbey.com; Penally; mains £25-31; 2-4.30pm & 6.30-9pm Wed-Sat), is one for special occasions, too.

Pembroke 8

Woodbine B&B $$

(01646-686338; www.pembrokebedandbreakfast.co.uk; 84 Main St; s/d £65/85;) This well-kept, forest-green Georgian town house presents a smart face to Pembroke's main drag. The three pretty guest rooms are tastefully furnished, with original fireplaces, sash windows and bold colour schemes. A 17th-century Welsh slate floor and inglenook fireplace grace the breakfast room.

Solva 9

MamGu Welshcakes Cafe $

(01437-454369; www.mamguwelshcakes.com; 20 Main St; lunch mains £5.50-7, box 6 welshcakes £4; 9.30am-5pm Mon-Sat, 10am-4pm Sun) You'll see the humble welshcake in a whole new light after a visit to MamGu. Friends Becky and Thea travelled the world before landing in the fishing village of Solva and working their magic with a griddle. At this rustic-cool coastal cafe, welshcakes traverse the entire taste spectrum, with flavours from leek and cheese to ginger and chilli-chocolate. All are delicious.

Haroldston House B&B $$

(01437-721404; www.haroldstonhouse.co.uk; 29 High St; 3-night stay from £264; P) Occupying a Georgian merchant's house, this eco-aware B&B has a dash of contemporary boutique style. The tasteful self-catering apartments feature art by owner Ian McDonald as well as other Wales-based artists. Quarters are big on charm, whether you opt for the deep-blue Blue Room, with original floorboards, shutters and log burner, or the Stable Studio in a stylishly converted 18th-century stable pigsty.

St Davids 10

Really Wild Emporium Cafe $

(01437-721755; www.thereallywildemporium.co.uk; 24 High St; cakes £2.50-3, mains £8.50; 10am-4pm) Foragers Julia and John from **Wild About Pembrokeshire** (01437-721035; www.wildaboutpembrokeshire.co.uk; foraging per person from £12; Apr-Oct;) have had fun converting a high-ceilinged art deco building into this fabulous emporium in central St Davids. Exposed brick, reclaimed wood and corrugated iron set an industro-cool scene for dishes peppered with foraged ingredients – from pad thai with wild garlic seeds to insanely delicious seaweed brownies.

Twr y Felin Hotel $$$

(01437-725555; www.twryfelinhotel.com; Caerfai Rd; d £250-290, ste £320-420; P) Pembrokeshire-born architect Keith Griffiths put his stamp on Twr y Felin, using a 19th-century windmill as the impetus for this slickly modern hotel in private landscaped grounds. A collection of specially commissioned, large-scale contemporary art (including works by Welsh street artist Pure Evil) enlivens the monochrome, distinctly minimalist interiors. All rooms are luxurious, but top billing goes to the spectacular three-level circular suite in the tower itself.

Enjoy an aperitif in the subtly lit, gallery-style lounge bar before dinner at **Blas** (01437-725555; www.blasrestaurant.com; Caerfai Rd; mains £22-34, 7-course tasting menu £69), hands down one of the top tables in town.

Snowdonia National Park

Great fortresses of rock rising steeply from glittering lakes and ancient forests: this drive takes you deep into the Wales you've always dreamt of.

TRIP HIGHLIGHTS

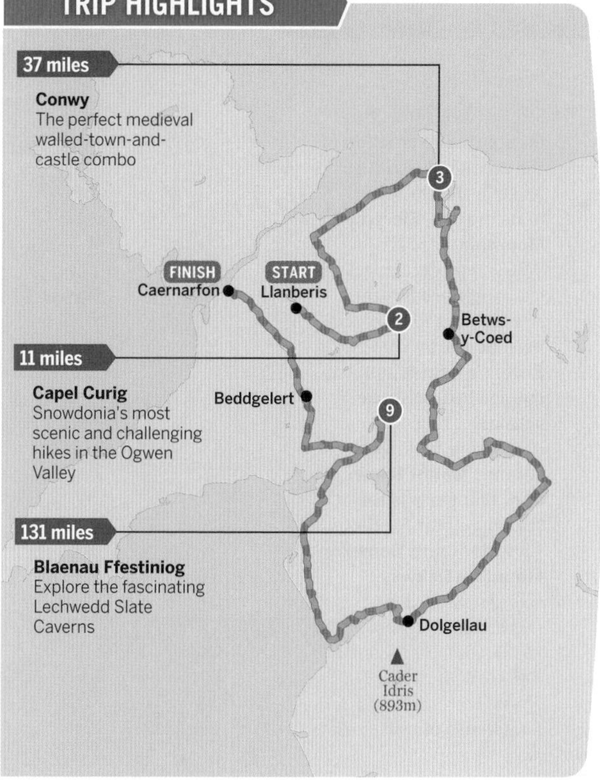

37 miles

Conwy
The perfect medieval walled-town-and-castle combo

FINISH Caernarfon

START Llanberis

Betws-y-Coed

11 miles

Capel Curig
Snowdonia's most scenic and challenging hikes in the Ogwen Valley

Beddgelert

131 miles

Blaenau Ffestiniog
Explore the fascinating Lechwedd Slate Caverns

Dolgellau

Cader Idris (893m)

4 DAYS
165 MILES / 266KM

GREAT FOR...

BEST TIME TO GO

Summer is best, although trails can get crowded during the school holidays (July and August).

ESSENTIAL PHOTO

The perfect medieval symmetry of Conwy's castle and walls.

BEST FOR OUTDOORS

The mountain ranges surrounding Capel Curig.

Conwy Conwy Castle

25 Snowdonia National Park

The treasures of the national park the Welsh call Eryri (The Highland) are laid before you, following this wild, winding route. You'll want to stop often to scramble up scree-scattered slopes, wander slate-built towns, venture down slate mines, and explore some of the mightiest castles in the British Isles. Pack your hiking boots, your camera and your sense of wonder: they'll all get a thorough workout.

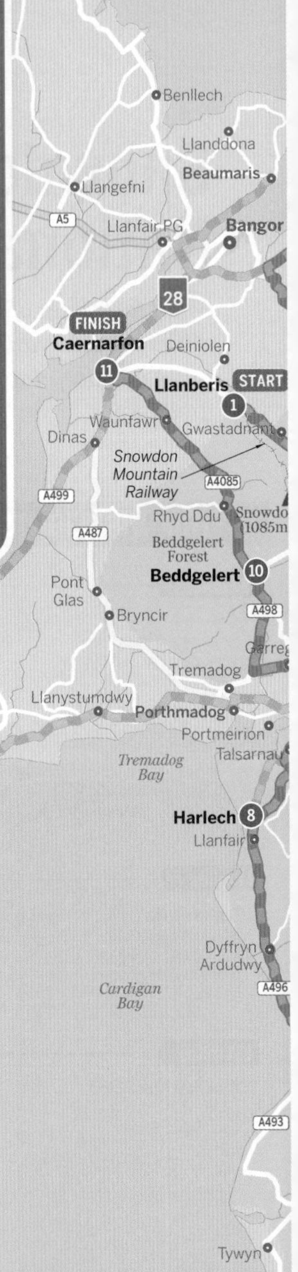

❶ Llanberis

Ground zero for rock climbers and mountain lovers, Llanberis is an offbeat little town that also offers a fantastic introduction to Snowdonia's industrial heritage. Climbers can sign up with a day stint with **Boulder Adventures** (☎01286-870556; www.boulderadventures.co.uk; Ty Du Rd; session/full day from £40/60), while history buffs are drawn by the atmospheric ruins of **Dobadarn Castle** (Castell Dolbadarn; Cadw; www.cadw.gov.wales; A4086; ⏲10am-4pm) and thc **National Slate Museum** (☎0300 111 2333; www.museum.wales/slate; off A4086; ⏲10am-4pm Sun, Mon, Wed & Thu; P), a fascinating re-creation of the area's industrial past. To get a similar sense of its present, **Electric Mountain** (☎01286-870636; www.electricmountain.co.uk) uncovers the science (and 16km of tunnels) of nearby Dinorwig, Europe's largest pumped-storage hydroelectric scheme.

If you're looking to summit **Mount Snowdon**, Llanberis is the starting point for the Victorian-built **Snowdon Mountain Railway** (☎01286-870223; www.snowdonrailway.co.uk; A4086; adult/child return diesel £29/20, steam £37/27; ⏲9am-5pm mid-Mar–Oct), a rack-and-pinion train

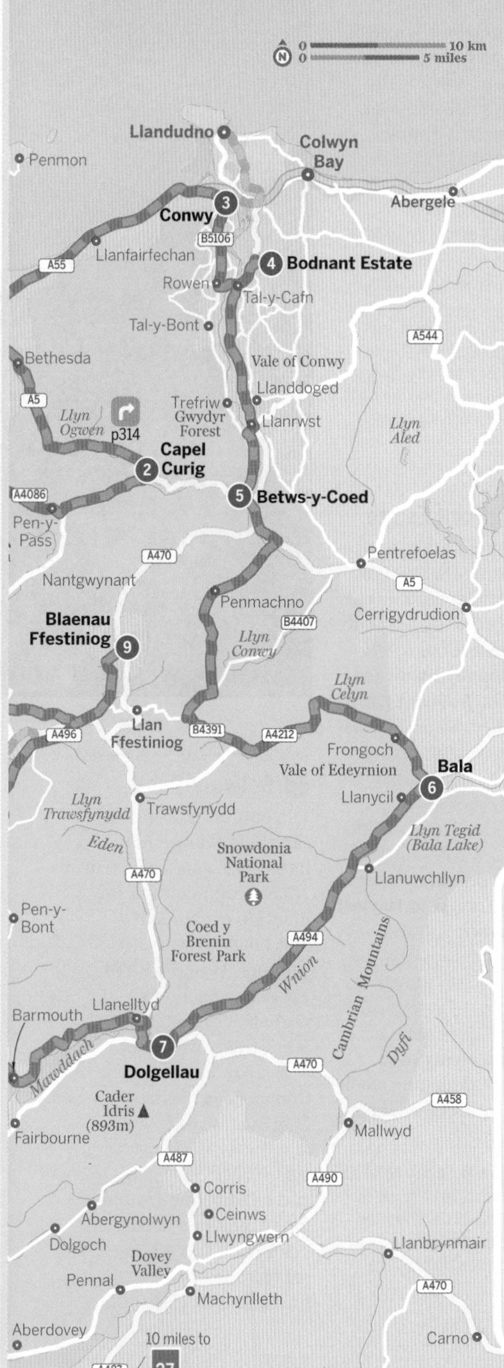

that scales Wales's highest peak; alternatively, just take the **Llanberis Path** to the top.

p316

The Drive » The 11-mile drive to Capel Curig offers an immediate introduction to Snowdonia's heady heights: the views from the Pen-y-Pass are impressive. Take the winding A4086 east out of Llanberis, then all the way to Capel Curig.

TRIP HIGHLIGHT

2 Capel Curig

Little more than an intersection, Capel Curig is a hugely popular walkers' base. From the hamlet, you can do a demanding half-day 5-mile ridge hike up **Moel Siabod**, or head for the nearby Ogwen Valley. Those seeking to polish their Bear Grylls skills should check out the excellent **Plas y Brenin National**

LINK YOUR TRIP

27 Wilderness Wales
Hop off the route at Dolgellau, heading 11 miles south on the A470 and 487 to Corris, to see another side of Wales's wild heart.

28 Northwest Wales
Jump ship at Conwy or Caernarfon to see more of what the northwest corner of Wales has to offer.

Mountain Sports Centre (01690-720214; www.pyb.co.uk; A4086;).

The Drive » The 26-mile drive to historic Conwy is worth it simply for the trip through the starkly beautiful Ogwen Valley, straddled by the Carneddau and Glyderau ranges. Take the A5 northwest from Capel Curig, then the North Wales Expressway northeast to Conwy.

TRIP HIGHLIGHT

3 Conwy

Ringed by medieval stone walls, Conwy is a banquet for medieval-history buffs. Its impressive **castle** (Cadw; 01492-592358; www.cadw..gov.wales; Castle Sq; adult/concession £8.80/5.40; 9.30am-5pm Mar-Jun, to 6pm Jul & Aug, shorter hours rest of year; P), commanding a narrow point in the mouth of the River Conwy, is complemented by the most complete set of **town walls** (Cadw; www.cadw.gov.wales; Rose Hill St) in Britain. Both were built in the late 13th century when this was an English garrison town lording it over the recently subdued Welsh.

Within the town, there are plenty more historical sights to be unearthed. **Plas Mawr** (Cadw; www.cadw.gov.wales; High St; adult/child £6.50/3.90; 9.30am-5pm Easter-Sep, to 4pm Oct) is one of the finest Elizabethan houses in Britain, while **Aberconwy House** is a merchant's house of the same vintage as the castle and town walls. And let's not skip over the excellent dining scene, either.

p316, p343

The Drive » The 7-mile hop from Conwy to Bodnant Estate takes you down the bucolic Conwy Valley. Take the Llanrwst Rd (B5106) south from near the castle, turning east onto the B5279 to cross the Conwy River, then north onto the A470, from which Bodnant Estate is signposted.

4 Bodnant Estate

Bodnant Estate is a beautiful estate that no fan of British landscaping should miss. Its horticultural collections are internationally renowned, while the **Bodnant Farm Shop** (01492-651931; www.bodnant-welshfood.co.uk; Furnace Farm, Tal-y-Cafn; farm shop 9.30am-5pm Mon-Sat, 10am-4pm Sun; P) is stocked with local and organic produce. There's also the excellent **Hayloft Restaurant** (01492-651102; www.bodnant-welshfood.co.uk; Bodnant Welsh Food, Furnace Farm, Tal-y-Cafn; mains £15-18; noon-3pm Sun), and plenty of courses (gardening, cooking, farming) throughout the year.

The Drive » Rejoin the A470, heading south to Llanrwst, then take the B5106 back over the Conwy and into Betws-y-Coed: about 13 miles all told.

EDDIE / 500PX ©

5 Betws-y-Coed

The outdoor-adventure capital of Snowdonia, Betws is a slate-coloured village commanding the junction of the Conwy and Llugwy rivers. In summer its many B&Bs are booked solid by walkers, climbers and other fresh-air fiends.

Nearby, check out the **Conwy Falls** (Rhaeadr Y Graig Lwyd; www.conwyfalls.com; A5, LL24 0PN; adult/child £1.50/1; 24hr;) and head below ground for adrenaline-packed via ferrata scrambles, subterranean zip-lining and freefalls into

Capel Curig Sheep in the hills surround this small village

darkness in a disused slate mine with **Go Below Underground Adventures** (01690-710108; www.go-below.co.uk; adventures £59-99; 9am-5pm). If you're looking for something more sedate, **Fairy Glen** (A470, LL24 0SH; 50p) is worth a walk and a swim, while **Gwydyr Forest** and **Swallow Falls** (Rhaeadr Ewynnol; A5, LL24 0DW; adult/child £1.50/50p) also attract their share of outdoorsy types. Finish off with some Spanish-Welsh tapas and an overnight stay at Olif.

p316

The Drive » The 27-mile drive to Bala is best appreciated taking narrow, winding B roads through ancient forest and past lakes: leave the A5 a few miles south of town, take the B4406 south through Penmachno, the B4391 east to the Tryweryn River, and the A4212 into Bala.

6 Bala

Quiet Bala is a jumping-off point for white-water rafting and kayaking with the **National White Water Centre** (Canolfan Dŵr Gwyn Genedlaethol; 01678-521083; www.ukrafting.co.uk; Frongoch, off A4212; rafting taster/full session £37/67; 9am-4.30pm Mon-Fri) on the River Tryweryn, and other forms of aquatic entertainment on Llyn Tegyn, Wales' largest natural lake, with **Bala Adventure & Watersports Centre** (01678-521059; www.balawatersports.com; Pensarn Rd; 9am-5pm, later in summer). Those preferring to keep dry might be tempted by a scenic ride on the narrow-gauge **Bala Lake railway** (01678-540666; www.bala-lake-railway.co.uk; adult/unaccompanied child return £12/6; Feb-Oct), or a blow-out meal at Michelin-starred **Tyddyn Llan** (01490-440264; www.tyddynllan.co.uk; B4401, Llandrillo; 3-/8-course dinner £75/95; lunch Fri-Sun,

DETOUR: OGWEN VALLEY TREKS

Start: 2 Capel Curig

If the wild calls when heading from Capel Curig to Conwy, give in to temptation to tackle some of Snowdonia's most scenic and challenging hikes. These are found in the Glyderau and Carneddau ranges, above the Ogwen Valley's glacial lakes, Llyn Ogwen and Llyn Idwal.

At the west end of Llyn Ogwen, **YHA Idwal Cottage** (0845 371 9744; www.yha.org.uk; A5, Nant Ffrancon LL57 3LZ; camping £12, dm/tw £25/59; daily Mar-Oct, Fri & Sat Nov-Feb) is the starting point for trails up the sharply angled **Tryfan** (918m) that take you high above **Llyn Idwal** (A5). Both Tryfan via Heather Terrace (4 miles) and Tryfan's North Ridge (4 miles) are demanding half-day treks; allow a full day to do the **Glyder Traverse** (6 miles) that takes in the other-worldly rock formations of the **Castle of the Winds** and **Devil's Kitchen**. On the other side of the A5, the spectacular 9-mile **Carnedd Loop** (A5, Tal-y-Llyn Ogwen Farm) awaits: a full-day adventure that comprises four mighty Carneddau peaks, including **Carnedd Llewelyn** (1064m), two highland lakes, and some scrambling.

From Capel Curig, head 5 miles northwest on the A5 to the bridge at Pont Pen-y-Benglog, where both lakes and walking trails begin. The YHA Idwal Cottage is your only overnighting option, but a good one. To rejoin the route, just continue up the A5 to Conwy.

---

dinner daily), a short drive from town.

The Drive » From Bala, it's a straightforward 18-mile drive southwest on the A494 (Bala Rd) to Dolgellau, skirting the northern shore of Llyn Tegyd.

7 Dolgellau

Built of handsome dark stone, Dolgellau boasts more than 200 heritage-listed buildings (the highest density of any town in Wales). With natural attractions such as the hikers' favourite Cader Idris on its doorstep, plus the bird-filled **Mawddach Estuary** (www.mawddachestuary.co.uk), and the mountain bikers' playground of **Coed y Brenin Forest Park** (01341-440747; www.naturalresources.wales/coedybrenin; A470; 9am-5pm Apr-Oct, shorter hours rest of year), it's well served with B&Bs, outlying farmstays and country houses, as well as imaginative restaurants, such as Tafarn y Gader (p316).

p316, p343

The Drive » The 20-mile drive to Harlech flanks the north side of the Mawddach Estuary, passing through the resort town of Barmouth and skirting the Cardigan Bay coast. Take the Cader Rd west out of town to the A493, head over the Mawddach to the A496 and follow it west through Barmouth, then north to Harlech.

8 Harlech

One of Wales's splendid 13th-century **castles** (Cadw; www.cadw.gov.wales; Castle St; adult/child £6.40/4.30; 10am-1pm & 2-5pm Wed-Sun) – and perhaps the most dramatically situated – commands the hill-town of Harlech. With views across Cardigan Bay to the Llŷn Peninsula in one direction, and towards Snowdonia's peaks in another, it's worth diverting up the steep road. Once there, you'll find top-notch B&Bs, cosy teashops, and some of the best bistros (p317) and Welsh comfort food – at **Castle Bistro Harlech** (01766-780416; www.castlebistroharlech.com; Stryd Fawr/High St; mains £12-17; 5.30-10pm Wed-Sun) – for miles around.

p317

The Drive » From Harlech, follow the Stryd Fawr (High St)/ B4573 northeast, merging with the A496 as it follows the River

Dwyryd further inland through woodlands. All up, this leg is 14 miles.

TRIP HIGHLIGHT

9 Blaenau Ffestiniog

Surrounded by striking mountains of shattered slate, Blaenau has made the most of its slate-mining heritage. It's the northern terminus of the former slate-carrying **Ffestiniog Railway** (Rheilffordd Ffestiniog; 01766-516024; www.festrail.co.uk; day ticket £25; daily Easter-Oct, reduced services rest of year;), which winds through the hills from coastal Porthmadog. Visitors may also explore the fascinating **Llechwedd Slate Caverns** (01766-830306; www.llechwedd.co.uk; A470; tours £20; 9.30am-5.30pm; P), **zip wire** (01248-601444; www.zipworld.co.uk; off A470, Llechwedd Slate Caverns; booking office 8am-6.30pm;) over vast open quarries, and tackle the seriously challenging mountain-bike trails of **Antur Stiniog** (01766-238007; www.anturstiniog.com; A470, Llechwedd Slate Caverns; 1 uplift £5, day pass from £31; 8am-5pm Thu-Mon Apr-Aug, Thu-Sun Sep-Mar) before hitting some creative Welsh-Greek fusion at **Caffi Kiki** (07450-325119; www.kikis-cafe.com; Lakeside Cafe, Tanygrisiau; mains £10; 5.30-8.30pm Fri & Sat;).

p317

The Drive » Backtrack southwest along the A496 to where the B4410 branches off to the west. Join the A498 at Prenteg, and follow its narrow curves north through dense forest and along the River Glaslyn to Beddgelert: all up a journey of 16 miles.

10 Beddgelert

Beautifully preserved Beddgelert, built of dark local stone at the junction of the Colwyn and Glaslyn rivers, is surrounded by photogenic hills and rolling farmland. This is prime walking country: consider dropping into the National Trust–owned **Craflwyn Farm** (NT; 01766-510120; www.nationaltrust.org.uk; A498) and taking on the 60-minute round-trip ramble to the hilltop of Dinas Emrys, legendary site of a castle built by King Vortigern. Alternatively, challenge yourself with a half-day ascent of **Moel Hebog Ridge** (off A4085), or take a gentle wander along the river to the legendary **Gelert's Grave** (24hr).

The Drive » Skirting the southern slopes of Snowdon and the northern shore of Llyn Cwellyn, the narrow valley road, A4085, winds its way 13 miles northwest to your last stop, Caernarfon.

11 Caernarfon

Any visit to Caernarfon inevitably focuses on its mighty **castle** (Cadw; www.cadw.gov.wales; adult/child £5.20/3.10; 10am-1pm & 2-5pm Mon-Wed, Sat & Sun;); its banded, hexagonal towers were designed in the 13th century to pay aesthetic tribute to the sturdy walls of Byzantium. Ironically for a town that figures strongly in both the Roman and English domination of Wales, Caernarfon is now a vibrant centre of Welsh language and culture. Well-stocked with characterful B&Bs, it also has some excellent pubs and restaurants – the Tuscan flavours of Osteria (p317) are standouts – and is the perfect base for forays across the Menai Strait to Anglesey, or along the less-trodden Llŷn Peninsula.

p317

Eating & Sleeping

Llanberis ❶

Beech Bank B&B $$

(01286-871085; www.beech-bank.co.uk; 2 High St; s/d from £70/80; P) First impressions of this double-gabled, wrought-iron-trimmed stone house are great, but step inside and it just gets better. A stylish renovation has resulted in beautiful bathrooms and exuberant decor, which matches the gregarious nature of the host. Breakfasts can be packed for early-rising hikers and climbers. Thoughtful touches, such as lending flasks to hikers, are a boon.

Conwy ❸

Watson's Bistro Welsh $$

(01492-596326; www.watsonsbistroconwy.co.uk; Bishop's Yard, Chapel St; 2-course lunch £15, mains £17-25; 5.30-8.30pm Wed, Thu & Sun, 5.30-9pm Fri, noon-2pm & 5.30-9pm Sat) In the lee of the town wall, Watson's holds the crown for the most imaginative cooking in Conwy proper, conjured out of locally sourced produce. Prepare to woo your sweetie over treacle-cured lamb with port and blackberry sauce, or perfectly seared steak with wild mushrooms. Everything is homemade, including the ice cream. An early-bird menu (three courses £25) is served before 6.30pm.

Amelie's French $$

(01492-583142; 10 High St; lunch mains £7-9.50, dinner mains £14-17; 11.30am-2.15pm & 6-9pm Tue-Sat;) Named after the Audrey Tautou film, and as friendly and beguiling as the film's star, this lovely boho bistro serves food that tastes as if it's been prepared by someone who really cares for you. This includes hearty homemade soup and open-faced crayfish sandwiches for lunch, and more substantial dinner mains, such as chicken cassoulet and other international dishes.

Y Capel Guesthouse $$

(01492-593535; www.ycapel.co.uk; Church St; s/d/f £100/120/220;) In its past incarnation, this welcoming guesthouse used to be the Bethesda Baptist Chapel (1846), which fell into disuse and disrepair in the 1970s. Lovingly restored, it is now an 11-room B&B. Rooms are compact and decorated in neutral colours, some with exposed wooden beams. Complimentary full Welsh breakfast is served at the Erskine Arms opposite.

Betws-y-Coed ❺

Olif Tapas $$

(01690-733942; www.olifbetws.wales; Holyhead Rd; tapas £5-7; 6-8.30pm Tue-Sun, noon-3pm Sat & Sun May-Oct, closed Mon-Wed Nov-Apr) Breakfast first up, burgers for lunch, and tapas and wine in the evening – Olif morphs to please throughout the day. The tapas have a distinctly Welsh flavour, without straying too far into fusion territory (the croquettes are made with Perl Wen cheese and the ham's from Camarthen) and fun finger foods, like popcorn cockles and cider-cooked mussels, abound.

Upstairs is a handful of bright boutique rooms, all en suite, with rain showers, and some with deep soaking tubs (rooms from £135).

Dolgellau ❼

Tafarn y Gader Tapas $$

(01341-421227; www.facebook.com/dolgellautapas; Smithfield St; tapas £5-11; 5-9pm Tue-Sat, 10am-2.30pm Sun;) Kicking Dolgellau's dining scene up a notch, this tapas bar is as ambitious as it is creative. There are some solid Spanish standards (*patatas bravas*, Serrano ham croquettes), but then dishes such as crispy rice with seared pigeon and marinated fennel and courgette carpaccio defy expectations, thrilling the tastebuds. A convivial atmosphere reigns amid the clinking of wine glasses.

Tyddyn Mawr Farmhouse Farmstay $$

(07979 377306; www.wales-guesthouse.co.uk; off A496, Tal-y-Bont; r incl breakfast £105; Feb-Nov; P) Two miles southwest of Dolgellau, off the A496, this oak-beamed 18th-century farmhouse nestles on the southern slopes of Cader Idris, and is mere steps away from the Pony Path. The two large, atmospheric bedrooms overlook the mountain, the owners make you feel like a family friend and the cooked breakfasts are excellent.

Harlech 8

As.Is

Bistro $

(01766-781208; www.asis-harlech.co.uk; The Square; mains £5-9.50; 5-9pm Mon-Sat) Overlooking the castle, this welcoming bistro features a short and sweet menu of solid, belly- and palate-pleasing food that doesn't bang on about 'taking you on a journey'. Highlights include sourdough pizza and jerk chicken wings, their crisp skin an allspice and chilli kick. The pared-down decor – naked wires, oversized light bulbs and rough timber tables – is equally pleasing.

Maelgwyn House

B&B $$

(01766-780087; www.maelgwynharlech.co.uk; Ffordd Isaf; r £98-135; Feb-Oct; P) A model B&B in an art-bedecked former boarding school, Maelgwyn has interesting hosts, delicious breakfasts and five elegant rooms (though attic Room 5 is rather snug) stocked with DVD players and tea-making facilities (ask for one of the three with sea views – they're definitely worth it). Bridget and Derek can also help arrange birdwatching trips and fungus forays.

Blaenau Ffestiniog 9

Bryn Elltyd Eco Guesthouse

Guesthouse $$

(01766-831356; www.ecoguesthouse.co.uk; Tanygrisiau; s/d from £60/90; P) Overlooking the Tanygrisiau reservoir, a mile south of Blaenau Ffestiniog, this wonderful guesthouse is 100% carbon-neutral, powered exclusively by renewables, and serving meals on request made from its own produce. Choose between the snug lake-view rooms in the main house or the two turf-roofed, sheep's-wool-insulated doubles in the garden. The location is great for bikers, hikers and canoe enthusiasts.

Caernarfon 11

Osteria

Tuscan $$

(01286-238050; 26 Hole in the Wall St; mains £12-15; 6-10pm Thu-Sat;) Two Tuscan partners opened this excellent addition to Caernarfon's dining scene in a compact building hard up against the city walls. Specialising in classic carpaccios and interesting bruschette (try the gorgonzola with walnuts and honey), they import many of their ingredients and wines from Tuscany and prepare daily specials such as stuffed vegetables and pasta with cod and cherry-tomato ragu.

Victoria House

B&B $$

(01286-678263; www.victoriahouse.wales; 13 Church St; s/d from £90/110; @) This is pretty much the perfect guesthouse – a delightful, solid Victorian building in Caernarfon's old town, run by exceptionally hospitable and attentive hosts. The four spacious, Victorian-style rooms include thoroughly contemporary touches, such as Chromecast. The Balcony Suite, with a private terrace looking across to Anglesey, is well worth the splurge, and breakfast is a joy.

Landscapes & Literature Across Southeast Wales

Take a magical journey along a splendid river valley flanked by graceful ruined abbeys and castles, before climbing through Brecon Beacons National Park to Britain's most bookish town.

TRIP HIGHLIGHTS

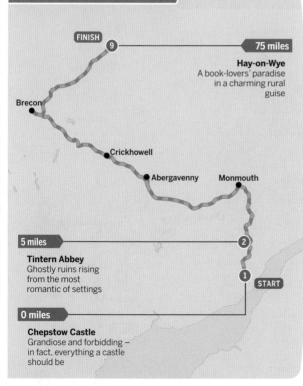

FINISH

9

75 miles

Hay-on-Wye
A book-lovers' paradise in a charming rural guise

Brecon

Crickhowell

Abergavenny

Monmouth

5 miles

2

Tintern Abbey
Ghostly ruins rising from the most romantic of settings

1

START

0 miles

Chepstow Castle
Grandiose and forbidding – in fact, everything a castle should be

3 DAYS
75 MILES / 121KM

GREAT FOR...

BEST TIME TO GO

This route is enjoyable year-round but consider May and June for spring flowers and the Hay Festival.

ESSENTIAL PHOTO

The spectral ruins of Tintern Abbey.

BEST FOR HISTORY

Exploring the hidden nooks of Chepstow and Raglan castles.

Tintern Tintern Abbey

26 Landscapes & Literature Across Southeast Wales

The Wye Valley was the very birthplace of British tourism. From as early as 1760, English high society flocked here to view artfully ruined Tintern Abbey and the many castles along the way. The romantic vistas that fired the likes of Turner, Coleridge and Wordsworth remain substantially intact today. The trip continues through the ravishing heart of rural Monmouthshire, then enters the starkly beautiful high country of Brecon Beacons National Park.

TRIP HIGHLIGHT

1 Chepstow

If you were in any doubt this was a border town, check out **Chepstow Castle** (Cadw; ☎01291-624065; www.cadw.gov.wales; Bridge St; adult/child £6.50/3.90; ⊙10am-1pm & 2-5pm Wed-Sun Mar-Oct, to 4pm Nov-Feb; 👪), standing guard over the River Wye, which still marks the divide between the two nations of Wales and England. This colossal fortress was founded by the Normans immedi-

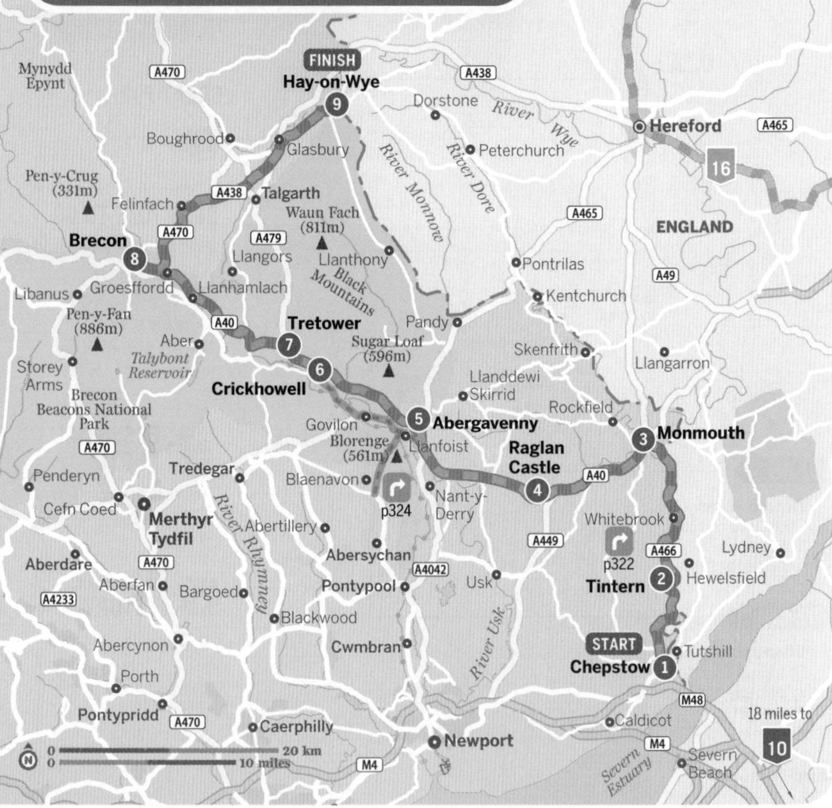

ately after their conquest of England, making it among Britain's oldest castles. It's a fascinating place to poke about in, but try not to wake King Arthur, who's believed to be snoozing in a cavern underneath the castle, until he's needed to save the day.

The town itself was once held in the castle's stony embrace by a surrounding wall, sections of which still remain. The old part of Chepstow is a likeable place to potter about in, with some good eateries, pubs and shops, and a little local **history museum** (01291-625981; www.visitmonmouthshire.com; cnr Bridge St & Gwy Ct; 11am-2pm Tue, to 4pm Sat).

p326

LINK YOUR TRIP

10 Winchester, Glastonbury & Bath

It's a 45-minute (30-mile) drive from Bath to Chepstow via the M4 and Severn Bridge.

16 Central England Industrial Powerhouse

From Great Malvern, it's 45 miles to Chepstow (allow 1¼ hours); head south to Gloucester and take the A48.

The Drive » From Chepstow, take the A466 north past Chepstow Racecourse and along the wooded Wye Valley to Tintern. It's an enchanting 5-mile drive, rendered rather mysterious when the morning mist, as it often does, lingers thickly.

TRIP HIGHLIGHT

2 Tintern

Immortalised by painters and poets down the ages, the enigmatic ruins of **Tintern Abbey** (Cadw; 0300 025 2239; www.cadw.gov.wales; Tintern; adult/child £5/2.30; 10am-1pm & 2-5pm Wed-Sun Mar-Oct, to 4pm Nov-Feb; P) are ridiculously picturesque. Part of it is the setting, with the River Wye on one side and forested hills fanning all around. The rest is down to the soaring grandeur of the Gothic architecture, made no less stirring by the lack of a roof or windows. Founded in 1131 by the Cistercian order, it was left to fall into elegant ruin after Henry VIII dissolved all of Britain's monasteries in the 16th century.

Tintern village spreads along the river for about a mile. There are some cracking local walks, including easy riverside tracks in the vicinity of the **Old Station** (01291-689566; www.visitmonmouthshire.com; parking per 3hr/day £2/4; 10am-5.30pm Apr-Oct; P) visitor centre-cum-cafe and the classic **Devil's Pulpit** (above Tintern; 24hr) hike up into those broccoli-green hills.

p326

The Drive » Beautiful landscapes keep unfurling as you progress up this tree-lined river valley. The road crosses the river into England and back before reaching Monmouth, a journey of 12 miles.

3 Monmouth

The county town of Monmouthshire is as English a town as you'll find in Wales. In fact, the border has shifted backwards and forwards over the centuries, shunting it between the two countries.

The rivers Monnow and Wye curl around the historic town centre, creating a natural moat to what was once a walled town attached to **Monmouth Castle** (www.monmouthcastlemuseum.org.uk; Castle Hill). All that remains of this august fortress – the birthplace of Henry V – is a small section of wall and part of a tower. In a much better state of repair is **Monnow Bridge**, the UK's only remaining medieval fortified bridge, which abuts the main street.

Monmouth's other famous son was Charles Stewart Rolls, co-founder of Rolls-Royce. Discover more about his life in the **Nelson Museum & Local History Centre**

DETOUR: WHITEBROOK

Start: 2 Tintern

The tiny hamlet of Whitebrook sits in peaceful seclusion on the Welsh side of the River Wye, reached only by extremely narrow country lanes. There's absolutely no reason to drive this way, as the main road hopped over to the easier English side of the river 2 miles earlier. Unless, of course, you're journeying to the **Whitebrook** (01600-860254; www.thewhitebrook.co.uk; Whitebrook, NP25 4TX; 3-course menu/lunch/dinner £35/55/85, d incl dinner from £330; noon-2pm & 7-9pm Wed-Sun; P), an exceptional restaurant awarded a Michelin star for its inventive approach to Modern British cuisine. If you are feeling indulgent, consider booking a room and making a night of it. To carry on to Monmouth, you're best backtracking along the same lane to rejoin the A466 at the bridge where it takes its English shortcut.

BILLY STOCK / SHUTTERSTOCK ©

(01600-710630; www.visitmonmouthshire.com; Priory St; 11am-2pm Tue, to 4pm Sat). The museum also has extensive displays on Admiral Horatio Nelson.

p326

The Drive » From Monmouth, take the busy A40 dual carriageway southwest for 9 miles. Raglan Castle rears into view to the right of the highway. Continue on to the roundabout near Raglan village before doubling back to enter the site.

4 Raglan Castle

Standing in majestic ruin beside a busy highway, **Raglan Castle** (Cadw; 01291-690228; www.cadw.gov.wales; Castle Rd, Raglan; adult/child £6.50/3.90; 10am-1pm & 2-5pm Wed-Sun Mar-Sep, 11am-4pm Wed-Sun Nov-Feb; P) is much more ornate than any castle needs to be. That's because defence was only part of its purpose – showing off the wealth, power and good taste of its owners was equally important. Much of the sandstone used in its construction has a pinkish hue, and elegant courtyards were backed by halls decorated with elaborate windows and fireplaces.

Raglan fell into disrepair after the Civil War of the 1640s. Still, much of the structure is intact and you should at allow an hour to fully explore the site.

The Drive » From the castle, backtrack down the highway to the nearest roundabout before swinging back past the castle on the A40 to Abergavenny. On the 11-mile trip, the mountains of Brecon Beacons National Park loom distractingly ever-nearer.

5 Abergavenny

Sitting on the doorstep of Brecon Beacons National Park, ringed by oddly shaped mountains, the Monmouthshire market town of Abergavenny makes a great base for walkers and other active types. It's also become a gastronomic hot spot, due to the quality of local farm produce and a handful of high-profile restaurants scattered about the surrounding countryside.

Raglan Raglan Castle

In the town itself, the main attraction is the imposing **St Mary's Priory Church** (01873-858787; www.stmarys-priory.org; Monk St; 9am-4pm Mon-Sat), filled with so many grand tombs that it's been dubbed the 'Westminster Abbey of Wales'. Once attached to a monastery, it survived Henry VIII's reforms by being converted into a parish church. The neighbouring 12th-century **Tithe Barn** (01873-858787; www.stmarys-priory.org; Monk St; 9am-4pm Mon-Sat) now holds a heritage centre and food hall showcasing Welsh products.

Abergavenny's castle is humble by Welsh standards, with only a few stretches of curtain wall and a local history **museum** (01873-854282; www.abergavennymuseum.co.uk; Castle St; 11am-2pm Thu, 1-4pm Sun) where the keep once stood.

On a literary note, contemporary writer Owen Sheers went to school in Abergavenny.

p326

The Drive » Leaving Abergavenny via the A40, you'll quickly enter Brecon Beacons National Park and cross into Powys. The highway shadows the River Usk, albeit from a distance, with the Sugar Loaf mountain to the right. You'll reach Crickhowell after 6 miles.

6 Crickhowell

Like Abergavenny, the picturesque, flower-festooned village of Crickhowell is encircled by contorted Black Mountains peaks, which form the eastern section of Brecon Beacons National Park. Aside from a crumbling castle, its main feature of interest is an elegant bridge over the River Usk, which has more arches on one side than the other. That is in addition to the proudly, prettily independent shops, restaurants and pubs that contributed towards this little honeypot winning 'Best Place to Live in Wales' in 2019 according to the *Sunday Times*.

Crickhowell takes its name from **Crug Hywel** (Table Mountain), a flat-topped mountain with the remains of an Iron Age fort at its summit. It makes an excellent target for a steep 3-mile-return walk. The **Crickhowell Walking Festival** (www.crickhowellfestival.com; ⊙Mar) in March throws further light on the region's delightful hikes.

🛏 p327

The Drive » It's under 3 miles from Crickhowell to Tretower, your next stop. Take the A40 out of town and then veer right onto the A479. Look for the sign to Tretower Court on your left.

7 Tretower

By the 15th century, the Vaughan family, like many toffs of the time, had tired of living in their drafty old castle and decided to build a more

DETOUR: BLAENAVON

Start: 5 Abergavenny

You have done pastoral, but industrial is just as much a defining landscape of this part of Wales. The coal mines of the South Wales Valleys once fuelled Britain's industrial revolution and powered the might of the British Navy. That all came to a standstill during the mine closures of the 1980s. The close-knit communities of the valleys took a major hit, unemployment soared and whole towns faced extinction.

One such place was Blaenavon, a town that came into being in the 18th century after the construction of the world's biggest ironworks. In the year 2000, 20 years after its Big Pit coal mine was closed, Blaenavon's unique conglomeration of industrial sites was awarded World Heritage status by Unesco, igniting a rebirth of sorts.

Start your visit at the excellent **Blaenavon World Heritage Centre** (☎01495-742333; www.visitblaenavon.co.uk; Church Rd; ⊙10am-5pm Tue-Sun) to put everything into perspective. The town's main attraction is the **Big Pit National Coal Museum** (☎0300 111 2333; www.museum.wales/bigpit; car park £3; ⊙10am-5pm Tue, Wed, Fri & Sat, guided tours 10am-3.30pm; P 👪), where you can get a feel for what life was like working the coal seam. The biggest attraction, heading 90m down into the pit depths under the guidance of former miners, was closed at the time of research but the above-ground museum is absolutely fascinating in its own right.

The historic **Blaenavon Ironworks** (Cadw; ☎01495-792615; www.cadw.gov.wales; North St; adult/child £5.20/3.10; ⊙10am-5pm daily Easter-Oct, 11am-4pm Fri-Sun Nov-Easter) are another must-see, the hulking ruins brought to life through audiovisual displays. A group of local enthusiasts has also resurrected a section of the **Pontypool & Blaenavon Railway** (☎01495-792263; www.bhrailway.co.uk; Furnace Sidings, Garn-Yr-Erw; per 8-person compartment £32), which once hauled coal down from the mines. Check online to see if/when steam trains are running to Whistle Stop, the highest station in both Wales and England.

Another byproduct of the town's reinvention is the **Blaenavon Cheddar Company** (☎01495-793123; www.chunkofcheese.co.uk; 80 Broad St; ⊙10am-3pm Mon-Fri), which produces award-winning cheeses, some of which are matured in the Big Pit itself.

Blaenavon is 7 miles southwest of Abergavenny via the B4246. From here you can continue back to the Head of the Valleys Rd and on through Llangattock to Crickhowell; 10 miles all told.

comfortable pad nearby. The result was **Tretower Court** (Cadw; www.cadw.gov.wales; Tretower; adult/child £6.50/3.90; ⏱10am-1pm & 2-5pm Mon-Wed, Sat & Sun), a large fortified house, still standing today in the unassuming hamlet of Tretower.

Most rooms have been left bare, but the kitchens and banquetting hall have been enlivened with period-style furnishings and implements. The house has also been used for period dramas including movies *Restoration* and *The Libertine*.

Don't forget to check out the medieval garden beside the house and to cross the fields to the Vaughan's old digs – the sturdy Norman motte-and-bailey castle, reminiscent of a giant's abandoned chess piece.

The Drive » Continue along the lane past Tretower Court to rejoin the A40, which leads to Brecon. It's a good, scenic road through the pastures that comprise the Brecon Beacons foothills. The journey is less than 12 miles; allow 20 minutes.

8 Brecon

At the confluence of the rivers Usk and Honddu, Brecon is a ruggedly handsome market town and major trailhead/activity hub for hiking and other outdoor pursuits in Brecon Beacons National Park.

When the Normans did their conquering hereabouts, inevitably they built a castle and a monastery. **Brecknock Castle** (Castle Sq) has largely been consumed by a hotel, but the monk's church has fared better, being subsequently converted into impressive **Brecon Cathedral** (☎01874-623857; www.breconcathedral.org.uk; Cathedral Close; ⏱11am-4pm Mon-Sat, to 3pm Sun). If you're interested in military history, don't miss the **Regimental Museum of the Royal Welsh** (☎01874-613310; www.royalwelsh.org.uk; The Barracks, The Watton; adult/child £5/2; ⏱10am-5pm Mon-Fri).

Brecon is the northern terminus of the **Monmouthshire & Brecon Canal**. Regular cruises depart from the Canal Basin, or you can hire your own boat for a self-guided trip. The canal towpath is a popular walking and cycling route. The bigger draw for walkers are the craggy summits of the Brecon Beacons, protruding like immense upturned antique irons near town. The key target is the summit of **Pen-y-Fan**.

✕ 🛏 p327

The Drive » For the 17-mile jaunt to Hay-on-Wye, bear east out of town along the Watton and then turn left onto the A470, which eventually becomes the A438. The road to Hay (the B4350) branches off at Glasbury.

TRIP HIGHLIGHT

9 Hay-on-Wye

If there's anywhere more bookish than Hay-on-Wye we'd be seriously surprised. Once a pretty but nondescript agricultural centre, Hay reinvented itself in the 1970s under the instigation of local maverick Richard Booth, who opened the world's largest bookshop in a defunct cinema, bought crumbling Hay Castle (www.haycastletrust.org), declared himself king, attracted national attention and saved the town from the decline facing many rural communities at the time.

Others took note and now there are literally dozens of new, secondhand, specialist and antiquarian bookshops in this small Powys town. On top of that, Hay-on-Wye is now the setting for the **Hay Festival** (☎box office 01497-822629; www.hayfestival.com; ticket prices vary; ⏱late May-early Jun), arguably the most famous literature event in the world and famously dubbed 'Woodstock of the mind' by former US president Bill Clinton.

Spend your Hay time alternating between bookshops, antique stores and pubs, and be sure to check out some of the excellent local eateries.

🛏 p327

Eating & Sleeping

Chepstow 1

Stonerock Pizza Pizza **$$**

(☎01291-621616; www.stonerockpizza.co.uk; 9-10 Upper Church St; pizzas £13-15; ⏱5-9pm Mon-Thu, to 9.30pm Fri, noon-9.30pm Sat, noon-9pm Sun) Those with a penchant for pizza will know that while you can grab a doughy, cheesy circle down at the supermarket for a pittance, it makes a world of difference having an artisan one cooked for you by people that have studied the art of Neapolitan pizza for 18 months. This little place's 'best pizzeria in the UK' awards stand testament.

Three Tuns Pub **$**

(☎01291-645797; 32 Bridge St; s/d from £45/65;) This mid-17th-century pub by the castle is Chepstow's best watering hole to grab a pint or take your pick from the pie-heavy pub menu (mains £10.50). With Tintern-based Kingstone Brewery beers, and an artful makeover, with rugs and antique furniture complementing the more rugged features of the ancient building, it's equally conducive to stay in one of the three en-suite guest rooms.

Tintern 2

Hop Garden Cabin **$$**

(☎01291-680111; www.thehopgarden.co.uk/glamping; Kingstone Brewery, NP16 7NX; d £115; P) The serene meadows and copses encompassing **Kingstone Brewery** (☎01291-680111; www.kingstonebrewery.co.uk; NP16 7NX; ⏱noon-4pm Mon-Wed, Fri & Sat; P) secrete five creaky glamping retreats, collectively called the Hop Garden: two shepherd's huts and three cabins, all isolated from each other, each sleeping two and abounding with their own fabulous quirks. Escaping the day-to-day is the point, so there's no wi-fi, but each has a wood-burning stove or outside firepit, which is much more fun!

Monmouth 3

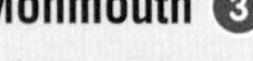

Stonemill Modern European **$$$**

(☎01600-716273; www.thestonemill.co.uk; B4233, Rockfield, NP25 5SW; lunch mains £13-27, 2-course dinner £27-31; ⏱noon-2pm & 6-9pm Wed-Sat, noon-2pm Sun) Housed in a 16th-century barn, 2.5 miles northwest of Monmouth, this upmarket restaurant showcases Welsh produce in Italian- and French-influenced dishes. It prides itself on making all of its own bread, pasta, pastries, jam, chutneys, ice cream and sorbets. The complex also has six stone and oak-beamed cottages for hire.

Abergavenny 5

Walnut Tree Modern British **$$$**

(☎01873-852797; www.thewalnuttreeinn.com; Old Ross Rd, Llanddewi Skirrid; mains £28-32, 2-/3-course lunch £30/35; ⏱noon-2.30pm & 6-10pm Wed-Sat; P) Established in 1963, the Michelin-starred Walnut Tree serves the cuisine-hopping meat and seafood creations of chef Shaun Hill, with a focus on fresh, local produce. If you're too full to move far after feasting on dishes such as middle white pork loin with glazed cheek and cauliflower, elegant cottage accommodation is available (from £175).

The Walnut Tree is 3 miles northeast of Abergavenny on the B4521.

Hardwick Modern British **$$$**

(☎01873-854220; www.thehardwick.co.uk; Old Raglan Rd; mains £17-27, 2-/3-course Sun lunch £26/30; ⏱noon-2.30 & 5.30-8pm Wed-Fri, noon-2.30pm & 6-9pm Sat, noon-3.30pm Sun; P) This traditional inn – with its old stone fireplace, low ceiling beams and burnished copper bar – has become head chef Stephen Terry's showcase for the best of unpretentious country cooking. Dishes such as braised rabbit with fried polenta are deeply satisfying, but you need to save room for the homemade ice cream. Attached are eight elegant rooms (from £135). The Hardwick is 2 miles south of Abergavenny on the B4598.

Angel Hotel Hotel **$$$**

(☎01873-857121; www.angelabergavenny.com; 15 Cross St; r £135-195, cottages £255-295; P) Abergavenny's top hotel is a fine Georgian building that was once a famous coaching inn. Choose between sleek, sophisticated rooms in the hotel itself, in an adjoining mews, in a Victorian lodge near the castle or in the 17th-century Castle Cottage (sleeping four). There's also a good restaurant and bar, serving modern British food and elaborate afternoon and high teas.

Crickhowell 6

Bear Pub **$$**

(01873-810408; www.bearhotel.co.uk; Beaufort St; incl breakfast s £99-192, d £123-248; P) If only every village in Wales had a pub like this… Looking back on 600 years of history, the Bear was once an overnight stop on the horse-drawn coach journey from London to West Wales. Now a delightfully old-school gastropub and hotel, it's full of creaky character, with blackened-oak beams, log fires and cosy nooks.

Brecon 8

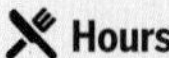

Hours Cafe **$**

(01874-622800; www.thehoursbrecon.co.uk; 15 Ship St; mains £5.75-8.25; 11am-4pm Tue-Sat;) You might happily linger for hours in this little dream of an indie bookshop and cafe, lodged in an endearingly wonky olive-green cottage. The cafe takes pride in local sourcing. Besides fair-trade coffee, it does a fine line in lunches and light bites, from homemade soups, quiche and sandwiches to halloumi with roasted veg. The cakes are delicious, too.

Peterstone Court Hotel **$$$**

(01874-665387; www.peterstone-court.com; Llanhamlach; d £155-235, ste £275; P) This elegant Georgian manor house on the banks of the Usk offers large rooms brimming with period charm and affording superb views across the valley to the Beacons. The spa is another big draw, with organic beauty treatments, a Moroccan-style relaxation room and a heated outdoor pool. There's also a separate three-bedroom cottage and an excellent restaurant.

Hay-on-Wye 9

By the Wye B&B **$$$**

(01497-828166; www.bythewye.uk; The Start; safari tents £130-195) Reclining in ancient native woodland on the banks of the River Wye, this eco-minded escape takes glamping to a whole new luxury level. Perched on stilts high in the tree canopy, the safari tents are sublime, with fantasy-like beds handmade from gnarly driftwood and lots of above-and-beyond details, including welcome baskets with local goodies, firepits, decks overlooking the river and binoculars for bird-spotting.

Wilderness Wales

From cetacean-rich Cardigan Bay to the great swelling upland of the Cambrian Mountains, Wales' wild heart will take your breath away.

TRIP HIGHLIGHTS

38 miles

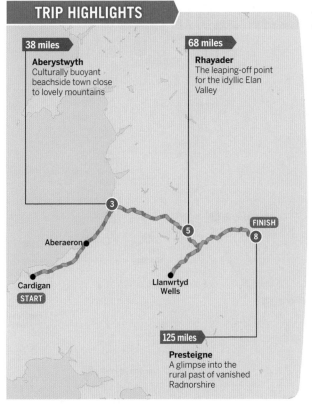

Aberystwyth
Culturally buoyant beachside town close to lovely mountains

68 miles

Rhayader
The leaping-off point for the idyllic Elan Valley

3
5
FINISH
8
Aberaeron
Cardigan
START
Llanwrtyd Wells

125 miles

Presteigne
A glimpse into the rural past of vanished Radnorshire

4 DAYS
125 MILES / 201KM

GREAT FOR ...

BEST TIME TO GO

Hiking, events and dolphin-spotting are best in summer. December to February brings snow to the Cambrian Mountains.

ESSENTIAL PHOTO

The mighty Victorian dams of the Elan Valley.

BEST FOR WILDLIFE

Red kites wheel over Rhayader and other locales in the Cambrian Mountains.

Devil's Bridge Three superimposed bridges over a cataract of the River Rheidol

27 Wilderness Wales

With cities to the south and outdoors magnet Snowdonia to the north, mid-Wales' natural grandeur is often ignored. This drive – from the historic port of Cardigan, through bright beach towns, Victorian spa country, pretty market towns, the great 'Desert of Wales' (as the empty Cambrian Mountains often get dubbed) and the forests and estuaries of the green northwest – shows how wrong this neglect is. We guarantee you won't forget this tour.

1 Cardigan

An important medieval and Elizabethan port, Cardigan is emerging from long obscurity to stake a claim as a major centre of culture in mid-Wales. Its riverside **castle** (Castell Aberteifi; ☎01239-615131; www.cardigancastle.com; cnr Bridge & Quay Sts; adult/child £6/3; ⏰10am-4pm; 👪) – where in the 12th century the first Eisteddfod was held – has been carefully restored, and serves once again as a bastion of Welsh culture, offering self-guided

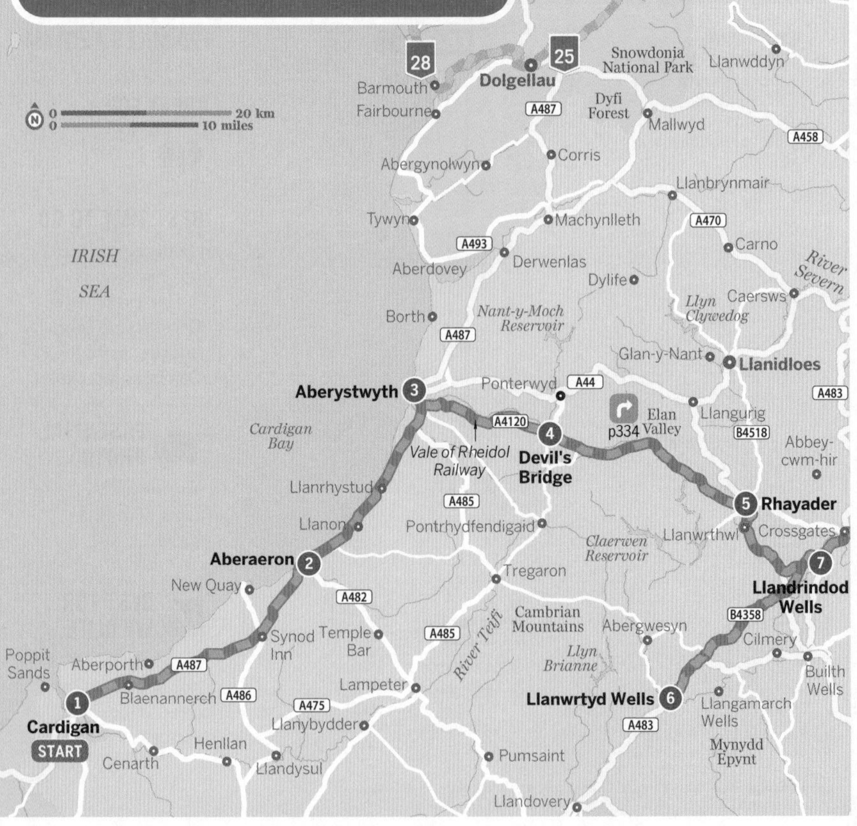

tours, performances, a sophisticated restaurant and more. Beyond, the vast sweep of Cardigan Bay promises stunning **encounters** (☎01239-623558; www.baytoremember.co.uk; Prince Charles Quay; adult/child from £26/13; ⌚Apr-Oct; 🐾) with dolphins, seals and birdlife (book boat trips online beforehand), whilst quiet sandy beaches like **Mwnt** (NT; www.nationaltrust.org.uk; SA43 1QH; parking per day £4) speckle the coastline heading north.

🛏 p335

The Drive » Take the A487 out of town as it heads northeast and inland for 22 miles, before rejoining the coast just outside the pretty harbour town of Aberaeron.

2 Aberaeron

With its colourful quayside rows of Georgian houses and shipping offices, many now occupied by top-notch B&Bs and hotels, Aberaeron makes a great stop alongside a tempestuous stretch of coast. Most of the appeal – such as the beautiful boutique hotel-restaurant Harbourmaster (p335) – is to be found along Pen Cei (Quay Parade, on the waterfront), but it's well worth the 2.5-mile trek out of town to visit **Llanerchaeron** (NT; ☎01545-570200; www.nationaltrust.org.uk; SA48 8DG; Ciliau Aeron; grounds only £5/2.50; ⌚garden & grounds 10.30am-5pm, shorter hours winter, woodland walks daily year-round; P), a lovely Georgian country estate.

🛏 p335

LINK YOUR TRIP

25 Snowdonia National Park

This is easily accessed from Aberystwyth by heading northeast on the A487, 24 miles to Corris.

The Drive » Continue cruising north up the coast until you hit the Mid-Wales metropolis of Aberystwyth (population under 20,000!); all up, the journey is 16 miles.

TRIP HIGHLIGHT

3 Aberystwyth

Not exactly the wilderness, but a very diverting place to spend an afternoon (or evening, or night) between your wild adventures, Aberystwyth is a lively student town lining a long, sandy beach with a big mix of attractions. Culturally, it's hard to go past the **National Library** (Llyfrgell Genedlaethol Cymru; ☎01970-632800; www.llgc.org.uk; Penglais Rd; ⌚9am-6pm Mon-Fri, to 5pm Sat), which surmounts a hill befitting its eminence behind the town, or the brilliant **Aberystwyth Arts Centre** (Canolfan Y Celfyddydau; ☎01970-623232; www.aberystwythartscentre.co.uk; Penglais Rd, SY23 3DE; ⌚box office 10am-8pm Mon-Sat, noon-5.30pm Sun). There's also a picturesque ruined **castle** (King St) and pubs aplenty to keep students and seaside drinkers happy. Dining-wise, there are many gems among Aber's twisting streets. Importantly, gorgeous countryside is also close: the northern Cambrian Mountains and Southern Snowdonia are extremely easy to access from town.

🛏 p335

The Drive » From Aberystwyth, it's a 12-mile climb on the A4120 to the wooded ravine of Devil's Bridge.

4 Devil's Bridge

The eponymous **bridge** (Pontarfynach; ☎01970-890233; www.devilsbridgefalls.co.uk; SY23 4QY; adult/child £4/2.50; ⏰24hr, staffed 9.30am-5pm Mar-Oct) is the main attraction at this otherwise out-of-the way corner of Mid-Wales. Spanning a cataract where the River Rheidol plunges into the homonymous gorge, it's actually a palimpsest of three overlapping bridges: the top built of iron in the early 20th century, the middle of stone in the mid-18th, and the first (also of stone) in the 11th.

It's worth paying the few pounds to descend into the gorge and the Coed Rheidol National Nature Reserve, with its dripping oaks and photogenic glimpses of the bridge. Devil's Bridge is also the inland terminus of the **Vale of Rheidol Railway** (☎01970-625819; www.rheidolrailway.co.uk; Park Ave; return adult/child £26/11; ⏰mid-Feb–Nov; 👪), a narrow-gauge industrial train preserved as a tourist attraction that clings to the slopes as it wends its picturesque way to coast-hugging Aberystwyth.

The Drive » From Devil's Bridge, you'll be venturing further into the back of beyond, skittering on narrow, remote lanes via Cwmystwyth, 18 miles to Rhayader.

TRIP HIGHLIGHT

5 Rhayader

An important agricultural centre, Rhayader is most appealing for its access to surrounding wild places. It's the closest centre to the delightfully dramatic

Elan Valley Craig Goch Dam

Elan Valley (p334), with its monumental Victorian and Edwardian dams, and is also handy for the beginning of the **Wye Valley Walk** (www.wyevalleywalk.org). Watch out for red kites wheeling overhead throughout these Cambrian uplands. For refreshment, try diminutive but characterful **Triangle Inn** (☎01597-810537; www.triangleinn.co.uk; Cwmdauddwr; mains £8-16; ⏲5-10pm Mon-Sat; 📶).

The Drive » From Rhayader, the next 20-mile stage snakes south and west on the A470 and A483 to Llanwrtyd Wells.

6 Llanwrtyd Wells

Mid-Wales' capital of kooky, little Llanwrtyd and its surrounding hills are home to a variety of weird and wonderful annual events, including **bog snorkelling** (www.green-events.co.uk; adult/child £15/12; ⏲bank holiday Aug) and a **fell-running competition** (www.green-events.co.uk; ⏲mid-Jun) that pits man against horse. Dining, drinking and sleeping options are also rich for such a tiny town, and include **Drovers Rest** (☎01591-610264; www.food-food-food.co.uk; The Square; 3 courses £35; ⏲noon-2pm & 7.30-9.30pm Wed-Sun; 📶) and the **Neuadd Arms** (☎01591-610236; www.neuaddarmshotel.co.uk; mains £8.50-14, 3-course meal £18.50; ⏲9am-10pm) – hub of the local community. The town is also a great base for forging out into the Cambrian Mountains to the north.

🛏 p335

The Drive » Jaunt along the A483 northeast from Llanwrtyd, switching to the B4358 at Beulah. Continue past Newbridge-on-Wye, joining the A4081 for a while to arrive at Llandrindod Wells; 17 miles all told.

DETOUR: THE ELAN VALLEY

Start: 5 Rhayader

From Rhayader, you really should head into the human-sculpted wilderness of the Elan Valley. It feels immediately wild once you leave civilisation behind, yet its defining features are the four mighty Victorian and Edwardian dams that were created to ensure water supplies to, ahem, Birmingham. Inevitably controversial, they've nonetheless created a 70-sq-mile chain of lake, forest and bog environments in Mid-Wales in which many rare plants and animals, and the totemic red kite, thrive. Nant-y-Gro, an early dam built here, was used in 1942 as target practice by Sir Barnes Neville Wallis, inventor of the 'dam-busting' bouncing bomb.

Elan Valley Visitor Centre (☎01597-810880; www.elanvalley.org.uk; B4518, Caban-coch Reservoir, LD6 5HP; ⊙9am-5pm Apr-Oct, 10am-4pm Nov-Mar) has all the information a visitor could need, including the specifics of many local hikes. In season, the **Penbont House** (☎01597-811515; LD6 5HS; s £65, d £90-130; ⊙tearoom 10am-6pm Apr-Sep, to 4.30pm winter; P 📶) makes for a delightful lunch or tea stop, and can provide accommodation too. From Rhayader, the visitor centre is less than 4 miles southwest on the B4518; backtrack to rejoin the main route.

7 Llandrindod Wells

The Victorian-Edwardian heyday of this spa town is still evident in the grand architecture of its hotels and terraces, however quiet they may be today. Hotel-spas still fly the flag of formal luxury, the mineral fountains and rambling gardens of **Rock Park** hint at bygone glory days, when visitors from around Britain would arrive to take the waters, and there is a 13-acre **lake** (LD1 5NU) with a Welsh water-spouting dragon at its centre for further ambles. For freewheeling fans there is also the **National Cycle Museum** (☎01597-825531; www.cyclemuseum.org.uk; cnr Temple St & Spa Rd East; adult/child £5/2; ⊙10am-4pm Tue & Wed, to 2pm Fri).

p335

The Drive » A 20-mile drive from here ushers you to Presteigne on the A483, A44, A488 and B4356 through the hills of historical Radnorshire. You journey via Crossgates and then Pilleth, site of an important battle victory for Owain Glyndŵr against the English under Sir Edward Mortimer, during the ultimately unsuccessful Welsh War of Independence.

TRIP HIGHLIGHT

8 Presteigne

The undemonstrative beauty of the former county of Radnorshire can be seen at something like its best in pretty little Presteigne with its winsome timber-framed buildings, independent shops and sophisticated air. In town, the **Judge's Lodging** (☎01544-260650; www.judgeslodging.org.uk; Broad St; adult/child £8.95/4.95; ⊙10.30am-4.30pm Wed-Sun Mar-Oct) reanimates a Victorian rural magistrate's household in exacting detail. Out of it, you have landed in a gentle chunk of unsung undulating Welsh countryside, with the **Offa's Dyke** (www.nationaltrail.co.uk) national trail on the doorstep. Bang on the border with England, it is also a fitting place to end your wild wanderings through Wales. Toast your trip in one of the nation's best real country pubs, the Harp Inn at Old Radnor, 6.5 miles southwest of town.

p335

Eating & Sleeping

Cardigan 1

Gwbert Hotel Hotel **$$**
(01239-612638; www.gwberthotel.com; Gwbert, SA43 1PP; s/d from £65/85; P) With unspoilt views from the cliff-lined inlet through which the Teifi flows into Cardigan Bay, and 21 comfortable, understated en-suite rooms (many better and higher priced than others), the Gwbert is among Cardigan's most appealing sleeps. There are hearty breakfasts and the Flat Rock bistro, which combines upmarket pub and bistro classics (mains £10 to £17). Located three miles north of Cardigan.

Aberaeron 2

Harbourmaster Hotel Boutique Hotel **$$$**
(01545-570755; www.harbour-master.com; Pen Cei, SA46 0BT; s/d from £140/150;) Standing proudly at Aberaeron's harbour entrance, this boutique hotel offers accommodation worthy of any chic city bolthole, besides its now famously fantastic food. The striking, indigo-painted Georgian buildings hold 13 singularly decorated rooms (seven in the main house) featuring Frette linens, Welsh blankets, bold colour schemes and high-tech bathrooms.

Rooms in the newly restored grain warehouse have the same contemporary styling, with excellent harbour views.

Downstairs, Harbourmaster's restaurant does delicious things with local seafood and Welsh beef, lamb and cheese (mains £12 to £28). Check the website for dinner-and-room packages and be aware that two-night minimums are sometimes in effect.

Aberystwyth 3

Bodalwyn B&B **$$**
(07969-298875; www.bodalwyn.co.uk; Queen's Ave; s/d from £49/69;) Simultaneously upmarket and full of home comforts, this handsome Edwardian B&B offers tasteful rooms with sparkling bathrooms and a hearty cooked breakfast (with vegetarian options). Three of the rooms have sea views, but ask for room 3, with the bay window.

Llanwrtyd Wells 

Lasswade Country House B&B **$$**
(01591-610515; www.lasswadehotel.co.uk; Station Rd; s/d from £70/85; P) This excellent country restaurant (with rooms) makes great use of a handsome, three-storey Edwardian house looking over the Irfon Valley towards the Brecon Beacons. Committed to green tourism (it's won multiple awards, sources hydroelectric power and offers electric-vehicle recharging), it's also big on gastronomy: the chef-owner's three-course menu (£36) features Cambrian lamb, Tally goats cheese and other delights.

Llandrindod Wells 7

The Cottage B&B **$$**
(01597-825435; www.thecottagebandb.co.uk; Spa Rd; s/d £48/75) A really class B&B in a rambling, Arts and Crafts–style Edwardian house, the Cottage exhibits comfortable period-style rooms with heavy wooden furniture and myriad original features, set within a winsome garden.

Presteigne 8

Harp Inn Pub Food **$$**
(01544-350655; www.harpinnradnor.co.uk; Old Radnor, LD8 2RH; mains £10-19; 6-10pm Wed & Thu, 5-10pm Fri, noon-2.30pm & 5-10pm Sat, noon-10pm Sun) One of the finest, most unspoilt rural pubs hereabouts, the Harp Inn is a treasure of a tavern in a stone-built Welsh longhouse commanding beautiful bucolic views over a melange of hiking trail-laced hills. Savour a thoughtful menu that is mainly pub food elevated several levels above standard whilst quaffing a local ale in snug, timber-framed, bare-stone-walled surrounds.

Northwest Wales

Shaped by pilgrims, conquerors and the restless sea, northwest Wales is an extraordinary corner of the British Isles that begs to be explored from behind the wheel.

TRIP HIGHLIGHTS

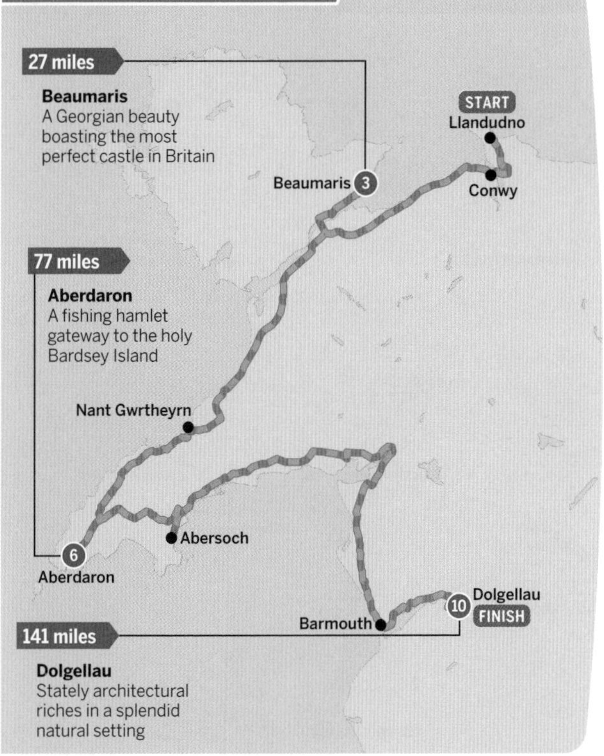

27 miles

Beaumaris
A Georgian beauty boasting the most perfect castle in Britain

77 miles

Aberdaron
A fishing hamlet gateway to the holy Bardsey Island

141 miles

Dolgellau
Stately architectural riches in a splendid natural setting

START
Llandudno
Conwy
Beaumaris 3
Nant Gwrtheyrn
Abersoch
6 Aberdaron
Barmouth
10 Dolgellau
FINISH

4 DAYS
141 MILES / 227KM

GREAT FOR...

BEST TIME TO GO

Flowers in bloom and warm weather make May a lovely time to visit.

ESSENTIAL PHOTO

Bardsey, the holy island of pilgrims, from Braich-y-Pwll at the tip of the Llŷn Peninsula.

BEST FOR HISTORY

The mock-Byzantine splendour of Caernarfon Castle.

Dolgellau Cycling in the town's natural surrounds

28 Northwest Wales

Starting from the bustling seaside resort of Llandudno, whose Victorian spirit lingers on, this trip takes in some of the mightiest castles and most dramatic coastline in the entire country. The medieval towns of Conwy, Beaumaris and Caernarfon give way to the Llŷn Peninsula's enchanting mix of pastoral landscapes and rugged cliffs, before the drive finishes among the heritage towns and bird-rich wetlands around the Mawddach River.

1 Llandudno

Strikingly situated below the towering limestone plateau of **Great Orme** (Y Gogarth), where you can explore the most extensive **Bronze Age mine** (☎01492-870447; www.greatormemines.info; Bishop's Quarry Rd; adult/child £8/5.50; ⏰9.30am-5.30pm mid-Mar–Oct; P 👪) yet discovered, Llandudno retains many of the attractions of its Victorian heyday: a grand promenade, a **Victorian pier** (www.llandudnopier.com; North Pde; ⏰9am-11pm summer, to 6pm rest of year;

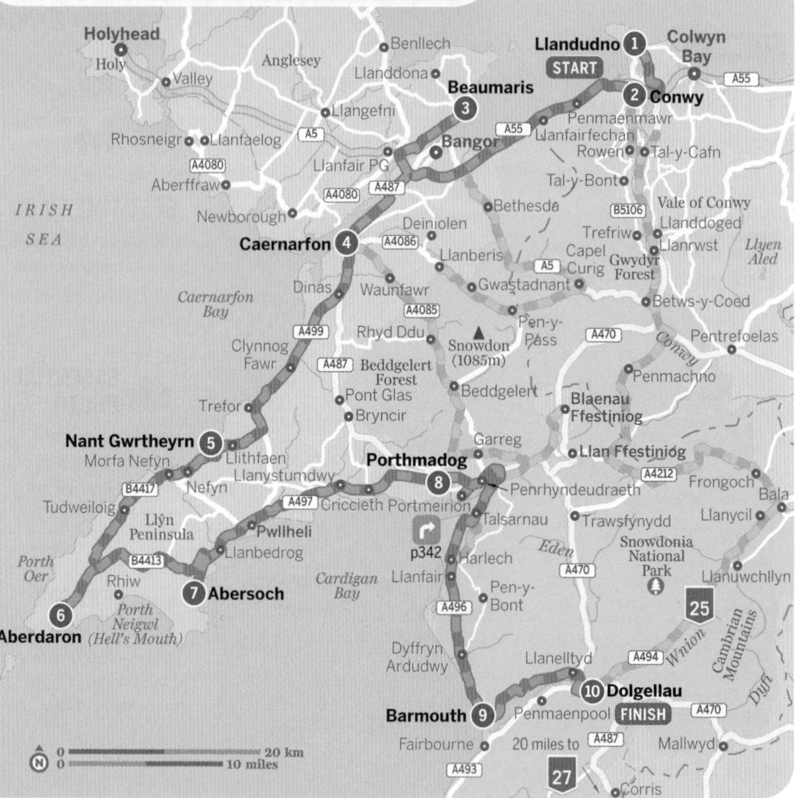

), a rack-and-pinion **tramway** (01492-577877; www.greatormetramway.co.uk; Victoria Station, Church Walks; adult/child return £8.10/5.60; 10am-6pm Easter-Oct), and even a **Punch and Judy show** (07900-555515; www.punchandjudy.com/codgal.htm; The Promenade; noon-4pm Sat & Sun year-round, daily school holidays Easter–mid-Sep). Add a huge range of B&Bs and restaurants, **Mostyn Gallery** (www.mostyn.org; 12 Vaughan St; 11am-4pm Tue-Sun), and this amounts to one of the highlights of the North Wales seaboard.

p343

The Drive » This first leg is just 4 miles, south down the A456 to Llandudno Junction, then west onto the A456 and through the tunnel under the River Conwy.

LINK YOUR TRIP

25 Snowdonia National Park

Join this circuit of Wales' most famous uplands at Dolgellau.

27 Wilderness Wales

Follow the A487 for 34 miles southwest of Dolgellau to start this tour of Wales' wild heart in reverse, at Aberystwyth.

2 Conwy

Conwy is a near-perfect medieval walled town with a superlative castle. Built in the 13th century as a key part of Edward I's 'Iron Ring', Conwy Castle (p312) has survived centuries of mixed fortunes; you stroll along sections of its mighty town wall for great views. The Old Town is studded with other historical and cultural attractions, such as Plas Mawr. Excellent accommodation, **real ale pubs** (01492-582484; www.albionalehouse.weebly.com; 1-4 Upper Gate St; noon-11pm Sun-Thu, to midnight Fri & Sat;), and fantastic eating options encourage you to linger longer.

p316, p343

The Drive » The Bangor Rd/A457 heads west out of Conwy to the A55. Cross the Menai Strait on the Pont Britannia, then take the A5 east into the town of Menai Bridge, following Dale St, then High St/Cadnant Rd until it joins Beaumaris Rd. It's 23 miles to your next stop.

TRIP HIGHLIGHT

3 Beaumaris

Beaumaris' broad streets, lined with handsome Georgian buildings, lead the visitor inevitably to the waterfront, and the town's unsurpassed **castle** (Cadw; www.cadw.gov.wales; Castle St; adult/child £6.50/3.90; 9.30am-5pm daily Mar-Jun, 10am-1pm & 2-5pm Mon-Wed, Sat & Sun Jul-Oct, shorter hours rest of year), a 13th-century masterpiece considered to be the most perfectly designed fortress in the British Isles. If you're not sated by history, there's also the 17th-century **courthouse** (Llys Biwmares; www.visitanglesey.co.uk; Castle St; adult/child £4/3; 10.30am-5pm Sat-Thu Apr-Oct) and Georgian **Gaol** (www.visitanglesey.co.uk; Steeple Lane; adult/child £7/5; 10am-5pm Apr-Oct, to 4pm Mar) to explore, as well as **Penmon Priory** (Cadw; www.cadw.gov.wales; B5109, Penmon; parking £3; 10am-4pm; P), a short drive north. It's also worth a **Seacoast Safaris** (07854 028393; www.seacoastsafaris.co.uk; Alma St, Pier House; Apr-Oct;) cruise to **Puffin Island** to view its clamouring bird population. Finish with a showstopper meal at the Michelin-starred **Sosban & the Old Butchers** (01248-208131; www.sosbanandtheoldbutchers.com; Trinity House, 1 High St; 8-course tasting menu £125; 7-11pm Wed-Sat) in nearby Menai Bridge.

p343

The Drive » Backtrack along the roads from Beaumaris to Menai Bridge, turn south over the eponymous bridge itself to join the A487, and head southwest for 13 miles to reach Caernarfon.

4 Caernarfon

Caernarfon's castle (p315), built during the same 13th-century push for English military consolidation as Conwy and Beaumaris, is just as impressive. Its hexagonal Byzantine-style walls are still pretty much complete, and tower over the Menai Strait and medieval town. Just outside the town walls are the remains of **Segontium** (Cadw; www.cadw.gov.wales; Ffordd Cwstenin; ⏲10am-4pm), a Roman fort from an earlier conquest, while inside there are excellent pubs, B&Bs and restaurants.

S-F / SHUTTERSTOCK ©

The Drive » The 18-mile leg to Nant Gwrtheyrn on the Llŷn Peninsula starts on the A487, south of Caernarfon. Take the A499 to the southwest, then the B4417 at Llanaelhaearn. The minor road over the hill to Nant Gwrtheyrn is signposted from Lithfaen.

5 Nant Gwrtheyrn

Reachable via the hairpin bends of a steep and narrow road, the 19th century buildings of Nant Gwrtheyrn have been revived as the **Welsh Language & Heritage Centre** (☎01758-750334; www.nantgwrtheyrn.org; Nant Gwrtheyrn, Llithfaen; 5-day course incl full board £495; ⏲call ahead for times), a bastion of Welsh culture. From the car park above the village, you can also do a wonderful hill walk to the **Tre'r Ceiri Hillfort** (⏲24hr), one of the best-preserved Iron Age forts in Europe, for tremendous views of the Llŷn from the top.

The Drive » Backtrack over the hill and then back down to Lithfaen, taking the B4417 west through Pistyll and Nefyn, and further west once you join the B4413. It's 19 miles to Aberdaron.

TRIP HIGHLIGHT

6 Aberdaron

It's worth persisting to the very end of the Llŷn Peninsula. The rocky tip of this barren outpost of Celtic Britain is starkly beautiful and the fishing hamlet of Aberdaron is the natural base from which to explore this unique landscape. You can detour to **Porthor** (Whistling Sands; NT; www.nationaltrust.org.uk; parking £4), aka Whistling Sands, to ride the waves there. And the view of the Pilgrims' Island of Bardsey across the gun-metal sea from the headland of **Mynydd Mawr** (NT; www.nationaltrust.org.uk; Lon Uwchmynydd), is one of north Wales' most arresting sights. In summer cross the treacherous waters on one of **Bardsey Boat Trips** (☎07971 769895; www.

Caernarfon Caernarfon Castle

bardseyboattrips.com; adult/child £35/25) to go birding or walking on the 'Isle of 20,000 Saints'.

The Drive » The narrow, scenic 13-mile drive to Abersoch follows the B4413 uphill and inland, then south along a signposted minor road into town.

7 Abersoch

Laid-back and lovely even in the colder months, with its Blue Flag beach and views across Cardigan Bay to Snowdonia, Abersoch gets particularly lively in summer, when crowds of visitors descend to swell its B&Bs, campsites and pubs. If you have the time to work on your sailing, wakeboarding, kitesurfing or surfing skills, try **Abersoch Sailing School** (☎07917-525540; www.abersochsailingschool.co.uk; LL53 7DP; ⏲8.30am-7pm Mar-Oct) or **Offaxis** (☎01758-713407; www.offaxis.co.uk; Lôn Engan; 2hr lessons incl equipment from £30; ⏲10am-5pm Mon-Fri, 9am-6pm Sat, 10.30am-4pm Sun). Abersoch's popularity sustains a number of well-above-par restaurants.

🛏 p343

The Drive » Take the A499 northeast, through Llanbedrog to Pwllheli. From there the A497 follows the coastal railway, through Criccieth to Porthmadog: all up, it's 20 miles.

8 Porthmadog

The former slate port of Porthmadog is a natural stopping point when driving from the Llŷn Peninsula to the northwest Welsh coast. It's also the start of two classic Welsh heritage railways – the **Welsh Highland** (☎01766-516000; www.festrail.co.uk; £40 return; ⏲Easter-Oct, limited service winter) and Ffestiniog

DETOUR: PORTMEIRION

Start: 8 Porthmadog

This fantasy village, created by visionary architect Sir Clough Williams-Ellis over five decades from 1925, is in a category of its own. Occupying a peninsula with a microclimate mild enough to encourage the growth of many exotic plants, it's a homage to what Williams-Ellis saw as the ideal human-made environments of the Mediterranean. Spend an hour or two wandering its fanciful Italianate piazzas, set-piece landscapes and visually delightful follies. The cult 1960s TV show *The Prisoner* was filmed here: every year the **PortmeiriCon** (Prisoner Convention; www.portmeiricon.com; Portmeirion; ⏲Apr) convention draws together its devotees.

Portmeirion is a 3-mile dash along High St/Britannia Tce from central Porthmadog, heading southeast over the broad Glaslyn River Estuary. When you reach Minfford, take the signposted road to Portmeirion. Just retrace your steps to recommence the itinerary.

(p315) lines – and a central point on the Cambrian Coast line to Pwllheli. Real ale fans will appreciate **Australia** (☎01766-515957; www.facebook.com/australiaporthmadog; 31 High St; ⏲noon-10pm Sun-Thu, to midnight Fri & Sat; 📶), a pub run by Purple Moose, a leading craft brewer in northern Wales.

The Drive » The 21 miles to Barmouth take in the sweep of Cardigan Bay. Take Porthmadog High St north, and join the A487 heading east. Leave the A487 at Penrhyndeudraeth, take the Briwet Bridge south, join the A496 and pass through Harlech on the way to Barmouth.

9 Barmouth

Barmouth may be a typical seaside resort, but its Victorian architecture and proximity to the walks and birdlife of the Mawddach Estuary (p314) make it special. Its impressive **railway bridge**, built in the town's heyday, spanning 699m of the Mawdach's mouth, is its most distinctive feature. It's well worth scrambling up **Dinas Oleu** hill for the panoramic views of the estuary and checking out **Tŷ Crwn Roundhouse** (www.barsailinst.org.uk/crwn.html; The Quay; ⏲10.30am-5pm), the former prison for drunk sailors and slatterns.

The Drive » The last, winding 10-mile stretch skirts the northern edge of the wide, sandy Mawddach Estuary. The A496 takes you to the junction with the A470, just north of the Mawddach River; from here, head south into Dolgellau.

TRIP HIGHLIGHT

10 Dolgellau

The charming market town of Dolgellau is one of the highlights of northwest Wales. This former wool and gold town has more than its share of listed buildings and an enviable natural setting. Dolgellau's proximity to **Cader Idris** (www.cadairidriswales.com), the walking and cycling trails passing through the Mawddach Estuary (p314) and the mountain-biking playground of Coed y Brenin Forest Park (p314) make it a natural base for fresh-air fiends. Exceptional B&Bs, coupled with creative tapas and wine bars such as **Gwin Dylanwad Wine** (☎01341-422870; www.dylanwad.co.uk; Porth Marchnad; snacks £1-5; ⏲10am-6pm Mon-Thu, to 8pm Fri & Sat) and Tafarn y Gader (p316), add to the appeal.

p316, p343

Eating & Sleeping

Llandudno 1

Escape B&B — B&B $$

(☎01492-877776; www.escapebandb.co.uk; 48 Church Walks; r from £110; P 📶) Escape is the original design B&B in Llandudno, with nine individually styled double bedrooms brimming with boutique-chic ambience and a host of ecofriendly and quirky features. Even if you're not an interior-design geek, you'll love the honesty-bar lounge, Bose iPod docks, DVD library, stand-alone roll-top baths, tasty breakfasts and atmosphere of indulgence. Suitable for kids over 10.

Conwy 2

Watson's Bistro — Welsh $$

(☎01492-596326; www.watsonsbistroconwy.co.uk; Bishop's Yard, Chapel St; 2-course lunch £15, mains £17-25; ⏲5.30-8.30pm Wed, Thu & Sun, 5.30-9pm Fri, noon-2pm & 5.30-9pm Sat) In the lee of the town wall, Watson's holds the crown for the most imaginative cooking in Conwy proper, conjured out of locally sourced produce. Prepare to woo your sweetie over treacle-cured lamb with port and blackberry sauce, or perfectly seared steak with wild mushrooms. Everything is homemade, including the ice cream. An early-bird menu (three courses £25) is served before 6.30pm.

Beaumaris 3

Bull — Historic Hotel $$

(☎01248-810329; www.bullsheadinn.co.uk; Castle St; d inn/Townhouse from £110/130, ste £166; 📶) These sister properties, the Bull and Townhouse, located across the road from each other, provide quite a contrast. Where the Bull – occupying an ancient coaching inn – is historic and retains original features, such as the heavy wooden beams (we love the suite with roll-top bath), the Townhouse is contemporary, high-tech and design driven. Breakfast is served at the inn.

Abersoch 7

Porth Tocyn — Historic Hotel $$$

(☎01758-713303; www.porthtocynhotel.co.uk; Bwlchtocyn, LL53 7BU; s/d incl breakfast from £105/168, cottage £200; ⏲mid-Mar–Oct; P 📶 🏊) Near the south end of Abersoch beach and overlooking Cardigan Bay, this country hotel comprises 17 beautifully appointed rooms, all decked out with luxury fabrics and king-sized beds, and a fine restaurant. Families are welcome, with a dedicated children's play area, but if you're looking for luxurious seclusion and solitary walks, consider renting Bwthyn Bach, a beautifully renovated stone cottage.

Barmouth 9

Celtic Cabin Cafe — Cafe $

(☎07775 331241; www.facebook.com/celticcabinbarmouth; Marine Pde; wraps £5-8; ⏲10am-6pm; 🖉) A wonderful addition to Barmouth's dining scene, this beachside cafe/takeaway joint specialises in terrific filled wraps, freshly made and served on the picnic tables with a view of the dunes and the sea. Try wraps with slow-roasted pork shoulder, falafel and hummus or locally caught mackerel and couscous...don't forget to finish with the homemade banana bread!

Dolgellau 10

Tan y Gader — B&B $$

(☎01341-421102; www.tanygader.co.uk; Meyrick St; s/d from £80/90; P 📶) There is much to love about this wonderful guesthouse. There are just three rooms, each playfully decorated to reflect a beloved children's classic (Alice, Secret Garden, Narnia); Narnia features a claw-footed tub. There are lots of thoughtful extras, and the owners go the extra mile when it comes to breakfast – a delicious gathering of locally sourced ingredients.

STRETCH YOUR LEGS CARDIFF

Start/Finish: The Hayes

Distance: 1.5 miles

Duration: 3 hours

The historic core of Wales' buzzy little capital is easily explored on foot. This route escorts you through busy shopping streets to the stunning castle and then through ravishing parkland to Cardiff's gleaming Civic Centre.

Take this walk on Trip

The Hayes

The Hayes is Cardiff's bustling car-free shopping strip, sporting a warren of dignified Victorian/Edwardian arcades on one side. At the end of the thoroughfare is Yr Hen Lyfrgell, or The Old Library, an ornate sandstone library building housing the very interesting **Museum of Cardiff** (029-2034 6214; www.cardiffmuseum.com; Yr Hen Lyfrgell, The Hayes; 10am-4pm). This is an excellent ambassador for city history and also a Welsh language hub.

The Walk » Directly behind Yr Hen Lyfrgell is a small park, with St John the Baptist Church on the other side.

St John the Baptist Church

This elegant 15th-century **church** (029-2039 5231; www.stjohnscardiff.wales; 3 St John St, CF10 1GL; 10am-3pm Mon-Sat, to 6pm Sun) is one of only a few medieval buildings left in central Cardiff. The delicate stonework on its fine Gothic tower is particularly impressive.

The Walk » Exit onto Trinity St and look for the entrance to Cardiff Market opposite the park.

Cardiff Market

Vibrant **Cardiff Market** (www.cardiffcouncilproperty.com/cardiff-market; St Mary St, CF10 1AU; 8am-4.30pm Mon-Sat) has been selling fresh produce and hardware since 1891, and the array of stalls here give a little insight into the city's soul. The cast-iron market hall still has the original market office in its centre, topped by a clock tower. It's great to gravitate here for a barter, a banter or a tasty snack.

The Walk » Exit via the opposite end of the market and turn right on to St Mary St, another blissfully car-free thoroughfare. Cardiff Castle is straight ahead.

Cardiff Castle

Cardiff Castle (029-2087 8100; www.cardiffcastle.com; Castle St; adult/child £14.50/10, incl guided tour £19.50/14; 9am-6pm Mar-Oct, to 5pm Nov-Feb) encompasses the city's entire history within its very grand fabric. The Normans built their

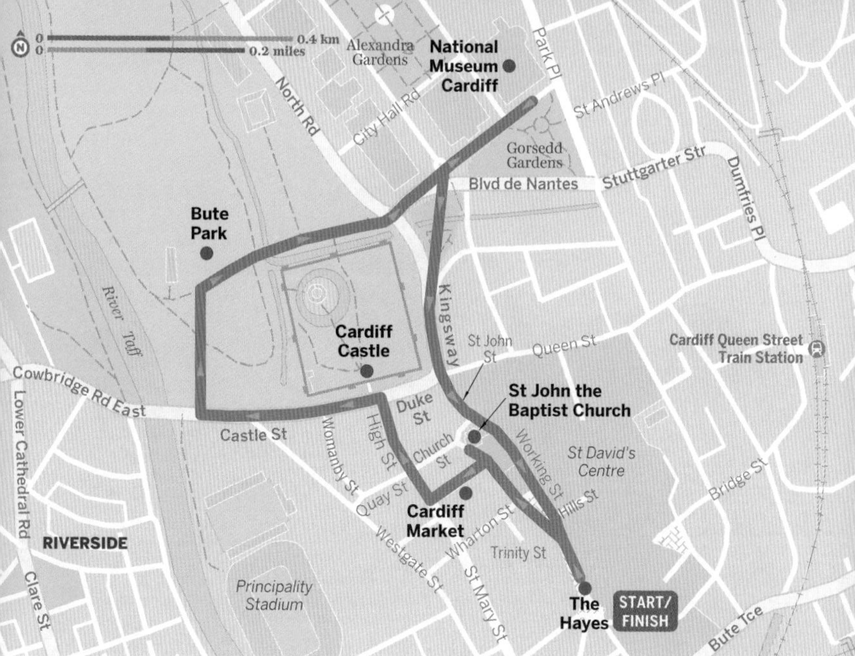

castle right on top of the walls of an ancient Roman fort. A Norman keep and gatehouse survives, flanked by a 15th-century manor house. Most of this fabulously ostentatious abode is testimony to the wealth and flamboyance of the Marquess of Bute, the family chiefly responsible for transforming Cardiff from sleepy backwater into the world's biggest coal port in the 18th and 19th centuries.

The Walk » Exit the castle and turn right. As you walk along, look for stone animals decorating the top of the walls. Continue until you reach pretty West Lodge containing the excellent Pettigrew Tea Rooms and enter Bute Park.

Bute Park

Edging the River Taff, resplendent **Bute Park** (www.bute-park.com; 7.30am-30min before sunset;) incorporates lawns, mature trees and flower-laced landscaped loveliness. Gifted to Cardiff, along with the castle, by the Bute family in 1947, it kicks off a nature corridor leading out of the city into the countryside. On sunny days, students drape themselves across the lawns while joggers endlessly circle the paths. West Lodge at the park entrance houses excellent **Pettigrew Tea Rooms** (029-2023 5486; www.pettigrew-tearooms.com; West Lodge, Castle St; mains £6-12, afternoon tea for one £17.50; 10am-6pm, closes 30min before dusk in winter).

The Walk » Cross behind the castle and exit the park, taking the underpass beneath North Rd to reach Cardiff's elegant Civic Centre. Built in the early 20th century, this neoclassical ensemble includes Cardiff Crown Court and City Hall.

National Museum Cardiff

Posing grandly beside City Hall, the **National Museum Cardiff** (0300 111 2333; www.museum.wales/cardiff; Gorsedd Gardens, CF10 3NP; 10am-5pm Tue, Thu, Sat & Sun; P) is treasure trove of art, including masterpieces by the likes of Monet, Renoir and Turner, and a significant collection of Welsh works. There's also a wonderful natural-history section.

The Walk » Wander back past the City Hall, looking for the underpass cutting below Blvd de Nantes. Head straight down the Kingsway, which leads to Working St and back to The Hayes.

Scotland

Scenery, history, atmosphere: Scotland simply spoils you. To drive here is to head deep into a captivating landscape fringed by vistas that stir the soul. A sense of something special is everywhere; from the pubs alive with live music, to spectacular shores and crisp, clear air. At its heart lie roller-coaster Highland roads, where ospreys soar above the pines. Nearby, Scotland's mighty glens deliver mountains, lochs and maybe a monster or two. A string of whisky distilleries tempt you to motor through historic Speyside. And all around the edges, majestic coast roads offer beauty, castles, villages and life at a gentler pace.

Skye Rugged and majestic landscapes
ELXENEIZE / SHUTTERSTOCK ©

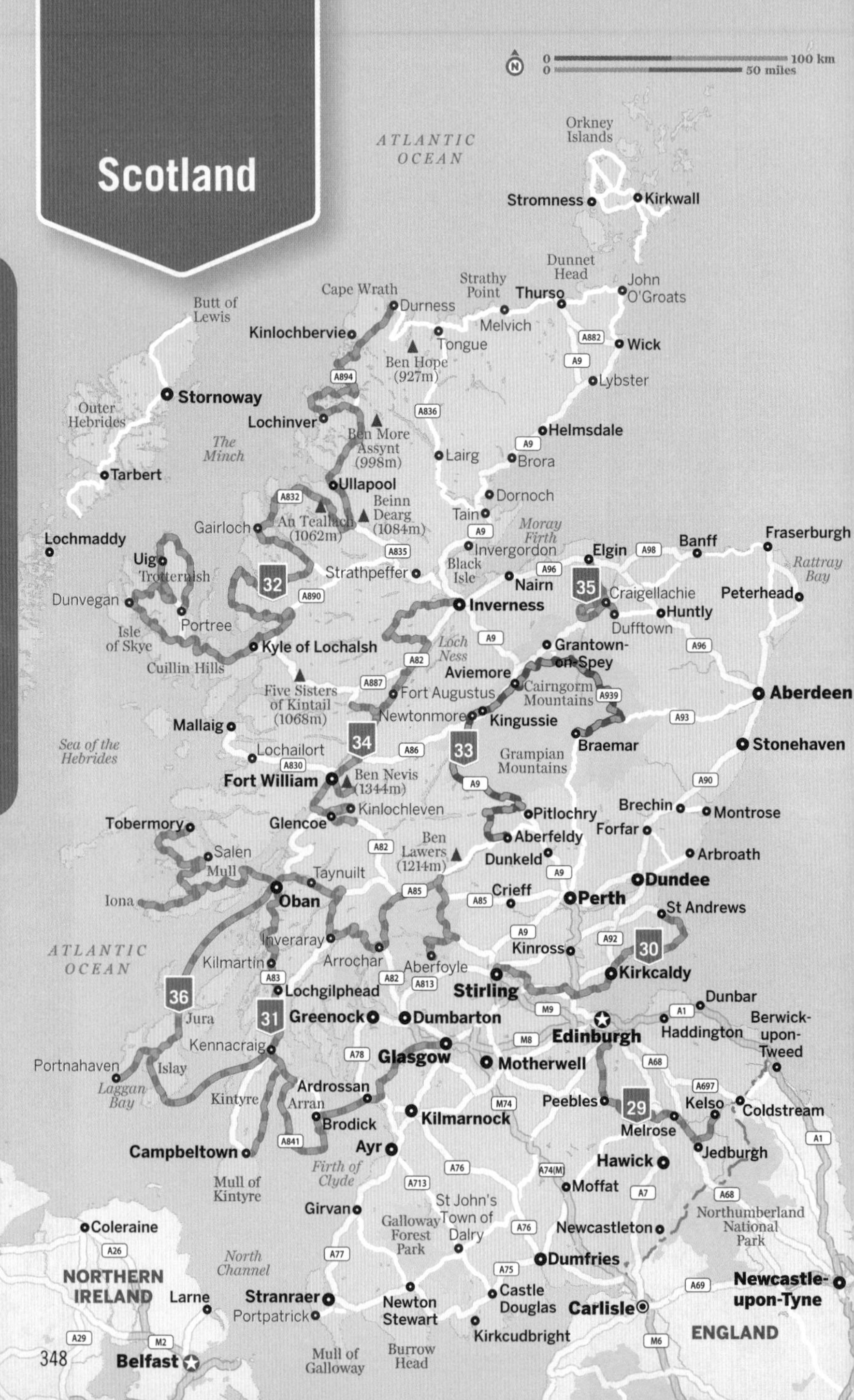
Scotland
0 100 km
0 50 miles
ATLANTIC OCEAN
Orkney Islands
Stromness
Kirkwall
Dunnet Head
Strathy Point
Thurso
John O'Groats
Cape Wrath
Durness
Melvich
Butt of Lewis
Kinlochbervie
Tongue
A882
Wick
Ben Hope (927m)
A9
A894
Lybster
Stornoway
A836
Outer Hebrides
Lochinver
Helmsdale
The Minch
Ben More Assynt (998m)
A9
Lairg
Brora
Tarbert
Ullapool
A832
Beinn Dearg (1084m)
Dornoch
An Teallach (1062m)
Tain
Gairloch
Moray Firth
A9
Lochmaddy
A835
Invergordon
Elgin
A98
Banff
Fraserburgh
Uig
Rattray Bay
Trotternish
32
Strathpeffer
Black Isle
A96
Nairn
35
Craigellachie
Peterhead
Dunvegan
A890
Inverness
Huntly
Portree
Dufftown
Isle of Skye
Kyle of Lochalsh
Loch Ness
A9
Grantown-on-Spey
A96
Cuillin Hills
A82
Aviemore
A887
Five Sisters of Kintail (1068m)
Fort Augustus
Cairngorm Mountains
A939
Aberdeen
Newtonmore
Kingussie
A93
Mallaig
34
33
Braemar
Stonehaven
Sea of the Hebrides
Lochailort
A86
Grampian Mountains
A830
Fort William
Ben Nevis (1344m)
A9
A90
Kinlochleven
Pitlochry
Brechin
Montrose
Tobermory
Glencoe
Aberfeldy
Forfar
Ben Lawers (1214m)
Salen
A82
Dunkeld
Arbroath
Mull
Taynuilt
A9
Dundee
Iona
Oban
A85
Crieff
Perth
A85
St Andrews
Inveraray
A9
A92
30
ATLANTIC OCEAN
Kinross
Kilmartin
Arrochar
Aberfoyle
Kirkcaldy
A83
A82
A813
Stirling
36
Lochgilphead
Dunbar
31
Greenock
Dumbarton
A9
A1
Jura
Edinburgh
Berwick-upon-Tweed
Kennacraig
A78
Glasgow
M8
Haddington
Portnahaven
Islay
Motherwell
A68
Laggan Bay
Ardrossan
A697
Kintyre
Arran
M74
Peebles
29
Kelso
Coldstream
Brodick
Kilmarnock
Melrose
A841
A1
Campbeltown
Ayr
Hawick
Jedburgh
Firth of Clyde
A76
A74(M)
Mull of Kintyre
A713
Moffat
A7
A68
Girvan
St John's Town of Dalry
Northumberland National Park
Coleraine
Galloway Forest Park
A76
Newcastleton
A26
A77
North Channel
Dumfries
NORTHERN IRELAND
A75
Larne
Stranraer
Newton Stewart
Castle Douglas
Carlisle
A69
Newcastle-upon-Tyne
Portpatrick
Kirkcudbright
A29
M2
M6
ENGLAND
Belfast
Mull of Galloway
Burrow Head

29 **The Borders 2–3 Days**
Ruined abbeys and Knights Templar tales amid a landscape of undulating hills.

30 **Stirling & Fife Coast 2–3 Days**
Shoreline drives taking in castles, golf links, medieval towns and golden sands.

31 **Lower West Coast 4–6 Days**
Photogenic touring along a coast of lochs, mountains and thundering waterfalls.

32 **Upper West Coast 3–5 Days**
The Highlands meet the Atlantic: imposing mountains, surging seas, and single-track roads.

Classic Trip 33 **Royal Highlands & Cairngorms 4–5 Days**
Where roads curve between majestic mountains and the Royals come to relax.

34 **Great Glen 2–3 Days**
Bewitching lakes and mountains – plus some monster-spotting at Loch Ness.

35 **Whisky Trails 2–3 Days**
A scenic tour of historic arts and crafts, taking in distilleries galore.

36 **Ferry-Hopping 6–8 Days**
A celebration of seafood and laidback lifestyles; enchanting island explorations.

DON'T MISS

Loch Garten
Watching Scotland's iconic ospreys diving for trout in this scenic, pine-fringed nature reserve. Trip 33

Quaich Bar
Settling deep into the armchairs at the Craigellachie Hotel to sample some of the 900-plus single malts. Trip 35

Kinlochleven Via Ferrata
Tackling the ladders and bridges of the 500m climbing route which weaves through the crags of Grey Mare's Tail. Trip 34

Holy Island
Breathing and thinking deeply on this rocky outcrop just off Arran – now run as a Buddhist retreat. Trip 36

Gairloch Marine Wildlife Centre
Keeping a look-out for basking sharks, porpoises and minke whales on an eco-friendly cruise. Trip 32

NEW
2019
BIKES
NEW
2019
BIKES
SEALSKINZ
Glentress
Peel Bikes

The Borders

On this drive through southeastern Scotland's enchanting Borders region, you'll take in market towns, ruins, castles and stately homes in a land of rolling hills redolent of history.

TRIP HIGHLIGHTS

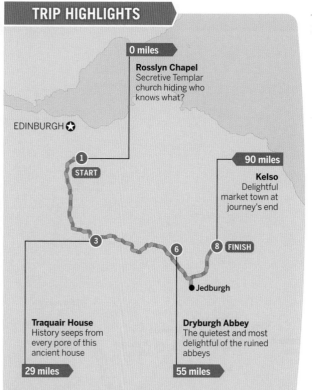

0 miles
Rosslyn Chapel
Secretive Templar church hiding who knows what?

EDINBURGH

1 START

90 miles
Kelso
Delightful market town at journey's end

3

6

8 FINISH

Jedburgh

Traquair House
History seeps from every pore of this ancient house
29 miles

Dryburgh Abbey
The quietest and most delightful of the ruined abbeys
55 miles

2–3 DAYS
90 MILES / 144KM

GREAT FOR...

BEST TIME TO GO

Late spring offers blooming flowers, green fields and local festivals.

ESSENTIAL PHOTO

Snapping Sir Walter's favourite vista from lovely Scott's View.

Mountain biking and forest zip lines at Glentress.

Peebles Cyclists at the mountain-biking hub of Glentress forest

29 The Borders

Romance and strife coincide in the Borders region, whose rough history of war and plunder is encapsulated by the magnificent ruins of four abbeys. Templar mysteries add an extra layer at atmosphere-packed Rosslyn Chapel, while a number of welcoming villages with ancient traditions pepper the countryside and grandiose mansions await exploration. Over it all is poised the benevolent ghost of Sir Walter Scott, quill in hand.

TRIP HIGHLIGHT

1 Roslin

It's only a 7-mile journey through city suburbs from central Edinburgh to Roslin, where the success of Dan Brown's novel *The Da Vinci Code* shot Scotland's most beautiful and enigmatic church, **Rosslyn Chapel** (Collegiate Church of St Matthew; ☎0131-440 2159; www.rosslynchapel.com; Chapel Loan, Roslin EH25 9PU; adult/child £9/free; ⏲9.30am-6pm Mon-Sat Jun-Aug, to 5pm Sep-May, noon-4.45pm Sun year-round;

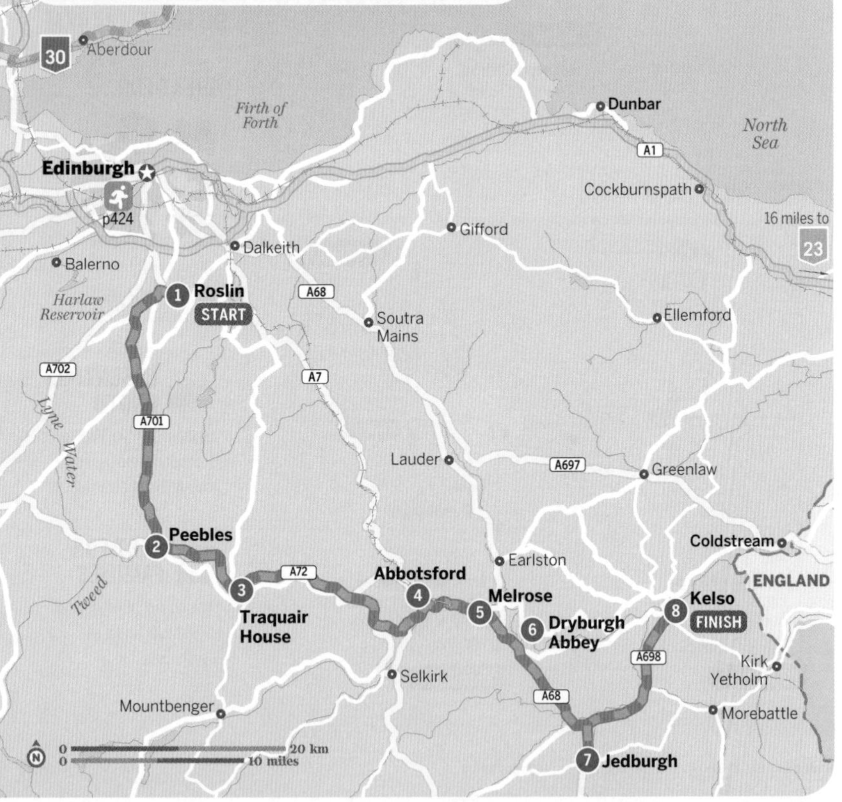

P; 37), to prominence. The chapel was built in the mid-15th century for William St Clair, third earl of Orkney, and the ornately carved interior – at odds with the architectural fashion of its time – is a monument to the mason's art, rich in symbolic imagery.

As well as flowers, vines, angels and biblical figures, the carved stones include many examples of the pagan 'Green Man'; other figures are associated with Freemasonry and the Knights Templar. Intriguingly, there are also carvings of plants from the Americas that predate Columbus' voyage of discovery. The symbolism has led some to conclude that Rosslyn is a secret Templar repository with hidden vaults concealing anything from the Holy Grail or the head of John the Baptist to the body of Christ himself.

LINK YOUR TRIP

23 Northumbria

It's a pleasantly leisurely drive along the Tweed from Kelso to reach the coast at Berwick, where you can take on the Northumbria route in reverse.

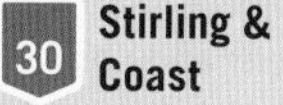

30 Stirling & Fife Coast

It's 80 miles northwest from Kelso via Edinburgh's southern bypass to Stirling and this coastal route.

The Drive » The A701 is easily accessed just outside Roslin, and it's an easy drive south along it and the A703 to Peebles, 15 miles away.

2 Peebles

With a picturesque main street set on a ridge between the lovely River Tweed and the Eddleston Water, Peebles is one of the most handsome of the Border towns. Though it lacks a major sight, the agreeable atmosphere, fine eating and snacking choices and good walking options in the rolling, wooded hills thereabouts will entice you to linger.

Two miles east of Peebles off the A72, **Glentress forest** (www.7stanesmountainbiking.com) has one of the best of the network of mountain-biking hubs known as the 7Stanes. The shop here hires rigs and will put you on the right trail for your ability. Classes are available also. These are some of Britain's best biking routes. There are also marked walking trails, forest **ziplines** (www.goape.co.uk; Glentress Forest; adult/child £33/25; Feb-Nov) and osprey-viewing available.

p357

The Drive » Cross the Tweed in Peebles and continue along the quiet country road B7062, or take the main A72 east and turn right in Innerleithen to reach Traquair House, which is well signposted. It's about a 7-mile drive whichever way you choose.

TRIP HIGHLIGHT

3 Traquair House

One of Scotland's great country houses, **Traquair House** (01896-830323; www.traquair.co.uk; Innerleithen; adult/child/family £10/5/27.50; 11am-5pm daily Easter-Sep, to 4pm daily Oct, to 3pm Sat & Sun Nov) has a powerful, ethereal beauty. Odd, sloping floors and a musty odour bestow a genuine feel, and parts of the building are believed to have been constructed long before the first official record of its existence in 1107. The massive tower house was gradually expanded but has remained virtually unchanged since the 17th century.

Since the 15th century, Traquair has belonged to the Stuart family, and the family's unwavering Catholicism and loyalty to the Stuart cause led to famous visitors including Mary, Queen of Scots and Bonnie Prince Charlie, but also to numerous problems as life as a Jacobite became a furtive, clandestine affair.

One of Traquair's most interesting places is the concealed room where priests secretly lived and

performed Mass. Other beautiful, time-worn rooms hold fascinating relics and letters.

In addition to the house, there's a garden maze, a small brewery producing the tasty Bear Ale, and a series of craft workshops.

The Drive » Head back to the A72 and head east towards Galashiels and Melrose. A couple of miles before Melrose, you'll reach Abbotsford, after a total drive of 17 miles.

4 Abbotsford

Just outside Melrose, **Abbotsford** (☎01896-752043; www.scottsabbotsford.com; visitor centre free, house adult/child £11.50/5; ⏲10am-5pm Apr-Oct, to 4pm Nov-Mar, house closed Dec-Feb) is the place to discover the life and works of Sir Walter Scott, to whom we arguably owe both the modern novel and our mind's-eye view of Scotland. This whimsical, fabulous house where he lived – and which ruined him when his publishers went bust – really brings this 19th-century writer to life. The grounds on the banks of the Tweed are lovely, and Scott drew much inspiration from rambles in the surrounding countryside.

A modern visitor centre displays memorabilia and gives an intriguing overview of the man, before a swish audioguide system – with one designed for kids – shows you around the house. In the house are some gloriously over-the-top features, with elaborate carvings, enough swords and dirks to equip a small army, a Chinese drawing room and a lovely study and library. There's a cafe-restaurant atop the visitor centre.

The Drive » It's just a couple of miles from Abbotsford to Melrose.

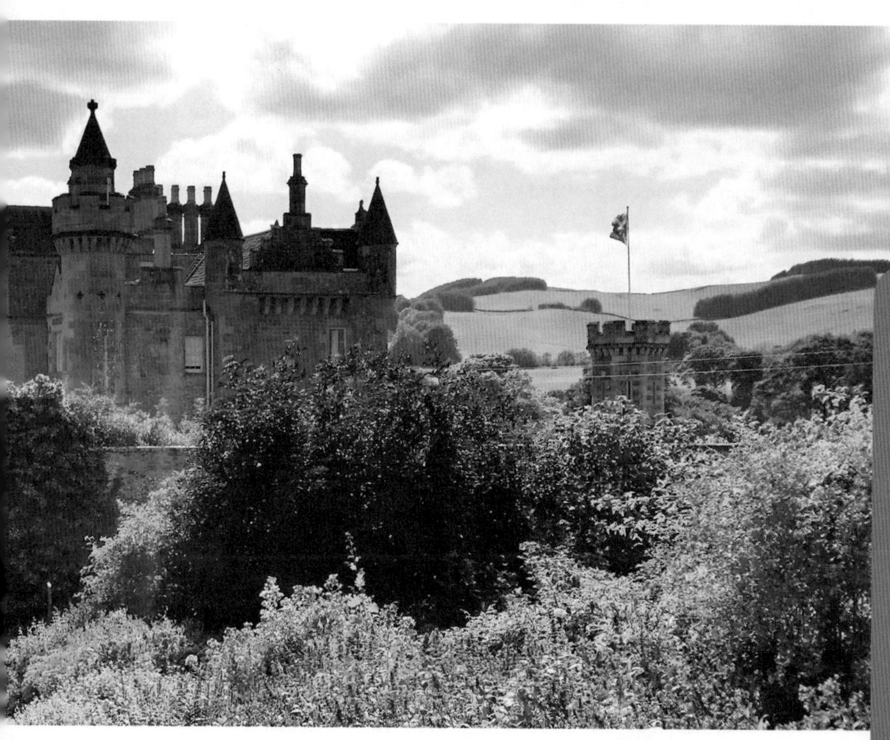

Abbotsford Once home to Sir Walter Scott

5 Melrose

Tiny, charming Melrose is a polished village running on the well-greased wheels of tourism. Sitting at the feet of the three heather-covered Eildon Hills, Melrose has a classic market square and one of the great abbey ruins.

Red-sandstone **Melrose Abbey** (HES; ☎01896-822562; www.historicenvironment.scot; adult/child £6/3.60; ⏲9.30am-5.30pm Apr-Sep, 10am-4pm Oct-Mar) was repeatedly destroyed by the English in the 14th century. The remaining broken shell is pure Gothic and the ruins are famous for their decorative stonework – look out for the pig gargoyle playing the bagpipes. Though Melrose had a monastery way back in the 7th century, this abbey was founded by David I in 1136 for Cistercian monks, and later rebuilt by Robert the Bruce, whose heart is buried here. Ask here for details of local walks.

In the immediate vicinity of the abbey, and all free to enter, it's worth exploring a couple of elegant gardens as well as an exhibition on local Roman heritage.

p357

The Drive » Dryburgh Abbey is a circuitous 7-mile drive from Melrose via the B6404. Head east from Melrose on the A72, then turn north up the A68, then turn right, following signposts for the abbey. Pause to admire the vistas from the famous Scott's View outlook.

TRIP HIGHLIGHT

6 Dryburgh Abbey

Dryburgh (HES; ☎01835-822381; www.historicenvironment.scot; adult/child £6/3.60; ⏲9.30am-5.30pm Apr-Sep, 10am-4pm Oct-Mar) is the most beautiful and complete of the Border abbeys, partly because

HISTORIC ENVIRONMENT SCOTLAND

Several of the attractions along this route are run by **Historic Environment Scotland** (HES; ☎0131-668 8999; www.historicenvironment.scot; annual membership adult/adult with children/family £58/63/106), a national heritage organisation. If you'll be visiting these and other highlights such as Stirling or Edinburgh Castles, consider joining up, as entry is free for members.

the neighbouring town of Dryburgh no longer exists (another victim of the wars) and partly for its lovely site by the Tweed in a sheltered birdsong-filled valley. Dating from about 1150, the abbey belonged to the Premonstratensians, a religious order founded in France, and conjures 12th-century monastic life more successfully than its nearby counterparts. The pink-hued stone ruins are the burial place of Sir Walter Scott.

The Drive » From Dryburgh Abbey, retrace your steps to the A68 and turn south on it. After 15 miles you'll reach Jedburgh.

---

7 Jedburgh

Attractive Jedburgh, where many old buildings and wynds (narrow alleys) have been intelligently restored, invites exploration by foot. It's centred on the noble skeleton of its ruined **abbey** (HES; ☎01835-863925; www.historicenvironment.scot; Abbey Rd; adult/child £6/3.60; ⏲9.30am-5.30pm Apr-Sep, 10am-4pm Oct-Mar; 👪).

Dominating the town, this was the first of the great Border abbeys to be passed into state care, and it shows – audio and visual presentations telling the abbey's story are scattered throughout the carefully preserved ruins (good for the kids). The red-sandstone ruins are roofless but relatively intact, and the ingenuity of the master mason can be seen in some of the rich (if somewhat faded) stone carvings in the nave.

✕ 🛏 p357

The Drive » It's 11 miles from Jedburgh to Kelso. Head north up the A68, then right on to the A698.

TRIP HIGHLIGHT

8 Kelso

Kelso, a prosperous market town with a broad, cobbled square flanked by Georgian buildings, has a cheery feel and historic appeal. During the day it's a busy little place, but after 8pm you'll have the streets to yourself. The town has a lovely site at the junction of the Tweed and Teviot, and is one of the most enjoyable places in the Borders.

Once one of the richest abbeys in southern Scotland, **Kelso Abbey** (HES; www.historicenvironment.scot; Bridge St; ⏲9.30am-5.30pm daily Apr-Sep, 10am-4pm Sat-Wed Oct-Mar) was reduced to ruins by English raids in the 16th century, though what little of it remains today is some of the finest surviving Romanesque architecture in Scotland.

Grandiose **Floors Castle** (☎01573-223333; www.floorscastle.com; adult/child castle & grounds £11.50/6; ⏲10.30am-5pm daily May-Sep, Sat & Sun Oct) is Scotland's largest inhabited mansion, home to the Duke of Roxburghe, and overlooks the Tweed about a mile west of Kelso. Built by William Adam in the 1720s, the original Georgian simplicity was 'improved' in the 1840s.

✕ 🛏 p357

Eating & Sleeping

Peebles 2

Coltman's Deli $$

(☎01721-720405; www.coltmans.co.uk; 71 High St; mains £14-17; ⏰10am-5pm Mon-Thu, to 10pm Fri & Sat, to 6pm Sun; 📶🌿) This main-street deli has numerous temptations, such as excellent cheeses and Italian smallgoods, as well as perhaps Scotland's tastiest sausage roll, with an equally toothsome vegetarian equivalent. Behind the shop, the good-looking dining area serves up confident bistro fare and light snacks with a variety of culinary influences, using top-notch local ingredients. Upstairs is a cosy bar.

Melrose 5

Provender Scottish $$

(☎01896-820319; www.provendermelrose.com; West End Lane; mains £15-20; ⏰11am-2.30pm & 6-9pm Mon-Fri, 10am-2.30pm & 6-9pm Sat, 10am-3pm & 6-8pm Sun; 🌿) Though a relative newcomer to the local scene, Provender feels very Melrose – classy but comfortable – already. It's a warmly decorated space with attractively low lighting, booth seating and solicitous service. Great seafood creations and other well-executed, appealing fare are complemented by a short but excellent wine list. Weekend brunches are another highlight.

Townhouse Boutique Hotel $$$

(☎01896-822645; www.thetownhousemelrose.co.uk; Market Sq; s/d/superior d £97/134/151; P📶) Classy Townhouse exudes warmth and professionalism, and has some of the best rooms in town, tastefully furnished with attention to detail. The superior rooms are enormous, with lavish furnishings and excellent en suites. Standard rooms are smaller but they're refurbished and comfortable. Well worth the price.

Jedburgh 7

Capon Tree Scottish $$

(☎01835-869596; www.thecapontree.com; 61 High St; mains £14-20; ⏰food 6-9pm; 📶) Attractively combining smart and casual, this welcoming bistro and bar does modern Scottish cuisine. Plates are beautifully, though not fussily, presented and ingredients are of high quality. The overall package is appealing, the service good and the ambience romantic.

Meadhon Guest House B&B $$

(☎01835-862504; www.meadhon.co.uk; 48 Castlegate; s/d/f £61/75/145; 📶) Very close to castle and abbey, this historic house on Jedburgh's main street dates back to 1653 and has lots of character. Bonnie Prince Charlie once stabled his horses here but the genial Danish owners offer more human comforts, with keypad locks, plush mattresses and impeccable standards. Home-cooked evening meals are available, as are attractive hand-knitted scarves.

Kelso 8

Cobbles Bistro $$

(☎01573-223548; www.cobbleskelso.co.uk; 7 Bowmont St; mains £10-17; ⏰food noon-2.30pm & 5.45-9pm Mon-Fri, noon-9pm Sat, noon-8.30pm Sun; 📶) This inn off the main square is so popular you will need to book a table at weekends. It's cheery, very welcoming and warm, and serves excellent upmarket pub food in generous portions. Pick and mix from bar menu, steaks, kebabs and gourmet options. Leave room for cheese and/or dessert. The bar's own microbrewed ales are excellent. A cracking place.

Old Priory B&B $$

(☎01573-223030; www.theoldpriorykelso.com; 33 Woodmarket; s/d £80/90; P📶) Fantastic rooms here are allied with numerous personal details – genial host Robin turns down the beds at night and makes you feel very welcome. Doubles are top-notch and the family room really excellent. The huge windows flood the rooms with natural light. The wonderful library room (£120) is huge and luxurious, with a super bathroom. Top-class B&B.

WE ARE
OPEN

Stirling & Fife Coast

Travelling from Scotland's most imposing castle to the hallowed home of golf, you'll visit a perfectly preserved medieval town, Fife's best beaches and a string of pretty fishing villages.

TRIP HIGHLIGHTS

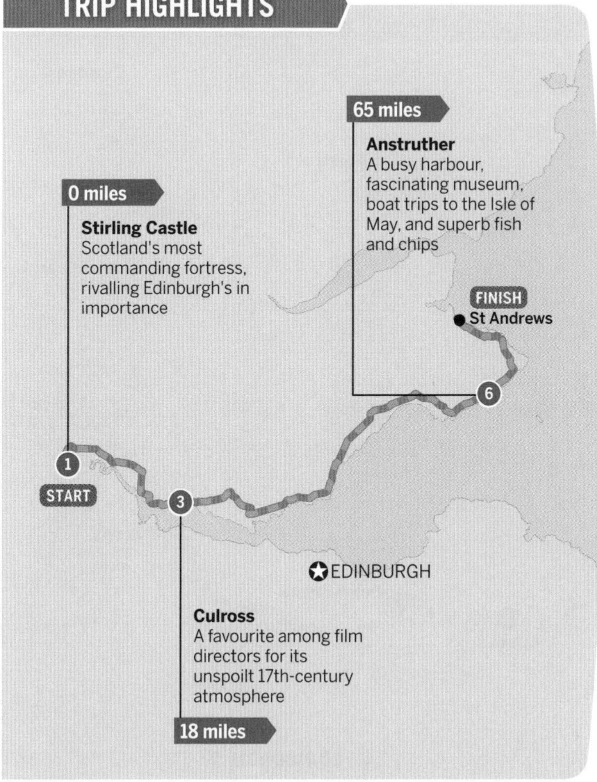

65 miles

Anstruther
A busy harbour, fascinating museum, boat trips to the Isle of May, and superb fish and chips

0 miles

Stirling Castle
Scotland's most commanding fortress, rivalling Edinburgh's in importance

FINISH
St Andrews

6

1

START

3

EDINBURGH

Culross
A favourite among film directors for its unspoilt 17th-century atmosphere

18 miles

2–3 DAYS
82 MILES / 131KM

GREAT FOR...

BEST TIME TO GO

July and August for summer fun on the beach at Elie.

ESSENTIAL PHOTO

Teeing off at St Andrews's, Old Course.

BEST FOR HISTORY

Exploring the beautifully preserved medieval village of Culross.

Culross Scotland's best-preserved example of a 17th-century town

30 Stirling & Fife Coast

Stirling and St Andrews, two of Scotland's top tourist magnets, bookend this trip along the less well known southwest coast of Fife, taking in the red pantiled roofs and crow-stepped gables of 17th-century Culross' cobbled lanes (regularly used as a film set), the golden-sand beaches and seaside walks of Elie and Earlsferry, and the pretty-as-a-picture fishing harbours of the East Neuk, one of central Scotland's most picturesque corners.

TRIP HIGHLIGHT

❶ Stirling

With an impregnable position atop a mighty wooded crag, Stirling's beautifully preserved Old Town is a treasure trove of historic buildings and cobbled streets winding up to the ramparts of its impressive castle, which offers views for miles around. Nearby is **Bannockburn**, scene of Robert the Bruce's pivotal triumph over the English in 1314.

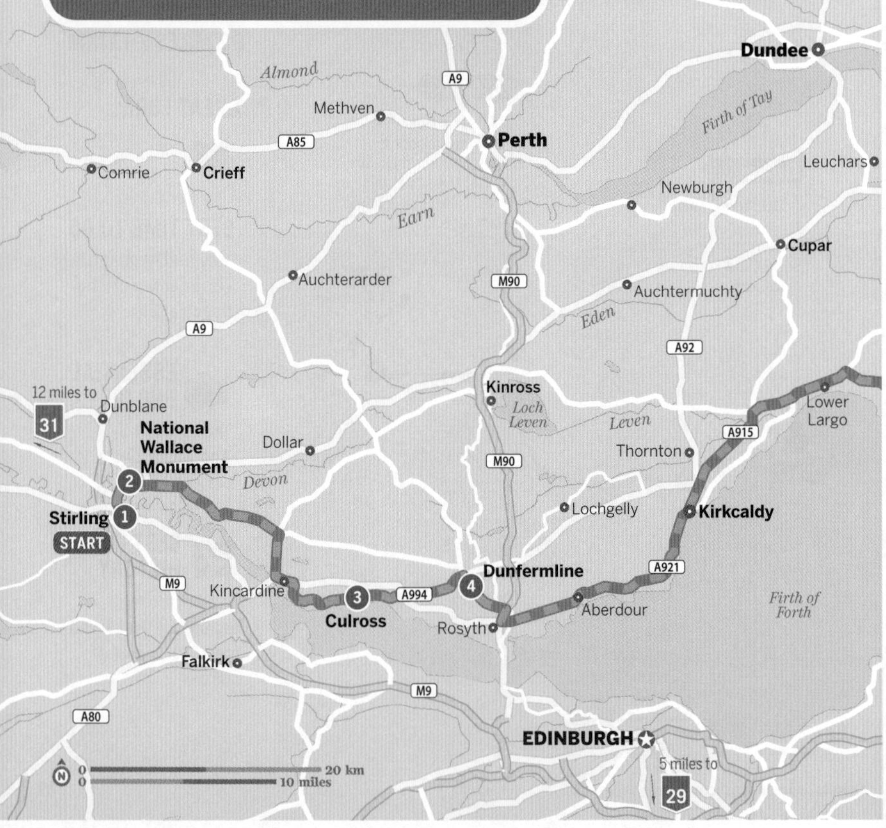

Many visitors find **Stirling Castle** (HES; www.stirlingcastle.scot; Castle Wynd; adult/child £16/9.60; ⌚9.30am-6pm Apr-Sep, to 5pm Oct-Mar, last entry 45min before closing; P) more atmospheric than Edinburgh – the location, architecture, historical significance and commanding views combine to make for a truly memorable experience. The undisputed highlight of a visit is the fabulous **Royal Palace**, its exterior studded with beautiful sculptures.

Sloping steeply down from Stirling Castle, the **Old Town** has a remarkably different feel to modern Stirling, its cobblestone streets packed with 15th- to 17th-century architectural gems, and surrounded by Scotland's best-surviving city wall.

p365

The Drive » Head north from Stirling city centre along Causewayhead Rd towards Bridge of Allan; at the junction with the A907 to Alloa, keep straight on and follow signs to the National Wallace Monument (total 2.5 miles). From the visitor centre car park, walk or shuttle-bus up the hill to the monument itself.

2 National Wallace Monument

Perched high on a crag above the floodplain of the River Forth, the Victorian **Wallace Monument** (☎01786-472140; www.nationalwallacemonument.com; Abbey Craig, FK9 5LF; adult/child £10.75/6.75; ⌚9.30am-5pm Apr-Jun, Sep & Oct, to 6pm Jul & Aug, 10am-4pm Nov-Feb, 10am-5pm Mar; P) is so Gothic it deserves circling bats and croaking ravens. Built in the shape of a medieval tower, it commemorates William Wallace, the hero of the bid for Scottish independence depicted in the film *Braveheart*. The view from the top over the flat, green gorgeousness of the Forth Valley, including the site of Wallace's 1297 victory over the English at Stirling Bridge, almost justifies the steep entry fee.

The climb up the narrow staircase inside leads through a series of galleries including the **Hall of Heroes**, a marble pantheon of lugubrious Scottish luminaries. Admire Wallace's 66in of broadsword and see the man himself re-created in a 3D audiovisual display.

The Drive » Return to the junction and head east on the A907 through Alloa and Clackmannan, then south on the A977 to Kincardine; at the junction with the A985, keep

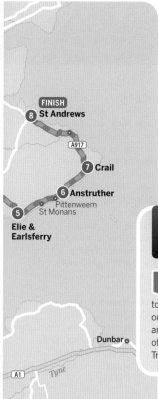

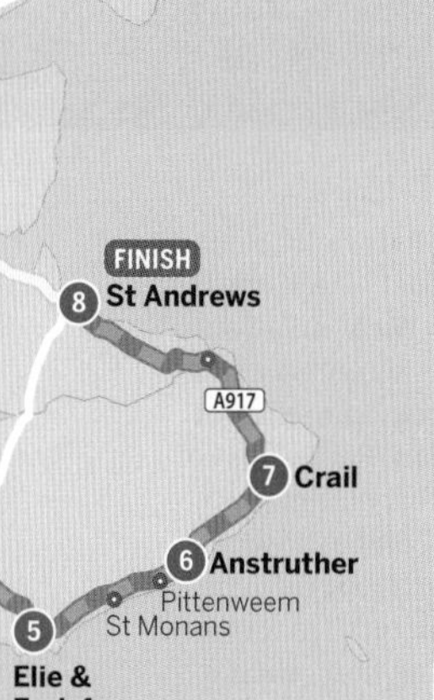

LINK YOUR TRIP

31 Lower West Coast
A short 20-mile hop to Callander links up with our trip around the scenic and historic highlights of the Loch Lomond, the Trossachs and Argyll.

29 The Borders
From St Andrews you can head south across the Forth to Rosslyn Chapel to begin our trip around the Borders' market towns, castles and stately homes.

straight, following signs for Fife Coastal Tourist Route until you reach Culross (16 miles).

TRIP HIGHLIGHT

3 Culross

Instantly familiar to fans of the TV series *Outlander,* in which it appears as the fictional village of Cranesmuir, Culross (*koo*-ross) is Scotland's best-preserved example of a 17th-century town. Limewashed white and yellow-ochre houses with red-tiled roofs stand amid a maze of cobbled streets; the winding Back Causeway to the abbey is lined with whimsical cottages.

Culross Palace (NTS; www.nts.org.uk; Low Causewayside, KY12 8JH; adult/child £10.50/7.50; ⏲11am-5pm Jul & Aug, to 4pm Apr-Jun, Sep & Oct) – more large house than palace – was the 17th-century residence of local laird Sir George Bruce and features an interior largely unchanged since his time. The decorative wood panelling and painted timber ceilings are of national importance, particularly the allegorical scenes in the **Painted Chamber**, which survive from the early 1600s. Don't miss the recreation of a 17th-century garden at the back, with gorgeous views from the top terrace.

✕ p365

The Drive » Continue east via the B9037 and A994 to Dunfermline (8 miles).

4 Dunfermline

Dunfermline is a large and unlovely town, but rich in history. The focus is evocative **Dunfermline Abbey** (HES; www.historicenvironment.scot; St Catherine's Wynd, KY12 7PE; adult/child £6/3.60; ⏲9.30am-5.30pm daily Apr-Sep, 10am-4pm Sat-Wed Oct-Mar), founded by King David I in the 12th century as a Benedictine monastery. The abbey and its neighbouring palace was already favoured by religious royals; Malcolm III married the exiled Saxon princess Margaret here in the 11th century, and both chose to be interred here. There were many more royal burials, none more notable than Robert the Bruce, whose remains were interred here in 1329.

The Drive » Take the M90 towards the Queensferry Crossing, but leave at Junction 1C (signposted A921 Inverkeithing) and continue east to the attractive seaside village of Aberdour. Stay on the A921 as far as Kirkcaldy, then take the faster A915 (signposted St Andrews) as far as Upper Largo, where you follow the A917 to Elie (35 miles).

5 Elie & Earlsferry

These two attractive villages have great sandy beaches, golf courses

and good walks along the coast – seek out the **Chain Walk**, an adventurous scramble along the rocky shoreline at Kincraig Point, west of Earlsferry (allow two hours, and ask local advice about tides before setting off). On a more relaxing note, there's nothing better than a lazy summer Sunday in Elie, watching the local team play cricket on the beach.

Elie Watersports (☎01333-330962; www.eliewatersports.com; Elie Harbour, Elie; ⏲May-Sep, ring ahead other times) hires out windsurfers (£30

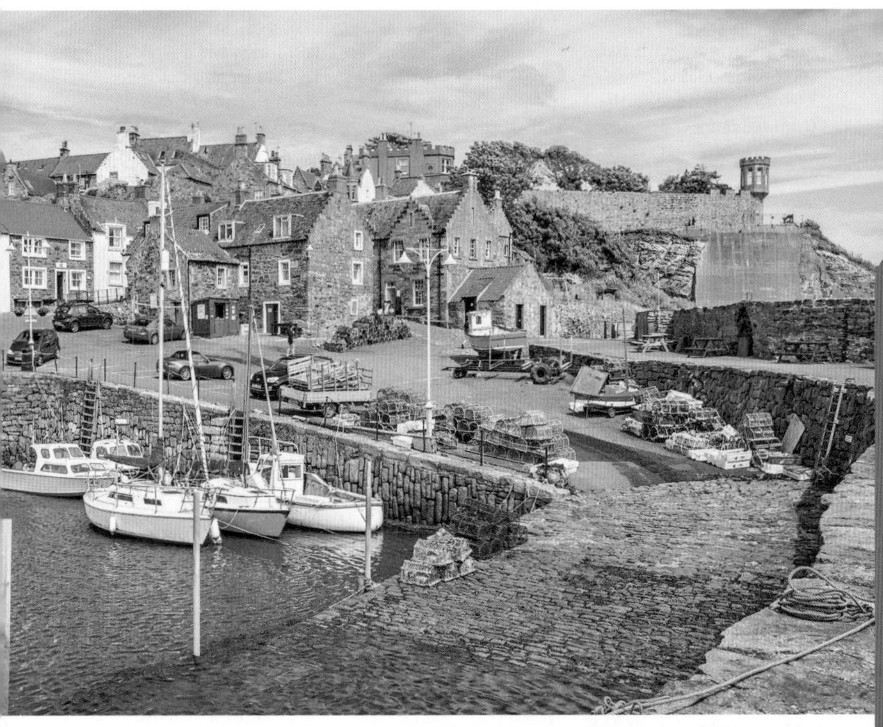

Crail Home to a peaceful, picturesque harbour

per two hours), sailing dinghies (from £25 per hour), canoes (from £15 per hour) and mountain bikes (£20 per day), and offers instruction (at extra cost).

p365

The Drive » Continue east along the Fife coast on the A917 through the pretty fishing villages of St Monans and Pittenweem to Anstruther (6 miles).

TRIP HIGHLIGHT

6 Anstruther

Once one of Scotland's busiest fishing ports, cheery Anstruther (pronounced *en*-ster by locals) offers a pleasant mixture of bobbing boats, historic streets and visitors ambling around the harbour grazing on fish and chips, or contemplating a boat trip to the **Isle of May** (www.nature.scot).

The excellent **Scottish Fisheries Museum** (www.scotfishmuseum.org; East Shore; adult/child £9/free; 10am-5.30pm Mon-Sat, 11am-5pm Sun Apr-Sep, 10am-4.30pm Mon-Sat, noon-4.30pm Sun Oct-Mar) covers the history of the Scottish fishing industry in fascinating detail, including plenty of hands-on exhibits for kids. Displays include the Zulu Gallery, which houses the huge, partly restored hull of a traditional Zulu-class fishing boat, redolent with the scents of tar and timber. Afloat in the harbour outside the museum lies the *Reaper,* a fully restored Fifie-class fishing boat built in 1902.

p365

The Drive » It's just a short 4-mile drive east to Crail.

7 Crail

Pretty and peaceful, little Crail has a much-photographed stone-built harbour surrounded by quaint cottages with red-tiled roofs. The village's history is outlined in the **Crail Museum** (www.crailmuseum.org.uk; 62 Marketgate, KY10 3TL; ⏲11am-4pm Mon-Sat, 1.30-4pm Sun Jun-Oct, Sat & Sun only Apr & May), but the main attraction is just wandering the winding streets and hanging out by the harbour.

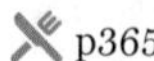 p365

The Drive » The A917 continues north for 10 miles to St Andrews, passing Kingsbarns Distillery and Cambo Walled Garden.

8 St Andrews

For a small town, St Andrews has made a big name for itself. Firstly as a religious centre and place of pilgrimage, then as Scotland's oldest (and Britain's third-oldest) university town. But it is its status as the home of golf that has propelled it to even greater fame, and today's pilgrims mostly arrive with a set of clubs in hand.

The Old Course, the world's most famous golf links, has a striking seaside location at the western end of town – it's a thrilling experience to stroll the hallowed turf. You are free to walk over the course on Sunday, or follow the footpaths around the edge at any time.

The ruins of **St Andrews Cathedral** (HES; www.historicenvironment.scot; The Pends, KY16 9QL; adult/child £6/3.60; ⏲9.30am-5.30pm Apr-Sep, 10am-4pm Oct-Mar) are testimony to what was once one of Britain's most magnificent medieval buildings. There's also a museum that contains the late-8th-century **St Andrews Sarcophagus**, Europe's finest example of early medieval stone carving.

St Andrews Castle (HES; www.historicenvironment.scot; The Scores, KY16 9AR; adult/child £9/5.40; ⏲9.30am-5.30pm Apr-Sep, 10am-4pm Oct-Mar) too is mainly in ruins, but the site itself is evocative and has dramatic coastline views.

p365

PLAYING THE OLD COURSE

The **Old Course** (☎reception 01334-466666, reservations 01334-466718; www.standrews.com; Golf Pl; green fees £95-195; ⏲Mon-Sat) is the oldest and most famous golf course in the world. Golf has been played here since the 15th century – by 1457 it was apparently so popular that James II had to ban it because it was interfering with his troops' archery practice. Although it lies beside the Royal & Ancient Golf Club, the Old Course is a public course.

To play the Old Course, you'll need to book in advance via the website, or by phoning the Reservations Department (or Reception, if just one day in advance or on the day). Reservations open on the last Wednesday in August the year before you wish to play. Fewer places than normal may be available in 2021 due to rescheduling of 2020 bookings cancelled because of COVID-19.

Unless you've booked months in advance, getting a tee-off time is literally a lottery; enter the ballot at the caddie office (or online, or by phoning Reception) before 2pm two days before you hope to play (there's no Sunday play). Be warned that applications by ballot are normally heavily oversubscribed, and green fees are £195 from April to October.

A caddie for your round costs £55 plus tip. If you play on a windy day, expect those scores to balloon: Nick Faldo famously stated, 'When it blows here, even the seagulls walk'.

Eating & Sleeping

Stirling 1

Victoria Square Guesthouse — B&B $$$

(01786-473920; www.victoriasquare.scot; 12 Victoria Sq, FK8 2QZ; s/d from £98/148; P) Though close to the centre of town, Victoria Sq is a quiet oasis of elegant Victorian buildings surrounding a verdant park. This luxury guesthouse's huge rooms, bay windows and period features make it a winner – there are two four-poster rooms (from £161) for romantic getaways, and some bedrooms have views to the castle towering above. No children under 12.

Culross 3

Bessie's Cafe — Cafe $

(07742-537301; www.facebook.com/culrosspalace; Main St; mains £5-9; 9am-5pm Mon-Fri, to 6pm Sat & Sun;) This cute coffee shop in the medieval courtyard next to Culross Palace caters to vegetarian tastes with dishes such as halloumi herb cakes with salad, or avocado on sourdough toast, but also serves versions with organic bacon or smoked salmon.

Elie & Earlsferry 5

Ship Inn — Pub Food $$

(01333-330246; www.shipinn.scot; The Toft, Elie; mains £9-19, steak £30; food served 11am-9pm;) Down by Elie harbour, this is a pleasant and popular place for a pint in the beer garden overlooking the wide sweep of the bay, but there's also a restaurant area with an above-average menu based on local seafood and steak.

Anstruther 6

Spindrift — B&B $$

(01333-310573; www.thespindrift.co.uk; Pittenweem Rd; s/d/f £80/135/150; P) Arriving from the west, there's no need to go further than Anstruther's first house on the left, a redoubt of Scottish cheer and warm hospitality. The rooms are elegant and extremely comfortable – some have views across to Edinburgh, and one is a wood-panelled re-creation of a ship's cabin, courtesy of the sea captain who once owned the house.

Crail 7

Lobster Store — Seafood $$

(01333-450476; www.facebook.com/reillyshellfish; 34 Shoregate; mains £6-15; noon-4pm Sat & Sun Easter-Jun, noon-4pm Tue-Sun Jul-Sep) This quaint little shack overlooking Crail harbour serves dressed crab and freshly boiled lobster that has been caught locally. You can have a whole lobster (split) or lobster rolls. This is no-fuss takeaway – there's a single table out the front, but you can find a place to sit and eat your catch anywhere around the harbour.

St Andrews 8

Haar — Scottish $$$

(01334-845750; www.haarrestaurant.com; 127 North St; 5-course tasting menu £60; 4-10pm Wed, noon-10pm Thu-Sun) Chef Dean Banks grew up in Arbroath, on the far side of the Tay estuary from St Andrews, and opened this atmospheric little restaurant after reaching the finals of Masterchef in 2018. Fresh local produce, with an emphasis on seafood, is treated to subtle Asian flavours – Dean's signature dish of lobster served with mirin butter is not to be missed.

34 Argyle St — B&B $$$

(07712 863139; www.34argylestreet.com; 34 Argyle St; r from £150;) Set in a fine old stone-built house just west of the town centre, the Argyle has four luxurious, hotel-quality bedrooms with huge modern bathrooms of dark tile, chrome and glass (two of the four have free-standing bath tubs). Little touches like drinks offered on arrival, fresh flowers and sweets add to the atmosphere of hospitality.

Lower West Coast

On this meandering drive you'll cruise through classic Highland scenery of lochs and mountains, forests and waterfalls, with perfectly placed castles to add that final touch to your photographs.

TRIP HIGHLIGHTS

158 miles

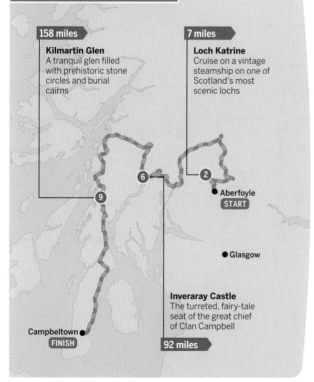

Kilmartin Glen
A tranquil glen filled with prehistoric stone circles and burial cairns

7 miles

Loch Katrine
Cruise on a vintage steamship on one of Scotland's most scenic lochs

Aberfoyle
START

Glasgow

Campbeltown
FINISH

Inveraray Castle
The turreted, fairy-tale seat of the great chief of Clan Campbell

92 miles

4–6 DAYS
222 MILES / 355KM

GREAT FOR...

BEST TIME TO GO

May and June have the best weather and the brightest roadside flowers.

ESSENTIAL PHOTO

The Falls of Dochart seen from the bridge in Killin.

BEST FOR FOODIES

Dining on seafood in Oban.

Killin Falls of Dochart

31 Lower West Coast

The scenery is the star of this trip, which winds its way from the shining waters, shady forests and foaming cascades of the Trossachs to the intricately fretted seaboard of Argyll, with its craggy hills and narrow, probing sea lochs. But history too is always close; you'll explore castles both medieval and Victorian, and touch the very heart of the nation at Kilmartin's ancient glen.

1 Aberfoyle

Aberfoyle is one of the gateways to **Loch Lomond & the Trossachs National Park**. Picturesque waymarked trails start from the nearby **Lodge forest visitor centre** (David Marshall Lodge; ☎0300 067 6615; www.forestryandland.gov.scot; A821; car park £1-3; ⏰10am-5pm Apr-Oct, to 4pm Nov, Dec, Feb & Mar, to 3pm Jan), ranging from a light 20-minute stroll to a nearby waterfall – with great interactive play options for kids – to a hilly 4-mile circuit. The

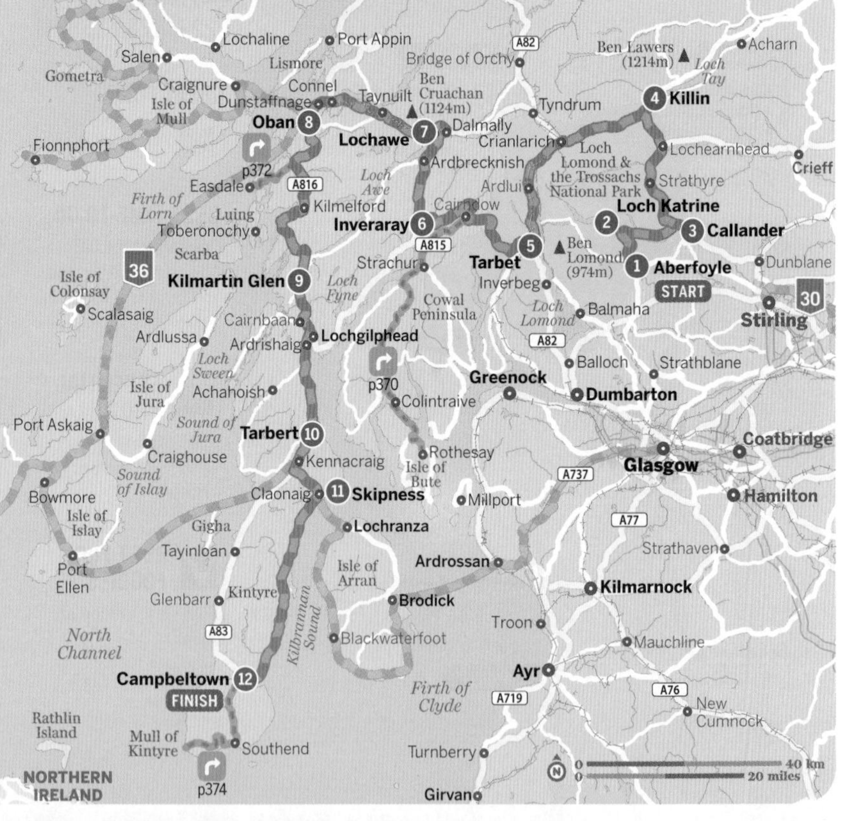

centre has a popular cafe as well as magnificent views and live wildlife cameras offering a peek at osprey and barn-owl nests among others. Also here, **Go Ape!** (☎0333 920 4859; www.goape.co.uk; Queen Elizabeth Forest Park; adult/child £35/28; ⏲Sat & Sun Nov & Feb-Easter, Wed-Mon Easter-Oct) will bring out the monkey in you on its exhilarating adventure course of long zip lines, swings and rope bridges among the trees. Look out, too, for the spooky mirror sculptures by local artist Rob Mulholland.

🛏 p377

The Drive » Head north on the A821 which leads high over the Duke's Pass, pausing for a photo opportunity at the crest of the hill, before descending to Loch Achray where a left turn leads along a narrow glen to a car park at Trossachs Pier on Loch Katrine (7 miles).

LINK YOUR TRIP

30 Stirling & Fife Coast

From Callander, the start of this castles and coastline tour in Stirling is just 20 miles to the southeast.

36 Ferry-Hopping

This trip intersects with the Ferry-Hopping one at Oban, from where you can take off on a tour of the islands.

TRIP HIGHLIGHT

2 Loch Katrine

Lovely Loch Katrine lies at the heart of the Trossachs, an area of outstanding natural beauty with thickly forested hills, romantic lochs, and excellent walking and cycling routes. **Cruises** (☎01877-376315; www.lochkatrine.com; Trossachs Pier, Loch Katrine; 1hr cruise adult £12-14, child £6.50-7.50) depart from Trossachs Pier at the loch's eastern end, including on the fabulous centenarian **steamship Sir Walter Scott**, or you can walk or cycle along the northern shore of the loch; **Katrinewheelz** (☎01877-376366; www.katrinewheelz.co.uk; Trossachs Pier, Loch Katrine; bike hire per half-/full day from £15/20; ⏲9am-5pm Apr-Oct, check for winter hours) hires out good bikes.

The Drive » Return to the A821 and drive east along the northern shores of Lochs Achray and Venachar, then turn right to arrive in the town of Callander (10 miles).

3 Callander

Callander, the principal Trossachs town, has been pulling in tourists for over 150 years, and has a laid-back ambience that quickly lulls visitors into lazy pottering. It's home to the **Hamilton Toy Collection** (☎01877-330004; www.thehamiltontoycollection.co.uk; 111 Main St; adult/child £3/1; ⏲10.30am-5pm Mon-Sat, noon-5pm Sun Apr-Oct; 👪), a powerhouse of 20th-century juvenile memorabilia, chock-full of dolls houses, puppets and toy soldiers.

Impressive **Bracklinn Falls** are reached by track and footpath from Bracklinn Rd (30 minutes each way from the car park). Also off Bracklinn Rd, a woodland trail leads up to **Callander Crags**, with great views over the surroundings; a return trip from the car park is about 4 miles.

🍴 p377

The Drive » The A84 leads north from Callander along Loch Lubnaig and Strathyre. Stop briefly at Balquhidder to pay respects at Rob Roy's grave; you might continue down the single-track road to Monachyle Mhor for a coffee or a posh lunch – the drive is worth it in any event. Back on the main road, continue north to Killin (22 miles).

4 Killin

This lovely village sits at the western end of Loch Tay and has a spread-out, relaxed feel, particularly around the scenic **Falls of Dochart**, which tumble through the centre. On a sunny day, people sprawl over the rocks by the bridge, pint or picnic in hand. There is fine walking around the town, and mighty mountains and glens close by.

Five miles northeast of Killin, Ben Lawers (1214m) rises above Loch Tay. Walking routes abound; one rewarding circular walk heads up into the Acharn forest south of town, emerging above the treeline to great views of Loch Tay and Ben Lawers. **Killin Outdoor Centre** (☎01567-820652; www.killinoutdoor.co.uk; Main St; bike per 24hr £25, kayak/canoe per 2hr £25; ⌚8.45am-5.45pm, hires available roughly Apr-Oct) provides walking advice as well as hiring bikes, canoes, kayaks and ice-climbing gear.

Glen Lochay runs westwards from Killin into the hills of Mamlorn. You can take a mountain bike up the glen; the scenery is impressive and the hills aren't too difficult.

Loch Tay is famous for its fishing – salmon, trout and pike are all caught here. **Fish 'n' Trips** (☎07967 567347; www.lochtayfishntrips.co.uk) can kit you out for a day's fishing with a boat, tackle and guide for £130 for two people, or rent you a boat for £65 a day.

The Drive » Head southwest from Killin, following the A85 along Glen Dochart to Crianlarich,

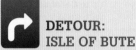

DETOUR: ISLE OF BUTE

Start: 5 Tarbet

Bute lies pinched between the thumb and forefinger of the Cowal peninsula, separated from the mainland by a narrow, scenic strait. The Highland Boundary Fault cuts through the middle of the island so that, geologically speaking, the northern half is in the Highlands and the southern half is in the central Lowlands.

Rothesay, the island's main town, was once one of Scotland's most popular holiday resorts, bustling with day-trippers disembarking from numerous steamers crowded around the pier. Cheap foreign holidays saw Rothesay's fortunes decline, but a nostalgia-fuelled resurgence of interest has seen many Victorian buildings restored. The grassy, flowery waterfront and row of noble villas make it a lovely place to be once again.

Splendid ruined 13th-century **Rothesay Castle** (HES; ☎01700-502691; www.historicenvironment.scot; King St; adult/child £6/3.60; ⌚9.30am-5.30pm daily Apr-Sep, 10am-4pm Sat-Wed Oct-Mar), with seagulls and jackdaws nesting in the walls, was once a favourite residence of the Stuart kings. It is unique in Scotland in having a circular plan, with four stocky round towers. The landscaped moat, with manicured turf, flower gardens and lazily cruising ducks, makes a picturesque setting.

The true jewel in Bute's crown is **Mount Stuart** (☎01700-503877; www.mountstuart.com; adult/child £13/7.50; ⌚11am-4pm Apr, May & Oct, to 5pm Jun-Sep, see website for winter hours, grounds 10am-6pm Mar-Oct), 5 miles south of Rothesay. The 19th-century family seat of the Stuart Earls of Bute is one of Britain's more magnificent stately homes, the first to have a telephone, underfloor heating and heated pool. Its eclectic interior, with a magnificent central hall and chapel in Italian marble, is heavily influenced by the third Marquess' interests in Greek mythology and astrology. The drawing room has paintings by Titian and Tintoretto among other masters.

From Tarbet, follow the A83 towards Inveraray. As you descend Glen Kinglas towards Loch Fyne, the A815 forks to the left just before Cairndow; follow it 10 miles south to Strachur, then take the A886 for another 24 miles to Colintraive; a five-minute ferry crossing (departs every 30 minutes) takes you to Bute.

PK289 / SHUTTERSTOCK ©

Inveraray Inveraray Castle

then turning south on the A82. Stop and stretch your legs at the Falls of Falloch, then continue to Tarbet (total 30 miles).

5 Tarbet

Tarbet is a tiny village at a road junction on the western shore of Loch Lomond. **Cruise Loch Lomond** (☎01301-702356; www.cruiselochlomond.co.uk; Tarbet; cruises adult/child from £12/7.50; ⏰8.30am-5.30pm late Mar-early Nov) offers boat trips from Tarbet and nearby Luss, including options exploring loch islands, Rob Roy's cave, the Arklet Falls, or walking a section of the West Highland Way from Inversnaid. The one-hour Northern Highlights cruise is a quick introduction from Tarbet, from where it also rents bikes.

The Drive » Strike west from Tarbet on the A83, which soon enters mountainous territory, climbing through Glen Croe and over the high pass known as the Rest and Be Thankful (a memorial stone in the car park at the top explains the name) to reach the sea at Loch Fyne. Continue around the head of this stunning loch to reach Inveraray (23 miles).

TRIP HIGHLIGHT

6 Inveraray

This historic planned village is all black and white – even the familiar logos of high-street chain shops conform. Spectacularly set on the shores of Loch Fyne, Inveraray was built by the Duke of Argyll in Georgian style in the 18th century. **Inveraray Jail** (☎01499-302381; www.inverarayjail.co.uk; Church Sq; adult/child £11.50/6.95; ⏰10am-5pm; 👪) has been turned into an interactive tourist attraction where you can sit in on a trial, try out a cell and discover the harsh tortures that were meted out to unfortunate prisoners.

The stunning **Inveraray Castle** (☎01499-302203; www.inveraray-castle.com; adult/child/family £12.50/8/35; ⏰10am-5.45pm Apr-Oct) has been the seat of the dukes of Argyll – chiefs of Clan Campbell – since the 15th century. The 18th-century building, with its fairy-tale turrets and fake battlements, houses an impressive armoury hall, its walls patterned with more than 1000 pole-arms, dirks, muskets and Lochaber axes.

Loch Fyne Oyster Bar (☎01499-600482; www.lochfyne.com; Clachan, Cairndow; mains £15-26; ⏰9am-7pm Mon-Sat, 10am-7pm Sun, to 5pm Nov-Mar, restaurant noon to 5pm or 6pm; 📶), 9 miles north of Inveraray, is a great place to try the local molluscs or other

DETOUR: ISLE OF SEIL

Start: 8 Oban

The small island of Seil is best known for its connection to the mainland – the graceful Bridge over the Atlantic, designed by Thomas Telford and opened in 1793.

On the west coast of the island is the pretty conservation village of **Ellenabeich**, with whitewashed cottages and rainwater barrels backed by a wee harbour and rocky cliffs. It was built to house local slate workers, but the industry collapsed in 1881 when the sea broke into the main quarry – the flooded pit can still be seen.

Just offshore is small, charming **Easdale Island**, which has more old slate-workers' cottages and an interesting **folk museum** (01852-300370; www.easdalemuseum.org; Easdale; suggested donation £3; 11am-4pm Apr–mid-Oct) with displays about the slate industry and social history. Once housing 450 people, the island's population fell to just seven old-timers by 1950 but now has a healthier few dozen after a program welcoming incomers. Climb to the top of the island (a 38m peak) for great views of the surrounding area. Confusingly, Ellenabeich is also referred to as Easdale, so 'Easdale Harbour', for example, is on the Seil side.

Seafari Adventures (01852-300003; www.seafari.co.uk; Ellenabeich; Apr-Oct) runs a series of exciting boat trips in high-speed rigid inflatables to Corryvreckan whirlpool (call for dates of 'Whirlpool Specials', when the tide is strongest), as well as summer whale-watching trips and several other excursions.

A ferry hop from Seil's southern end takes you to neighbouring **Isle of Luing**, a quiet backwater that has no real sights but is appealing for wildlife walks and easy-going bike rides.

To reach Seil, 10 miles south of Oban, follow the A816 to Kilninver and turn right on the B844. To rejoin the main trip, retrace your route to the A816.

Scottish seafood, eat in or take away. Nearby **Fyne Ales** (01499-600120; www.fyneales.com; Achadunan, Cairndow; tours £7.50-10; 10am-6pm) is an excellent craft brewery with tours and a lovely bar-cafe where you can taste the beers; our favourite is the light, citrussy Jarl.

p377

The Drive » A ceremonial arch at the east end of town marks the beginning of the A819, which snakes north through low hills and dense forest to reach the shores of Loch Awe. When you reach the A85 junction, turn left and continue around the head of the loch to Lochawe village (16 miles).

7 Lochawe

Loch Awe is one of Scotland's most beautiful lochs, with rolling forested hills around its southern end and spectacular mountains in the north. It is the longest loch in Scotland – about 24 miles – but is less than 1 mile wide for most of its length. At its northern end, it escapes to the sea through the narrow Pass of Brander, where Robert the Bruce defeated the MacDougalls in 1309.

Just east of Lochawe village are the scenic ruins of the much-photographed **Kilchurn Castle** (HES; www.historicenvironment.scot; Dalmally; 9.30am-5.30pm Apr-Sep). Built in 1440, it enjoys one of Scotland's finest settings. It's a scenic stroll to it from the (unmarked) car park on the A85, just west of the Inveraray turn-off between Dalmally and Lochawe.

You can climb to the top of the four-storey castle tower for impressive views of Loch Awe and the surrounding hills.

Three miles west of the village you can visit **Cruachan power station** (☎01866-962630; www.visitcruachan.co.uk; A85; adult/child £7.50/2.50; ⏰9.15am-4.45pm Mon-Fri Apr-Oct, to 3.45pm Mon-Fri Nov-Mar), where electric buses take you more than half a mile inside Ben Cruachan to see the hydroelectric scheme which occupies a vast cavern hollowed out of the mountain.

A further 6 miles will bring you Taynuilt, where you can visit the fascinating **Bonawe Furnace** (HES; ☎01866-822432; www.historicenvironment.scot; Taynuilt; adult/child £6/3.60; ⏰9.30am-5.30pm Apr-Sep), a picturesque historical iron smelting complex. It's now a tranquil, beautiful place, with the old buildings picturesquely arranged around a green hillside, and there's great background information on the iron industry. Take a picnic!

The Drive » Continue west on the A85 to Oban (21 miles from Lochawe), stopping at Bridge of Connel to see the Falls of Lora, whitewater rapids under the bridge caused by the tide flowing in and out through the narrow rocky mouth of Loch Etive (depends on tide times).

8 Oban

Oban, the main ferry terminal for crossings to the Scottish islands, enjoys a fine setting on a broad bay with glorious views west to the hills of Mull. Some of Britain's standout places to enjoy fish and shellfish are to be found here, whether you go for no-frills crab shacks like the **Oban Seafood Hut** (☎07881-418565; www.facebook.com/obanseafood.hut.9; Railway Pier; mains £3-14; ⏰10am-6pm mid-Mar–Oct), or more upmarket restaurants such as **Ee-usk** (☎01631-565666; www.eeusk.com; North Pier; mains £14-24; ⏰noon-3pm & 5.45-9.30pm

LOCH LOMOND

The 'bonnie banks' and 'bonnie braes' of Loch Lomond have long been Glasgow's rural retreat – a scenic region of hills, water and healthy fresh air within easy reach of Scotland's largest city. Today the loch's popularity shows no sign of decreasing.

Loch Lomond is mainland Britain's largest lake and, after Loch Ness, the most famous of Scotland's lochs. Its proximity to Glasgow (20 miles away) means that the tourist honeypots of Balloch, Loch Lomond Shores and Luss get pretty crowded in summer. The eastern shore, which is followed by the West Highland Way long-distance footpath, is quieter and offers a better chance to appreciate the loch away from the busy main road.

Loch Lomond straddles the Highland border. The southern part is broad and island-studded, fringed by woods and Lowland meadows. However, north of Luss the loch narrows, occupying a deep trench gouged out by glaciers during the Ice Age, with 900m mountains crowding either side.

There are around 60 islands, large and small, in the loch. Most are privately owned, and only two (Inchcailloch and Inchmurrin) can be reached without your own boat or canoe. **Inchcailloch** is a nature reserve reached by boats from Balmaha or Luss, while privately owned **Inchconnachan** is only accessible by boat or canoe. Unusually, it is home to a herd of wallabies, introduced by a previous owner; the rare capercaillie nests here too.

Inchmurrin is reached by passenger ferry from Arden on the loch's western shore and has walking trails, beaches, self-catering cottages and a restaurant that is open from Easter to October. See www.inchmurrin-lochlomond.com.

Apr-Oct, noon-2.30pm & 5.45-9pm Nov-Mar;) or **Waterfront Fishouse** (01631-563110; www.waterfrontfishouse.co.uk; 1 Railway Pier; mains £15-23; noon-2pm & 5.30-9pm, extended hours Jun-Aug;). Sustainable sourcing is an important element that's widely practised.

In the centre of town, handsome **Oban Distillery** (01631-572004; www.malts.com; Stafford St; tours £10; 9.30am-7.30pm Mon-Fri & 9.30am-5pm Sat & Sun Jul-Sep, 9.30am-5pm Mar-Jun & Oct-Nov, noon or 12.30-4.30pm Dec-Feb) has been producing since 1794. The standard guided tour leaves regularly (worth booking) and includes a dram, a take-home glass and a taste straight from the cask.

Crowning the hill above town is a Colosseum-like Victorian folly, **McCaig's Tower** (cnr Laurel & Duncraggan Rds; 24hr), commissioned in 1890 by a local with the philanthropic intention of providing work for unemployed stonemasons. To reach it on foot, make the steep climb up Jacob's Ladder (a flight of stairs) from Argyll St; the bay views are worth the effort.

A pleasant 1-mile stroll north along the coast road leads to **Dunollie Castle** (01631-570550; www.dunollie.org; Dunollie Rd; adult/child £6/3; 10am-5pm Mon-Sat, noon-5pm Sun Apr-Oct), built by the MacDougalls of Lorn in the 13th century and unsuccessfully besieged for a year during the 1715 Jacobite rebellion. It's ruined, but ongoing conservation work is offering increasing access. The nearby 1745 House – seat of Clan MacDougall – is an intriguing museum of local and clan history, and there are pleasant wooded grounds and a cafe. Free tours run twice daily.

p377

The Drive » Head south from Oban for 29 miles on the A816 to Kilmartin Glen.

TRIP HIGHLIGHT

9 Kilmartin Glen

This magical glen is the focus of one of the biggest concentrations of **prehistoric sites** in Scotland. Burial cairns, standing stones, stone circles, hill forts and cup-and-ring-marked rocks litter the countryside. Within a 6-mile radius of Kilmartin village there are 25 sites with standing stones and over 100 rock carvings. In the 6th century, Irish settlers arrived in this part of Argyll and founded the kingdom of Dál Riata (Dalriada), which eventually united with the Picts in 843 to create the first Scottish kingdom.

Their seat of power was the hill fort of **Dunadd**, on the plain 3.5 miles to the south of Kilmartin. Rising out of the boggy plain of Moine

ROB ROY

Nicknamed Red (*'ruadh'* in Gaelic, anglicised to 'roy') for his ginger locks, Robert MacGregor (1671–1734) was the wild leader of the wildest of Scotland's clans, outlawed by powerful neighbours, hence their sobriquet, Children of the Mist. Incognito, Rob became a prosperous livestock trader, before a dodgy deal led to a warrant for his arrest.

A legendary swordsman, the fugitive from justice then became notorious for daring raids into the Lowlands to carry off cattle and sheep. Forever hiding from potential captors, he was twice imprisoned, but escaped dramatically on both occasions. He finally turned himself in and received his liberty and a pardon from the king. He lies buried – perhaps – in the churchyard at Balquhidder; his uncompromising later epitaph reads 'MacGregor despite them'. His life has been glorified over the years due to Walter Scott's novel and the 1995 film. Many Scots see his life as a symbol of the struggle of the common folk against the inequitable ownership of vast tracts of the country by landed aristocrats.

Mhor Nature Reserve, it's an atmospheric spot. A slippery path leads to the summit, where you can gaze out on much the same view that the ancient kings of Dál Riata enjoyed 1300 years ago. Atop the hill, a footprint, faint rock carvings of a boar and an ogham inscription may have been used in inauguration ceremonies.

Though **Kilmartin House Museum** (01546-510278; www.kilmartin.org; Kilmartin) will be closed until 2023, it's worth dropping in here first because an outdoor display will introduce you to the various ancient sites of the area; grab a coffee here, too, to help with the worthwhile redevelopment project.

The Drive » Continue south on the A810 and A83 through Lochgilphead and Ardrishaig to Tarbert (21 miles). If you fancy a longer and more scenic route, turn right on the B8024 south of Ardrishaig, which follows the west coast of Knapdale with views to the hills of Jura (42 miles).

10 Tarbert

The attractive fishing village and yachting centre of Tarbert is the gateway to Kintyre, and most scenic, with buildings strung around its excellent natural harbour. A crossroads for nearby ferry routes, it's a handy stepping stone to Arran or Islay, but is well worth a stopover on any itinerary.

CORNFIELD / SHUTTERSTOCK ©

Kilmartin Glen Temple Wood prehistoric site

The picturesque harbour is overlooked by the crumbling, ivy-covered ruins of **Tarbert Castle** (24hr), rebuilt by Robert the Bruce in the 14th century. You can hike up via a signposted footpath beside **Loch Fyne Gallery** (01880-820390; www.facebook.com/LochFyneGallery; Harbour St; 10am-5pm Mon-Sat, 11am-4pm Sun), a shop which showcases the work of local artists.

Try to time your trip to fit in a meal at the simple but stylish **Starfish** (01880-820733; www.starfishtarbert.com; Castle St; mains £14-21; 5-8.30pm Tue-Thu, 12.30-2pm & 5-8.30pm Fri & Sat Mar-Oct;) seafood restaurant, where a great variety of specials are prepared with whatever's fresh off the Tarbert boats that day. There are options for vegetarians and meat-eaters, too, and decent cocktails. Best to book.

p377

The Drive » Continue south from Tarbert on the A83 and, just past the ferry terminal at Kennacraig, turn left on the B8001 to Claonaig and another left to the road end at Skipness (13 miles).

11 Skipness

Tiny Skipness is pleasant and quiet with great views of Arran. Beyond the village rise the substantial remains of 13th-century **Skipness Castle** (HES; www.historicenvironment.scot; castle & chapel 24hr, tower 9.30am-5.30pm Apr-Sep, 10am-4pm Oct), a former possession of the Lords of the Isles. It's a striking building, composed of dark-green local stone trimmed with contrasting red-brown sandstone from Arran. The tower

DETOUR: MULL OF KINTYRE

Start: ⓬ Campbeltown

A narrow winding road, 15 miles long, leads south from Campbeltown to the Mull of Kintyre, passing some good sandy beaches near Southend. This remote headland was immortalised in Paul McCartney's famous song – the former Beatle owns a farmhouse in the area. From where the road ends, a 30-minute steep downhill walk leads to a clifftop lighthouse, with Northern Ireland, only 12 miles away, visible across the channel. Don't leave the road when the frequent mists roll in as it's easy to become disoriented.

house was added in the 16th century and was occupied until the 19th century. From the top you can see the roofless, 13th-century St Brendan's Chapel down by the shore. The kirkyard contains some excellent carved grave slabs.

Attached to Skipness House, near the castle, is the **Seafood Cabin** (☎01880-760207; www.skipnessseafoodcabin.co.uk; dishes £3-18; ⏲11am-7pm Sun-Fri late May-Sep), a great place for lunch on a fine summer day, serving no-frills but delicious local fish and shellfish at outdoor picnic tables with grand views over the grassy coast. It's famous for crab rolls, which are on the small side: add on a pot of mussels or plate of gravadlax.

Continuing the theme, nearby **Skipness Smokehouse** (☎01880-760378; www.skipnesssmokehouse.com; ⏲noon-5pm Sun-Fri Mar-Dec) produces sensational hot smoked salmon among other goodies.

The Drive » Return to Claonaig and turn left to follow the B842 down the eastern shore of the Kintyre peninsula to Campbeltown (30 miles), a twisting roller-coaster of a road that climbs high above the sea then swoops down to remote bays, with breathtaking views across the water to the rocky peaks of Arran.

⓬ Campbeltown

Blue-collar Campbeltown, set around a beautiful harbour, still suffers from the decline of its fishing and whisky industries but is rebounding on the back of golf tourism and a ferry link to Ayrshire. The spruced-up seafront backed by green hills lends the town a distinctly optimistic air.

There were once no fewer than 32 distilleries around Campbeltown, but most closed in the 1920s. Today **Springbank** (☎01586-555468; www.springbank.scot; 85 Longrow; tours from £10; ⏲tours Mon-Sat) is one of only three operational. It is also one of the few around that distills, matures and bottles all its whisky on the one site, making for an interesting tour. It's a quality malt, one of Scotland's finest. Various premium tours take you deeper into the process.

Campbeltown's most unusual sight awaits in a cave on the southern side of Davaar island, at the mouth of Campbeltown Loch. On the wall of the cave is an eerie painting of the **Crucifixion** by local artist Archibald MacKinnon, dating from 1887. You can walk to the island at low tide: check tide times with the tourist office.

Near Campbeltown, the **Machrihanish Golf Club** (☎01586-810277; www.machgolf.com; Machrihanish; green fee £75) is a classic links course, designed by Old Tom Morris. It's remarkably good value compared to courses of a similar standard elsewhere in Scotland. The famous first hole requires a very decent drive across the bay, or you'll literally end up on the beach. Close by is the much newer **Machrihanish Dunes** (☎01586-810000; www.machrihanishdunes.com; Machrihanish; green fee £110), an impressive seaside experience and very welcoming: the clubhouse is a convivial little hut, it's child-friendly and there are often website offers.

Eating & Sleeping

Aberfoyle 1

Lake of Menteith Hotel Hotel $$$

(01877-385258; www.lake-hotel.com; Port of Menteith; r £150-255; P) Soothingly situated on a lake (yes, it's the only non-loch in Scotland) 3 miles east of Aberfoyle, this genteel retreat makes a great romantic getaway. Though all rooms are excellent, with a contemporary feel, it's worth an upgrade to the enormous 'lake heritage' ones with a view of the water: it really is a sensational outlook. Even if you're not staying, head down to the waterside bar-restaurant (mains £15 to £19). Check the website for packages.

Callander 3

Callander Meadows Scottish $$

(01877-330181; www.callandermeadows.co.uk; 24 Main St; dinner mains £13-19; 10am-2.30pm & 6-8.30pm Thu-Sun year-round, plus Mon May-Sep;) Informal and cosy, this well-loved restaurant in the centre of Callander occupies the front rooms of a Main St house. It's truly excellent; there's a contemporary flair for presentation and unusual flavour combinations, but a solidly British base underpins the cuisine. There's a great beer/coffee garden out the back, where you can also eat. Lighter lunches such as sandwiches are also available.

Inveraray 6

Samphire Seafood $$

(01499-302321; www.samphireseafood.com; 6a Arkland; dinner mains £14-23; noon-2.30pm & 5-8.45pm Wed-Sun;) There's lots to like about this compact restaurant that makes an effort to source sustainable local seafood. It does a delicious seafood stew and you can expect to see lobster, oysters and langoustines from the loch regularly featuring as specials.

George Hotel Inn $$

(01499-302111; www.thegeorgehotel.co.uk; Main St E; d £100-145; P) The George boasts a magnificent choice of opulent, individual rooms decorated with sumptuous period furniture. Some feature four-poster beds, Victorian roll-top baths and/or private Jacuzzis (superior rooms and suites cost £165 to £225 per double; the library suite is quite a sight). Some rooms are in an annexe opposite and there are also self-catering options. The cosy wood-panelled bar, with rough stone walls, flagstone floor and peat fires, is a delightful place for all-day bar meals, and has a beer garden.

Oban 8

Elderslie Guest House B&B $$

(01631-570651; www.obanbandb.com; Soroba Rd; s £55, d £78-92; Apr–mid-Oct; P) A B&B can be a difficult balancing act: making things modern without losing cosiness, being friendly and approachable without sacrificing privacy. At this spot a mile south of Oban, the balance is absolutely right, with a variety of commodious rooms with big showers, large towels and lovely outlooks over greenery. Breakfast is great, there's outdoor lounging space and the hosts are excellent.

Tarbert 10

Knap Guest House B&B $$

(01880-820015; www.knapguesthouse.co.uk; Campbeltown Rd; d £90-99;) This cosy upstairs spot at the bend in the main road offers faultless hospitality, luxurious furnishings and an attractive blend of Scottish and Far Eastern decor, with wooden elephants especially prominent. The welcome is warm, and there are great harbour views from the breakfast room, where the open kitchen allows you to admire the host at work. Prices drop in low season. Rooms are plush, with the owner's years in hospitality paying dividends for guests. One is a suite (£135 to £180), which has an excellent, spacious lounge area with vistas.

Upper West Coast

32

Experience the most stirring of Scottish highland and island scenery, with majestic mountains looming over shimmering lochs and stunning coastlines.

TRIP HIGHLIGHTS

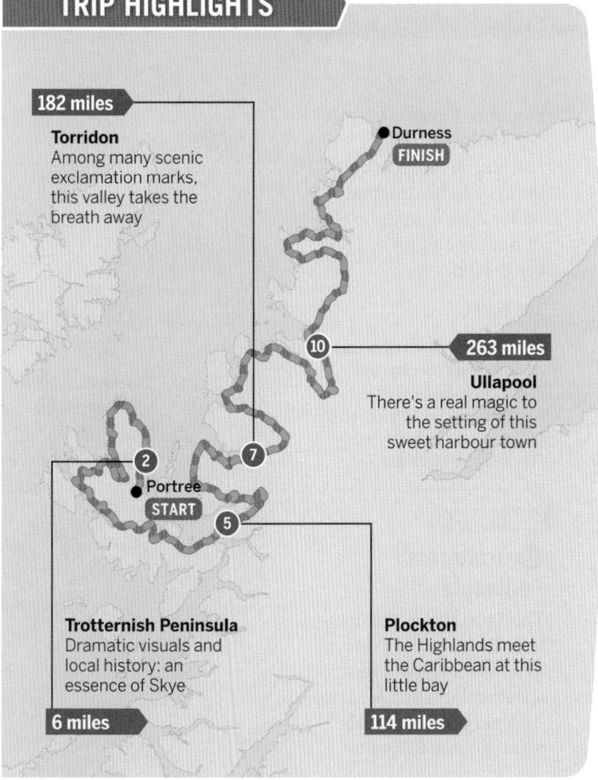

182 miles
Torridon
Among many scenic exclamation marks, this valley takes the breath away

Durness
FINISH

10
263 miles
Ullapool
There's a real magic to the setting of this sweet harbour town

2
7
Portree
START
5

Trotternish Peninsula
Dramatic visuals and local history: an essence of Skye
6 miles

Plockton
The Highlands meet the Caribbean at this little bay
114 miles

3–5 DAYS
360 MILES / 575KM

GREAT FOR...

BEST TIME TO GO

June is busy but offers long evenings and dreamy light. September is quieter, with fewer midges.

ESSENTIAL PHOTO

Sunset from Applecross, with the hills of Raasay and Skye silhouetted.

BEST FOR FOODIES

The local seafood is sublime.

Plockton Boats moored in the town harbour

32 Upper West Coast

Quintessential highland country such as this, marked by single-track roads, breathtaking emptiness and a wild, fragile beauty, leaves an indelible imprint on the soul. Scotland's far northwest coastline is a feast of deep inlets, forgotten beaches and surging peninsulas; looming inland are some of Scotland's most imposing and emblematic peaks. Whether it's blazing sunshine or murky greyness, the character of the land is totally unique and constantly changing.

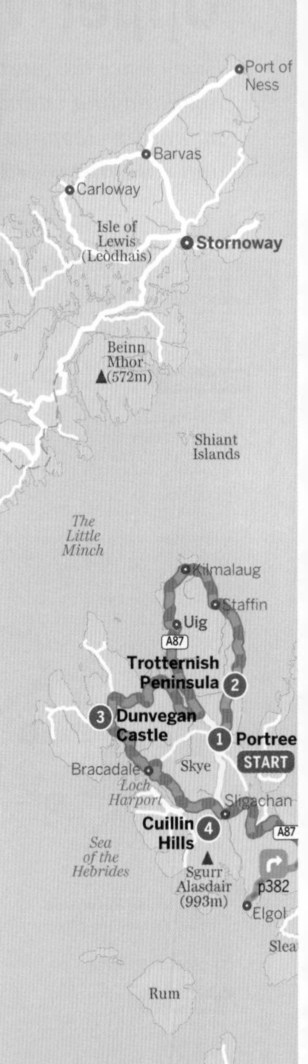

1 Portree

Portree is Skye's largest and liveliest town. It has a pretty harbour lined with brightly painted houses, and there are great views of the surrounding hills. Its name (from the Gaelic for King's Harbour) commemorates James V, who came here in 1540 to pacify the local clans.

MV Stardust (☎07795-385581; www.skyeboat-trips.co.uk; Portree Harbour; adult/child £20/10) offers 1½-hour boat trips around Portree Bay, with the chance to see seals, porpoises and – if you're lucky – white-tailed sea eagles. There are also two-hour cruises to the Sound of Raasay (£25/15 per adult/child). You can also arrange fishing trips, or to be dropped off for a hike on the Isle of Raasay and picked up again later.

🛏 p389

The Drive » Follow the road north through the centre of Portree to leave town on the A855, which after about 6 miles brings you to the Trotternish Peninsula's first sights.

TRIP HIGHLIGHT

2 Trotternish Peninsula

The Trotternish Peninsula to the north of Portree has some of Skye's most spectacular – and bizarre – scenery. Whatever the weather, it is difficult not to be blown away by the savage beauty of this place.

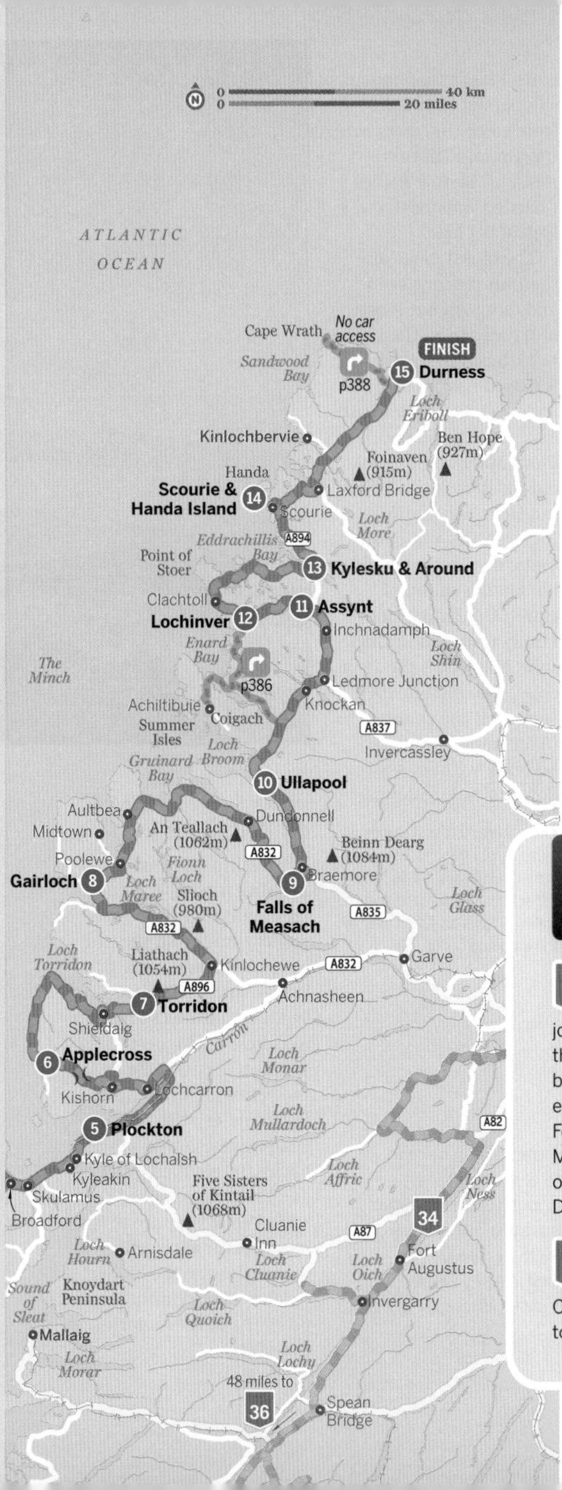

The 50m-high, pot-bellied pinnacle of crumbling basalt known as the **Old Man of Storr** (P) is prominent above the road 6 miles north of Portree. Walk up to its foot from the car park at the northern end of Loch Leathan (round trip 2 miles). Past the Old Man is a popular clifftop lookout over spectacular **Kilt Rock**.

At the northern end of the peninsula at Kilmuir, the peat-reek of crofting life in the 18th and 19th centuries is preserved in the thatched cottages, croft houses, barns and farm implements of the evocative **Skye Museum of Island Life** (☎01470-552206; www.skyemuseum.co.uk; Kilmuir; adult/child

LINK YOUR TRIP

34 Great Glen

Allowing a day's journey between them, this trip can be tackled before or after this drive, either by heading from Fort William to the ferry at Mallaig and thence to Skye, or by dropping down from Durness to Inverness.

36 Ferry-Hopping

Link these trips via Oban and the Mallaig ferry to Skye.

£4/50p; ⏲9.30am-5pm Mon-Sat Easter-late Sep; P). Behind the museum is Kilmuir Cemetery, where a tall Celtic cross marks the grave of Flora MacDonald.

🛏 p389

The Drive » Keep following the road around the peninsula, through the ferry port of Uig and on to Borge, where you take a right on to the A850 to Dunvegan. From the Old Man of Storr it's about 54 miles via this route.

3 Dunvegan Castle

Skye's most famous historic building, and one of its most popular tourist attractions, **Dunvegan Castle** (☎01470-521206; www.dunvegancastle.com; adult/child £14/9; ⏲10am-5.30pm Easter–mid-Oct; P) is the seat of the chief of Clan MacLeod. In addition to the usual castle stuff – swords, silver and family portraits – there are some interesting artefacts, including the Fairy Flag, a diaphanous silk banner that dates from some time between the 4th and 7th centuries, and Bonnie Prince Charlie's waistcoat and a lock of his hair.

The oldest parts are the 14th-century keep and dungeon but most of it dates from the 17th to 19th centuries, when it played host to Samuel Johnson, Sir Walter Scott and, most famously, Flora MacDonald. Look out for Rory Mor's Drinking Horn, a beautiful 16th-century vessel of Celtic design that could hold half a gallon of claret. Upholding the family tradition in 1956, John Macleod – the 29th chief, who died in 2007 – downed the contents in one minute and 57 seconds 'without setting down or falling down'.

The Drive » It's 24 scenic miles across the heart of the island along the A863 to Sligachan, a crossroads and walkers' haven watched over by the brooding Cuillin Hills.

JAROSLAV SEKERES / SHUTTERSTOCK ©

4 Cuillin Hills

The Cuillin Hills are Britain's most spectacular mountain range (the name comes from the Old Norse *kjöllen*, meaning 'keel-shaped'). Though small in stature (Sgurr Alasdair, the highest summit, is only 993m), the peaks are near-alpine in character, with knife-edge ridges, jagged pinnacles, scree-filled gullies and hectares of naked rock. While they are a paradise for experienced mountaineers, the higher reaches of the Cuillin are off limits to the majority of walkers.

DETOUR: ELGOL

Start: 4 Cuillin Hills

On a clear day, the 15-mile journey along the road from Broadford to Elgol is one of the most scenic on Skye. It takes in two classic postcard panoramas – the view of Bla Bheinn across Loch Slapin (near Torrin), and the superb view of the entire Cuillin range from Elgol pier. Elgol itself is a tiny settlement with a shop and cafe at the end of this long, single-track road.

Skye Old Man of Storr

The good news is that there are also plenty of good low-level hikes within the ability of most walkers, several leaving from Sligachan.

The Drive » It's a 30-mile drive from Sligachan on the A87 along the Skye coast, past the Raasay ferry at Sconser, through Broadford and over the bridge onto the mainland at Kyle of Lochalsh. In town, take a left up the hill and follow this road to Plockton.

TRIP HIGHLIGHT

5 Plockton

Idyllic little Plockton, with its perfect cottages lining a perfect bay, looks like it was designed as a film set. And it has indeed served as just that – scenes from *The Wicker Man* (1973) were filmed here, and the village became famous as the location for the 1990s TV series *Hamish Macbeth*.

With all this picture-postcard perfection, it can get busy in summer, but there's no denying its appeal, with 'palm trees' (actually hardy New Zealand cabbage palms) lining the waterfront, a thriving small-boat sailing scene and several good places to stay, eat and drink. The local langoustines (Plockton prawns) are famous.

It's fun to get out on the water here. **Calum's Seal Trips** (☎07761-263828; www.calums-sealtrips.com; adult/child £14/6; ⊙Apr-Oct) runs friendly seal-watching cruises – there's a seal colony just outside the harbour, and the trip comes with an excellent commentary. **Sea Kayak Plockton** (☎01599-544422; www.seakayakplockton.co.uk; 1-day beginner course adult/child £85/65), meanwhile, offers everything from beginners' lessons to multiday trips around Skye to highly challenging odysseys.

p389

The Drive » Head to the A890, running northeast beside Loch Carron. Turn left along the A896 along the loch's opposite side and through likeable Lochcarron village before taking a left turn to Applecross. The magnificent Bealach na Ba (Pass of the Cattle; 626m) climbs steeply and hair-raisingly via hairpin bends (not suitable for caravans or large motorhomes), then drops dramatically to the village with views of Skye (36 miles total).

6 Applecross

The delightfully remote seaside village of Applecross feels like an island retreat due to its isolation and magnificent views of Raasay and the hills of Skye that set the pulse racing, particularly at sunset. On a clear day, it's an unforgettable place. Book ahead for a bed or meal at the inn.

The Drive » It's 25 winding miles of single-track road from Applecross around the north coast of the peninsula to the pretty waterside village of Shieldaig, where you rejoin the A896 and head east for the majestic 7 miles to Torridon, along the shore of the sea loch of the same name.

7 Torridon

The road running through Glen Torridon is dwarfed by some of Britain's most dramatic mountain scenery. Carved by ice from massive layers of ancient sandstone that takes its name from the region, the mountains here are steep, shapely and imposing, whether flirting with autumn mists, draped in dazzling winter snows, or reflected in the calm blue waters of Loch Torridon on a summer day.

The road from lovely Shieldaig, which boasts an attractive main street of whitewashed houses right on the waterfront, reaches the head of the sea loch at spectacularly sited Torridon village. It's a base for excursions to the Torridon peaks: **Liathach** (1054m; pronounced 'lee-agakh', Gaelic for 'the Grey One'), **Beinn Eighe** (1010m; 'ben ay', 'the File') and **Beinn Alligin** (986m; 'the Jewelled Mountain'). These are big, serious mountains for experienced hill walkers only.

The Drive » Follow the A896 northeast to Kinlochewe, then turn left along the A832, which continues to Gairloch (27 miles total). The road follows the shore of beautiful Loch Maree. From a car park 1.5 miles past Beinn Eighe visitor centre, there's a great waymarked 4-mile return walk to a plateau and cairn on the side of Beinn Eighe, offering magnificent views.

8 Gairloch

Gairloch is a knot of villages around the inner end of the loch of the same name. It's a good base for whale- and dolphin-watching excursions, and the surrounding area has beautiful sandy beaches, good trout fishing and birdwatching.

Gairloch Marine Wildlife Centre & Cruises (☎07751-992666; www.porpoise-gairloch.co.uk; Pier Rd, IV21 2BQ; cruises adult/child £30/25; ⏲10am-4pm Easter-Oct) has audiovisual and interactive displays, lots of charts, photos and knowledgeable staff. From here, cruises run three times daily (weather permitting); during the two-hour trips you may see basking sharks, porpoises and minke whales. The crew collects data on

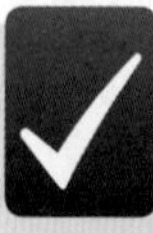

TOP TIP: SINGLE-TRACK ROADS

Along much of this drive you will find single-track roads that are only wide enough for one vehicle. Passing places (usually marked with a white diamond sign, or a black-and-white striped pole) are used to allow oncoming traffic to get by. Remember that passing places are also for overtaking – you must pull over to let faster vehicles pass. Be wary, too, of sheep straying onto the road.

THE NORTH COAST 500

The drive around Scotland's far northern coastline is one of Europe's finest road trips. Words fail to describe the sheer variety of scenic splendour which unfolds as you cross this empty landscape of desolate moorlands, brooding mountains, fertile coastal meadows and stunning white-sand beaches.

In a clever piece of marketing, it's been dubbed the North Coast 500, as the round trip from Inverness is roughly that many miles, though you'll surely clock up a few more if you follow your heart down narrow byroads and seek perfect coastal vistas at the end of dead-end tracks.

In our opinion, the scenery is best viewed by travelling anticlockwise, heading north from Inverness up the east coast to Caithness, then turning west across the top of Scotland before descending down the west coast. This way, you'll make the most of the coastal vistas, the light and the awesome backdrop of the Assynt mountains.

While the drive hasn't actually changed, the new name has caught the imagination of tourists, so visitor numbers are well up. The villages along the way aren't overstocked with accommodation, so it's well worth reserving everything in advance if you're travelling the route in the spring or summer months. In winter lots of accommodation is closed so it's a good idea to book then, too.

water temperature and conditions, and monitors cetacean populations, so you are subsidising important research.

Six miles north of Gairloch, splendid **Inverewe Garden** (NTS; ☎01445-712952; www.nts.org.uk; IV22 2LG; adult/concession £13/11.50; ⏰9.30am-6pm Jun-Aug, to 5.30pm May, to 5pm Mar, Apr & Sep, to 4pm Oct, 10am-4pm Nov-Feb) is a welcome splash of colour on this otherwise bleak coast. The climate here is warmed by the Gulf Stream, which allowed Osgood MacKenzie to create this exotic woodland garden in 1862.

The Drive » It's a slow, winding 42 miles along the A832 from Gairloch north and east to the junction with the A835. Take your time and enjoy the scenic solitude.

9 Falls of Measach

Just west of the junction of the A835 and A832, a car park gives access to the **Falls of Measach**, which spill 45m into spectacularly deep and narrow Corrieshalloch Gorge. You can cross the gorge on a swaying suspension bridge, and walk west for 250m to a viewing platform that juts out dizzyingly above a sheer drop. The thundering falls and misty vapours rising from the gorge are very impressive.

The Drive » From the road junction, it's 12 miles northwest on the good A835 to Ullapool.

TRIP HIGHLIGHT

10 Ullapool

This pretty port on the shores of Loch Broom is the largest settlement in Wester Ross and one of the most alluring spots in the Highlands, a wonderful destination in itself as well as a gateway to the Western Isles. Offering a row of whitewashed cottages arrayed along the harbour and special views of the loch and its flanking hills, the town has a very distinctive appeal. The harbour served as an emigration point during the Clearances, with thousands of Scots watching Ullapool recede behind them as the diaspora cast them across the world.

Housed in a converted Telford church, **Ullapool Museum** (☎01854-612987; www.ullapoolmuseum.co.uk; 7 West Argyle St, IV26 2TY; adult/child £5/free; ⏰11am-4pm Mon, Tue, Thu & Fri, 10am-5pm

Sat Apr-Oct) relates the prehistoric, natural and social history of the town and Lochbroom area, with a particular focus on the emigration to Nova Scotia and other places. Leaving from Ullapool's harbour, **Seascape** (☎07511-290081; www.sea-scape.co.uk; adult/child £30/20; ⏰May-Sep) runs enjoyable two-hour tours out to the Summer Isles in an orange rigid inflatable boat (RIB). It also runs shorter trips, plus excursions to nearby Isle Martin, with time ashore.

🛏 p389

The Drive » It's 26 miles north along the A835 then A837 to the Skiag Bridge road junction at the heart of the Assynt region. Stop along the way to appreciate the mountainscapes and keep an eye out in the rear-view mirror, as many of the best perspectives unfold behind you.

11 Assynt

With its other-worldly scenery of isolated peaks rising above a sea of crumpled, lochan-spattered gneiss, Assynt epitomises the northwest's wild magnificence. Glaciers have sculpted the Torridonian sandstone into spectacular peaks, including Suilven's distinctive sugarloaf and ziggurat-like Quinag. The area is the centrepiece of what has been designated the **Northwest Highlands Geopark** (www.nwhgeopark.com).

Half a mile south of the Skiag Bridge road junction, perched on an island at the edge of Loch Assynt, are the romantic ruins of **Ardvreck Castle**, a 15th-century stronghold of the MacLeods of Assynt. There are rumoured to be several ghosts at Ardvreck, including the daughter of a MacLeod chieftain who was sold in marriage to the devil by her father. Thanks Dad! Nearby are the ruins of a barrack house built by the MacKenzies in the 1720s. There are wonderful summer sunsets over the castle and loch.

The Drive » Head west 10 miles from Skiag Bridge along the A837 to reach Lochinver. The road runs along the northern shore of wild and moody Loch Assynt.

12 Lochinver

Lochinver is Assynt's main settlement, a busy little fishing port that's a popular port of call with its laid-back atmosphere, good facilities and striking scenery.

Using local landscapes as inspiration, **Highland Stoneware** (☎01571-844376; www.highlandstoneware.com; Baddidarroch, Lochinver; ⏰9am-6pm Mon-

DETOUR: COIGACH

Start: 10 Ullapool

The region west of the main A835 road from Ullapool to Ledmore Junction is known as Coigach (www.coigach.com). A lone, single-track road off the A835 9 miles north of Ullapool penetrates this wilderness, leading through gloriously wild scenery to remote settlements.

Coigach is a wonderland for walkers and wildlife enthusiasts, with a patchwork of sinuous silver lochs dominated by the isolated peaks of Cul Mor (849m), Cul Beag (769m), Ben More Coigach (743m) and Stac Pollaidh (613m). The main settlement is the straggling township of Achiltibuie, 15 miles from the main road, with the gorgeous Summer Isles moored just off the coast, and silhouettes of mountains skirting the bay.

You could head back to the main road to continue your journey, or, at the western end of Loch Lurgainn, a branch road leads north to Lochinver, a scenic backroad so narrow and twisting that it's nicknamed the Wee Mad Road (not suitable for caravans or large motorhomes).

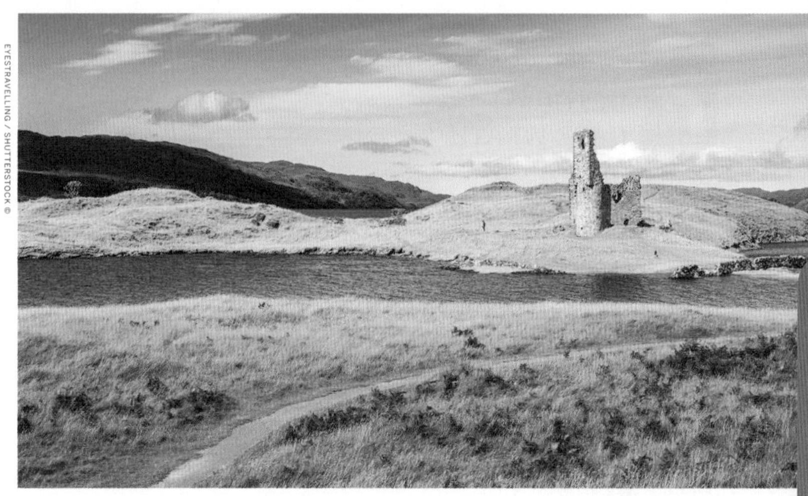

Assynt Ruins of Ardvreck Castle

Fri, 9am-5pm Sat, 11am-3pm Sun Easter-Oct, 9am-5.30pm Mon-Fri Nov-Easter) ensures you can relive the north-west's majesty every time you have a cuppa. Even better are the mosaics outside, especially the car.

Cam-Mac Boat Trips (☎07498-973094; www.cam-mac-boat-trips.co.uk; Lochinver; adult/child £30/15; ⏰Apr-Sep) give a good taste of this spectacular coastline.

Just north of Lochinver (or if coming from the north, not far south of Kylesku), a 23-mile detour on the narrow B869 rewards with spectacular views and fine beaches. From the lighthouse at Point of Stoer, a one-hour cliff walk leads to the **Old Man of Stoer**, a spectacular sea stack.

✕ p389

The Drive » Head north from Lochinver up the narrow B869 coastal route, which rewards with spectacular views and fine beaches. From the lighthouse at Point of Stoer, a one-hour cliff walk leads to the Old Man of Stoer, a spectacular sea stack. After 23 miles, you join the A894 just south of Kylesku.

⓭ Kylesku & Around

Hidden away on the shores of Loch Glencoul, tiny Kylesku served as a ferry crossing until it was made redundant by beautiful Kylesku Bridge in 1984. It's got an excellent inn and is a good base for walks; you can hire bikes here too.

Five miles southeast, in wild, remote country, lies 213m-high **Eas a'Chuil Aluinn**, Britain's highest waterfall. You can hike to the top of the falls from a parking area at a sharp bend in the main road 3 miles south of Kylesku (6 miles return). It can also be seen on **boat trips** (☎01971-502231; Kylesku; adult/child £30/20; ⏰Apr-Sep) from Kylesku.

The Drive » It's 10 spectacular miles up the A894 from Kylesku to Scourie. Look behind you for the best views.

⓮ Scourie & Handa Island

Scourie is a pretty crofting community with decent services, halfway between Durness and Ullapool. A few miles north lies **Handa Island** (www.scottishwildlifetrust.org.uk), a nature reserve run by the Scottish Wildlife Trust. The island's western sea cliffs provide nesting sites for important breeding populations of great skuas, arctic skuas, puffins, kittiwakes, razorbills and guillemots. Reach

DETOUR: CAPE WRATH

Start: ⑮ Durness

Though its name actually comes from the Norse word *hvarf* (turning point), there is something daunting and primal about Cape Wrath, the remote northwesternmost point of the British mainland.

The danger of the hazardous, stormy seas led to the building of the lighthouse at the cape by Robert and Alan Stevenson in 1828. The last keepers had left by 1998, when people were replaced by automation. Three miles to the east are the seabird colonies of Clo Mor, the British mainland's highest vertical sea cliffs (195m).

Part of the moorland has served for decades as a bombing range. The island of An Garbh-Eilean, 5 miles from the cape, has the misfortune to be around the same size as an aircraft carrier and is regularly ripped up by RAF bombs and missiles. There is no public access when the range is in use; restrictions are described at www.visitcapewrath.com/mod.

Getting to Cape Wrath involves a **boat ride** (☎07719-678729; www.capewrathferry.wordpress.com; return £10, bike £15; ⏱10am-4.30pm May-Sep) – passengers and bikes only – across the Kyle of Durness (10 minutes), connecting with a **minibus** (☎07742-670196; www.visitcapewrath.com; return £13; ⏱May-Sep) running 11 miles to the cape (50 minutes). This combination is a friendly but eccentric and sometimes shambolic service with limited capacity, so plan on waiting in high season, and call ahead to make sure the ferry is running. The ferry leaves from 2 miles southwest of Durness, and runs twice or more daily from Easter to mid-October. If you eschew the minibus, it's a spectacular 11-mile ride or hike from boat to cape over bleak scenery.

the island from Tarbet, 6 miles north of Scourie, via a **ferry** (☎07780-967800; www.handa-ferry.com; Tarbet Pier; adult/child return £15/5; ⏱outbound 9am-2pm Mon-Sat Apr-Aug, last ferry back 5pm).

The Drive » Continue 7 miles northeast from Scourie on the A894, then north 19 miles on the A838 to reach Scotland's north coast at Durness.

⑮ Durness

Scattered Durness is wonderfully located, strung out along cliffs rising from a series of pristine beaches. When the sun shines, the effects of blinding white sand, the cry of seabirds and the spring-green-coloured seas combine in a magical way.

Walking around the sensational sandy coastline is a highlight, as is a visit to Cape Wrath. Durness' beautiful beaches include **Rispond** (also known as Ceannabeinne) to the east, **Sango Sands** below town and **Balnakeil** to the west. At Balnakeil, a craft village occupies a one-time early-warning radar station. A walk along the beach to the north leads to Faraid Head, where you can see puffin colonies in early summer.

A mile east of the village is a path down to **Smoo Cave**. From the vast main chamber, you can head through to a smaller flooded cavern where a waterfall sometimes cascades from the roof. There's evidence the cave was inhabited about 6000 years ago. You can take a **boat trip** (☎01971-511704; www.smoocavetours.weebly.com; adult/child £6/3; ⏱11am-4pm Apr, May, Sep & Oct, 10am-5pm Jun-Aug) to explore a little further into the interior.

🛏 p389

Eating & Sleeping

Portree 1

Bosville Hotel Hotel $$$

(01478-612846; www.bosvillehotel.co.uk; 9-11 Bosville Tce; r from £220;) The Bosville brings a little bit of metropolitan style to Portree with its locally made designer fabrics and handcrafted furniture, fluffy bathrobes and bright, spacious bathrooms. It's worth splashing out a bit for the 'premium' rooms, with views over the town and harbour.

Trotternish Peninsula 2

Flodigarry Hotel Heritage Hotel $$$

(01470-552203; www.hotelintheskye.co.uk; Flodigarry; r £215-450, ste £640-730; Easter-Oct; P) From 1751–59, Flora MacDonald lived in a cottage that is now part of this atmospheric country-house hotel, given a new lease of life by adventurous owners. You can stay in the cottage itself (there are four bedrooms), or in the more spacious rooms and suites in the main hotel. Nonguests are welcome at the stylish bar and restaurant, with great sea views.

Plockton 5

Plockton Hotel Inn $$$

(01599-544274; www.plocktonhotel.co.uk; 41 Harbour St; s/d £100/150, cottage s/d £65/100;) The Plockton Hotel is one of those classic Highland spots that manages to make everyone happy, whether it's thirst, hunger or weariness that brings people knocking. Assiduously tended rooms are a real delight, with a homely atmosphere and thoughtful touches. Those without a sea view are consoled with more space and a balcony with rock-garden perspectives. The cottage nearby offers simpler comfort.

Ullapool 10

Ceilidh Place Hotel $$$

(01854-612103; www.theceilidhplace.com; 14 West Argyle St, IV26 2TY; r £130-180; P) This hotel is a celebration of Scottish culture: we're talking literature and traditional music, not tartan and Nessie dolls. Rooms go for character over modernity; instead of TVs they come with a selection of books chosen by Scottish literati, plus eclectic artwork and cosy touches. The sumptuous lounge has sofas, chaise longues and an honesty bar. There's a bookshop here, too.

Lochinver 12

Lochinver Larder & Riverside Bistro Bistro $

(01571-844356; www.lochinverlarder.com; 3 Main St, Lochinver; pies £5-6, mains £7-13; 10am-7.45pm Mon-Sat, to 5.30pm Sun Apr-Oct, 10am-4pm Mon-Sat Nov-Mar;) An outstanding menu of inventive food made with local produce is on offer here. The bistro turns out delicious seafood dishes in the evening, while the takeaway counter sells tasty pies with a wide range of gourmet fillings (try the venison and cranberry). It also does quality meals to take away and heat up: great for hostellers and campers.

Durness 15

Mackays Rooms Hotel $$$

(01971-511202; www.visitdurness.com; d standard £149, deluxe £169-210; May-Oct; P) You really feel you're at the furthest-flung corner of Scotland here, where the road turns through 90 degrees. But whether heading south or east, you'll go far before you find a better place to stay than this haven of Highland hospitality. With its big beds, soft fabrics and contemporary colours, it's a romantic spot with top-notch service.

Classic Trip

Royal Highlands & Cairngorms

The heart of the Scottish Highlands features a feast of castles and mountains, wild roller-coaster roads, ancient Caledonian pine forest, and the chance to see Highland wildlife up close and personal.

TRIP HIGHLIGHTS

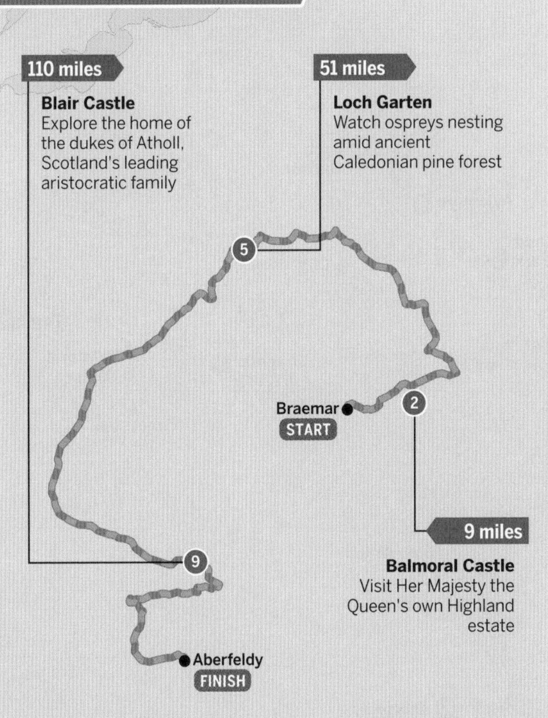

4–5 DAYS
149 MILES / 238KM

GREAT FOR...

BEST TIME TO GO

July and August mean good weather and all attractions are open.

ESSENTIAL PHOTO

The gorgeous view of Schiehallion mountain from Queen's View on Loch Tummel.

BEST FOR WILDLIFE

Watching the nesting ospreys at Loch Garten.

Braemar Braemar Castle

Classic Trip

33 Royal Highlands & Cairngorms

You'll tick off the highlights of Royal Deeside and the central Highlands as you make this circuit around Cairngorms National Park. Queen Victoria kick-started the Scottish tourism industry when she purchased Balmoral Castle in the middle of the 19th century, and her descendants still holiday here. Later, heed the call of the great outdoors with a visit to an osprey nesting site.

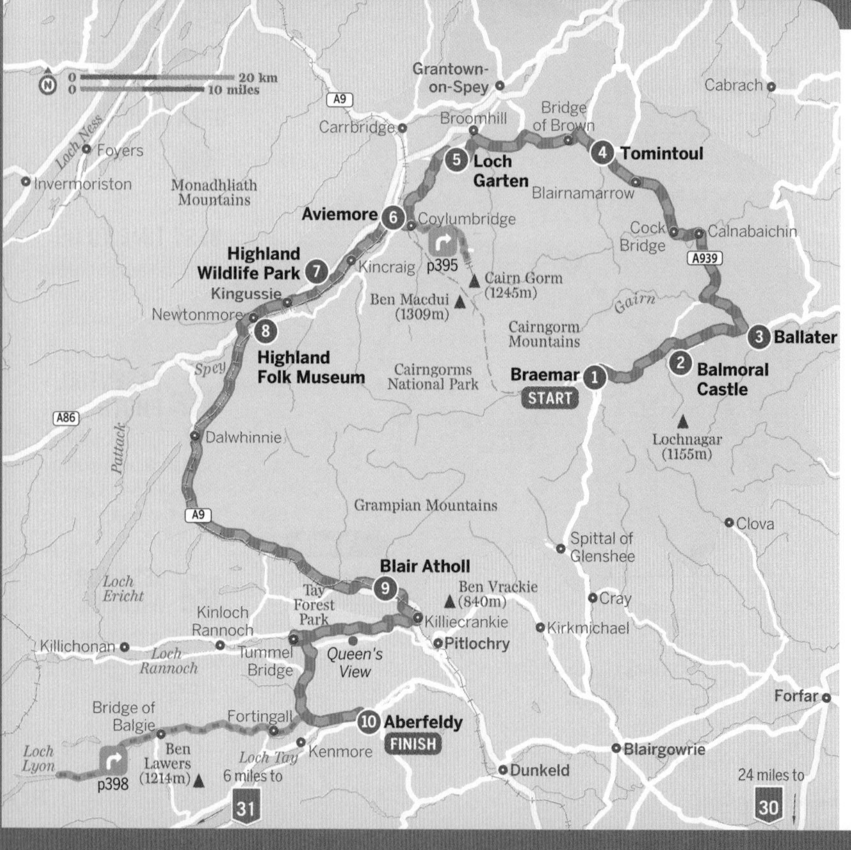

1 Braemar

Braemar is a pretty little village with a grand location on a broad plain ringed by mountains where the Dee valley and Glen Clunie meet. In winter this is one of the coldest places in the country – temperatures as low as -29°C have been recorded.

Just north of the village, turreted **Braemar Castle** (www.braemarcastle.co.uk; adult/child £10/4; 10am-5pm daily Jul & Aug, Wed-Sun Apr-Jun, Sep & Oct; P) dates from 1628 and served as a government garrison after the 1745 Jacobite rebellion. It was taken over by the local community in 2007, and now offers guided tours of the historic castle apartments.

There are Highland games in many towns and villages throughout the summer, but the best known is the **Braemar Gathering** (www.braemargathering.org), which takes place on the first Saturday in September.

p399

The Drive » The upper valley of the River Dee stretches east from Braemar to Aboyne. Made famous by its long association with the monarchy, the region is often called Royal Deeside. Head east from Braemar on the A93 for 9 miles to the car park at the entrance to Balmoral Castle.

TRIP HIGHLIGHT

2 Balmoral Castle

Built for Queen Victoria in 1855 as a private residence for the royal family, **Balmoral Castle** (01339-742534; www.balmoralcastle.com; Crathie; guided tour adult/child £15/6; 10am-5pm Apr-Jul, limited dates Oct-Dec; P) kicked off the revival of the Scottish Baronial style of architecture that characterises so many of Scotland's 19th-century country houses. Admission is by guided tour (book ahead); the tour is interesting and well-thought-out but very much an outdoor one through garden and grounds.

As for the castle itself, only the ballroom, which displays a collection of Landseer paintings and royal silver, is open to the public. Don't expect to see the Queen's private quarters! The main attraction is learning about Highland estate management, rather than royal revelations.

You can buy a booklet that details several waymarked walks within Balmoral Estate; the best is the climb to **Prince Albert's Cairn**.

The Drive » Continue east on the A93 for another 8 miles to Ballater.

3 Ballater

The attractive village of Ballater owes its 18th-century origins to the curative waters of nearby Pannanich Springs (now bottled commercially as Deeside Natural Mineral Water), and its prosperity to nearby Balmoral Castle.

After the original station was destroyed by fire in 2015, the **Old Royal Station** (01339-755306; Station Sq; tourist office 10am-3pm) building – newly restored to exactly replicate the one built in 1866 to receive Queen Victoria when she visited Balmoral by train – reopened in 2018. It houses a tourist office, a tearoom and a cafe-bistro. Behind the tourist office is a replica of Queen Victoria's carriage.

There are many pleasant walks in the surrounding area. The steep woodland walk up **Craigendarroch** (400m) takes

LINK YOUR TRIP

31 Lower West Coast

From Aberfeldy it's a lovely 23-mile drive along Loch Tay to Killin, where you can pick up our tour of the Argyllshire coast.

30 Stirling & Fife Coast

A scenic 46 miles lead south from Aberfeldy to Stirling, the start of our tour of the historic and cultural jewels of Fife.

just over one hour; ask at the tourist office for more info. You can hire bikes from **CycleHighlands** (☎01339-755864; www.cyclehighlands.com; The Pavilion, Victoria Rd; Santa Cruz mountain-bike hire per day £80; ⌚9am-5pm Mon-Thu & Sat, to 4pm Fri & Sun) and **Bike Station** (☎01339-754004; www.bikestationballater.co.uk; Station Sq; bicycle hire per day adult/child £20/10; ⌚9am-6pm), which also offer guided bike rides and advice on local trails.

🛏 p399

The Drive » The A939 strikes north through the mountains from Ballater to Tomintoul (25 miles). The section beyond Cock Bridge is a magnificent roller-coaster of a road, much loved by motorcyclists, summiting at the Lecht pass (637m) where there's a small skiing area (it's usually the first road in Scotland to be blocked by snow when winter closes in).

❹ Tomintoul

Tomintoul (tom-in-towel) is a pretty, stone-built village with a grassy, tree-lined main square. It was built by the Duke of Gordon in 1775 on the old military road that leads over the Lecht pass from Corgarff, a route now followed by the A939. The **Tomintoul & Glenlivet Discovery Centre** (☎01807-580760; discovery@tgdt.org.uk; The Square; ⌚10am-5pm Apr-Oct) celebrates local history, with reconstructions of a crofter's kitchen and a blacksmith's forge.

There's excellent mountain biking at the **BikeGlenlivet** (www.glenlivetestate.co.uk; trails free, parking £3) trail centre, 4.5 miles north of Tomintoul, off the B9136 road.

🍴 🛏 p399

The Drive » Continue northwest from Tomintoul on the A939 for 8.5 miles before turning left on a minor road to the village of Nethy Bridge. In the village, turn left towards Aviemore on the B970 then, after 600m, turn left again on a minor road to Loch Garten (total 17 miles).

TRIP HIGHLIGHT

❺ Loch Garten

A car park on the shores of Loch Garten, amid beautiful open forest of Scots pine, gives access to the **RSPB Loch Garten Osprey Centre** (☎01479-831694; www.rspb.org.uk/lochgarten; Tulloch; osprey hide adult/child £5/2.50; ⌚osprey hide 10am-6pm Apr-Aug). Ospreys nest in a tall pine tree on the reserve – you can watch from a hide as the birds feed their young, and see live CCTV feeds from the nest. These rare and beautiful birds – the only bird of prey in the world that eats only fish – migrate here each spring from Africa, arriving in April and leaving in August (check the website to see if they're in residence).

The Drive » The minor road leads back to the B970, where you turn left along the banks of the River Spey to Coylumbridge; turn right here to reach Aviemore (11 miles).

❻ Aviemore

The gateway to the Cairngorms, Aviemore may not be the prettiest town in Scotland – the main attractions are in the surrounding area – but when bad weather puts the hills off limits, Aviemore fills up with hikers, cyclists and climbers (plus skiers and snowboarders in winter) cruising the outdoor-equipment shops or recounting their latest adventures in the cafes and bars.

Strathspey Steam Railway (☎01479-810725; www.strathspeyrailway.co.uk; Station Sq; adult/child return £16.25/8.10) runs steam trains on a section of restored line between Aviemore and Broomhill, 10 miles to the northeast, via Boat of Garten. There are four or five trains daily from June to August, and a more limited service in April, May, September, October and December, with the option of eating afternoon tea, Sunday lunch or a three-course dinner on board.

🛏 p399

The Drive » From Aviemore, drive south on the B9152, which follows the valley of the River Spey; after 8.5 miles, soon after passing through the village of Kincraig, you'll see a sign on the right for the Highland Wildlife Park.

7 Highland Wildlife Park

The **Highland Wildlife Park** (01540-651270; www.highlandwildlifepark.org; Kincraig; adult/child £18.50/12.50; 10am-6pm Jul & Aug, to 5pm Apr-Jun, Sep & Oct, to 4pm Nov-Mar; P) features a drive-through safari park and animal enclosures that offer the chance to view rarely seen native wildlife, such as Scottish wildcats, capercaillies, pine martens and red squirrels. It is also home to species that once roamed the Scottish hills but have long since disappeared, including wolves, lynx, wild boars, beavers and European bison. Last entry is two hours before closing.

The Drive » Continue southwest on the B9152 through Kingussie to the Highland Folk Museum (6.5 miles).

8 Highland Folk Museum

The old Speyside towns of Kingussie (kin-yew-see) and Newtonmore sit at the foot of the great heather-clad humps known as the Monadhliath Mountains. Newtonmore is best known as the home of the excellent **Highland Folk Museum** (01540-673551; www.highlandfolk.com; Kingussie Rd, Newtonmore; 10.30am-4pm Wed-Sun; P), an open-air collection of historical buildings and artefacts revealing many aspects of Highland culture and lifestyle. Laid out like a farming township, it has a community of traditional thatch-roofed cottages, a sawmill, a schoolhouse, a shepherd's bothy (hut) and a rural post office.

DETOUR: CAIRNGORM MOUNTAIN

Start: 6 Aviemore

Cairngorm Mountain (1245m), 10 miles southeast of Aviemore, is the sixth-highest summit in the UK and home to Scotland's biggest ski area. From Aviemore, it's a 10-mile drive to Coire Cas car park at the end of Ski Rd; from here the climb to the summit of Cairn Gorm (1245m) is 2 miles and takes about two hours to the top (a challenging climb that requires a map and compass; beware of changeable weather conditions). The old funicular railway here closed in 2018.

From Aviemore, the road to Cairngorm Mountain passes through the **Rothiemurchus Estate**, famous for having one of Scotland's largest remnants of Caledonian forest, the ancient forest of Scots pine that once covered most of the country. The **Rothiemurchus Centre** (01479-812345; www.rothiemurchus.net; Ski Rd, Inverdruie; 9.30am-5.30pm; P) has maps detailing more than 50 miles of footpaths and cycling trails, including the 4-mile trail around **Loch an Eilein**, with its ruined castle and peaceful pine woods.

Six miles east of Aviemore, the road passes **Loch Morlich**, surrounded by some 8 sq miles of pine and spruce forest that make up the Glenmore Forest Park. Its attractions include a sandy beach (at the east end) and a water-sports centre.

Nearby, the **Cairngorm Reindeer Centre** (01479-861228; www.cairngormreindeer.co.uk; Glenmore; adult/child £17.50/12.50;) runs guided walks to see and feed Britain's only herd of reindeer, which are free-ranging but very tame. Walks take place at 11am daily (weather-dependent), plus another at 2.30pm from May to September. Book tickets in advance by phone.

Classic Trip

WOLLERTZ / SHUTTERSTOCK ©

JAMES ALEX DUNCAN / SHUTTERSTOCK ©

WHY THIS IS A CLASSIC TRIP

ISABEL ALBISTON, WRITER

The wild and romantic landscape of the Cairngorms is ever changing: tempestuous skies flit from ominous grey to dazzling sunshine, whipping winds give way to moments of serene calm, snow melts and the mountains turn purple with heather that carpets the forest floors in summer. This trip reveals the area's haunting beauty, packing in wildlife encounters, castles and even a whisky distillery.

Above: Blair Castle
Left: Red squirrel, RSPB Loch Garten Osprey Centre
Right: Balmoral Castle

PITSCH22 / SHUTTERSTOCK ©

The Drive » Join the main A9 Inverness to Perth road and follow it south for 35 miles to Blair Atholl, passing through bleak mountain scenery and climbing to a high point of 460m at the Pass of Drumochter.

TRIP HIGHLIGHT

9 Blair Atholl

The picturesque vllage of Blair Atholl dates only from the early 19th century, built by the Duke of Atholl, head of the Murray clan, whose seat – magnificent **Blair Castle** (☎01796-481207; www.blair-castle.co.uk; house & gardens adult/child £14/8.50, gardens only £7.70/3.50; ⏰10am-5.30pm Easter-Oct, to 4pm Sat & Sun Nov-Easter; P 👪) – is one of the most popular tourist attractions in Scotland.

Thirty rooms are open to the public and they present a wonderful picture of upper-class Highland life from the 16th century on. The original tower was built in 1269, but the castle underwent significant remodelling in the 18th and 19th centuries. Highlights include the 2nd-floor **Drawing Room** with its ornate Georgian plasterwork and Zoffany portrait of the 4th duke's family, complete with a pet lemur called Tommy; and the **Tapestry Room** draped with 17th-century wall hangings created for Charles I. The **dining room** is sumptuous – check out the 9-pint wine glasses.

There are more than 50 miles of cycling trails through the estate; hire a bike from **Blair Atholl Bike Hire** (☎0845-548 2270; www.segway-ecosse.com/bike-hire; Blair Castle Caravan Pk; per day adult/child £28/20; ⏲9am-6pm).

p399

The Drive » Follow the B8079 southeast out of Blair Atholl for a few miles, past the historic battle site of Killiecrankie, and turn right on the B8019 Strathtummel road. This gloriously scenic road leads along Loch Tummel (stop for photographs at Queen's View) to Tummel Bridge; turn left here on the B846 over the hills to Aberfeldy (29 miles).

---

⑩ Aberfeldy

Aberfeldy is the gateway to Breadalbane (the historic region surrounding Loch Tay), and a good base: adventure sports, angling, art and castles all feature on the menu here. It's a peaceful, pretty place on the banks of the Tay, but if it's moody lochs and glens that steal your heart, you may want to push further west into **Glen Lyon**.

You arrive in the town by crossing the River Tay via the elegant **Wade's Bridge**, built in 1733 as part of the network of military roads designed to tame the Highlands. At the eastern end of town is **Aberfeldy Distillery** (www.dewarsaberfeldydistillery.com; tours adult/child from £9/free; ⏲10am-6pm Mon-Sat, noon-4pm Sun Apr-Oct, 10am-4pm Mon-Sat Nov-Mar; P), home of the famous Dewar's whisky; entertaining tours of the whisky-making process are followed by a tasting of venerable Aberfeldy single malts and others.

🛏 p399

DETOUR: GLEN LYON

Start: ⑩ Aberfeldy

The 'longest, loneliest and loveliest glen in Scotland', according to Sir Walter Scott, stretches for 32 unforgettable miles of rickety stone bridges, native woodland and heather-clad hills, becoming wilder and more uninhabited as it snakes its way west. The ancients believed it to be a gateway to Faerieland, and even the most sceptical of visitors will be entranced by the valley's magic.

There are no villages in the glen – the majestic scenery is the main reason to be here – just a cluster of houses at Bridge of Balgie, where the **Glenlyon Tearoom** (☎01887-866221; Bridge of Balgie; snacks £3-4; ⏲10am-5pm Apr-Oct; P 📶), with a suntrap of a terrace overlooking the river, serves as a hub for walkers, cyclists and motorists. The owner is a fount of knowledge about the glen, and her pistachio and almond cake is legendary.

There are several waymarked woodland walks beginning from a car park a short distance beyond Bridge of Balgie, and more challenging hill walks into the surrounding mountains (see www.walkhighlands.co.uk/perthshire).

From Abefeldy, the B846 leads to the pretty village Fortingall, famous for its ancient yew tree, where a narrow minor road strikes west up the glen; another steep and spectacular route from Loch Tay crosses the hills to meet it at Bridge of Balgie. The road continues west as far as the dam on Loch Lyon, passing a memorial to Robert Campbell (1808–94), a Canadian explorer and fur trader who was born in the glen.

Eating & Sleeping

Braemar 1

Craiglea B&B $$

(01339-741641; www.craigleabraemar.com; Hillside Rd; d/tr £90/115; P) Craiglea is a homely B&B set in a pretty stone cottage with double, twin and family rooms, all en suite. Packed lunches are available for a day in the hills and the owners can give advice on local walks. Minimum stay of two nights.

Braemar Lodge Hotel Hotel $$$

(01339-741627; www.braemarlodge.co.uk; Glenshee Rd; dm/s/d from £25/85/140, 3-bed cabin per week from £770; P) This Victorian shooting lodge on the southern outskirts of Braemar has bags of character, not least in the wood-panelled Malt Room bar, which is as well stocked with mounted deer heads as it is with single malt whiskies. There's a good restaurant with views of the hills (mains £11 to £35), plus a 12-bed hikers' bunkhouse (book in advance).

Ballater 3

Auld Kirk B&B $$$

(01339-755762; www.theauldkirk.com; Braemar Rd; s/d from £130/140; P) Here's something a little out of the ordinary – a seven-bedroom B&B and coffee lounge housed in a converted 19th-century church. The interior blends original features with sleek modern decor – the pulpit now serves as the reception desk, while the lounge is bathed in light from leaded Gothic windows.

Tomintoul 4

Clockhouse Restaurant Scottish $$

(01807-580378; www.clockhouserestaurant.com; The Square; mains £13-24; 11am-9pm Apr-Oct) Serves light lunches and bistro dinners made with fresh Highland lamb, beef, venison and salmon.

Argyle Guest House B&B $$

(01807-580766; www.argyletomintoul.co.uk; 7 Main St; s/d/f £45/72/99;) Well-run B&B offering six comfortable rooms of varying sizes (two rooms share a bathroom) and the best porridge in the Cairngorms.

Aviemore 6

Cairngorm Hotel Hotel $$

(01479-810233; www.cairngorm.com; Grampian Rd; s/d £75/110; P) Better known as 'the Cairn', this long-established hotel is set in the fine old granite building with the pointy turret opposite the train station. It's a welcoming place with comfortable rooms and a determinedly Scottish atmosphere, with tartan carpets and stags' antlers. There's live music on weekends, so it can get a bit noisy – not for early-to-bedders.

The restaurant serves traditional Highland comfort food such as fish pie, fillet of venison and haggis, neeps and tatties (£10 to £23).

Blair Atholl 9

Blair Atholl Watermill Cafe $

(01796-481321; www.blairathollwatermill.com; Ford Rd; mains £4-7; 9.30am-4pm Apr-Oct; P) This working watermill grinds its own flour and bakes its own bread, and serves it up in this atmospheric cafe as deliciously fresh sandwiches. You can watch the mill at work, and even sign up for bakery courses.

Aberfeldy 10

Tigh'n Eilean Guest House B&B $$

(01887-820109; www.tighneilean.co.uk; Taybridge Dr; s/d from £48/80; P) Everything about this property screams comfort. It's a gorgeous place overlooking the Tay, with individually designed rooms – one has a Jacuzzi, while another is set on its own in a cheery yellow summer house in the garden, giving you a bit of privacy. The garden itself is fabulous and the riverbank setting is delightful.

Great Glen

This lake-and-mountain themed trip leads you through some of the Highlands' scenic hot spots, and along the shores of world-famous Loch Ness – here be monsters!

TRIP HIGHLIGHTS

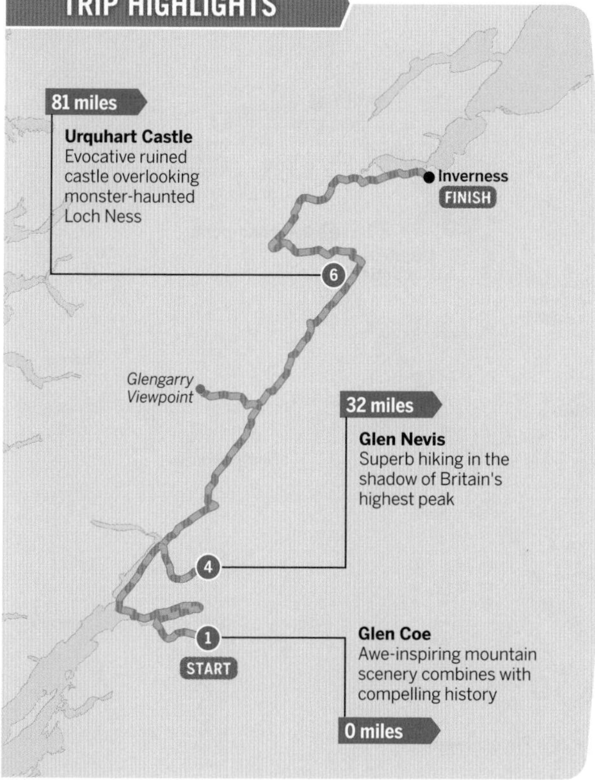

81 miles

Urquhart Castle
Evocative ruined castle overlooking monster-haunted Loch Ness

Inverness
FINISH

6

Glengarry Viewpoint

32 miles

Glen Nevis
Superb hiking in the shadow of Britain's highest peak

4

1
START

Glen Coe
Awe-inspiring mountain scenery combines with compelling history

0 miles

2–3 DAYS
147 MILES / 235KM

GREAT FOR...

BEST TIME TO GO

April to see snow on the mountains, October for autumn colours in the forests.

ESSENTIAL PHOTO

Failing a shot of the Loch Ness monster, crossing the wire bridge at Steall Falls.

BEST FOR FAMILIES

Taking a Nessie-hunting cruise from Fort Augustus.

Glen Nevis Steall Falls

34 Great Glen

The Great Glen is a geological fault running in an arrow-straight line across Scotland, filled by a series of lochs including Loch Ness. This trip follows the A82 road along the glen (completed in 1933 – a date that coincides with the first sightings of the Loch Ness monster!) and links two areas of outstanding natural beauty – Glen Coe to the south, and Glen Affric to the north.

TRIP HIGHLIGHT

1 Glen Coe

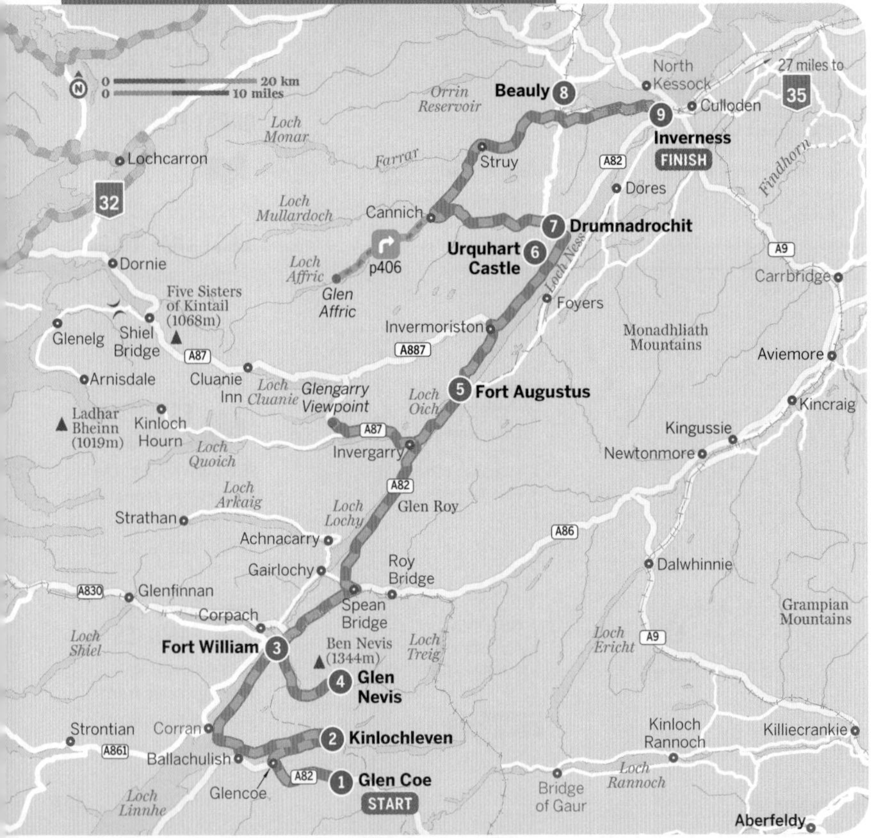

Scotland's most famous glen is also one of its grandest. The A82 road leads over the **Pass of Glencoe** and into the narrow upper glen. The southern side is dominated by three massive, brooding spurs, known as the **Three Sisters**, while the northern side is enclosed by the continuous steep wall of the knife-edged **Aonach Eagach** ridge, a classic mountaineering challenge.

Glencoe Visitor Centre (NTS; ☎01855-811307; www.nts.org.uk; parking £4; ⏲9.30am-4pm; P) provides comprehensive information on the geological, environmental and cultural history of Glencoe, charts the development of mountaineering in the glen, and tells the story of the Glencoe Massacre in all its gory detail.

 p407

The Drive » From Glencoe village at the foot of the glen, head east on the B863 for 7 miles along the southern shore of Loch Leven to Kinlochleven.

2 Kinlochleven

Kinlochleven is hemmed in by high mountains at the head of beautiful Loch Leven, where the West Highland Way brings a steady stream of hikers through the village. It is also the starting point for walks up the glen of the River Leven, through pleasant woods to the **Grey Mare's Tail** waterfall, and harder mountain hikes into the Mamores.

Scotland's first **Via Ferrata** (☎01397-747111; www.verticaldescents.com; Unit 3, Kinlochleven Business Park; per person/family £65/240) – a 500m climbing route equipped with steel ladders, cables and bridges – snakes through the crags around the Grey Mare's Tail, allowing non-climbers to experience the thrill of climbing (you'll need a head for heights, though!).

p407

The Drive » Return west along the north side of Loch Leven, perhaps stopping for lunch at the excellent Lochleven Seafood Cafe, then head north on the A82 to Fort William (22 miles).

3 Fort William

Basking on the shores of Loch Linnhe amid magnificent mountain scenery, Fort William has one of the most enviable settings in the whole of Scotland. If it wasn't for the busy dual carriageway crammed between the less-than-attractive town centre and the loch, and one of the highest rainfall records in the country, it would be almost idyllic. Even so, the Fort has carved out a reputation as Outdoor Capital of the UK (www.outdoorcapital.co.uk).

The small but fascinating **West Highland Museum** (☎01397-702169; www.westhighlandmuseum.org.uk; Cameron Sq; ⏲10am-2pm Tue-Fri) is packed with all manner of Highland memorabilia. Look out for the secret portrait of Bonnie Prince Charlie – after the Jacobite rebellions, all things Highland were banned, including pictures of the exiled leader, and this tiny painting looks like nothing more than a smear of paint until viewed in a cylindrical mirror.

p407

The Drive » At the roundabout on the northern edge of Fort William, take the minor road that runs into Glen Nevis; it leads to a car park at the far end of the glen, 6.5 miles away.

TRIP HIGHLIGHT

4 Glen Nevis

Scenic Glen Nevis – used as a filming location for *Braveheart* and the Harry Potter movies – wraps around the base of Ben Nevis, Britain's highest mountain. The **Glen Nevis Visitor Centre** (☎01349-781401; parking £4; ⏲8.30am-4pm, longer hours Jul & Aug) is situated 1.5 miles up the glen, and

LINK YOUR TRIP

32 Upper West Coast

The stirring wilderness of the northwest Highlands awaits – Skye lies 60 miles northwest of Fort Augustus along the A87.

35 Whisky Trails

A short drive east from Inverness to Elgin (39 miles) links to our trip around the heartland of Scotland's whisky distilleries.

provides information on hiking, weather forecasts, and specific advice on climbing **Ben Nevis**.

From the car park at the end of the road, 5 miles beyond the visitor centre, there is an excellent 1.5-mile walk through the spectacular, verdant **Nevis Gorge** valley to **Steall Falls**, a 100m-high bridal-veil waterfall. You can reach the foot of the falls by crossing the river on a wobbly, three-cable wire bridge – one cable for your feet and one for each hand – a real test of balance!

The Drive » Return down Glen Nevis and head north on the A82. At Invergarry, turn left onto the A87 which climbs high above Loch Garry; stop at the famous Glengarry Viewpoint (layby on left). By a quirk of perspective, the lochs to the west appear to form the map outline of Scotland. Return to the A87 and continue to Fort Augustus (44 miles).

5 Fort Augustus

Fort Augustus, at the junction of four old military roads, was originally a government garrison and the headquarters of General George Wade's road-building operations in the early 18th century. Today, it's a neat and picturesque little place bisected by the Caledonian Canal.

Boats using the canal are raised and lowered 13m by a 'ladder' of five consecutive locks. It's fun to watch, and the neatly landscaped canal banks are a great place to soak up the sun. The **Caledonian Canal Centre** (Ardchattan House, Canalside; ⌚10am-4pm Wed-Sun), beside the lowest lock, has information on the history of the canal.

Cruise Loch Ness (☎01320-366277; www.cruiselochness.com; adult/child £15/9; ⌚10am, noon, 2pm & 4pm daily Apr-Nov, fewer sailings Dec-Mar), at the jetty beside the canal bridge, operates one-hour cruises on Loch Ness accompanied by the latest high-tech sonar equipment so you can keep an underwater eye open for the Loch Ness monster.

The Drive » It's a straightforward but scenic 17-mile drive along the shores of Loch Ness to Urquhart Castle.

TRIP HIGHLIGHT

6 Urquhart Castle

Commanding a superb location with outstanding views over Loch Ness, **Urquhart Castle** (HES; ☎01456-450551; www.historicenvironment.scot; adult/child £9.60/5.80; ⌚9.30am-6pm Apr-Oct, to 4.30pm Nov-Mar; P) is a popular Nessie-hunting hotspot. The castle was repeatedly sacked and rebuilt (and sacked and rebuilt) over the centuries; in 1692 it was blown up to prevent the Jacobites from using it. The five-storey tower house at the northern point is the most impressive remaining fragment and offers wonderful views across the water.

SUSANNE POMMER / SHUTTERSTOCK ©

The visitor centre includes displays of medieval items discovered in the castle and a video theatre: the film, with a dramatic 'reveal' of the castle at the end, can be downloaded onto

Urquhart Castle Overlooking Loch Ness

your phone using a QR code if the visitor centre is closed.

The Drive » A short hop of 2 miles leads to Drumnadrochit.

7 Drumnadrochit

Deep, dark and narrow, Loch Ness stretches for 23 miles between Inverness and Fort Augustus. Its bitterly cold waters have been extensively explored in search of Nessie, the elusive Loch Ness monster, but most visitors see her only in the form of a cardboard cutout at Drumnadrochit's monster exhibitions.

The **Loch Ness Centre** (☎01456-450573; www.lochness.com; adult/child £8.45/4.95; ⏰9.30am-6pm Jul & Aug, to 5pm Easter-Jun, Sep & Oct, 10am-4pm Nov-Easter; P 👪) adopts a scientific approach that allows you to weigh the evidence for yourself. Exhibits include the original equipment – sonar survey vessels, miniature submarines, cameras and sediment coring tools – used in various monster hunts, as well as original photographs and film footage of sightings. You'll find

DETOUR: GLEN AFFRIC

Start: 7 Drumnadrochit

Glen Affric, one of the most beautiful glens in Scotland, extends deep into the hills beyond Cannich, halfway between Drumnadrochit and Beauly. The upper reaches of the glen, now designated as **Glen Affric Nature Reserve**, is a scenic wonderland of shimmering lochs, rugged mountains and native Scots pine forest, home to pine martens, wildcats, otters, red squirrels and golden eagles.

A narrow, dead-end road leads southwest from Cannich; about 4 miles along is **Dog Falls**, a scenic spot where the River Affric squeezes through a narrow, rocky gorge. A circular walking trail (red waymarks) leads from Dog Falls car park to a footbridge below the falls and back on the far side of the river (2 miles, allow one hour).

The road continues beyond Dog Falls to a parking area and picnic site at the eastern end of **Loch Affric**, where there are several short walks along the river and the loch shore. The circuit of Loch Affric (10 miles, allow five hours walking, two hours by mountain bike) follows good paths right around the loch and takes you deep into the heart of some very wild scenery.

out about hoaxes and optical illusions, as well as learning a lot about the ecology of Loch Ness – is there enough food in the loch to support even one 'monster', let alone a breeding population?

The Drive » Head west on the A831 which leads to the village of Cannich – jumping-off point for the Glen Affric detour – before turning north along lovely Strathglass to reach Beauly (30 miles).

8 Beauly

Mary, Queen of Scots is said to have given this village its name in 1564 when she visited, exclaiming in French: 'Quel beau lieu!' (What a beautiful place!). Founded in 1230, the red-sandstone **Beauty Priory** is now an impressive ruin, haunted by the cries of rooks nesting in a magnificent centuries-old sycamore tree.

Corner on the Square makes a good place to break your journey; it's well worth the stop.

 p407

The Drive » Drive east on the A862 for 12 miles to Inverness.

9 Inverness

Inverness has a great location astride the River Ness at the northern end of the Great Glen. In summer it overflows with visitors intent on monster hunting at nearby Loch Ness, but it's worth a visit in its own right for a stroll along the picturesque River Ness, a cruise on Loch Ness, and a meal in one of the city's excellent restaurants.

The main attraction in Inverness is a leisurely stroll along the river to the **Ness Islands**. Planted with mature Scots pine, fir, beech and sycamore, and linked to the riverbanks and each other by elegant Victorian footbridges, the islands make an appealing picnic spot. They're a 20-minute walk south of the castle – head upstream on either side of the river (the start of the Great Glen Way), and return on the opposite bank.

p407

Eating & Sleeping

Glen Coe 1

✕ Glencoe Café — Cafe $

(☎01855-811168; www.glencoecafe.co.uk; Lorn Dr, Glencoe village; mains £4.50-10; ⏰11am-5pm Fri-Wed May-Oct, to 4pm Nov-Apr; P 📶) This friendly cafe is the social hub of Glencoe village, serving breakfast fry-ups (including vegetarian versions) till 11.30am, light lunches based on local produce and the best cappuccino in the glen.

🛏 Clachaig Inn — Hotel $$$

(☎01855-811252; www.clachaig.com; s/d £78/155; P 📶 🐾) The Clachaig, 2 miles southeast of Glencoe village, has long been a favourite haunt of hill walkers and climbers. As well as comfortable accommodation (opt for a room with a Glen Coe view), there's a lounge bar with snug booths and high refectory tables serving good food (mains £11 to £20) from noon to 9pm.

Kinlochleven 2

✕ Lochleven Seafood Cafe — Seafood $$

(☎01855-821048; www.lochlevenseafoodcafe.co.uk; mains £11-40, whole lobster £40; ⏰ meals noon-3pm & 6-9pm, coffee & cake 10am-noon & 3-5pm mid-Mar–Oct; P 👪) This place serves superb shellfish freshly plucked from live tanks – oysters, razor clams, scallops, lobster and crab – plus a daily fish special and some non-seafood dishes. For warm days, there's an outdoor terrace with a view across the loch to the Pap of Glencoe. The cafe is 5 miles west of Kinlochleven, on the north shore of the loch.

Fort William 3

✕ Lime Tree — Scottish $$

(☎01397-701806; www.limetreefortwilliam.co.uk; Achintore Rd; mains £19-22.50, set menu £30; ⏰6.30-9.30pm; P 📶) The restaurant at this small **hotel** (☎01397-701806; www.limetreefortwilliam.co.uk; Achintore Rd; d £155-175; P 📶) and art gallery has put the UK's Outdoor Capital on the gastronomic map. The chef turns out delicious dishes built around fresh Scottish produce, such as Loch Fyne oysters, Loch Awe trout and Ardnamurchan venison.

🛏 Grange — B&B $$$

(☎01397-705516; www.grangefortwilliam.com; Grange Rd; d £195-225; ⏰ closed Sun; P 📶) An exceptional 19th-century villa set in its own landscaped grounds, the Grange is crammed with antiques and warmed by log fires. It has two luxury suites fitted with leather sofas, handcrafted furniture and roll-top baths, one situated in a charming self-contained cottage in the sprawling gardens, all with a view over Loch Linnhe. No children.

Beauly 8

✕ Corner on the Square — Cafe $

(☎01463-783000; www.corneronthesquare.co.uk; 1 High St; dishes £2.50-8.50; ⏰8.30am-5pm Mon-Fri, to 8pm Sat, 9am-5pm Sun) Beauly's best lunch spot is this superb little delicatessen and cafe that serves breakfast (till 11.30am), daily lunch specials (11.30am to 4.30pm) and excellent coffee.

Inverness 9

🛏 Heathmount Hotel — Boutique Hotel $$$

(☎01463-235877; www.heathmounthotel.com; Kingsmills Rd; d from £170; P 📶) Small and friendly, the Heathmount combines a popular local bar and restaurant with eight designer hotel rooms, each one different, ranging from a boldly coloured family room in purple and gold to a slinky black velvet four-poster double. Five minutes' walk east of the city centre.

Whisky Trails

As well as visiting half a dozen famous whisky distilleries, you'll discover ancient crafts and traditions such as barrel-making, wool-spinning and hand-loom weaving on this tour of historic Speyside.

TRIP HIGHLIGHTS

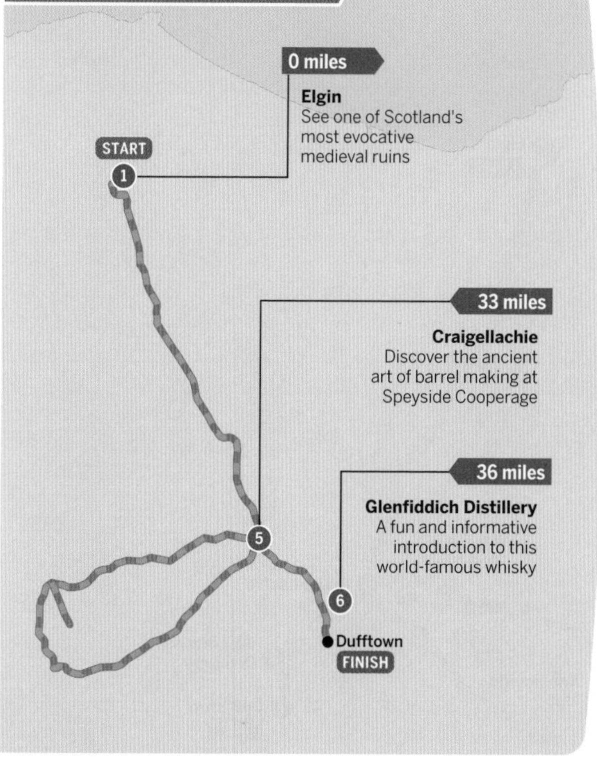

START

1

0 miles

Elgin
See one of Scotland's most evocative medieval ruins

33 miles

Craigellachie
Discover the ancient art of barrel making at Speyside Cooperage

5

36 miles

Glenfiddich Distillery
A fun and informative introduction to this world-famous whisky

6

Dufftown

FINISH

2–3 DAYS
39 MILES / 62KM

GREAT FOR...

BEST TIME TO GO

Early May or late September, when the Spirit of Speyside festivals take place.

ESSENTIAL PHOTO

A whisky-barrel maker at work in the Speyside Cooperage.

BEST FOR SHOPPING

Stocking up on gourmet goodies at Elgin's Gordon & Macphail.

Craigellachie Restoring barrels at Speyside Cooperage

35 Whisky Trails

The old county of Moray, centred on the town of Elgin, lies at the heart of an ancient Celtic earldom and is famed for its mild climate and rich farmland – the barley fields here traditionally provided the raw material for Speyside's whisky distilleries. This trip leads from Elgin's historic cathedral into the heart of Speyside to experience the magic of Scotch whisky at its source.

TRIP HIGHLIGHT

1 Elgin

Elgin, dominated by a hilltop monument to the 5th Duke of Gordon, has been the provincial capital of Moray for more than eight centuries. Many people think that the ruins of **Elgin Cathedral** (HES; www.historicenvironment.scot; King St; adult/child £9/5.40; ⏲9.30am-5.30pm Apr-Sep, 10am-4pm Oct-Mar), known as the 'lantern of the north', are the most beautiful and evocative

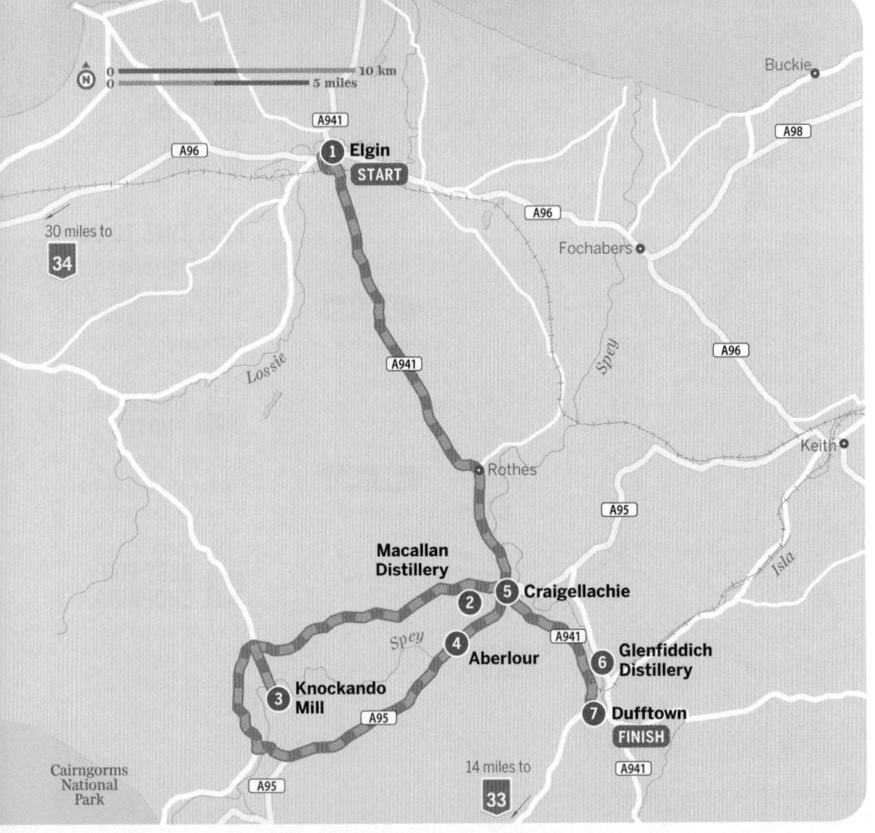

in Scotland; its octagonal chapter house is the finest in the country.

The town is also home to Scotland's oldest independent **museum** (www.elginmuseum.org.uk; 1 High St; donations accepted; ⏲10am-5pm Mon-Fri, 11am-4pm Sat Apr-Oct), a captivating collection beautifully displayed in a purpose-built Victorian building. Exhibits range from Ecuadorian shrunken heads to Peruvian mummies, and include internationally important fish and reptile fossils discovered in local rocks, and mysterious Pictish carved stones.

Look out for **Gordon & MacPhail** (☎01343-545110; www.gordonandmacphail.com; 58-60 South St; ⏲8.30am-5pm Mon-Sat, alcohol on sale from 10am), the world's largest specialist malt-whisky dealer. Over a century old and offering around 450 different varieties, this Elgin shop is a place of pilgrimage for whisky connoisseurs.

p415

The Drive » Follow the A941 south from Elgin to reach the River Spey at Rothes, where a welter of distillery signs announce that you have arrived in Speyside, the heart of Scotland's whisky industry. South of Rothes, turn right on the B9102 which soon leads to the Macallan Distillery (14 miles).

2 Macallan Distillery

The Macallan – king of Speyside malts – is produced in a range of sherry and bourbon finishes. The **Macallan Distillery** (☎01340-318000; www.themacallan.com; Easter Elchies, Craigellachie; visitor centre free, distillery tours from £50; ⏲10am-6pm; P) enjoys a lovely location 1 mile west of Craigellachie and is housed in a spectacular turf-roofed visitor centre made from engineered timber that also contains an exhibition, restaurant, whisky bar and gift boutique. Tours must be pre-booked.

The Drive » Continue west on the B9102 for 7 miles to the Knockando Woolmill. It's down a short side road on the left – look out for the signpost.

3 Knockando Mill

Hidden in a fold of the hills beneath Cardhu distillery, **Knockando Woolmill** (☎01340-810345; www.kwc.co.uk; Knockando; ⏲10am-4pm Tue-Sun Apr-Oct) is a rare survival of an 18th-century woollen mill that has been lovingly restored to full working order. The ancient looms clank away Monday to Friday, turning out plaid and tweed textiles that can be purchased in the neighbouring shop. Guided tours cost £5.

Beyond the mill, on the banks of the Spey, lie two more distilleries, **Tamdhu** and **Knockando**.

SHOPPING FOR CASHMERE

Founded in 1797, **Johnstons of Elgin** (☎01343-554009; www.johnstonsofelgin.com/visit-us/elgin-mill; Newmill, IV30 4AF; ⏲10am-4.30pm) is famous for its cashmere woollen clothing, and is the only UK woollen mill that still sees the manufacturing process through from raw fibre to finished garment. There's a retail outlet with restaurant on the edge of town, and free guided tours of the works.

LINK YOUR TRIP

34 Great Glen

Inverness, the final stop on our tour of Highland highlights, is 39 miles west of Elgin along the A96.

33 Royal Highlands & Cairngorms

You can extend your explorations into the Cairngorms national park by following the second half of this trip: join it at Tomintoul, 19 miles southwest of Dufftown.

HIGHLAND_LOON / SHUTTERSTOCK ©

The Drive » Return to the B9102 and turn left. After 4 miles, turn left again to cross the River Spey, and once more on the A95. You will soon pass the small, friendly and independent Glenfarclas Distillery before arriving in Aberlour (total 11 miles).

❹ Aberlour

Aberlour (www.aboutaberlour.co.uk) – or Charlestown of Aberlour, to give it its full name – is a pretty village straggling along the banks of the River Spey. **Aberlour Distillery** (☎01340-881249; www.aberlour.com; tours from £20; ⏰9.30am-5pm daily Apr-Oct, 10am-4pm Mon-Fri Nov-Mar; Ⓟ) is right on the main street, and offers an excellent, detailed tour with a proper tasting session. Other attractions include salmon fishing on the Spey, and some lovely walks along the Speyside Way.

As the home of Walkers shortbread and Aberlour single malt, the village is rightly proud of its local produce, and you can browse a huge selection of Scottish food and drink in the village's own Spey Larder (p415), or sit down to a meal and a few nips of whisky at the Mash Tun (p415).

🍴🛏 p415

The Drive » From Aberlour, it's a short hop of just under 2 miles to Craigellachie.

TRIP HIGHLIGHT

❺ Craigellachie

Craigellachie Hotel (p415) is famous for its wonderfully old-fashioned, hunting-lodge atmosphere, from the wood-panelled lobby to the opulent drawing room where you can sink into a sofa in front of the log fire. Its **Quaich Bar**, lined with more

Macallan Distillery Producer of the king of Speyside malts

than 900 varieties of single malt whisky, is a particularly compelling drawcard.

On the southern edge of the village is the **Speyside Cooperage** (☎01340-871108; www.speysidecooperage.co.uk; tours from £4; ⏰9am-5pm Mon-Fri, closed Christmas-early Jan; P), where you can watch the fascinating art of barrel-making during a 45-minute guided tour.

The Drive » Drive south along the A941 for 4 miles to Glenfiddich Distillery.

🛏 p415

TRIP HIGHLIGHT

6 Glenfiddich Distillery

Along with Glenmorangie, Glenfiddich is among the most famous of single malt whisky brands, and kept the flame of whisky appreciation alive during the dark years of the 1970s and '80s, before the revival of interest in all things distilled.

Glenfiddich Distillery (☎01340-820373; www.glenfiddich.co.uk; admission free, tours from £10; ⏰9.30am-4.30pm; P) is big and bustling. The standard tour (£10) starts with an overblown video, but it's fun and informative; an in-depth half-day Pioneer's Tour (£95) must be pre-booked.

The Drive » Continue into the centre of Dufftown, just 0.75 miles south.

7 Dufftown

Rome may be built on seven hills, but Dufftown's built on seven stills, say the locals. Founded in 1817 by James Duff, 4th earl of Fife, Dufftown lies at the heart of the Speyside whisky-distilling region. With seven working

HOW TO BE A MALT-WHISKY BUFF

'Love makes the world go round? Not at all! Whisky makes it go round twice as fast.' *Whisky Galore,* Compton Mackenzie (1883–1972).

Whisky tasting today is big news: being able to tell your Ardbeg from your Edradour is de rigueur among the whisky nosing set, so here are some pointers to help you impress your friends.

What's the difference between malt and grain whiskies? Malts are distilled from malted barley – that is, barley that has been soaked in water, then allowed to germinate for around 10 days until the starch has turned into sugar – while grain whiskies are distilled from other cereals, usually wheat, corn or unmalted barley.

So what is a single malt? A single malt is a whisky that has been distilled only from malted barley and is the product of a single distillery. A pure (or vatted) malt is a mixture of single malts from several distilleries, and a blended whisky is a mixture of various grain whiskies (about 60%) and malt whiskies (about 40%) from many different distilleries.

Single malts vs blends? A single malt, like a fine wine, somehow captures the terroir or essence of the place where it was made and matured – a combination of the water, the barley, the peat smoke, the oak barrels in which it was aged and (in the case of certain coastal distilleries) the sea air and salt spray. Each distillation varies from the one before, like different vintages from the same vineyard.

How should a single malt be drunk? Either neat, or with a little water added. To appreciate the aroma and flavour to the utmost, a measure of malt whisky can be cut (diluted) with one-third to two-thirds as much spring water. Ice, tap water and (God forbid) mixers are for philistines. Would you add lemonade to a glass of Chablis?

distilleries nearby, Dufftown has been dubbed Scotland's malt-whisky capital and is host to the biannual **Spirit of Speyside** (www.spiritofspeyside.com) whisky festival.

As well as housing a selection of distillery memorabilia (try saying that after a few drams), the town's **Whisky Museum** (☎01340-821097; www.whisky.dufftown.co.uk; 12 Conval St; ⏰10am-4pm Apr-Oct) holds 'nosing and tasting evenings' where you can learn what to look for in a fine single malt (£20 per person; 8pm Wednesday July and August). You can then test your newfound skills at the nearby Whisky Shop, which stocks hundreds of single malts.

The **Keith & Dufftown Railway** (☎01340-821181; www.keith-dufftown-railway.co.uk; Dufftown Station; adult/child return £11/5) sees trains hauled by 1950s diesel motor units running on weekends from May to September, plus Fridays in July and August.

p415

Eating & Sleeping

Elgin 1

Cafe Kombucha — Vegan $$

(01343-551093; www.cafekombucha.co.uk; 239 High St; mains £7-13; noon-4pm & 5-10pm Mon-Sat;) Elgin's first 100% vegan eatery has been pulling in the crowds with inventive dishes such as pakora burgers served with brioche, guacamole and mango sauce, and tortilla wraps filled with black beans, sweetcorn, spring onions and salsa. There's also pizza to go, and a range of daily specials.

Moraydale — B&B $$

(01343-546381; www.moraydaleguesthouse.com; 276 High St; s/d/f from £60/80/100; P) The Moraydale is a spacious Victorian mansion filled with period features – check out the stained glass and the cast-iron and tile fireplaces. The bedrooms are all en suite and equipped with modern bathrooms – the three large family rooms are particularly good value.

Southbank Guest House — B&B $$

(01343-547132; www.southbankguesthouse.co.uk; 36 Academy St; d/tr from £80/150; P) The family-run, 15-room Southbank is set in a large Georgian town house in a quiet street south of Elgin's centre, just five minutes' walk from the cathedral and other sights. There may be a three-night minimum stay in high season.

Aberlour 4

Spey Larder — Food & Drinks

(01340-871243; www.speylarder.com; 96-98 High St; 9.30am-5pm Mon-Sat) This deli is the place to shop for picnic goodies to eat on the banks of the River Spey. Choose from a great selection of Scottish artisan cheeses, smoked salmon, venison charcuterie, delicious home-baked bread and local craft beers.

Mash Tun — B&B $$

(01340-881771; www.mashtun-aberlour.com; 8 Broomfield Sq; s/d from £85/120;) Housed in a curious stone building made for a sea captain in the outline of a ship, this luxurious B&B has a famous whisky bar – a place of pilgrimage for whisky enthusiasts – which has a collection of old and rare single malts. There's also an excellent restaurant (mains £12 to £25, lunch and dinner daily) that serves top-notch pub grub.

Craigellachie 5

Craigellachie Hotel — Hotel $$$

(01340-881204; www.craigellachiehotel.co.uk; Craigellachie; r from £150; P) This country house hotel has been beautifully refurbished but retains a wonderful old-fashioned atmosphere, from the wood-panelled lobby to the opulent drawing room where you can sink into a sofa in front of the log fire. The big attraction for whisky connoisseurs is the **Quaich Bar**, a cosy nook filled with handcrafted furniture and lined with more than 900 varieties of single malt whisky.

Dufftown 7

Whisky Shop — Food & Drinks

(01340-821097; www.whiskyshopdufftown.co.uk; 1 Fife St; 10am-6pm Mon-Sat year-round, plus Sun Easter-Oct) A fantastic shop that stocks hundreds of single malts and runs tasting sessions and other events.

Davaar B&B — B&B $$

(01340-820464; www.davaardufftown.co.uk; 17 Church St; d/f £70/85;) This sturdy Victorian villa has three smallish but comfy rooms. The breakfast menu is superb, offering the option of Portsoy kippers as well as the traditional fry-up (which uses eggs from the owner's own chickens).

Caledonian MacBrayne

Ferry-Hopping

Jumping around the islands of the west coast on the ferry network – munching seafood and sipping whisky along the way – is one of Scotland's iconic pleasures.

TRIP HIGHLIGHTS

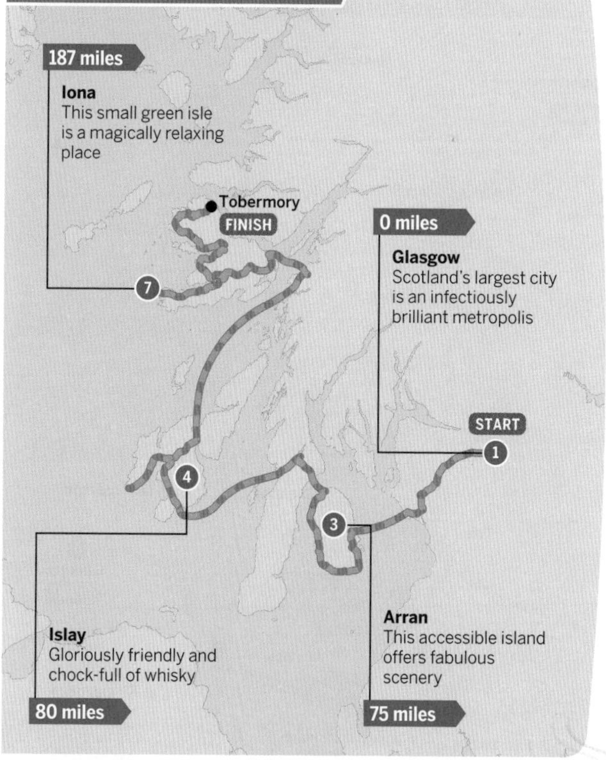

6–8 DAYS
255 MILES / 410KM (PLUS FERRIES)

GREAT FOR...

BEST TIME TO GO

May is often great, with a whisky festival on Islay and surprisingly good weather.

ESSENTIAL PHOTO

The colourful, pretty shorefront cottages of Tobermory.

Mull's white-tailed eagles and whale watching.

Oban Ferry leaving Oban harbour

36 Ferry-Hopping

Taking in four of Scotland's most enticing islands plus the vibrant city of Glasgow, this is an in-depth exploration of southwestern Scotland. The route covers stunningly scenic Arran, Islay's welcoming distilleries, Oban's seafood scene, Mull's heart-lifting landscapes and the enchanting holy isle of Iona. The ferry trips themselves – offering sensational coastal perspectives and wildlife-spotting opportunities – are part of the adventure.

TRIP HIGHLIGHT

1 Glasgow

Full of excellent art, design, food and pubs, Glasgow is an intoxicatingly vibrant place with a legendary live-music scene and loads to see.

The city's cathedral is one of Scotland's most interesting and atmospheric; don't miss a stroll in the adjacent Necropolis.

West of the centre, Kelvingrove Art Gallery & Museum is a fabulous display of paintings and

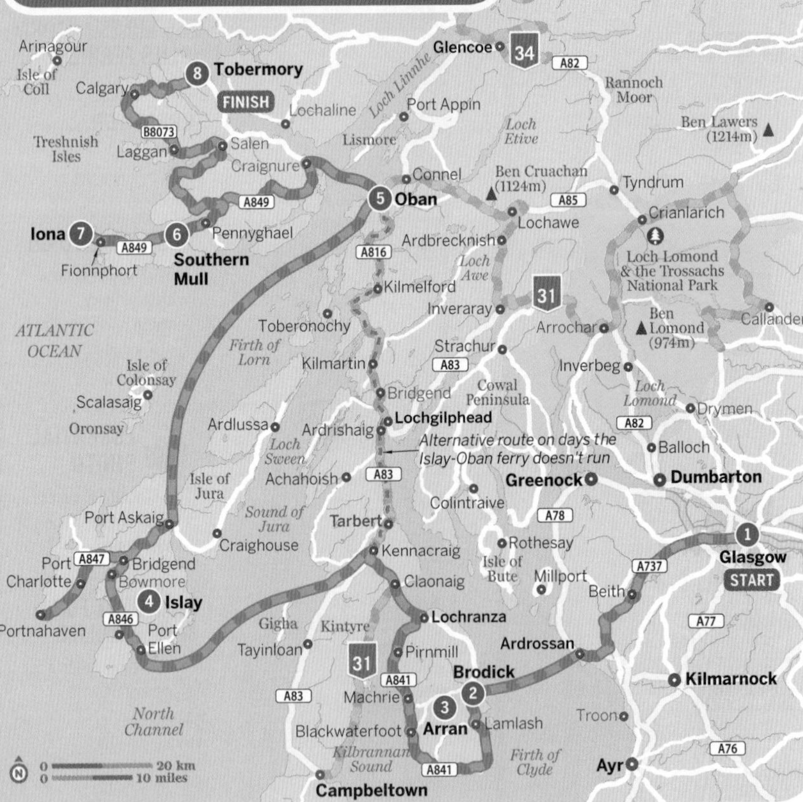

much more, while the Burrell Collection, due to reopen in 2021 after a five-year revamp, has a soothing parkland setting and a great art collection.

Look out for the work of architecture and design genius Charles Rennie Mackintosh at places such as Mackintosh House.

Glasgow is a shopping paradise, with the boutiques of the central pedestrianised area counterbalanced by the vintage shops and delis of the bohemian West End.

The Drive » Take the M8 out of Glasgow to the west, then exit for the A737, which runs down to the Ayrshire coast, where you pick up the A78 northwest the last few miles to Ardrossan and the Arran ferry. The total drive is 33 miles.

LINK YOUR TRIP

31 Lower West Coast

Once you've visited Mull, head back to Oban and explore the Kintyre peninsula on this trip.

34 Great Glen

From Tobermory, you can get a ferry across to Kilchoan and approach Fort William by a lonely, scenic route.

2 Brodick

The Ardrossan ferry arrives at Brodick, beating heart of the Isle of Arran, rising from a coastal road that follows the long curving bay. On a clear day it's a spectacular vista, with Goatfell looming over the forested shore.

Two miles north, elegant **Brodick Castle** (NTS; ☎01770-302202; www.nts.org.uk; castle & park adult/child £13.50/9.50, park only £7/5; ⏰castle 11am-4pm Apr-Oct, park 9.30am-sunset year-round) evolved from 13th-century origins into a stately home and hunting lodge for the dukes of Hamilton. The extensive grounds, now a country park with various trails among the rhododendrons, justify the entry fee. Nearby, the walk up and down **Goatfell**, the island's highest point, is 8 miles return (up to eight hours).

p423

The Drive » Take the A841 southbound to do a leisurely clockwise near-circuit of the island. It's 42 miles this way right around to Lochranza, otherwise only 14 miles away heading north.

TRIP HIGHLIGHT

3 Arran

Lamlash, just 3 miles south of Brodick, is in a dazzling setting, strung along the beachfront. Just offshore is Buddhist-run **Holy Island** (www.holyisle.org), which you can visit.

The landscape in the south of Arran is gentler than in the north; the road drops into little wooded valleys, and Kildonan has pleasant sandy beaches, basking seals and a gorgeous water outlook. Another spectacular coastal setting is at the **Lagg Distillery** (☎01770-870565; www.laggwhisky.com; Lagg; tours adult/child £10/free; ⏰10am-5.30pm daily Apr-Sep, 10am-4pm Tue-Sat Oct-Mar), a modern set-up producing a robust, peaty style.

On the western side of the island is **Machrie Moor Stone Circle** (Machrie; ⏰24hr), a pleasant 1.25-mile stroll from the parking area on the coastal road.

The village and ferry port of Lochranza is characterised by numerous red deer and a picturesque ruined 13th-century **castle** (HES; www.historicenvironment.scot; ⏰24hr).

p423

The Drive » From April to October, a ferry runs from Lochranza to Claonaig on Kintyre; in winter this goes to more sheltered Tarbert. From Claonaig, the B8001 crosses the peninsula to Kennacraig (5 miles) and the ferry to Islay, which docks at either Port Askaig in the island's east, or Port Ellen in the south. From Tarbert, it's 5 miles south on the A83 to Kennacraig.

4 Islay

The home of some of the world's greatest and peatiest whiskies, whose names reverberate on the tongue like a pantheon of Celtic deities, Islay (eye-lah) is a wonderfully friendly place and the birdlife, fine seafood, turquoise bays and basking seals are ample non-whisky reasons to visit.

Islay has nine working distilleries, with a 10th on the way. All welcome visitors and run tours. It's worth booking ahead; you'll certainly need to for the more involved premium tours. Pick up the invaluable pamphlet listing tour times from the tourist office.

The island's 'capital', Bowmore, has a round church to leave the devil no corners to hide in, and the **Bowmore distillery** (01496-810441; www.bowmore.com; School St; tours from £10; 9.30am-6pm Mon-Sat, noon-4pm Sun Mar-Oct, 10am-5pm Mon-Sat Nov-Feb), which malts its own barley.

Three of the biggest, peatiest names in single malt are close together near Port Ellen in the south: **Laphroaig** (01496-302418; www.laphroaig.com; tours from £10; 9.45am-5pm daily Mar-Oct, to 4.30pm daily Nov & Dec, to 4.30pm Mon-Fri Jan & Feb), **Lagavulin** (01496-302749; www.lagavulindistillery.com; tours from £15; 9.15am-5pm daily Mar-Sep, 9.45am-5pm Mon-Sat Oct-Dec, 10.15am-4pm Mon-Sat Jan-Feb) and **Ardbeg** (01496-302244; www.ardbeg.com; tours from £8; 9.30am-5pm Mon-Fri year-round, plus Sat & Sun Apr-Oct). On the western side of the island, two excellent distilleries are **Bruichladdich** (01496-850190; www.bruichladdich.com; Bruichladdich; tours from £7.50; 9am-6pm Mon-Fri, to 5pm Sat, 10am-4pm Sun Apr-Sep, reduced hours Oct-Mar), near Port Charlotte, and boutique-sized **Kilchoman** (01496-850011; www.kilchomandistillery.com; Rockfield Farm, Kilchoman; tours from £10; 9.45am-5pm Apr-Oct, closed Sat & Sun Nov-Mar). Head past Port Charlotte to Portnahaven to watch seals on the harbour rocks.

Three miles from Port Askaig, tumbledown ruins of houses and a chapel on an islet in a shallow loch mark **Finlaggan** (01496-840644; www.finlaggan.org; adult/child £4/2; ruins 24hr, museum 10.30am-4.15pm Mon-Sat Apr-Oct), what remains of the stronghold of the Lords

JOOST VAN UFFELEN / SHUTTERSTOCK ©

FERRY IMPORTANT

Scotland's west-coast ferries are operated by **Caledonian MacBrayne** (CalMac; 0800 066 5000; www.calmac.co.uk). A comprehensive timetable booklet is available from tourist offices and on the website. There's a summer timetable and one for winter, when services are somewhat reduced. It's important to book car spaces ahead online or by phone; several days ahead for Islay, Mull and Arran is best. If there are no spaces left, you can still turn up and wait in the standby queue; you'll often but not always squeeze on. Downloading the Calmac app is also a good idea, as it has the latest information on cancelled services etc.

Tobermory Fish traps beside the village harbour

of the Isles. Start your exploration at the visitor centre. The islet itself is open at all times.

p423

The Drive » Try and time your exit from Islay for a day when there's a ferry from Port Askaig to Oban via Colonsay. Otherwise, head back to Kennacraig then north up the A83, turning left on to the A816 at Lochgilphead. It's 56 miles from Kennacraig to Oban. If going this way, stop at Kilmartin's interesting museum and prehistoric sights.

5 Oban

Oban, main gateway to many of the Hebridean islands, is a waterfront town on a delightful bay, with sweeping views to Kerrera and Mull. In summer the town centre is crowded with holidaymakers and travellers headed for the archipelago. But the setting is still lovely, and Oban's brilliant seafood restaurants are marvellous places to be as the sun sets over the bay.

Basking Shark Scotland (07975-723140; www.baskingsharkscotland.co.uk; Mar-Oct) runs entertaining boat trips with optional snorkelling, focused on finding and observing basking sharks – the world's second largest fish – and other notable marine species. Book these weeks or months ahead.

Sea Kayak Oban (National Kayak School; 01631-565310; www.seakayakoban.com; Argyll St; 10am-5pm Mon-Fri, 9am-5pm Sat, 10am-4pm Sun, winter hours greatly reduced) has a well-stocked shop, rental, great route advice and sea-kayaking courses, including an all-inclusive two-day intro for beginners.

The Drive » From the centre of Oban, get the ferry across to Craignure on the island of Mull. It takes about an hour.

6 Southern Mull

Mull can lay claim to some of the finest and most varied scenery in the Inner Hebrides. Noble birds of prey soar over mountain and coast, while the western waters provide good whale-watching.

Near the Craignure ferry slip, **Duart Castle** (☎01680-812309; www.duartcastle.com; adult/child £8/4; ⏰10.30am-5pm daily May–mid-Oct, 11am-4pm Sun-Thu Apr), the ancestral seat of the Maclean clan, enjoys a spectacular position on a rocky outcrop overlooking the Sound of Mull.

Contact **Mull Eagle Watch** (☎01680-812556; www.mulleaglewatch.com; adult/child £10/5; ⏰Apr-Sep) to observe the white-tailed eagle, Britain's largest bird of prey. Tours run in the mornings and afternoons.

Great walks in the southern part of the island include the popular climb of Ben More and the spectacular trip to Carsaig Arches.

The Drive » From the ferry at Craignure, it's 37 miles of imposing scenery along the A849 to Mull's southwestern tip at Fionnphort. From here, a passenger ferry zips to Iona, just across the strait.

TRIP HIGHLIGHT

7 Iona

Like an emerald teardrop off Mull's western shore, enchanting, idyllic Iona, holy island and burial ground of kings, is a magical place that lives up to its lofty reputation.

Iona's ancient but heavily reconstructed **abbey** (HES; ☎01681-700512; www.historicenvironment.scot; adult/child £9/5.40; ⏰9.30am-5.30pm Apr-Sep, 10am-4pm Oct-Mar) is the spiritual heart of the island. The spectacular nave, dominated by Romanesque and early Gothic vaults and columns, is a powerful space; a door on the left leads to the beautiful cloister, where medieval grave slabs sit alongside modern religious sculptures. Out the back, the museum displays fabulous carved high crosses. Next to the abbey is an ancient graveyard where there's an evocative Romanesque chapel as well as a mound that marks the burial place of 48 of Scotland's early kings, possibly including Macbeth.

Trips from Iona run to the spectacular accordion-like island of Staffa and its awe-inspiring basalt-columned Fingal's Cave.

🛏 p423

The Drive » Get the ferry back to Fionnphort and drive back up the A849 for 18 miles before taking a left onto the B8035. Follow this then the B8073 along the coast, a spectacular drive along the Mull coastline for a slow, single-track 50 miles to the capital, Tobermory.

8 Northern Mull & Tobermory

The highlights of northern Mull, apart from the spectacular drive, are the glorious beach and gallery-cafe complex at Calgary; and the pretty capital, Tobermory, with colourful houses arrayed along a pretty harbour like a village in a picture book. It makes a great base, with a good selection of accommodation and fine seafood.

Sea Life Surveys (☎01688-302916; www.sealifesurveys.com; Ledaig; ⏰Apr-Oct) runs whale-watching trips that head out from Tobermory harbour to the waters north and west of Mull. Shorter seal-spotting jaunts are also available.

🍴 🛏 p423

Eating & Sleeping

Brodick 2

Glenartney B&B $$

(01770-302220; www.glenartney-arran.co.uk; Mayish Rd; d £80-110; Easter-Oct; P) Uplifting bay views and genuine, helpful hosts make this a cracking option. Airy, stylish rooms make the most of the natural light at the top of the town. Comfortable lounges, help-yourself home baking and pod coffee plus a sustainable ethos make for a very pleasurable stay. Top facilities for cyclists, plus drying rooms and trail advice for hikers are added bonuses.

Arran 3

Cafe Thyme Cafe $

(01770-840227; www.oldbyre.co.uk; Old Byre Visitor Centre, Machrie; dishes £10-14; 10am-5pm, reduced hours winter;) At the Old Byre Visitor Centre, this is a very pleasant spot, with chunky wooden tables, outdoor seating and sweeping views from its elevated position. It has home baking, a wide tea selection and decent coffee. Less predictably, the food menu features great Turkish pizza, meze boards and smartly priced daily specials. Lunches are served from noon to 3pm.

Islay 4

SeaSalt Bistro $$

(01496-300300; www.seasalt-bistro.co.uk; 57 Frederick Cres, Port Ellen; mains £10-16; noon-2.30pm & 5-8.45pm) This buzzy modern place represents an unusual combination in Port Ellen: a takeaway doing kebabs, pizzas and bacon rolls, but also a classy bistro. High-backed dining chairs are comfortable for devouring delicious local seafood off a menu of daily specials. The owner and staff are very friendly. It also opens from 10am to noon for coffee and breakfasty fare.

Lambeth House B&B $$

(01496-810597; www.lambeth-guesthouse.co.uk; Jamieson St; s/d £75/100;) Cheerily welcoming, and with smart modern rooms with top-notch en suite bathrooms, this is a sound option in the centre of town. The host is a long-time expert in making guests feel at home, and her breakfasts are reliably good. Rooms vary substantially in size but their prices are the same, so ask for a larger one when booking.

Iona 7

Argyll Hotel Hotel $$

(01681-700334; www.argyllhoteliona.co.uk; s £80, d £100-118; mid-Mar–mid-Oct;) This lovable, higgledy-piggledy warren of a hotel has great service and appealing snug rooms (those with sea views cost more – £176 for a double), including good-value family options. The rooms offers simple comfort and relaxation rather than luxury. Most look out to the rear, where a huge organic garden supplies the restaurant. This is a relaxing and amiably run Iona haven.

Tobermory 8

Café Fish Seafood $$

(01688-301253; www.thecafefish.com; The Pier; mains £12-26; noon-3pm & 5.30-11pm mid-Mar–Oct;) Seafood doesn't come much fresher than the stuff served at this warm and welcoming little restaurant overlooking Tobermory harbour. Crustaceans go straight from boat to kitchen to join rich seafood stew, fat scallops, fish pie and catch-of-the-day on the daily-changing menu, where confident use of Asian ingredients adds an extra dimension. Book ahead.

Highland Cottage Boutique Hotel $$$

(01688-302030; www.highlandcottage.co.uk; Breadalbane St; d £175-190; Apr–mid-Oct; P) Antique furniture, four-poster beds, embroidered bedspreads, fresh flowers and candlelight lend this small hotel (only six rooms) an appealingly old-fashioned cottage atmosphere, but with all mod cons, including full-size baths and room service. There's also an excellent restaurant here (dinner £49.50), and the personable owners are experts in guest comfort.

STRETCH YOUR LEGS EDINBURGH

Start/Finish: Castle Esplanade

Distance: 1 mile

Duration: 2–3 hours

This walk explores the alleys and side streets around the Royal Mile, leading you away from the main tourist trail and into hidden corners and historic nooks. It involves a bit of climbing up and down steep stairs.

Take this walk on Trip

Castle Esplanade

Begin on the Castle Esplanade, which provides a grandstand view south over the city to the Pentland Hills.

The Walk » Head towards Castlehill and the start of the Royal Mile.

Cannonball House

The 17th-century house on the right is known as Cannonball House because of the iron ball lodged in the wall. It was not fired in anger, but marks the gravitation height to which water would flow naturally from the city's first piped water supply. The building now houses an excellent **restaurant** (0131-225 1550; www.contini.com/cannonball; 356 Castlehill, EH1 2NE; mains £15-30; noon-3pm & 5.30-10pm Tue-Sat; 23, 27, 41, 42), a good place to sample classic Scottish cuisine.

The Walk » Continue down Castlehill for barely 100m to the Camera Obscura.

Camera Obscura

Edinburgh's **Camera Obscura** (www.camera-obscura.co.uk; Castlehill, EH1 2ND; adult/child £16.50/12.50; 9am-10pm Jul & Aug, 9.30am-8pm Apr-Jun, Sep & Oct, 9.30am-7pm Nov-Mar; 23, 27, 41, 42) is a curious 19th-century device – in constant use since 1853 – that uses lenses and mirrors to throw a live image of the city onto a large horizontal screen. Stairs lead up through various displays to the **Outlook Tower**, which offers great views over the city.

The Walk » Go down Ramsay Lane past Ramsay Garden – one of Edinburgh's most desirable addresses – and around to the right to the towers of New College.

New College

This neo-Gothic building is home to Edinburgh University's Faculty of Divinity. Nip into the courtyard to see the **statue of John Knox**, a firebrand preacher who led the Protestant Reformation in Scotland, and was instrumental in the creation of the Church of Scotland in 1560.

The Walk » Turn right and climb the stairs into Milne's Court, a student residence belonging to

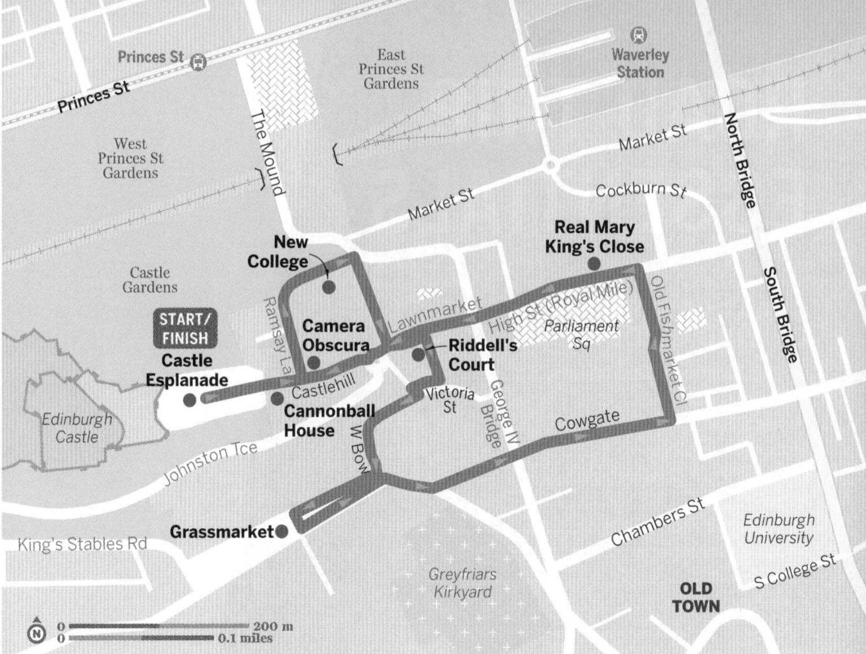

Edinburgh University. Exit into Lawnmarket, cross the street (bearing slightly left) and duck into Riddell's Court at No 322–8.

Riddell's Court

Riddell's Court is a typical Old Town close. You'll find yourself in a small courtyard, but the house in front of you (built in 1590) was originally the edge of the street (the building you just walked under was added in 1726 – look for the inscription in the doorway on the right). The arch with the inscription *Vivendo discimus* (we live and learn) leads into the original 16th-century courtyard.

The Walk ›› Turn right down Fisher's Close, which leads to Victoria Tce; Maxie's Bistro, at the far end, is a great place to stop for a drink. Descend the stairs at the foot of Upper Bow and continue downhill to the Grassmarket.

Grassmarket

The site of a cattle market from the 15th century until the start of the 20th century, the Grassmarket was once the city's main place of execution, and over 100 martyred Covenanters are commemorated by a monument at the eastern end, where the gallows used to stand.

The Walk ›› Head east along the Cowgate, passing under the arch of George IV Bridge. Turn left and climb up Old Fishmarket Close, a typical cobbled Old Town wynd, and emerge onto the Royal Mile; bear left across the street.

Real Mary King's Close

Edinburgh's 18th-century City Chambers were built over the sealed-off remains of **Real Mary King's Close** (☎0131-225 0672; www.realmarykingsclose.com; 2 Warriston's Close, EH1 1PG; adult/child £17.95/11.25; ⏰hours vary, approx 9.30am-9pm Apr-Oct, 10am-5.30pm Nov-Mar; 🚌23, 27, 41, 42), and the lower levels of this medieval Old Town alley have survived almost unchanged amid the foundations for 250 years. Now open to the public, this spooky, subterranean labyrinth gives a fascinating insight into the everyday life of 17th-century Edinburgh.

The Walk ›› Walk back up the Royal Mile to the Castle Esplanade.

ROAD TRIP ESSENTIALS

Great Britain Driving Guide

Driving in Great Britain opens up everything from country lanes to mountain roads. Downsides include traffic jams, high fuel costs and parking bills.

Driving Fast Facts

- **Right or left?** Left
- **Manual or automatic?** Manual
- **Legal driving age** 17
- **Top speed limit** 70mph (112km/h) on motorways and some (but not all) dual carriageways
- **Signature cars** MG, Morris Minor and Mini

DRIVING LICENCE & DOCUMENTS

At the time of writing, if you're an EU national, from the European Economic Area or from Northern Ireland you can drive any type of vehicle listed on your licence. It's not clear if or how Britain's decision to leave the EU (Brexit) will affect this (the rules are slightly different if you're from the Channel Islands or the Isle of Man).

If you're from any other country, you can drive any small vehicle (such as a car or motorcycle) listed on your licence for up to 12 months.

If asked by the police, you must be able to produce a valid driving licence and insurance documents within seven days.

INSURANCE

It's illegal to drive a car or motorbike in Britain without (at least) third-party insurance. This will be included with all rental cars. If you're bringing your own vehicle, check whether your insurance will cover you in Britain.

HIRING A CAR

Compared with many countries (especially the USA), hire rates can be expensive in Britain: the smallest cars start at about £120 per week, and it's around £190 and upwards per week for a medium car. You will require a credit card and a copy of your driving licence; drivers from some countries may also need an International Drivers' Permit (IDP).

Using a rental-broker or comparison site such as Auto Europe (www.autoeurope.co.uk), UK Car Hire (www.ukcarhire.net) or Kayak (www.kayak.com) can also help find bargains, but beware of cheap agencies that often have hidden terms and/or limited mileages.

Occasionally, local car-hire firms can offer more competitive prices.

Basic third-party insurance is included, which covers liability to other drivers should you have an accident. Standard rental contracts usually have an excess payable in the event of damage to the vehicle, which can be £1000 or more depending on the vehicle you're driving. All car-hire firms will offer you the option of paying extra to waive this excess – but this is usually an expensive option.

Check whether your own car insurance covers you for excess on hire cars, or consider a stand-alone policy that covers you specifically for the excess (try comparing prices at www.moneymaxim.co.uk). If you damage the car, you will generally have to pay the excess when you return it, and then reclaim it later from your insurance company.

The main players:

Avis (www.avis.co.uk)

Budget (www.budget.co.uk)

Europcar (www.europcar.co.uk)

Sixt (www.sixt.co.uk)

Thrifty (www.thrifty.co.uk)

MOTORHOME RENTAL

Hiring a motorhome or camper van (£650 to £1200 a week) is more expensive than hiring a car, but saves on accommodation costs and gives almost unlimited freedom. Sites to check include the following:

Just Go (www.justgo.uk.com)

Wicked Campers (www.wickedcampers.co.uk)

Wild Horizon (www.wildhorizon.co.uk)

BRINGING YOUR OWN VEHICLE

You can usually use a non-GB car without registering or taxing it in the UK if all of the following rules apply:

➡ You're just visiting, and have no plans to live in the country.

➡ The vehicle is registered and taxed in your own country.

➡ You only use the car for up to six months in total (either on one visit or a number of shorter visits over a year).

For more details see www.gov.uk/importing-vehicles-into-the-uk.

Road Trip Websites

Automobile Association (AA; www.theaa.com) The UK's largest motoring organisation; also provides breakdown cover

RAC (www.rac.co.uk) Another key motoring organisation and breakdown cover provider

UK Government (www.gov.uk/browse/driving) Official advice on driving in Great Britain

AA Route Planner (www.theaa.com/route-planner) Directions and maps from the AA

Traffic Report (www.trafficengland.com) Government-run, searchable database of current congestion and planned roadworks

MAPS

You'll need good road maps – we recommend getting them even if you have a satnav system.

For countrywide cover, the AA's excellent atlas series includes the spiral-bound *AA Road Atlas Britain* (£11.99) with a scale of 1:200,000. It also produces 9 indexed regional maps covering the whole of Britain (£4.99) on scales ranging from 1:200,000 to 1:300,000.

These and a broad range of other, reliable maps and atlases are widely available at petrol stations and bookshops.

MOTORING ORGANISATIONS

Motoring organisations in Britain include the Automobile Association (www.theaa.com) and the RAC (www.rac.co.uk). For both, annual membership starts at around £45, including 24-hour roadside breakdown assistance.

Britannia (www.lv.com/breakdown-cover) offers better value from £30 a year, while a greener alternative is the Environmental Transport Association (www.eta.co.uk); it provides breakdown assistance but doesn't campaign for more roads.

ROADS & CONDITIONS

Motorways and main A roads deliver you quickly from one end of the country to another. Motorways feature service stations (signed as 'Services') where you can buy fuel, food and often a meal at a fast-food eatery. Services are regularly spaced but it's still worth keeping an eye on the fuel gauge and being aware of the distance to the next one.

Lesser A roads, B roads and minor roads are usually more scenic and are ideal for car or motorcycle touring. You can't travel fast, but you won't care.

Toll routes are rare. The M6 (Toll) runs for a 27-mile stretch near Birmingham,

Driving Problem-Buster

What should I do if my car breaks down? Call the service number of your car-hire company and one of their roadside assistance vehicles will arrive or a local garage will be contacted. If you're bringing your own car, it's a good idea to join breakdown cover providers, such as the AA (www.theaa.com), Britannia (www.lv.com/breakdown-cover) or the RAC (www.rac.co.uk). If you're not a member they can still organise assistance (it'll just cost you more).

What if I have an accident? Hire cars usually have a leaflet in the glovebox about what to do in case of an accident. Exchange basic information with the other party (name, insurance details, driver's licence number, company details if the car is a rental). No discussion of liability needs to take place at the scene. It's a good idea to photograph the scene of the accident, noting key details (damage sustained, car positions on the road, any skid markings). Call the police (999) if required.

What should I do if I get stopped by the police? Always remain calm and polite; officers are generally courteous and helpful. They may want to see your passport or other valid form of ID, licence and proof of insurance – you're not required by law to carry these, but must be able to produce them, if asked, at a police station within seven days.

What if I can't find anywhere to stay? If you're travelling during the summer months, always book accommodation in advance. If you're stuck, call the local tourist office's accommodation hotline. If they're closed, many offices have lists of places to sleep posted in the window,

Will I be able to find ATMs? You'll find ATMs in all cities, and in most towns and at many service stations. Most are free to use, some though may be subject to a small charge – they will be labelled as such. Local shops often offer 'cash back' – where in exchange for a purchase over £5 you can effectively debit cash from your account.

Will I need to pay tolls in advance? Many toll routes offer a pre-paid service but you can also usually pay on site – follow the signs ushering you into lanes specifying pre-paid, cash or card.

and costs up to £6.70 per car; payment is either in advance or on-site, by cash or card. There are also tolls to cross bridges such as the Dartford Crossing, the Humber Bridge, the Mersey Tunnels, the Tamar Bridge and the Tyne Tunnel.

In winter (usually December to March), snow and ice frequently affect routes in parts of Scotland, higher ground in Wales and often to a lesser extent northern England. It can also affect the rest of the country and occur outside those months. When it does, disruption can be significant.

Rush hours can stretch from 6am to 9am and 4pm to 7pm around London and the bigger cities, but tend to be shorter in smaller cities and towns. School summer holidays bring congestion around national parks, popular cities such as Oxford, Bath Edinburgh and York, and in coastal areas – the peak-time bank-holiday queues down to the West Country are notorious.

ROAD RULES

Drink driving is taken very seriously; you're allowed a maximum blood-alcohol level of 80mg/100mL (0.08%) in England and Wales, or 50mg/100mL (0.05%) in Scotland.

Some other important rules:

- drive on the left (!)
- wear fitted seat belts in cars
- wear helmets on motorcycles
- give way to your right at junctions and roundabouts

Approximate Road Distances (miles)

	Bath	Birmingham	Brighton	Cambridge	Canterbury	Cardiff	Durness	Edinburgh	Heathrow Airport	Llanberis	London	Manchester	Newcastle	Norwich	Oxford	Penzance	Portsmouthance	Stonehenge	Torquay
Birmingham	110																		
Brighton	160	170																	
Cambridge	170	100	120																
Canterbury	180	190	90	110															
Cardiff	55	110	200	200	220														
Durness	640	550	720	610	710	650													
Edinburgh	380	290	460	350	450	390	260												
Heathrow Airport	100	110	70	70	90	140	660	400											
Llanberis	250	125	330	250	330	170	560	300	260										
London	120	120	50	60	60	155	660	400	20	260									
Manchester	180	210	260	180	260	190	470	220	200	100	200								
Newcastle	310	200	340	230	330	315	380	120	280	250	280	150							
Norwich	230	160	170	60	160	270	630	370	150	310	115	185	250						
Oxford	70	70	110	85	130	105	620	360	50	200	70	160	260	150					
Penzance	210	270	280	360	340	220	810	550	270	400	310	350	480	425	260				
Portsmouth	80	150	50	135	125	155	700	440	70	280	80	240	340	205	85	240			
Stonehenge	35	130	120	140	140	90	660	400	70	260	100	220	330	200	70	200	55		
Torquay	120	190	190	250	250	130	720	460	200	330	220	260	390	310	170	110	150	110	
York	240	140	270	160	260	240	470	200	230	17	200	80	90	180	180	400	275	270	310

➡ always use the left lane on motorways and dual carriageways unless overtaking (although so many people ignore this rule, you'd think it didn't exist)

➡ don't use a mobile phone while driving unless it's fully hands-free (another rule frequently flouted)

Drivers often flash their hazard lights once or twice as an informal way to say 'thank you' for road courtesies extended to them.

Speed Limits

Speed limits are usually 30mph (48km/h) in built-up areas, 60mph (96km/h) on main roads and 70mph (112km/h) on motorways and most (but not all) dual carriageways.

PARKING

Many cities have short-stay and long-stay car parks; the latter are cheaper though may be less convenient. 'Park & Ride' systems allow you to park on the edge of the city then ride to the centre on frequent nonstop buses for an all-in-one price. Roadside parking in villages and in city residential areas can be free – but everywhere it's worth checking carefully for signs indicating charges.

Yellow lines (single or double) along the edge of the road indicate restrictions. Nearby signs spell out when you can and can't park. In London and other big cities, traffic wardens operate with efficiency; if you park on the yellow lines at the wrong time, your car will be clamped or towed away, and it'll cost you £130 or more to get driving again. In some cities there are also red lines, which mean no stopping at all. Ever.

Driving Tips

Don't rely solely on your satnav. Although often highly reliable, they have been known to route cars across rivers where there are no bridges and down country tracks only wide enough for animals. Having a good map and being aware of your broader location is always wise.

Some parts of rural Britain have unfenced grazing. You'll be tipped off by warning signs and often cattle grids (bars set into the road to stop animals crossing). After that, watch your speed and expect to see sheep, ponies and even cows on the roads.

The real fun of driving in Britain is away from the motorways and on country, coastal and mountain routes. Here it's best to make journey time calculations bearing in mind the 'tractor factor' – how much longer it'll take if travelling behind a farm vehicle moving painfully slowly...

FUEL

Cities and towns have numerous petrol stations; you'll also find service stations cropping up regularly beside motorways and the more important A roads. In rural areas, petrol stations are much less plentiful; you'll also find the prices in these tend to be higher – it's a good idea to fill up before heading into the wild.

Prices vary but you can expect to pay around £1.25 per litre.

RADIO

Radio stations offer up-to-date traffic news, top tunes and good company. Local radio (both BBC and independent) has the most detailed travel news and weather information. National stations also include the following:

BBC Radio 1 (98–99.6MHz FM) Music radio, targeted at 15- to 29-year-olds.

BBC Radio 2 (88–92MHz FM) Hits, easy listening and chat; aimed at adults.

BBC Radio 3 (90–92.2MHz FM) Classical, often highbrow.

BBC Radio 4 (92–94.4MHz FM) Quality, diverse, imaginative speech radio.

BBC Radio 5 Live (909 or 693 AM) All speech, news and sports-focused.

Classic FM (100–102MHz FM) Accessible classical music.

Virgin Radio (1215Hz MW) Music, showbiz and chat.

GREAT BRITAIN PLAYLIST

The Bonnie Banks o' Loch Lomond (Traditional) Catchy folk ditty about Scotland's 'low' and 'high' roads.

Road to Nowhere (Talking Heads) Oddly not prompted by Birmingham's scary Spaghetti Junction, but by fears of an apocalypse.

Road to Hell (Chris Rea) Variously attributed to being inspired by the M25, the A63 and the A19.

A13, Trunk Road to the Sea (Billy Bragg) The British version of *Route 66*.

The Combine Harvester (The Wurzels) For when you're stuck behind one.

Great Britain Travel Guide

GETTING THERE & AWAY

Flights, cars and rail tickets can be booked online at lonelyplanet.com/bookings.

AIR

Most visitors reach Britain by air, with London a global transport hub. The massive growth of budget ('no-frills') airlines has increased the number of routes – and reduced the fares – between Britain and other countries in Europe.

Airports

London's main airports:

Heathrow (www.heathrow.com) Britain's main airport for international flights; often chaotic and crowded. About 15 miles west of central London.

Gatwick (www.gatwickairport.com) Britain's number-two airport, mainly for international flights, 30 miles south of central London.

Stansted (www.stanstedairport.com) About 35 miles northeast of central London, mainly handling charter and budget European flights.

Luton (www.london-luton.co.uk) Some 35 miles north of central London, well known as a holiday-flight airport.

London City (☎020-7646 0088; www.londoncityairport.com; Hartmann Rd, E16; 📶; ⓤLondon City Airport) A few miles east of central London, specialising in flights to/from European and other UK airports.

Some planes on European and long-haul routes avoid London and use major regional airports including Manchester and Glasgow. Smaller regional airports such as Southampton, Cardiff and Birmingham are served by flights to and from continental Europe and Ireland.

CAR & MOTORCYCLE

If you want to drive or ride to Britain you'll have to bring your car by ferry or use the Channel Tunnel.

SEA

Ferry travel can be via port-to-port routes or combined with a long-distance bus trip, although journeys can be long and financial savings not huge compared with budget airfares. You can travel as a foot passenger or bring your car.

Ferry Fares

Most ferry operators offer flexible fares, meaning great bargains at quiet times of day or year. For example, short cross-channel routes such as Dover to Calais or Boulogne can be as low as £50 for a car plus two passengers, although around £75 to £120 is more likely. If you're a foot passenger there's less need to book ahead; fares on short crossings cost about £30 to £50 each way.

Ferry Routes

The main ferry routes between Great Britain and other European countries include the following:

- Dover–Calais (France)
- Dover–Boulogne (France)
- Newcastle–Amsterdam (Netherlands)
- Newhaven–Dieppe (France)
- Harwich–Hook of Holland (Netherlands)
- Hull–Zeebrugge (Belgium)
- Hull–Rotterdam (Netherlands)
- Liverpool–Dublin (Ireland)
- Portsmouth–Santander (Spain)
- Portsmouth–Bilbao (Spain)

- Holyhead–Dublin (Ireland)
- Fishguard–Rosslare (Ireland)
- Pembroke Dock–Rosslare (Ireland)

Ferry Bookings

Book direct with one of the operators listed below, or use the very handy www.directferries.co.uk – a single site covering all sea-ferry routes.

Brittany Ferries (www.brittany-ferries.com)

DFDS Seaways (www.dfdsseaways.co.uk)

Irish Ferries (www.irishferries.com)

P&O Ferries (www.poferries.com)

Stena Line (www.stenaline.com)

TRAIN

International trains are a comfortable, 'green' option; the Channel Tunnel allows direct rail services between Britain, France and Belgium, with onward connections to many other European destinations. Options include transporting your car.

Channel Tunnel Passenger Service

High-speed Eurostar (www.eurostar.com) passenger services shuttle at least 10 times daily between London and Paris (2½ hours) or Brussels (two hours). Buy tickets from travel agencies, major train stations or the Eurostar website.

The normal one-way fare between London and Paris/Brussels costs around £150; advance booking and off-peak travel gets cheaper fares as low as £35 one way.

Channel Tunnel Car Service

Drivers use Eurotunnel (www.eurotunnel.com). At Folkestone in England or Calais in France, you drive onto a train, get carried through the tunnel and drive off at the other end.

Trains run about four times an hour from 6am to 10pm, then hourly through the night. Loading and unloading takes an hour; the journey lasts 35 minutes.

Book in advance online or pay on the spot. The standard one-way fare for a car and up to nine passengers is between £75 and £100 depending on time of day; promotional fares often bring it down to £60 or less.

DIRECTORY A–Z

ACCESSIBLE TRAVEL

All new buildings have wheelchair access, and even hotels in grand old country houses often have lifts, ramps and other facilities. Hotel and B&Bs in historic buildings are often harder to adapt, so you'll have less choice here.

Modern city buses and trams have low floors for easy access, but few have conductors who can lend a hand when you're getting on or off. Many taxis take wheelchairs, or just have more room in the back.

For tips on travel and thoughtful insight on traveling with a disability, download Lonely Planet's free Accessible Travel guide from www.shop.lonelyplanet.com/categories/accessible-travel.

Useful organisations:

Accessible Britain (www.visitbritain.com/au/en/plan-your-trip/getting-around-britain/accessible-britain) Tourist-office guide to accessible travel in Britain.

Disability Rights UK (www.disabilityrightsuk.org) Published titles include a Holiday Guide. Other services include a key for 7000 public disabled toilets across the UK.

Tourism for All (www.tourismforall.org.uk) Travel advice and a useful travel planner.

ACCOMMODATION

Accommodation in Britain is as varied as the sights you visit. From hip hotels to basic barns, the wide choice is all part of the attraction. Expect prices to be unpredictable in the aftermath of the Covid-19 pandemic.

Book Your Stay Online

For more accommodation reviews by Lonely Planet authors, check out http://hotels.lonelyplanet.com. You'll find independent reviews, as well as recommendations on the best places to stay. Best of all, you can book online.

Practicalities

Newspapers Tabloids include the *Sun*, *Evening Standard*, *Mirror* and *Daily Record* (in Scotland); quality 'broadsheets' include (from right to left, politically) the *Telegraph*, *Times*, *Independent* and *Guardian*.

TV Leading broadcasters include BBC, ITV and Channel 4. Satellite and cable TV providers include Sky and Virgin Media.

Radio National BBC stations are Radio 1 (98–99.6MHz FM), Radio 2 (88–92MHz FM), Radio 3 (90–92.2MHz FM), Radio 4 (92–94.4MHz FM) and Radio 5 Live (909 or 693 AM). National commercial stations include Virgin Radio (1215Hz MW) and Classic FM (100–102MHz FM).

Weights & Measures Britain uses a mix of metric and imperial measures (eg petrol is sold by the litre but beer by the pint; mountain heights are in metres but road distances in miles).

Smoking Forbidden in all enclosed public places in Britain. Most pubs have a smoking area outside.

Hotels

There's a massive choice of hotels in Britain, from small town houses to grand country mansions, and no-frills locations to boutique hideaways. At the bargain end, single/double rooms cost from £45/60. Move up the scale and you'll pay £100/150 or way beyond.

If all you want is a place to put your head down, budget chain hotels can be a good option, although most are lacking in ambience. Prices vary on demand: at quiet times twin-bed rooms start from £30; at the height of the tourist season you'll pay £60 or more. Some options:

Ibis Hotels (www.ibis.com)

Premier Inn (www.premierinn.com)

Travelodge (www.travelodge.co.uk)

Rates

There's no such thing as a 'standard' hotel rate in Britain. Many hotels, especially larger places or chains, vary prices according to demand – or have different rates for online, phone or walk-in bookings – just like airlines and train operators. So if you book early for a night when the hotel is likely to be quiet, rates are cheap. If you book late, or aim for a public-holiday weekend, you'll pay a lot. But wait until the very last minute, and you can *sometimes* get a bargain as rates drop again. The end result: you can pay anything from £25 to £200 for the very same hotel room. With that in mind, the hotel rates we quote are often guide prices only. (In contrast, B&B prices tend to be much more consistent.)

B&Bs

The B&B (bed and breakfast) is a great British institution. At smaller places it's pretty much a room in somebody's house; larger places may be called a 'guesthouse' (halfway between a B&B and a full hotel). Prices start from around £30 per person for a simple bedroom and shared bathroom; for around £35 to £50 per person you get a private bathroom – either down the hall or en suite.

Prices Usually quoted per person, based on two people sharing a room. Single rooms for solo travellers are harder to find, and attract a 20% to 50% premium. Some B&Bs simply won't take single people (unless you pay the full double-room price), especially in summer.

Booking Advance reservations are preferred at B&Bs and are essential during popular periods. You can book many B&Bs via online agencies but rates may be cheaper if you book direct. If you haven't booked in advance, most towns have a main drag of B&Bs; those with spare rooms hang up a 'Vacancies' sign. Many B&Bs require a minimum two-night stay at weekends. Some places reduce rates for longer stays (two or three nights) midweek. If a B&B is full, owners may recommend another place nearby (possibly a private house taking occasional guests, not in tourist listings).

Food Most B&Bs serve enormous breakfasts; some offer packed lunches (from around £7) and evening meals (around £15 to £20).

Bed & Breakfast Nationwide (www.bedandbreakfastnationwide.com)

Pubs & Inns

As well as selling drinks, many pubs and inns offer lodging, particularly in country areas. For bed and breakfast, you'll pay around £30 per person for a basic room, around £45 for something better. An advantage for solo tourists: pubs often have single rooms.

Hostels

There are two types of hostel in Britain: those run by the Youth Hostels Association (www.yha.org.uk) and Scottish Youth Hostels Association (www.hostellingscotland.org.uk); and independent hostels, most listed in the *Independent Hostel Guide* (www.independenthostels.co.uk).

Hostels can be found in rural areas, towns and cities, and they are aimed at all types of traveller, young and old. Some hostels occupy converted cottages, country houses and even castles – often in wonderful locations. Traditionally, sleeping in hostels usually meant sleeping in dormitories, although the future of dorm accommodation remains uncertain as a result of the coronavirus pandemic. Most hostels also have twin or four-bed rooms.

Camping

Campsites range from farmers' fields with a tap and basic toilet, costing from £5 per person per night, to smarter affairs with hot showers and many other facilities, charging up to £15. You usually need all your own kit.

A few campsites also offer self-catering accommodation in chalets, caravans, tepees, yurts and stylish wooden camping 'pods', often dubbed 'glamping'.

If you're touring Britain with a tent or campervan (motorhome), consider joining the Camping & Caravanning Club (www.campingandcaravanningclub.co.uk), which provides up to 30% discount on its sites for an annual membership fee of £41. The club owns almost 100 campsites and lists thousands more in the invaluable Big Sites Book (free to members).

ELECTRICITY

FOOD

Britain has enjoyed something of a culinary revolution over the past two decades. London is recognised as having one of the best restaurant scenes in the world, while all over the country stylish eateries and gourmet gastropubs are making the most of a new-found passion for quality local produce.

Where to Eat

It's wise to book ahead for midrange restaurants, especially at weekends. Top-end restaurants should be booked at least a couple of weeks in advance.

Cafes Traditional cafes are simple eateries serving simple food – sandwiches, pies, sausage and chips. Quality varies enormously: some cafes definitely earn their 'greasy spoon' handle, while others are prim and clean.

Tearooms The tearoom is a British institution, serving cakes, scones and sandwiches accompanied by pots of tea (coffee is usually available too). Upmarket tearooms may also serve afternoon or high tea.

Coffee shops In most cities and towns you'll also find coffee shops – both independents and international chains – serving decent lattes, cappuccinos and espressos, and

Eating Price Ranges

In reviews, the following price ranges refer to a main dish.

£ less than £12 (London less than £15)

££ £12–£22 (London £15–£25)

£££ more than £22 (London more than £25)

continental-style snacks such as bagels, panini or ciabattas.

Restaurants London has scores of excellent restaurants that could hold their own in major cities worldwide, while eating places in other British cities can give the capital a run for its money (often for rather less money).

Pubs Many British pubs serve a wide range of food, and it's often a good-value option whether you want a toasted sandwich between museum visits in London, or a three-course meal in the evening after touring the castles of Wales and elsewhere.

Gastropubs The quality of food in some pubs is now so high that they have created a whole new genre of eatery – the gastropub. The finest are almost restaurants (a few have been awarded Michelin stars) but others go for a more relaxed atmosphere.

When to Eat

Breakfast Served in most hotels and B&Bs between 7am and 9am, or perhaps 8am to 10am on weekends. In cafes, the breakfast menu might extend to 11am through the week.

Lunch Generally taken between noon and 2pm, and can range from a sandwich and a bag of crisps to a three-course meal with wine. Many restaurants offer a set menu two-course lunch at competitive prices on weekdays. Cafes often have a daily lunch special, or offer soup and a sandwich.

Afternoon tea A tradition inherited from the British aristocracy and eagerly adopted by the middle classes, afternoon tea is a between-meals snack now enjoying a revival in country hotels and upmarket tearooms. It consists of dainty sandwiches, cakes and pastries plus, of course, a cup of tea, often poured from a silver teapot and sipped politely from fine china cups.

Dinner The main meal of the day, usually served in restaurants between 6pm and 9pm, and consisting of two or three courses – starter, main and dessert. Upmarket restaurants might serve a five-course dinner, which may include a fish course between starter and main.

Sunday lunch Another great British tradition. This is the main meal of the day, normally served between noon and 4pm. Many pubs and restaurants offer Sunday lunch, where the main course usually consists of roast beef, lamb or pork, accompanied by roast and mashed potatoes, gravy, and boiled vegetables such as carrots and peas.

In parts of Britain, notably northern England and Scotland, many people use the word 'dinner' for their main midday meal, and 'tea' for a light evening meal. However, this terminology is rarely, if ever, used in restaurants.

British Classics

Fish and chips Long-standing favourite, best sampled in coastal towns.

Haggis Scottish icon, mainly offal and oatmeal, traditionally served with 'tatties and neeps' (potatoes and turnips).

Sandwich Global snack today, but an English 'invention' from the 18th century.

Laverbread Laver is a type of seaweed, mixed with oatmeal and fried to create this traditional Welsh speciality.

Ploughman's lunch Bread and cheese – pub menu regular, perfect with a pint.

Roast beef and Yorkshire pudding Traditional lunch on Sunday for the English.

Cornish pasty Savoury pastry, southwest speciality, now available countrywide.

INTERNET ACCESS

- Mobile broadband coverage is good in large population centres, but limited or nonexistent in rural areas. However, beware high charges for data roaming – check with your mobile/cellphone provider before travelling.
- Most hotels, B&Bs, hostels, stations and coffee shops (even some trains and buses) have wi-fi access, charging anything from nothing to £6 per hour.

➡ Internet cafes are surprisingly rare in Britain, especially away from big cities and tourist spots. Most charge from £1 per hour, but out in the sticks you can pay £5 per hour.

➡ Public libraries often have computers with free internet access, but only for 30-minute slots, and demand is high. All the usual warnings apply about keystroke-capturing software and other security risks.

LGBT+ TRAVELLERS

Britain is a generally tolerant place for gay and lesbian travellers. London, Manchester and Brighton have flourishing gay scenes, and in other sizeable cities (even some small towns) you'll find communities not entirely in the closet. That said, you'll still find pockets of homophobic hostility in some areas. Resources include the following:

Diva (www.divamag.co.uk)

Gay Times (www.gaytimes.co.uk)

Switchboard LGBT+ Helpline (www.switchboard.lgbt; ☎0300 330 0630)

MONEY

ATMs (usually called 'cash machines') are common in cities and towns, but watch out for tampering; a common ruse is to attach a card reader to the slot. Visa and MasterCard are widely accepted in Britain, except at some smaller B&Bs which take cash or cheque only. Other credit cards, including Amex, are not so widely accepted.

Cities and larger towns have banks and exchange bureaux for changing money into pounds, but some bureaux offer poor rates. You can change money at some post offices, which is very handy in country areas; exchange rates are fair.

OPENING HOURS

Opening hours may vary throughout the year, especially in rural areas where many places have shorter hours, or close completely, from October or November to March or April.

Banks 9.30am to 4pm or 5pm Monday to Friday; some are open 9.30am to 1pm Saturday.

Pubs & Bars 11am to 11pm Monday to Thursday, 11am to 1am Friday and Saturday, 12.30pm to 11pm Sunday.

Restaurants Lunch is noon to 3pm, dinner 6pm to 9pm/10pm (or later in cities).

Shops 9am to 5.30pm (or 6pm in cities) Monday to Saturday, and often 11am to 5pm Sunday. London and other cities have convenience stores open 24/7.

PUBLIC HOLIDAYS

Holidays for the whole of Britain:

New Year's Day 1 January (plus 2 January in Scotland)

Easter March/April (Good Friday to Easter Monday inclusive)

May Day First Monday in May

Spring Bank Holiday Last Monday in May

Summer Bank Holiday Last Monday in August

Christmas Day 25 December

Boxing Day 26 December

In England and Wales most businesses and banks close on official public holidays. In Scotland, bank holidays are just for the banks, and many businesses stay open.

On public holidays, some small museums and places of interest close, but larger attractions have their busiest times. If a place closes on Sunday, it'll probably be shut on bank holidays as well.

Virtually everything – attractions, shops, banks, offices – closes on Christmas Day, although pubs are open at lunchtime. There's usually no public transport on Christmas Day, and a very minimal service on Boxing Day.

SAFE TRAVEL

Britain is a remarkably safe country, but crime is not unknown in London and other cities.

➡ Watch out for pickpockets and hustlers in crowded areas popular with tourists such as around Westminster Bridge in London.

➡ When travelling by tube, tram or urban train services at night, choose a carriage containing other people.

➡ Many town centres can be rowdy on Friday and Saturday nights when the pubs and clubs are emptying.

➡ Unlicensed minicabs (a bloke with a car earning money on the side) are best avoided.

Sleeping Price Ranges

Reviews of places to stay use the following price ranges, all based on double room with private bathroom in high season. Hotels in London are more expensive than the rest of the country, so have different price ranges.

£ less than £65 (London less than £100)

££ £65–£130 (London £100–£200)

£££ more than £130 (London more than £200)

TELEPHONE

Mobile Phones

The UK uses the GSM 900/1800 network, which covers the rest of Europe, Australia and New Zealand, but isn't compatible with the North American GSM 1900. Most modern mobiles can function on both networks, but check before you leave home just in case.

Roaming charges within the EU were eliminated in June 2017 but, after the UK's decision to leave the EU (Brexit), it's not yet clear whether this will also be the case in Britain. Other international roaming charges can be prohibitively high, and you'll probably find it cheaper to get a UK number by buying a SIM card (from £5 including calling credit) for your own phone. Or buy a cheap pay-as-you-go phone (from £10 including calling credit).

Pay-as-you-go phones can be recharged by buying vouchers from shops.

Phone Codes

Dialling into the UK Dial your country's international access code then 44 (the UK country code), then the area code (dropping the first 0) followed by the telephone number.

Dialling out of the UK The international access code is 00; dial this, then add the code of the country you wish to dial.

Making a reverse-charge (collect) international call Dial 155 for the operator. It's an expensive option, but not for the caller.

Area codes in the UK Do not have a standard format or length, eg Edinburgh 0131, London 020, Ambleside 015394.

Directory Assistance A host of agencies offer this service – numbers include 118 118, 118 500 and 118 811 – but fees are extortionate (around £6 for a 45-second call); search online for free at www.thephonebook.bt.com.

Mobile phones Codes usually begin with 07.

Free calls Numbers starting with 0800 or 0808 are free.

National operator (100)

International operator (155)

TOURIST INFORMATION

Most British cities and towns, and some villages, have a tourist information centre or visitor information centre – for ease we've called all of these places 'tourist offices'.

Tourist offices tend to have helpful staff, books and maps for sale, leaflets to give away, and advice on things to see or do. Some can also assist with booking accommodation. Some are run by national parks and often have small exhibits about the area.

Most tourist offices keep regular business hours; in quiet areas they tend to close from October to March.

Visit Britain (www.visitbritain.com) is the country's official tourism website.

VISAS

➡ At the time of writing, if you're a citizen of the European Economic Area (EEA) nations or Switzerland, you don't need a visa to enter or work in Britain – you can enter using your national identity card. It's not yet clear if or how this may be affected by Brexit.

➡ Visa regulations are always subject to change, so it's essential to check with your local British embassy, high commission or consulate before leaving home.

➡ Currently, if you're a citizen of Australia, Canada, New Zealand, Japan, Israel, the USA and several other countries, you can stay for up to six months (no visa required), but you are not allowed to work.

➡ Nationals of many countries, including South Africa, will need to obtain a visa: for more info, see www.gov.uk/check-uk-visa.

➡ The Youth Mobility Scheme, for Australian, Canadian, Japanese, Hong Kong, Monégasque, New Zealand, South Korean and Taiwanese citizens aged 18 to 31, allows working visits of up to two years, but must be applied for in advance.

➡ Commonwealth citizens with a UK-born parent may be eligible for a Certificate of Entitlement to the Right of Abode, which entitles them to live and work in the UK.

➡ Commonwealth citizens with a UK-born grandparent could qualify for a UK Ancestry Employment Certificate, allowing them to work full time for up to five years in the UK.

➡ British immigration authorities have always been tough; dress neatly and carry proof that you have sufficient funds with which to support yourself. A credit card and/or an onward ticket will help.

BEHIND THE SCENES

SEND US YOUR FEEDBACK

We love to hear from travellers – your comments help make our books better. We read every word, and we guarantee that your feedback goes straight to the authors. Visit **lonelyplanet.com/contact** to submit your updates and suggestions.

Note: We may edit, reproduce and incorporate your comments in Lonely Planet products such as guidebooks, websites and digital products, so let us know if you don't want your comments reproduced or your name acknowledged. For a copy of our privacy policy visit lonelyplanet.com/privacy.

ACKNOWLEDGMENTS

Climate map data adapted from Peel MC, Finlayson BL & McMahon TA (2007) 'Updated World Map of the Köppen-Geiger Climate Classification', *Hydrology and Earth System Sciences*, 11, 163344.

Front cover photographs (clockwise from top): Grassington, albinoni/Shutterstock ©; Lavenham, Michael Brooks/Alamy Stock Photo ©; Motorist at the Atlantic coast, Dougal Waters/Getty Images ©

Back cover photograph: Winnats Pass, Derbyshire, England, R A Kearton/Getty Images©

THIS BOOK

This 2nd edition of Lonely Planet's *Great Britain's Best Trips* guidebook was researched and written by Anthony Ham, Isabel Albiston, Oliver Berry, Joe Bindloss, Fionn Davenport, Belinda Dixon, Damian Harper, Anna Kaminski, Catherine Le Nevez, Andy Symington, Tasmin Waby, Kerry Walker, Luke Waterson, Neil Wilson. This guidebook was produced by the following:

Senior Product Editor Sandie Kestell

Senior Cartographer Mark Griffiths

Product Editor Joel Cotterell

Book Designer Virginia Moreno

Assisting Editors Andrew Bain, Nigel Chin, Carly Hall, Victoria Harrison, Trent Holden, Charlotte Orr, Brana Vladisavljevic

Assisting Cartographers Rachel Imeson, Julie Sheridan

Cover Researcher Brendan Dempsey-Spencer

Thanks to Sasha Drew, Paul Harding, Karen Henderson, Genna Patterson, Karyn Noble, Lyahna Spencer, Amanda Williamson

INDEX

C

D

E

F

G

H

I

J

K

L

M

N

O

P

R

S

T

U

V